# Bed Breakfast Stops 2001

## Value for money accommodation in England, Scotland, Wales & Ireland

### Special Supplements for
### Non-Smokers
### Disabled
### & Special Diets

FHG Publications
Paisley

Part of IPC Country and Leisure Media Ltd

**LONDON**

## FALCON HOTEL

- Central London
- ★★ B&B Hotel
- Family friendly • Est. 30 years
- Tranquil position
- Set in a garden square.
- 2 mins Paddington Station
- Airlines check-ins 15 mins Heathrow on Express Link

- En-suite facilities
- Very clean and comfortable
- Close to tourist attractions and shops
- Triple and Family rooms
- Full freshly cooked English breakfasts

E-mail: info@aafalcon.co.uk
Website: www.aafalcon.co.uk
Tel: +44 (0) 20 7723 8603
Fax: +44 (0) 20 7402 7009
11 Norfolk Sq., Hyde Park North, London W2

*Our guests first and always*

Affordable prices from: Singles £35, Doubles £55
*For latest seasonal prices please call*

---

## THE VEGAS HOTEL
104 Warwick Way, Victoria, London SW1V 1SD
Telephone 0207-834 0082; Fax: 0207-834 5623;
e-mail: info@vegashotel.co.uk • web: www.vegashotel.co.uk

We are a friendly Bed & Breakfast hotel in Victoria at a convenient location in the city of London near Buckingham Palace and other sights. Only a few minutes' walk to British Airways Terminal, Victoria Coach, Railway and Underground Station. All rooms are with shower/wc, hairdryer, satellite TV, telephone and alarm clock. Reception open 24 hours.

Rates: single room with shower/wc £35-£49; Double/twin room with shower/wc from £40-£69.
All rates inclusive of full English Breakfast and VAT    ETC

---

## Haven Hotel
6-8 Sussex Gardens, Paddington, London W2 1UL
Tel: 020 7723 5481/2195; Fax: 020 7706 4568

Very centrally situated Bed and Breakfast. First hotel in Sussex Gardens from Edgware Road. Parking available. Reasonable rates. Major shops and attractions nearby.

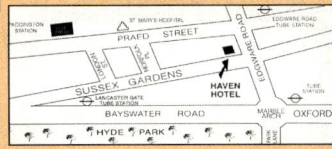

🚇 EDGWARE ROAD, PADDINGTON, MARBLE ARCH, LANCASTER GATE 🚇

---

## PUBLISHER'S NOTE

While every effort is made to ensure accuracy, we regret that FHG Publications cannot accept responsibility for errors, omissions or misrepresentations in our entries or any consequences thereof. Prices in particular should be checked because we go to press early. We will follow up complaints but cannot act as arbiters or agents for either party.

# LONDON

## The Hotel Columbus

141 Sussex Gardens, Hyde Park, London W2 2RX
Tel: 020-7262 0974; Fax: 020-7262 6785
E-mail: hotelcolumbus@compuserve.com
Website: http://www.delmerehotels.com

This charming Bed and Breakfast hotel is the ideal choice for individuals and families who seek both value for money and a quality B & B in the "Heart of London".

Situated in an elegant tree-lined avenue close to Hyde Park and Oxford Street, it is a former residence of the aristocracy and has now been converted to provide modern, comfortable accommodation. All rooms have en suite shower, telephone, TV, etc.

**Look no further for London's Best B&B !**

## MACDONALD AND DEVON HOTELS
### 43-46 ARGYLE SQUARE, KING'S CROSS, LONDON WC1H 8AL

Macdonald and Devon Hotels are centrally located right in London's heartland and well served by public transport. Short walk from St. Pancras and King's Cross and Thameslink mainline railway stations. These provide lines to Heathrow and Gatwick Airports, they are also the main lines in the North South and West of England. In these family run hotels, bed and English breakfast is offered in a friendly and clean environment. Competitive prices attract both business people and tourist alike. The Hotels comprise of 60 rooms. Single, double and triples and family size rooms. All rooms are equipped with washbasins, colour TV. Tea/coffee making facilities. En suite facilities are in some rooms. Central heating throughout.

TEL: 020 7837 3552
FAX: 020 7278 9885

For further information, visit our website: www.macdonaldhotel.com

## The Royal Park Hotel

Very comfortable 3 star accommodation in central London. Ideally situated for shopping, sightseeing and business. Close to Harrods, Hyde Park and the rest of Knightsbridge. T.V, tea and coffee facilities and telephone in every room.

**All major credit cards are accepted**

email: info@theroyalpark.com

2-5 Westbourne Terrace,
London, W2 3UL
www.theroyalpark.com

Tel: 020 7402 6187
Fax: 020 7224 9426

LONDON/CHESHIRE/CORNWALL

# ELIZABETH HOTEL

Quiet, convenient Townhouse overlooking the magnificent gardens of Eccleston Square. Only a short walk from Buckingham Palace and other tourist attractions. Easy access to Knightsbridge, Oxford Street and Regent Street. Extremely reasonable rates in a fantastic location. Visa, Mastercard, Switch, Delta & JCB are all accepted

37 Eccleston Square,
Victoria, London,
SW1V 1PB
www.elizabeth-hotel.com

info@elizabethhotel.com
Tel: 020 7828 6812
Fax: 020 7828 6814

## APLAS GUEST HOUSE

Patricia and Michael Aplas welcome you to the Aplas Guest House. We are a small family-run guest house and have been established for 15 years.

We are ideally located, some five minutes' walk to the city centre and about the same to the railway station. For those coming by car, parking is available. Most of our rooms are en suite and can be booked on a 'room only' or 'B&B' basis.

★ Our prices range from £13.00 to £17.50 per person. ★
★ Discounts are available for long stays and children. ★

*For more information contact:*
Aplas Guest House, 106 Brook Street, Chester, Cheshire CH1 3DU
**TELEPHONE 01244 312401**

## TRENCREEK

**St Gennys, Bude, Cornwall EX23 0AY**
**Tel: (01840) 230219**

Comfortable farmhouse which offers a homely and relaxed family atmosphere. Situated in quiet and peaceful surroundings yet within reach of Crackington Haven. Well placed for easy access to coastal and countryside walks. Family, double and twin-bedded rooms, most en suite, all with tea and coffee making facilities. Two comfortable lounges. Games Room. Separate dining room. Generous portions of home-cooked farmhouse food are always freshly prepared. Children welcome, special rates for under twelves. Spring and Autumn breaks available.
Non-Smoking. Sunday lunches and evening meals available. Contact Richard and Margaret Heard.

Please mention Bed and Breakfast Stops when enquiring

CORNWALL

# MARCORRIE HOTEL

### 20 FALMOUTH ROAD, TRURO TR1 2HX

Victorian town house in conservation area, five minutes' walk from the city centre and cathedral. Centrally situated for visiting country houses, gardens and coastal resorts. All rooms are en suite and have central heating, colour TV, telephone, tea-making facilities. Ample parking. Credit cards: Visa, Access, Amex. Open all year. B&B from £23.25 pppn.

**Tel: 01872 277374   Fax: 01872 241666**

## Glenthorne

Glenthorne is set in its own grounds with ample parking area. Within five minutes' walk of the picturesque village with its quaint little harbour, a photographer's paradise. If you like walking there is the beautiful Valency Valley which leads to St. Juliot Church for the Thomas Hardy fans, also spectacular coastal walks. It's an ideal base for touring. Accommodation – one double with washbasin and one twin room, both with tea/coffee making facilities. Own lounge with colour TV. Pets welcome if well behaved. Own front door key.
Bed and Breakfast from £15.50

**Mrs Sheila M. Smith, Glenthorne, Penally Hill, Boscastle PL35 0HH (01840 250502)**

## ROCKLANDS

"Rocklands" is situated overlooking part of Cornwall's superb coastline and enjoys uninterrupted sea views. The Lizard is well known for its lovely picturesque scenery, coastal walks and enchanting coves and beaches, as well as the famous Serpentine Stone which is quarried and sold locally. Open Easter to October. The Hill family have been catering for visitors on the Lizard since the 1850's. Three bedrooms with sea views, one en suite, tea/coffee making facilities and electric heaters; sittingroom with TV and video; sun lounge; diningroom with separate tables. Bed and Breakfast weekly terms from £126 per person. NO VAT. Children and well trained pets welcome.

**Mrs D. J. Hill, "Rocklands", The Lizard, Near Helston TR12 7NX Tel: 01326 290339**

## Elder Grove Lake Road, Ambleside, Cumbria

Enjoy quality accommodation and service in our Victorian house, conveniently situated for walking or sightseeing and close to Ambleside with many shops and restaurants. We offer 10 comfortable bedrooms, all with private bathrooms, also colour televisions, kettle tray, hair dryers and radios. Start the day with a choice of breakfast from a full Cumbrian breakfast to a lighter bite served in our unique Lakeland dining room, and in the evenings relax in our bar or lounge. We have parking, central heating and ask for no smoking please.

Contact Paul and Vicky McDougall for brochure and tariff on 015394 32504
e-mail: info@eldergrove.co.uk  Website: www.eldergrove.co.uk

**Please mention Bed and Breakfast Stops when enquiring**

CORNWALL

# White Lodge Hotel

### Mawgan Porth Bay, Near Newquay, Cornwall TR8 4BN
### Tel: St. Mawgan (STD 01637) 860512

## GIVE YOURSELVES & YOUR DOGS A BREAK

at our family-run White Lodge Hotel overlooking beautiful Mawgan Porth Bay, near Newquay, Cornwall

★ Dogs most welcome- FREE OF CHARGE
★ Your dogs sleep with you in your bedroom.
★ Direct access to sandy beach and coastal path.
★ Dog loving proprietors with 18 years' experience in catering for dog owners on holiday with their dogs
★ ALL bedrooms with colour TV, tea/coffee makers, alarm clocks, radios, intercoms, heaters etc.
★ Some en suite bedrooms
★ Fantastic sea views from most rooms
★ Well-stocked residents' lounge bar, diningroom and sun patio with outstanding sea views across the bay.
★ Games room with pool table and dart board etc.
★ Large free car park within hotel grounds

| SPECIAL 6 DAYS (5 NIGHTS) CHRISTMAS HOUSE PARTY ONLY £250 | SPECIAL 6 DAYS (5 NIGHTS) NEW YEAR (HOGMANAY) BREAK ONLY £210 | SPECIAL 6 DAYS (5 NIGHTS) BREAKS ONLY £160-£175 BB & Evening Meal | WEEKLY TERMS FROM £210-£230 FOR 5-COURSE EVENING DINNER, BED AND 4-COURSE BREAKFAST WITH CHOICE OF MENU |

### Phone 01637 860512  John or Diane Parry for free colour brochure

ALL PRICES INCLUDE VAT AT 17½%
E-mail: dogfriendlyhotel@redhotant.com
Website: www.dogfriendlyhotel.co.uk

Please mention Bed and Breakfast Stops when enquiring

**CUMBRIA**

### Colin and Rosemary Haskell
# Borwick Lodge

*Silver* SILVER AWARD

Outgate, Hawkshead, Ambleside, Cumbria LA22 0PU
Tel & Fax: Hawkshead (015394) 36332
e-mail: borwicklodge@talk21.com • website: www.borwicklodge.com

Award-winning delightful 17th century house nestling in three acres of secluded gardens. Breathtaking panoramic lake and mountain views. Ideally situated. Close to Hawkshead village with good choice of restaurants and inns. Beautiful en suite rooms with colour televisions and tea-making facilities. King-size four-poster rooms. Somewhere special in this most beautiful corner of England. Ample parking. NON-SMOKING THROUGHOUT. Bed and Breakfast from £25 Residential licence.

*See Board Section – Ambleside, Cumbria*

## The Ferndale Hotel
Lake Road, Ambleside, Cumbria LA22 0DB
Tel: 015394 32207

The Ferndale Hotel is a small, family run Hotel where you will find a warm, friendly welcome and personal attention at all times. Offering excellent accommodation with good home cooked English or Vegetarian breakfast. Our ten attractive bedrooms have all been individually decorated and furnished, each with full en suite facilities, colour television and tea/coffee making tray, most having individually designed canopy/draped beds. Full central heating throughout, several rooms having views of the fells, and including ground floor bedrooms. The Ferndale is open all year round with a car park, is licensed, offers packed lunches, hair dryer, clothes/boot drying and ironing facilities. A wide choice of places to dine, within minutes' walking distance, ranging from excellent pub food to superb restaurants of many varied cuisines will complete your day.

Bed and Breakfast £19 - £25 pppn. Weekly £125 - £155 pp. **Please phone for brochure.**

### BROOKLANDS
GUEST HOUSE
**2 PORTLAND PLACE, PENRITH, CUMBRIA CA11 7QN**

AA ♦♦♦♦

Charming elegant surroundings await any visitor to Brooklands Guest House. Conveniently situated in the heart of historic Penrith, this beautifully restored Victorian terraced house provides an excellent base for exploring the many and various delights of the English Lakes. Debbie and Leon will make it their business to ensure that your stay is as enjoyable as possible and that you will want to return to repeat the experience time and again. Bed and Breakfast from £17.

**Tel: 01768 863395 • Fax: 01768 864895**
website: www.SmoothHound.co.uk

**CUMBRIA**

## THE GATE HOTEL & ORCHID SIAM RESTAURANT

An attractive family-run business on the outskirts of Appleby within easy reach of the town centre with its shops, castle and swimming pool and approximately one mile from the golf course. It is tastefully decorated with panelling from the steam ship 'The Berengaria'. A traditional log fire enhances the warm and friendly service offered all year round. Our rooms are en suite and well furnished with colour TV and tea/coffee trays. There is ample parking, a pleasant enclosed garden and play area. Pets welcome by arrangement. Specialising in Thai food we also offer conventional English food. Licensed. Bed and Breakfast from £25 to £30 per person; Evening Meal from £4.95 to £12.50.

*Mrs Souter*

THE GATE HOTEL, BONGATE, APPLEBY CA16 6LH TEL: 017683 52688; FAX: 017683 53858 WEBSITE: WWW.APPLEBY/WEB.CO.UK/GATE

## THE SWAN HOTEL KESWICK

A family-run 17th century former coaching inn set in idyllic surroundings twixt lake and mountains. For a true sense of beauty, history and relaxation, cossetted by polite friendly, staff catering for your every need. Enjoy an open fire, lake walks, imaginative home-cooking and real ales. Bed and Breakfast from £29 per person per night; Dinner, Bed and Breakfast from £45 per night. Three nights Dinner, Bed and Breakfast from £130 per person. Children and pets welcome. Open all year. Excellent restaurant and bar food. Winter Breaks November to March from £65 per person for 3 nights.

Please call Colin or Joy Harrison for a brochure. Website: www.swan-hotel-keswick.co.uk
The Swan Hotel, Thornthwaite, Keswick, Cumbria CA12 5SQ  Tel: 017687 78256

## DUNMAIL HOUSE

Keswick Road, Grasmere LA22 9RE • Tel: 015394 35256
e-mail: enquiries@dunmailhouse.freeserve.co.uk
website: www.dunmailhouse.com

ETC ♦♦♦♦

Dunmail House is traditionally built from local stone on the northern edge of the village, it is ideally situated for a wide variety of walks to suit all abilities. The garden is a particular feature of the house with magnificent views and our guests are encouraged to enjoy its beauty with us. Standard and en suite rooms are available, all of which enjoy wonderful views of the surrounding fells. All rooms contain a colour TV, hair dryer and hostess tray. The comfort of homely, country style hospitality, cleanliness and personal service combined with a traditional English Breakfast make Dunmail House an ideal choice for a relaxing holiday. Ample car parking is available for guests' cars. We are a non-smoking establishment and must therefore request that our guests do not smoke. Sorry, no children or pets.

## LYNDHURST HOTEL

Wansfell Road, Ambleside, Cumbria LA22 0EG
Tel: 015394 32421

Attractive small Victorian hotel, quietly situated in its own garden with private car park. Only two minutes from Ambleside centre.
Lovely bedrooms, all en suite. Four-poster bedroom or luxury bedroom for that special occasion. Scrumptious food, friendly service.
Cosy bar. Winter and Summer Breaks.
Please phone or write for our colour brochure.

**BED & BREAKFAST FROM £20.00**

Please mention Bed and Breakfast Stops when enquiring

**CUMBRIA**

## Wanslea Guest House

Telephone: 015394 33884    ETC ♦♦♦♦
E-mail: wanslea.guesthouse@virgin.net

Wanslea is a spacious family-run Victorian non-smoking guest house with fine views, situated just a stroll from the village and Lake shore with walks beginning at the door. We offer a friendly welcome and comfortable rooms, all of which have colour TV and tea/coffee tray; most rooms are en suite. A good breakfast will start your day before enjoying a fell walk or maybe a more leisurely stroll by the lake. Relax in our licensed residents' lounge with a real fire on winter evenings. Children are welcome and pets accepted by arrangement.

Wanslea Guest House, Liz, Mary & Craig, Lake Road, Ambleside. LA22 0DB

Bed and Breakfast from £17.50 per person.
Evening Meal also available to party bookings.
Autumn, Winter, Spring Breaks at reduced rates.
Brochure on request.

## The Knoll Country Guest House
### Lakeside, Near Newby Bridge, Cumbria LA12 8AU
### Tel: 015395 31347

e-mail: info@theknoll.co.uk • website: www.theknoll.co.uk

• Refurbished en suite rooms with TV, telephone, tea and coffee
• Comfortable lounge with bar, open fire, games, books and magazines
• Rich habitats with wide variety of wildlife
• Convenient paths for long and short walks

The Knoll is set amidst wooded countryside at the south end of Lake Windermere, just five minutes' walk from the attractive village of Lakeside and the pier. Within easy driving distance of many Lakeland attractions.

## SANDOWN
### Lake Road, Windermere, Cumbria LA23 2JF   Tel & Fax: 015394 45275

Superb Bed and Breakfast accommodation. All rooms en suite with colour TV and tea/coffee making facilities. Situated two minutes from Lake Windermere, shops and cafes. Many lovely walks. Open all year. Special out of season rates, also two-day Saturday/Sunday breaks. From £22 to £30 per person, excluding Bank Holidays. Well behaved dogs welcome. Each room has own safe private car parking. SAE or telephone for further details

**Proprietors: Irene and George Eastwood**

## Holly-Wood Guesthouse                ETC ♦♦♦♦
Holly Road, Windermere, Cumbria LA23 2AF • Telephone 015394 42219

Holly-Wood is a beautiful Victorian house offering clean comfortable accommodation in a quiet position, a three minute walk from the village centre.
A perfect location for your visit to the Lake District and within reach of the Dales and Morecambe Bay.
Traditional or vegetarian breakfast.
Cosy residents' lounge. Bus and station transfer.
En suite and budget rooms available, with central heating, tea/coffee making facilities, television and hairdryer. Low season and short break reductions
Bed & Breakfast from £16 to £25 per person.
**No Smoking • No Pets**

**DERBYSHIRE**

# SIDESMILL FARM

Mrs Catherine Brandrick

Snelston, Ashbourne, Derbyshire DE6 2GQ
Telephone: 01335 342710
Website: www.sidemill.demon.co.uk

Peaceful dairy farm located on the banks of the River Dove. A rippling mill stream flows quietly past the 18th century stone-built farmhouse. Traditional English breakfast, excellent local pubs and restaurants. One double room en suite, one twin-bedded room with private bathroom, tea/coffee making facilities. Ideal base for touring: within easy reach of Dovedale, Alton Towers, stately homes and many other places of interest.

Open February-November. Car necessary, parking available.
Bed and Breakfast from £20 per person. A non-smoking establishment. ETC ♦♦♦♦

## WINDY HARBOUR FARM HOTEL

**Woodhead Road, Glossop SK13 7QE**
**Tel: 01457 853107**

Situated in the heart of the Peak District on the B6105, approximately one mile from Glossop town centre and adjacent to the Pennine Way. Our 10-bedroom hotel with outstanding views of Woodhead and Snake Passes and the Longdendale Valley is an ideal location for all outdoor activities. A warm welcome awaits you in our licensed bar and restaurant serving a wide range of excellent home-made food. Bed and Breakfast from £20 per night, singles to £42 per night, family.

## Stone Cottage

A charming cottage in the quiet village of Clifton, one mile from the Georgian market town of Ashbourne.

Each bedroom is furnished to a high standard with all rooms en suite, two with four-poster bed. TV and coffee making facilities.
A warm welcome is assured and a hearty breakfast in this delightful cottage. There is a large garden to relax in.

Ideal for visiting Chatsworth House, Haddon Hall, Dovedale, Carsington Waters and the theme park of Alton Towers.

Good country pubs nearby serving evening meals.
Enquiries to: *Mrs A. M. Whittle, Stone Cottage, Green Lane, Clifton, Ashbourne, Derbyshire DE6 2BL • Telephone: 01335 343377 Fax: 01335 347117 • E-mail: info@stone-cottage.fsnet.co.uk*

**Tel: 01629 813521 • e-mail: gm@rowson99.freeserve.co.uk**

At almost 1000ft above sea level, the village nestles at the head of Lathkill Dale, a National Nature Reserve, and is surrounded by the stunning scenery of the White Peak. Miles of footpaths spread out in all directions from the village. Cycle hire and fantastic horse riding are available locally. Rooms (single, double and twin) have en suite facilities, tea/coffee, colour TV, radio, and hairdryers and are centrally heated and double glazed. Laundry facilities are also available to guests. Rowson Farm dates from the late 1700s; the land has been farmed traditionally for generations and has many acres of ancient haymeadows. A variety of Aga-cooked breakfasts are served daily. Children and pets welcome by arrangement. Ample private parking.

*Clean and comfortable accommodation awaits you. Ask about our Drive and Hike service. B&B from £20 to £25.*
**Mr G. Mycock, Rowson House Farm, Monyash, Bakewell, Derbyshire DE45 1JH**

## DERBYSHIRE/DEVON

### THORNHILL HOTEL
**Sea Front, Teignmouth TQ14 8TA**
Tel 01626 773460 • website: www.english-riviera.co.uk/hotels/thornhill/index.htm

An elegant and immaculate 10 bedroomed licensed Georgian Hotel. Convenient parking. Level, quiet location on sea front, close to all amenities. En suite, colour Tv's. Non-smoking. Superb food. Large comfortable lounge. Ground floor bedroom. Teignmouth has a long level Promenade, beautiful flowers and 'Den Lawns'. Safe, sandy beach. Cliff walks. Bowling, tennis, golf, fishing, sailing, theatre and shops. Good public transport. Ideal base for exploring country villages, Dartmoor, diverse resorts, Cities of Exeter and Plymouth. Come to the Thornhill and enjoy yourselves. Bed & Breakfast £25.00, Half Board £36.50. Reductions for 3 or more nights.

### FOLLY FOOT

A warm welcome awaits you at "Folly Foot", a modern bungalow 50 metres from a sandy beach and the South West Way coastal footpath. The beach is safe for swimming, surfing and body-boarding. There is a lifeguard in season. Well known area for divers. Golf course two miles. The picturesque towns of Salcombe, Totnes, Modbury and Kingsbridge are within easy reach. Bigbury on Sea and Burgh Island only a few minutes walk. Four excellent local pubs. A high standard of decoration in all bedrooms, one double en suite, one double and single en suite, one double room and one single room with washing facilities in large bathroom. All bedrooms have TV, clock radio, tea/coffee facilities and central heating. Hearty breakfast, vegetarians welcome. Partially heated swimming pool. Children over eight years preferred. Sorry no smoking in the house. Parking. Drying facilities for walkers and wetsuits. Bed and Breakfast from £20 per night, reduced rates for children under 12. Brochure available.

**Mrs Carol Walsh, Folly Foot, Challaborough, Bigbury on Sea, Kingsbridge TQ7 4JB Tel: 01548 810036**

### Varley House, Chambercombe Park, Ilfracombe EX34 9QW
Tel: 01271 863927 • Fax: 01271 879299 • e-mail: info@varleyhouse.co.uk • website: www.varleyhouse.co.uk

Built at the turn of the century for returning officers from the Boer War, Varley generates a feeling of warmth and relaxation, combined with an enviable position overlooking Hillsborough Nature Reserve. Winding paths lead to the Harbour and several secluded coves. Our attractive, spacious, fully en suite, non-smoking bedrooms all have colour TV, central heating, generous beverage tray, hairdryer and clock radio alarm. Superb food, beautiful surroundings and that special friendly atmosphere so essential to a relaxing holiday. Cosy separate bar. Car Park. Children over five years of age. Dogs by arrangement. Bed and Breakfast from £24 per person. Weekly from £160 per person. Dinner available £12.

### Recommended SHORT BREAK HOLIDAYS IN BRITAIN

*Introduced by John Carter, TV Holiday Expert and Journalist*
Specifically designed to cater for the most rapidly growing sector of the holiday market in the UK. Illustrated details of hotels offering special "Bargain Breaks" throughout the year.

*Available from newsagents and bookshops for £4.99 or direct from the publishers for £5.50 including postage (UK only)*

**FHG PUBLICATIONS LTD**
**Abbey Mill Business Centre, Seedhill, Paisley, Renfrewshire, Scotland PA1 1TJ**

**DEVON**

# BRADDON HALL HOTEL

70 Braddons Hill Road East, Torquay TQ1 1HF
Telephone/Fax: 01803 293908
E-mail: braddonhall@tinyworld.co.uk
Website: www.braddonhall.co.uk
**Proprietors: Peter and Carol White**

This delightful personally run hotel is situated in a peaceful yet convenient position, only a few minutes from the harbour, shopping centre, beaches and entertainments.

★ All rooms are en suite, individual in character and tastefully decorated

★ All have remote control colour TVs and tea/coffee making facilities

★ Romantic four-poster bed available for that special occasion

★ Full central heating for those early and late breaks

★ Discounts for the over 55's on weekly bookings out of season

★ Friendly relaxed atmosphere

★ Parking

★ Bed and breakfast per person per night from £16 low season to £20 high season

*Please write or telephone for our brochure and book with confidence.*

Please mention Bed and Breakfast Stops when enquiring

# DEVON

## Leworthy Farmhouse on the North Cornwall/Devon Border

A charming Georgian farmhouse nestling in an unspoilt backwater, with lawns, orchard, meadow, fishing lake. A genuinely warm, friendly and discreet peaceful haven. Beautifully prepared en suite guest rooms, ample fresh milk, quality teas, pretty china and bed linen. Chintzy curtains, luxury carpets. Peaceful lounge. The ticking of chiming clocks, sparkling old china, Victoriana. Big comfy old sofas, books, games, puzzles. Also spacious dining room. Breakfast traditional farmhouse, or prunes, porridge, fresh fruit, yogurt, free range eggs, kippers, black pudding. Nearby spectacular North Cornish coast (20 mins). Good walking, fishing, cycling. Quiet pastoral enjoyment. No smoking. No pets.

**Phil and Pat Jennings, Leworthy Farmhouse, Lower Leworthy, Pyworthy, Holsworthy, North Devon EX22 6SJ.**
**Telephone: 01409 259469**

## WENTWORTH HOUSE

Wentworth House, a friendly family run private hotel built as a gentlemans residence in 1857, standing in lovely gardens only a stone's throw from the town.. and minutes from the sea, harbour and Torrs Walks. En-suite rooms with colour TV and tea/coffee making facilities. Family rooms sleeping up to four persons. Home cooked food with packed lunches on request. Spacious bar/lounge. Secure storage for bicycles etc. Private parking in grounds. Open all year. Bed & Breakfast from £17.00. Bed, Breakfast & Evening Meal from £23.50. Stay a few days or a week, we will make your visit a pleasant one.

**2 Belmont Road, Ilfracombe EX34 8DR Tel & Fax: 01271 863048**

## Sunnymeade Country Hotel West Down, North Devon EX34 8NT

Small friendly family run country hotel. Close to Woolacombe's Blue Flag Beach and Exmoor
Many local activities eg: golf, horse riding, surfing, cycling & walking and clay pigeon shooting
Award winning home cooked food using local Devon produce
Special Diets can be accommodated
Licensed bar, 2 ground floor rooms
Large enclosed gardens. Secure car park

**Tel: 01271 863668**
**Web: www.sunnymeade.co.uk**

David and Marianna invite you to relax, smoke-free in the comfort of their elegant, lovingly restored period Victorian house, near lovely Bicclescombe Park in Ilfracombe, on Devon's romantic Atlantic Coast. We offer delightful spacious, individually designed, en suite bedrooms. We also have a reputation for scrumptious homemade fare. Private car park.

**"Lyncott" Guest House, 56 St Brannock's Road, Ilfracombe, North Devon EX34 8EQ**
**Tel/Fax: 01271 862425**
**Website: www.s-h-systems.co.uk/hotels/lyncott.html**

ETC ♦♦♦♦

*Relax in elegant smoke-free surroundings*

**Please mention Bed and Breakfast Stops when enquiring**

### DEVON/DORSET

## Willow Bridge

★ Lovely beaches ★ sailing ★ fishing ★ golf ★ bowls ★ tennis ★ swimming in a modern indoor pool ★ theatre ★ cinema ★ concerts ★ art festivals-Sidmouth Carnival ★ Many wonderful gardens to visit and relax in!

**Millford Road, Sidmouth, Devon EX10 8DR**
**Tel/Fax: 01395 513599**

The Willow Bridge has an enviable reputation for good food, comfort and a happy atmosphere. Picturesque riverside setting overlooking Byes Park, yet only five minutes' level walk from Regency Town and esplanade. Bedrooms en suite with colour TV etc. Dining room, licensed bar. Private car park. Non smoking. Full Fire certificate. Brochure on request.

## Lyme Bay House Hotel

Lyme Bay House is on the sea front, near to rail and coach stations and shops. Teignmouth is a popular holiday resort with a long sandy beach and pier.

• En suite available • Lift – no steps • Bed & Breakfast from £18

**Teignmouth, Seafront, South Devon TQ14 8SZ  Tel: 01626 772953**

## Silverlands Hotel
**27 Newton Road, Torquay TQ2 5DB**
**Telephone: 01803 292013**

Situated on a main route to town and beach (approximately half-a-mile). Superb family-run guest house. Eleven superior rooms furnished and decorated to a high standard, mostly en suite. Relaxed and homely atmosphere. Satellite TV, hot and cold wash facilities, tea and coffee making, full central heating available in all rooms. Ample car parking. Full English breakfast.

Open all year. From £14 to £20 per person
• ETB COMMENDED • AA QQQ •

## MARSHWOOD MANOR

ETC ♦♦♦♦
Near Bridport, Near Charmouth
Dorset DT6 5NS
Tel: Broadwindsor (01308) 868442
Website: www.marshwoodmanor.co.uk

Five tastefully furnished en suite rooms. Close to Charmouth and Lyme Regis. Bed and Breakfast. Evening meal on request. Speciality home cooking. Weekly or Short Breaks available. Brochure on request. AA listed.

Please mention Bed and Breakfast Stops when enquiring

## DURHAM/GLOUCESTERSHIRE

### Highview Country House

Standing in 1 acre of gardens, in open and rolling countryside, peace and tranquillity awaits. Private and safe parking, situated on the edge of a delightful village with all amenities. Good access from A1m and a springboard for the North of England with Durham City only 12 minutes away. Our spacious ground floor rooms are all en suite and furnished to a high standard with colour TV and hospitality tray. Residents lounge with open balcony and view for miles. Open log fires are a feature of the dining room with fresh fruit and a full English breakfast (grilled). Bed & Breakfast rates from £23 per person per night. (reduced for children) also 3 bedroomed apartment - ring for brochure.

**Durham - John and Jean Thompson, Highview Country House**
Kirk Merrington, near Spennymoor DL16 7JT • Tel: 01388 811005 • e-mail: highviewhouse@genie.co.uk

---

### THE PLAISTERERS ARMS
**Abbey Terrace, Winchcombe, Near Cheltenham, Gloucestershire GL54 5LL**
**Tel and Fax: 01242 602358**

Set in the heart of historic Winchcombe (the capital of Mercia in the Middle Ages), and close to Sudeley Castle, the Plaisterers Arms is an unusual split-level Cotswold stone inn with oak-beamed ceilings and a wonderful traditional atmosphere. The inn serves a varied selection of hand-pulled real ales and a wide range of meals, including delicious home-made pies, daily specials and a traditional roast lunch on Sundays. Upstairs are five well appointed and attractively decorated en suite bedrooms, all with colour television and tea/coffee facilities. At the rear is a large beer garden with attractive patios which overflow with spectacular floral displays during spring and summer.

---

**WOODGREEN FARM**
Bulley, Churcham, Gloucester GL2 8BJ
Mrs Ellie Wiltshire                ETC ♦♦♦♦

A 300-year-old homely farmhouse which has recently been refurbished to a high standard. Situated in a peaceful countryside location, ideal for exploring Gloucester, Forest of Dean, Wye Valley and the Cotswolds on foot, by bike or by car. We offer three attractive, comfortable bedrooms, each with en suite bathroom, tea and coffee making facilities, and colour television. Full central heating, open fires, a cosy guests' sitting room, and a large garden which guests can use. Secure off-road parking for cars and bikes. You are assured of an excellent breakfast. We also offer traditional home-cooked evening meals from a varied menu. Open all year. No smoking or pets. B&B from £19pp.

**Tel: 01452 790292 • Fax: 01452 790107**
e-mail: woodgreen_farm@hotmail.com
website: www.fweb.org.uk/woodgreenfarm
*We promise you a comfortable, warm, friendly atmosphere from which to enjoy your holiday.*

---

### Lamfield   Mrs Caroline Garrett
**Rodborough Common, Stroud, Gloucestershire GL5 5DA**

Delightful Cotswold stone house altered over the years from a row of cottages dating back to 1757. Situated 500ft above sea level bordering National Trust Common land two miles south east of Stroud between A46 and A419, we enjoy superb views across the valley. Lamfield offers one room with a double bed and one with twin beds. Both with washbasin. Shared bathroom. Sittingroom for guests with TV. Set in three-quarters of an acre of secluded garden. Ample off road parking. Excellent pubs locally for evening meals. Bed and Breakfast from £38 per room for two sharing. Come and share my home for a night or two.

**Telephone: 01453 873452**

## GLOUCESTERSHIRE

# The Ragged Cot Inn

The Ragged Cot Inn is a beautiful 17th Century Cotswold Coaching Inn set in attractive gardens high on top of Minchinhampton Common which forms part of 600 acres of National Trust land some two miles from Gatcombe Park and Minchinhampton Golf Club, which has two 18 hole courses and where the Inn's guests enjoy preferential green fees.

The Historic Inn serves numerous real ales as well as the more well known brands and offers a choice of 75 malt whiskies from its traditional beamed bars, with its open fires and exposed Cotswold stone walls. It offers succulent home cooked food complete with fresh vegetables and locally supplied free range meat. There is a non-smoking restaurant if preferred. The ten superb double or twin en-suite bedrooms make the Inn the perfect base to explore the Cotswolds and is a haven for lovers of country pursuits. Dogs and horses are welcome (but please advise beforehand). Located virtually central between Stratford and Bath with Cheltenham just 15 miles away and Cirencester ten miles, there are just too many places and things of interest to list here. The Ragged Cot Inn is recommended in a range of guides including the Millennium Edition of the Good Pub Guide and the Good Beer Guide and is Three Crowns commended by the English Tourist Board. http://home.btclick.com/ragged.cot

*The Ragged Cot Inn,
Cirencester Road, Hyde, Near Stroud,
Gloucestershire GL6 8PE
Telephone 01453 884323   Fax 01453 731166*

### Your Inn For All Seasons

## FROGFURLONG COTTAGE

**Frogfurlong Lane,
Down Hatherley
GL2 9QE
Tel: 01452 730430**

At Frogfurlong Cottage we have two self-contained suites offering tranquillity and a truly 'get away from it all' break. The Pool Room: a double en suite with jacuzzi and direct access to the 30ft indoor heated swimming pool, £24 per person per night. The Garden Room: a twin/king size room with en suite shower bathroom, £22 per person per night. Prices include full breakfast. Both have colour TV and tea/coffee tray facilities. The 18th century cottage, surrounded by fields, is situated in the green-belt area within the triangle formed by Cheltenham, Gloucester and Tewkesbury. Local attractions include the Cotswolds, Malverns and Forest of Dean. Dinner £14.50 (three course) plus coffee, by arrangement. Sorry, no pets or children.

## Edgewood House

Penny and Peter Stevens

**Churcham, Gloucester GL2 8AA
Tel: 01452 750232**

Family-run country guest house set in two acres of lovely gardens. Ideal for visiting Forest of Dean, Wye Valley, Cotswolds and Malverns. Close to RSPB Reserve and viewpoint for Severn Bore Tidal Wave. Spacious, centrally heated double, family and twin rooms tastefully furnished with comfortable beds and colour televisions. Most rooms are en suite and have tea/coffee making facilities. Spacious dining room and lounge. Ample parking. Generous cooked breakfasts. Several excellent eating places nearby. Bed and Breakfast from £22 to £25. Children over ten years welcome with reductions if sharing with two adults. Sorry no smoking or pets. Open all year. Recommended by the "WHICH?" guide.

**AA ♦♦♦♦**

Please mention Bed and Breakfast Stops when enquiring

## HAMPSHIRE/HEREFORDSHIRE

### Harts Lodge
**AA ♦♦♦♦**

242 Everton Road
Everton, Lymington, Hampshire SO41 OHE

Bungalow (non smoking), set in three acres. Large garden with small lake and an abundance of bird life. Quiet location. Three miles west of Lymington. Friendly welcome and high standard. Accommodation comprising double, twin and family en suite rooms, each with tea/coffee making facilities and colour TV. Delicious four-course English breakfast. The sea and forest are five minutes away by car. Horse riding, golf and fishing are nearby. The village pub, serving excellent homemade meals is half-a-mile away. Children and pets welcome. Bed and Breakfast from £21 per person.

**Telephone: 01590 645902**

---

### Our Bench
**Guest House**

Tel & Fax: 01590 673141
e-mail: enquiries@ourbench.co.uk
website: www.ourbench.co.uk

Proprietors: Roger and Mary Lewis

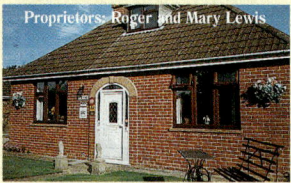

♦ Walking Disabled Welcome.
♦ Indoor Heated pool, Jacuzzi and Sauna.
♦ Non-Smokers only.
♦ No Children or Pets.
♦ National Accessibility Scheme three.
♦ Optional Evening Meals.
♦ Quiet Situation between New Forest and Coast.
♦ Large Bungalow.
♦ Four course breakfast, special diets catered for.
♦ Mountain bikes available.

9 Lodge Road, Pennington, Lymington. SO41 8HH

---

### The Old Vicarage

This Victorian vicarage - set in the heart of the breathtakingly beautiful Golden Valley, with a back drop of the Black Mountains and Welsh Border - was once the home of Lewis Carroll's brother. Come and tarry awhile, stay in our home - share its family treasures and warm hospitality. Our breakfasts are brilliant! Our candlelit dinners are most imaginative - the real taste of fresh, local and home grown produce is a premium. Go on - be pampered!.

Vowchurch, Hereford HR2 0QD  Tel/Fax: 01981 550357
website: www.golden-valley.co.uk/vicarage
Bed and Breakfast: £21 per person per night for four night stay,
£28 per person for single night stay.
Dinner Bed and Breakfast from £36 per person per night.

*Award Winners of creative cooking with local foods.*
ETC ♦♦♦♦ Silver Award

---

### Leadon House Hotel

For brochure contact resident owners -
**JAN AND MIKE WILLIAMS**

Ross Road, Ledbury, Herefordshire HR8 2LP

Comfortable accommodation, good food and a warm welcome await you in our recently refurbished Edwardian Country House Hotel. Situated in open countryside, approx 1 mile from the town centre, an ideal base from which to explore England's most rural Country, the Malvern Hills and Wye Valley. Country walks abound, starting at our own front door.

♦ Gracefully appointed en suite bedrooms ♦ Ample off-road parking
♦ Elegant Lounge Bar, Conservatory & Dining Room ♦ Children welcome
♦ A la carte, bar meals & special diets ♦ Smoking restricted to the bar
♦ B&B from £24.50 pp ♦ Short breaks available all year round

Tel: 01531 631199     Fax: 01531 631476     E-mail: leadonho@lineone.net

**Please mention Bed and Breakfast Stops when enquiring**

# KENT

## RENVILLE OAST
Bridge, Canterbury CT4 5AD  Tel & Fax: 01227 830215
E-mail: renville.oast@virgin.net

Renville Oast is a 150 year old building previously used for drying hops for the brewery trade. It is situated in beautiful Kentish countryside only two miles from the cathedral city of Canterbury; 10 miles from the coast and one-and-a-half-hour's drive from London. Many interesting castles, historic houses, gardens and Howletts Wildlife Park within easy reach. All rooms are comfortably furnished, with tea making facilities. One family room en suite, one double en suite and one twin-bedded room with private bathroom. TV lounge for guests. Ample parking space. Friendly welcome. Excellent pub food nearby. Bed and Breakfast from £22.50 per person.

## The White House
6 St. Peter's Lane,
Canterbury,
Kent.
CT1 2BP
♦♦♦♦

A gracious Regency townhouse in an ideal location within the old city walls. We are situated in a quiet lane, yet adjacent to the Marlowe Theatre and the High Street, and only five minutes' walk from the Cathedral, all attractions and the bus/rail stations.
Nearby is a delightful mix of shops, restaurants and parks.
Our nine spacious bedrooms are all en suite with colour television and tea/coffee trays. We provide an excellent English breakfast, but cater happily for vegetarian and special diets by arrangement.
The MacDonald family will do their best to make your stay comfortable and enjoyable.
Open all year. Bed and breakfast from £45-£55 for double/twin, £55-£70 for family room and £30 single.
Telephone (01227) 761836
E-mail: WHWelcome@aol.com

## Chrislyn's Guest House
15 Park Avenue, Dover CT16 1ES
Tel: 01304 202302 • Fax: 01304 203317

A warm welcome awaits you at Chrislyn's Victorian Guest House, internationally renowned for its hospitality and cleanliness. Full English breakfast, or vegetarian on request. Two family rooms, two twin and one double available. All rooms have washbasins, some have showers, all have colour TV, tea/coffee making facilities, radio alarms and hairdryers. Central heating throughout. Situated in quiet residential part of the town, only five minutes' drive from the docks and five minutes' walk from the town centre, Castle and parks. French and Dutch spoken by Chris. Children welcome. Regret, no pets.
Bed only from £16 per person; Bed & Breakfast from £19 to £25 per person.    ETC ♦♦♦

## Penny Farthing Guest House
Member of the White Cliffs of Dover Hotel & Guest House Group    RAC ♦♦♦  AA ♦♦♦

Spacious and comfortable Victorian Guest House privately owned, minutes away from the ferries, hoverport, trains and 10 minutes from the tunnel. Ideally situated for restaurants, banks, shops and all other amenities. We cater for both overnight and short term stays offering a high standard at reasonable prices. All of our rooms feature en suite or with private shower, colour TV, tea/coffee making facilities. Guests have a wide choice of breakfasts, provision is made for early departures. Quotes for family rooms or 'room only' are available on request. Parking space available on the forecourt.

Proprietors: Annette and Keith McPherson 109 MAISON DIEU ROAD, DOVER CT16 1RT
Tel: 01304 205563 • Fax: 01304 204439

Please mention Bed and Breakfast Stops when enquiring

## KENT/LANCASHIRE

### Bolden's Wood
**Fiddling Lane, Stowting, Near Ashford TN25 6AP**

Between Ashford/Folkestone. Friendly atmosphere on a working smallholding set in unspoilt countryside. Modern centrally heated accommodation built for traditional comforts. No smoking throughout. One double, one twin, two single rooms. Log burning stove in TV lounge. Full English breakfast. Evening meals by arrangement. Country pub nearby. Children love the old-fashioned farmyard, the free range chickens and friendly sheep and cattle. Our paddocks, ponds, stream and small wood invite relaxation. Nearby, our private secluded woodland and downland allow quiet visitors to observe bird life, rabbits, foxes, badgers and occasionally deer. To round off your stay you could even book a short sightseeing or fishing trip on our Folkestone fishing boat! Easy access to Channel Tunnel and Ferry Ports. Bed and Breakfast £17.50 per person.

**Tel & Fax: 01303 812011**

### Southgate – Little Fowlers
**Rye Road, Hawkhurst, Near Cranbrook, Kent TN18 5DA**

Large 17th century country house on the Kent/Sussex border. Near Sissinghurst, Dixter, Bodiam, Rye, Battle, Leeds, Tunbridge Wells and coast. All en suite bedrooms are furnished with antiques and have beautiful views. One oak four-poster, one double\twin\triple, each with TV, tea\coffee making facilities, and hairdryer. Choice of breakfast in our original Victorian flower conservatory. Guests' own cosy oak-beamed sittingroom and use of lovely one-acre gardens. Warm hospitality. Few minutes' walk for excellent evening meals. **ETC** Private parking. Non-smoking throughout. ♦♦♦♦

**Tel & Fax: 01580 752526**
e-mail: Susan.Woodard@southgate.uk.net
website: www.southgate.uk.net/

AA ♦♦♦♦

### CASTLEMERE HOTEL
13 Shaftesbury Avenue, North Shore, Blackpool FY2 9QQ  Tel: 01253 352430  Fax: 01253 350116
E-mail: bookings@hotelcastlemere.co.uk or sue@hotelcastlemere.co.uk  Web: www.hotelcastlemere.co.uk

**FHG DIPLOMA WINNER**          **AA ♦♦♦**

The Castlemere is a licensed family run hotel. The resident proprietors Dave and Sue Hayward have been running the Castlemere for the past 11 years and have established an excellent clientele. The hotel is situated in the very pleasant North Shore area of Blackpool, adjacent to the delightful Queen's Promenade with its lovely views across the Irish Sea. The busy town centre, bus and train stations are convenient and a range of entertainment opportunities for all ages and tastes, including a Casino and Golf Course, are within an easy walk or a short tram ride. Blackpool is ideally situated for visiting the Dales, Lake District, "Bronte" Country and the Fylde Coast. Easy access to M55. All rooms are en suite with central heating, colour TV, alarm clock radios, tea-making facilities and hairdryers. Ironing facilities are also available. The Castlemere has a cosy bar, where evening snacks are available. Evening Dinner is optional. Open all year. Car Park. All major credit cards accepted.

**Terms from £22 per day per person, bed & breakfast.**

---

**Mark and Claire Smith,
50 Dean Street, Blackpool FY4 1BP
Tel: 01253 349195**

*The Award-winning*
### Old Coach House

An historic detached house surrounded by its own award winning gardens in the heart of Blackpool; one minute from the sea and The Pleasure Beach. Free car parking. All bedrooms are non-smoking and fully en suite with all usual facilities and more! Four-poster beds available. Open all year for Bed and Breakfast from £27.50. Licensed restaurant. Private outside jaccuzzi in Japanese style garden leading from large conservatory where smoking is permitted.

*Blackpool Tourism Award 1998/99
NWTB B&B of the Year 1998/9
RAC Small Hotel of the Year 1998/9
Booker Prize of Excellence 2000*

**ETC ♦♦♦♦ Silver Award**

**LINCOLNSHIRE/NORFOLK/NORTHUMBERLAND**

# CLEE HOUSE
### 31-33 Clee Road, Cleethorpes DN35 8AD

Clee House is a magnificent Edwardian property that stands in its own grounds just a few minutes walk from the sea front and many other attractions of Cleethorpes. We have 10 bedrooms, mostly en suite with tea/coffee making facilities, direct dial telephones and satellite TV. Some rooms have wheelchair access. On site parking. All major credit cards accepted. Open all year round. ETC/AA ◆◆◆◆

Tel & Fax: 01472 200850 • E-mail: cleehouse@pobox.com • Website: www.cleehouse.com

---

# MACHRIMORE
### Burnt Street, Wells-next-the-Sea NR23 1HS
### Tel: 01328 711653
### EETB ◆◆◆◆

A warm welcome awaits you at this attractive barn conversion. Set in quarter-of-an-acre in quiet location close to the shops and picturesque harbour of Wells. En suite guest bedrooms at ground floor level overlook their own patio and garden area. Ample car parking. Sorry no smoking in the bedrooms. Ideal for the bird watching sanctuaries at Cley, Salthouse and Titchwell. Close to Sandringham, Holkham and the Shrines at Walsingham. Prices from £22 to £24 daily; £140 to £155 weekly. 10% reduction for 3 nights or more.

---

### Station Road, Docking, King's Lynn PE31 8LS
### Tel/Fax: 01485 518273
### ETC ◆◆◆

# JUBILEE LODGE

Jubilee Lodge offers high standard bed and breakfast accommodation. All bedrooms are en-suite, with colour TV, and complement the comfortable residents' lounge and the unique dining room. Choice of English or Continental breakfasts. Packed lunches are also available on request. Good food and a friendly welcome is assured. Many local eating places offer varied menus for evening meals. The house is situated only four miles from a glorious, sandy beach, convenient for golf, sailing, walking, birdwatching. Close to Sandringham and other places of historic interest. Smoke and pet free establishment. B&B £17.50 p.p.p.n.

E-mail: marjoryhoward@hotmail.com

---

# Westlea

We invite you to relax in the warm, friendly atmosphere of "Westlea" situated at the side of the Aln Estuary. We have an established reputation for providing a high standard of care and hospitality. Guests start the day with a hearty breakfast of numerous choices and in the evening a varied and appetising four-course traditional meal is prepared using local produce. All bedrooms are bright, comfortable and en suite with colour TVs, hot drinks facilities. Large visitors' lounge and diningroom overlooking the estuary. Ideal for exploring castles, Farne Islands, Holy Island, Hadrian's Wall. Fishing, golf, pony trekking, etc within easy reach. Bed and Breakfast from £20; Bed, Breakfast and Evening Meal from £32.

Numerous Hospitality awards.
Private parking Two bedrooms on ground floor ETC ◆◆◆
Janice and Norman Edwards, Westlea, 29 Riverside Road, Alnmouth NE66 2SD Tel: 01665 830730

---

Please mention Bed and Breakfast Stops when enquiring

## NORTHUMBERLAND/OXFORDSHIRE/SHROPSHIRE

### Beck 'N' Call

Mo & Brian Halliday look forward to welcoming you to Beck 'N' Call.

Situated on the outskirts of the picturesque village of Warkworth in rural Northumberland, Beck 'N' Call is an outstanding traditional country cottage (over 200 years old) where guests receive a warm and friendly welcome.
Set in large terraced gardens with a stream, it is within five minutes' walk of the village, river walks, and the most beautiful sandy beach and dunes.
The cottage itself has traditional features including beamed ceilings and lounge with open fire etc. Accommodation consists of one family room and two double bedrooms, all of which have heating, washbasin, tea/coffee maker and colour television.
En suite facilities are available. Throughout the summer months the gardens provide a truly idyllic setting with a wealth of colour. In addition to a charming diningroom, the cottage also offers a comfortable residents' lounge with open log fire. B & B from £18.50

Beck 'N' Call,
Birling West Cottage,
Warkworth, Morpeth,
Northumberland NE65 0XS
Tel: (01665) 711653

• Children are most welcome. • Private parking. • Baby listening service.
E-mail: beck-n-call@lineone.net • Website: www.beck-n-call.co.uk

### Charlton House

*'We think you will remember 'Charlton House' fondly, long after your stay has ended'*

2 AYDON GARDENS, SOUTH ROAD, ALNWICK NE66 2NT
**TELEPHONE: 01665 605185**

Awarded 'Lion Heart Award' Given by Alnwick District Council for most popular guest house.
Recommended by 'Which?' in their 'Good Bed & Breakfast' Guide.

Charlton House is a very special Victorian town house, where our guests are always welcomed in a friendly, relaxed atmosphere. Our guests have five of our rooms, 3 doubles, 1 twin, and 1 single. All rooms are beautifully decorated, some with original fireplaces and patchwork quilts. All bedrooms have private facilities, hospitality trays and colour T.Vs. There is also a comfortable guest lounge. Breakfasts can be a light snack or a banquet. You may choose from Traditional English, Vegetarian or Continental.

**TARIFF FROM £20 PER PERSON PER NIGHT (INCLUDES BREAKFAST)**

---

Mr and Mrs N. Hamilton
Gorselands Hall, Boddington Lane,
North Leigh, Witney, Oxon OX8 6PU
Tel 01993 882292 • Fax 01993 883629
e-mail: hamilton@gorselandshall.com
website: www.gorselandshall.com

Lovely old Cotswold stone farmhouse with oak beams and flagstone floors in delightful rural setting. Large secluded garden, grass tennis court and croquet lawn. Ideal for Blenheim Palace, the Cotswolds and Oxford. Roman villa close by. Good walking country. Comfortable, attractively furnished bedrooms with views of the garden or the surrounding countryside. All rooms en-suite, with colour television and tea/coffee making facilities. Non-smoking. Lounge with snooker table for residents' use. A choice of excellent pubs within easy reach. B&B from £22.50. Winter discounts available.

### *Gorselands Hall*

---

## PEARTREE FARMHOUSE

Farm Grove, Newport TF10 7PX
Tel: 01952 811193

Charming farmhouse set in picturesque gardens, enjoying the best of both worlds on the very edge of historic market town yet in country setting. Immaculate modern accommodation, non-smoking environment, TV lounge. All rooms satellite TV, tea/coffee making facilities, controllable central heating, mostly en suite. Ample private parking. Very convenient for Telford, Ironbridge etc. Bed and Breakfast from £20 per person.

**SHROPSHIRE/SOMERSET**

## Willowfield
### COUNTRY GUEST HOUSE

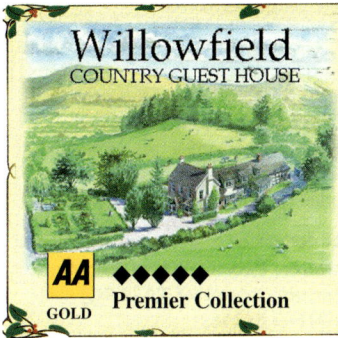

Quiet and idyllic, in its own grounds with beautiful rural views. An interesting house from Elizabethan to Edwardian. All bedrooms en suite with posture sprung beds, settee, TV and Beverages. Guest lounge with open fire. Elizabethan dining-room, individual tables, candlelit dinners. Delicious home-cooking, home grown and local produce. Ideal central location for days out, visiting the many places of interest.

★ **Willowfield is fully licensed.** ★ **Non smoking.**
★ **No pets.** ★ **Fire certificated.** ★ **Ample parking**
**Spring and Autumn breaks.**
Philip and Jane Secrett offer you a warm and friendly welcome to enjoy their hospitality. All is revealed in our colour brochure:

Lower Wood, All Stretton, CHURCH STRETTON
Telephone: **(01694) 751471**

**AA** ◆◆◆◆◆
**GOLD** Premier Collection

---

## *Staddlestones*

3 Standards Road, Westonzoyland, Somerset TA7 0EL
Tel: 01278 691179 • Fax: 01278 691333
e-mail: staddlestones@euphony.net

Relax in the spacious comfort of our elegant Georgian-converted 17th century farmhouse. Centrally located in the historic village of Westonzoyland, close to J23 of the M5 motorway, *Staddlestones* provides an ideal base for exploring Somerset. The area is renowned for walking, fishing, cycling and wildlife and also has some excellent golf courses.

• Double or twin rooms with en suite facilities or private bathroom. • Tea/coffee making facilities in all rooms. • Guest sitting room with inglenook fireplace, TV and video. • Large secluded garden with pond. • Good local pubs/restaurants for evening meals. • Business facilities available. • Open all year. Private parking. Full central heating.
Please note that we have a 'No Smoking' policy at *Staddlestones* and regrettably cannot accept small children or pets.

---

## THE EXMOOR WHITE HORSE INN
### Exford West Somerset TA24 7PY

Situated in the delightful Exmoor village of Exford, overlooking the River Exe, this family-run 16th century Inn is an ideal spot for that well-earned break. The public rooms are full of character with beams, log fires and Exmoor stone throughout. All bedrooms have en suite facilities, colour television, tea-making and central heating, and are furnished in keeping with the character of the Inn. The restaurant serves a variety of local dishes and the bar is renowned for its carvery. This is excellent walking country with a selection of circular walks from the Inn. The village is also noted for its excellent riding facilities.

Tel: 01643 831229 • Fax: 01643 831246 • E-mail: exmoorwhitehorse@demon.co.uk

---

## The Gainsborough Hotel
### Weston Lane - Bath - BA1 4AB
Tel: 01225 311380    Fax: 01225 447411

A very spacious and comfortable country house style bed and breakfast hotel, situated in our own grounds with nice views, near the Botanical Gardens, municipal golf course and centre.
The Abbey, Roman Baths, pump room and shops are a very pleasant walk through Victoria Park. The hotel provides a warm and relaxing atmosphere for our guests, as well as a large attractive residents' lounge overlooking the hotel's lawns.
All our 17 individual and tastefully furnished bedrooms are ensuite with colour and satellite TV, direct dial telephone, hairdryer and complimentary beverage facilities. A delicious five course breakfast is served each day. We also have a small friendly bar, two sun terraces and private car park.
Singles: £45-£59 high season;  Doubles/Twins: £58 - £90 high season.
(all room rates include English breakfast and VAT)

 ◆◆◆◆

Please mention Bed and Breakfast Stops when enquiring

## SOMERSET

Situated in the village of Porlock in Exmoor National Park in deepest Somerset.

Car parking • En suite facilities • Open all year round • Non-smoking • Full central heating • Packed meals on request • Private guest lounge • Radio, TV, tea/coffee making facilities in each room • Ideal base for visiting Exmoor and to see the beautiful countryside.

Telephone or write for brochure or the booking of a room:
Richard and Gill Growden, Parsons Street, Exmoor National Park, Porlock, Somerset TA24 8QJ
Tel: 01643 862563

### NORTH DOWN FARM
Pyncombe Lane, Wiveliscombe, Taunton TA4 2BL
Tel & Fax: 01984 623730

In tranquil secluded surroundings on the Somerset/Devon border. Traditional working farm set in 100 acres of natural beauty with panoramic views of over 40 miles. M5 motorway seven miles and Taunton 10 miles. All rooms tastefully furnished to high standard include en suite, TV, and tea/coffee making facilities. Family room, double or single available. Dining room and lounge with log fires for guests comfort; centrally heated and double glazed. Drying facilities. Delicious home produced food a speciality. Fishing, golf, horse riding and country sports nearby. Dogs welcome. Bed and Breakfast from £30 per person per night generous discounts on seven or more nights stay. North Down Break: three nights bed and breakfast and evening meal £80 per person.

The Old Rectory is situated next to the village church, a few minutes' walk from five miles of sandy beaches. An ideal base from which to explore local places of interest such as Cheddar Caves, Wookey Hole, Secret World and Animal Farm. Fishing, golf, swimming and horse-riding all nearby.

Most rooms are en suite and ground floor rooms are available. All rooms have colour TV and tea/coffee making facilities. We have large walled gardens with children's play area, as well as a private car park. Restaurants available nearby.

Keith and Helen Perrett
Church Road, Brean, Burnham-on-Sea TA8 2SF
Tel: 01278 751447 • Fax 01278 751800

# White Horse Inn

This popular local inn has newly refurbished en suite rooms. It is situated within easy walking distance of the town centre and local amenities. Guests are assured of home-cooked inn food in comfortable surroundings, and the day starts with a full English breakfast. Open all year. Three bedrooms, all with shower and toilet. Children welcome. Bar meals, real ale. Taunton 21 miles.

**10 St Michael's Avenue, Yeovil, Somerset BA21 4LB**
Tel: 01935 476471; Fax: 01935 476480

## THE POACHER'S TABLE
### Cliff Street, Cheddar BS27 3PT
### Tel: 01934 742271
### Tony and Caroline Rymell

A friendly and warm welcome to all at our family run guest house and licensed restaurant built in the 17th century and featuring many exposed oak beams. Situated at the foot of Cheddar Gorge within walking distance of caves and gorge, ideally placed to visit the many local places of interest including Bath, Wells, Glastonbury and Bristol. Three double en suite bedrooms and one twin standard bedroom, all have colour TV and tea/coffee making facilities. Bed and full English Breakfast from £20 per person per night. Evening Meal also available in our candlelit restaurant.

## "MOORLANDS"
### Hutton, Near Weston-super-Mare
### Tel and Fax: 01934 812283

**Resident host: Mrs Margaret Holt**

Enjoy fine food and warm hospitality at this impressive late Georgian house set in landscaped gardens below the slopes of the Western Mendips. A wonderful touring centre, perfectly placed for visits to beaches, sites of special interest and historic buildings. Families with children particularly welcome; reduced terms and pony rides. Full central heating, open fire in comfortable lounge. Licensed. Open all year. Bed and Breakfast from £19 per person.     ETC ♦♦♦

**Hungerford Farm** is a comfortable 13th century farmhouse on a 350-acre mixed farm, three-quarters of a mile from the West Somerset Steam Railway. Situated in beautiful countryside on the edge of the Brendon Hills and Exmoor National Park. Within easy reach of the North Devon coast, two-and-a-half miles from the Bristol Channel and Quantock Hills. Marvellous country for walking, riding, and fishing on the reservoirs. Family room and twin-bedded room, both with colour TV; own bathroom, shower, toilet. Own lounge with TV and open fire. Children welcome at reduced rates, cot and high chair. Sorry, no pets. Open February to November.

### Hungerford Farm, Washford, Watchet TA23 0JZ
### Tel: 01984 640285 • e-mail: sarah.richmond@virgin.net

## Infield House

36 Portway, Wells, BA5 2BN  Tel: 01749 670989  Fax: 01749 679093

Victorian townhouse beautifully restored with period decor and portraits. A short walk to the city centre, Cathedral and Bishop's Palace. Short drive to Cheddar, Wookey Hole and Glastonbury and 40 minutes to Bath. Wonderful walks on Mendip Hills. Double or twin bedrooms, all en suite with colour TV, tea and coffee making facilities. Evening meals on request. Bed and Full English/Vegetarian/continental breakfasts £21 to £24.50 per person per night.   AA ♦♦♦♦

## SOMERSET/STAFFORDSHIRE/EAST SUSSEX

# Highercombe Farm
Dulverton, Exmoor, Somerset TA22 9PT.
**Tel: 01398 323616    ETC ♦♦♦♦ Silver Award**

Relax and enjoy our special hospitality on a 450 acre working farm (including 100 acres of woodland), in an outstanding, peaceful, situation on **Exmoor**. Off the beaten track yet only four miles from Dulverton. We are an ideal base for exploring coast and moor. There is an abundance of wildlife on the farm including wild red deer. We are happy to take you on a farm tour. The farmhouse enjoys spectacular views, central heating, large visitors' lounge and log fires. Pretty rooms with generous en suite bathrooms. Delicious farmhouse cooking, fresh produce, home-made marmalade, etc. Bed and Breakfast from £19.50, Dinner, Bed and Breakfast from £34. Private, well equipped self-catering wing of farmhouse also available (ETC ★★★). Brochure available. Contact: Abigail Humphrey

**e-mail:** abigail@highercombe.demon.co.uk • **website:** www.highercombe.demon.co.uk

---

## *Butterton House*                                       ETC ♦♦♦

One-and-a-half miles from Junction 15 on M6, in beautiful gardens and countryside, (tennis court and croquet lawn). Visit Pottery Factory shops, Alton Towers, Chester and Peak District. Large comfortable en suite rooms. Voted 'Best B&B in England' by Country Rover Brochure Guests. Great English breakfasts. Vegetarians catered for.

*Directions: After leaving M6 at Junction 15 turn right three times. It is first house on the right down small country lane.*

Park Road, Butterton, Newcastle-under-Lyme, Staffordshire ST5 4DZ
TEL 01782 619085 • E-MAIL sjtoast@aol.com
WEB touristnetuk/wm/butterton.com

*Bed &Breakfast £20 - £30 pp*
*Evening Meal £12.50 - £15*

---

## *Jeake's House Hotel*

Dating from 1689, Jeake's House stands on one of the most beautiful cobbled streets in Rye's medieval town centre. Each stylishly restored bedroom with brass, mahogany or four-poster bed combines traditional elegance and luxury with every modern comfort. A roaring fire greets you on cold mornings in the elegant galleried chapel, which is now the dining room. There is a comfortable sitting room and bar with books and pictures lining the walls. Private car park nearby.

**Mermaid Street, Rye, East Sussex TN31 7ET**
**Tel: 01797 222828 • Fax: 01797 222623**
e-mail: jeakeshouse@btinternet.com    website: www.jeakeshouse.com

AA ♦♦♦♦♦ Premier Collection Award • RAC ♦♦♦♦♦ Sparkling Diamond and Warm Welcome Award
ETC ♦♦♦♦♦ Silver Award • Good Hotel Guide – Cesar Award

---

## *Bolebroke Castle*

Henry VIII's hunting lodge, Bolebroke Castle is set on a beautiful 30 acre estate with lakes, woodlands and views to Ashdown Forest, where you will find 'Pooh Bridge'. Antiques and beamed ceilings add to the atmosphere. four-poster suite available. B&B or Self-Catering options. Please call for our brochure.

**In the heart of "Winnie the Pooh" country.**
ETC ♦♦♦

Bolebroke Castle, Hartfield,
East Sussex TN7 4JJ
**Tel: 01892 770061**

Please mention Bed and Breakfast Stops when enquiring

### EAST SUSSEX/WEST SUSSEX/WARWICKSHIRE

**C**LEAVERS LYNG is a privately owned family-run hotel with a history dating back to the reign of Queen Elizabeth 1. Set amidst elegant secluded gardens, it offers panoramic views across unspoilt Sussex countryside.
*A perfect retreat in the heart of beautiful & historic East Sussex*
Good traditional English cooking is enjoyed in the intimate restaurant, and the spacious lounge bar offers a wide selection of spirits, liqueurs and draught beers in a relaxed and friendly atmosphere.
All our en suite bedrooms are extremely comfortable and are centrally heated with tea/coffee making facilities and direct dial telephones. Lots of excellent walks.

Church Road, Herstmonceux,
Hailsham, East Sussex BN27 1QJ
• Telephone: 01323 833131
• Fax: 01323 833617
• E-Mail: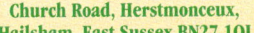

## CLEAVERS LYNG
*16th Century Country Hotel & Restaurant*

---

## Armani Guest house(Gatwick)

Are you flying to and from Gatwick Airport?
Need a clean, comfortable and convenient place to stay?
We are only 12 minutes away from Gatwick Airport.
We cater for travellers and business people.

**ALL TYPES OF ROOMS WITH PRIVATE FACILITIES AVAILABLE ALL YEAR ROUND AT REASONABLE RATES.**

Tel: 01293 511938/ 07973 897675 • Fax: 01293 425172 • E-Mail: Bookings@ArmaniGuestHouses.com

*"Terricon", Ifield Green, Ifield, Crawley, West Sussex RH11 0NU*

---

# THE SQUIRRELS
Henfield, Albourne Road, Woodmancote BN5 9BH

The Squirrels is a country house with lovely large garden set in a secluded area convenient for south coast and downland touring. Brighton and Gatwick 20 minutes. Good food at pub five minutes' walk. One family, one double, one twin and one single rooms, all with colour TV, washbasin, central heating and tea/coffee making facilities. Ample parking space. A warm welcome awaits you. Open all year. Directions: from London take M25, M23, A23 towards Brighton, then B2118 to Albourne. Turn right onto B2116 Albourne/Henfield Road - Squirrels is approximately one-and-a-half miles on left. Bed and Breakfast £20.

Tel: 01273 492761

---

# The Old Rectory

Charming Georgian Grade II Listed old rectory, jutting out onto the green in the beautiful, peaceful village of Warmington. Spacious, well-furnished bedrooms. Oak-panelled drawing room in which to relax.
Convenient for Blenheim Palace, the Cotswolds, Oxford, Stratford, Silverstone, Warwick Castle and the Fairport Convention!
Also many fine gardens, including Brook Cottage, nearby. Good restaurants close to hand, including 'The Plough' in the village itself.

Warmington - Banbury - OX17 1BU
Tel: 01295 690531; Fax: 01295 690526
e-mail: sirwhcockcroft@clara.co.uk

Please mention Bed and Breakfast Stops when enquiring

## WARWICKSHIRE/WORCESTERSHIRE

### Penryn Guest House
**126 ALCESTER ROAD • STRATFORD-UPON-AVON CV37 9DP**
Telephone: +44(0)1789 293718 • Fax: +44(0)1789 266077
e-mail: penrynhouse@btinternet.com
website: www.smoothHound.co.uk/hotels/penryn.html

Penryn Guest house is personally run by Andrew and Gill Carr, who provide a comfortable and friendly environment. Most bedrooms en suite with colour TV, hairdryer and tea/coffee making facilities. Situated one mile from town centre, convenient for all major Shakespearean attractions, with Warwick Castle and Cotswolds villages within easy reach. Private car park. Full English or Continental breakfast served. All major credit cards accepted.

**STRICTLY NON SMOKING**

ETC/RAC ♦♦♦♦

### ♦♦ Linhill ♦♦

**35 Evesham Place, Stratford-upon-Avon CV37 6HT**
Tel: 01789 292879 • Fax: 01789 299691
• E-mail: linhill@bigwig.net • Web: Linhillguesthouse.co.uk

Linhill is a comfortable Victorian Guest House run by a friendly young family. It is situated only five minutes' walk from Stratford's town centre with its wide choice of fine restaurants and world famous Royal Shakespeare Theatre. Every bedroom at Linhill has central heating, colour TV, tea/coffee making facilities and washbasin. En suite facilities are also available, as are packed lunches and evening meals. Bicycle hire and babysitting facilities if desired. Leave the children with us and re-discover the delight of a candlelit dinner in one of Stratford's inviting restaurants. Bed and Breakfast from £16 to £30; Evening Meal from £6.50 to £8. Reduced rates for Senior Citizens.

### THE GLOBE HOTEL & LICENSED RESTAURANT
**54 Birmingham Road, Alcester B49 5EG • Tel & Fax: +44 (0)1789 763287**

Situated in the historic market town of Alcester with its many timber-framed buildings from as early as the 16th century. The Globe Hotel offers the best in hospitality, luxury accommodation, outstanding cuisine and service. All centrally heated bedrooms are en suite with colour TV and hospitality trays. Our conservatory lounge-bar provides a perfect atmosphere to relax. Local to Bagley Hall and Coughton Court we are ideally placed for Stratford-upon-Avon (seven miles) historic Warwick, motorway networks M40/M42, NEC, airport 30 minutes and touring the Cotswolds with its many places of interest and beauty. Open all year. Colour brochure available.

**ETC grading applied for. Ground Floor Room and Disabled Access**

### Hidelow House
**Acton Green, Acton Beauchamp, Worcester WR6 5AH**
**Near Malvern.** Lovely small stone country house amongst peaceful pastureland on the Herefordshire/Worcestershire borders. Central for many places of historical interest, walking and golf. Tastefully refurbished en suite rooms; magnificent residents' lounge with grand piano; log fires on cooler days, sun-terrace overlooking extensive gardens, fishpool, waterfall and stunning open views across unspoilt Herefordshire countryside. **Suite with four poster bed.** Disabled persons accommodation in adjoining adapted cottage. Home cooked evening meals by arrangement. Personal transport service. Self-catering cottages nearby in converted stone and timber hop and tithe barns.

**Silver SILVER AWARD**

Tel: 01886 884547 • Fax: 01886 884060 • E-mail: fhg@hidelow.co.uk • Web: www.hidelow.co.uk

**NORTH YORKSHIRE**

## THE RED HOUSE
**OSWALDKIRK, YORK, YO62 5XY**
Tel/Fax: 01439 788063 • Email: d.matthias@themutual.net

An attractive period property located on the edge of the beautiful North Yorkshire Moor National Park. It is within easy driving distance of the London/Edinburgh A1 motorway and is situated 20 miles north of York, with easy access to the coast and the historic towns of Harrogate, Whitby and Scarborough.

The Red House is close to Ampleforth Abbey and is set in ¾ acre offering good en-suite accommodation. The village has a 16th century coaching inn serving evening meals. There are many excellent restaurants and places of interest close by, including Castle Howard as featured in Brideshead Revisited TV series. A warm welcome, log fires in the winter and home cooking guaranteed.

## Browson Bank Farmhouse Accommodation

A newly converted granary set in 300 acres of farmland. The accommodation consists of three very tastefully furnished double/twin rooms all en suite, tea and coffee making facilities, colour TV and central heating. A large, comfortable lounge is available to relax in. Full English breakfast served. Situated six miles West of Scotch Corner (A1). Ideal location to explore the scenic countryside of Teesdale and the Yorkshire Dales and close to the scenic towns of Barnard Castle and Richmond. Terms from £18.00 per night.

**Browson Bank Farmhouse, Browson Bank, Dalton, Richmond DL11 7HE**
**Tel: (01325) 718504 or (01325) 718246**

## SUNNYSIDE

Sunnyside is a large and relaxing home, facing south, and overlooking open countryside on the edge of the pretty village of Middleton. The famous Steam Railway runs from the nearby market town of Pickering and travels through the magnificent Moors National Park to the moorland villages of Goathland and Grosmont. Also of interest in the area is the Eden Camp World War II museum, and of course Castle Howard, which has featured in many TV series. Sunnyside has comfortable and tastefully furnished guest lounge and dining room. All bedrooms are en suite, furnished with antique pine with tea/coffee making facilities, TV, hair dryer and complimentary toiletries. Delicious imaginative breakfasts. Double single and family rooms, some ground floor rooms. Private parking. Gardens for guests' use. Evening dinner can be provided if required. Bed and Breakfast £26-£28 single room, £46-48 double room.   **ETC ♦♦♦♦**

**Carr Lane, Middleton, Pickering, North Yorkshire YO18 8PD**
**Tel & Fax: 01751 476104 • website: www.smoothhound.co.uk/hotels/sunny.html**

## Walburn Hall

Mrs D. Greenwood, Downholme,
Richmond, N.Yorks. DL11 6AF

**Tel & Fax 01748 822152**

Walburn Hall is one of the few remaining fortified farmhouses dating from the 14th Century. It has an enclosed courtyard and terraced garden. Accommodation: two Doubles (one Four Poster bed), one Twin, all with en suite facilities. A guests' lounge and dining room have beamed ceilings and stone fireplaces with log fires (as required). Your stay at Walburn Hall in the heart of the Yorkshire Dales of Swaledale and Wensleydale gives the opportunity to visit Richmond, Middleham and Bolton Castles and numerous Abbeys. York, Durham and Harrogate are one hour away. Sorry no pets, Non-smoking. Open March - November. Self-catering Dales Farmhouse available. Sleeps seven+ cot. Brochure on request.

**BED & BREAKFAST FROM £25 PER PERSON.**   **ETC ♦♦♦♦ SILVER AWARD**

## NORTH YORKSHIRE

### KISMET GUEST HOUSE

147 Haxby Road, York YO31 8JZ
Tel: 01904 621056
e-mail: kismetguesthouse@yahoo.com
website: www.ksmetguesthouse.com

A warm welcome waits you at the Victorian "Kismet Guest House". Relax and enjoy your stay with Nigel and Barbara. Close to all city centre amenities and with easy access to the Yorkshire Dales and coast. 10 minute walk to the city walls, restaurants and shops. 10 minute drive to the railway station. Most rooms en suite, all centrally heated with colour TV, tea/coffee making facilities. Substantial full English breakfast is served. Vegetarians catered for. Secure off road parking is available, as is an evening meal upon request. No pets. Non-smoking. Open all year. Bed and Breakfast from £22.50 per person.

### The Hazelwood
ETC/AA/RAC ♦♦♦♦

24-25 Portland St, Gillygate, York YO31 7EH
TEL: (01904) 626548  FAX: (01904) 628032
E-mail: reservations@thehazelwoodyork.com
Website: www.thehazelwoodyork.com

Luxury and elegance in the very heart of York. Situated only 400 yards from York Minster yet in an extremely quiet residential area and having its own car park, The Hazelwood is a Victorian townhouse retaining many original features where the atmosphere is friendly and informal. Our bedrooms are individually styled: they are all en suite and centrally heated and have been fitted to the highest standard using designer fabrics. We offer a wide choice of high quality breakfasts including vegetarian ranging from traditional English to croissants and Danish pastries. Completely non-smoking. Bed and Breakfast from £32.00

## Other FHG holiday and accommodation guides

**FHG Publications** are available in most bookshops and larger newsagents but we will be happy to post you a copy direct if you have any difficulty. We will also post abroad but have to charge separately for post or freight.

*The inclusive cost of posting and packing the guides in the UK is as follows:*

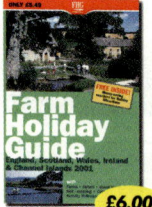 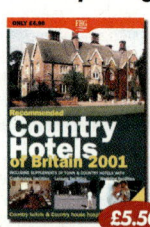   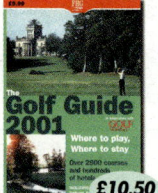

£6.00 — £5.50 — £5.50 — £6.00 — £10.50

  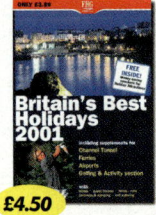  

£4.00 — £5.50 — £4.50 — £4.50 — £6.50

Please mention Bed and Breakfast Stops when enquiring

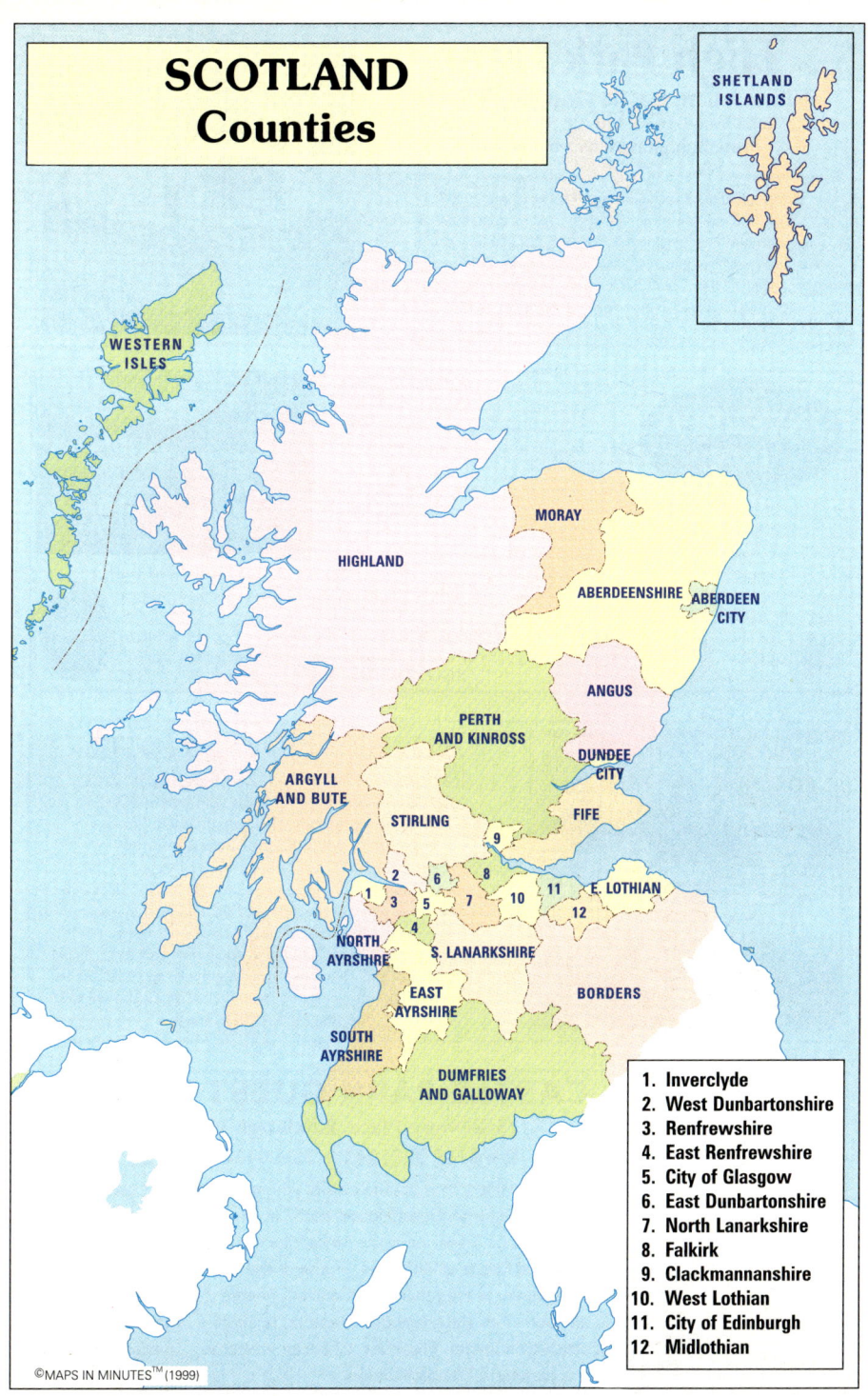

**DUMFRIES & GALLOWAY/DUNBARTONSHIRE/EDINBURGH & LOTHIANS**

# High Park Farm
**Balmaclellan, Castle Douglas DG7 3PT**
Tel & Fax: 01644 420298  STB ★★ B&B
e-mail: high.park@farming.co.uk

Enjoy a holiday amidst beautiful scenery while staying at our comfortable farmhouse situated by Loch Ken. High Park is a family-run dairy, beef and sheep farm offering accommodation in one family room, one twin bedroom (upstairs), one double bedroom (ground floor); all have washbasins, shaver points and tea/coffee making facilities. Central heating, home baking. Comfort, cleanliness and good food guaranteed.
Open Easter to October. Bed and Breakfast from £16;
Brochure on request.

---

## INVERBEG INN

The Inverbeg Inn, stands on the banks of Scotland's most famous stretch of water, Loch Lomond, just beyond the village of Luss. Surrounded by breathtaking scenery, history and culture, and only 30 minutes from Glasgow. Bordering on Rob Roy country, and en route to the West Coast through Arrochar, and the North by Rannoch Moor the location for touring and sightseeing is second to none. The hotel offers a choice of accommodation from comfy individuality to sheer luxury. The three suites in the lodge are perfect for that special occasion. Eat in style in the traditional dining room, offering fresh local produce or take a snack in the Caledonian Bar with Scottish real ale, or one of our fine range of whiskies. Open all year excluding Christmas. 20 en suite rooms. All major Credit Cards accepted.

Inverbeg, Luss, Loch Lomond G83 8PD  Tel: 01436 860678 • Fax: 01436 860686
e-mail: inverbeg@onyxnet.co.uk • website: www.scottish-selection.co.uk
**SCOTLAND'S BEST**

---

## ALLISON HOUSE HOTEL
15/17 Mayfield Gardens, Edinburgh EH9 2AX
Tel: 0131 667-8049 • Fax: 0131 667-5001
• e-mail: enquiry@allisonhousehotel.com
• website: www.allisonhousehotel.com

Personal service is assured at the Allison House Hotel where David and Anne-Marie Hinnrichs take great pride and care in the welcome their guests receive. Situated close to the major air, road and rail links around Edinburgh yet only 10 minutes from the city centre.
The hotel boasts an elegant restaurant, comfortable residents' lounge with honesty bar, and 23 bedrooms all with private shower-room en-suite, offering the essentials you will need to make your stay enjoyable
AA/RAC ★★    STB ★★★

---

## CASTLE PARK GUEST HOUSE
75 Gilmore Place, Edinburgh EH3 9NU
Tel: 0131 2291215 • Fax: 0131 2291223

A warm and friendly welcome awaits you at Castle Park Guest House, a charming Victorian Guest House ideally situated close to King's Theatre and city centre. Travel along the Royal Mile with Edinburgh Castle at one end and the Palace of Holyrood, House of the Official Scottish Residence of the Queen, at the other end. Centrally heated throughout, colour TV in all rooms, en suite facilities available, tea/coffee hospitality tray, full Scottish/Continental breakfast. Children welcome - special prices. Off street parking. STB classification.

**FIFE/HIGHLANDS/PERTH & KINROSS**

## Newton of Nydie Farmhouse Bed & Breakfast

A working Scottish farm situated in the Kingdom of Fife. Three miles from St Andrews, ideally situated for Perth, Edinburgh and Dundee, not forgetting the picturesque fishing villages of East Fife. St Andrews boasts several golf courses including the famous Old & Royal Ancient clubhouses. Beautiful sandy beaches with Blue Flag awards and historic castles. This area also boasts one of the driest and sunniest climates in the UK. A warm welcome awaits all who stay.

*Self-catering bungalow sleeps six in rural position on the farm, see brochure for details.*

**Sam and Doreen Wood, Newton of Nydie, Strathkinness, St Andrews, Fife KY16 9SL**

STB ★★★   Tel: 01334 850204   e-mail: nydiefarmhouse@talk21.com

---

A warm friendly welcome awaits you at this family-run B&B. Five minutes' drive from Dundee, 15 minutes' drive to St Andrews. Good bus service. Near many local attractions and surrounded by golf courses. An ideal touring base – one hour drive from Edinburgh, two hours to Inverness. Cyclists and walkers welcome. Situated on River Tay, one minute to the picturesque harbour. A short walk to the Tentsmuir Forest and four-mile sandy beach – ideal for birdwatchers and walkers. Five minutes' drive to Kinshaldy Riding Stables.
Good traditional home-cooked Scottish breakfast. Special diets catered for. Evening meals on request. Children free when sharing with adults. Discounts available for longer stays. Smoking outside.
Two twin, one double room, all with washbasins, tea-making facilities, colour TV and video.

**Welcome Host Scotland's Best**
B&B from £15 to £19.

**Mrs M. Forgan B&B**
**23 Castle Street, Tayport, Fife DD6 9AE**
Tel: 01382 552682
Fax: 01382 552692

website: www.forgan.ukf.net/

---

Jim and Judy Bennett welcome you to Mossgiel. We are situated in a beautiful countryside setting between the Cathedral city of Dunblane and Doune Castle, yet conveniently placed for access to the A9 and M9. Mossgiel is an ideal base for touring Stirling, Loch Lomond and the Trossachs; Perth, Glasgow and Edinburgh are also within easy reach. The house is furnished to a high standard and all bedrooms are equipped with hairdryers, clock radios and tea/coffee making facilities. We have one double and one family room with en suite facilities and one twin room with private facilities. The guest lounge has a colour TV and is available at all times. All rooms are on the ground floor, and there is safe off road parking within spacious grounds. Centrally heated throughout and operating a no-smoking policy, ensuring you a comfortable, relaxing holiday.

## MOSSGIEL
### Bed and Breakfast

**Doune Road, Dunblane, Perthshire FK15 9ND**
Tel: 01786 824325 • e-mail: judy@mossgiel.com

---

### HAYFIELD COTTAGE

We welcome you to Hayfield Cottage. Situated in our tranquil four-acre garden with the River Farg flowing through, 'The Garden Room' has a self-contained twin bedded room with sitting area around a wood-burning stove. Colour TV, radio, tea-making facilities and en suite shower room. Breakfast is served in our conservatory at a time to suit you.

The 'Best Kept' award-winning village of Glenfarg is ideally situated for touring Edinburgh, St Andrews and the Highlands and boasts the highly acclaimed Glenfarg Hotel to supply your dinner/supper requirements.

Come and breathe a sense of peace and history with a walk around our idyllic garden with its very own derelict corn-mill and say hello to the ducks, goose and hens.

The price of £20 per person includes home baking on arrival

Peter & Marion Dickson
Hayfield Road, Glenfarg PH2 9QH
Tel: 01577 830431
e-mail: pdickson@talk21.com

---

Please mention Bed and Breakfast Stops when enquiring

# HIGHLANDS

# Dreamweavers
## The holiday centre where dreams come true

**Artist's Palette**
Scenery to inspire. Create your masterpiece in beautiful quiet surroundings.

**Birdwatcher's Hide**
From Golden Eagle to tiny Wren, this is the place to see the birds of Scotland.

**Photographer's Dream**
Tranquil lochs, stunning sunsets, mountain views, sea scapes, for the keen photographer.

**Walker's Haven**
Walking the Great Glen? Rest your aching muscles and re-charge yourself in aromatherapy luxury.

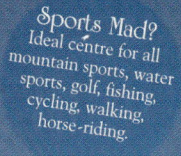

**Sports Mad?**
Ideal centre for all mountain sports, water sports, golf, fishing, cycling, walking, horse-riding.

**Special Theme Weeks**
Explore your Celtic Roots with heritage weeks. Learn ancient crafts with skilled craftsmen.

**Catch of a Lifetime**
If fishing is your sport this is the ideal location for river, loch and sea fishing..

**Disabled**
Specially adapted to meet the needs of all disabled. Easy access and range of aids available.

**Children Welcome**
Active children can let off steam and test their courage exploring the adventure playground or learn new skills in the indoor activity centre.

Come to the heart of the Highlands and experience the ultimate in Scottish hospitality. Comfortable spacious accommodation, plentiful home cooking in beautiful surroundings.

Dreamweavers, Earendil, Mucomir, By Spean Bridge PH34 4EQ
Tel/Fax: 01397 712548   E-mail: helen@dreamweavers.co.uk

34   Please mention Bed and Breakfast Stops when enquiring

### PERTH & KINROSS/NORTH WALES/PEMBROKESHIRE

## RIVERVIEW HOUSE
### Leny Road, Callander FK17 8AL
### Tel & Fax: 01877 330635

Excellent value for money accommodation in the Trossachs area which forms the most beautiful part of Scotland's first proposed National Park. Ideal centre for walking and cycling holidays with cycle storage being available. Guest House: all rooms en-suite, TV and tea/coffee making facilities. Bed and breakfast from £21, dinner by arrangement £10. Low season and long stay discounts available. Private parking, STB ★★★.

Self catering: Stone cottage, sleeps three to four people, from £225 per week, STB ★★★★.

Call Drew or Kathleen Little for details. Sorry no smoking and no pets.

e-mail: auldtoll@netscapeonline.co.uk • website: www.nationalparkscotland.co.uk

---

### FRON HEULOG COUNTRY HOUSE
Betws-y-Coed, North Wales LL24 0BL
Tel: 01690 710736; Fax: 01690 710920
E-mail: jean&peter@fronheulog.co.uk
Website: www.fronheulog.co.uk
*Jean & Peter Whittingham welcome house guests*

*"The Country House in the Village!"*

### *Betws-y-Coed – "Heart of Snowdonia"*
We invite you to visit our home where you will enjoy real hospitality. Fron Heulog is an elegant Victorian stone-built house facing south in quiet, peaceful, wooded riverside scenery, which offers de luxe accommodation, completely non-smoking, with full facility bedrooms, en suite bathrooms, spacious lounges, a pleasant dining room and private parking. Sorry no pets. Highly recommended for friendly atmosphere, warmth, comfort, and hostess' home cooking. Full central heating. In Betws-y-Coed, in the heart of the wonderfully picturesque Snowdonia National Park – with so much to see and do – Fron Heulog is an ideal touring and walking centre. Bed and Breakfast from £20 – £28

Fron Heulog has been Highly Commended by WTB.
★★★ Country House. • Tourism Award
Welcome Host Gold. • Recommended by "Which?"
Welcome – Croeso!

---

### TYDDYN CHAMBERS  Pwllglas, Ruthin, Denbighshire LL15 2LS
### Tel: 01824 750683

A traditional sheep and dairy working farm set in scenic countryside with close proximity to Snowdonia and many other North Wales attractions. Your hosts are a traditional Welsh-speaking musical family. Your stay will be enhanced by tasting our home-fare cooking and enjoyment of the peaceful surroundings. One double room, one twin room and one family room - all en suite. Croeso/welcome. Open all year except Christmas and New Year. Evening Meal from £10. Bed and Breakfast from £18 to £22.   **WTB ★★ FARM**

---

## PENYCASTELL FARM HOTEL
### Llanrhystud, Ceredigion SY23 5BZ     Tel: 01974 272622

Penycastell has a fantastic central location in Wales which makes it an ideal place for exploring the Cardigan Bay Marine Heritage Coast, Aberystwyth and Aberaeron. Situated well above sea level the farm enjoys spectacular panoramic views. Cosy and relaxing atmosphere, antiques and paintings abound, along with beams and old panelling. All bedrooms are en suite and centrally heated, and each is individually designed with lots of little extras. One twin available on ground floor, suitable for partially disabled. One four-poster room. Car parking. Sorry, no children or pets. Bed and Breakfast £25 to £45. Special Breaks available.

Please mention Bed and Breakfast Stops when enquiring

# Other FHG Holiday and Attractions Guides

## SELF-CATERING HOLIDAYS

One of the best and perhaps the widest selection of self-catering accommodation, covering the whole of the UK. Established 30 years, and with over 1,000 entries it is firmly established as the market-leader for self-catering holiday choices throughout Britain.

From modern apartment complexes to hidden forest cabins, there is a holiday to suit every need. There is also a large selection of caravan holidays. The guide has proved popular with families and couples who enjoy the freedom of a direct-booked self catering holiday.

## CARAVAN & CAMPING HOLIDAYS

This handy sized guide is one of our most popular titles and has been a best-seller for over 20 years. This guide covers every type of caravan and camping facility with user-friendly symbols to show grading of standards and facilities. As a longtime best-seller our Guide to Caravan & Camping Holidays continues to offer advertisers low cost year-long exposure to the largest single category of holiday-maker throughout the UK.

## BRITAIN'S BEST HOLIDAYS

An extremely popular and inexpensive quick reference guide for all kinds of holiday opportunities throughout Britain. The extensive range of holidays is split into four main categories – Board (hotels, guest houses, farms, bed & breakfast, etc); Self-Catering (houses, cottages, flats, chalets); Caravans (solus sites, parks and camping sites); Activity holidays (camping, golfing, sporting holidays) This guide is very user-friendly with self-explanatory symbols to show services and amenities. It is most popular amongst families and those looking for the easiest route to making a direct booking.

Guides available from most bookshops and larger newsagents. or direct from
FHG Publications Ltd. Abbey Mill Business Centre, Seedhill, Paisley PA1 1TJ
Prices (inc. post and packing), Caravan & Camping £4.50
Britains Best Holidays £4.50 and Self Catering Holidays £5.50

# BED AND BREAKFAST STOPS 2001

Hotels, Guest Houses, Farmhouses, Private Homes, for food and accommodation throughout Britain

FHG

# CONTENTS

**Guide to Tourist Board Ratings** ..41
**Readers' Offer Vouchers** ............43-60
**Website Directory** .....................420-428
**Index of Towns/Counties** ............429-434

## ENGLAND

| | | | |
|---|---|---|---|
| Bedfordshire | 71 | London (Greater) | 61 |
| Berkshire | 72 | Norfolk | 224 |
| Buckinghamshire | 73 | Northamptonshire | 236 |
| Cambridgeshire | 73 | Northumberland | 236 |
| Cheshire | 78 | Nottinghamshire | 241 |
| Cornwall | 83 | Oxfordshire | 243 |
| Cumbria | 105 | Shropshire | 248 |
| Derbyshire | 130 | Somerset | 257 |
| Devon | 139 | Staffordshire | 274 |
| Dorset | 163 | Suffolk | 276 |
| Durham | 176 | Surrey | 278 |
| Essex | 178 | East Sussex | 280 |
| Gloucestershire | 179 | West Sussex | 285 |
| Hampshire | 190 | Warwickshire | 289 |
| Herefordshire | 197 | West Midlands | 296 |
| Hertfordshire | 201 | Wiltshire | 296 |
| Isle of Wight | 202 | Worcestershire | 300 |
| Kent | 204 | East Yorkshire | 304 |
| Lancashire | 212 | North Yorkshire | 305 |
| Leicestershire | 217 | West Yorkshire | 327 |
| Lincolnshire | 219 | | |

# CONTENTS

## SCOTLAND

| | |
|---|---|
| Aberdeen, Banff & Moray ..........330 | Glasgow & District ......................361 |
| Argyll & Bute ...............................331 | Highlands (Mid) .........................363 |
| Ayrshire & Arran ........................335 | Highlands (South) ......................365 |
| Borders ........................................338 | Lanarkshire ................................370 |
| Dumfries & Galloway ..................340 | Perth & Kinross .........................371 |
| Dunbartonshire ..........................344 | Stirling & District .......................376 |
| Dundee & Angus .........................344 | Scottish Islands...........................377 |
| Edinburgh & Lothians .................346 | |
| Fife...............................................357 | |

## WALES

| | |
|---|---|
| Anglesey & Gwynedd...................382 | Pembrokeshire ............................395 |
| North Wales ................................386 | Powys...........................................398 |
| Cardiganshire..............................393 | South Wales ................................402 |
| Carmarthenshire ........................394 | |

## NORTHERN IRELAND

Co. Down......................................405

## REPUBLIC OF IRELAND

| | |
|---|---|
| Co. Kerry .....................................406 | Co. Kildare .................................406 |

## Special Welcome Supplements

Non-Smoking ........................................................................407
Disabled ................................................................................414
Special Diets .........................................................................416

# FOREWORD

We are pleased to introduce readers of this year 2001 edition of *Bed and Breakfast Stops* to a large selection of overnight accommodation. You will find well over 1000 entries each with a clear description, many illustrated and all with full contact details, offering town or country hospitality for the holiday or the business traveller. Our Supplements will direct you quickly to accommodation for Non-smokers, the Disabled or those with Special Diets. To add to your holiday enjoyment we have arranged with the proprietors and managers of a range of holiday attractions to offer our readers FREE or REDUCED RATE entry during 2001. We hope that you will find this useful.

Anne Cuthbertson
*Editor*

ISBN 185055 320 3
© IPC Media Ltd 2001
Cover photographs: Still Moving Picture Co.
Cover design: Oliver Dunster, Focus Network

No part of this publication may be reproduced by any means or transmitted without the permission of the Publishers.

Maps: ©MAPS IN MINUTES™ (1999)

Typeset by FHG Publications Ltd. Paisley.
Printed and bound in Great Britain by William Clowes, Beccles, Suffolk.

Distribution. Book Trade: WLM, Unit 11, Newmarket Court, Newmarket Drive, Derby DE24 8NW
(Tel: 01332 573737. Fax: 01332 573399).
News Trade: Market Force (UK) Ltd, 247 Tottenham Court Road, London W1P 0AU
(Tel: 020 7261 6809; Fax: 020 7261 7227).

Published by FHG Publications Ltd., Abbey Mill Business Centre,
Seedhill, Paisley PA1 ITJ (Tel: 0141-887 0428 Fax: 0141-889 7204).
e-mail: fhg@ipcmedia.com

US ISBN 1-55650 916 2
Distributed in the United States by
Hunter Publishing Inc., 130 Campus Drive, Edison, N.J. 08818, USA

*Bed & Breakfast Stops* is an FHG publication, published by
IPC Country & Leisure Media Ltd, part of IPC Media Group of Companies.

# Ratings You Can Trust

## ENGLAND

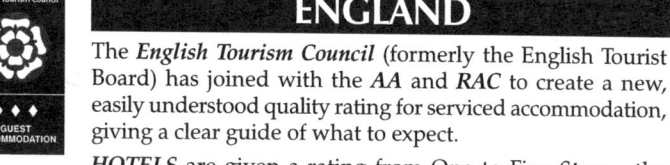

The *English Tourism Council* (formerly the English Tourist Board) has joined with the *AA* and *RAC* to create a new, easily understood quality rating for serviced accommodation, giving a clear guide of what to expect.

*HOTELS* are given a rating from One to Five *Stars* – the more Stars, the higher the quality and the greater the range of facilities and level of services provided.

*GUEST ACCOMMODATION*, which includes guest houses, bed and breakfasts, inns and farmhouses, is rated from One to Five *Diamonds*. Progressively higher levels of quality and customer care must be provided for each one of the One to Five Diamond ratings.

*HOLIDAY PARKS, TOURING PARKS and CAMPING PARKS* are now also assessed using *Stars*. Standards of quality range from a One Star (acceptable) to a Five Star (exceptional) park.

Look out also for the new *SELF-CATERING* Star ratings. The more *Stars* (from One to Five) awarded to an establishment, the higher the levels of quality you can expect. Establishments at higher rating levels also have to meet some additional requirements for facilities.

NB *Some self-catering properties had not been assessed at the time of going to press and in these cases the old-style KEY symbols will still be shown.*

## SCOTLAND

*Star Quality Grades* will reflect the most important aspects of a visit, such as the warmth of welcome, efficiency and friendliness of service, the quality of the food and the cleanliness and condition of the furnishings, fittings and decor.

**THE MORE STARS, THE HIGHER THE STANDARDS.**

The description, such as Hotel, Guest House, Bed and Breakfast, Lodge, Holiday Park, Self-catering etc tells you the type of property and style of operation.

*In England, Scotland and Wales, all graded properties are inspected annually by Tourist Authority trained Assessors.*

## WALES

Places which score highly will have an especially welcoming atmosphere and pleasing ambience, high levels of comfort and guest care, and attractive surroundings enhanced by thoughtful design and attention to detail

**STAR QUALITY GUIDE FOR SERVICED ACCOMMODATION AND HOLIDAY PARKS**

★★★★★ Exceptional quality
★★★★ Excellent quality
★★★ Very good quality
★★ Good quality
★ Fair to good quality

**SELF-CATERING ACCOMMODATION**

The *DRAGON GRADES* spell out the quality. They range from Grade 1 (simple and reasonable) to Grade 5 (excellent quality). The grades reflect the overall quality, not the range of facilities.

# FHG Diploma Winners 2000

Each year we award a small number of diplomas to holiday proprietors whose services have been specially commended by our readers. The following were our FHG Diploma Winners for 2000.

## England

**CUMBRIA**
- Mr & Mrs Haskell, Borwick Lodge, Outgate, Hawkshead, Cumbria LA22 0PU (015394 36332).

- Mrs Val Sunter, Higher House Farm, Oxenholme Lane, Natland, Kendal, Cumbria LA9 7QH (015395 61177).

**DEVON**
- Jenny Fox, Highstead Farm, Bucks Cross, Bideford, Devon EX39 5DX (01237 431201).

**DORSET**
- Mr & Mrs Reynolds, The Vine Hotel, 22 Southern Rd, Southbourne, Bournemouth, Dorset BH6 3SR (01202 428309).

**HAMPSHIRE**
- Mrs Ellis, Efford Cottage Guest House, Milford Road, Everton, Lymington, Hampshire SO41 0JD (015906 42315).

**KENT**
- Pam & Arthur Mills, Cloverlea, Bethersden, Ashford, Kent TN26 3DU (01233 820353)

## Wales

**ANGLESEY & GWYNEDD**
- Jim & Marion Billingham, Preswylfa, Aberdovey, Gwynedd LL35 0LE (01654 767239)

**NORTH WALES**
- Bob & Nesta Wivell, Pen-Y-Bont Fawr, Cynwyd, Near Corwen, North Wales LL21 0ET (01490 412663)

## Scotland

**ABERDEENSHIRE, BANFF & MORAY**
- Garth Hotel, Grantown on Spey, Morayshire PH26 3HN (01479 872836)

**PERTH & KINROSS**
- The Windlestrae Hotel, The Muirs, Kinross, Tayside KY13 7AS (01577 863217)

# HELP IMPROVE BRITISH TOURIST STANDARDS

*Why not write and tell us about the holiday accommodation you have chosen from one of our popular publications?*

*Complete a nomination form giving details of why you think YOUR host or hostess should win one of our attractive framed diplomas.*

## FHG READERS' OFFER 2001 | Bekonscot Model Village

Warwick Road, Beaconsfield, Buckinghamshire HP9 2PL

Tel: 01494 672919

One child FREE when accompanied by full-paying adult

valid February to Octber 2001

**NOT TO BE USED IN CONJUNCTION WITH ANY OTHER OFFER**

---

## FHG READERS' OFFER 2001 | Trinity House National Lighthouse Centre

Wharf Road, Penzance, Cornwall TR18 4BN

Tel: 01736 360077    website: www.trinityhouse.co.uk

10% discount off all admissions when accompanied by a responsible pet.

valid from April to October 2001

**NOT TO BE USED IN CONJUNCTION WITH ANY OTHER OFFER**

---

## FHG READERS' OFFER 2001 | Windermere Steamboat Museum

Rayrigg Road, Windermere, Cumbria LA23 1BN

**Tel: 015394 45565**

Two for the price of one (adults) OR 25% off family ticket

valid March to October 2001

**NOT TO BE USED IN CONJUNCTION WITH ANY OTHER OFFER**

---

## FHG READERS' OFFER 2001 | Cars of the Stars Motor Museum

Standish Street, Keswick, Cumbria CA12 5HH

Tel: 017687 73757    e-mail: cotsmm@aol.com
website: www.carsofthestars.com

One child free with two paying adults

Valid 2001

**NOT TO BE USED IN CONJUNCTION WITH ANY OTHER OFFER**

---

## FHG READERS' OFFER 2001 | Treak Cliff Cavern

HOME OF BLUE JOHN STONE

Castleton, Hope Valley, Derbyshire S33 8WP

Tel: 01433 620571

10% discount

valid during 2001

**NOT TO BE USED IN CONJUNCTION WITH ANY OTHER OFFER**

*Be a giant in a magical miniature world of make-believe depicting rural England in the 1930's. "A little piece of history that is forever England."*

**Open:** 10am to 5pm daily 17th February to 28th October.

**Directions:** Junction 16 M25, Junction 2 M40.

FHG PUBLICATIONS, ABBEY MILL BUSINESS CENTRE, PAISLEY PA1 1TJ

---

*The world's leading collection of lighthouse equipment. AV theatre and reconstructed living quarters.*

DOGS ON LEADS

**Open:** Sunday to Friday 10.30am to 4.30pm Easter to 31st October 2001

**Directions:** A30 into Penzance

FHG PUBLICATIONS, ABBEY MILL BUSINESS CENTRE, PAISLEY PA1 1TJ

---

*World's finest steamboat collection and premier all-weather attraction. Swallows and Amazons exhibition, model boat pond, tea shop, souvenir shop. Free guided tours "Dolly": 1850-2000 Exhibition.*

**Open:** 10am to 5pm 3rd weekend in March to last weekend October

**Directions:** on A592 between Windermere and Bowness-on-Windermere

FHG PUBLICATIONS, ABBEY MILL BUSINESS CENTRE, PAISLEY PA1 1TJ

---

*A collection of cars from film and TV, including Chitty Chitty Bang Bang, James Bond cars, Del Boy's van, Fab1 and many more.*

PETS MUST BE KEPT ON LEAD

**Open:** Daily 10am-5pm. Closed February half term. Weekends only in December.

**Directions:** In centre of Keswick close to car park

FHG PUBLICATIONS, ABBEY MILL BUSINESS CENTRE, PAISLEY PA1 1TJ

---

*An underground wonderland of stalactites, stalagmites, rocks, minerals and fossils. Home of the unique Blue John stone – see the largest single piece ever found. Suitable for all ages.*

**Open:** March to October opens 9.30am, November to February opens 10am. Enquire for last tour of day and closed days.

**Directions:** ½ mile west of Castleton on A6187 (old A625)

FHG PUBLICATIONS, ABBEY MILL BUSINESS CENTRE, PAISLEY PA1 1TJ

| **FHG** READERS' OFFER 2001 | **The Gnome Reserve & Wild Flower Garden** <br> West Putford, Near Bradworthy, Devon EX22 7XE <br> Tel: 01409 241435  e-mail: info@gnomereserve.co.uk <br> website: www.gnomereserve.co.uk <br> One free child with full paying adult <br> NOT TO BE USED IN CONJUNCTION WITH ANY OTHER OFFER | Valid during 2001 |

| **FHG** READERS' OFFER 2001 | **Plymouth Dome (and Smeaton's Tower)** <br> The Hoe, Plymouth, Devon PL1 2NZ <br> Tel: 01752 600608 <br> One child FREE with one full-paying adult <br> NOT TO BE USED IN CONJUNCTION WITH ANY OTHER OFFER | valid during 2001 |

| **FHG** READERS' OFFER 2001 | **The Big Sheep** <br> Bideford, Devon EX39 5AP <br> Tel: 01237 472366 <br> Admit one child FREE with each paying adult <br> NOT TO BE USED IN CONJUNCTION WITH ANY OTHER OFFER | valid uduring 2001 |

| **FHG** READERS' OFFER 2001 | **Coldharbour Mill Working Wool Museum** <br> Coldharbour Mill, Uffculme, Cullompton, Devon EX15 3EE <br> Tel: 01884 840960   e-mail: info@coldharbourmill.org.uk <br> website: www.coldharbourmill.org.uk <br> Two adult tickets for the price of one <br> NOT TO BE USED IN CONJUNCTION WITH ANY OTHER OFFER | valid during 2001 |

| **FHG** READERS' OFFER 2001 | **Killhope Lead Mining Museum** <br> Cowshill, Upper Weardale, Co. Durham DL13 1AR <br> Tel: 01388 537505 <br> One child FREE with full-paying adult (not valid for Park Level Mine) <br> NOT TO BE USED IN CONJUNCTION WITH ANY OTHER OFFER | valid April to October 2001 |

| | |
|---|---|
| Visit 1000+ gnomes and pixies in two acre beech wood. Gnome hats are loaned free of charge - so the gnomes think you are one of them - don't forget your camera! Also 2-acre wild flower garden with 250 labelled species. | **Open:** daily 10am to 6pm 21st March to 31st October<br><br>**Directions:** Between Bideford and Bude; follow brown tourist signs from A39/A388/A386 |

**FHG PUBLICATIONS, ABBEY MILL BUSINESS CENTRE, PAISLEY PA1 1TJ**

| | |
|---|---|
| Award-winning centre sited on Plymouth's famous Hoe telling the story of the city, from the epic voyages of Drake, Cook and the Mayflower Pilgrims to the devastation of the Blitz. A must for all the family | **Open:** Summer daily 9am - 6pm; Winter Tuesday- Sunday 9am - 5pm. For current information Tel: 01752 600608<br><br>**Directions:** follow signs from Plymouth City Centre to the Hoe and seafront |

**FHG PUBLICATIONS, ABBEY MILL BUSINESS CENTRE, PAISLEY PA1 1TJ**

| | |
|---|---|
| "England for Excellence" award-winning rural attraction combining traditional rural crafts with hilarious novelties such as sheep racing and duck trialling, Indoor adventure zone for adults and children. | **Open:** daily, 10am to 6pm April - Oct Phone for Winter opening times and details<br><br>**Directions:** on A39 North Devon link road, two miles west of Bideford Bridge |

**FHG PUBLICATIONS, ABBEY MILL BUSINESS CENTRE, PAISLEY PA1 1TJ**

| | |
|---|---|
| An exciting working wool museum with machinery that spins yarn and weaves cloth, including the Devon tartan. Mill machinery, restaurant, gardens in a waterside setting. Home of the giant New World tapestry. | **Open:** April to November daily 10.30am to 5pm; November to April Monday to Friday 10.30am to 5pm<br><br>**Directions:** Two miles from Junction 27 M5; follow signs to Willand (B3181) then brown tourist signs to Museum |

**FHG PUBLICATIONS, ABBEY MILL BUSINESS CENTRE, PAISLEY PA1 1TJ**

| | |
|---|---|
| Britain's best preserved lead mining site – and a great day out for all the family, with lots to see and do. Underground Experience – Park Level Mine now open. | **Open:** April 1st to October 31st 10.30am to 5pm daily<br><br>**Directions:** alongside A689, midway between Stanhope and Alston in the heart of the North Pennines. |

**FHG PUBLICATIONS, ABBEY MILL BUSINESS CENTRE, PAISLEY PA1 1TJ**

## FHG NATIONAL WATERWAYS MUSEUM

Llanthony Warehouse, Gloucester Docks, Gloucester GL1 2EH

Tel: 01452 318054   e-mail: info@nwm.demon.uk
website: www.nwm.org.uk

**READERS' OFFER 2001**

20% off all museum tickets (Single)

valid during 2001

NOT TO BE USED IN CONJUNCTION WITH ANY OTHER OFFER

---

## FHG Verulamium Museum

St Michael's, St Albans, Herts AL3 4SW

Tel: 01727 751810

**READERS' OFFER 2001**

"Two for One"

valid from 1/8/01 until 31/12/01

NOT TO BE USED IN CONJUNCTION WITH ANY OTHER OFFER

---

## FHG Museum of Kent Life

Sandling, Maidstone, Kent ME14 3AU

Tel: 01622 763936 e-mail: enquiries@museum-kentlife.co.uk website: www.museum-kentlife.co.uk

**READERS' OFFER 2001**

Free entry for child when accompanied by full-paying adult

Valid 1/3/01 to 31/10/01

NOT TO BE USED IN CONJUNCTION WITH ANY OTHER OFFER

---

## FHG DONINGTON GRAND PRIX COLLECTION

DONINGTON PARK
Castle Donington, Near Derby, Leics DE74 2RP

Tel: 01332 811027

**READERS' OFFER 2001**

One child FREE with each full-paying adult

valid until 01/01/02

NOT TO BE USED IN CONJUNCTION WITH ANY OTHER OFFER

---

## FHG Butterfly & Wildlife Park

Long Sutton, Spalding, Lincs PE12 9LE

Tel: 01406 363833

**READERS' OFFER 2001**

One FREE child with one full-paying adult

valid April to October 2001 (Not Bank Holiday weekends)

NOT TO BE USED IN CONJUNCTION WITH ANY OTHER OFFER

On three floors of a Listed Victorian warehouse telling 200 years of inland waterway history. • Historic boats • Painted boat gallery • Blacksmith • Archive film • Hands-on displays "A great day out"

**Open:** Summer 10am to 5pm
Closed Christmas Day

**Directions:** Junction 11A or 12 off M5 – follow brown signs for Historic Docks. Railway and bus station 10 minute walk. Free coach parking.

FHG PUBLICATIONS, ABBEY MILL BUSINESS CENTRE, PAISLEY PA1 1TJ

---

The museum of everyday life in Roman Britain. An award-winning museum with re-created Roman rooms, hands-on discovery areas, and some of the best mosaics outside the Mediterranean

**Open:** Monday to Saturday
10am-5.30pm
Sunday 2pm-5.30pm

**Directions:** St Alban's

FHG PUBLICATIONS, ABBEY MILL BUSINESS CENTRE, PAISLEY PA1 1TJ

---

Open-air museum with historic buildings housing exhibitions on Kent life over past 100 years. Sample Kentish fare in the tearoom. Medway boat trip, adventure playground, free parking.

DOGS MUST BE KEPT ON LEAD

**Open:** daily March to November 4th
10am to 5.30pm

**Directions:** just off Junction 6 M20, A229 to Maidstone

FHG PUBLICATIONS, ABBEY MILL BUSINESS CENTRE, PAISLEY PA1 1TJ

---

The world's largest collection of Grand Prix racing cars – over 130 exhibits within five halls, including McLaren Formula One cars.

**Open:** daily 10am to 5pm (last admission 4pm). Closed Christmas/New Year.

**Directions:** 2 miles from M1 (J23a/24) and M42/A42; to north-west via A50.

FHG PUBLICATIONS, ABBEY MILL BUSINESS CENTRE, PAISLEY PA1 1TJ

---

Large wildlife park with Reptile Land, Tropical House, Insectarium, Birds of Prey Centre, farm animals, wallaby enclosure, llamas; adventure playground, tea room and gift shop.

**Open:** daily from 10am
April to end October

**Directions:** off A17 at Long Sutton

FHG PUBLICATIONS, ABBEY MILL BUSINESS CENTRE, PAISLEY PA1 1TJ

**FHG READERS' OFFER 2001**

**Cleethorpes Humber Estuary Discovery Centre**

Lakeside, King's Road, Cleethorpes, N.E. Lincolnshire DN35 8LN
Tel: 01472 323232    e-mail: discovery.centre@nelincs.gov.uk
website: www.time-discoverycentre.co.uk

One child free with every full-paying adult/senior citizen

*Valid during 2001 (exhibition only, not special events)*

NOT TO BE USED IN CONJUNCTION WITH ANY OTHER OFFER

---

**FHG READERS' OFFER 2001**

**Southport Zoo and Conservation Trust**

Princes Park, Southport, Merseyside PR8 1RX
Tel: 01704 538102

FREE Zoo Pack per family

*valid during 2001 except Bank Holidays*

NOT TO BE USED IN CONJUNCTION WITH ANY OTHER OFFER

---

**FHG READERS' OFFER 2001**

**Tales of Robin Hood**

30-38 Maid Marian Way, Nottingham, Notts NG1 6GF
Tel: 0115 948 3284    website: www.robinhood.uk.com

One child FREE with each paying adult

*valid until end September 2001*

NOT TO BE USED IN CONJUNCTION WITH ANY OTHER OFFER

---

**FHG READERS' OFFER 2001**

**The Caves of Nottingham**

Drury Walk, Broadmarsh Centre, Nottingham NG1 7LS
Tel: 0115 924 1424    e-mail: info@cavesofnottingham.co.uk

One child free when accompanied by two full paying adults

*Valid during 2001 except Bank Holidays and August.*

NOT TO BE USED IN CONJUNCTION WITH ANY OTHER OFFER

---

**FHG READERS' OFFER 2001**

**Wookey Hole Caves & Papermill**

Wookey Hole, Wells, Somerset BA5 1BB
Tel: 01749 672243

£1 per person OFF full admission price (up to max. 5 persons)

*valid during 2001*

NOT TO BE USED IN CONJUNCTION WITH ANY OTHER OFFER

Visit the Discovery Centre and you'll become a time traveller, experiencing extinct creatures, submerged forests, Viking raids and the Victorian seaside along your voyage of discovery. TIME is an exciting interactive exhibition.

**Open:** Open daily 10am to 5pm (Please check for seasonal variations), except Christmas/Boxing/New Year's Days

**Directions:** Follow Lakeside signs from Cleethorpes seafront, A180 or A15 through Grimsby

FHG PUBLICATIONS, ABBEY MILL BUSINESS CENTRE, PAISLEY PA1 1TJ

---

Lions, snow leopards, chimpanzees, penguins, reptiles, aquarium and lots more, set amidst landscaped gardens. Gift shop, cafe and picnic areas.

**Open:** all year round from 10am

**Directions:** on the coast 16 miles north of Liverpool; follow the brown and white tourist signs

FHG PUBLICATIONS, ABBEY MILL BUSINESS CENTRE, PAISLEY PA1 1TJ

---

Come to the world's greatest medieval adventure and enter our world of mystery and merriment. Jump on the magical 'Travel Back in Time' and ride in search of Robin.

**Open:** daily 10am to 6pm (last admission 4.30pm)

**Directions:** near Nottingham Castle in city centre – follow brown tourist signs

FHG PUBLICATIONS, ABBEY MILL BUSINESS CENTRE, PAISLEY PA1 1TJ

---

750-year old man-made cave system beneath a modern day shopping centre. Discover how the caves were used with a unique 40-minute audio tour.

**Open:** daily Mon-Sat 10am to 4.15pm, Sundays 11am to 4pm

**Directions:** In Nottingham city centre, within Broadmarsh Shopping Centre

FHG PUBLICATIONS, ABBEY MILL BUSINESS CENTRE, PAISLEY PA1 1TJ

---

* Britain's most spectacular caves
* Traditional paper-making
* Penny Arcade
* Magical Mirror Maze *

**Open:** Summer 10am to 5pm; Winter 10.30am to 4.30pm. Closed 17-25 Dec.

**Directions:** from M5 J22 follow brown-and-white signs via A38 and A371. Two miles from Wells.

FHG PUBLICATIONS, ABBEY MILL BUSINESS CENTRE, PAISLEY PA1 1TJ

## FHG READERS' OFFER 2001

**Exmoor Falconry & Animal Farm**
Allerford, Near Porlock, Minehead, Somerset TA24 8HJ
Tel: 01643 862816    e-mail: exmoorfalcon@freenet.co.uk
website: www.exmoorfalconry.co.uk
10% off entry to Falconry Centre

*Valid during 2001*

NOT TO BE USED IN CONJUNCTION WITH ANY OTHER OFFER

---

## FHG READERS' OFFER 2001

**Royal Doulton Visitor Centre**
Nile Street, Burslem, Stoke-on-Trent, Staffs ST6 2AJ
Tel: 01782 292434
Two admissions for the price of one – does not apply to factory tours

*valid during 2001*

NOT TO BE USED IN CONJUNCTION WITH ANY OTHER OFFER

---

## FHG READERS' OFFER 2001

**PARADISE PARK**
Avis Road, Newhaven, East Sussex BN9 0DH
Tel: 01273 512123 • Fax: 01273 616005
Website: www.paradisepark.co.uk
Admit one FREE adult or child with one adult paying full entrance price

*valid during 2001*

NOT TO BE USED IN CONJUNCTION WITH ANY OTHER OFFER

---

## FHG READERS' OFFER 2001

**Buckley's Yesterday's World**
High Street, Battle, East Sussex TN33 0AQ
Tel: 01424 775378    e-mail: info@yesterdaysworld.co.uk
website: www.yesterdaysworld.co.uk
50p off each admission

*Valid until end 2001*

NOT TO BE USED IN CONJUNCTION WITH ANY OTHER OFFER

---

## FHG READERS' OFFER 2001

**Wildfowl & Wetlands Trust**
District 15, Washington, Tyne & Wear NE38 8LE
Tel: 0191 416 5454
One FREE admission with full-paying adult

*valid from 1st Jan 2001 to 30th Sep 2001*

NOT TO BE USED IN CONJUNCTION WITH ANY OTHER OFFER

*Falconry centre with animals - flying displays, animal handling, feeding and bottle feeding - in 15th century NT farmyard setting on Exmoor. Also falconry and outdoor activities, hawk walks and riding*

**Open:** 10.30am to 4.30pm

**Directions:** A39 west of Minehead, turn right at Allerford, half-mile along lane on left

**FHG PUBLICATIONS, ABBEY MILL BUSINESS CENTRE, PAISLEY PA1 1TJ**

---

*The world's largest display of Royal Doulton figures past and present. Video theatre, demonstration room, museum, restaurant and shop. Factory Tours by prior booking weekdays only.*

**Open:** Monday to Saturday 9.30am to 5pm; Sundays 10.30am to 4.30pm
Closed Christmas week

**Directions:** from M6 Junction 15/16; follow A500 to junction with A527. Signposted.

**FHG PUBLICATIONS, ABBEY MILL BUSINESS CENTRE, PAISLEY PA1 1TJ**

---

*Discover one of Britain's best indoor Botanic Gardens and Paradise Water Gardens, an inspiration for garden lovers. Other attractions include the Planet Earth Exhibition with amazing fossils and moving dinosaurs, the Sussex History Trail and Pleasure Gardens.*

**Open:** Open daily, except Christmas Day and Boxing Day.

**Directions:** signposted off A26 and A259

**FHG PUBLICATIONS, ABBEY MILL BUSINESS CENTRE, PAISLEY PA1 1TJ**

---

*Experience history and nostalgia at its very best at one of the South of England's favourite attractions. Over 30 room and shop displays bring the park to life*
PETS NOT ALLOWED IN CHILDRENS PLAY AREA

**Open:** 10am to 6pm (last admission 4.45pm, one hour earlier in winter)

**Directions:** Just off A21 in Battle High Street opposite the Abbey

**FHG PUBLICATIONS, ABBEY MILL BUSINESS CENTRE, PAISLEY PA1 1TJ**

---

*100 acres of parkland, home to hundreds of duck, geese, swans and flamingos. Discovery centre, cafe, gift shop; play area.*

**Open:** every day except Christmas Day

**Directions:** signposted from A19, A195, A1231 and A182

**FHG PUBLICATIONS, ABBEY MILL BUSINESS CENTRE, PAISLEY PA1 1TJ**

## FHG READERS' OFFER 2001

**Stratford Butterfly Farm**

Swans Nest Lane, Stratford-upon-Avon, Warwickshire CV37 7LS

Tel: 01789 299288 e-mail: stratford_butterfly_farm@compuserve.com
website: www.butterflyfarm.co.uk

One child free with each paying adult

*Valid during 2001*

NOT TO BE USED IN CONJUNCTION WITH ANY OTHER OFFER

---

## FHG READERS' OFFER 2001

**Atwell-Wilson Motor Museum**

Stockley Lane, Calne, Wiltshire SN11 0NF

Tel: 01249 813119

2 admissions for the price of one

*Valid during 2001*

NOT TO BE USED IN CONJUNCTION WITH ANY OTHER OFFER

---

## FHG READERS' OFFER 2001

**Yorkshire Dales Falconry and Conservation Centre**

Crows Nest, Giggleswick, Settle, North Yorkshire LA2 8AS

Tel: 01729 822832

One FREE adult admission with every full-paying adult

*valid 1/4 to 30/9/2001 (not Bank Holidays)*

NOT TO BE USED IN CONJUNCTION WITH ANY OTHER OFFER

---

## FHG READERS' OFFER 2001

**Embsay & Bolton Abbey Steam Railway**

Bolton Abbey Station, Skipton, N. Yorkshire BD23 6AF

Tel: 01756 710614

One adult travels FREE when accompanied by a full fare paying adult
(does not include Special Event days)

*valid during 2001*

NOT TO BE USED IN CONJUNCTION WITH ANY OTHER OFFER

---

## FHG READERS' OFFER 2001

**Museum of Rail Travel**

Ingrow Railway Centre, Near Keighley, West Yorkshire BD22 8NW

Tel: 01535 680425

"One for one" free admission

*Valid during 2001 except during special events (ring to check)*

NOT TO BE USED IN CONJUNCTION WITH ANY OTHER OFFER

Wander through a lush landscape of exotic foliage where a myriad of multi-coloured butterflies sip nectar from tropical blossoms. Stroll past bubbling streams and splashing waterfalls; view insects and spiders all safely behind glass.

**Open:** 10am to 6pm summer, 10am to dusk winter

**FHG PUBLICATIONS, ABBEY MILL BUSINESS CENTRE, PAISLEY PA1 1TJ**

---

Around 100 vintage and classic cars, motorbikes and commercials, with over 30 taxed. Superb view of Wiltshire Downs; children's play and picnic area

**Open:** Sunday to Thursday 11am to 5pm (1st April to 31st Oct); 11am to 4pm (1st Nov to 31st March)

**Directions:** A4 from Calne to Marlborough, follow brown tourist signs

**FHG PUBLICATIONS, ABBEY MILL BUSINESS CENTRE, PAISLEY PA1 1TJ**

---

Award-winning bird of prey centre featuring free-flying demonstrations daily. 30 species on permanent display including the largest bird of prey in the world – the Andean Condor. Children's adventure playground. Tea-room and gift shop.

**Open:** daily 10am to 5pm

**Directions:** just outside Settle on the A65 Skipton to Kendal road.

**FHG PUBLICATIONS, ABBEY MILL BUSINESS CENTRE, PAISLEY PA1 1TJ**

---

Steam train operate over a 4½ mile line from Bolton Abbey Station to Embsay Station. Many family events including Thomas the Tank Engine take place during major Bank Holidays.

**Open:** steam trains run every Sunday throughout the year and up to 7 days a week in summer. 11am to 4.15pm

**Directions:** Embsay Station signposted from the A59 Skipton by-pass; Bolton Abbey Station signposted from the A59 at Bolton Abbey.

**FHG PUBLICATIONS, ABBEY MILL BUSINESS CENTRE, PAISLEY PA1 1TJ**

---

A fascinating display of railway carriages and a wide range of railway items telling the story of rail travel over the years.

**ALL PETS MUST BE KEPT ON LEADS**

**Open:** daily 11am to 4.30pm

**Directions:** Approximately one mile from Keighley on A629 Halifax road. Follow brown tourist signs

**FHG PUBLICATIONS, ABBEY MILL BUSINESS CENTRE, PAISLEY PA1 1TJ**

## FHG READERS' OFFER 2001

**The Grassic Gibbon Centre**
Arbuthnott, Laurencekirk, Aberdeenshire AB30 1PB
Tel: 01561 361668   e-mail: lgginfo@grassicgibbon.com
website: www.grassicgibbon.com
Two for the price of one entry to exhibition

*Valid during 2001 (not groups)*

**NOT TO BE USED IN CONJUNCTION WITH ANY OTHER OFFER**

---

## FHG READERS' OFFER 2001

**STORYBOOK GLEN**
Maryculter, Aberdeen, Aberdeenshire AB12 5FT
Tel: 01224 732941
10% discount on all entries

*valid until end 2001*

**NOT TO BE USED IN CONJUNCTION WITH ANY OTHER OFFER**

---

## FHG READERS' OFFER 2001

**Kelburn Castle & Country Centre**
Fairlie, Near Largs, Ayrshire KA29 0BE
Tel: 01475 568685 e-mail: info@kelburncountrycentre.com
website: www.kelburncountrycentre.com
One child free for each full paying adult

*Valid until October 2001*

**NOT TO BE USED IN CONJUNCTION WITH ANY OTHER OFFER**

---

## FHG READERS' OFFER 2001

**CREETOWN GEM ROCK MUSEUM**
Chain Road, Creetown, Near Newton Stewart, Kirkcudbrightshire DG8 7HJ
Tel: 01671 820357 • E-mail: gem.rock@btinternet.com
Website: www.gemrock.net
10% off admission prices

*valid during 2001*

**NOT TO BE USED IN CONJUNCTION WITH ANY OTHER OFFER**

---

## FHG READERS' OFFER 2001

**MYRETON MOTOR MUSEUM**
Aberlady, East Lothian EH32 0PZ
Tel: 01875 870288
One child FREE with each paying adult

*valid during 2001*

**NOT TO BE USED IN CONJUNCTION WITH ANY OTHER OFFER**

| | |
|---|---|
| Visitor centre dedicated to the much-loved Scottish writer Lewis Grassic Gibbon. Exhibition, cafe, gift shop. Outdoor children's play area. Disabled access throughout. | **Open:** daily April to October 10am to 4.30pm. Groups by appointment including evenings.<br><br>**Directions:** On the B967, accessible and signposted from both A90 and A92. |

FHG PUBLICATIONS, ABBEY MILL BUSINESS CENTRE, PAISLEY PA1 1TJ

| | |
|---|---|
| 28-acre theme park with over 100 nursery rhyme characters, set in beautifully landscaped gardens. Shop and restaurant on site. | **Open:** 1st March to 31st Oct: daily 10am-6pm; 1st Nov to end Feb: Sat/Sun only 11am- 4pm<br><br>**Directions:** 6 miles west of Aberdeen off B9077 |

FHG PUBLICATIONS, ABBEY MILL BUSINESS CENTRE, PAISLEY PA1 1TJ

| | |
|---|---|
| The historic home of the Earls of Glasgow. Waterfalls, gardens, famous Glen, unusual trees. Riding school, stockade, play areas, exhibitions, shop, cafe and The Secret Forest.<br><br>**PETS MUST BE KEPT ON LEAD** | **Open:** daily 10am to 6pm Easter to October<br><br>**Directions:** On A78 between Largs and Fairlie, 45 mins drive from Glasgow |

FHG PUBLICATIONS, ABBEY MILL BUSINESS CENTRE, PAISLEY PA1 1TJ

| | |
|---|---|
| Worldwide collection of gems, minerals, crystals and fossils<br>•Erupting Volcano•Audio Visual•<br>•Crystal Cave•Unique Giftshop•<br>•Relax in our themed tea room•<br>•Internet Cafe • | **Open:** Open daily Easter to 30th November; Dec/Feb – weekends only.<br><br>**Directions:** 7 miles from Newton Stewart, 11 miles from Gatehouse of Fleet; just off A75 Carlisle to Stranraer road. |

FHG PUBLICATIONS, ABBEY MILL BUSINESS CENTRE, PAISLEY PA1 1TJ

| | |
|---|---|
| Motor cars from 1896, motorcycles from 1902, commercial vehicles from 1919, cycles from 1880, British WWII military vehicles, ephemera, period advertising etc | **Open:** daily October to Easter 10am to 5pm; Easter to October 10am to 6pm. Closed Christmas Day and New Year's Day<br><br>**Directions:** off A198 near Aberlady. two miles from A1 |

FHG PUBLICATIONS, ABBEY MILL BUSINESS CENTRE, PAISLEY PA1 1TJ

## FHG Almond Valley Heritage Centre

**READERS' OFFER 2001**

Millfield, Livingston, West Lothian EH54 7AR
Tel: 01506 414957  e-mail: almondheritage@cableinet.co.uk
Free child with adult paying full admission

Valid during 2001

**NOT TO BE USED IN CONJUNCTION WITH ANY OTHER OFFER**

---

## FHG EDINBURGH CRYSTAL VISITOR CENTRE

**READERS' OFFER 2001**

Eastfield, Penicuik, Midlothian EH26 8HB
Tel: 01968 675128
Two for the price of one (higher ticket price applies)

valid April 2001 until April 2002

**NOT TO BE USED IN CONJUNCTION WITH ANY OTHER OFFER**

---

## FHG Deep Sea World

**READERS' OFFER 2001**

North Queensferry, Fife KY11 1JR
Tel: 01383 411880/0906 941 0077 (24hr info line, calls cost 10p per minute)
One child FREE with a full-paying adult

valid until end 2001

**NOT TO BE USED IN CONJUNCTION WITH ANY OTHER OFFER**

---

## FHG Highland and Rare Breeds Farm

**READERS' OFFER 2001**

Elphin, Near Ullapool, Sutherland IV27 4HH
Tel: 01854 666204
One FREE adult or child with adult paying full entrance price

valid May to September 2001

**NOT TO BE USED IN CONJUNCTION WITH ANY OTHER OFFER**

---

## FHG New Lanark Visitor Centre

**READERS' OFFER 2001**

New Lanark Mills, Lanark, Lanarkshire ML11 9DB
Tel: 01555 661345
One child FREE with each full paying adult

valid during 2001

**NOT TO BE USED IN CONJUNCTION WITH ANY OTHER OFFER**

*An innovative museum exploring the history and environment of West Lothian on a 200-acre site packed full of things to see and do, indoors and out.*

**Open:** daily (except Christmas and New Year) 10am to 5pm

**Directions:** 15 miles from Edinburgh, follow "Heritage Centre" signs from A899

**FHG PUBLICATIONS, ABBEY MILL BUSINESS CENTRE, PAISLEY PA1 1TJ**

---

*Visitor Centre with Exhibition Room, factory tours (children must be able to wear safety glasses provided), Crystal Bargains, gift shop, licensed tea room. Facilities for disabled visitors.*

**Open:** Visitor Centre open daily; Factory Tours weekdays (9am-3.30pm) all year, plus weekends (11am-2.30pm) April to September.

**Directions:** 10 miles south of Edinburgh on the A701 Peebles road; signposted a few miles from the city centre

**FHG PUBLICATIONS, ABBEY MILL BUSINESS CENTRE, PAISLEY PA1 1TJ**

---

*Scotland's award-winning aquarium where you can enjoy a spectacular diver's eye view of our marine environment through the world's longest underwater safari. New 'Amazing Amphibians' display, behind the scenes tours. Aquamazing entertainment for all the family*

**Open:** daily except Christmas Day and New Year's Day

**Directions:** from Edinburgh follow signs for Forth Road Bridge, then signs through North Queensferry. From North, follow signs through Inverkeithing and North Queensferry.

**FHG PUBLICATIONS, ABBEY MILL BUSINESS CENTRE, PAISLEY PA1 1TJ**

---

*Highland croft open to visitors for "hands-on" experience with over 35 different breeds of farm animals – "stroke the goats and scratch the pigs". Farm information centre and old farm implements. For all ages, cloud or shine!*

**Open:** daily mid-May to third week in September 10am to 5pm

**Directions:** on A835 15 miles north of Ullapool

**FHG PUBLICATIONS, ABBEY MILL BUSINESS CENTRE, PAISLEY PA1 1TJ**

---

*200-year old conservation village with award-winning Visitor Centre, set in beautiful countryside*

**Open:** daily all year round 11am to 5pm

**Directions:** one mile south of Lanark; well signposted from all major routes

**FHG PUBLICATIONS, ABBEY MILL BUSINESS CENTRE, PAISLEY PA1 1TJ**

## FHG READERS' OFFER 2001

### Bala Lake Railway
The Station, Llanuwchllyn, Bala, Gwynedd LL23 7DD
Tel: 01678 540666 website: www.bala-lake-railway.co.uk
Two adults for the price of one with voucher. Dogs are free!

*Valid during 2001 season*

**NOT TO BE USED IN CONJUNCTION WITH ANY OTHER OFFER**

---

## FHG READERS' OFFER 2001

### MUSEUM OF CHILDHOOD MEMORIES
1 Castle Street, Beaumaris, Anglesey LL58 8AP
Tel: 01248 712498  website: www.nwi.co.uk/museumofchildhood
One child FREE with two adults

*valid during 2001*

**NOT TO BE USED IN CONJUNCTION WITH ANY OTHER OFFER**

---

## FHG READERS' OFFER 2001

### Alice in Wonderland Centre
3/4 Trinity Square, Llandudno, Conwy, North Wales LL30 2PY
Tel: 01492 860082  e-mail: alice@wonderland.co.uk
website: www.wonderland.co.uk
One child FREE with two paying adults. Guide Dogs welcome

*valid uduring 2001*

**NOT TO BE USED IN CONJUNCTION WITH ANY OTHER OFFER**

---

## FHG READERS' OFFER 2001

### Celtica
Y Plas, Machynlleth, Powys SY20 8ER
Tel: 01654 702702
Child FREE when accompanied by full-paying adult

*valid during 2001*

**NOT TO BE USED IN CONJUNCTION WITH ANY OTHER OFFER**

---

## FHG READERS' OFFER 2001

### Rhondda Heritage Park
Lewis Merthyr Colliery, Coed Cae Road, Trehafod, Near Pontypridd CF37 7NP
Tel: 01443 682036  e-mail: rhonpark@netwales.co.uk
website: www.netwales.co.uk/rhondda-heritage
Two adults or children for the price of one.

*Valid until end 2001 for full tours only. Not validon special event days.*

**NOT TO BE USED IN CONJUNCTION WITH ANY OTHER OFFER**

A delightful ride by narrow gauge steam train along the shore of Wales largest natural lake through the beautiful scenery of Snowdonia National Park

**Open:** Easter to end September; daily except some Mondays and Fridays early/late season

**Directions:** Easily accessible via A55 and A494

FHG PUBLICATIONS, ABBEY MILL BUSINESS CENTRE, PAISLEY PA1 1TJ

---

Nine rooms in a Georgian house filled with items illustrating the happier times of family life over the past 150 years. Joyful nostalgia unlimited.

**Open:** March to end October

**Directions:** opposite Beaumaris Castle

FHG PUBLICATIONS, ABBEY MILL BUSINESS CENTRE, PAISLEY PA1 1TJ

---

Walk through the Rabbit Hole to the colourful scenes of Lewis Carroll's classic story set in beautiful life-size displays. Recorded commentaries and transcripts available in several languages

**Open:** 10am to 5pm daily (closed Sundays Easter to November); closed Christmas/Boxing/New Year's Days.

**Directions:** situated just off the main street, 250 yards from coach and rail stations

FHG PUBLICATIONS, ABBEY MILL BUSINESS CENTRE, PAISLEY PA1 1TJ

---

A unique theme attraction presenting the history and culture of the Celts. Audio-visual exhibition, displays of Welsh and Celtic history, soft play area, tea room and gift shop. Events throughout the year.

**Open:** 10am to 6pm daily (last admission to exhibitions 4.40pm)

**Directions:** in restored mansion just south of clock tower in town centre; car park just off Aberystwyth road

FHG PUBLICATIONS, ABBEY MILL BUSINESS CENTRE, PAISLEY PA1 1TJ

---

Make a pit stop whatever the weather! Join an ex-miner on a tour of discovery, ride the cage to pit bottom and take a thrilling ride back to the surface. AV presentations, period village street, children's adventure play area, restaurant and gift shop. Full disabled access.

**Open:** Open daily 10am to 6pm (last tour 4.30pm). Closed Mondays October to Easter, also Christmas/Boxing days

**Directions:** Exit Junction 32 M4, signposted from A470 Pontypridd. Trehafod is located between Pontypridd and Porth

FHG PUBLICATIONS, ABBEY MILL BUSINESS CENTRE, PAISLEY PA1 1TJ

# ENGLAND

## GREATER LONDON

### Adria Hotel

44 Glenthorne Road,
Hammersmith, London W6 0LS
Tel: 020 7602 6386 • Fax: 020 7602 9226
e-mail: george@adria.demon.co.uk

This newly refurbished hotel is conveniently situated just 100 metres from the Underground, making it ideal for exploring all the historic, cultural, leisure and entertainment amenities of the capital. Accommodation is available in 15 comfortable bedrooms, all en suite, and offering superb value for money. Major credit cards accepted. Parking available.

*Singles £39.   Doubles £59.*

**SEND FOR BROCHURE**

### Lincoln House Hotel London W1

33 Gloucester Place, London W1U 8HY
Tel: 020-7486 7630 (3 lines), Fax: 020-7486 0166

LONDON
Tourist Board and
Convention Bureau

Built in the days of King George III, this hotel offers Georgian charms and character. En suite rooms with modern comforts. Competitively priced. Located in the heart of London's West End, next to Oxford Street and most famous shopping attractions, close to Theatreland. Ideal for business and leisure.

The Lincoln House Hotel is recommended by British and European consumer associations and motoring organisations. It is also commended by many world distinguished guide books for its good value and very competitive tariff.

e-mail: reservations@lincoln-house-hotel.co.uk
Website: www.lincoln-house-hotel.co.uk

*"Georgian Hotel With Modern Comfort"* **WHICH?**

For reservations call free 0500-007 208

**HAMMERSMITH. Anne and Sohel Armanios, 67 Rannoch Road, Hammersmith, London W6 9SS (020 7385 4904; Fax: 020 7610 3235).** Comfortable, centrally located, quiet Edwardian family home. Great base for sightseeing. Close to river, traditional pubs, many local restaurants. Excellent transport facilities, three minute walk to buses, 12 minutes' walk to Underground, direct line to West End, theatres, shopping, Harrods, museums, galleries, Albert Hall, Earl's Court and Olympia exhibition centres. Direct line to Heathrow, Victoria (Gatwick), Liverpool Street (Stansted) Airports. We have double/twin and triple rooms with central heating and TV. Smoking only in garden. Bed and Continental Breakfast £22 per person per night. Reductions for children. Single occupancy £32 per night.

**HARROW. Mrs P. Giles, Oak Lodge, Brookshill, Harrow Weald, Middlesex HA3 6RY (020 8954 9257).** If you are looking for Ghoulies and Ghosties I'm afraid you won't find them in this lovely 200 year old lodge, or in the large garden. But you will find a warm welcome and pleasant surroundings and a genuine piece of old England. Rooms have washbasins, TV, tea/coffee facilities and central heating. Car ideal, we have car park, but we are also on bus route. A short drive to Harrow, Watford, Wembley, or train journey to London very easy; six miles M25, four miles M1. Single from £19.50, double from £39 including full English breakfast. Non smoking guests appreciated.

**HARROW. Harrow Guest House, 48 Butler Road, Harrow, Middlesex HA1 4DR.** Family guesthouse near Underground, buses and BR station. 20 minutes from central London, 30 minutes Heathrow. In quiet residential area yet near all amenities. Traditional breakfast. Bed and Breakfast from £25 single; double from £45 . Lunch and Evening Meal available. Central heating. TV and tea making facilities. Non-smoking. **Contact Steve Miller (Tel: 0208 621 9090).**

**KENSINGTON. Mowbray Court Hotel, 28-30 Penywern Road, Earls Court, London SW5 9SU (0207 370 2316; Fax: 0207 370 5693).** Listed Bed and Breakfast Tourist Class Hotel with nearly all the services of a four star hotel. Majority of rooms with bath/WC, direct dial phone, hair dryer, trouser press, iron and colour satellite TV. Non-smoking rooms available. There is a comfortable residents' bar and a lift to all floors. Babysitting service on request. the hotel is close to all the major shopping areas and tourist sights and is situated in a residential tree-lined street. we are open 24-hours-a-day all year round. We accept well behaved pets. Family rooms for four/six persons with or without facilities available. Frommers recommended. All credit cards accepted. 5% discount on presentation of this advert. (excluding VAT).
e-mail: mowbraycourthotel@mcmail.com
website: http://www.M-C-Hotel.mcmail.com

**KEW GARDENS. Mrs L. Gray, 1 Chelwood Gardens, Kew TW9 4JG (020 8876 8733).** Situated in quiet cul-de-sac, private newly renovated luxury bed and breakfast accommodation in friendly family home. Seven minutes' walk to underground station with easy access by bus or tube to all parts of London, museums, theatres, shopping, etc. Convenient for Twickenham, Wembley, Heathrow Airport, M3 and M4, Hampton Court, Kew Gardens, Public Records Office, Wimbledon, Windsor Castle, Chessington World of Adventure and River Thameside walks. Comfortable, friendly house with TV, central heating, tea and coffee facilities. Varied selection of English pubs and restaurants nearby. Unrestricted street parking. Regret no pets. We welcome tourists and business people looking for an economical alternative to hotel life in relaxed informal surroundings. Open all year.

**FHG**

Visit the FHG website
**www.holidayguides.com**
for details of the wide choice of accommodation
featured in the full range of FHG titles

**KING'S CROSS. Macdonald and Devon Hotels, 43-46 Argyle Square, King's Cross, London WC1H 8AL (020 7837 3552; Fax: 020 7278 9885).** Macdonald and Devon Hotels are centrally located right in London heartland and well served by public transport. Short walk from St. Pancras and King's Cross and Thames link mainline railway stations. These provide lines to Heathrow and Gatwick Airports, they are also the main lines in the North, South, and West of England. In these family-run hotels, bed and English breakfast is offered in a friendly and clean environment. Competitive prices attract both business people and tourists alike. The Hotels comprise 60 rooms – single, double, triples and family-size. All rooms are equipped with washbasins, colour TV, tea/coffee making facilities. En suite facilities are in some rooms. Central heating throughout. Please write or telephone for our brochure and further information.

**LONDON. Mr J.H. Todd, The Hotel Columbus, 141 Sussex Gardens, Hyde Park, London W2 2RX (020 7262 0974; Fax: 020 7262 6785).** This charming Bed & Breakfast hotel is the ideal choice for individuals and families who seek both value for money and a quality B&B in the "heart of London". Situated in an elegant tree-lined avenue close to Hyde Park and Oxford Street it was a former residence of the aristocracy and has now been converted to provide modern, comfortable accommodation. All rooms now have en suite shower and w.c. Telephone, TV, etc. Look no further for London's best B&B!
e-mail: hotelcolumbus@compuserve.com
website: www.delmerehotels.com

**LONDON. Compton Guest House, 65 Compton Road, Wimbledon SW19 7QA (Tel & Fax: 020 8947 4488 and Tel: 020 8879 3245).** Situated just five minutes from Wimbledon station and within easy reach of Wimbledon Tennis Courts, Wimbledon Common, Golf and squash clubs. Easy access to the West End and central London, and close to many first class restaurants, theatre and cinema. All rooms are comfortably furnished with washbasin, colour TV, shaver light points, central heating and tea/coffee making facilities. We have room service, and if you decide to have breakfast it is served in the rooms for your own comfort and privacy. Hairdryers and irons available, free of charge, on request. Please contact Mrs A Haq for details of prices.

**LONDON. Falcon Hotel, 11 Norfolk Square, Hyde Park W2 1RU (020 7723 8603; Fax: 020 7402 7009).** Situated in central London this 2 star B&B Hotel is family friendly. Established for 30 years and set in a tranquil position within a garden square. Two minutes from Paddington Station, 15 minutes from Heathrow on Express Link. En suite facilities, very clean and comfortable. Triple and Family rooms available. Close to tourist attractions and shops. Full freshly cooked English breakfasts. Affordable prices from: Singles £35, Doubles £55.
e-mail: info@aafalcon.co.uk
website: www.aafalcon.co.

---

Readers are requested to mention this guidebook when seeking accommodation (and please enclose a stamped addressed envelope).

# ATHENA HOTEL

**110-114 SUSSEX GARDENS, HYDE PARK, LONDON W2 1UA**
**Tel: 0207 706 3866    Fax: 0207 262 6143**
e-mail: athena@stavrouhotels.co.uk    website: www.stavrouhotels.co.uk

## TREAT YOURSELVES TO A QUALITY HOTEL AT AFFORDABLE PRICES

The Athena is a newly completed family run hotel in a restored Victorian building. Professionally designed, including a lift to all floors and exquisitely decorated, we offer our clientele the ambience and warm hospitality necessary for a relaxing and enjoyable stay. Ideally located in a beautiful tree-lined avenue, extremely well-positioned for sightseeing London's famous sights and shops; Hyde Park, Madame Tussaud's, Oxford Street, Marble Arch, Knightsbridge, Buckingham Palace and many more are all within walking distance.

Travel connections to all over London are excellent, with Paddington and Lancaster Gate Stations, Heathrow Express, A2 Airbus and buses minutes away. Our tastefully decorated bedrooms have en suite bath/shower rooms, satellite colour TV, bedside telephone, tea/coffee making facilities. Hair dryer, trouser press, laundry and ironing facilities available on request. Ample car parking.

Single Room £50 - £65
Double/Twin Room £66 - £89
Family Room from £25 per person

***All prices include a full traditional English Breakfast and VAT***

---

# LONDON HOTEL

**BEST RATES**

SINGLES from £23 – £42 pp
DOUBLES from £19 – £32 pp
FAMILIES 3/4/5/6 from £12 – £24 pp

WINDSOR HOUSE HOTEL, 12 PENYWERN ROAD, LONDON SW5 9ST
Tel: 44 (0)20 7373 9087  Fax: 44 (0)20 7385 2417

## 5 mins to Piccadilly

INCLUDES BIG BREAKFAST, USE OF KITCHEN, GARDEN

# CENTRAL LONDON!

## FIVE KINGS GUEST HOUSE

Five Kings is a family-run guest house and member of the English Tourism Council with Two Diamonds awarded. 16 rooms, seven en suite. All rooms have colour TV. Situated in a quiet area yet only 15 minutes to Central London, Oxford Street, Leicester Square, Camden Lock, London Zoo, Kings Cross and St Pancras Stations are only two miles away.

No parking restriction in Anson Road.

Single £24-£30                Double/twin £36-£46,
Family 1x3 £52-£56        Family 1x4 £62-£66
All prices include English breakfast and VAT

**Five Kings Guest House**
59 Anson Road, Tufnell Park, London N7 0AR
Telephone: 020 7607 3996  Fax: 020 7609 5554

---

## WHITE LODGE HOTEL   ETC ♦♦♦

White Lodge Hotel is situated in a pleasant North London suburb, with easy access via tube and bus to all parts of London. Alexandra Palace is the closest landmark and buses pass the front door. Prices are kept as low as possible for people on low budget holidays, whilst maintaining a high standard of service and cleanliness. Many guests return year after year which is a good recommendation. Six single, ten double bedrooms, four family bedrooms (eight rooms en suite), all with washbasins; three showers, six toilets; sittingroom; diningroom

Cot, high chair, babysitting and reduced rates for children.

No pets, please. Open all year for Bed and Breakfast from £28 single, from £38 double, from £44 double ensuite.

Mrs Nancy Neocleous, White Lodge Hotel, No. 1 Church Lane, Hornsey, London N8. Tel: 020 8348 9765 Fax: 020 8340 7851

---

## BOKA HOTEL
### 35 EARDLEY CRESCENT, LONDON SW5 9JT
### Tel: 020 7370 1388   Fax: 020 7912 0515

A medium sized, smart family-style hotel situated a few minutes' walk from Earls Court Tube Station. We offer budget accommodation for tourists and students.

♦ Single from £18 - £25  ♦ Double from £28 - £40  ♦ Sharing from £10

---

### Barry House Hotel
*"We believe in family-like care"*

We are a small family-run Bed and Breakfast in the heart of London close to Hyde Park and Marble Arch. The bedrooms have en suite shower/toilet, colour TV, telephone and tea/coffee making facilities.
Rates include Full English Breakfast.
Closest Rail/Underground Stations: Paddington and Lancaster Gate.

**Tel: 020 7723 7340 ; Fax: 020 7723 9775**
**12 Sussex Place, Hyde Park, London W2 2TP**
e-mail: hotel@barryhouse.co.uk
website: www.barryhouse.co.uk

## Greater London

**LONDON. Mr C. Crias, The Rhodes Hotel, 195 Sussex Gardens, Hyde Park, London W2 (020 7262 5617; Fax: 020 7262 0537).** This elegant late Georgian house is 200 metres from the beautiful Hyde Park and Kensington Gardens. For shopping it is close to Marble Arch and the famous Oxford Street and the West End. For travelling it is conveniently situated for Heathrow Express and Kensington Gate Tube – the Airbus A2 for Heathrow stops nearby. The hotel is air-conditioned. All our rooms have satellite TV, telephone, hairdryer, refrigerator and tea/coffee making facilities. For your budget, en suite rooms rates from £50 single, £70 double. All rates inclusive of VAT and include a generous Continental breakfast. Families are specially catered for. ETC ♦♦♦
e-mail: chris@rhodeshotel.co.uk OR chris@rhodeshotel.com
website: www.rhodeshotel.co.uk also rhodeshotel.com

---

**LONDON. Mrs B. Merchant, 562 Caledonian Road, Holloway, London N7 9SD (020 7607 0930).** Comfortable well furnished rooms in small private home, full central heating. Two double and one single rooms, all non-smoking. Extra single beds for double rooms available. Eight bus routes; one minute for Trafalgar Square, Westminster, St Paul's. Piccadilly Line underground few minutes' walk. Direct Piccadilly and Heathrow. One-and-a-half miles King's Cross, Euston and St. Pancras Main Line Stations. Four and a half miles Piccadilly, three miles London Zoo and Hampstead Heath. Two minutes A1. Kings Cross for Gatwick. Central for all tourist attractions. Full English Breakfast. Terms: £18.50 per person per night. Children under 10 years £16.00 per night. Minimum stay two nights. Unrestricted street parking. SAE, please.

---

**LONDON. Europa House Hotel, 151 Sussex Gardens, Hyde Park, London W2 (020 7723 7343; Fax: 020 7224 9331).** Europa House is a small privately-owned hotel which aims to give personal service of the highest standard. Full central heating, all rooms en suite. Within easy reach of the West End. Situated close to Paddington Station. Double and twins. Singles. Family rooms available. Special rates for children under 10 years. Full English breakfast. Terms available on request. ETC ♦♦.
e-mail: europahouse@enterprise.net

---

## Dalmacia Hotel

71 Shepherds Bush Road, Hammersmith, London W6 7LS

Tel: 020 7603 2887
Fax: 020 7602 9266

e-mail: george@adria.demon.co.uk

We offer comfortable and value for money accommodation

SINGLES £37
DOUBLE/TWINS £57
- All rooms en suite
- Listed by Les Routiers and L.T.B.
- Direct-dial telephones
- All major credit cards accepted
- Satellite TV and Remote
- Brochure available

---

## The Royal Park Hotel

2-5 Westbourne Terrace, London, W2 3UL

www.theroyalpark.com

Very comfortable 3 star accommodation in central London. Ideally situated for shopping, sightseeing and business. Close to Harrods, Hyde Park and the rest of Knightsbridge. T.V, tea and coffee facilities and telephone in every room.

All major credit cards are accepted    email: info@theroyalpark.com

**Tel: 020 7402 6187**
**Fax: 020 7224 9426**

# QUEENS HOTEL

**33 Anson Road, Tufnell Park, London N7**
**Telephone: 020 7607 4725**
**Fax: 020 7697 9725**
**e-mail: queens@stavrouhotels.co.uk**
**website: www.stavrouhotels.co.uk**

The Queens Hotel is a large double-fronted Victorian building standing in its own grounds five minutes' walk from Tufnell Park Station. Quietly situated with ample car parking spaces; 15 minutes to West End and close to London Zoo, Hampstead and Highgate. Two miles from Kings Cross and St Pancras Stations. Many rooms en suite. ETC ♦♦

Singles from £23-£34 - Double/Twins from £30-£44 Triples and Family Rooms from £16 per person.

All prices include full English Breakfast plus VAT. Children half price. Discounts on longer stays.

**LONDON. Rose Court Hotel, 1 Talbot Square, London W2 1TR (020 7723 5128; Fax: 020 7723 1855).** The Rose Court Hotel is located close to Hyde Park, Park Lane and the major shopping street of London, Oxford Street. Other famous attractions such as Madame Tussauds, Buckingham Palace, museums and theatres are within easy reach. Pleasantly situated in a quiet garden square the hotel is privately run and offers comfort, courteous service, friendliness and hospitality. The bedrooms have en suite facilities, satellite TV, telephone and fridge. Hairdryer and ironing facilities are also available. Single room £35 to £56, double/twin rooms £56 to £72, triple rooms £70 to £88, family rooms £90 to £100. Credit cards are accepted. Rates are inclusive of taxes and English breakfast.

**LONDON. Hazelwood House, 865 Finchley Road, Golders Green, London NW11 8LX (020 8458 8884).** Enjoy luxury in a friendly atmosphere at our RAC and SRAC listed establishment. Whether on holiday or business, this hotel is famous for its "home from home" atmosphere in London's exclusive district of Golders Green. Private forecourt parking for five/six cars. Children over five years, animals accepted. Single room with breakfast from £28 per night, double room with breakfast from £38 per night.

**See also Colour Display Advertisement** **LONDON. Mr S. Mehra, Haven Hotel, 6-8 Sussex Gardens, Paddington, London W2 1UL (020 7723 5481; Fax: 020 7706 4568).** Very centrally situated Bed and Breakfast. First hotel in Sussex Gardens from Edgware Road. Reasonable rates. Parking available. Nearest underground stations: Edgware Road, Paddington, Marble Arch and Lancaster Gate. Major shops and attractions all nearby.

**LONDON. Mrs Anne Scott, Holiday Hosts, 59 Cromwell Road, Wimbledon, London SW19 8LF (020 8540 7942; Fax: 020 8540 2827).** We offer Bed and Breakfast accommodation in selected friendly private homes. Our homes are chosen for their comfort and location in good residential areas of South and West London. They are convenient for transport, restaurants, museums, art galleries, theatres, shopping, Wimbledon Tennis, Hampton Court, Kew Gardens, Public Records Office, Heathrow and Gatwick Airports, M3/M4, A3, River Thames boat trips and interesting riverside walks. An economical alternative for business people, tourists and students. An excellent base for touring Southern England. TV and tea/coffee facilities. £14.50 to £35 per person per night. *MEMBER OF LONDON TOURIST BOARD.*
e-mail: holiday.hosts@btinternet.com

---

**Ringelblume**
89 Somerton Rd, London NW2 1RU
Tel: 0181-830 6589 Fax: 0181-830 7389

In a quiet Edwardian street (close to Hampstead Heath, the poet Keats' house and Kenwood House), find our green garden and wild rose porch. See the colourful light reflected through leaded windows onto a terra cotta hallway floor; enter by the grand oak staircase to our private rooms.

*Some with four-posters and real fires; ensuite rooms with Victorian gold showers and basins. Experience silent nights here!*

Enjoy breakfast of home-baked bread, English cheeses, fruit juice and Swiss Muesli; or cooked British Breakfast. A short Tube ride takes you to Baker Street, Oxford Street, Regents Park, Wembley Stadium, Camden Lock and Market. London tours and walks. Local attractions include live theatre, poetry recitals, pubs, sports centres. M1, A5, A40 one minute. Free parking. From £20. ACCESS, VISA accepted. Cheques payable to Ms T. Stobbe

**LONDON. The Vegas Hotel, 104 Warwick Way, Victoria, London SW1V 1SD (0207-834 0082; Fax: 0207-834 5623)** We are a friendly Bed & Breakfast hotel in Victoria at a convenient location in the city of London near Buckingham Palace and other sights. Only a few minutes' walk to British Airways Terminal, Victoria Coach, Railway and Underground Station. All rooms are with shower/wc, hairdryer, satellite TV, telephone and alarm clock. Reception open 24 hours. Rates: single room with shower/wc £35-£49; Double/twin room with shower/wc from £40-£69. All rates inclusive of full English Breakfast and VAT.
e-mail: info@vegashotel.co.uk
website: www.vegashotel.co.uk

# ELIZABETH HOTEL

Quiet, convenient Townhouse overlooking the magnificent gardens of Eccleston Square. Only a short walk from Buckingham Palace and other tourist attractions. Easy access to Knightsbridge, Oxford Street and Regent Street. Extremely reasonable rates in a fantastic location. Visa, Mastercard, Switch, Delta & JCB are all accepted

info@elizabethhotel.com
Tel: 020 7828 6812
Fax: 020 7828 6814

37 Eccleston Square, Victoria,
London, SW1V 1PB
www.elizabeth-hotel.com

## SHAKESPEARE HOTEL

22 - 28 Norfolk Square, Paddington,
London W2 1RS
Tel: 020 7402 4646 Fax: 020 7723 7233
website: www.shakespearehotel.co.uk
e-mail: info@shakespearehotel.co.uk

A 65 bedroom hotel in a quiet garden square, offering inexpensive accommodation in Central London. Single, Double, Triple and Family rooms available with or without private facilities. Telephone, Fax, e-mail or write to us for a brochure and price list and get a Shakespeare touch while in London.

## Dolphin Hotel

*32-34 Norfolk Square, Paddington Station*
*London W2 1RT*
*Tel: 020 7402 4943; 020 7402 4949*
*Fax: 020 7723 8184*
*e-mail: info@dolphinhotel.co.uk*
*website: www.dolphinhotel.co.uk*

A budget hotel located in a tree lined square within walking distance of Oxford Street and Hyde Park, just two minutes from Paddington Station.

| | |
|---|---|
| *Single Room* | £40.00-£42.00 |
| *Double Room* | £50.00-£55.00 |
| *Double Room with bathroom* | £65.00-£70.00 |

*Triple & Family Rooms also available*

# London Hotel Group

## For Hostels and Hotels in the Heart of London

2 Pembridge Square, Notting Hill Gate, London W2 4EW  Tel: 020 7727 1316  Fax: 020 7229 0803
e-mail: info@lhhotels.co.uk    Bookings: nottinghill@lhghotels.co.uk    A small chain of hotels and Student Hostels situated in the heart of London (Holland Park, Belgravia and Victoria).

### Notting Hill Hotel
All rooms en suite. Large continental Breakfast. From £45.00 per night. Open 24 hours
2 Pembridge Square, Notting Hill Gate
London W2 4EW
Tel: 020 7727 1316
Fax: 020 7229 0803

### Granada Hotel
Sharing four-six a room, most rooms with en suite facilities. From £10.00 per night.
73 Belgrave Road, Victoria, London SW1V 2BG
Tel: 020 7821 7611

Groups of all sizes and ages welcome. Groups from £9.00 pppn.
Situated in the heart of London, all Hostels and Hotels are near mainline stations and underground stations.

For details please ring +44 020 7727 1316
and ask for Michael Harrison or Simon Perry.

---

# FOR THE MUTUAL GUIDANCE OF GUEST AND HOST

Every year literally thousands of holidays, short breaks and overnight stops are arranged through our guides, the vast majority without any problems at all. In a handful of cases, however, difficulties do arise about bookings, which often could have been prevented from the outset.

It is important to remember that when accommodation has been booked, both parties – guests and hosts – have entered into a form of contract. We hope that the following points will provide helpful guidance.

**GUESTS:** When enquiring about accommodation, be as precise as possible. Give exact dates, numbers in your party and the ages of any children. State the number and type of rooms wanted and also what catering you require – bed and breakfast, full board etc. Make sure that the position about evening meals is clear – and about pets, reductions for children or any other special points.

Read our reviews carefully to ensure that the proprietors you are going to contact can supply what you want. Ask for a letter confirming all arrangements, if possible.

If you have to cancel, do so as soon as possible. Proprietors do have the right to retain deposits and under certain circumstances to charge for cancelled holidays if adequate notice is not given and they cannot re-let the accommodation.

**HOSTS:** Give details about your facilities and about any special conditions. Explain your deposit system clearly and arrangements for cancellations, charges etc. and whether or not your terms include VAT.

If for any reason you are unable to fulfil an agreed booking without adequate notice, you may be under an obligation to arrange suitable alternative accommodation or to make some form of compensation.

*While every effort is made to ensure accuracy, we regret that FHG Publications cannot accept responsibility for errors, omissions or misrepresentations in our entries or any consequences thereof.*
*Prices in particular should be checked because we go to press early. We will follow up complaints but cannot act as arbiters or agents for either party.*

# BEDFORDSHIRE

**PULLOXHILL. Mrs A. Lawrence, "Tower House", 74 Church Road, Pulloxhill MK45 5HE (01525 714818).** "Tower House", a welcoming, friendly artist's home is situated in a quiet lane backing onto open countryside. All en suite bedrooms have central heating, TV and tea/coffee making facilities. Full English and Continental breakfasts are served in a farmhouse style kitchen. Guests are invited to use the garden and conservatory, where smoking is permitted. Off-road parking. Mainline station - Flitwick three miles - London 50 minutes. Seven miles to Woburn Abbey, nine miles to Luton Airport. Three miles from A6, five miles from Junction 12 of M1. Village pub serving food. Lovely walks.

**SANDY. Mrs M. Codd, Highfield Farm, Great North Road, Sandy SG19 2AQ (01767 682332; Fax: 01767 692503).** Tranquil welcoming atmosphere on attractive arable farm. Set well back off A1 giving quiet, peaceful seclusion yet within easy reach of the RSPB, the Shuttleworth Collection, the Greensand Ridge Walk, Grafham Water and Woburn Abbey. Cambridge 22 miles, London 50 miles. All rooms have tea/coffee making facilities, most have bathroom en suite and two are on the ground floor. There is a separate guests' sittingroom with TV. Family room. Dogs welcome by arrangement. No smoking. Guestaccom "Good Room" Award. Most guests return! Prices from £25 per person per night. **ETC** ◆◆◆◆◆

**SANDY. Mrs Anne Franklin, Village Farm, Thorncote Green, Sandy SG19 1PU (01767 627345)** Village Farm is a family-run working farm, mixed arable with a flock of 1000 free range laying hens, plus turkeys and geese for Christmas trade. Accommodation comprises one double bedroom, two twin/family rooms, both en suite. Full farmhouse breakfast plus beverages in room. Thorncote Green is a picturesque hamlet within easy reach of many interesting places:- Shuttleworth Collection, Swiss Gardens, RSPB headquarters, Greensand Ridge walk, Woburn Abbey, Wimpole Hall and Cambridge. Bed and Breakfast from £20 per person per night. **ETC** ◆◆

# FHG PUBLICATIONS

**FHG** publish a large range of well-known accommodation guides. We will be happy to send you details or you can use the order form at the back of this book.

*When making enquiries or bookings,
a stamped addressed envelope is always appreciated*

# BERKSHIRE

**ASCOT. Graham and Sue Chapman, Lyndrick Guest House, The Avenue, Ascot SL5 8LS (01344 883520; Fax: 01344 891243).** Lyndrick is a five bedroom Victorian house in a tree lined avenue. All bedrooms have colour TV and tea/coffee making facilities, most are en suite. Breakfast is served in a pleasant conservatory. Windsor four miles, Ascot Racecourse and Mill Ride Golf Club are two minutes and Wentworth and Sunningdale Golf Clubs are within 10 minutes. London/Waterloo 40 minutes by train; Heathrow Airport 25 minutes, easy access to M3, M4, M25 and A30. Open all year.

**READING, Three Mile Cross. Mrs M.S. Erdwin, Orchard House, Church Lane, Three Mile Cross, Reading RG7 1HD (01189 884457).** Orchard House is well situated close to M4 Motorway, Heathrow 30 minutes away, Gatwick 45 minutes; Oxford 30 miles and London 35 miles (just 29 minutes by train); five minutes' from Arborfield Garrison. Wealth of holiday interest to suit all tastes in the area. Ideal halt for that long journey to Cornwall or Wales. Accommodation all year round in this modern, large, homely house close to the Chilterns and Berkshire Downs. Children welcome. Babysitting can be arranged; high chair available. Evening drink; English or Continental Breakfast; Evening Meal/Light Supper available; Packed Lunches on request. Pets permitted at extra charge. Close to Thames, Kennet and Avon Canal/River for coarse fishing. Also close to Digital and Racal training centres, Reading Rock Festival, and the new Reading football/rugby stadium. Tourist Board registered. Terms from £17.50 for Bed and Breakfast. Taxi service at moderate rates. SAE, please.

**WINDSOR. Mr Robert Sousa, Netherton Hotel, 96 St Leonards Road, Windsor SL4 3DA (01753 855508; Fax: 01753 621267).** This recently refurbished hotel offers a comfortable and friendly atmosphere. All rooms are en suite, with colour TV, direct-dial telephone, tea/coffee making facilities. Also available are hairdryers and iron facilities. There is a TV lounge for guests' use. Full English breakfast. We have a private car park and are easy to find. Walking distance to Windsor Castle, town centre, train stations and Legoland is only one-and-a-half miles away. Central London can be reached in 35 minutes by train. M4 only two miles, Heathrow seven miles. Children welcome. **ETC/AA/RAC ◆◆◆**
e-mail: netherton@btconnect.com

---

Visit the **FHG** website
# www.holidayguides.com
for details of the wide choice of accommodation featured in the full range of FHG titles

# BUCKINGHAMSHIRE

**AYLESBURY. Anita and John Cooper, Poletrees Farm, Ludgershall Road, Brill, Near Aylesbury HP18 9TZ (Tel: 01844 238276; Fax: 01844 238462).** We would like to welcome you to our home and working farm. We rear British beef and sheep. Our three grandchildren can be hilarious; we understand your needs when travelling with children. We have one family room so please bring them; you will be made very comfortable. We provide spacious, comfortable accommodation in our historic house with oak-beamed ceilings, wattle and daub walls. Guests have their own diningroom and TV lounge where we can sit and chat to you. Perhaps you would like a cup of tea in our lovely garden. We can cater for dietary requirements if you let us know. Evening Meals or cold suppers can be booked. Winners of Roy Castle Award for a smoke-free house. Bed and Breakfast from £23 - £28. **ETC** ♦♦♦.

**BEACONSFIELD. Mr and Mrs Ben Dickinson, Beacon House, 113 Maxwell Road, Beaconsfield HP9 1RF (Tel & Fax:01494 672923).** Located in Beaconsfield New Town, five minutes from M40, Junction 2, easy five minute walk to station, with 40 minutes train to London, (Wembley Central en route). Rail links to Oxford and Warwick. Windsor/Legoland are only 12 miles away and on bus route, as are Oxford and Heathrow airport. The surrounding Chilterns are well-supplied with picturesque villages, lovely old pubs and restaurants. Good walking country with splendid scenery, including Burnham Beeches. All rooms have colour TV, tea/coffee facilities. Guests are welcome to use garden. Early breakfast possible. Non-smoking. Regret no pets. German and some French spoken. Bed and Breakfast single £25, double £36, single en suite £30, twin en suite £42 per night.
**e-mail: ben.dickinson@tesco.net**

# CAMBRIDGESHIRE

**CAMBRIDGE. Paul and Alison Tweddell, Dykelands Guest House, 157 Mowbray Road, Cambridge CB1 7SP (01223 244300; Fax: 01223 566746).** Enjoy your visit to Cambridge by staying at our lovely detached guesthouse. Ideally located for city centre and for touring the secrets of the Cambridgeshire countryside. Easy access from M11 Junction 11, but only one-and-a-half miles from the city centre, on a direct bus route. Near Addenbrookes Hospital. All bedrooms have colour TV, clock radio, tea/coffee making facilities; heating and double glazing; seven en suite; ground floor rooms available. Bed and full English Breakfast from £27 singles, £38 doubles. Ample car parking. Most major credit/debit cards welcome. Open all year. Brochure on request. Non-smoking establishment.**ETC/AA** ♦♦♦.

**CAMBRIDGE near. Vicki Hatley, Manor Farm, Landbeach, Cambridge CB4 4ED (01223 860165).** Five miles from Cambridge and 10 miles from Ely. Vicki welcomes you to her carefully modernised Grade II Listed farmhouse, which is located next to the church in this attractive village. All rooms are either en suite or have private bathroom and are individually decorated. TV, clock radios and tea/coffee making facilities are provided in double, twin or family rooms. There is ample parking and guests are welcome to enjoy the walled gardens. Bed and Breakfast from £20 per person double, and £30 single.

## Cambridgeshire

**CAMBRIDGE. Cristina's Guest House, 47 St. Andrews Road, Cambridge CB4 1DH (01223 365855/327700; Fax: 01223 365855).** Guests are assured of a warm welcome here, quietly located in the beautiful city of Cambridge, only 15 minutes' walk from the City Centre and colleges. All rooms have colour TV, hairdryer, alarm/clock radio and tea/coffee making equipment, some rooms have private shower and toilet. Centrally heated with comfortable TV lounge. Private car park, locked at night. No smoking house. **ETC/AA** ♦♦♦

**CAMBRIDGE. Mrs Debbie Sills, Chequer Cottage, Streetly End, Horseheath CB1 6RP (01223 891522).** Set in a quiet hamlet of 16th century period properties on the Cambridgeshire/Suffolk border, ideally situated for touring the surrounding countryside. Cambridge is 14 miles away, and other local places of interest include Ely Cathedral, The Fens, Newmarket Races, Duxford War Musuem, local gardens and stately homes (National Gardens Scheme). Local pubs serve good food and beer. Spacious double room with en suite bathroom, TV tea making facilities, central heating and parking space. Home cooked country breakfast. Non-smoking, no pets. £45 double, £30 single. Open all year.

**CAMBRIDGE. Mrs Julie Webb, Redby Lodge, 15 Queen Ediths Way, Cambridge CB1 4PH (01223 566686; Fax: 01223 414307)** Delightful detached cottage-style house with very large gardens, situated in very select area south side of the city. A very secluded and quiet house awaits you, with warm comfortable rooms. Tea/coffee making facilities, colour TV , radio and shaver point in all rooms. One single en suite, one double en suite and one family en suite. We are approximately two miles from city centre and near world famous Addenbrookes Hospital. Private off-street parking. Prices from £28 per person single, £48 double, £65 family.. Tom and Julie are very helpful hosts.
e-mail: redbylodge@15qewcb.freeserve.co.uk
website: www.cambridge-bedandbreakfast.co.uk

**CAMBRIDGE. Mrs Jean Wright, White Horse Cottage, 28 West Street, Comberton, Cambridge CB3 7DS (01223 262914).** A 17th century cottage with all modern conveniences situated in a charming village four miles south-west of Cambridge. Junction 12 off M11 - A603 from Cambridge, or A428 turn off at Hardwick turning. Accommodation includes one double room, twin and family rooms. Own sittingroom with colour TV; tea/coffee making facilities. Full central heating; parking. Golfing facilities nearby. Excellent touring centre for many interesting places including Cambridge colleges, Wimpole Hall, Anglesey Abbey, Ely Cathedral, Imperial War Museum at Duxford, and many more. Bed and Breakfast from £20 per person. Children welcome.

---

# FREE or REDUCED RATE entry to Holiday Visits and Attractions — see our READERS' OFFER VOUCHERS on pages 43-60

## Cambridgeshire

**CAMBRIDGE. Victorian Guest House, 57 Arbury Road, Cambridge CB4 2JB (Tel & Fax: 01223 350086).** Victorian Guest House is an extremely comfortable Victorian house situated off Milton Road, within walking distance of the City Centre, River Cam and Colleges, with easy access to the M14, M11 and the Cambridge Science Park. All our rooms are en suite or have private facilities. Colour TV, iron, ironing board, hair dryer, payphone, tea and coffee making facilities; good parking to the front available. Our guests can enjoy a lovely breakfast served in the diningroom, overlooking picturesque gardens to the rear; there we can cater for all your needs. Mr and Mrs Fasano strive very hard to offer all their guests a very warm welcome and comfortable stay, which is why guests return to us over and over again. **ETC ◆◆◆◆.**
e-mail: vicmaria@globalnet.co.uk

**ELY. Jenny Farndale, Cathedral House, 17 St. Mary's Street, Ely CB7 4ER (Tel & Fax: 01353 662124).** Cathedral House is situated in the centre of Ely and within the shadow of its famous cathedral. A Grade II Listed house, it retains many original features and has a delightful walled garden. One twin, one double and one family bedrooms, all overlook the garden, are comfortably furnished and have tea/coffee facilities, TV, central heating and en suite bathrooms. In cold months there is a log fire in the dining room. An ideal base for touring East Anglia, within easy reach of Cambridge, Welney and Wicken Fen Wildlife Reserves, Newmarket, Bury St. Edmunds and several National Trust properties. Open all year except Christmas and New Year. No smoking. Based on two persons sharing twin/double: two nights midweek £90, weekends £95; three nights midweek £135, weekends £144. One week £300 to £320. Offers not applicable Bank Holidays or High Season. **ETC ◆◆◆◆** *SILVER AWARD.*
e-mail: farndale@cathedralhouse.co.uk
website: www.cathedralhouse.co.uk

**ELY. Mrs Linda Peck, Sharps Farm, Twenty Pence Road, Wilburton, Ely CB6 3PX (01353 740360).** Between Ely (six miles) and Cambridge (12 miles) our modern farmhouse offers guests a warm welcome and a relaxed atmosphere. All rooms have en suite or private bathrooms, central heating, colour TV, radio alarm, tea/coffee making facilities, hair dryer and views over surrounding countryside. Breakfast is served in the conservatory, with home-made preserves and free range eggs. Special diets catered for. Disabled facilities. Ample parking. No smoking. Bed and Breakfast from £19. Short Breaks available.

**ELY. Mrs Val Pickford, Rosendale Lodge, 223 Main Street, Witchford, Ely CB6 2HT (01353 667700; Fax: 01353 667799).** A friendly atmosphere awaits you at Rosendale Lodge. Enjoy breakfast in our galleried dining room – relax on sofas around the inglenook, on sunnier days in the south-facing garden. Elegant bedrooms, one of which is on the ground floor, are furnished with thought and care and have large double or twin beds, central heating, sofa, colour TV, generous beverage tray and individually designed en suites. Visit Ely's magnificent Cathedral, Stained Glass Museum or stroll along the riverside. Cambridge, Newmarket Racecourse, Thetford Forest, stately homes, Duxford Air Museum and Welney Wildlife Reserve are a short drive away – an ideal touring base for East Anglia and a haven for anglers, cyclists and walkers. Directions: at A10/A142 Ely/Cambridge roundabout take A142 to Witchford, left into village and we are approximately one mile on the left opposite a restaurant. B&B from £35 single/£50 Double. Non-smoking. **ETC ◆◆◆◆◆** *SILVER AWARD,* **AA ◆◆◆◆,** *CATEGORY 1 ACCESSIBLE.*

*Please mention Bed & Breakfast Stops when writing to enquire about accommodation*

**HEMINGFORD GREY. Maureen and Tony Webster, The Willow Guest House, 45 High Street, Hemingford Grey, St. Ives (Cambs.) PE28 9BJ (01480 494748; Fax: 01480 464456).** Large private house in the centre of this picturesque village. 100 yards from a much photographed section of the Great Ouse River, and oldest (1150) inhabited house in England. One mile from 15th century bridge west of St. Ives, 15 minutes' drive from Cambridge City Centre. Family rooms, twin rooms, doubles and singles. All bedrooms are en-suite and have colour TV, tea/coffee making facilities, hairdryers, clock radios, central heating. Private parking. Guest phone. Bed and Breakfast from £21 including VAT (full English Breakfast). Sorry no pets or smoking. Ideally situated for north/south and east/west travel being only one mile from A14 dual carriageway connecting M1-A1 and M11.

**HUNTINGDON. Mr and Mrs R. Williams, Apple Tree House, 4 Vinegar Hill, Alconbury Weston, Huntingdon PE17 5JA (01480 890285).** Apple Tree House is a relaxed and stylish Edwardian home, set in the peace and beauty of this historic corner of Cambridgeshire. Conveniently located close to the main junction of the A1, A1(M) and A14, there is excellent access to Cambridge, Peterborough and Huntingdon. We offer a full English breakfast, wherever possible including locally produced fare. Continental breakfasts and vegetarian alternatives are always available. For an evening meal, the pub next door offers a wide choice. All rooms are equipped with TV, clock radio and tea/coffee making facilities. Two rooms with en suite bathroom (one with shower, one with bath). Bed and Breakfast from £20 to £50. **AA ♦♦♦**
e-mail: appletreeh@aol.com

**OVER. David and Julia Warren, Charter Cottage, Horse Ware, Over CB4 5NX (01954 230056; Fax: 01954 232300).** A warm welcome and a friendly atmosphere await you in our peaceful cottage accommodation in an interesting corner of the village. Open all year, we offer two ground floor, centrally heated bedrooms, one twin bedded and one double, both with hot and cold water, tea/coffee making facilities and TV. Fully equipped bathroom also adjacent. Full English breakfast. Ample off-road parking, pleasant country garden with patio. Easy reach of Cambridge, Ely and St. Ives. Bed and Breakfast £20 single, £32 double. Directions: A14 Cambridge to Huntingdon, follow signs to Over, then first left immediately after Over Church.
e-mail: chartercottage@talk21.com

**ST. NEOTS. Mrs Eileen Raggatt, The Ferns, Berkley Street, Eynesbury, St. Neots PE19 2NE (01480 213884).** An 18th century house (private family home) in large garden situated on Eynesbury Green. Two rooms available with double bed plus single bed, one with private bathroom, the other with washbasin. Central heating. Charges from £18 per person for Bed and Breakfast, reduced rates for children under 10. St. Neots is a market town on the River Ouse just off the A1; one-and-a-half hours north of London, 16 miles west of Cambridge.

**WICKEN. Mrs Valerie Fuller, Spinney Abbey, Wicken, Ely CB7 5XQ (01353 720971). Working farm.** Spinney Abbey is an attractive Grade II Listed Georgian stone farmhouse with views across pasture fields. It stands in a large garden with tennis court next to our dairy farm which borders the National Trust Nature Reserve Wicken Fen. One double and one family room, both en suite, and twin-bedded room with private bathroom, all with TV, hospitality tray, etc. Full central heating, guests' sittingroom. Regret no pets and no smoking upstairs. Situated just off A1123, half a mile west of Wicken. Open all year. Bed and Breakfast from £22 per person.
**ETC ♦♦♦♦**
e-mail: spinney.abbey@tesco.net

**WISBECH. Jayne Best, Four Winds, Mill Lane, Newton, Wisbech PE13 5HZ (01945 870479; Fax: 01945 870274).** Charming country house situated in the midst of the Fens countryside, although only four miles from Wisbech and close to King's Lynn, Norfolk coast (28 miles). Ideally situated for touring, fishing and cycling. Accommodation comprises one double en suite with shower, one twin en suite with bath, two singles with washbasins and one main bathroom with Airspa. Private parking. Terms from £17.

**WYTON. Robin and Marion Seaman, The Elms, Banks End, Wyton, Huntingdon PE28 2AA (01480 453523).** Rambling Edwardian house close to picturesque village of Houghton and Wyton, off the A1123 two miles between historic market towns of Huntingdon and St. Ives; five minutes from A1 and A14; M11 15 minutes. One double en suite room, one twin en suite room, and two single rooms with washbasins and private bathroom. All have tea/coffee making facilities and colour TV. Central heating. Bed and Breakfast from £20 per person. Non-smoking. No pets. Friendly personal service and a warm welcome assured.

# FHG

Other specialised

# FHG PUBLICATIONS

Published annually: Please add 50p postage (UK only) when ordering from the publishers

- Recommended COUNTRY HOTELS OF BRITAIN   £4.99
- Recommended WAYSIDE & COUNTRY INNS OF BRITAIN   £4.99
- PETS WELCOME!   £5.99
- B&B IN BRITAIN   £3.99
- THE GOLF GUIDE Where to Play / Where to Stay   £9.99

## FHG PUBLICATIONS LTD
### Abbey Mill Business Centre, Seedhill, Paisley, Renfrewshire PA1 1TJ

Tel: 0141-887 0428 • Fax: 0141-889 7204
e-mail: fhg@ipcmedia.com • website: www.holidayguides.com

# CHESHIRE

**ALTRINCHAM. Dr Yau, Oasis Hotel, 46/48 Barrington Road, Altrincham WA14 1HN (0161-928 4523; Fax: 0161-928 1099).** The Oasis Hotel is situated within walking distance of Altrincham Town Centre with Metrolink direct to Manchester City Centre and a short distance from Manchester International Airport with easy access from M6, M56, M63. All bedrooms are en suite and include colour TV, tea/coffee making facilities and telephone. Terms: Single room £30 - £40 per night; Double/Twin £40 - £48 per night; Family room £50 - £60 per night. Prices include full English breakfast.

**BALTERLEY (near Crewe). Mrs Joanne Hollins, Balterley Green Farm, Deans Lane, Balterley, near Crewe CW2 5QJ (01270 820214). Working farm, join in.** Jo and Pete Hollins offer guests a friendly welcome to their home on a 145 acre dairy farm in quiet and peaceful surroundings. Green Farm is situated on the Cheshire/Staffordshire border and is within easy reach of Junction 16 on the M6. An excellent stop-over place for travellers journeying between north and south of the country. We also offer a pets' corner and pony rides for young children. One family room en suite, one single and one twin-bedded room on ground floor suitable for disabled guests. Tea making facilities and TV in all rooms. Children welcome cot provided. Pets welcome. This area offers many attractions; we are within easy reach of historic Chester, Alton Towers and the famous Potteries of Staffordshire. Open all year. Caravans and tents welcome. Bed and Breakfast from £19 per person. **ETC** ♦♦♦♦

**CHESTER CITY. Frank and Maureen Brady, Holly House, 41 Liverpool Road, Chester CH2 1AB (01244 383484).** Holly House is a Victorian townhouse on the A5116, offering a friendly welcome in quiet, elegant surroundings. Comfort and high standards are our priority. Only five minutes' walk from the famous Roman walls which encircle this historic city with its 11th century Cathedral, castle, museum of Roman artifacts, buildings of architectural interest, Amphitheatre, walks by the river, shopping in "The Rows". Spacious accommodation comprises two double/family rooms fully en suite and a double with full private facilities. TV, tea/coffee facilities, own keys. Parking. Bed and Breakfast from £38 to £40 for two sharing, or as family rooms at £12 per additional person supplement. Vegetarians catered for. Non-smoking. A warm welcome from Frank and Maureen Brady.

*See also Colour Display Advertisement*

**CHESTER. Mr & Mrs M. Aplas, Aplas Guest House, 106 Brook Street, Chester CH1 3DU (01244 312401).** Patricia and Michael Aplas welcome you to the Aplas Guest House. We are a small family run guest house and have been established for 15 years. We are ideally located some five minutes' walk from the city centre and about the same distance from the railway station. For those coming by car, parking is available. Most of our rooms are en suite and can be booked on a "Room Only" or "Bed & Breakfast" basis. Our prices range from £13 to £17.50 per person and discounts are available for long stays and children.

Cheshire 79

**CHESTER. Helen and Colin Mitchell, Mitchell's of Chester, 28 Hough Green, Chester CH4 8JQ (01244 679004; Fax: 01244 659567).** Relax in this tastefully restored Victorian residence set in compact landscaped gardens and forecourt. The tall well appointed corniced rooms are complemented by a sweeping staircase and antique furniture. This small family run guest house has all en suite rooms with hospitality tray, alarm clock, hair dryer and many other comforts. It is within walking distance of the ancient Roman walled city with its wealth of historic buildings and its famous race course. It is also the gateway to North Wales. Guests have the convenience of a pay phone, off street parking and being on a main bus route. We are situated on the south side of Chester on the A5104. Bed and breakfast from £24 per person. **ETC** ◆◆◆◆. *SILVER AWARD.*
e-mail: mitoches@dialstart.net

**CHESTER. Mrs Anne Arden, Newton Hall, Tattenhall. Chester CH3 9NE (01829 770153; Fax: 01829 770655).** Part 16th century oak-beamed farmhouse set in large well kept grounds, with fine views of historic Beeston and Peckforton Castles and close to the sandstone Trail. Six miles south of Chester off A41 and ideal for Welsh hills. Rooms are en suite or have adjacent bathroom. Colour TV in all bedrooms. Guests' own Lounge. Fully centrally heated. See our rare Shropshire Downs sheep and pedigree cattle. Bed and Breakfast from £20. Children and pets welcome. Open all year. **ETC** ◆◆◆
e-mail: newton.hall@farming.co.uk

**CHESTER. Hotel Romano, 51 Lower Bridge Street, Chester CH1 1RS (01244 325091/321139; Fax: 01244 315628).** Hotel Romano is ideally situated within the city's Roman walls, close to many historical features including Chester's famous Rows with their interesting and quaint shops. All bedrooms offer comfort and luxury with en suite bathrooms, satellite TV, telephone, tea and coffeee making facilities, also laundry services. Four-poster and family rooms available. We have two restaurants to choose from: an à la carte restaurant and our excellent pizzeria. Terms: Bed and Breakfast from £45 single, £65 double. Mini breaks from £110.

**CHESTER. Brian and Hilary Devenport, White Walls, Village Road, Christleton, Chester CH3 7AS (Tel/Fax: 01244 336033).** White Walls, a 100 year old converted stables, in the heart of Award-Winning village Christleton, two miles Chester, off the A41, close to A55, M53 and North Wales. Walking distance to village pub and two canalside pub/restaurants, church, Post Office, Hairdresser and bus stop. Half hourly bus service to Chester. The village pond is home to swans, mallards, Aylesbury ducks and moor hens. En suite double bedroom at £45 per night, twin bedded room with washbasin at £36 per night all including English Breakfast. Single from £20. Colour TV, tea/coffee making facilities, central heating, overlooking garden. Non-smoking. Sorry, no children or pets
e-mail: h.h.devenport@talk21.com

**CHESTER. Mr D.R. Bawn, The Gables Guest House, 5 Vicarage Road, Hoole, Chester CH2 3HZ (01244 323969).** Guests are welcomed to this pleasant Victorian family house situated in a quiet residential area just off the main bus route, one mile from City centre. Near park and tennis courts. Makes an ideal base for touring with easy access to all major roads. The guest house offers accommodation in family, double and twin bedrooms; hot and cold, central heating, colour TV and tea-making facilities, hairdryer, clock radio, Television lounge. Open from January to December. Open parking. Bed and Breakfast from £17 per person; weekly terms available. Reductions for children

*When making enquiries or bookings, a stamped addressed envelope is always appreciated*

**CHESTER near. Beryl and John Milner, Green Cottage, The Green, Higher Kinnerton, Chester CH4 9BZ (Tel & Fax: 01244 660137).** A homely, friendly, peaceful and comfortable country retreat just over the Welsh border, ideally situated for exploring the historic City of Chester under seven miles away. Easy access to all routes (five minutes from the A55) make this an ideal base for touring North Wales, West Cheshire and North Shropshire. Beryl and John, previous winners of a Prince of Wales' Award, will offer you warm hospitality and invite you into their home, which has recently been renovated and furnished to a high standard. A double room and a twin room are available, overlooking open countryside. Tea/coffee making facilities, TV, shared private bathroom with bath and shower, central heating, off-road parking, pleasant gardens. There are two pubs within the village offering excellent cuisine. Non-smoking. Bed and Full English Breakfast from £19 per person, with reductions for weekly stays. Please send or telephone for our brochure. **WTB ★★★** *GUEST HOUSE.*

**CHURCH MINSHULL. Brian and Mary Charlesworth, Higher Elms Farm, Minshull Vernon, Crewe CW1 4RG (01270 522252).** A 400-year-old farmhouse on working farm. Oak-beamed comfort in dining and sittingrooms, overlooking Shropshire Union Canal. No dinners served but four pubs within two miles. Interesting wildlife around. Convenient for M6 but tucked away in the countryside; from M6 Junction 18, off A530 towards Nantwich. Family room, double, twin and single rooms are all en suite, with colour TV and tea/coffee facilities. Well behaved pets welcome. Within 15 miles of Jodrell Bank, Oulton Park, Bridgemere Garden World, Stapeley Water Gardens, Nantwich and Chester. Bed and Breakfast from £23. Half price for children under 12 years.

**CONGLETON. Mrs Sheila Kidd, Yew Tree Farm, North Rode, Congleton CW12 2PF (01260 223569; Fax: 01260 223328).** Discover freedom, relaxation, wooded walks and beautiful views. Meet a whole variety of pets and farm animals on this friendly working farm. Your comfort is our priority and good food is a speciality. Generous scrummy breakfasts and traditional evening meals. A true taste of the countryside — just for you! Bed and Breakfast from £19; optional Evening Meal £10. Brochure on request. **ETC ♦♦♦♦**
e-mail: kidyewtreefarm@netscapeonline.co.uk

**CREWE. Little Heath Farm, Audlem, Near Crewe CW3 0HE (Tel & Fax: 01270 811324). Working farm.** Hilary and Bob Bennion welcome you to their warm and spacious farmhouse which is over 200 years old, with oak-beamed TV lounge and dining room, and furnished in traditional style. The accommodation consists of warm spacious no-smoking bedrooms, one double en suite, one double and one twin, all with washbasin and tea making facilities. Every effort is made to make your stay enjoyable, comfortable and relaxing. We provide a full farmhouse breakfast; in the evening a three-course meal of good country food with fresh meat and vegetables and locally baked bread. Little Heath makes an ideal base for visiting Cheshire, Shropshire and Staffordshire. Bed and Breakfast from £18 per person, Evening Meal available.

**FREE or REDUCED RATE entry to Holiday Visits and Attractions — see our READERS' OFFER VOUCHERS on pages 43-60**

**FRODSHAM. Mrs Susan Ward, Long Croft, Dark Lane, Kingsley WA6 8BW (01928 787193).** In a delightful secluded country lane and standing in its own grounds, Long Croft offers a wealth of charm and character together with modern conveniences. Double and twin-bedded rooms, both with en suite facilities, TV and tea/coffee making facilities; guests' own sitting room with private dining room overlooking secluded patio. Plenty of good pubs in the area and reasonably priced restaurants in Frodsham, a pretty market town just two miles away. Within striking distance of Chester, Manchester, Liverpool and North Wales and on the doorstep of Oulton Park racing circuit and Delamere Forest. Children welcome. Home cooked traditional English breakfast with own free range eggs. Evening meals specially prepared as requested. From £18 to £25 per person; reductions for children.

**HYDE, near Manchester. Mrs Charlotte R. Walsh, Needhams Farm, Uplands Road, Werneth Low, Gee Cross, near Hyde SK14 3AQ (0161 368 4610; Fax: 0161 367 9106). Working farm.** A cosy 16th century farmhouse set in peaceful, picturesque surroundings by Werneth Low Country Park and the Etherow Valley, which lie between Glossop and Manchester. The farm is ideally situated for holidaymakers and businessmen, especially those who enjoy peace and quiet, walking and rambling, golfing and riding, as these activities are all close by. At Needhams Farm everyone, including children and pets, receives a warm welcome. Good wholesome meals available in the evenings. Residential licence and Fire Certificate held. Open all year. Bed and Breakfast from £20 single minimum to £34 double maximum; Evening Meal £7. **ETC/AA ♦♦♦, RAC ACCLAIMED.**
e-mail: charlotte@needhamsfarm.demon.co.uk
website: www.needhamsfarm.demon.co.uk

**KINGSLEY. Mrs Susan Klin, Charnwood, Hollow Lane, Kingsley, Near Frodsham WA6 8EF (01928 787097; Fax: 01928 788566).** Charnwood provides spacious accommodation, set in its own landscaped grounds in the delightful village of Kingsley. Close by are Delamere Forest and Oulton Park Racing Circuit. Also ideally situated for historic Chester and McArthur Glen Designer Outlet Village. A wide range of luxury accommodation is available from £18 per person including a private suite sleeping up to five people. Each room adjoins a private comfortable sitting room with TV. All room have colour TV, tea/coffee making facilities and hairdryer. Full traditional English breakfast is served in a comfortable dining room overlooking the garden. Secure parking provided. **AA ♦♦♦♦.**
e-mail: susan.klin@talk21.com

**MACCLESFIELD. Mrs P.O. Worth, Rough Hey Farm, Leek Road, Gawsworth, Macclesfield SK11 0JQ (01260 252296).** Featured in "Which?" B&B Guide. Delightfully situated overlooking the Cheshire Plain and on the edge of the Peak National Park in an area of outstanding natural beauty, Rough Hey is an historic former hunting lodge dating from before the 16th century, tastefully modernised yet retaining its old world character. This 300 acre sheep farm, with long horn cattle, consists of wooded valleys and hills with plenty of wildlife and lovely walks. In the locality there are numerous old halls and villages to visit. Double room en suite, twin room en suite and two single rooms, all with washbasins, TV and tea/coffee making facilities. Large comfortable lounge with TV. No smoking. A warm and friendly welcome is assured. Terms from £20. **ETC ♦♦♦♦.**

---

# FHG

## Visit the FHG website
## www.holidayguides.com
for details of the wide choice of accommodation
featured in the full range of FHG titles

**NANTWICH. Mrs West, Stoke Grange Mews, Stoke Grange Farm, Chester Road, Nantwich CW5 6BT (01270 625525).** Comfortable canal side farmhouse B&B with en suite rooms, colour TV, tea/coffee facilities plus a four-poster bed. Balcony giving panoramic views of canal and countryside. Log burning fire in diningroom and wonderful antique tapestry in the lounge. We also have a two-bedroomed self-catering cottage with all mod cons in a converted barn across from the farmhouse. Shared garden. Pets corner. Meals can be obtained from two pubs in the village of Barbridge only a ten minute walk away along the canal or road. Bed and Breakfast from £25 - £30 single, £50 - £60 double. Self-catering from £225 - £375 per week. **ETC ♦♦♦**

**TATTENHALL. Mrs B. Willoughby, The Pheasant Inn, Higher Burwardsley, Tattenhall CH3 9PF (01829 770434; Fax: 01829 771097).** The Pheasant Inn is a 300-year-old inn nestling on the top of the Peckforton Hills, with magnificent views over the Cheshire Plain to Wales. It has a well-earned reputation for good food and fine wines, with a range of real ales and a well-stocked bar. All the bedrooms are situated in a converted barn, sympathetically modernised to the highest standard, with en suite bathrooms, colour TV, radio and tea/coffee making facilities. Being away from the main building, your privacy and peace are assured. Ideally placed for visiting Chester, Nantwich, Wrexham and Wales. Terms on request. **ETC ★★, AA** *LISTED.*

# PLEASE NOTE

All the information in this book is given in good faith in the belief that it is correct. However, the publishers cannot guarantee the facts given in these pages, neither are they responsible for changes in policy, ownership or terms that may take place after the date of going to press. Readers should always satisfy themselves that the facilities they require are available and that the terms, if quoted, still apply.

# FHG

PLEASE MENTION THIS GUIDE WHEN YOU WRITE OR PHONE TO ENQUIRE ABOUT ACCOMMODATION

IF YOU ARE WRITING, A STAMPED, ADDRESSED ENVELOPE IS ALWAYS APPRECIATED

# CORNWALL

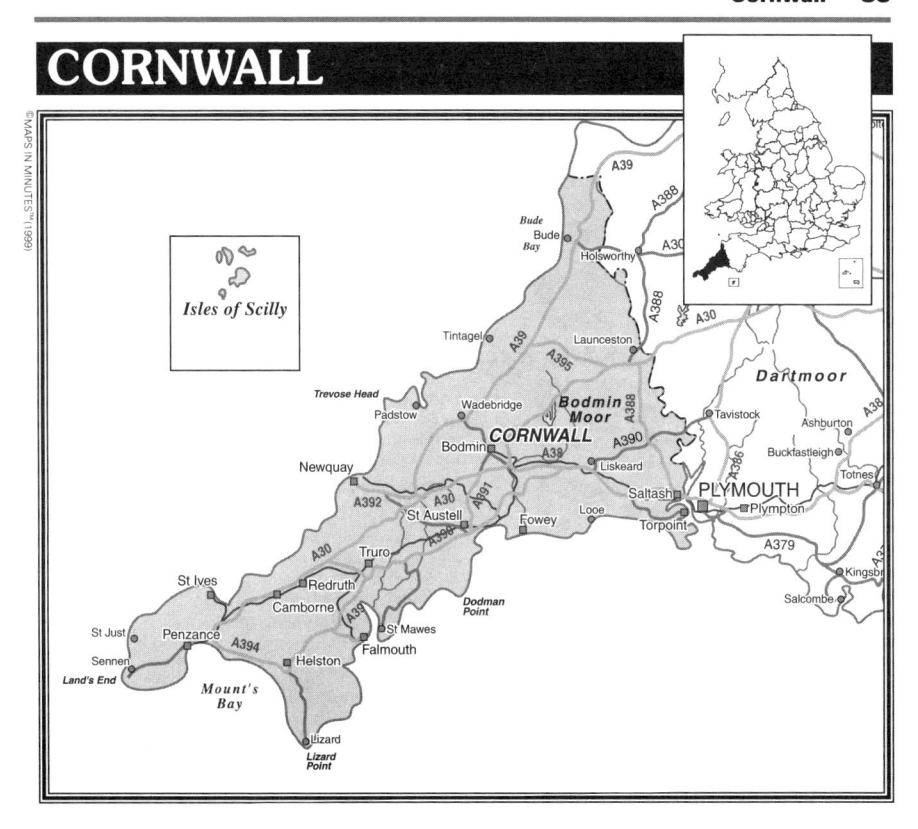

**BODMIN. Mrs Jenny Bass, Trehannick Farm, St. Teath, Bodmin PL30 3JW (01208 850312). Working farm.** Mentioned in the Domesday Book in 1086, Trehannick is a family farm situated in the beautiful Allen Valley. Safe sandy beaches, coastal walks, golf, sailing and fishing are all within easy reach of this peaceful farmhouse. All rooms have beautiful south-facing views and the usual amenities (tea/coffee making facilities, etc). One double room is en suite. Non-smoking throughout. Ample parking. Sorry no pets. Please telephone for further details.

**BODMIN. Mrs Joy Rackham, High Cross Farm, Lanivet, Near Bodmin PL30 5JR (01208 831341).** Traditional granite farmhouse circa 1890 on a 91 acre working farm. The village of Lanivet is the geographical centre of Cornwall and is therefore ideal for the north and south coastal beaches ad the moor. Riding, fishing and cycle tracks are close by also new Eden Project. The bedrooms have washing facilities and shaver points. There is a separate lounge and dining room for guests with tea and coffee making facilities. Bed and Breakfast £15 daily. Evening Meal optional.

**BODMIN near. Mrs Dolly Ellis, Mena Barn, Lanivet, Bodmin PL30 5HW (01208 831271).** Mena Barn is situated in the tiny hamlet of Mena, one mile from the Lanivet Junction of the A30. Mena offers easy access to both north and south coasts and The Moors. The area is ideal for walking, riding, golf, fishing and cycling, with lots of places of interest close by. One double, one twin, one single and one guests' bathroom. Central heating. Tea/coffee making facilities in rooms. Children over 10 welcome. Dogs welcome, by arrangement. Bed and Breakfast from £15 per person. Stabling available for two horses, by arrangement.

**BOSCASTLE. Ruth and Michael Parsons, The Old Coach House, Tintagel Road, Boscastle PL35 0AS (01840 250398; Fax: 01840 250346).** Relax in a 300 year old former coach house now tastefully equipped to meet the needs of the new millennium with all rooms en suite, colour TVs, radios, tea/coffee makers and central heating. Accessible for disabled guests. Good cooking. This picturesque village is a haven for walkers with its dramatic coastal scenery, a photographer's dream, and an ideal base to tour both the north and south coasts. The area is famed for its sandy beaches and surfing whilst King Arthur's Tintagel is only three miles away. Come and enjoy a friendly holiday with people who care. Brochure on request. Bed and Breakfast from £18 to £25. **AA ♦♦♦♦**
e-mail: parsons@old-coach.demon.co.uk
website: www.old-coach.co.uk

**BOSCASTLE. Mrs P. E. Perfili, Trefoil Farm, Camelford Road, Boscastle PL35 0AD (01840 250606).** Trefoil is non-smoking accommodation only, a short walk to the picturesque village of Boscastle. En suite rooms, tea/coffee making facilities. Colour TV's. Comfortable accommodation, good home cooking, vagetarians catered for. Sandy beaches, a haven for walkers and a photographer's dream. The ideal base for North and South Cornish coasts. Reductions for weekly bookings and children. A warm welcome awaits you. Bed and Breakfast from £19.

**BOSCASTLE. Mrs Cheryl Nicholls, Trerosewill Farmhouse, Paradise, Boscastle PL35 0DL (01840 250545). Working Farm.** Luxurious Bed and Breakfast accommodation in modern farmhouse on working farm, only a short walk from the picturesque village of Boscastle. Rooms have spectacular coastal and rural views; all en suite, with tea making facilities. Colour TV and telephone available if required. Mineral water and bathrobes provided. Licensed, centrally heated. Seasonal log fires. Large gardens. Traditional farmhouse fayre. Feed the calves. Superb coastal and countryside walks. One way walks arranged. Packed Lunches available. Spring and Autumn breaks. Bed and Breakfast from £19. Strictly non-smoking. FHG Diploma Award. Good food Award Winner of Farmhouse Bed and Breakfast for Cornwall 2000. **ETC ♦♦♦♦** *SILVER AWARD.*

See also Colour Display Advertisement

**BOSCASTLE. Mrs Sheila M. Smith, Glenthorne, Penally Hill, Boscastle PL35 0HH (01840 250502).** Glenthorne is set in its own grounds with ample parking area. Within five minutes' walk of the picturesque village with its quaint little harbour, a photographer's paradise. If you like walking there is the beautiful Valency Valley which leads to St. Juliot Church for the Thomas Hardy fans, also spectacular coastal walks. It's an ideal base for touring. Accommodation - one double with washbasin and one twin room, both with tea/coffee making facilities. Own lounge with colour TV. Pets welcome if well behaved. Own front door key. Bed and Breakfast from £15.50.

**Cornwall** 85

# Stamford Hill Hotel
*"A Country House Hotel"*

Set in five acres of gardens and woodland overlooking open countryside yet only a mile from the sandy beaches of Bude, our spacious Georgian Manor House with 15 en suite bedrooms with TV and tea/coffee making facilities, outdoor heated pool, tennis court, badminton court, games room and sauna is the ideal place for a relaxing holiday or short break. Daily Bed and Breakfast from £27.50; Three Day Break Dinner, Bed and Breakfast from £112.50. Pets welcome.   **AA ★★** 
Ian & Joy McFeat, Stamford Hill Hotel, Stratton, Bude, Cornwall EX23 9AY (01288) 352709

**BOSCASTLE. Mrs Jackie Haddy, Home Farm, Minster, Boscastle PL35 0BN (Tel & Fax: 01840 250195).** Home Farm is a beautifully situated working farm overlooking picturesque Boscastle and its heritage coastline. The farm is surrounded by National Trust countryside and footpaths through unspoilt wooded valleys to Boscastle village, restaurants and harbour. Traditional farmhouse with beautiful furnishings has three charming en suite rooms with colour TV with satellite link, tea-making facilities; cosy guest lounge with log fire. Good home cooking; walled garden; plenty of friendly farm animals. Beaches, golf courses, riding stables, coastal paths and many other activities for you to enjoy. A warm welcome awaits you. **ETC ♦♦♦**
e-mail: jackie.haddy@btclick.com

**BUDE. Mrs S.A. Trewin, Lower Northcott Farm, Poughill, Bude EX23 9EQ (01288 352350). Working farm.** Elegant Georgian farmhouse, magnificently situated one mile north of Bude, with outstanding views of rugged heritage coastline. Spacious en suite bedrooms with colour TV, four-poster beds and tea/coffee facilities. A warm welcome, personal attention assured. Home cooking our speciality. Central heating throughout. Bed and Breakfast from £18. Open all year. **AA ♦♦♦**
e-mail: sally@coast-countryside.co.uk
website: www.coast-countryside.co.uk

See also Colour Display Advertisement

**BUDE. Margaret and Richard Heard, Trencreek Farmhouse, St Gennys, Bude EX23 0AY (01840 230219).** Comfortable small farmhouse which offers a homely and relaxed family atmosphere. Situated in quiet and peaceful surroundings yet within reach of Crackington Haven. Well placed for easy access to coastal and countryside walks. Family, double and twin-bedded rooms, most en suite, all with tea and coffee making facilities. Two comfortable lounges. Games Room. Separate dining room. Generous portions of home-cooked farmhouse food are always freshly prepared. Children welcome, special rates for under twelves. Spring and Autumn breaks available. Non-smoking. Sunday lunches and midday lunches optional.

**FREE or REDUCED RATE entry to Holiday Visits and Attractions — see our READERS' OFFER VOUCHERS on pages 43-60**

## Cornwall

**BUDE. Mrs Pearl Hopper, West Nethercott Farm, Whitstone, Holsworthy (Devon) EX22 6LD (01288 341394). Working farm, join in.** Personal attention and a warm welcome await you on this dairy and sheep farm. Watch the cows being milked, help with the animals. Free pony rides, scenic farm walks. Short distance from sandy beaches, surfing and the rugged North Cornwall coast. Ideal base for visiting any part of Devon or Cornwall. We are located in Cornwall though our postal address is Devon. The traditional farmhouse has washbasin and TV in bedrooms; diningroom and separate lounge with colour TV. Plenty of excellent home cooking. Access to the house at anytime. Bed and Full English Breakfast from £15, Evening Meal and packed lunches available. Children under 12 years reduced rates. Weekly terms available.

**BUDE. Mrs Christine Nancekivell, Dolsdon Farm, Boyton, Launceston PL15 8NT (01288 341264).** Dolsdon was once a 17th century coaching inn, now modernised, situated on the Launceston to Bude road within easy reach of sandy beaches, surfing, Tamar Otter Park, leisure centre with heated swimming pool, golf courses, fishing, tennis and horse riding and is ideal for touring Cornwall and Devon. Guests are welcome to wander around the 260 acre working farm. All bedrooms have washbasins and tea making facilities (en suite family room available). Comfortably furnished lounge has colour TV. Plenty of good home cooking assured - full English breakfast. Parking. Bed and Breakfast from £15; reductions for children. Brochure available.

**CADGWITH COVE. Mrs A. Betty, High Massetts, Cadgwith Cove, Helston TR12 7LA (01326 290571).** Situated in Cadgwith Cove, the most south-westerly point of the UK. A delightful unspoilt quaint fishing village with safe bathing, boating, superb Inn with folk, jazz and fisherman singing evenings. Bed and Breakfast in Edwardian house with relaxed atmosphere and panoramic views over water and cove, 200 yards from beach. Large sub-tropical garden. Convenient for National Trust Gardens, Falmouth, Truro and Penzance. The Helford River, riding and golf are available nearby. A self-catering studio is also available in the house. There is also available a waterside property at Helford which sleeps six.

**CALLINGTON. Mrs W.E. Trewin, Higher Manaton, Callington PL17 8PX (Tel & Fax: 01579 370460).** You are guaranteed a warm welcome at Higher Manaton, a 90-acre farm set in rolling Cornish countryside. Two-and-half miles north-west of Callington on the B3257, central for the historic towns of Launceston, Tavistock and Plymouth. Ideal touring centre for Bodmin Moor, Dartmoor, sandy beaches, golf, riding, fishing, swimming and designated footpaths. The 18th century farmhouse has spacious roooms. Separate diningroom and lounge with TV/video. Family, twin and double rooms, all with private facilities. Bed and Breakfast £19 per night; reductions for children. Extensive range of handcrafted wood-turning displayed.
**ETC ♦♦♦**

**EAST LOOE. Jenny and John Jenkin, Sea Breeze, Lower Chapel Street, East Looe PL13 1AT (01503 263131).** A small, comfortable and friendly Guest House situated in the old part of the town. Conveniently situated on level ground very close to the beach, harbour, shops and restaurants. Our mostly en suite, colour co-ordinated bedrooms all have colour TV, hair dryer, tea and coffee making facilities and are fully centrally heated to make your winter breaks more comfortable. We serve a generous traditional full English Breakfast as well as catering for vegetarians. Come and enjoy a holiday where nothing is too much trouble. Senior Citizen discounts. Brochure and tariff available on request.
e-mail: johnjenkin@sbgh.freeserve.co.uk
website: www.cornwallexplore.co.uk/seabreeze

**FALMOUTH. Heritage House, 1 Clifton Terrace, Falmouth TR11 3QG (01326 317834).** We offer visitors a warm friendly welcome at our comfortable family-run guesthouse. Centrally located for town and beaches. All bedrooms are tastefully decorated with colour TV, free tea/coffee, vanity basins and central heating, with access available at all times throughout the day. Children are welcome, with cot and highchair available. Bed and full English or vegetarian breakfast from £16 per person nightly. Reduced rates for longer stays. Accommodation includes single, twin, double and family bedrooms. On street parking available with no restrictions. Open all year (except Christmas). Resident proprietors: **Lynn and Ken Grimes.** 
e-mail: heritagehouse@tinyonline.co.uk

**FALMOUTH. Bos-Sclewys Guest House, 97 Dracaena Avenue, Falmouth TR11 2EP (01326 314592).** A friendly, Cornish family-run guest house. Family, double and twin en suite bedrooms are available on ground and first floors. The comfortable rooms have central heating, colour TV and tea/coffee making facilities. A varied full English breakfast is served in a spacious diningroom with separate tables. Bos-Sclewys is open all year. Large private car park. This is a non-smoking establishment. Reservations from and to any day. Bed and Breakfast from £18. Reductions for weekly bookings. Cornwall Tourist Board Approved Accommodation. Please write or phone for brochure to **Yvonne Eddy.**

**FALMOUTH. "Wickham", 21 Gyllyngvase Terrace, Falmouth TR11 4DL (01326 311140).** A small, friendly, non-smoking guest house situated between the harbour and beach with views over Falmouth Bay. We are close to the railway station and within easy reach of the town. Wickham is the ideal base for exploring Falmouth and South Cornwall's gardens, castles, harbour, coastal footpath and much more. All rooms have television and beverage facilities, some have sea views. We specialise in home-cooked meals and offer a varied breakfast menu. Evening meals are served with fresh seasonal vegetables. Bed and Breakfast from £19 nightly, £120 weekly. Evening meal £9. Discount for children. Single overnight stays welcome/
e-mail: enquiries@wickhamhotel.freeserve.co.uk 

**FALMOUTH. Mrs Waddington, 'Trevaylor', 8 Pennance Road, Falmouth TR11 4EA (01326 313041; Fax: 01326 316899).** 'Come as a stranger, leave as a friend,' - you are assured of a warm welcome in pleasant surroundings. Small detached hotel situated between town and beach. En suite rooms with TV, tea/coffee making facilities and full central heating. Full English Breakfast or vegetarian alternative. Evening meals by arrangement, special diets catered for. Walking, sailing, tennis, golf and fishing nearby. Bed and Breakfast from £18, special weekly and winter rates. Open all year. Non-smoking establishment. Children welcome. Pets by arrangement. 
e-mail: stay@trevaylor.co.uk

**FALMOUTH. Mrs Val Condliffe, Inow House, Port Navas, Falmouth TR11 5RQ (Tel & Fax : 01326 340113).** Tranquil cottage adjacent to our lovely country house, set in three-acre gardens of magnolias, camellias and rhododendrons overlooking a beautiful wooded valley on the north bank of the Helford River. Close to Trebah and Glendurgan gardens and within easy reach of Lost Gardens of Heligan, Eden Project and many National Trust properties. The two-bedroomed cottage, which is non-smoking, sleeps six (double, twin, double sofa-bed). Regrettably we are unable to accommodate children or pets. Bed linen, towels, electricity and heating are all included. Self-catering or Bed and Breakfast. Short breaks available. Further information and brochure on request.

**FALMOUTH. Mrs D. Nethercot, "Telford", 47 Melvill Road, Falmouth TR11 4DG (01326 314581).** 
"Excellent accommodation, good food – see you again" – an actual quote from our Visitors' Book. Why don't YOU try our guest house this year for your annual holiday or out-of-season break? We really do try and make your holiday a happy one and many guests return annually. We are Cornwall Tourist Board registered and mentioned in Arthur Eperon's "Travellers' Britain". Singles, doubles and twin rooms are available, all with colour TV and complimentary tea-making facilities. En suite rooms. Central heating. Private parking. Open March to November. Tariff: Bed and Breakfast from £115 weekly.

**FALMOUTH. Celia and Ian Carruthers, The Clearwater, 59 Melvill Road, Falmouth TR11 4DF (01326 311344).** Enjoy quality bed and breakfast accommodation, in a perfect location. Clean, comfortable, tastefully decorated bedrooms with TVs and hot drink making facilities. Ten rooms, some en suite. Delicious home cooking. Bar. Close to excellent restaurants, idyllic walks, secluded coves, creekside pubs, watersports, ancient castles and country houses. Two minutes' walk to Falmouth's main beach. Drying and storage facilities for sailing, diving, walking gear, etc. Large car park and near railway station. We welcome guests for short or long stays almost all year, from a very reasonable £18 per night. Please call for a brochure, directions or to check availability. **AA** *RECOMMENDED.* 
e-mail: clearwater@lineone.net
website: www.clearwaterhotel.co.uk

**FALMOUTH. Mrs J. Eustice, Trevu House Hotel, 45 Melvill Road, Falmouth TR11 4DG (01326 312852; Fax: 01326 318631).** Trevu House is a small family-run hotel with a friendly home from home atmosphere, with special emphasis on comfort, cleanliness and personal service. The situation is ideal for a seaside holiday being only about two minutes' walk from Gyllyngvase Beach and within easy reach of the town, harbour and railway station. Spacious accommodation is tastefully furnished with bright modern decor. Large comfortable lounge/reading room. Bedrooms are en suite and have modern divan beds, some 6' wide, colour TV, tea/coffee facilities and central heating. We pride ourselves on our high standard of breakfast cuisine which is well presented and served at separate tables. Trevu House is a non-smoking establishment. Full Fire Certificate held. Small car park. Bed and breakfast from £17.50. No single room supplement. Brochure available upon request. 
e-mail: elaine.eddy@lineone.net
website: www.trevu-house-hotel.co.uk

**FALMOUTH (Near). Mrs A. Hunter, 'Broad Reach', Trewen Road, Budock Water, Near Falmouth TR11 5EB (01326 313469).** 'Broad Reach' is situated two miles from Falmouth. All bedrooms enjoy peaceful country views over fields to Falmouth Bay, as does our warm, light conservatory where breakfast is served. We are ideally placed for visiting Cornwall's gardens, Helford River and The Carrick Roads. Coastal path, golf and sailing are all nearby. The Eden Project, Lizard, Penzance, St Ives and north coast can all be reached within an hour. Bed and Breakfast from £17.50 with weekly rates. All rooms are comfortable, light and well equipped. There is a large garden to enjoy, and ample parking. Pets welcome, reductions for children.

Please mention *Bed and Breakfast Stops* when making enquiries about accommodation featured in these pages.

**HELSTON. Mr Joe Gormley, Alma House, Mullion, Helston TR12 7BZ (01326 240509).** A warm and friendly family owned guest house with fully licensed restaurant offering bed and breakfast with evening meal available. Situated in the centre of the village with sea views; car parking at the rear of the building. Each room offers en suite bathrooms, remote-control colour TV and tea/coffee making facilities. We have a large lounge with a well stocked bar. Alma House is within easy walking distance of nearby beaches and Great Britain's most southerly 18 hole golf course. There are many coastal walks to be enjoyed with fabulous views looking over Mounts Bay and beyond, with the Lizard Point only a short drive away. A warm and friendly welcome and comfortable stay is assured at Alma House. Rooms range from £22 to £25 per person. Reduced rates out of season.
**AA ♦♦♦♦** 
e-mail: alma_house@freenet.co.uk

**HELSTON. Mrs P. Roberts, Hendra Farm, Wendron, Helston TR13 0NR (01326 340470).** Hendra Farm, just off the main Helston/Falmouth road, is an ideal centre for touring Cornwall; three miles to Helston, eight to both Redruth and Falmouth. Safe sandy beaches within easy reach - five miles to the sea. Beautiful views from the farmhouse of the 60 acre beef farm. Two double, one single, and one family bedrooms; bathroom and toilets; sittingroom and two diningrooms. Cot, babysitting and reduced rates offered for children. No objection to pets. Car necessary, parking space. Enjoy good cooking with roast beef, pork, lamb, chicken, genuine Cornish pasties, fish and delicious sweets and cream. Open all year except Christmas. Evening Dinner, Bed and Breakfast from £125 per week which includes cooked breakfast, three course evening dinner, tea and homemade cake before bed. Bed and Breakfast only from £14.00 per night also available.

**HELSTON. Mrs M. Jenkin, Tregea, Wendron, Helston TR13 0NS (01326 573885).** Tregea is a peaceful country cottage three miles from Helston, seven miles from Redruth, just off B3297 road. Ideal centre for touring towns and beauty spots, Falmouth 11 miles, Penzance 14 miles, Truro 16 miles, The Lizard 11 miles, six miles to the sea. Tregea is situated in the centre of the farm with its own drive. Lovely country views, pretty cottage garden and comfortable accommodation. One double bedroom with vanity unit. One twin bedded room. Bathroom and toilet, for visitors use only. Lounge/diner with TV/video. Coffee/tea facilities in bedrooms. Bed and Breakfast £15 per night £16 for one night only. Evening Meal £7. Car necessary/parking. A warm welcome and good food is assured.

**HELSTON. Mrs Moira Bevan, The Manse, St. Keverne, Helston TR12 6LY (Tel & Fax: 01326 281025).** The Manse is a comfortable Victorian house in a small friendly village. It is an ideal base for walking, including the south west coast path, diving, fishing and exploring the beautiful Lizard Peninsula. Double rooms (one en suite) have vanity unit, colour TV and beverage tray. Food is home-cooked using mainly local and/or organic produce. Vegetarian options. An Evening Meal is available, also Packed Lunches on request. The Manse is a non-smoking house and we welcome children over 12 years and well behaved dogs. Bed and Breakfast from £17.50 to £20. Discounts for week bookings and low season Short Breaks. Brochure on request. *CORNWALL TOURIST BOARD APPROVED.*
e-mail: themanse@classicfm.net

**HELSTON. Mrs Penny Jenkin, Barton Farm, Gweek, Helston TR13 0QH (01326 572557).** Barton Farm is a family-run dairy farm situated in a quiet location just above Gweek. The charming open beamed farmhouse is surrounded by gardens. The accommodation consists of three attractive bedrooms with tea/coffee facilities, clock, radio, hairdryer and heating. Two bathrooms/showers, dining room and open fired lounge with TV. A warm welcome, good food and comfort are a priority. Ideal for touring South West Cornwall including the beautiful Helford River and the Lizard. Excellent beaches and coastline to explore just a short drive away. Tourist attractions include the Seal Sanctuary, Flambards and Poldark Mine only five minutes away.

## 90  Cornwall

**See also Colour Display Advertisement**

**HELSTON near. Mrs D. J. Hill, Rocklands, Pentreath Road, The Lizard, Near Helston TR12 7NX (01326 290339).** "Rocklands" is situated overlooking part of Cornwall's superb coastline and enjoys uninterrupted sea views. The Lizard is well known for its lovely picturesque scenery, coastal walks and enchanting coves and beaches, as well as the famous Serpentine Stone which is quarried and sold locally. Open Easter to October. The Hill family have been catering for visitors on the Lizard since the 1850's. Three bedrooms with sea views, one en suite, tea/coffee making facilities and electric heaters; sittingroom with TV and video; sun lounge; diningroom with separate tables. Bed and Breakfast weekly terms from £126 per person. NO VAT. Children and well trained pets welcome.

**HELSTON near. Mark and Christine Channing, Parc-an-Ithan House Hotel, Sithney, Near Helston TR13 0RN (Tel & Fax: 01326 572565).** Chris and Mark welcome you to their peaceful country hotel set in its own grounds. We have six individually decorated en suite bedrooms, including a four-poster bedroom. All rooms enjoy panoramic open country views. Each room has remote-control colour TV, tea and coffee making facilities, clock/radio. Some rooms have sofas for that extra comfort. We are ideally located for exploring the Lizard and Land's End peninsulas, and all of West Cornwall's attractions, and just five minutes' drive from sandy beaches. We serve freshly prepared home-cooked food, dinners are served by candlelight, always with a choice of menu. There is a fully stocked licensed bar and cosy residents' guest lounge. Bed and Breakfast from £20, Bed, Breakfast and Evening Meal £32. Weekly rates and short break specials out of season. Ample private off-road parking. Call for free colour brochure. **ETC ♦♦♦** 
e-mail: parchotel@btinternet.com
website: www.s-h-systems.co.uk/hotels.parcanit.html

**LAND'S END. Corinne & Allan Collinson, Bosavern House, St Just-in-Penwith, Penzance TR19 7RD (Tel & Fax: 01736 788301).** Modernised 17th century country house in two acres of garden, one mile from the coast, four miles from sandy beach, Penzance six miles, near Land's End. Convenient for airport. An ideal walking and touring centre. The house is well appointed, double glazed and all rooms have their own showers and toilets. Home cooking, log fires and friendly personal service ensure your comfort. Open all year, except Christmas. Bed and Breakfast from £19.00. Write or phone for brochure. **ETC ♦♦♦.** 
e-mail: marcol@bosavern.u-net.com
website: www.bosavern.u-net.com

**LAUNCESTON. Mrs Mary Rich, "Nathania", Altarnun, Launceston PL15 7SL (01566 86426).** A warm welcome awaits you, for accommodation on a small farm on Bodmin Moor within easy reach of coast, moors, towns, lakes and fishing. Visit King Arthur country – Tintagel, Dozmary Pool, the famous Jamaica Inn, Wesley Cottage and cathedral of the moors. One mile from A30, very quiet, ideal for overnight stop for West Cornwall. Double room en suite, twin rooms with bathroom adjoining. Tea making facilities and TV. Payphone. Conservatory and lounge for quiet relaxation. We look forward to meeting you for one night, or why not book your holiday with us and tour Cornwall. You will enjoy the quiet, happy, relaxing atmosphere. Prices from £10.50 per person per night. Please telephone, or write, for details – SAE, thank you.

---

*Please mention Bed & Breakfast Stops when writing to enquire about accommodation*

**Cornwall**  91

**LAUNCESTON (near Bodmin Moor). Mrs Barbara Sleep, Trevadlock Farm, Trevadlock, Launceston PL15 7PW (Tel & Fax: 01566 782239).** A truly Cornish welcome awaits you at Trevadlock. a working farm set within 230 acres on the edge of Bodmin Moor. Just one-and-a-half miles from the main A30. Ideally placed for breaking your journey, or staying longer and touring both north and south coasts, or both counties. We offer a traditional farmhouse breakfast in a friendly relaxing atmosphere. Large comfortable rooms. One double en suite, one twin with bathroom. All rooms have tea/coffee making facilities, colour TV, hairdryer. Bed and Breakfast from £19. **ETC ♦♦♦♦** SILVER AWARD.
e-mail: trevadlockfarm@compuserve.com

**LISKEARD. Mrs Stephanie Rowe, Tregondale Farm, Menheniot, Liskeard PL14 3RG (Tel & Fax: 01579 342407). Working farm, join in.** Feeling like a break near the coast? Come and relax, join our family with the peace of the countryside — breathtaking in Spring — on a 200 acre mixed farm, situated near Looe between A38 and A390. See pedigree South Devon cattle and sheep naturally reared, explore the woodland farm trail amidst wildlife and flowers. This stylish, characteristic farmhouse, which dates back to the Domesday Book, has featured in the Daily Telegraph, and is a Cream of Cornwall member, provides exceptional comfort with en suite bedrooms all with colour TV, tea/coffee making facilities, lounge diningroom with log fires. A conservatory to enjoy each day's warmth capturing a beautiful view over the farm, set in an original walled garden including picnic table, tennis court and play area. Special activities can be arranged — golf, fishing, cycling and walking. Home local produce a speciality, full English Breakfast, enjoy a delicious optional evening meal from £11. Bed and Breakfast from £21. Open all year. A warm welcome awaits you to discover the beauty of Cornwall. Please phone for a brochure and discuss your requirements. **ETC/AA ♦♦♦♦** SILVER AWARD. Self-catering character cottage also available (**ETC★★★★** )

**LISKEARD. Daphne A. Rogers, Hotel Nebula, Liskeard PL14 3JU (Tel & Fax: 01579 343989).** A warm welcome awaits you at our friendly and comfortable hotel. All our bedrooms are non-smoking and en suite with colour TV and tea and coffee making facilities. Enjoy a hearty breakfast before exploring beaches, moors (Bodmin and Dartmoor nearby), playing golf or wind-surfing on a nearby lake. Relax by our wood-burning fire, lit on colder days, in our comfortable well-stocked bar. Evening Meals available on request, special diets catered for; full central heating, ample parking, open all year. Bed and Breakfast from £26. Ring for details. *SECTA, CORNWALL TOURIST BOARD.*

**LISKEARD. Mrs C. Copplestone, Trethevy Farm, Darite, Liskeard PL14 5JX (01579 343186).** Relax in beautiful and peaceful surroundings in a delightful spacious 16th century Listed farmhouse on the edge of Bodmin Moor in the heart of Cornish countryside. Ideal for walking, touring and visiting places of local historical interest, such as National Trust properties, ancient monuments and quaint fishing villages of Looe, Polperro. Within walking distance of local 17th century pub. Enjoy tasteful decoration - one en suite room and one double room with adjoining bathroom. All with colour TV, tea/coffee making facilities. Strictly no smoking in the bedrooms. Sorry no pets. Full traditional farmhouse breakfast. Evening Meal also available with advanced bookings. Details on request.

---

**FHG**

Visit the FHG website
**www.holidayguides.com**
for details of the wide choice of accommodation
featured in the full range of FHG titles

## Cornwall

**LIZARD PENINSULA. Bob and Jackie Royds, Colvennor Farmhouse, Cury Cross Lanes, Helston TR12 7BJ (01326 241208).** Colvennor, a part 17th century Grade II Listed former farmhouse offers a welcoming and peaceful retreat. Approached by a long driveway and set in an acre of garden with far reaching rural views. The comfortable en suite bedrooms, two double and one twin, each have TV and hospitality tray. Relax in the guest lounge with its beamed ceiling and pore over the many maps and books on hand. Explore the coast down to the breathtaking Lizard Point and round to the lovely Helford River. Bed and full Farmhouse Breakfast £18 to £22 per person. Special breaks. Non-smoking. No reductions for children. **AA** ◆◆◆◆

**LOOE. Mrs D. Eastley, Bake Farm, Pelynt, Looe PL13 2QQ (Tel & Fax: 01503 220244). Working farm**
This is an old farmhouse, bearing the Trelawney Coat of Arms (1610), situated midway between Looe and Fowey. There are three double bedrooms all with washbasins, one with en suite, bathroom/toilet, shower room/toilet; sittingroom/diningroom. Children welcome at reduced rates. Sorry, no pets. Open from April to October. A car is essential for touring the area, ample parking. There is much to see and do here – horse riding, coastal walks, golf, National Trust properties within easy reach. The sea is only five miles away and there is shark fishing at Looe. Bed and Breakfast from £17. Cleanliness guaranteed. Brochure available on request. **ETC** ◆◆◆

**LOOE. Mrs Lynda Wills, Polgover Farm, Widegates, Looe PL13 1PY (01503 240248). Working farm.**
Polgover Farm is situated in picturesque countryside, four miles from Looe on the B3252 and ideally situated to explore Cornwall and South Devon. Local attractions include horse riding, golf, fishing, water sports, Monkey Sanctuary and many beaches. There is always a warm welcome at Polgover's spacious 16th century Listed farmhouse, where you can have a peaceful and relaxing holiday. There are three tastefully decorated bedrooms, all with washbasins, colour TV and tea/coffee facilities. Guests' bathroom. Lounge with colour TV incorporating breakfast room with separate tables. Sorry, no pets. Open Easter to October. Ample parking. Bed and Breakfast from £16. Weekly and child reductions. Brochure available. Also luxury six-berth fully equipped self-catering caravan in its own garden available at the farm.
website: www.polgoverfarm_homestead.com

**LOOE. Mrs Angela Eastley, Little Larnick Farm, Pelynt, Looe PL13 2NB (01503 262837).** Little Larnick is situated in a sheltered part of the West Looe river valley. Walk to Looe from our working dairy farm and along the coastal path to picturesque Polperro. The character farmhouse and barn offers twin, double and family en suite rooms. The bedrooms are superbly equipped and decorated to a high standard. The family room is in a downstairs annexe overlooking the garden. Our newly renovated barn offers three self-contained bedrooms with their own lounge areas. Cycling shed, drying room and ample parking. No pets, no smoking. Bed and Breakfast from £20 to £23. Open all year. **ETC** ◆◆◆◆

---

Readers are requested to mention this guidebook when seeking accommodation (and please enclose a stamped addressed envelope).

## Talehay Farm
### Pelynt Nr Looe PL13 2LT
### A Quiet Haven in the Countryside near the sea

Talehay farmhouse is an ancient 17th Century Grade II Listed Cornish farmstead. It is located between Looe & Polperro and makes an ideal touring base. This quiet haven offers top class accommodation. Many of the farm's original features - exposed oak beams, slate windowsills, open log fires - add a grace and charm enhanced by the antique furniture and tasteful decor. The views across open countryside are superb. Our large double, family and twin rooms are all en suite with colour TV and tea/coffee making facilities. The delicious breakfasts make use of local produce, including our own free-range eggs and such delights as home made marmalade. Bed & Breakfast from £20 open all year. Cornwall Tourist Board approved. Non Smoking.

Let our brochure convince you – Tel/Fax Mrs Ann Brumpton 01503 220252
E-mail: pr.brumpton@ukonline.co.uk  Website: www.cornwallexplore.co.uk/talehay

---

**MARAZION near. Jenny Birchall, Mount View House, Varfell, Ludgvan, Penzance TR20 8AH (01736 710179).** Mount View House is a Victorian former farmhouse standing in half an acre of gardens overlooking St. Michael's Mount. The house is furnished in traditional style and offers one room with sea views and another with rural views. Rooms have washbasins, central heating and tea/coffee making facilities. Guests' WC and shower room; sitting/diningroom with open fire. Children welcome, cot available. Situated approximately three miles from Penzance and five miles from St. Ives. We are the ideal touring stopover. Our close proximity to the heliport (one mile) makes us an ideal stopover en route to the Scilly Isles. Bed and Breakfast from £16 per person per night. Four night low season breaks at £100 for two people sharing. Self-catering accommodation also available.

---

**MEVAGISSEY. Mrs Anne Hennah, Treleaven Farm, Mevagissey PL26 6RZ (01726 842413). Working farm.** Treleaven Farm is situated in quiet, pleasant surroundings overlooking the village and the sea. The 200-acre mixed farm is well placed for visitors to enjoy the many attractions of Mevagissey with its quaint narrow streets and lovely shops. Fishing and boat trips are available and very popular. Also, visit the Lost Gardens of Heligan. The house offers a warm and friendly welcome with the emphasis on comfort, cleanliness and good food using local produce. A licensed bar and solar heated swimming pool add to your holiday enjoyment, together with a games room and putting green. Tastefully furnished throughout, with central heating, there are five double bedrooms and one family bedroom, all en suite with tea/coffee making facilities and TV; bathroom, two toilets. Sittingroom and diningroom. Open February to November for Bed and Breakfast from £22. Dinner £12. Sorry, no pets. SAE, please, for particulars or telephone.

---

**NEWQUAY. Terri and Dave Clark, Trewerry Mill, Trerice, St Newlyn East TR8 5GS (Tel & Fax: 01872 510345).** A 17th Century watermill which ground corn for the nearby Trerice Manor, now National Trust. Four miles from the north coast in the peaceful Gannel valley; very central for exploring Cornwall. In seven acres of beautiful grounds with river and wildlife pond. Enjoy Cornish cream teas in the tranquil gardens. The large, beamed mill-room is now the residents' lounge, with TV and bar. Non-smoking throughout. Comfortable bedrooms: two double, one triple, one twin and two single. Some are en suite and all have washbasin and tea making facilities. Large car park. Bed and full Breakfast from £18. Please phone for colour brochure or view our website.
e-mail: trewerry.mill@which.net
website: www.connexions.co.uk/trewerry.mill

---

**PLEASE SEND A STAMPED ADDRESSED ENVELOPE WITH ENQUIRIES**

**NEWQUAY. Mike and Mel Morgan, Kallacliff Hotel, Lusty Glaze Road, Newquay TR7 3AD (01637 871704).** Kallacliff is a nine bedroomed detached hotel situated in a peaceful area on the outskirts of Newquay with what must be some of the finest panoramic sea views in the locality. The hotel is next to the Coastal Path, overlooking Lusty Glaze Beach and within easy walking distance of the town centre. The atmosphere is friendly and relaxed and we offer en suite rooms including ground floor, all with colour TV, tea/coffee making facilities and hair dryer. Residents' car park and lounge/bar. A traditional breakfast is served with optional Evening Meal available. Bed and Breakfast from £17.50 nightly. Please ring for brochure.

**NEWQUAY. Mrs Lavery, Pensalda, 98 Henver Road, Newquay TR7 3BL (01637 874601).** Take a break in the 'heart of Cornwall'. A warm and friendly welcome awaits you at our family-run guest house, an ideal location from which to explore the finest coastline in Europe. Situated on the main A3058 approximately half-a-mile from the town and close to beaches and amenities. Single, double and family rooms available, including two chalets situated in pleasant and peaceful garden. En suite rooms available. All rooms have colour TV and tea making facilities. We have a reputation for serving good food with a choice of menu. Licensed bar, central heating. Car park. Fire certificate. Some pets welcome. Bed & Breakfast from £16, Evening Meal available. Reduced rates October to March. Open all year.

**NEWQUAY. Margaret and Alan Bird, The Philadelphia, 19 Eliot Gardens, Newquay TR7 2QE (01637 877747; Fax: 01637 876860).** Newquay's premier smoke-free guest house. Bright and spacious quality accommodation in six individually themed rooms, superbly refurbished and decorated with luxury en suite facilities, colour TV and complimentary beverages. Quiet tree-lined avenue, own car park, award winning gardens and private patio with spa pool. Only 200 yards to the seafront; town, station etc. five minutes' walk. For excellent food, comfort and great hospitality in a relaxed and friendly atmosphere, stay at the Philadelphia. Bed and Breakfast from £23 per person per night. Children welcome. Regret, no pets. Recommended by "Which?" in 'Top 20 UK Guest Houses' as seen on TV.
e-mail: stay@thephiladelphia.co.uk
website: www.thephiladelphia.co.uk

**NEWQUAY. Mike and Alison Limer, Alicia, 136 Henver Road, Newquay TR7 3EQ (Tel & Fax: 01637 874328).** Relax on the Cornish Peninsula in our friendly 'home from home' Guest House. Mike and Alison will be pleased to welcome you to their home where you can unwind in the sun lounge or enjoy the last rays of the sun in the porch. There is also a comfortable lounge to relax in which is adjacent to the dining room where traditional home cooking is served. All bedrooms are centrally heated and comfortably furnished with colour TV and tea/coffee making facilities. Some rooms are en suite. Alicia is ideally situated near Porth and Lusty Glaze beaches and only a short walk to Newquay town centre. Bed and Breakfast from £15 daily. Please telephone or write for brochure.

**NEWQUAY. Pauline and Brian Budd, Fairview House, 2 Fairview Terrace, Newquay TR7 1RJ (Tel & Fax: 01637 871179).** Fairview House offers a warm and friendly welcome where every effort is made to make your stay as relaxing and enjoyable as possible. Our comfortable bedrooms are mostly en suite with colour TV and tea/coffee making facilities. We endeavour to serve the best traditional English food using fresh local produce and special dietary needs may be catered for by arrangement. Situated enviably close to the centre of town and sandy beaches but also within easy reach of all that Newquay has to offer, we are ideally placed to discover the charms of Cornwall. Cosy licensed bar, unrestricted parking, open all year.

# White Lodge Hotel
Mawgan Porth Bay, Near Newquay,
Cornwall TR8 4BN
Tel: St. Mawgan (STD 01637) 860512
e-mail: dogfriendlyhotel@redhotant.com
website: www.dogfriendlyhotel.co.uk

**GIVE YOURSELVES AND YOUR DOGS A BREAK** at our family-run White Lodge Hotel overlooking beautiful Mawgan Porth Bay, near Newquay, Cornwall

ALL PRICES INCLUDE VAT AT $17^1/_2$%

| SPECIAL 6 DAYS (5 NIGHTS) CHRISTMAS HOUSE PARTY ONLY £250 | SPECIAL 6 DAYS (5 NIGHTS) NEW YEAR (HOGMANAY) BREAK ONLY £210 | SPECIAL 6 DAYS (5 NIGHTS) BREAKS ONLY £160-£175 BB&EM | WEEKLY TERMS FROM £210-£230 FOR 5-COURSE EVENING DINNER, BED AND 4-COURSE BREAKFAST WITH CHOICE OF MENU |
|---|---|---|---|

* Dogs most welcome- FREE OF CHARGE
* Your dogs sleep with you in your bedroom.
* Dog loving proprietors with 18 years' experience in catering for dog owners on holiday with their dogs
* ALL bedrooms with colour TV, tea/coffee makers, alarm clocks, radios, intercoms, heaters etc.
* Some en suite bedrooms
* Fantastic sea views from most rooms.
* Well-stocked residents' lounge bar, dining room and sun patio with outstanding sea views across the bay.
* Games room with pool table and dart board etc.
* Large free car park within hotel grounds
* Direct access to sandy beach and coastal path

**Phone John or Diane Parry 01637 860512 for free colour brochure**

*See also Colour Advertisement on page 7*

**NEWQUAY. Crantock Bay Hotel, West Pentire, Crantock, Near Newquay, TR8 5SE (01637 830229; Fax: 01637 831111).** This long-established family-run hotel is beautifully situated on West Pentire headland overlooking Crantock Bay, with four acres of landscaped grounds leading directly onto the beach. The spacious and comfortable public rooms all face the sea, and a major refurbishment has now provided an outstanding indoor swimming pool and other leisure facilities. Meals in the bright and spacious restaurant are a high spot of each day and are skilfully prepared using only the freshest ingredients. Voted one of the 'Top 50' hotels in Europe by The Observer. Children and pets welcome.
e-mail: stay@crantockbayhotel.co.uk
website: www.crantockbayhotel.co.uk

**PADSTOW. Mrs A. Woosnam-Mills, Mother Ivey Cottage, Trevose Head, Padstow PL28 8SL (Tel & Fax: 01841 520329).** In 1870 Mother Ivey Cottage was a 'fish cellars' used for processing the catches, landed on the beach below, from the fishing fleet. In 1920 the house was altered to its present layout. We have two guest bedrooms each with twin beds and private bathrooms. Evening meals are also usually available. The house is situated on the clifftop on Trevose head and looks across Mother Ivey Bay towards the Padstow Life Boat Station. The coastal footpath runs behind the property and nearby are Trevose Golf Course and many swimming and surfing beaches.

*Please mention Bed & Breakfast Stops when writing to enquire about accommodation*

**Cornwall**

**PADSTOW. Mrs Sandra May, Trewithen Farm, St Merryn, Near Padstow PL28 8JZ (01841 520420).** Trewithen farmhouse is a newly renovated Cornish Roundhouse, set in a large garden and situated on a working farm enjoying country and coastal views. The picturesque town of Padstow with its pretty harbour and narrow streets with famous fish restaurants is only three miles away. St Merryn Parish boasts seven beautiful sandy beaches and bays. Also coastal walks, golf, fishing and horse riding on neighbouring farm. Hire a bike or walk along the Camel Trail cycle and footpath - winding for 18 miles along the River Camel. The accommodation has been tastefully decorated to complement the exposed beams and original features. All bedrooms are en suite or have vanity units, with hot drink facilities. Parking. Full English breakfast. TV lounge. Bed and Breakfast from £22 per person per night. Evening meal optional. Weekly rates and Winter weekend breaks available. **ETC** ♦♦♦

**PAR. Mr and Mrs Rowe, Tregaminion Farm House, Menabilly, Par PL24 2TL.** En suite and self contained family B&B throughout the year. Our farm nestles in the hollows of the South Cornish Coast set deep within the Du Maurier countryside. We can offer you a peaceful, relaxed and friendly holiday in our family-run farmhouse. We are within easy walking distance of Polkerris and Polridmouth Bays, both beautiful, small, safe beaches for you and your children to enjoy. The ancient port of Fowey is also within walking distance, approximately two to three miles. Stay with us for as little or as long as you like. For more information and prices please contact **Jill Rowe (01726 812442).**

**PENZANCE. Rosemary and Bill Wooldridge, Camilla House Hotel, Regent Terrace, Penzance TR18 4DW (Tel & Fax: 01736 363771).** We would like to welcome you to this lovely Listed building (with own car park) in a quiet terrace close to the harbour and town centre and within easy reach of bus and coach stations. Penzance is an ideal base from which you can explore West Cornwall at any time of year. Single, double, twin and triple rooms availabale, many en suite, some with sea views. We hope that the warm welcome and excellent breafast plus central heating for your out-of-season visit will make this one of your favourite places. For the safety and comfort of all our guests, smoking is not allowed in the hotel. Bed and Breakfast from £20 to £28 per person per night. **AA** ♦♦♦♦.
website: www.camillahouse-hotel.co.uk

**PENZANCE. Mr and Mrs B.M. Smyth, Carnson House, East Terrace, Penzance TR18 2TD (01736 365589).** A friendly welcome awaits you in our centrally situated, licensed Private Hotel. We specially cater for rail and coach travellers being only yards from the station. A high standard of comfort is maintained together with a reputation for excellent food. We have a comfortable lounge, attractive diningroom with separate dining tables, and eight bedrooms, all with heating, tea-makers and colour TV and some with en suite facilities. Penzance is a lively and interesting town with plenty of shops, gardens and promenade, and is the natural centre for exploring the Land's End Peninsula with its beaches, cliffs, coves and villages. We arrange many local excursions, including some to the Isles of Scilly as well as coach tours and car hire. . Bed and Breakfast from £18 to £24 daily. **RAC** *LISTED*

**PENZANCE. Mr and Mrs G. W. Buswell, Penalva Private Hotel, Alexandra Road, Penzance TR18 4LZ (01736 369060).** The hotel is TOTALLY NON-SMOKING, offering full central heating, fresh immaculate interior, en-suite facilities, excellent food and a real welcome with courteous service. Penalva is a well positioned imposing late Victorian hotel set in a wide tree-lined boulevard with ample parking, close to promenade and shops. Perfect centre for enjoying the wealth of beautiful sandy coves, historical remains and magnificent walks. Large guest lounge and separate diningroom. Colour TV and tea/coffee making facilities in bedrooms. Open all year. Special diets by prior arrangement. Sorry, no pets. Bed and Breakfast from £15 to £21. Weekly reductions. Children 6 to 12 half-price if sharing family rooms. Highly recommended. SAE, please, for brochure. **AA** ♦♦♦

**Cornwall** 97

**PENZANCE. John and Andrea Leggatt, Cornerways Guest House, 5 Leskinnick Street, Penzance TR18 2HA (01736 364645)**. A Listed Town House close to rail/bus stations and car parks. All rooms are en suite with tea/coffee making facilities and colour TV. Bed and Breakfast from £19.00 per person; optional evening meal £8.50 per person. Weekly terms avialable. Open all year.
e-mail: cornerways@penzance90.fsnet.co.uk

**PENZANCE. Mr and Mrs Adams, Homefields Guest House, Sennen, Near Penzance TR19 7AD (01736 871418)**. Michael and Sandra offer you a warm welcome at our small and friendly licensed guest house overlooking Cornwall's rugged north coast. Close to beautiful sandy beaches, Land's End and the Minack Open Theatre. The South-West Coastal Path and Cycle Way are on our doorstep. All rooms have colour TV, tea/coffee, and heating. All have en suite or private facilities; some have sea views. Four-poster available. Pets welcome. Terms from £15 to £19 per person per night.
**RAC ♦♦♦** *SPARKLING DIAMONDS AWARD, RECOMMENDED BY WHICH? MAGAZINE.*

**PENZANCE. Mrs Rosalind Wyatt, South Colenso Farm, Goldsithney, Penzance TR20 9JB (01736 762290). Working farm.** South Colenso Farm is a 76 acre working arable farm. The spacious Georgian style farmhouse is set in beautiful unspoilt countryside, peaceful and secluded, yet not isolated. Ideally situated between Marazion and Praa Sands, a perfect location for touring both coasts of Cornwall, with sandy beaches and pretty coves nearby. The large en suite bedrooms (two double and one family room) have tea/coffee making facilities and a lovely country view. Relax in our comfortable lounge with colour television and log fire. Full English Breakfast is served in our sunny diningroom with separate tables. Ample private parking. Non-smoking. Children over six years welcome. Please write or call for terms.
e-mail: damian@dcwyatt.freeserve.co.uk

**PENZANCE. Mrs M. D. Olds, Mulfra Farm, Newmill, Penzance TR20 8XP (01736 363940)**. This hill farm, with cows and calves, high on the edge of the Penwith moors, offers superb accommodation which attracts many of our guests to return year after year. The 17th century, stone built, beamed farmhouse has far reaching views, is attractively decorated and furnished and offers two double en suite bedrooms with tea and coffee facilities, TV, shaver socket;comfortable lounge with inglenook fireplace, diningroom with separate tables and conservatory. Car essential, ample parking, warm friendly atmosphere, good food, beautiful walking country, ideal centre for exploring west Cornwall. Bed and Breakfast £130 per person per week. Evening Meal by arrangement. Further details with pleasure.

**PENZANCE. Carol and Keith Richards, Con Amore, 38 Morrab Road, Penzance TR18 4EX (Tel & Fax: 01736 363423)**. Con Amore was once a Victorian Gentleman's residence, situated opposite sub-tropical gardens, just off the sea front, Promenade and town centre. We wish to show you Cornish hospitality that will make you want to return to us again. All of our rooms have their own character and each has colour TV central heating and tea/coffee making facilities. Keys are provided for unrestricted access at all times. A full English breakfast is included, but we cater for all tastes, and vegetarian and special diets are well catered for. Children under 10 years of age are half price when sharing with two adults. For more information, please call Carol or Keith.
e-mail: KRich30327@aol.com

# Boscean Country Hotel
## St Just, Penzance, Cornwall TR19 7QP

The Boscean Country Hotel, located amidst some of the most dramatic scenery in West Cornwall, is somewhere very special just waiting to be discovered. This country house offers a wonderful combination of oak panelled walls, a magnificent oak staircase and open log fires. The natural gardens, extending to nearly three acres, are a haven for wildlife including foxes and badgers.

Situated on the heritage coast in an area of outstanding natural beauty close to Cape Cornwall and the coastal footpath, this is an ideal base from which to explore the Land's End Peninsula. The moors of Penwith are rich in Iron and Bronze Age relics dating back to 4000BC. Penzance, St Michael's Mount, St Ives, Land's End and the Minack Theatre are all a short distance away.

12 en suite rooms, centrally heated throughout, licensed bar. Excellent home cooking using fresh local produce. *Unlimited Desserts!!* Open all year.

*English Tourism Council* ◆◆◆

*Bed & Breakfast £22.00   Dinner, Bed & Breakfast £35.00*

Tel/Fax 01736 788748   E-mail: Boscean@aol.com
Website: www.bosceancountryhotel.co.uk

## EDNOVEAN HOUSE
**Perranuthnoe, Near Penzance, Cornwall TR20 9LZ**
*Clive & Jacqueline Whittington*
**Tel: 01736 711071**
e-mail: ednoveanhouse.fsnet.co.uk

A warm welcome awaits you at our beautifully situated Victorian Country House, offering nine letting rooms, most having en-suite facilities and panoramic sea views. Situated in one acre of lovely gardens surrounded by farmland and overlooking St. Michaels Mount and Mounts Bay, it has one of the finest views in Cornwall. TV lounge, diningroom/bar, small library/writing room, putting green and ample parking. Pets welcome by arrangement. Bed and Breakfast from £20 to £27.50 per person. A peaceful and tranquil setting with the coast path and beach a short walk away. **AA** ◆◆◆

**PENZANCE ( near Porthcurno). Mrs P. M. Hall, Treen Farmhouse, Treen, St. Levan, Penzance TR19 6LF (01736 810253).** Just off the South West coastal footpath, Treen Farm is a family-run dairy farm in the village of Treen, set in 80 acres of pasture land by the sea, near Lands End (four miles). Visitors are welcome to use the gardens, walk around the farm or watch milking. Pub, shop, cafe, campsite and beaches nearby. Ideal for walking and sightseeing. Comfortable farmhouse Bed and Breakfast accommodation - single, twin and double (en suite) rooms with tea/coffee making facilities, views of gardens, pasture land and sea. Some with TV. Traditional English Breakfast served. Guests' lounge with open fire and television. Private parking. Pets welcome. Reductions for children. Sorry, no smoking. Bed and Breakfast from £15. Self-catering also available for two people (plus cot) from £150.

## FREE or REDUCED RATE entry to Holiday Visits and Attractions — see our READERS' OFFER VOUCHERS on pages 43-60

**PERRANPORTH. Chy an Kerensa, Cliff Road, Perranporth TR6 0DR (01872 572470).** Licensed Guest House situated by Coastal Path, directly overlooking miles of rolling surf, golden sands, rocks and heathland. Only 200 metres from beach and village centre, which has various restaurants, shops and pubs to suit all tastes and ages. Also tennis, bowls, wetsuit and surfboard hire, with golf and horse riding nearby. Our comfortable bedrooms, most en suite, have colour TV, central heating and tea/coffee making facilities. Many have panoramic sea views, as do our lounge/bar and diningroom. Bed and Breakfast from £17 to £24 per person. Weekly rates and other reductions. A warm welcome from Wendy Woodcock all year. Please write or telephone for further details. **ETC ◆◆◆**.

**POLZEATH. Mrs P. White, Seaways, Polzeath PL27 6SU (01208 862382).** Seaways is a small family guest house, 250 yards from safe, sandy beach. Surfing, riding, sailing, tennis, squash, golf all nearby. All bedrooms with en suite or private bathrooms, comprising one family, two double, two twin and a single room. Sittingroom; diningroom. Children welcome (reduced price for under 10's). Cot, high chair available. Comfortable family holiday assured with plenty of good home cooking. Lovely cliff walks nearby. Padstow a short distance by ferry. Other places of interest include Tintagel, Boscastle and Port Isaac. Non-smoking establishment. Open all year round. Bed and Breakfast from £20; Evening Meal £8.50.

**PORTHLEVEN. Mrs Mary Fuhrmann, Tamarind, Shrubberies Hill, Porthleven, Helston TR13 9EA (01326 574303).** Situated on the Looe Bar side of Porthleven on Lizard Peninsula. Sea views from bedrooms. Four-course English breakfast taken in sun lounge with panoramic views over Mounts Bay. 264 yards from beach and costal path. Five minutes' walk from harbour, shops, restaurants and inns. Colour TV, tea and coffee making facilities in bedrooms. Guests welcome to use garden; facilities for drying swimwear etc. Off road parking on property. Knowledge of German. Bed And Breakfast from £18 per person, sharing bathroom with one other couple, or £20 with private bathroom. Smoking in sun lounge only.

**PORTHLEVEN. Mrs M.A. Woodward, Greystones, 40 West End, Porthleven TR13 9JL (Tel & Fax: 01326 565583).** Bed and Breakfast in comfortable Guesthouse situated near coastal path. Ideal for touring. Dogs accommodated free, children half-price. All rooms overlooking the sea. A few minutes' walk from harbour, beaches, shops, pubs and restaurants. Full English breakfast or cooked to your requirements. Colour TV, tea/coffee making facilities.Bed and Breakfast from £15 per person per night and from £95 per person per week.

**PORT ISAAC. Long Cross Hotel & Victorian Gardens, Trelights, Port Isaac, Cornwall PL29 3TF (Tel: 01208 8802430O).** Stay in one of Cornwall's most unusual hotels set in our own magnificent gardens, visited by thousands of garden lovers annually. We also have our own Free House Tavern for your enjoyment. Area of Outstanding Natural Beauty. Spacious en suite rooms. Pets' corner with animals to feed. Children's adventure play area. Only £55 for three nights September to June.

Terms quoted in this publication may be subject to increase if rises in costs necessitate

## 100    Cornwall

**PRAA SANDS. Marian Foy, Mzima, Penlee Close, Praa Sands, Penzance TR20 9SR (01736 763856).** Comfortable Cornish family-run, non-smoking Bed and Breakfast accommodation. Friendly atmosphere in large modern bungalow with garden and patio for visitors' use. One kilometre to beach which is a two kilometre long sweep of sand and surf popular for bathing and watersports. The south west coastal path in close proximity provides miles of walks along the spectacular Cornish coastline. Central for touring West Cornwall, Lizard Peninsula, Lands End, St. Michaels Mount. Tea and coffee making facilities, colour TV, washbasin central heating in all rooms.

**ROSELAND PENINSULA. Mrs Shirley E. Pascoe, Court Farm, Philleigh, Truro TR2 5NB (01872 580313). Working farm, join in.** Situated in the heart of the Roseland Peninsula at Philleigh, with its lovely Norman church and 17th century Roseland Inn, this spacious and attractive old farmhouse set in over an acre of garden offers Bed and Breakfast accommodation. There are double, single and family bedrooms with washbasin and tea-making facilities; bathroom, separate toilet; large comfortable lounge with colour TV. Enjoy a full English breakfast in the traditional farmhouse kitchen. Children welcome, cot, high chair, babysitting available. Sorry, no pets indoors. Car essential – ample parking. The family livestock and arable farm includes 50 acres of woodlands which border the beautiful Fal Estuary providing superb walking, picnic areas and bird-watching opportunities, while the nearest beaches are just over two miles away. Please write or telephone for brochure and terms.

**ROSELAND PENINSULA. Mrs Ann Palmer, Trenestrall Farm, Ruan High Lanes, Truro TR2 5LX (01872 501259). Working farm, join in.** A family-run farm offers accommodation in 200-year-old stone built barn. Centrally situated in the beautiful and peaceful Roseland Peninsula close to St. Mawes. Accommodation comprises one double and one twin-bedded rooms with washbasin and one further twin room, all with tea/coffee making facilities; bathrooms and shower rooms for guests' use only; en suite available, sittingroom with TV. Children welcome. A friendly personal service assured. Pets welcome by arrangement. Bed and Breakfast from £16 per person per night.

TRENESTRALL FARM

**ST AGNES. The Sunholme Hotel, Goonvrea Road, St Agnes TR5 0NW (01872 552318).** Situated in extensive grounds on the south-facing slope of St Agnes Beacon. The Sunholme Hotel enjoys some of the finest views in the South West. Ideal for touring; cliff walks and beaches. Good food and service. All bedrooms en suite. Pets welcome (£1.50 per night). Write or telephone for brochure. **AA ★★**

**ST AGNES. Dorothy Gill-Carey, Penkerris, Penwinnick Road, St. Agnes TR5 0PA (Tel & Fax: 01872 552262).** An enchanting Edwardian licensed residence in garden with large lawn in unspoilt Cornish village. Penkerris has fields on one side yet there are pubs, shops, etc. only 150 yards away on the other side. Attractive diningroom, lounge with colour TV, video, piano, and log fires in winter. Bedrooms with washbasin, TV, kettle, shaver point, radio; en suite if required. There is a shower room as well as bathrooms. Beaches, swimming, surfing, gliding and magnificent cliff walks nearby. Children welcome; dogs by arrangement. From £15 to £22.50 per night Bed and Breakfast; Dinner available from £10. Open all year. **ETC ◆◆ AA, RAC** *AND LES ROUTIERS RECOMMENDED.*

PENKERRIS

**ST AUSTELL. Mrs Liz Berryman, Polgreen Farm, London Apprentice, St. Austell PL26 7AP (01726 75151).** Polgreen is a family-run dairy farm nestling in the Pentewan Valley in an Area of Outstanding Natural Beauty. One mile from the coast and four miles from the picturesque fishing village of Mevagissey. A perfect location for a relaxing holiday in the glorious Cornish countryside. Centrally situated, Polgreen is ideally placed for touring all of Cornwall's many attractions. Cornish Way Leisure Trail adjoining farm. Within a few minutes' drive of the spectacular Eden Project and Heligan Gardens. All rooms with private facilities,, colour TV, tea/coffee making facilities. Guest lounge. Children welcome. Terms from £18 per night. **ETC** ♦♦♦.
e-mail: polgreen.farm@btclick.com

**ST IVES. Mrs C.E. Quick, Menwidden Farm, Ludgvan, Penzance TR20 8BN (01736 740415).** Menwidden Farm is centrally situated in West Cornwall, five miles from St. Ives (north coast) and three miles from Marazion (south coast). Within easy reach of Land's End and the Lizard Peninsula. Comfortable bedrooms and good home cooking including roast meats, pasties and Cornish cream. Three double (one en suite), one twin bedded and one single bedrooms all with tea/coffee making facilities; bathroom and shower room; sittingroom and diningroom. Children welcome and pets allowed. Open March to October. Car essential – parking. Fire Certificate and basic Hygiene Certificate held. Past winner of Farm Holiday Guide Diploma. Evening Meal, Bed and Breakfast from £145 per week, or from £17 per night. **ETC** ♦♦♦

**ST IVES. Mrs N.I. Mann, Trewey Farm, Zennor, St. Ives TR26 3DA (01736 796936). Working farm.** On the main St. Ives to Land's End road, this attractive granite-built farmhouse stands among gorse and heather-clad hills, half-a-mile from the sea and five miles from St. Ives. The mixed farm covers 300 acres, with Guernsey cattle and fine views of the sea; lovely cliff and hill walks. Guests will be warmly welcomed and find a friendly atmosphere. Five double, one single and three family bedrooms (all with washbasin); bathroom, toilets; sittingroom, diningroom. Cot, high chair and babysitting available. Pets allowed. Car essential, parking. Open all year. Electric heating. Bed and Breakfast only. SAE for terms, please.

**ST IVES. Miss B. Delbridge, Bella Vista Guest House, St. Ives Road, Carbis Bay, St. Ives TR26 2SF (01736 796063).** First class accommodation, highly recommended, satisfaction guaranteed. Extensive views of sea and coastline, close to golf courses and only a short walk to the beach. Washbasins, colour TV, Central heating, Radio intercom, baby listening service, tea/coffee making facilities in all rooms. Own key to rooms. Free parking on premises. Personal supervision. Fresh farm produce. Fire Certificate held. Bed and Breakfast from £18. Open all year. Non-smokers welcome. SAE for brochure.

**ST IVES. Carlyon Guest House, 18 The Terrace, St Ives TR26 3BP (01736 795317).** Situated in the picturesque fishing village of St Ives, this attractive Guest House enjoys sea views and offers a warm, friendly atmosphere. The comfortable, attractive bedrooms all have colour TV and tea/coffee making facilities. All rooms fully en suite. Good English cooking can be enjoyed in the diningroom (separate tables). Children welcome. Bed and Breakfast with four-course Evening Meal optional. Illustration shows view from the house. SAE for terms and further details.

**ST IVES.** Mrs S. Britnell, Little Pengelly Farmhouse, Trenwheal, Leedstown, Hayle TR27 6BP (01736 850452). Picturesque 17th century farmhouse located within easy reach of Land's End and Lizard Peninsula midway between St. Ives and Helston off the B3302. Guest TV lounge and conservatory. Early morning tea and generous breakfast with home-baked bread. Hot and cold savouries and sweets served from 1pm to 7pm daily. Considerate pet owners welcome. Sorry non-smoking and not suitable for young children. Open Easter to end of October - terms £17 per person per night. SELF CATERING COTTAGE - sleeps two - open all year. Quiet and private with its own patio and garden. Pets welcome. Non-smoking. Three-day off-peak breaks. Please write or phone for full details and photographs. 
e-mail: britnell@littlepengelly.co.uk
website: www.littlepengelly.co.uk

**SENNEN.** Mr and Mrs R.A. Comber, Sunny Bank Hotel, Sea View Hill, Sennen TR19 7AR (01736 871278). Sunny Bank is a Highly Recommended hotel standing in large gardens overlooking Sennen Cove. There are 11 bedrooms, all centrally heated with tea and coffee making facilities, some rooms have showers, all have sea or country views. There is a large TV lounge and separate reading room. The grounds provide ample parking. The food is all home prepared and cooked using local produce whenever possible. The breakfasts, evening meals and 'Minack Theatre' picnics are delicious. Lands End, the Minack Theatre, sandy beaches and cliff or countryside walks are all within easy reach. Open January – November. Bed and Breakfast from £15.

**TINTAGEL.** Cate West, Chilcotts, Bossiney, Tintagel PL34 0AY (Tel & Fax: 01840 770324). Without stepping onto a road, slip through the side gate of this 16th Century listed cottage into a landscape owned by the National Trust and designated as an Area of Outstanding Natural Beauty. Closest cottage to nearby Bossiney beach for rock pools, surfing, safe swimming and caves to explore. Walk the airy cliff path north to nearby Rocky Valley or on to picturesque Boscastle Harbour. Southwards takes you to the ruins of King Arthur's Castle and onwards to busy Trebarwith Strand. Notice you have not stepped onto a road yet? Detached traditional country cottage ideal for a small number of guests. Home cooking, warm informal atmosphere, large bright double/family bedrooms with beamed ceilings and olde worlde feel. All rooms have TV, tea/coffee makers. Self-catering annexe available. May I send you a brochure? Bed and Breakfast from £16. Directions: Bossiney adjoins Tintagel on the B3263 (coast road), Chilcotts adjoins large lay-by with telephone box.

**TREGONY.** Mrs Sandra R. Collins, Tregonan, Tregony, Truro TR2 5SN (Tel & Fax 01872 530249). **Working farm.** Tregonan is tucked away down a half-mile private lane amidst its 300 acre farm, a spacious house in a secluded garden. A former home of the Tremayne family, founders of Heligan Gardens just three miles away. Six miles west of Mevagissey on the threshold of the Roseland Peninsula. A good selection of walks, gardens, beaches and eating places locally. Car essential, ample parking. Heated bedrooms, two double en suite and one twin, all with TV, radio and beverage making facilities. Guest sittingroom. Limited to six guests. Regret no pets. Bed and English Breakfast menu from £19. OS Ref: SW 955 452.
ETC ♦♦♦♦

---

*Please mention Bed & Breakfast Stops when writing to enquire about accommodation*

# MARCORRIE HOTEL

**20 FALMOUTH ROAD, TRURO TR1 2HX**

Victorian town house in conservation area, five minutes' walk from the city centre and cathedral. Centrally situated for visiting country houses, gardens and coastal resorts. All rooms are en suite and have central heating, colour TV, telephone, tea-making facilities. Ample parking. Credit cards: Visa, Access, Amex. Open all year.
B&B from £37.50 single, £47.50 double

**Tel: 01872 277374   Fax: 01872 241666**

*See also Colour Advertisement*

---

**TRURO. Mrs Shirley Wakeling, Rock Cottage, Blackwater, Truro TR4 8EU (01872 560252).** 18th century beamed cob cottage, formerly the village schoolmaster's home. A haven for non-smokers. Two double/one twin, en suite. Rooms with beverage tray, toiletries,clock/radio, colour TV, hairdryer and shaver point. Centrally heated. Attractive guest sittingroom with colour TV. Cosy dining room with antique Cornish range. Private parking. Garden. Village location three miles from ocean and six miles from Truro. Sorry, no children or pets. Open all year except Xmas and New Year. Bed and Breakfast from £22. Mastercard/Visa/Switch/Delta/JCB. Telephone for colour brochure. **ETC/AA ♦♦♦♦**

*Rock Cottage*

---

**TRURO. Andrew and Catherine Webb, Tregony House, 15 Fore Street, Tregony, Truro TR2 5RN (01872 530671).** Grade II Listed building on main street of Tregony, nine miles Truro, many beaches close by. Ideally situated for exploring all of Cornwall. Accommodation comprises front: double with en suite facilities, twin and single room sharing bathroom; back: double with en suite facilities and twin with private bathroom, both overlooking garden. All have tea/coffee making facilities. Guests' sitting room with colour TV and open fire. Breakfast and dinner served in low beamed 18th century dining room. Private and off-road parking available. Access and Visa cards accepted. Children over 12 years welcome. Terms from £19.50 Bed and Breakfast, £11.50 for four-course Dinner. Brochure available.

---

**TRURO. Mrs M.A. Hutchings, Lands Vue Country House, Three Burrows, Truro TR4 8JA (01872 560242).** You will find a warm welcome at our peaceful country home, set in two acres of garden where you may relax or enjoy a game of croquet. There are three lovely bedrooms all with en suite facilities, TV and tea making facilities. There is a cosy lounge with open fire and the large diningroom, where we serve a delicious farmhouse breakfast, has superb views over the Cornish countryside. Being very central for all Cornwall's famous gardens and coastline, Lands Vue is an ideal base highly recommended by many of our guests who return year after year. Write or phone Molly Hutchings for brochure. **AA ♦♦♦♦**

---

*Visit the FHG website www.holidayguides.com for a wide choice of holiday accommodation*

## Cornwall

**TRURO. Pam and Reg Wells, Grey Rocks, Penstraze Irish Wolfhounds, Truro TR4 8PE (01872 560231).** Small, 100 year old Cornish Farmhouse in country setting. Central heating. Own car park. Half-acre garden. Two double rooms with washbasin, colour TV and courtesy tray. One very small single room. Ideally situated for touring the whole of Cornwall. South coast 10 miles approximately, north coast five miles approximately, four miles from the beautiful, quaint city of Truro. Dogs welcome, free, sleep in your room or in large outdoor kennel if preferred. Many lovely walks for dogs nearby and throughout Cornwall. Please telephone for brochure.

**WADEBRIDGE. Mrs E. Hodge, Pengelly Farm, Burlawn, Wadebridge PL27 7LA (01208 814217).** A Listed Georgian farmhouse situated in quiet location on a 150 acre farm overlooking wooded valleys, approximately one and a half miles from Wadebridge. Ideal location for touring or walking and cycling to the Camel Trail. There are a number of beaches plus sailing, golf, horse-riding and much more within 20 minutes' close drive. Large garden for relaxing or for children to play. Three prettily decorated bedrooms all with vanity units, tea and coffee making facilities, colour TV and hairdryers. Traditional English breakfast or special requests by prior arrangement. Lounge with colour TV. Children welcome, cot and highchair available, babysitting on request. Bed and Breakfast £18. **ETC ♦♦♦,** *CORNWALL TOURIST BOARD REGISTERED ACCOMMODATION.*

**ZENNOR. Sue and John Wilson, Tregeraint House, Zennor, St. Ives TR26 3DB (Tel & Fax: 01736 797061).** Traditional cottage in an acre of gardens overlooking the Atlantic coastline in one of the most beautiful parts of Cornwall. The house has been lovingly restored, providing a base from which to explore this fascinating area. Each bedroom (one twin, one double, one family) is comfortably furnished with a plumbed-in traditional pine washstand and central heating. Tea and coffee making facilities. Vegetarian and other diets can be catered for and there are nearby pubs where reasonable meals can be had while St. Ives and Penzance offer excellent eating, artistic and other facilities. Open all year except at Christmas. £20 per person (£2 single supplement).
**e-mail: sueewilson@yahoo.co.uk**

---

*The* **FHG**
# GOLF GUIDE
*Where to Play
Where to Stay*
**2001**

Available from most bookshops, the 2001 edition of
**THE GOLF GUIDE** covers details of every UK golf course – well over 2500 entries – for holiday or business golf. Hundreds of hotel entries offer convenient accommodation, accompanying details of the courses – the 'pro', par score, length etc.

In association with 'Golf Monthly' and including the Ryder Cup Report as well as Holiday Golf in Ireland, France, Portugal, Spain, The USA, South Africa and Thailand.

**£9.99 from bookshops or £10.50 including postage (UK only) from FHG Publications,
Abbey Mill Business Centre, Paisley PA1 1TJ**

# CUMBRIA

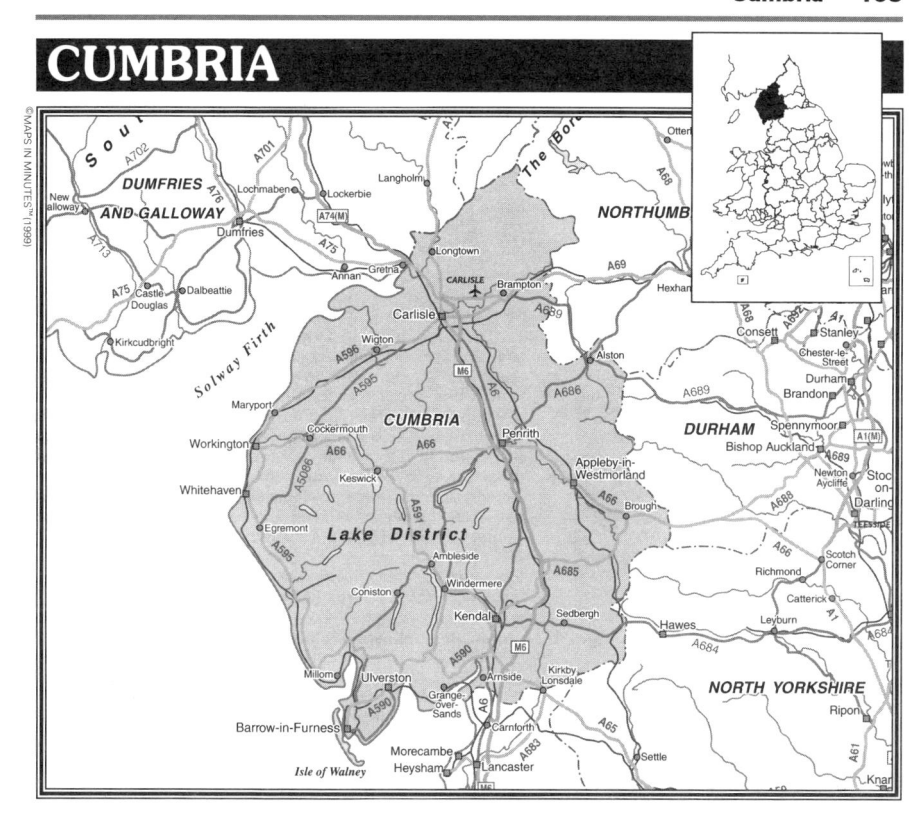

**ALSTON. Clare and Mike Le Marie, Brownside House, Leadgate, Alston CA9 3EL (01434 382169 or 01434 382100).** Alston, England's highest market town, is in the heart of the unspoilt North Pennines, an ideal centre for walking, cycling, birdwatching and exploring old lead mines. Easy reach for Lake District, Hadrian's Wall, Northumberland. A warm welcome awaits you at Brownside House, dating back to 1849, set in open country with superb views. One double and two twin bedded rooms all with washbasins and tea/coffee facilities. Shared bathroom with bath and shower. Residents' lounge with log fire, TV. Full central heating. Children and pets welcome (babysitting available). Bed and Breakfast £18.00; Evening Meal £6.50. Weekly and Short Break terms available. ETC ♦♦♦

**AMBLESIDE. Peter & Anne Hart, Bracken Fell, Outgate, Ambleside LA22 0NH (015394 36289).** A delightful country residence with two acres of gardens, situated in beautiful open countryside between Ambleside and Hawkshead in the picturesque hamlet of Outgate. This comfortable home with its lovely accommodation and friendly service is ideally located for exploring the Lake District. Each bedroom has its own private facilities, colour TV, hairdryer, complimentary tea and coffee and a superb view. There is a comfortable lounge, diningroom and ample private parking. Two country inns where evening meals are available are within walking distance. Bed and Breakfast from £23.00. No pets or children under 12 years. Non-smoking. Self-catering accommodation also available. Write or phone for brochure.
ETC ♦♦♦
e-mail: hart.brackenfell@virgin.net
website: www.brackenfell.com

**AMBLESIDE. Mrs Maureen Rushby, Fern Cottage, 6 Waterhead Terrace, Ambleside LA22 0HA (015394 33007).** Homely Lakeland stone terraced house situated on the edge of Ambleside only two minutes' walk from the head of Lake Windermere and the Steamer Piers and one mile from the village. Ideal base for touring the Lakes. Kendal approximately 12 miles, Bowness-on-Windermere five miles, Hawkshead and Grasmere about 20 minutes' drive away. The accommodation comprises two double rooms and one twin room, all with tea/coffee making facilities and vanity unit; shared bathroom, lounge/diner with TV. Brochure available. Bed and Breakfast £15 – £17 per person.

*See also Colour Display Advertisement*

**AMBLESIDE. Elder Grove, Lake Road, Ambleside LA22 0DB (015394 32504).** Enjoy quality accommodation and service in our Victorian house, conveniently situated for walking or sightseeing and close to Ambleside with many shops and restaurants. We offer 10 comfortable bedrooms, all with private bathroom, also colour television, kettle tray, hair dryer and radio. Start the day with a choice of breakfast from a full Cumbrian Breakfast to a lighter bite served in our unique Lakeland diningroom, and in the evenings relax in our bar or lounge. We have parking, central heating and ask for no smoking please. Contact Paul and Vicky McDougall for brochure and tariff. **ETC ♦♦♦♦**
e-mail:info@eldergrove.co.uk
website: www.eldergrove.co.uk

**AMBLESIDE. Mrs Sheila Briggs, High Wray Farm, High Wray, Ambleside LA22 0JE (015394 32280).** Charming 17th century olde worlde farmhouse with Beatrix Potter connections. Original oak beams, cosy lounge with log burning fire. Pretty colour co-ordinated bedrooms, all with en suite facilities. Heating and tea/coffee trays are in all rooms. Situated in a quiet unspoilt location, panoramic views and lake shore walks close by. A warm welcome awaits all who visit us where comfort, cleanliness and personal attention are assured. Follow the B5286 from Ambleside toward Hawkshead, turn left for Wray. Follow road to High Wray, the farm is on the right. Families welcome. Terms from £20. FHG Diploma Winner. **ETC ♦♦♦♦**

**AMBLESIDE. Mrs Margaret Rigg, The Dower House, Wray Castle, Ambleside LA22 0JA (015394 33211).** Lovely old house, quiet and peaceful, stands on an elevation overlooking Lake Windermere, with one of the most beautiful views in all Lakeland. Its setting within the 100-acre Wray Castle estate (National Trust), with direct access to the Lake, makes it an ideal base for walking and touring. Hawkshead and Ambleside are about ten minutes' drive away and have numerous old inns and restaurants. Ample car parking; prefer dogs to sleep in the car. Children over five years welcome, reduced rates if under 12 years. Bed and Breakfast from £25; optional Evening Meal from £13. Open all year round.

**AMBLESIDE. Bob and Anne Jeffrey, The Anchorage, Rydal Road, Ambleside LA22 9AY (015394 32046).** Situated two minutes' walk from the centre of Ambleside, with its many shops, restaurants and inns, this modern guest house has a private car park, comfortable lounge, tastefully furnished bedrooms with colour TV, tea/coffee making facilities and central heating. Each bedroom has pleasant views over parkland or surrounding fells. En suite rooms available. Choice of English, vegetarian or Continental breakfast. Ideal base for walkers or those wishing to tour the Lake District. Non-smoking. Sorry, no pets. Open February to mid December. Weekly rates/mid-week breaks available at various times. Bed and Breakfast from £18 to £27. **ETC ♦♦♦**

## Cumbria

**See also Colour DIsplay Advertisement**
Tel: 015394 36332

### BORWICK LODGE
Outgate, Hawkshead, Ambleside LA22 0PU
website: www.borwicklodge.com

A leafy driveway entices you to the most enchantingly situated house in the Lake District, a very special 17th century country lodge with magnificent panoramic lake and mountain views, quietly secluded in beautiful gardens. Ideally placed in the heart of the Lakes and close to Hawkshead village with its good choice of restaurants and inns. Beautiful en suite bedrooms with colour television and tea/coffee facilities, including "Special Occasions" and "Romantic Breaks", two king-size four-poster rooms. Colin and Rosemary welcome you to their "haven of peace and tranquillity" in this most beautiful corner of England. Ample parking. NON-SMOKING. Bed and Breakfast from £25. May we send our brochure? Tourist Board ♦♦♦♦ and SILVER AWARD. Four times winner of FHG Diploma for Accommodation and Service.

## ELTERWATER PARK
Skelwith, Ambleside, Cumbria
♦♦♦♦ Licensed Guest House
### At the Gateway to Langdale

Elterwater Park is a traditional Lakeland house, high on the hills above Langdale. Situated 3 miles from Ambleside and 1 mile from Skelwith Bridge. Its parkland borders Elterwater, the lake of Swans, a leisurely 10 minute walk away. At Elterwater Park great care has been taken to preserve traditional features while ensuring every modern comfort.

Each elegantly furnished room is spacious and airy, warm in winter and cool in summer, with lovely views. All bedrooms are en suite. Colour TV, radio, hair dryers, hospitality trays, fresh flowers and lots of storage space make this a home from home.

At Elterwater Park all meals are freshly prepared, from local ingredients wherever possible.

**B&B fr £28   DB&B fr £43**

**Tel: 015394 32227**
email: enquiries@elterwater.com
www.elterwater.com

---

**AMBLESIDE. Doug and Pat Callen, Kingswood, Old Lake Road, Ambleside LA22 0AE (015394 34081).** Kingswood is a charming, Victorian Lakeland house offering first class en suite accommodation and a superb breakfast, including vegetarian. The house is only a two minute walk from the town centre and a short distance from the lake. Kingswood is a non-smoking establishment with ample private parking. All rooms have tea and coffee making facilities together with colour TV and central heating for all year comfort. Bed and Breakfast rates are from £20 to £30. Please call or e-mail us for further information.
e-mail: doug@kingswood.f9.co.uk

**See also Colour Display Advertisement** **AMBLESIDE. Mr O' Brian, Ferndale Hotel, Lake Road, Ambleside LA22 0DB (015394 32207).** The Ferndale Hotel is a small, family-run Hotel where you will find a warm, friendly welcome and personal attention at all times. Offering excellent accommodation with good home cooked English or Vegetarian breakfast. Our ten attractive bedrooms have all been individually decorated and furnished, each with full en suite facilities, colour TV and tea/coffee making tray, most having individually designed canopy/draped beds. Full central heating throughout; several rooms have views of the fells, including ground floor bedrooms. Open all year round with car park, licensed, offering packed lunches, hair dryer, clothes/boot drying and ironing facilities. A wide choice of places to dine within minutes' walking distance, ranging from excellent pub food to superb restaurants of many varied cuisines will complete your day. Bed and Breakfast £19 to £25 per person per night. Weekly £125 to £155. Please phone for brochure. **ETC** ♦♦♦

---

**FHG**

Visit the FHG website
## www.holidayguides.com
for details of the wide choice of accommodation
featured in the full range of FHG titles

## Cumbria

**See also Colour Display Advertisement**

**AMBLESIDE. Liz, Mary and Craig, Wanslea Guest House, Lake Road, Ambleside LA22 0DB (015394 33884).** Wanslea is a spacious family-run Victorian non-smoking guest house with fine views, situated just a stroll from the village and Lake shore with walks beginning at the door. We offer a friendly welcome and comfortable rooms, all of which have colour TV and tea/coffee tray; most rooms are en suite. A good breakfast will start your day before enjoying a fell walk or maybe a more leisurely stroll by the lake. Relax in our licensed residents' lounge with a real fire on winter evenings. Children are welcome and pets accepted by arrangement. Bed and Breakfast from £17.50 per person. Evening Meal also available to party bookings. Autumn, Winter, Spring Breaks at reduced rates. Brochure on request. **ETC** ◆◆◆◆.
e-mail: **wanslea.guesthouse@virgin.net**

**See also Colour Display Advertisement** **AMBLESIDE. Helen and Chris Green, Lyndhurst Hotel, Wansfell Road, Ambleside LA22 0EG (015394 32421).** Attractive small Victorian hotel quietly situated in its own garden with private car park. Only two minutes from Ambleside centre. Lovely bedrooms, all en suite. Four poster bedroom or luxury bedroom for that special occasion. Scrumptious food, friendly service. Full central heating for all-year comfort. Cosy bar. Winter and Summer Breaks. A delightful base from which to explore the Lakes either by car or as a walker. Bed and Breakfast from £20. Phone or write for colour brochure, please. **ETC** ◆◆◆.

**APPLEBY. Mrs K.M. Coward, Limnerslease, Bongate, Appleby CA16 6UE (017683 51578).** Limnerslease is a family run guest house five minutes' walk from the town centre. A good half-way stopping place on the way to Scotland. There is a good golf course and an indoor heated swimming pool. Many lovely walks are all part of the charm of Appleby. Two double and one twin bedrooms, all with washbasin, colour TV, tea/coffee making facilities at no extra charge; bathroom, toilet; diningroom. Open January to November with gas heating. Ample parking. Bed and Breakfast from £17.

**APPLEBY. Mrs Diana Dakin, Morningside, Morland, Penrith CA10 3AZ (01931 714393).** Morningside is idyllically situated in the pretty village of Morland, midway between Appleby and Penrith, in the beautiful Eden Valley. Convenient for touring all of Cumbria and only 10 miles from Ullswater, it is perfect for a relaxing break. Friendly, personal service is assured in the beautifully appointed, ground floor twin-bedded room with en suite shower room, colour TV, hot drinks facilities plus the advantage of own entrance from private patio. A delicious breakfast is served in the bedroom overlooking the garden and village views. Central heating. Parking. Bed and Breakfast £20 per person. No smoking please.

---

# FHG

### PLEASE MENTION THIS GUIDE WHEN YOU WRITE OR PHONE TO ENQUIRE ABOUT ACCOMMODATION

IF YOU ARE WRITING, A STAMPED, ADDRESSED ENVELOPE IS ALWAYS APPRECIATED

## Cumbria

**See also Colour Display Advertisement**

**APPLEBY. The Gate Hotel, Bongate, Appleby CA16 6LH (017683 52688).** An attractive family-run business on the outskirts of Appleby in easy reach of the town centre with its shops, castle and swimming pool and approximately one mile from the golf course. It is tastefully decorated with panelling from the steam ship 'The Berengaria'. A traditional log fire enhances the warm and friendly service offered all year round. Our rooms are en suite and well furnished with colour TV and tea/coffee trays. There is ample parking, a pleasant enclosed garden and play area. Pets welcome by arrangement. Specialising in Thai food we also offer conventional English food. Licensed. Bed and Breakfast from £25 to £30 per person; Evening Meal from £4.95 to £12.50.
website: www.appleby/web.co.uk/gate

**APPLEBY near. Mrs M. Neilson, Tarka House, Bolton, Appleby CA16 6AW (Tel & Fax: 01768 361422).** Looking for an overnight stop with comfort and hospitality, when going north or south? Please look at your map, we are only one mile off the A66 and only a short distance from the M6 in a very peaceful village. Here we can offer you en suite bedrooms and a three course dinner if you wish at very reasonable cost! Please phone or write for a brochure. Bed and Breakfast from £20 per person per night. **ETC** ♦♦♦

**APPLEBY-IN-WESTMORLAND. Barbara and Derick Cotton, Glebe House, Bolton, Appleby-in-Westmorland CA16 6AW (017683 61125);** Our 17th century former farmhouse is ideally located for exploring the Eden Valley, an area waiting to be discovered by those who seek tranquillity in an area of outstanding natural beauty. Very quiet location with outstanding views of the Pennines. Approximately one mile from the A66 and four miles west of Appleby, and very convenient for visits to the Lake District, Yorkshire Dales and Scottish Borders. Centrally heated accommodation includes two double (one en suite) and one twin room all with tea-making facilities. Hearty breakfasts are served, with special diets catered for. Children welcome. Non-smoking. Bed and Breakfast £15 to £22. Please send SAE for brochure.
e-mail: derick.cotton@btinternet.com

**BOWNESS-ON-WINDERMERE. Biskey Howe Villa, Craig Walk, Bowness-on-Windermere LA23 3AX (015394 43988; Fax: 015394 88379).** This detached Victorian villa stands in an elevated position on the slopes of Biskey Howe (a noted Lakeland viewpoint) in a quiet area of Bowness, away from traffic and the busy Lake road yet within a few minutes' walk of the Lake and shops. You will find a friendly atmosphere in this family-run small Hotel. All bedrooms have en suite facilities, colour TV, telephone, clock/alarm, hairdryer and tea/coffee making equipment. There is a TV lounge, sun lounge and bar. Terraced rock gardens and private car parking front and rear. Open April to October. Bed and Breakfast from £26 per night according to season and length of stay. Children £16. Illustrated brochure and tariff sent on request.
e-mail: rooms@biskey-howe-hotel.co.uk
website: www.biskey-howe-hotel.co.uk

---

**FREE or REDUCED RATE entry to Holiday Visits and Attractions — see our READERS' OFFER VOUCHERS on pages 43-60**

## 110 Cumbria

**BOWNESS-ON-WINDERMERE. Vivien and Howard Newham, Langthwaite, Crook Road, Ferry View, Bowness-on-Windermere LA23 3JB (015394 43329).** Langthwaite is a large bungalow set in delightful gardens, part of which are for our guests own use with an elevated patio area. Our double and twin rooms are en suite and furnished to a high standard with TV, etc. Your comfort is assured. A wholesome breakfast is served in the conservatory. We are close to Bowness with pleasant walks and within a short drive of some of the best restaurants, pubs, golf, boating in Lakeland. An ideal base for your holiday. Bed and Breakfast £20 to £26. Open mid February to mid November. Sorry no pets or smoking. **AA** ◆◆◆
e-mail: howard.t.newham@amserve.net

**BRAMPTON. Mrs Ann Thompson, Low Rigg Farm, Walton, Brampton CA8 2DX (016977 3233).** We are a family-run dairy farm in beautiful Hadrian's Wall country, three miles Brampton, nine miles Carlisle. Conveniently situated for the Scottish Borders, Northumberland and the Lake District. The farmhouse is comfortably furnished with guests' own lounge, diningroom. The bedrooms have king-size or twin beds, tea/coffee facilities and clock-radios. Free-range eggs, home-made bread rolls and preserves are served for breakfast. Evening Meals are available by arrangement. There is a large garden and ample parking space. Guests are welcome to view the farm activities including milking. Bed and Breakfast from £16; Evening Meals from £10. Reductions for children and more than one night's stay. **ETC** ◆◆◆
e-mail: lowrigg@lineone.net

**CALDBECK. Mr and Mrs A. Savage, Swaledale Watch, Whelpo, Caldbeck CA7 8HQ (016974 78409).** Ours is a mixed farm of 300 acres situated in beautiful countryside within the Lake District National Park. Easy reach of Scottish Borders, Roman Wall, Eden Valley. Primarily a sheep farm (everyone loves lambing time). Visitors are welcome to see farm animals and activities. Many interesting walks nearby or roam the peaceful Northern fells. Enjoyed by many Cumbrian Way walkers. Very comfortable accommodation with excellent home cooking. All rooms have private facilities. Central heating. Tea making facilities. Bed and Breakfast from £18 to £24; Evening Meal from £12, Tuesday, Wednesday, Thursday and Saturday only. **AA/ETC** ◆◆◆◆.

**CARLISLE. James and Elaine Knox, The Steadings, Townhead, Houghton, Carlisle CA6 4JB (01228 23019).** We offer you a warm welcome to our new self-contained barn conversion adjoining our Grade II Listed Georgian house circa 1700. Exposed beams, tastefully decorated. Eight rooms, six en suite, two standard, all are centrally heated, double glazed and with colour TV and tea/coffee making facilities. Private parking. Excellent breakfasts. Tearoom on site. Situated minutes from M6 Junction 44; rural location yet only three miles from Carlisle city centre. Extremely easy to find. Ideal location for visiting historic Carlisle, Lake District, Roman Wall, Scottish Borders. To find us leave Junction 44, take A689 Hexham Road for three-quarters of a mile, first on right. Bed and Breakfast £16 to £18 double/twin, £20 to £22 single.

**CARLISLE. Mrs L. Young, 7 Hether Drive, Lowry Hill, Carlisle CA3 0ED (01228 527242; Mobile: 07855 642925).** Detached bungalow in quiet location with easy access English Lake District and Scottish Border country (M6 Junction 44). One room specially adapted for disabled guests - ramped access, wheel-in shower, six grab rails, adjustable toilet seat, all light switches and sockets at wheelchair height. Also family room, sleeps five, cot available, French window into garden play area. Both rooms have TV and tea making facilities. Central heating throughout. Well-behaved dogs welcome. Tariff: £18 twin or double room, half price for children sharing with adults. £20 for single occupancy.
e-mail: Liljonmeg@aol.com

**Cumbria** **111**

**CARLISLE. Eric and Daphne Houghton, Cherry Grove, 87 Petteril Street, Carlisle CA1 2AW (Tel & Fax: 01228 541942).** A warm welcome awaits you at Cherry Grove where Eric and Daphne offer a friendly, comfortable, family-run guest house. The five family/double/twin bedded en suite rooms are all decorated to a high standard and contain colour television with satellite, welcome tray, hairdryer and radio alarm clock. Built at the turn of the century, this lovely red brick town house is situated one mile from Carlisle city, is within easy reach of the M6 and only eight miles from the Scottish Border. Within 18 miles of Carlisle, on the A69 you can find the ever popular Hadrian's Wall and also Birdoswald Roman Fort and Visitor Centre.
e-mail: petteril87@aol.com

**CARLISLE. Ronnie and Jackie Fisher, Cornerways Guest House, 107 Warwick Road, Carlisle CA1 1EA (01228 521733).** Ronnie and Jackie welcome you to their family-run Guest House. A Grade II Listed building situated in the heart of historic Carlisle just two minutes' walk from city centre with castle, cathedral, bus and railway stations. An ideal base for visiting the Lake District, Hadrian's Wall and Gretna Green. Colour TV, welcome tray, shaver points and central heating in all rooms; en suite rooms available. Payphone and off-street parking. Reasonable rates from £14 per person with reductions for children. To reach us by car turn off M6 at Junction 43. **ETC** ◆◆◆◆.

**CARLISLE. Mr G. Shipp, Naworth House, 33 Victoria Place CA1 1HP (01228 521645).** An imposing town house offering informal, comfortable high standard en suite rooms with TV, tea and coffee facilities and private parking. We are only a short walk from the excellent town centre with its fine variety of shops, restaurants, pubs and of course the cathedral, castle and award winning Tullie House museum. Also close by is Stoney Holme and Swift golf courses, the Sands sports and leisure centre and the splendid River Eden. A short drive takes you to historic Hadrian's Wall, the magnificent Lake District and romantic Gretna Green. Our rates start from only £19 per person which includes English breakfast and taxes. **ETC** ◆◆◆◆.
e-mail: bbs@naworth.com
website: www,naworth.com

**CARLISLE. Mrs Georgina Elwen, New Pallyards, Hethersgill, Carlisle CA6 6HZ (01228 577308). Working farm, join in.** Farmhouse filmed for BBC TV. Relax and see beautiful North Cumbria and the Borders. A warm welcome awaits you in our country farmhouse tucked away in the Cumbrian countryside, yet easily accessible from M6 Junction 44. In addition to the surrounding attractions there is plenty to enjoy, including hill walking, peaceful forests and sea trout/salmon fishing or just nestle down and relax with nature. Two double en suite, two family en suite rooms and one twin/single bedroom, all with tea/coffee making equipment. Bed and Breakfast from £21 per person, Dinner £13; Dinner, Bed and Breakfast weekly rates from £160 to £175. Menu choice. Self-catering offered. Disabled facilities. We are proud to have won a National Salon Culinaire Award for the "Best Breakfast in Britain". **ETC** ◆◆◆ *GOLD AWARD WINNER.*
e-mail: info@newpallyards.freeserve.co.uk
website: www.newpallyards.freeserve.co.uk

---

*Please mention* **Bed and Breakfast Stops** *when making enquiries about accommodation featured in these pages.*

**CARLISLE. Mrs M. Sisson, Bessiestown Farm Country Guest House, Catlowdy, Near Longtown, Carlisle CA6 5QP (Tel & Fax: 01228 577219).** Guests return year after year to enjoy the warm welcome, peace and quiet, pretty en suite bedrooms, delightful public rooms and simply delicious home cooking. Indoor heated pool. Courtyard cottages and new honeymoon suite. Bed and Breakfast from £24.50, Evening Meal £12.50. Exit 44 M6 – Longtown and follow signs to Catlowdy. **ETC ♦♦♦♦♦** *SILVER AWARD. CUMBRIA AND ENGLAND BEST BED AND BREAKFAST AWARD WINNER.*
e-mail: bestbb2000@cs.com

**CARLISLE. Mrs Dorothy Nicholson, Gill Farm, Blackford, Carlisle CA6 4EL (01228 675326; mobile: 07808 571586).** In a delightful setting on a beef and sheep farm, this Georgian style farmhouse dated 1740 offers a friendly welcome to all guests breaking journeys to or from Scotland or having a holiday in our beautiful countryside. Near Hadrian's Wall, Gretna Green and Lake District. Golf, fishing, swimming and large agricultural auction markets all nearby; also cycle path passes our entrance. Accommodation is in one double room en suite, one family and one twin/single bedrooms. All rooms have washbasins, shaver points and tea/coffee making facilities. Two bathrooms, shower; lounge with colour TV; separate diningroom. Open all year. Reductions for children; cot provided. Central heating. Car essential, good parking. Pets permitted. Bed and Breakfast from £18. Telephone for further details or directions.

**COCKERMOUTH. George and Isobel Kerr, Link House, Bassenthwaite Lake, Cockermouth CA13 9YD (017687 76291; Fax: 017687 76670).** Link House, a warm and friendly, family-run, late Victorian country house set in the quieter part of the Lake District National Park at the northern end of Lake Bassenthwaite with stunning views of both the surrounding forests and fells. Conveniently situated minutes from Keswick and Cockermouth. All the attractive bedrooms have en suite facilities, colour TV and tea/coffee making. Conservatory Bar, lounge and private car park exclusively for guests. Bed and Breakfast from £20 per person. Two single, two twin, three doubles and one family room, all en suite. Further single with separate bathroom. Restricted smoking. Children over seven; well-behaved pets by arrangement. Open all year. **ETC/AA ♦♦♦♦.**
e-mail: gfkerr@totalise.co.uk

**COCKERMOUTH. Mrs V. A. Waters, The Rook Guesthouse, 9 Castlegate, Cockermouth CA13 9EU (01900 828496).** Interesting 17th century town house, adjacent to historic castle, we offer comfortable accommodation with full English, vegetarian or Continental breakfast served in rooms which are equipped with washbasin, colour TV, tea/coffee facilities and central heating. En suite and standard rooms available. Cockermouth is an unspoilt market town located at the North Western edge of the Lake District within easy reach of the Lakes, Cumbrian Coast and Border country. We are ideally situated as a base for walkers, cyclists and holidaymakers. Bed and Breakfast from £16 per person sharing room, single occupancy £20. Open all year, except Christmas.

**COCKERMOUTH. Mrs Chester, Birk Bank Farm, Brandlingill, Cockermouth CA13 0RB (01900 822326).** Birk Bank is a traditional Lakeland farmhouse situated up a short drive from the public road, four miles from Cockermouth. Within easy reach of Lakes and coast on a working beef and sheep farm; Enjoy home cooking using local produce and free range eggs served in guests' diningroom with separate tables. Lounge with TV and log fire on chilly evenings, tea/coffee in lounge with homemade biscuits. Morning tea if requested. One double room, one triple, electric blankets. Bathroom and shower room. Bed and Breakfast from £16 to £18. Evening Meal if booked in advance £9. Children over five welcome. Sorry no pets. Open March to October.

## HUNDITH HILL HOTEL
**Lorton Vale, Cockermouth CA13 9TH**
Tel: 01900 822092
Fax: 01900 828215

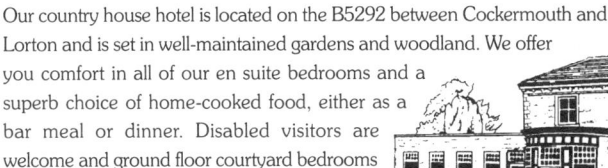

Our country house hotel is located on the B5292 between Cockermouth and Lorton and is set in well-maintained gardens and woodland. We offer you comfort in all of our en suite bedrooms and a superb choice of home-cooked food, either as a bar meal or dinner. Disabled visitors are welcome and ground floor courtyard bedrooms with private parking facilities are available.

Full colour brochure and tariff on request.

## *Prospect House Hotel*, Kents Bank Road, Grange-over-Sands, Cumbria LA11 7DJ Tel: 015395 32116

*A warm welcome awaits you at Prospect House. Seven bedrooms, six with private facilities, all have TV, radio, tea/coffee making facilities. Noted for our cuisine using fresh produce – no junk food. Car parking, Residents' bar. Our best advertisement is the many return visits we receive each year. Independently inspected to local authority approved criteria. Bed and Breakfast from £24.00, Dinner (served at 7pm) £12.50. Please telephone Mr W. Lambert for brochure and full tariff.*

**DALTON-IN-FURNESS. Mrs Nicholson, Park Cottage, Dalton-in-Furness LA15 8JZ.** Over 300 years old, Park Cottage overlooks Burlington Lake and has four acres of grounds - mainly woodland and garden with 31 types of wild birds feeding and nesting. Surrounded by public footpaths in open countryside and farmland we enjoy a very peaceful location. Two lounges cater for smokers and non-smokers, with a separate dining room. All bedrooms have splendid views, are en suite and have co-ordinated furnishings, TV/video, tea/coffee making facilities and central heating. Wide choice for breakfast, evening meals available. Packed lunches, suggested itineraries and maps. Ideally situated for walking, fishing (trout and coarse) and birdwatching. Excellent standards and value at £18 per person Bed and Breakfast. Phone **01229 462850** for brochure.

*See also Colour Display Advertisement*

**GRASMERE. Dunmail House, Keswick Road, Grasmere LA22 9RE (015394 35256).** A traditional Lakeland stone house on the edge of the village and set in spacious gardens with outstanding views. Ideally located for all the activities for which this area of Lakeland is noted. Personally run by Trevor and Lesley Bulcock who aim to provide a friendly family atmosphere. Guest lounge with TV. All rooms have tea/coffee facilities, central heating, TV and beautiful views. Some en suite. Non smoking. Ample parking. No pets. Easily accessible by public transport. Weekly rates and special winter breaks available. **ETC ♦♦♦♦**.
e-mail: enquiries@dunmailhouse.freeserve.co.uk
website: www.dunmailhouse.com

---

*Please mention Bed & Breakfast Stops when writing to enquire about accommodation*

**HADRIAN'S WALL. Pauline and Brian Staff, Holmhead Guest House on Thirlwall Castle Farm, Hadrian's Wall, Greenhead, Via Brampton CA8 7HY (Tel & Fax: 016977 47402).** This former farmhouse is not only built on Hadrian's Wall but also of it. It has stone arches, exposed beams and antique furnishings. Your host was a former Tour Guide and is an expert on Hadrian's Wall. Guests dine together for fantastic breakfasts and candlelit evening meals. A good wine list is available. Guide books, tea/coffee etc are available in the upstairs lounge which has an open fire. Four cosy bedrooms with shower/toilet. No smoking. Bed and Breakfast from £26, Evening Meal £20. Special breaks and discount ticket available. Winter Ghost Trail weekends. **ETC ♦♦♦♦**
e-mail: Holmhead@hadrianswall.freeserve.co.uk
website: www.bandbhadrianswall.com

**HAWKSHEAD. Peter & Anne Hart, Bracken Fell, Outgate, Ambleside LA22 0NH (015394 36289).** A delightful country residence with two acres of gardens, situated in beautiful open countryside between Ambleside and Hawkshead in the picturesque hamlet of Outgate. This comfortable home with its lovely accommodation and friendly service is ideally located for exploring the Lake District. Each bedroom has its own private facilities, colour TV, hairdryer, complimentary tea and coffee and a superb view. There is a comfortable lounge, diningroom and ample private parking. Two country inns where evening meals are available, are within walking distance. Bed and Breakfast from £23.00. No pets or children under 12 years. Non-smoking. Self-catering accommodation also available. Write or phone for brochure. **ETC ♦♦♦**
e-mail: hart.brackenfell@virgin.net
website: www.brackenfell.com

*See also Colour Display Advertisement*

**HAWKSHEAD. Colin and Rosemary Haskell, Borwick Lodge, Outgate, Hawkshead, Ambleside LA22 0PU (015394 36332).** A leafy driveway entices you to the most enchantingly situated house in the Lake District, a very special 17th century country lodge with magnificent panoramic lake and mountain views, quietly secluded in beautiful gardens. Ideally placed in the heart of the Lakes and close to Hawkshead village with its good choice of restaurants and inns. Beautiful en suite bedrooms with colour television and tea/coffee facilities, including "Special Occasions" and "Romantic Breaks", two king-size four-poster rooms. 3 times winner of FHG Diploma for Accommodation and Service. Colin and Rosemary welcome you to their "haven of peace and tranquillity" in this most beautiful corner of England. Ample parking. NON SMOKING. Bed and Breakfast from £25. May we send our brochure? **ETC ♦♦♦♦**

**HAWKSHEAD (Near). Paul and Fran Townsend, Pepper House, Satterthwaite, Cumbria LA12 8LS (Tel & Fax: 01229 860206).** A warm welcome awaits in 16th century former farmhouse with elevated position in tranquil valley on edge of Grizedale Forest, four miles from Hawkshead. Red and roe deer and other wildlife abound. Trout fishing nearby. Excellent, peaceful base for exploring the Lakes, close to Beatrix Potter's farm and Ruskin's Brantwood. Miles of forest trails for walking and cycling. Sympathetically updated, all bedrooms have en suite facilities. Two comfortable lounges, one with TV. Central heating, log fires; diningroom and terraces with wonderful views. Licensed bar, generous home cooking. Non-smoking. Bed and Breakfast from £23.50; with Dinner from £34. Weekly rates and special winter rates available.

---

**FHG**

Visit the FHG website
**www.holidayguides.com**
for details of the wide choice of accommodation
featured in the full range of FHG titles

**Cumbria    115**

**KENDAL. Glynis Byrne, Marwin House, Duke Street, Holme, Near Carnforth LA6 1PY (01524 781144).** Marwin House is a delightful country cottage situated in the small unspoilt village of Holme, gateway to the Lake District and Yorkshire Dales, yet only five minutes from M6 Junction 36. We are an ideal base for walking. Bedrooms are comfortable and tastefully decorated with colour TV, tea/coffee making facilities and central heating. Private lounge with colour TV/video. Children are most welcome. Off-road parking. Breakfast a speciality served in a warm friendly atmosphere. Bed and Breakfast from £16 to £18. Open all year. **ETC** ♦♦

**KENDAL. Mrs A. Taylor, Russell Farm, Burton-in-Kendal, Carnforth, Lancs. LA6 1NN (01524 781334; Fax: 01524 782511).** Why not spend a few days at Russell Farm? The proprietors pride themselves on trying to give guests an enjoyable holiday with good food, friendly atmosphere, relaxing surroundings away from the hustle and bustle. The 150-acre dairy farm is set in a quiet hamlet one mile from the village of Burton-in-Kendal, and five miles from the old market town of Kirkby Lonsdale. An ideal centre for touring Lakes and Yorkshire Dales, or going to the coast. Ideal stopover for people travelling south or to Scotland, only five minutes from M6 Motorway. One double, one single and one family bedrooms; bathroom, toilet; sittingroom and diningroom. Children welcome; cot, high chair and babysitting offered. Pets accepted, if well-behaved. Open from March to November for Evening Dinner, Bed and Breakfast or Bed and Breakfast. Reductions for children. Car essential, parking. Send large SAE, please, for terms and brochure.

**KENDAL. Mrs Jean Bindloss, Grayrigg Hall, Grayrigg, Near Kendal LA8 9BU (01539 824689). Working farm.** Comfortable, peaceful 18th century farmhouse set in a beautiful country location, ideal for touring the Lakes and famous Yorkshire Dales. We run a beef and sheep farm only four-and-a-half miles from Kendal and with easy access to the M6 motorway, Junction 38. Guests are assured of the finest accommodation and a friendly welcome. One spacious family room and one double bedroom, tasteful lounge/dining room with colour TV; bathroom. Children most welcome, cot, babysitting if required. Open March to November. Bed and Breakfast from £16 per person; Evening Meal £10. Further information gladly supplied.

**KENDAL near. Mrs Olive M. Knowles, Cragg Farm, New Hutton, Near Kendal LA8 0BA (Tel/Fax: 01539 721760). Working farm.** Cragg Farm is a delightful 17th century oak beamed farmhouse which retains its character yet has all the modern comforts. This 280 acre working dairy/sheep farm is set in peaceful countryside and ideally positioned for exploring the Lake District and Yorkshire Dales. Located four miles from Kendal on A684 road and three miles M6 Junction 37. This makes an ideal stopover between England and Scotland. We have one double, one family and one single bedrooms, all with tea/coffee making facilities; bathroom with shower and toilet; lounge/diningroom with colour TV. Full central heating. Full English Breakfast served. Families are welcome, reduced rates for children. Weekly terms and Short Breaks available. Open March to November for Bed and Breakfast from £17 to £19 per person. Self-catering caravan also available; weekly terms.
e-mail: knowles.cragg@ukgateway.net
website: www.cragg-farm.sagenet.co.uk

Terms quoted in this publication may be subject to increase if rises in costs necessitate

## 116 Cumbria

**KENDAL near. Mrs Pat Metcalfe, Crook Hall, Crook, Near Kendal, Cumbria LA8 8LF (Tel & Fax: 01539 821352).** Lovely, spacious farmhouse dating from the 15th century, with oak beams and beautiful old panelling in guest lounge. The poet, William Wordsworth, used to visit here. Working ORGANIC dairy and sheep farm. We also keep water buffalo! Magnificent scenery abounds; good walking areas. Conveniently situated between Kendal and Lake Windermere, in quiet situation half-a-mile up our pretty country lane. A warm welcome awaits you. Bed and Breakfast from £18.00 to £22.50 per person. Two double and one family room. No smoking. No pets. Open April to December.

**KENDAL near. Jean Macbeth, Low Plain Farmhouse, Brigsteer, Near Kendal LA8 8AX (015395 68464; Fax: 015395 68916).** Tucked away in the Lyth Valley, Low Plain is a lovely former farmhouse, set in the heart of picturesque countryside where guests are assured of a peaceful and relaxing stay. Each beautifully decorated bedroom has an en suite showerroom, TV and hostess tray and all have wonderfull views. There are many good pubs and restaurants in the area, in particular the local village inn which is within walking distance. Bed and Breakfast from £22.50 per person.
**ETC ♦♦♦♦**
e-mail: farmhouse@lowplain.co.uk
website: www.lowplain.co.uk

**KESWICK. Mrs Deborah Mawson, Dalton Cottage, Bassenthwaite CA12 4QG (017687 76952).** Dalton Cottage is a traditional Lakeland farm cottage nestling at the foot of Skiddaw. Its situation is idyllic, with spectacular views over Bassenthwaite Lake to the front, Ullock Pike and Skiddaw to the rear, making it an ideal base for walking and touring the Lakes. Both bedrooms are tastefully decorated and are en suite with tea/coffee making facilities. We serve hearty English breakfasts and local inns provide good food nearby in the evenings. Dalton Cottage is typical of the period, with beams, open log fires and antiques. It is the perfect place to relax and unwind and is ideal for families – cot and high chair available. Open all year. Bed and Breakfast from £22, £145 weekly. Friday/Saturday/Sunday Special Breaks £63. Deborah and Martyn look forward to meeting you.
e-mail: deborah.dalt.cottage@talk21.com
website: www.daltoncottage.co.uk

**KESWICK. Linda & Stuart Robertson, Clarence House, 14 Eskin Street, Keswick CA12 4DQ (017687 73186; Fax: 017687 72317).** A lovely Victorian house ideally situated for the lake, theatre, parks and market square. Good centre for walking or touring holidays. Bedrooms are decorated to a high standard and have full en suite facilities (single room has separate private bathroom), colour TVs, hospitality trays and central heating. Four-poster and ground floor rooms are available. A warm, friendly welcome and hearty breakfasts await you. Vegetarian and other dietary needs catered for. Evening meal available in our licensed diningroom. Cycle store. Open all year. We accept Visa, Mastercard, Switch, Delta etc. Non-smoking. Bed and Breakfast from £23 per person. Brochure on request. **ETC ♦♦♦♦**
e-mail: ClarenceHo@aol.com

**KESWICK. Val and Alan Hewer, The Paddock Guest House, Wordsworth Street, Penrith Road, Keswick-on-Derwentwater CA12 4HU (017687 72510).** Personally run by Val and Alan this delightful residence of charm and character dates from the mid 1800's. With six guest bedrooms (all en suite) including family room. All rooms have tea/coffee facilities, colour TV, hairdryers, clock radios and central heating. Enjoy our guest lounge with an open log fire. Built from Lakeland slate stone and minerals. A hearty English, vegetarian or Continental breakfast is served between 8.15 and 8.45am. In a quiet residential area only five minutes' walk back to the centre and ten minutes to the lake, close by the beautiful and tranquil Fitz Park. No smoking. Off street parking available.

**KESWICK. Ian and Janice Picken, Lynwood House Licensed Guest House, 35 Helvellyn Street, Keswick CA12 4EP (017687 72398).** Fantastic scenery, fabulous fell-walking; five minutes from town centre, 10 minutes to Lake Derwentwater. Free from smoke. Full Fire Certificate held. Full breakfast menu. Finest cuisine. Facilities for tea/coffee making, heating; TV; washbasins and shaver points. Furnished distinctively. Friendly welcome. In short absolutely fabulous! Bed and Breakfast from £16.50 to £20.50 per person per night. **ETC** ♦♦♦♦ *SILVER AWARD*.

**KESWICK. J.W. and S. Miller, Acorn House Hotel, Ambleside Road, Keswick CA12 4DL (017687 72553; Fax: 017687 75332).** Georgian house situated in gardens with private car parks yet only a few minutes from town centre, ideal for touring the Lake District. Traditional furniture enhances the character of each of the 10 spacious bedrooms complemented by the co-ordinated decor. All have en suite bath/shower rooms, colour TV and tea/coffee making facilities; four-poster beds also available. The generous full English Breakfast will set you up for the day whether walking, climbing or sightseeing, and after the day's exertions you can relax in the large comfortable, elegant lounge. The Hotel is open most of the year and you can be sure of a warm welcome. Bed and Breakfast from £26 per person. Reduced rates for children. Directions, from M6 take A66 to Keswick. **AA** *LISTED,* **RAC** *HIGHLY ACCLAIMED.*

**KESWICK. Ken and Heather Armstrong, Kiln Hill Barn, Bassenthwaite, Keswick CA12 4RG (017687 76454).** Kiln Hill Farm is set in open countryside with beautiful views. It offers single, twin and family bedrooms. TV. Lounge with a log fire for cooler evenings and central heating throughout. Coffee and tea making facilities in each room. En suite available. Evening meals and packed lunches on request. Terms and further details available on application.
**website: www.kilnhillbarn.co.uk**

**KESWICK. Allerdale House, 1 Eskin Street, Keswick CA12 4DH (017687) 73891; Fax: 017687 74068).** Allerdale House was designed and built for the chief architect of Allerdale council in the late 19th century, and although still furnished with many antiques it now offers comfortable accommodation with facilities associated with a small hotel in the 21st century. En suite rooms with TV, hairdryer, telephone and radio. Private parking and drying room (for the occasional wet day). Both proprietors are life long Keswickians with extensive local knowledge, and with over 20 years' experience in the hospitality industry provide a family atmosphere with a professional approach. Please contact us for a brochure and tariff. B&B £24 per person. DB&B from £35.50 and bargain breaks. No smoking throughout the house. **AA** ♦♦♦♦
**website: www.SmoothHound.co.uk/hotels/allerdale.html**

**KESWICK. Mrs Burns, Lindisfarne Guest House, 21 Church Street, Keswick CA12 4DX (017687 73218).** A cosy, friendly guest house with home cooking and hearty breakfasts. Situated within a residential area close to the town centre of Keswick and within easy walking distance of Lake Derwentwater and Fitz Park. We have some en suite rooms and all bedrooms have colour TV, tea/coffee facilities, central heating and washbasin. Bed and Breakfast from £19; Evening Meal optional. Chris and Alison Burns look forward to welcoming you. **ETC** ♦♦♦.

## 118    Cumbria

**KESWICK. Mr Birtwistle, Kalgurli Guest House, 33 Helvellyn Street, Keswick, Cumbria CA12 4EP (017687 72935).** Situated in a quiet residential part of Keswick, yet only a few minutes' walk from the town centre, parks and the lake. Ideal centre for those wishing to explore the beauty of the Lake District. All bedrooms have washbasin (en suite available), colour TV, tea/coffee making facilities, shaver point and bedside lamps; full central heating. Lounge available, separate from the diningroom, and guests have their own key and access to the lounge and bedrooms at all times. Our aim is to provide a high standard of accommodation and over the years we have built up a valued reputation for excellent home cooking and a warm and friendly atmosphere. Whether you wish just bed and breakfast or dinner, bed and breakfast we hope the personal service we offer will make your stay with us a happy one. **ETC ♦♦♦**

**KESWICK. Linda and Ronnie Walker, Watendlath, 15 Acorn Street, Keswick CA12 4EA (017687 74165).** Small, tasteful and renowned for its superb traditional English Breakfasts, Watendlath provides a perfect base for that truly unforgettable Lakeland holiday. Boasting facilities associated with much larger establishments, Proprietors Linda and Ronnie Walker offer a warm and friendly welcome to their lovely home. Just a few minutes from Keswick town centre, Watendlath is a quiet and relaxed retreat. The attractive rooms have colour TV, tea/coffee making facilities, radio-alarm clocks, heating and hairdryers, in fact everything to make your holiday a home-from-home experience. Rooms with en suite shower and toilet are available. Children are especially welcome. Cot, high chair and babysitting service are all available. Bed and Breakfast from £18 per person per night. Weekly from £125.

**KESWICK. Mrs D. Bell, Lyndhurst Guest House, 22 Southerby Street, Keswick CA12 4EF (017687 72303).** Family-run guest house just two minutes from Keswick town centre, near park and lake. Open all year. Children welcome. En suite rooms. Non-smoking. Pets welcome. All rooms are fully en suite and have colour TV, central heating and tea/coffee making facilities. Family, twin and double rooms available. Children and groups welcome; child discount applies. Cyclists welcome and cycle storage available. Packed lunches available. Bed and full English Breakfast £19.50 per person, two or more nights £18.50 per person per night.

**KESWICK. Mrs J. Cowie, Craglands, Penrith Road, Keswick-on-Derwentwater CA12 4LJ (017687 74406)** Craglands is a charming Victorian house ten minutes' walk from Keswick town centre. All rooms en suite, with views towards Grisedale Pike and Latrigg. Ideally situated for walking and cycling. Close to historic stone circle. Private parking, cycle storage. Bed and Breakfast from £19.per person to £25per person. Optional evening meal. No pets, Children over six. Open all year. Non smoking. **AA ♦♦♦♦**
e-mail: keswick@craglands.freeserve.co.uk

*See also Colour Display Advertisement*   **KESWICK. The Swan Hotel & Country Inn, Thornthwaite, Keswick CA12 5SQ (017687 78256).** A family-run 17th century former coaching inn set in idyllic surroundings twixt lake and mountains. For a true sense of beauty, history and relaxation, cossetted by polite, friendly, staff catering for your every need. Enjoy an open fire, lake walks, imaginative home-cooking and real ales. Bed and Breakfast from £29 per person per night; Dinner, Bed and Breakfast from £45 per night. Three nights Dinner, Bed and Breakfast from £125 per person. Children and pets welcome. Open all year. Excellent restaurant and bar food. Winter Breaks November to March from £65 per person for three nights. Please call Colin or Joy Harrison for a brochure.
website: www.swan-hotel-keswick.co.uk

---

*Please mention Bed & Breakfast Stops when writing to enquire about accommodation*

**Cumbria**

**KESWICK. Mrs S. Park, Langdale, 14 Leonard Street, Keswick CA12 4EL (017687 73977).** Victorian town house, quietly situated, yet close to town, park, lake and fells. All rooms furnished to a very high standard, having quality en suite facilities, central heating, colour TV, tea/coffee making facilities throughout. We have a pleasant, comfortable residents' lounge with colour TV and video. Enjoy a good home cooked English or vegetarian breakfast or our popular Continental breakfast. We have a non smoking policy throughout the house. We will ensure your stay is a pleasant one. Bed and Breakfast from £21; Theatre Breaks. Special three nights midweek/weekend breaks September to April.

**KESWICK. Mr and Mrs Ray and Sally Newton, Sunnyside Guest House, 25 Southey Street, Keswick CA12 4EF (017687 72446; Fax: 017687 74447).** We refurbished this Victorian guest house in 1998 to provide five tastefully decorated en suite rooms and two standard double rooms with adjacent private facilities. A comfortable guest lounge is located on the first floor with good views of Skiddaw. Sunnyside is five minutes' walk from the town centre, ten minutes' walk from Derwentwater and Theatre by the Lake. We are friendly and flexible and provide a relaxing environment for our guests to enjoy their stay, with substantial breakfasts to set them up for a day walking the fells or visiting local attractions. Our car park accommodates eight vehicles. Children welcome. Dogs by arrangement. Bed and Breakfast from £19. **AA/RAC/CTB ♦♦♦♦**
e-mail: raynewton@survey.u-net.com 
website: www.survey.u-net.com

**KESWICK. Mrs M.A. Illman, Beckstones Farm, Thornthwaite, Keswick CA12 5SQ (017687 78510).** Beneath the forest and looking over fields to the magnificent mountain scenery of Skiddaw and the Helvellyn Ranges, Beckstones is peacefully situated off the beaten track and within a short stroll of the southern shores of Bassenthwaite Lake. Built in 1726, the Georgian Farmhouse has been extended into the barn, providing quality, centrally heated en suite bedrooms with hospitality trays. Beckstones has a cosy oak beamed diningroom, TV lounge, ample parking, a large garden and a cycle store. Dogs by arrangement. Bar meals three minutes' walk away, Keswick 10 minutes' drive. Excellent touring and walking base. B&B from £21.50. Brochure available. **ETC ♦♦♦.**

**KESWICK. Annie Scally and Ian Townsend, Latrigg House, St. Herbert Street, Keswick CA12 4DF (017687 73068).** An attractive Victorian house in a quiet area, only a few minutes' walk from the town centre and Lake, providing an excellent base for visiting the Lake District. We promise a very warm welcome, good food, comfort and hospitality (vegetarian and vegan meals provided if required). We offer a no-smoking environment for the well being and comfort of guests, comfortable rooms, (all with en suite facilities), colour TVs, tea/coffee facilities and central heating. Comfortable residents' lounge with TV. Bed and Breakfast from £19.00 to £20.00. Children under 12 special rate if sharing adult room. Sorry no pets. **ETC ♦♦♦♦**

---

All the information in this book is given in good faith in the belief that it is correct. However, the publishers cannot guarantee the facts given in these pages, neither are they responsible for changes in policy, ownership or terms that may take place after the date of going to press. Readers should always satisfy themselves that the facilities they require are available and that the terms, if quoted, still apply.

**KESWICK. Mr and Mrs Sharpe, Foye House, 23 Eskin Street, Keswick CA12 DQ (017687 73288; Fax: 017687 80220).** Richard and Judy offer you a warm welcome to Foye House. A small Victorian guest house close to the town centre, lake and fells and a few minutes' walk from The Theatre by The Lake. Our centrally heated rooms are decorated and furnished to a high standard with cleanliness and comfort a priority. All have remote-controlled colour TVs, hair dryers, radio alarm clocks and a hospitality tray. We serve a hearty traditional or vegetarian breakfast. An ideal base for exploring the beautiful Lake District National Park. Non-smoking. Please contact Richard and Judy Sharpe for a brochure and details of Special Offers. All major Debit and Credit cards accepted.
e-mail: Foye_House@Keswick98.freeserve.co.uk

**KESWICK. Mrs M.A. Relph, Littletown Farm, Newlands, Keswick CA12 5TU (017687 78353; Fax: 017687 78437). Working farm.** Littletown Farm, situated in a peaceful part of the beautiful Newlands Valley has all the facilities of a small hotel. Although fully modernised, the farmhouse retains a traditional character with comfortable lounge, diningroom and licensed bar. Most bedrooms are en suite with tea-making facilities, heating and washbasins. Traditional four-course dinner served six nights a week. Excellent walking and climbing nearby. The market towns of Keswick and Cockermouth and the Lakes are all within easy distance. Ample parking. Dinner Bed & Breakfast from £38 to £42 per person. Bed and Breakfast from £26 to £30 per person. SAE please.

**KESWICK. Mrs Marion Robinson, "Thelmlea" Country Guest House, Braithwaite, Keswick CA12 5TD (017687 78305).** Friendly family-run guest house set in one and three-quarter acres of grounds commanding superb views in Lakeland village two miles from Keswick. Boating, fishing, bowling, tennis, golf and horse riding available nearby. Central heating throughout. All bedrooms have full facilities including tea/coffee, colour TV and radio alarms. Packed lunches available. Access to rooms at all times including guests' lounge. A hairdryer, iron/ironing board and drying facilities are provided for use by guests. Children and pets welcome. Car park and garden area for guests' use. £16 to £21 per person per night. Reductions for weekly bookings. Brochure on request.

**KESWICK. Mrs Elizabeth Scott, Woodside, Penrith Road, Keswick CA12 4LJ (017687 73522).** Situated on the outskirts of Keswick, "Woodside" is an ideal centre for sightseeing in the picturesque Lake District. This is a family-run bed and breakfast establishment offering the very highest of standards. Bedrooms with en suite, TV, tea making facilities and central heating. Large car park and lovely gardens. Many local attractions and country walks. 15 minutes' walk to town centre. Open all year round. Full English Breakfast. Bed and Breakfast from £18. Reduced rates in winter.

**KESWICK/BORROWDALE. Mrs S. Bland, Thorneythwaite Farm, Borrowdale, Keswick CA12 5XQ (017687 77237).** Thorneythwaite Farm has a beautiful, peaceful position in the Borrowdale Valley standing half-a-mile off the road. The 220 acre sheep farm is seven miles from Keswick and half-a-mile from Seatoller. The 18th century farmhouse has great character inside and out, several rooms having oak beams and panelling and being furnished to suit. Two double and one family bedrooms, all with tea/coffee making facilities; sittingroom with open or electric fire; diningroom; bathroom and toilet. Cot, high chair and reduced rates for children. Sorry no pets. Open from April to November, mid-week bookings accepted. A perfect base for fell walking; Scafell, Great Gable, Glaramara are all within walking distance from the farm. Bed and Breakfast from £18.

**KESWICK (Lake District). Tony and Ann Atkin, Glencoe Guest House, 21 Helvellyn Street, Keswick CA12 4EN (017687 71016).** Cycling, walking or touring, a warm welcome is guaranteed. Our renovated Victorian Guest House situated in a quiet area of town yet only five minutes' stroll from the centre of Keswick and its amenities. Glencoe offers spacious en suite and standard rooms, all decorated and furnished to a high standard, each offering its own colour TV, hospitality tray and radio-alarm. Double, twin and single rooms available. In the interest of all our guests "Glencoe" is a totally non-smoking guesthouse. Local knowledge and maps are available to those wishing to explore the Northern Lakes and Fells. Bed and Breakfast from £18 per person.
e-mail: enquiries@glencoeguesthouse.co.uk
website: www.glencoeguesthouse.co.uk


**KIRKBY LONSDALE. Mrs Pauline Bainbridge, Tossbeck, Middleton, Kirkby Lonsdale LA6 2LZ (015242 76214).** A warm welcome awaits you at Tossbeck, a working farm situated in the unspoilt Lune Valley, within easy reach of the M6, the Lake District, the Yorkshire Dales and England's largest showcave is 10 miles away. The farmhouse is a 17th century Listed building. Rooms available are one double/twin en suite and a family room with separate private facilities. Both bedrooms have televisions and drink making facilities. The dining room has individual tables. Bed and Breakfast from £17 with Short Break offers. Children welcome. No smoking. Please ring for a brochure.


**KIRKBY STEPHEN. Mrs Sylvia Capstick, Duckintree House, Kaber, Kirkby Stephen CA17 4ER (017683 71073).** Duckintree is a working family farm set in the quiet Eden Valley countryside just off the A685 Kirkby Stephen to Brough road. Easy access to the Lakes and Yorkshire Dales or ideal for breaking your journey from the south of England/Midlands to Scotland. Car essential, ample parking. The rooms comprise family, double and twin (cot available) with tea/coffee making facilities. Lounge/dining-room with colour TV. All rooms overlook a large garden and countryside. Bed and Breakfast from £16. Reductions for children under 12 years. Pets welcome by arrangement. Evening Meal can be provided. Open from March to October. Campsite available for tourers and tents. Write or phone for details.

**LAKE DISTRICT/HAWKSHEAD. Grizedale Lodge, Hawkshead, Ambleside LA22 0QL (015394 36532; Fax:015394 36572).** Set in the heart of the South Lakeland National Park, Grizedale Lodge is one of the most beautiful bed and breakfast locations. Within easy reach are the famous sculpture trails, sailing on Windermere or Coniston, Brantwood, Beatrix Potter country, trout fishing,and other attractions; Hawkshead five minutes. All rooms are en suite, centrally heated, and have colour TV, tea and coffee making facilities and hairdryers. Some have the added luxury of four-poster beds. Ample parking, a winter log fire, TV lounge and sun terrace. Residential licence. Open all year, rates start from £25 per person per night.
e-mail: enquiries@grizedale-lodge.com
website: www.grizedale-lodge.com

**LOWESWATER. Mrs Vickers, Askhill Farm, Loweswater, Cockermouth CA13 0SU (01946 861640).** Askhill is a family-run farm which has beef and sheep. Situated on the hillside overlooking Loweswater Lake. The area is ideal for fell-walkers; there are plenty of walks (high fells or low walks) to suit everyone's level of ability; we are handy for all the western lakes, Crummock Water, Buttermere, Ennerdale (with lots of woodland walks), Wast Water (the deepest lake). Loweswater is handy for Keswick (10 miles approximately), Cockermouth (eight miles), the city of Carlisle with Roman connections (30 miles approximately), Maryport, steeped in Roman history (12 miles), and we are roughly 12 miles from the Solway coast. **ETC** ◆◆◆

---

*Please mention Bed & Breakfast Stops when writing to enquire about accommodation*

## Cumbria

**NEWBIGGIN ON LUNE. Mrs Brenda Boustead, Tranna Hill, Newbiggin-on-Lune, Kirkby Stephen CA17 4NY (015396 23227 or 07989 892368).** Tranna Hill offers a relaxing and friendly atmosphere in a non-smoking environment. Five miles from M6 Junction 38, ideal base for walkers, fishermen & golfers with Howeill Fells, nature reserve, fish farm and golf course only minutes away. Well placed for breaking your journey or touring the Lakes and Dales. En suite rooms with TV, refreshment trays, central heating and beautiful views. Private parking and large gardens. Delicious breakfasts. All for £18 per person per night. **ETC** ♦♦♦

*See also Colour Display Advertisement* **NEWBY BRIDGE. Mr Alastair Rushton, The Knoll Country Guest House, Lakeside, Near Newby Bridge LA12 8AU (015395 31347).** The Knoll is set amidst wooded countryside at the south end of Lake Windermere, just five minutes' walk from the attractive village of Lakeside and the pier, but within easy driving distance of many Lakeland attractions. If you enjoy walking there are convenient paths at the back of the Knoll, taking you on an all day walk with pub stop for lunch, or a 20 minute evening stroll. All bedrooms have en suite, central heating, TV, direct-dial telephones, tea and coffee making facilities and have recently been refurbished to a high standard. Our residents' lounge offers a relaxing atmosphere for you to put your feet up and take it easy. With residents' bar, board games, light reading, TV and open coal fire. To reserve a room at The Knoll telephone (015395 31347). **ETC** ♦♦♦♦

**PENRITH. Mrs Jean Ashburner, Lattendales Farm, Berrier Road, Greystoke, Penrith CA11 0UE (017684 83474). Working farm, join in.** Comfortable 17th century farmhouse in quiet attractive village five miles from Penrith. Ideal for touring the Northern Lakes. Accommodation comprises one twin room and two double rooms; lounge with colour TV. Children and pets welcome; reductions for children. Non-smoking. Bed and Breakfast from £16 to £17 per person. Directions, follow B5288 from Penrith, in Greystoke take Berrier Road and Lattendales Farm is first B&B on left.

**PENRITH. Norcroft Guest House, Graham Street, Penrith CA11 9LQ (Tel & Fax: 01768 862365).** Conveniently situated for M6 and just five minutes' walk from town centre, our delightful Victorian house boasts an ideal location. All en suite with a variety of rooms ranging from single, twin, double, triple to family suites with separate connecting children's accommodation. Also available our recently completed ground floor room with disabled access. Awarded the RAC Warm Welcome Award and renowned for our delicious Cumbrian breakfast – why not treat yourself to a stay? Non-smoking. Private parking. Credit cards accepted. Rates from £15 per person Bed and Breakfast. Children welcome. Regret, no pets. For brochure and details please contact **Mrs Sylvia Jackson. ETC/RAC** ♦♦♦♦ *WARM WELCOME AWARD.*

**PENRITH. Mrs Margaret Taylor, Tymparon Hall, Newbiggin, Stainton, Penrith CA11 0HS (Tel and Fax: 017684 83236).** Enjoy a relaxing break in the beautiful North Lakes and explore the Eden Valley. A delightful 18th century Manor House and colourful summer garden situated on a 150 acre sheep farm in a peaceful rural area close to Lake Ullswater. Enjoy old-fashioned hospitality, home cooked farmhouse breakfasts and three-course dinners. Guests' bedrooms, en suite or standard, offer space and tranquillity with every facility for a memorable time. Evening Dinner, Bed and Breakfast. Brochure on request with SAE. **ETC** ♦♦♦♦.
e-mail: margaret@peeearson.freeserve.co.uk
website: www.peeearson.freeserve.co.uk

**PENRITH. Barbara and David Hughes, Blue Swallow Guest House, 11 Victoria Road, Penrith CA11 8HR (Tel & Fax: 01768 866335).** A comfortable Victorian house set in the attractive market town of Penrith, ideally situated to explore the delightful Eden Valley, the wonderful scenery of the Lake District and the Yorkshire Dales National Park. For the golfing enthusiast Penrith boasts an 18 hole golf course and there are several more within easy driving distance. Resident proprietors Barbara and David Hughes look forward to welcoming you whether you are on holiday, just breaking a long journey or in the area for business - you'll be made to feel at home. All rooms have colour TV, tea tray and central heating. Full and varied English breakfast served. Bed and Breakfast from £17 to £20 per person. **ETC ◆◆◆**.

**PENRITH. Mrs Ann Toppin, Gale Hall, Melmerby, Penrith CA10 1HN (01768 881254). Working farm.** Mrs Ann Toppin welcomes guests to her home on a working beef/sheep farm 10 miles east of Penrith and the M6, a mile-and-a-half from the peaceful village of Melmerby. Beautiful setting at the foot of the Pennines and with extensive views of the Lakeland Fells. Ideal for walking, convenient for the Lake District. Single, double, twin or family rooms available; cot and babysitting. Residents' lounge. Pets welcome by arrangement. Bed and Breakfast from £15; reduction for children under 12 years. Special diets catered for. Full English or Vegetarian Breakfast served. Excellent bar meals available locally.

**PENRITH. Mrs Marion Barrit, Low Garth Guest House, Penruddock, Penrith CA11 0QU (017684 83492).** A warm welcome awaits you at this small family-run guest house, which is situated on high ground surrounded by open farmland on the edge of Penruddock Village just off the A66. The building is a traditional 18th century barn built from local stone which has been sympathetically converted to provide a charming house with magnificent views over the fells. Open all year, accommodation is available in two bedrooms with en suite shower/toilet, comfortable beds, colour TV and tea/coffee making facilities. Full English breakfast is provided and freshly home cooked dinner is available if required. Bed and Breakfast from £18 per person; Dinner £12 per person. Brochure.

**PENRITH. Mrs Brenda Preston, Pallet Hill Farm, Penrith CA11 0BY (017684 83247).** Pallet Hill Farm is pleasantly situated two miles from Penrith on the Penrith-Greystoke-Keswick road (B5288). It is four miles from Ullswater and has easy access to the Lake District, Scottish Borders and Yorkshire Dales. There are several sports facilities in the area - golf club, swimming pool, pony trekking; places to visit such as Lowther Leisure Park and the Miniature Railway at Ravenglass. Good farmhouse food and hospitality with personal attention. Double, single, family rooms; dining/sittingroom. Children welcome, cot, high chair. Sorry no pets. Car essential, parking. Open Easter to November. Bed and Breakfast from £10.50 (reduced weekly rates). Reduced rates for children.

*See also Colour Display Advertisement*

**PENRITH. Leon and Debbie Kirk, Brooklands Guest House, 2 Portland Place, Penrith CA11 7QN (01768 863395; Fax: 01768 864895).** Charming and elegant surroundings await any visitor to Brooklands Guest House. Conveniently situated in the heart of historic Penrith, this beautifully restored Victorian terraced house provides an excellent base for exploring the many and various delights of the English Lakes. Debbie and Leon will make it their business to ensure that your stay is as enjoyable as possible and that you will want to return to repeat the experience time and again. Charming, elegant surroundings await any visitor to Brooklands Guest House in the heart of historic Penrith. Every effort will be made to ensure an enjoyable stay, including catering for specific dietary requirements and the provision of non-smoking rooms. Bed and Breakfast from £17.
**website: www.SmoothHound.co.uk**

---

Terms quoted in this publication may be subject to increase if rises in costs necessitate

**PENRITH near. Mrs Barbara Booth, Ullswater House, Pooley Bridge, Near Penrith CA10 2NN (017684 86259).** Situated in the delightful village of Pooley Bridge, close to Lake Ullswater and the Steamer Pier, the house has a residential licence; full central heating; ample car parking space. All bedrooms have private facilities, television, refrigerator, and tea and coffee making facilities. The tariff is £21 per person per night, with reductions for four-nightly and weekly stays. Please telephone for any further details. **ETC ♦♦♦.**

**PENRITH. Angela and Ivor Davies, Woodland House Hotel, Wordsworth Street, Penrith CA11 7QY (01768 864177; Fax: 01768 890152).** Small, friendly and elegant licensed private hotel situated at the foot of Beacon Hill, and only five minutes' walk from the centre of the town. Large car park. All rooms are en suite and have tea/coffee making facilities and colour TV. Whether on business or pleasure an ideal base for exploring Lakes, Borders, Pennines, Eden Valley or stopover to/from Scotland. Library of maps and books for walkers, nature lovers and sightseers. Open all year. Sorry, no pets. The Hotel is NO SMOKING throughout. Bed and Breakfast from £24.00. Brochure. **ETC ♦♦♦ AA, RAC** 
e-mail: **ivordavies@woodlandhouse.co.uk**
website: **www.woodlandhouse.co.uk**

**PENRITH. Mrs C. Blundell, Albany House, 5 Portland Place, Penrith CA11 7QN (Tel & Fax: 01768 863072).** Close to town centre, Albany House is a large mid-Victorian terraced house. A high standard of cleanliness, comfort and personal friendly attention is assured at all times. Five spacious nicely decorated bedrooms (one double, three triple, all with washbasins; one family en suite). All have central heating, colour/satellite TV and tea/coffee making facilities. Situated close to M6, A6 and A66, ideal base for touring Lake District, Eden Valley, Hadrian's Wall, Scottish Borders and an excellent stopover between England and Scotland. Within easy reach of Lowther Leisure Park, sailing, wind surfing, fell walking, pony trekking, golf and swimming. Bed and Breakfast from £17.50. **AA QQQ.**

**PENRITH. Eileen Reid and Peter Sowerby, Brandlehow Guest House, 1 Portland Place, Penrith CA11 7QN (01768 864470).** A warm welcome assured at our guest house offering a high standard of comfort and cleanliness. Five spacious, tastefully decorated bedrooms, all with washbasins, central heating, double glazing, colour TV and tea/coffee facilities. Twin, double and family rooms available, including one excellent family room for five. Ideally situated, close to M6, A6, for touring the Lake District, Scottish Borders, Hadrian's Wall and for overnight stops en route to and from Scotland. Local amenities include Lowther Fun Park, golf, sailing and pony trekking. Bed and Breakfast from £17 double, £19 single inclusive. Reductions for longer stays. Weekly terms available. **AA ♦♦♦.**

**PENRITH. Mrs C Bousfield, Trainlands, Maulds Meaburn, Penrith CA10 3HX (017683 51249).** This 17th/18th century farmhouse and working farm is situated away from busy roads between the Eden and Lyvennet Valleys, but within easy reach of the M6 and A66. Five miles west of Appleby and 13 miles south of Penrith. Guest TV lounge/diningroom with a real fire await those who need to get away from it all, but with plenty of walking for those with the energy. Evening meal by arrangement. For bookings or further information contact Carol Bousfield on the above number or by
e-mail: **bousfield@trainlands.u-net.com**

*When making enquiries or bookings,
a stamped addressed envelope is always appreciated*

**SHAP. Mr and Mrs D. L. and M. Brunskill, Brookfield, Shap, Penrith CA10 3PZ (01931 716397).** Situated one mile from M6 motorway (turn off at Shap interchange No. 39), first accommodation off motorway. Excellent position for touring Lakeland, or overnight accommodation for travelling north or south. Central heating throughout, renowned for good food, comfort and personal attention. All bedrooms are well-appointed and have en suite facilities, remote-control colour TV, hospitality tray and hairdryer. Diningroom where delicious home cooking is a speciality. Well-stocked bar. Residents' lounge. Sorry, no pets. Open from January to December. Terms sent on request, ample parking. Full Fire Certificate. **AA** ◆◆◆◆.

---

**TEBAY. Carmel House Guest House, Mount Pleasant, Tebay CA10 3TH (015396 24651).** Ideally situated between the beautiful Lune and Eden Valleys, quarter-of-a-mile from M6 Junction 38. Ideal stopover or base for touring - midway between Lakes and Yorkshire Dales - or fishing the River Lune and walking the lovely surrounding countryside. Three double, one twin and two singles, all en suite with colour TV, central heating and tea/coffee facilities. Full Fire Certificate. Private parking. Bed and Breakfast from £17.50. **AA** *QQQ*, **RAC** *ACCLAIMED*.

---

**TROUTBECK. Gwen and Peter Parfitt, Hill Crest, Troutbeck, Penrith CA11 0SH (017684 83935).** Gwen and Peter assure you of a warm and friendly welcome at Hill Crest, their unique Lakeland home which offers two en suite double/family rooms, one twin room. Home cooking, choice of menu including vegetarian; non-smoking establishment, early morning tea, bedtime drinks; packed lunches. Panoramic mountain views. Aira Force waterfalls, Ullswater 10 minutes, Keswick 15 minutes, a good base for walking, boating, touring, Lakes, Hadrian's Wall and the Borders. Books, maps and hints from Gwen on what to see. Walkers, children and dogs welcome. Bed and Breakfast £14 per person twin room, £16 per person en suite rooms. Children half-price sharing. Dinner from £5 (optional). Weekly rates. 10 minutes Junction 40 M6. At Hill Crest we aim to create a relaxed and informal atmosphere where guests are treated as part of the family. Highly recommended by previous guests.

---

**ULLSWATER. Geoff and Steph Mason, Knotts Mill Country Lodge, Watermillock, Penrith CA11 0JN (Tel & Fax: 017684 86699)**. Spacious guesthouse close to magical Ullswater, in peaceful, scenic surroundings. Ideal for walking, boating or touring the Lake District. Eight en suite bedrooms with stunning views, including family rooms and facilities for the disabled. Our large dining room and lounge have picture windows that overlook the fells. Delicious Evening Meals with generous servings and quality home cooked food and choice of wines. Only 10 minutes from junction 40 M6 with private grounds and parking. Low season discounts when the Lake District is at its most beautiful with snow on the peaks and you can relax by our log fire. **ETC** ◆◆◆.
website: www.knottsmill.cwc.net

---

# FREE or REDUCED RATE entry to Holiday Visits and Attractions — see our READERS' OFFER VOUCHERS on pages 43-60

## Cumbria

**WHITEHAVEN. Robin Bailey, Corkickle Guest House, 1 Corkickle, Whitehaven CA28 8AA (Tel & Fax: 01946 692073).** An elegant Grade II Listed late Georgian town house situated close to the town centre and the start of the C-2-C cycle way. Ideal base for exploring the delights of the West Cumbrian coast and only a short distance from the Lake District National Park. All six bedrooms have en suite/private facilities and are furnished to a high standard to include colour television, tea and coffee making facilities, radio and central heating. There is a residents' lounge and diningroom complete with many original decorative features. Open all year. Children welcome, pets by arrangement. Licensed. Non-smoking. Bed and Breakfast from £22.50 per person, Evening Meal £10. Please write or telephone for brochure. **ETC/AA** ◆◆◆◆.

**WINDERMERE. Mrs J. Seal, Brook House, 30 Ellerthwaite Road, Windermere LA23 2AH (015394 44932).** A friendly welcome awaits you at Brook House which is convenient for village and lake. Ideal touring centre. We offer personal service, together with excellent English cooking, under the personal supervision of the proprietors. All rooms are decorated to a high standard; residents' lounge with colour TV; full central heating. All bedrooms have private showers/baths, colour TV, tea/coffee making facilities, and most have private toilets. Access to rooms at all times. Guests' parking. Full Fire Certificate. RAC Acclaimed. Open all year. Bed and Breakfast from £17 to £25. **ETC** ◆◆◆

*See also Colour Display Advertisement*

**WINDERMERE. Mr and Mrs Tyson, Holly-Wood Guest House, Holly Road, Windermere LA23 2AF (015394 42219).** Holly-Wood is a beautiful Victorian house offering clean comfortable accommodation in a quiet position, three minutes' walk from the village centre. A perfect location for your visit to the Lake District and within reach of the Dales and Morecambe Bay. Central heating, tea/coffee makers, television and hair dryer. Traditional or vegetarian breakfasts. Cosy residents' lounge. Bus/station transfer. En suite and budget rooms available. Low season and short break reductions. Bed and Breakfast from £16 to £25 per person. Non-smoking. No pets. **ETC** ◆◆◆◆

**WINDERMERE. Mrs P. Wood, The Haven Guest House, Birch Street, Windermere LA23 1EG (015394 44017).** The Haven is a comfortable Victorian Guest House centrally located in the attractive village of Windermere, a short walk from the railway station, restaurants, shops and all local amenities. Sports such as walking, mountaineering, pony trekking and water skiing can be enjoyed in the area. All rooms have TV and tea/coffee making facilities. Open all year. Bed and Breakfast from £17. Vegetarians and special diets catered for. Reductions for children. Non smoking. Parking. Brochure on request. **AA** ◆◆◆

**WINDERMERE. Applethwaite House, 1 Upper Oak Street, Windermere LA23 2LB (015394 44689).** We offer you a warm welcome to our family-run guest house, where we provide clean and comfortable accommodation within a relaxed and friendly atmosphere. Situated in a quiet cul-de-sac, only five minutes' walk from the village centre, it is conveniently placed for the bus and train stations, being a 10 minute walk away. A hearty breakfast is our promise. Pets and families most welcome. Vegetarians catered for. All rooms have colour TV and complimentary hot drinks. Garage facilities for storage of bikes. No smoking. Bed and Breakfast from £16 depending on season. **ETC** ◆◆◆
e-mail: applethwaitehouse@btinternet.com
website: www.btinternet.com/~applethwaitehouse

## BOSTON HOUSE

*A Lakeland Guest House*

♦♦♦♦

*Exclusively for non-smokers*

Boston House, the perfect choice for sincere attentive hospitality.
Romantic en suite bedrooms with four-poster beds.
The joyful experience of AGA cooked breakfasts. Private Parking.
And only a short stroll to all the amenities in Windermere.
Including restaurants shops and public transport.
**The Terrace, Windermere, Cumbria LA23 1AJ**
**Telephone 015394 43654**
e-mail: info@bostonhouse.co.uk   web: www.bostonhouse.co.uk
Your Hosts: John and Pauline MacDonald

---

## Oldfield House

Stuart and Pat Reeves
Oldfield House, Oldfield Road
Windermere
Cumbria LA23 2BY
Telephone: (015394) 88445
Fax: (015394) 43250
E-mail: pat.reeves@virgin.net
Website: www.oldfieldhouse.co.uk

We would like to welcome you to Oldfield House, which has a friendly, informal atmosphere within a traditionally-built Lakeland stone residence. Eight bedrooms, all en suite, four-poster room, all with Colour TV, Radio, Hairdryer, Telephone and Tea/Coffee Making.
• Quiet, central location
• Free use of Leisure Club facilities
• Reductions for three nights/children
• Non-smoking establishment
• Most major credit cards accepted

AA ♦♦♦♦      ETC ♦♦♦♦

EUROCARD   VISA   MasterCard

---

**WINDERMERE. Mylne Bridge House, Brookside, Lake Road, Windermere LA23 2BX (015394 43314; Fax: 015394 48052).** Mylne Bridge House is the ideal location for your Lakeland break, situated off the main road between Windermere village and the Lake. There is a large private car park with easy access from Lake Road. There are eight bedrooms, seven of which offer en suite facilities – Room eight has its own private facilities. There is a good mix of single, double, twin and family rooms; all have colour television and tea/coffee making facilities. Most rooms have south-facing windows to capture the sunshine and all are centrally heated for winter comfort. Special diets can be catered for. Non-smoking. No pets. Children welcome. Free fishing permits. Bed and Breakfast from £20 to £25 per person per night. 
e-mail: mylnebridgehouse@talk21.com
website: www.s/h/systems.co.uk/hotels/mylne.html

---

**WINDERMERE. Mr and Mrs Mick Rooney, Villa Lodge, Cross Street, Windermere LA23 1AE (Tel & Fax: 015394 43318).** Friendliness and cleanliness guaranteed. Extremely comfortable accommodation in peaceful area overlooking Windermere village, yet two minutes from bus and rail stations. All eight bedrooms are tastefully decorated, all en suite (one four-poster for that special occasion), with remote-control colour TV, hairdryer, tea/coffee making facilities and full central heating. Most have magnificent views of the Lake and mountains. Superb English Breakfast served in our delightful diningroom. Vegetarian and special diets catered for. Open all year. Special offers November-March. Safe, private parking for eight cars. Evening meal optional with residential licence. Pets welcome by prior arrangement. An excellent base for exploring the whole of the Lake District. Bed and Breakfast from £23per person per night. **ETC ♦♦♦♦** 
e-mail: rooneym@btconnect.com
website: www.villa-lodge.co.uk

## Cumbria

**WINDERMERE. Brian and Margaret Fear, Cambridge House, 9 Oak Street, Windermere LA23 1EN (015394 43846).** Cambridge House is a traditional, family run Lakeland guesthouse situated in the middle of Windermere village convenient for all amenities including buses and trains. It is also central for all South Lakes beauty spots. One hour to Keswick and the Northern Lakes and only 20 minutes from M6 Junction 36. Double, twin and family rooms are available; all are modern and comfortable and include en suite facilities, colour TV and tea/coffee making. A full English, Continental or vegetarian breakfast is provided. Centrally heated throughout. Bed and Breakfast from £16. Open all year.
e-mail: reservations@cambridge-house.fsbusiness.co.uk
website: www.cambridge-house.fsbusiness.co.uk

**WINDERMERE. Mr J. A. Bowe, Greenriggs Guest House, 8 Upper Oak Street, Windermere, Cumbria LA23 2LB (Tel & Fax: 015394 42265).** A traditional Lakeland stone Victorian terraced house quietly situated on a level walk just a couple of minutes from the centre of Windermere off the main Windermere to Bowness road, close to a bus route, shops, restaurants, park with children's play area and all the other amenities of Windermere village. Seven letting bedrooms, choose from single, double, twin or family room, the majority of which are en suite. All rooms centrally heated with colour TV, complimentary tea/coffee and biscuits tray, shaver point and washbasin. Some rooms non-smoking. A full home-cooked traditional English breakfast is served - Continental or vegetarian breakfast available on request. No smoking in diningroom. Private parking. Access to rooms at all times. Prices from £14 low season, to £25 high season.

**WINDERMERE. Mick & Angela Brown, Haisthorpe House, Holly Road, Windermere LA23 2AF (015394 43445; Fax: 015394 48875).** Set in a quiet secluded area of Windermere, close to the village centre, Haisthorpe offers high standatds at reasonable prices. For those special occasions we have our 'Victorian Room', 'Four-Poster Room' and 'Jacuzzi Room'. All rooms are en suite and to our high, four diamond standard. One of only two establishments to receive a 'Highly Commended' accolade in the Cumbria Tourist Board 'Bed and Breakfast of the Year Awards' in 1999 and 2000. Private parking available. En suite rooms £19 to £22, special en suite rooms £21 to £27. **ETC** ♦♦♦♦ *SILVER AWARD*
e-mail: haisthorpe@clara.net
website: www.haisthorpe.clara.net

**WINDERMERE. Adrian and Elizabeth Legge, Pinethwaite Holiday Cottages, Lickbarrow, Windermere, The Lake District LA23 2NQ (015394 44558; Fax: 015394 44556).** SELF CATERING AND BED AND BREAKFAST. Pinethwaite offers a new concept for a totally relaxing Short Break. Enjoy the freedom of self-catering with a breakfast package to start your day. Our unique cottages and apartments nestle in the heart of a ten-acre private woodland, the haunt of roe deer, red squirrels and extensive bird life, just one mile from Windermere and Bowness villages. Our accommodation is well-equipped and we have a sauna and laundry on site. For walking weekends, we offer a range of our own easy to follow guides for long or short, high or low level walks. Relax in the Country Club, be pampered in the beauty salon, dine at our favourite pubs and restaurants. Inclusive weekends from £120, budget weekends from £88. For details request our brochure or visit our website.
e-mail: legge@pinethwaite.freeserve.co.uk
website: www.pinecottages.co.uk

---

Terms quoted in this publication may be subject to increase if rises in costs necessitate

**Cumbria** 129

**WINDERMERE. Mr and Mrs Harvey, College House, College Road, Windermere LA23 1BU (015394 45767).** A non-smoking, spacious Victorian family home offering a warm and friendly welcome, in a quiet area close to village centre and railway station. Some rooms have superb mountain views, all are either en suite or have private bathroom, colour TV, tea/coffee making facilities and full central heating. We have plenty of interesting local guides, maps, books, pictures and fresh flowers plus a small private garden with furniture for guests' use. We can pre-arrange local minibus tours, hire of mountain bikes or horse riding facilities. Bed and Breakfast from £18 to £28. Vegetarians welcome. Private car spaces and garage for bikes. **ETC ♦♦♦**.

*See also Colour Display Advertisement*

**WINDERMERE. Irene and George Eastwood, Sandown, Lake Road, Windermere LA23 2JF (015394 45275).** Superb bed and breakfast accommodation. All rooms en suite with colour TV, tea/coffee making facilities. Situated two minutes from Lake Windermere, shops and cafes. Many lovely, scenic walks. Open all year. Special out of season rates, also two-day Saturday –Sunday breaks. Well behaved dogs welcome. Each room has own safe, private car parking. SAE or telephone for further details. Member of Lakeland Catering Association. Terms from £30 per person.

**WINDERMERE. Mrs S. Coleman, Rockside Guest House, Ambleside Road, Windermere LA23 1AQ (Tel & Fax: 01539 445343).** Rockside is built of traditional Lakeland stone and slate, and is full of character yet with all modern amenities. Two minutes' walk from town centre and ideal for touring the whole of the Lake District. Help given to plan routes and walks. Singles, twins, doubles and family rooms available, all with colour TV, telephone, clock/radio and central heating. Most have en suite bathroom, tea/coffee making facilities and hairdryer. Choice of breakfast. Large car park. Open all year as every season in the Lake District has its own magic. Credit cards accepted. Bed and Breakfast from £18.50 to £26.50 per person, half price for children sharing. Reductions for longer stays. Open all year. **RAC** ACCLAIMED. *"BED AND BREAKFAST GREAT BRITAIN" AGENCY TOP 50.*

---

*PLEASE MENTION THIS GUIDE WHEN YOU WRITE*

*OR PHONE TO ENQUIRE ABOUT ACCOMMODATION.*

*IF YOU ARE WRITING, A STAMPED,*

*ADDRESSED ENVELOPE IS ALWAYS APPRECIATED.*

---

**FHG**

Visit the FHG website
**www.holidayguides.com**
for details of the wide choice of accommodation
featured in the full range of FHG titles

# DERBYSHIRE

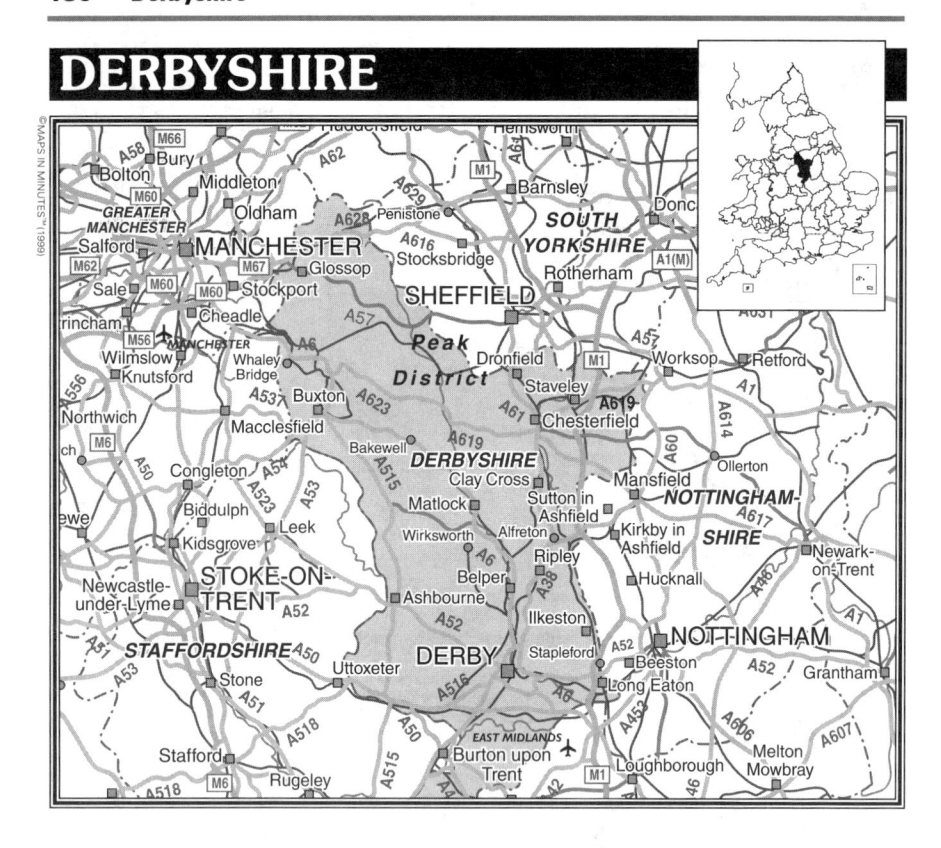

**AMBERGATE. Mrs Carol Oulton, Lawn Farm, Whitewells Lane, off Holly Lane, Ambergate DE56 2DN (01773 852352). Working farm, join in**. Enjoy comfortable bed and breakfast accommodation on a working beef and sheep farm, one mile from the A6 at Ambergate. Ambergate has many woodland walks and a picturesque canal which leads to nearby Cromford, home of the Arkwright Mill. Matlock Bath is 10 miles away and offers many attractions including the Cable Cars. Within easy travelling distance of Haddon Hall, Chatsworth House and Gardens, the Peak District National Park and the National Tramway Museum at Crich. Accommodation comprises double en-suite room and family room with handbasin. Terms on request from £17.50 per night. Children welcome at reduced rates. Pets welcome by arrangement. Non-smokers preferred.
e-mail: caroloulton@farming.co.uk

**ASHBOURNE. Alan and Liz Kingston, Old Boothby Farm, The Green, Ashbourne DE6 1EE (01335 342044).** In an idyllic Gateway to the Peak location, this stable conversion to a romantic holiday home offers perfect accommodation for couples. Situated on the green in Ashbourne it is conveniently located near the shops and pubs of this charming market town. Alton Towers, Dovedale, Buxton, Matlock and numerous stately homes close by. Superb walking country. May be booked together with adjoining property to accommodate larger parties (separate entrances). Shops and pubs one mile. Accommodation consists of lounge/bedroom with double bed, kitchen with breakfast bar, shower room with toilet and basin. Bed linen and towels included in price. Elecricity by £1 meter. Parking for one car. Use of owners' large garden with patio and barbecue. Suitable for partially disabled. Self catering also available.

**Derbyshire** **131**

## The Dog and Partridge Country Inn

With rooms in the grounds.....

Mary and Martin Stelfox welcome you to a family-run seventeenth century inn and motel set amidst five acres. Close to Alton Towers, Dovedale and Ashbourne. We specialise in family breaks, special diets and vegetarians are catered for. All bedrooms are en suite with colour TV, direct-dial telephone, tea making facilities and baby listening service. It is ideally situated for touring Stoke Potteries, Derbyshire Dales and Staffordshire moorlands. The restaurant is open all day, and non-residents are welcome. Open at Christmas and New Year.

**The Dog and Partridge Country Inn, Swinscoe, Ashbourne, Derbyshire DE6 2HS**
**Telephone: 01335 343183 • Fax: 01335 342742**
**website: www.dogandpartridge.co.uk**

**ASHBOURNE. The Courtyard, Dairy House Farm, Alkmonton, Longford, Ashbourne DE6 3DG (Tel & Fax: 01335 330187). Grazing farm.** Victorian cowshed tastefully converted and furnished to a very high standard. Tranquil location, yet within easy reach of Alton Towers (eight miles), Chatsworth House, Calke Abbey and many other historic houses. The Potteries are close to hand, as is the American Adventure Theme Park. We are surrounded by beautiful countryside which includes Dovedale and the many other lovely Dales which make up the Derbyshire Dales. A newly opened 18 hole, par-three golf course is only four miles away. Good farmhouse fare served on our 18 acre farm. Stay in one of our seven rooms – five double, one twin and a family suite, all with en suite facilities. Category 1 Wheelchair Access. Children welcome. Regret, no pets. Bed and Breakfast from £24; family suite from £75. Winter breaks October 20–March 20: Dinner, Bed and Breakfast £34 per person per night, minimum two nights. **AA/RAC ♦♦♦♦, RAC** *SPARKLING DIAMOND AWARD, CATEGORY 1 DISABLED.* 
e-mail: andy@dairyhousefarm.force9.co.uk
website: www.digitalpages.co.uk/courtyard

*See also Colour Display Advertisement*

**ASHBOURNE. Mrs Catherine Brandrick, Sidesmill Farm, Snelston, Ashbourne DE6 2GQ (01335 342710).** Peaceful dairy farm located on the banks of the River Dove. A rippling mill stream flows quietly past the 18th century stone-built farmhouse. Traditional English breakfast, excellent local pubs and restaurants. One double room en suite, one twin-bedded room with private bathroom, tea/coffee making facilities. Ideal base for touring: within easy reach of Dovedale, Alton Towers, stately homes and many other places of interest. Open February-November. Car necessary, parking available. Bed and Breakfast from £20 per person. A non-smoking establishment. **ETC ♦♦♦♦**
website: www.sidemill-demon.co.uk

**ASHBOURNE. A. and D. Harris, Dairy House Farm, Alkmonton, Longford, Ashbourne. DE6 3DG (Tel & Fax: 01335 330359).** This old redbrick farmhouse is situated on an 18-acre stock grazing farm in the tranquil countryside of the Derbyshire Dales, famous for its beautiful dales. Original features still exist including oak beams and a inglenook fireplace which is in the guests' lounge. There are five bedrooms, one twin and four single, with tea/coffee making facilities; four are en suite, one has a private bathroom. Guests have their own dining room and lounges, large colour TV, log fire. Warm welcome and hospitality guaranteed in a comfortable atmosphere with good food and a residential licence. Sorry, no pets, no smokers and no children under 16. Bed and Breakfast from £25 per person; Dinner, Bed and Breakfast £40 per person. Winter breaks from £36 per person Dinner, Bed and Breakfast. Minimum two nights – October 20th to March 20th. **ETC/AA ♦♦♦♦.**
e-mail: andy@dairyhousefarm.force9.co.uk
website: www.digitalpages.co.uk/dairyhousefarm

*When making enquiries or bookings, a stamped addressed envelope is always appreciated*

# 132 Derbyshire

**ASHBOURNE. Mrs E. J. Harrison, Little Park Farm, Mappleton, Ashbourne DE6 2BR (01335 350 341). Working farm.** This 125 acre dairy farm is situated in the peaceful Dove Valley, ideally placed for the Derbyshire Dales, National Trust properties and Alton Towers. Nearby cycle hire, five minutes' ride from Ashbourne, and within walking distance of the village local, where bar meals are served. Plenty of wildlife and beautiful walks, ideal place for unwinding. The oak beamed listed farmhouse is over 300 years old and is tastefully furnished with lounge (colour TV), diningroom (separate tables), tea making facilities, two double and one twin-bedded rooms with washbasin, bathroom and toilet. Sorry, no pets. Open April to October. Bed and Breakfast from £18. Non-smoking establishment. **ETC ♦♦♦**.

*See also Colour Display Advertisement*

**ASHBOURNE. Mrs A.M. Whittle, Stone Cottage, Green Lane, Clifton, Ashbourne DE6 2BL (01335 343377; Fax: 01335 347117).** A charming cottage in the quiet village of Clifton, one mile from Georgian market town of Ashbourne. Ideal for visiting Chatsworth House, Haddon Hall, Dovedale, Carsington Waters and the theme park of Alton Towers. Each bedroom is furnished to a high standard with all rooms en suite and having TV and coffee making facilities. Large garden to relax in. A warm welcome is assured and a hearty breakfast in our delightful cottage. Nearby good country pubs serving evening meals. Please write or telephone for further details. **AA** *QQQ RECOMMENDED*.
e-mail: info@stone-cottagefsnet.co.uk

**ASHBOURNE. Mrs E.M. Smail, New House Farm, Kniveton, Ashbourne DE6 1JL (01335 342429). Working farm.** Organically managed, this traditional family farm is in the South Peak District. Carsington Water is two miles, Ashbourne three miles and Dovedale a lovely five mile walk; Alton Towers 10 miles. There are pets, free-range livestock, archaeological features and farm shop. Guided farm walks. We serve organic, free-range and fair-traded foods. Vegetarians and other diets welcome. Children's teas, light suppers, babysitting and play area available. Pets welcome. Tea/coffee facilities, central heating, TV and radio in rooms. We also arrange FREE WORKING HOLIDAYS, individual/group camping and a venue for courses. Bed and Breakfast from £8 to £15.

**ASHBOURNE near. Tony and Linda Stoddart, Cornpark Cottage, Upper Mayfield, Near Ashbourne DE6 2HR (Tel & Fax: 01335 345041).** If you want tea and coffee making facilities, stale biscuits, UHT milk and a TV in your bedrooms, we don't have them. We will however make you endless real coffee or tea in your own lounge with a log fire, while you watch TV or videos or read from our vast collection of books. If you want a shower cubicle in the bedroom masquerading as 'en suite' we don't have it. We have got a bathroom with hot and cold water and a toilet (and we can pronounce en suite). We have got an en suite tennis court, off road parking, duvets, pillows, beds and towels. We are friendly, witty and our breakfasts are cooked on the same day. All this from £17, children £12. Self-catering in barn also available. Phone, write, fax or e-mail for a brochure. Open all year.
e-mail: stoddart@clara.co.uk

**BAKEWELL. Gayle and Hugh Tyler, Sheldon House, Chapel Street, Monyash, Near Bakewell DE45 1JJ (01629 813067).** An 18th century listed building in the picturesque village of Monyash (five miles from Bakewell), in the heart of the Peak National Park. Renovated to a high standard, we offer comfortable accommodation and a friendly atmosphere. Three doubles with en-suite facilities (two with colour TV, one with bath), guests' sittingroom with colour TV. All rooms have central heating and tea/coffee making facilities. Ideal base for visits to Chatsworth House, Haddon Hall, Hardwick Hall and excellent for cycling and walking. Open all year round except Christmas. No smoking. Bed and Breakfast from £21. **ETC ♦♦♦♦**
e-mail: tyler.family@lineone.net

## ROWSON HOUSE FARM  ETC

*Tel & Fax: 01629 813521* • *e-mail: gm@rowson99.freeserve.co.uk*  ★★

At almost 1000ft above sea level, the village nestles at the head of Lathkill Dale, a National Nature Reserve, and is surrounded by the stunning scenery of the White Peak. Cycle hire and fantastic horse riding are available locally. Rooms (single, double and twin) have en suite facilities, tea/coffee, colour TV, radio, and hair dryer and are centrally heated and double glazed. Laundry facilities are also available to guests. A variety of Aga-cooked breakfasts are served daily. Children and pets welcome by arrangement. Ample private parking. Clean and comfortable accommodation awaits you. Drive and Hike service. B&B from £20 to £25. **Mr G. Mycock, Rowson House Farm, Monyash, Bakewell, Derbyshire DE45 1JH**

See also Colour Display Advertisement

**BAKEWELL. Mrs Julia Finney, Mandale House, Haddon Grove, Bakewell DE45 1JF (01629 812416).** Relax in the warm and friendly atmosphere of our peaceful farmhouse situated on the edge of Lathkill Dale, now a nature reserve managed by English Nature. Our rooms have en suite facilities, colour TV and tea making equipment, and two are on the ground floor making them suitable for disabled visitors. A varied breakfast menu is offered and packed lunches are available. Excellent local inns and restaurants a short drive away. Bed and Breakfast from £19.25 to £22. 10% reductions for weekly bookings. Three night Bargain Breaks available in March, April and October. No smoking in the house. Telephone for brochure.
**ETC ◆◆◆◆**
e-mail: julia.finney@virgin.net
website: www.mandalehouse.co.uk

**BAKEWELL. Mrs Jenny Spafford, Barleycorn Croft, Sheldon, Near Bakewell DE45 1QS (01629 813636).** A well converted small attached barn with private bathroom and TV lounge. Accommodates two, three or four people in a twin and/or double room with washbasin, shaver point, thermostatically controlled heater and tea/coffee making facilities, creating a pleasant private apartment. Also provided: full English or vegetarian breakfast, ironing facilities, hairdryer; independent access with own key and private parking. Sheldon is a unique, unspoilt farming village with no through traffic or public transport, only three miles from Bakewell and ideal for visiting Chatsworth House, Haddon Hall, Matlock, Buxton and all parts of the Peak District. Open all year. Non-smokers only please and unsuitable for pets and children under seven years. Bed and Breakfast from £18.50. **AA ◆◆◆**

**BAKEWELL near. Mr and Mrs Clarke, Upperdale House, Monsal Dale, Buxton SK17 8SZ (01629 640536).** Idyllic riverside guesthouse enjoying a unique setting in the prettiest of Derbyshire Dales. Accommodation includes two double and one twin-bedded rooms, all en suite, with colour TV, tea/coffee facilities, full central heating and river views. Splendid local walks, numerous outdoor activities including trout fishing available. Closed Christmas and New Year. No pets. Sorry no smoking in the bedrooms. Monsal Dale signposted from A6 near Bakewell. Bed and Breakfast from £22 per person. Special off-peak breaks available. Vegetarians/medical diets catered for.

---

**FREE or REDUCED RATE entry to Holiday Visits and Attractions — see our READERS' OFFER VOUCHERS on pages 43-60**

## THE CHARLES COTTON HOTEL

The Charles Cotton is a small, comfortable hotel. The hotel lies in the heart of the Derbyshire Dales, pleasantly situated in the village square of Hartington, with nearby shops catering for all needs. It is renowned throughout the area for its hospitality and good home cooking. Pets and children are welcome and special diets are catered for. The Charles Cotton makes the perfect centre to relax and enjoy the area, whether walking, cycling, brass rubbing, pony trekking or even hang gliding. Open Christmas and New Year.

**Hartington, Near Buxton SK17 0AL**
**Tel & Fax: 01298 84229 • e-mail: info@charlescotton.co.uk • website: www.charlescotton.co.uk**

---

**BUXTON. Mrs Ann Oliver, "Westlands", Bishop's Lane, St. John's Road, Buxton SK17 6UN (01298 23242).** Close to Staffordshire and Cheshire borders, this well established Bed and Breakfast is for non-smokers. Situated on country lane one mile from town centre and Opera House, Westlands offers three rooms with central heating, washbasins, TV and drinks making facilities. Full English Breakfast provided. Ample off-road parking available. Very convenient for Chatsworth House, the Potteries, etc. An excellent centre for walking in the Peak District. Golf facilities available locally. Rates from £17.50 per person per night for Bed and Breakfast. Reductions for three nights, special rates for parties of four. Special diets catered for by arrangement.

**BUXTON. Pat and Trevor Cotton, The Old Manse, 6 Clifton Road, Silverlands, Buxton SK17 6QL (Tel & Fax: 01298 25638).** A spacious Victorian house quietly situated, yet within easy walking distance of the town centre, noted for its ancient architecture, Opera House and beautiful Pavilion Gardens. Buxton is ideally situated for visiting the delights of the Peak District, Alton Towers and the Trafford Centre. At the end of the day you can enjoy a delicious home cooked evening meal or just a quiet drink in our television lounge or bar. After a good nights sleep start your day with a freshly cooked full English Breakfast. Special dietary needs catered for. Bed and Breakfast from £18 per person. Three nights Dinner, Bed and Breakfast from £87.

**BUXTON. Buxton View, 74 Corbar Road, Buxton SK17 6RJ (01298 79222).** A friendly welcome awaits you at this stone built guesthouse with its pleasing garden and splendid views over Buxton and the surrounding hills. Only a short walk from this spa town's Georgian centre, the Peak National Park surrounds you with its glorious scenery and a host of varied attractions. Comfortable en suite rooms are provided with every thoughtful touch and a spacious guest lounge is stocked with maps and guide books. Delicious English breakfasts are served in the conservatory and you will be warmed by the interest we take in our guests; you will leave wishing you had stayed longer! Bed and Breakfast from £20 per person per night; Evening Meals available. Children and pets welcome. **ETC/AA** ♦♦♦♦

---

# FHG

Visit the FHG website
## www.holidayguides.com
for details of the wide choice of accommodation
featured in the full range of FHG titles

Derbyshire 135

## Ye Olde Cheshire Cheese Inn
### How Lane, Castleton, Sheffield, Derbyshire S30 2WJ
Telephone: 01433 620330 Fax: 01433 621847
Website: www.peakland.com/cheshirecheese • E-mail: kslack@btconnect.com

This delightful 17th century free house is situated in the heart of the Peak District and is an ideal base for walkers and climbers; other local attractions include cycling, golf, swimming, gliding, horse riding and fishing. All bedrooms are en suite with colour TV and tea/coffee making facilities. A "Village Fayre" menu is available lunchtimes and evenings, all dishes home cooked in the traditional manner; there is also a selection of daily specials. Large car park. Full Fire Certificate. **B&B from £25.00.**

---

**BUXTON. Roger and Maria Hyde, Braemar, 10 Compton Road, Buxton SK17 9DN (01298 78050).** Guests are warmly welcomed all the year round into the friendly atmosphere of Braemar, situated in a quiet residential part of this spa town. Within five minutes' walk of all the town's many and varied attractions i.e., Pavilion Gardens, Opera House, swimming pool; golf courses, horse riding, walking, fishing, etc are all within easy reach in this area renowned for its scenic beauty. Many of the Peak District's famous beauty spots including Chatsworth, Haddon Hall, Bakewell, Matlock, Dovedale and Castleton are nearby. Accommodation comprises comfortable double and twin bedded rooms fully en suite with colour TV and hospitality trays, etc. Full English Breakfast served and diets catered for. Non-smokers preferred. Terms £22.50 inclusive for Bed and Breakfast. Weekly terms available. **ETC ♦♦♦♦**

---

**BUXTON. Mr Andrew McKerrow, Cotesfield Farm, Parsley Hay, Buxton SK17 0BD (01298 83256).** A quiet, easily accessible, Listed farmhouse on a working farm overlooking the High Peak Trail and Upper Long Dale and less then one mile to the cycle hire centre. Guests have the benefit of accommodation separate from the farmhouse, allowing them to go "free range" yet still have the use of TV lounge, bathroom with shower and tea making facilities. The farm is central to some of the main natural attractions of the Peak District - Hartington Dale two miles, Bakewell eight miles, Lathkill six miles, Dovedale four miles, the Roaches eight miles, Monsal Dale 11 miles, Buxton eight miles; the High Peak Trail is 100 yards and accessible from the farm.

---

*The* **FHG**
# GOLF GUIDE
*Where to Play*
*Where to Stay*
## 2001

Available from most bookshops, the 2001 edition of **THE GOLF GUIDE** covers details of every UK golf course – well over 2500 entries – for holiday or business golf. Hundreds of hotel entries offer convenient accommodation, accompanying details of the courses – the 'pro', par score, length etc.

*In association with 'Golf Monthly' and including the Ryder Cup Report as well as Holiday Golf in Ireland, France, Portugal, Spain, The USA, South Africa and Thailand.*

**£9.99 from bookshops or £10.50 including postage (UK only) from FHG Publications,
Abbey Mill Business Centre, Paisley PAI ITJ**

## 136  Derbyshire

**CHESTERFIELD. Ms Elaine Harper, Abbeydale Hotel, Cross Street, Chesterfield S40 4TD (01246 277849).** Quiet town centre location within walking distance of historic Market Square and Crooked Spire. Chatsworth House, Haddon Hall, Hardwick Hall and Peak District all within easy reach. This comfortable small hotel is great for short breaks and a good stopping off place - close to M1 and mainline rail station. All rooms are en suite with TV and tea/coffee making facilities. Some rooms on ground floor, some non-smoking. Freshly prepared evening meals. Licensed. Car park. Bed & Breakfast from £25 per person per night. **ETC/AA ★★**
e-mail: elaine@abbey66.freeserve.co.uk
website: www.derbyshire.org/accommodation/abbeydale

**DERBY. Mrs Catherine Dicken, Bonehill Farm, Etwall Road, Mickleover DE3 5DN (01332 513553).** This 120 acre mixed farm with Georgian farmhouse is set in peaceful rural surroundings, yet offers all the convenience of being only three miles west of Derby, on the A516 between Mickleover and Etwall. Within 10 miles there is a choice of historic houses to visit; Calke Abbey, Kedleston Hall, Sudbury Hall. Peak District 20 miles, Alton Towers 20 miles. Accommodation in three bedrooms (one twin, one double en suite, one family room with en suite facilities), all with tea/coffee making facilities. Cot and high chair provided. Open all year. Bed and Breakfast from £20. Tennis, croquet available. A warm and friendly welcome awaits you.

**DERBY. Mr and Mrs J. Richardson, Rangemoor Park Hotel, 67 Macklin Street, Derby DE1 1LF (01332 347252; Fax: 01332 369319).** Long established family-run Hotel. Privately owned and run by the present owners since the late 70s. The hotel is modern with traditional standards offering outstanding hospitality and comfort. All 24 bedrooms have colour TV and tea/coffee making with 13 also having en suite facilities, direct-dial telephone and hair dryer. Ideally situated just a few minutes' walk from the centre of Derby. For your convenience there is ample free car parking, own front door key and night porter. Whether for business or holiday the proprietors pride themselves on personal and attentive service.

**See also Colour Display Advertisement** **GLOSSOP. Graham and Julie Caesar, Windy Harbour Farm Hotel, Woodhead Road, Glossop SK13 7QE (01457 853107).** Situated in the heart of the Peak District on the B6105, approximately one mile from Glossop town centre and adjacent to the Pennine Way. Our 10-bedroom hotel with outstanding views of Woodhead and Snake Passes and the Longdendale Valley is an ideal location for all outdoor activities. A warm welcome awaits you in our licensed bar and restaurant serving a wide range of excellent home-made food. Bed and Breakfast from £18 per night (singles) to £40 per night (family).

**HARTINGTON near Buxton. Bridgette and Frank Lipp, The Manifold Inn, Hulme End, Hartington, Near Buxton SK17 0EX (01298 84537).** The Manifold Inn is a 200-year-old coaching inn now owned by Frank and Bridgette Lipp. It offers warm hospitality and good "pub food" at sensible prices. This lovely mellow stone inn nestles on the banks of the River Manifold opposite the old toll house that once served the turnpike and river ford. All of the guests' accommodation is in the converted old stone blacksmith's shop in the secluded rear courtyard of the inn. The bedrooms have en suite shower, colour TV, tea/coffee making facilities and telephones. Bed and Breakfast £24 to £36. Brochure availble. **ETC ◆◆◆**

**Derbyshire** 137

**HATHERSAGE. Mrs Jean Wilcockson, Hillfoot Farm, Castleton Road, Hathersage, Hope Valley S32 1EG (01433 651673).** Newly built accommodation onto existing farmhouse offering comfortable, well appointed, en suite rooms. All with central heating, colour TV, tea/coffee making facilities,hair dryer and comfortable easy chairs. We have a large car park and public telephone for guests' use. Excellent home cooked food including vegetarian meals. Bed and Breakfast from £19 to £25 per person. We are situated in the heart of the Peak District, ideal for walking or visiting Chatsworth House, Bakewell, Castleton, Edale and many more places of interest. Current Fire Certificate held. Open all year. Non-smokers. **ETC/AA ◆◆◆◆** *WELCOME HOST*
e-mail: lorna@wilcockson0.fsnet.co.uk
website: www.hillfootfarm.com

HILLFOOT FARM

**ILAM. Mrs M. Richardson, Throwley Hall Farm, Ilam, Ashbourne DE6 2BB (01538 308202 or 308243).** Situated on a working beef and sheep farm in quiet countryside near the Manifold Valley, on the public road from Ilam to Calton. Within easy reach of Dovedale and Alton Towers, also stately homes. Accommodation comprises two double and two twin rooms, two rooms en suite, all with washbasins and TVs. Dining/sitting room with colour TV. Full central heating, also open fire. Tea/coffee making facilities. Bed and Breakfast from £20. Reduced rates for children, cot and high chair available.

**MATLOCK. Mrs Whitehead, Mount Tabor House, Bowns Hill, Crich, Matlock DE4 5DG (01773 857008; Mobile: 07977 078266).** High in the Derbyshire Dales lies the village of Crich, and Crich Stand, a memorial to the Sherwood Foresters, which can be seen from miles around. In the centre of this traditional village is Mount Tabor House, a former Methodist chapel which served the community for more than a hundred years. Converted several years ago, this fine Victorian building with its Gothic windows, most retaining their original stained glass, now offers extremely comfortable guest accommodation with a homely atmosphere. The two en suite bedrooms both have garden views, hospitality tray, TV/video, antique Scandinavian king-size pine bed and twin beds, corner bath and power shower. A family suite is also available. Candlelit dinners are served in the large living/dining area upstairs or on the new balcony overlooking the wooded Amber Valley. The atmosphere is peaceful and the views stunning. Fay uses local and organic produce in the freshly prepared meals. Non-smoking throughout. Local attractions include National Tramway Museum, Chatsworth, Haddon, Kedleston and Wingfield Manor. Double room £25 per person; £30 single; three-course dinner £17. **AA ◆◆◆◆**
e-mail: mountabor@email.msn.com 

**MATLOCK. Mrs D. Wootton, Old School Farm, Uppertown Lane, Uppertown, Ashover, Near Chesterfield S45 0JF (01246 590813). Working farm, join in.** This working farm in a small hamlet on the edge of the Peak District enjoys unspoilt views. Ashover is three miles away and mentioned in the Domesday Book; Chatsworth House, Haddon Hall, Hardwick Hall, Matlock Bath and Bakewell all within seven miles. Accommodation comprises two family rooms with en suite facilities, one double, one single room. Guests have their own bathroom; washbasin in three of the large rooms. Plenty of hot water; fitted carpets; large livingroom/diningroom with colour TV. Car essential. No smoking in bedrooms. NO PETS. Disabled guests welcome. Children welcome. Open from April to October. Bed and Breakfast from £22 per person per night; Bed, Breakfast and Evening Meal £30 per person per night. Evening meal minimum two persons. Reductions for children. Take the B5057 Darley Dale Road off the A632 Chesterfield to Matlock main road. Take second left. Keep on this road for approximately one mile. Old School Farm is on left opposite the stone water trough. **ETC/RAC ◆◆◆◆** *SPARKLING DIAMOND AWARD.*

**MATLOCK. Mrs G. Parkinson, Dimple House, Dimple Road, Matlock DE4 3JX (01629 583228).** 19th Century family house with large mature garden, views of Riber Castle and surrounding hills. Within walking distance of town with pubs, restaurants, buses and trains. Spacious rooms all have TV and tea making facilities, guests sitting room and conservatory. Pets very welcome (no extra charge), good dog walks close by. No smoking, car parking. Matlock is surrounded by wonderful countryside, the Peak Park is close, as are many stately homes including Chatsworth and Haddon Hall. Bed & Breakfast from £20. **ETC ◆◆◆**

## 138   Derbyshire

**MATLOCK. Mrs Linda Lomas, Middlehills Farm Bed and Breakfast, Grange Mill, Matlock DE4 4HY (01629 650368).** We know the secret of contentment - we live in the most picturesque part of England. Share our good fortune, breathe the fresh air, absorb the peace, feast your eyes on the beautiful scenery that surrounds our small working farm, with our pot bellied pig who just loves to have her ears scratched, and Bess and Ruby who are ideal playmates for children of all ages. Retire with the scent of honeysuckle and waken to the aroma of freshly baked bread and sizzling bacon then sample the delights of the Peak District and Derbyshire Dales such as Dovedale, Chatsworth and Haddon Hall.

**MATLOCK. Mrs S. Elliott, "Glendon", Knowleston Place, Matlock DE4 3BU (01629 584732).** Warm hospitality and comfortable accommodation in this Grade II Listed building. Conveniently situated by the Hall Leys Park and River Derwent, it is only a short level walk to Matlock town centre. Large private car park. Rooms are centrally heated and have washbasin, colour TV and tea/coffee making facilities. En suite available. No smoking in the diningroom. An ideal base for exploring the beautiful Peak District of Derbyshire, with easy access to many places of interest including Chatsworth House, Haddon Hall, National Tramway Museum and Heights of Abraham cable car. Bed and Breakfast from £19 per person. **AA ♦♦♦♦**

**TIDESWELL. Pat and David Harris, Laurel House, The Green, Litton, Tideswell, Near Buxton SK17 8QP (01298 871971).** A warm welcome awaits you in this elegant Victorian house overlooking the green in the pretty village of Litton. There are many lovely dales and rivers virtually on the doorstep, yet Tideswell is only one mile away. We are ideally situated for discovering all Derbyshire has to offer. One double with en-suite facilities and a twin with washbasin and private use of bathroom and toilet; tea/coffee making facilities in both rooms. A lounge with colour TV is available. Bed and Breakfast from £16. Non-smoking establishment. Directions: Off A623 at Tideswell. We look forward to seeing you. **ETC ♦♦♦♦**

**TIDESWELL. Mr D.C. Pinnegar, "Poppies", Bank Square, Tideswell, Buxton SK17 8LA (01298 871083).** "Poppies" is situated in the centre of an attractive Derbyshire village in the Peak District. Ideal walking country and within easy reach of Castleton, Bakewell, Matlock and Buxton. Accommodation comprises one family room and twin room with washbasins, one double room en suite, all with TV and tea/coffee making facilities. Bathroom and two toilets. Evening meals available by arrangement. Children welcome. Non smoking establishment. Bed and Breakfast from £17.50; Evening Meal from £11. **ETC ♦♦♦**
e-mail: poptidza@dialstart.net

**WINSTER. Mrs Jane Ball, Brae Cottage, East Bank, Winster DE4 2DT (01629 650375).** In one of the most picturesque villages in the Peak District National Park this 300-year-old cottage offers independent accommodation across the paved courtyard. Breakfast is served in the cottage. Rooms are furnished and equipped to a high standard; both having en suite bathrooms, tea/coffee making facilities, TV and heating. The village has two traditional pubs which provide excellent food. Local attractions include village (National Trust) Market House, Chatsworth, Haddon Hall and many walks from the village in the hills and dales. Ample private parking, Non-smoking throughout. Bed and Breakfast from £20 per person (reduced rates for children). **ETC ♦♦♦♦**

# DEVON

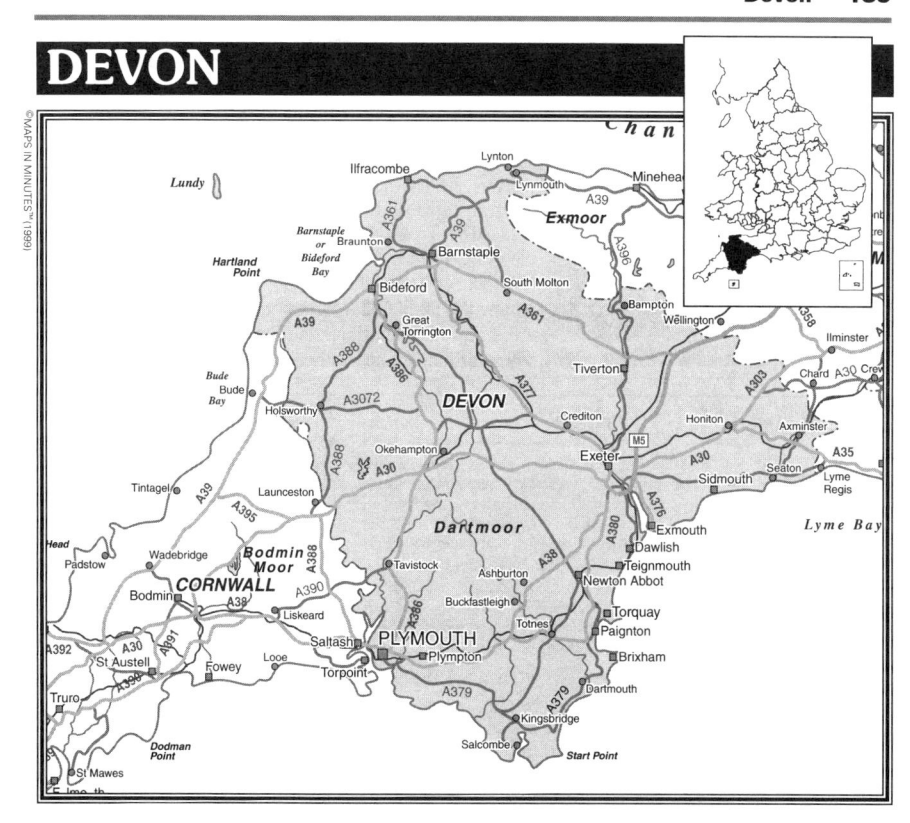

**ASHBURTON. Chris and Annie Moore, Gages Mill, Buckfastleigh Road, Ashburton TQ13 7JW (Tel & Fax: 01364 652391).** Relax in the warm and friendly atmosphere of our lovely 14th century former wool mill, set in over an acre of gardens on the edge of the Dartmoor National Park. Eight delightful en suite rooms, one on the ground floor; all with tea and coffee making facilities, central heating, radio-alarm clock and country views. Cooking to a very high standard using local produce wherever possible. Licensed. Ample parking. We are one mile from the ancient Stannary town of Ashburton, with its slate-hung buildings, antique shops and book shops. This is an ideal base for exploring South Devon with its many National Trust properties, pretty villages, coastal towns and, of course, Dartmoor itself. We are sorry, we do not take children under 12 years of age, or pets. **ETC, AA, RAC** ♦♦♦♦ plus **ETC** *SILVER AWARD FOR EXCELLENCE, "GUIDE TO GOOD FOOD IN THE WEST COUNTRY".* 
e-mail: moore@gagesmill.co.uk
website: www.gagesmill.co.uk

**ASHBURTON. (Dartmoor). Mrs Joy Hasler, Riversmead, Newbridge, Near Ashburton TQ13 7NT (01364 631224).** Riversmead, situated in the picturesque River Dart valley between Holne and Poundsgate and only four miles from Ashburton, offers peace and tranquillity with far reaching views from all windows. Set in one acre of garden with a stream running through, Riversmead is only two minutes' walk from the River Dart where you can enjoy walks on the river bank. Accommodation consists of one double and one twin, both en suite, and one king double with private bathroom. Guests' sitting room with colour TV and tea/coffee making facilities. Ample parking. Open all year. Bed and Breakfast from £20 per person.

A warm welcome to our Traditional English house standing on its own in a quiet countryside setting with panoramic views across the Taw valley. Pretty cottage garden. AA ♦♦♦♦♦ confirms we offer something special in the way of B&B accommodation. Three en suite rooms furnished with care, with good quality beds, easy chairs, bath/shower rooms with powerful thermostatic showers. Plenty of hot water. Tea fac., C/H, col. TV. Fridge for your own use, fresh milk. Relaxing lounge. Perfect North Devon touring base, 20 mins coast. Near RHS Rosemoor, Clovelly, Woolacombe, Lynmouth, Exmoor. No-smoking. En suite B&B £18-£25. Dinner available. Open all year.

Phone 01769 560034. Springfield-Garden, Atherington, Umberleigh, N. Devon EX37 9JA.
www.broadgdn.eurobell.co.uk

## Manor Mill House

Relax in our welcoming 16th century miller's house situated in historic Bampton, winner of many "Britain in Bloom" awards. Set in a peaceful, attractive riverside location, yet close to all amenities. There are three double/twin rooms, two with four-poster beds, and one on the ground floor, all en suite, with TV, tea and coffee making facilities, and full central heating. There are beamed ceilings, log fires in winter and delicious breakfasts using local produce.

Manor Mill House is in an ideal location, being close to Exmoor and centrally situated for Dartmoor, North and South coasts, Exeter, Taunton, National Trust properties, cycling routes, walks and many other places of interest. Bed and Breakfast (non smoking) £21 to £24 per person per night. Please enquire for brochure. ETC ♦♦♦♦

*Silver AWARD*

Chris and Kathy Ayres, Manor Mill House, Bampton EX16 9LP
Tel: 01398 332211 • E-Mail: stay@manormill.demon.co.uk • Website: www.manormill.demon.co.uk

---

**AXMINSTER. Ms C. M. Putt, Highridge Guest House, Lyme Road, Axminster EX13 5BQ (01297 34037).** Let me make you feel at home, pamper you with good food and make you comfortable in pretty, clean rooms, all with vanity units, colour TV and tea/coffee facilities. Take tea in our beautiful gardens with ponds and ornamental ducks. Nearby there are six lovely beaches, and several golf courses and a wild life park are easily accessible. We can provide maps and details of no less than 15 fishing venues, encompassing sea fishing, fly fishing, and coarse fishing. Enjoy a day on Dartmoor or a trip to Exeter, Taunton or Yeovil for shopping, or walk the Coastal Path from Lyme Regis to Seaton. End your day with a well-cooked three-course meal for only £8.50. Bed and Breakfast £16.50. Reduced rates for under 10 year olds. Pets welcome.

---

**BARNSTAPLE. Mrs Sheelagh Darling, Lee House, Marwood, Barnstaple EX31 4DZ (01271 374345).** Stone-built Elizabethan Manor House dating back to 1256, standing in its own secluded gardens and grounds with magnificent views over rolling Devon countryside. James II ceilings, an Adam fireplace, antiques and the work of resident artist add interest. Easy access to coast and moor. Family-run, friendly and relaxing atmosphere. Walking distance to local pub with excellent food. Marwood Gardens one mile. Open April to October. One double, one twin room and one four-poster room, all en suite with colour TV and tea/coffee making facilities. Bed and Breakfast from £20. No children under 12 years. Well-behaved pets welcome.

---

*When making enquiries or bookings, a stamped addressed envelope is always appreciated*

**BARNSTAPLE. C & M. Hartnoll, Little Bray House, Brayford, Near Barnstaple EX32 7QG (Tel & Fax: 01598 710295).** Situated nine miles east of Barnstaple, Little Bray House is ideally placed for day trips to East Devon, Somerset and Cornwall, the lovely sandy surfing beaches at Saunton Sands and Woolacombe, and many places of interest both coastal and inland. Exmoor also has great charm out of season! Come and share the pace of life and fresh air straight from the open Atlantic, and be sustained by a good healthy breakfast. Able to cater for two to ten people staying in a cottage and/or pretty twin-bedded rooms with bathroom. Lovely gardens, walks. Prices from £16–£18 per person per night.

**BARNSTAPLE. Mr and Mrs D. Woodman, The Old Rectory, Challacombe, Barnstaple EX31 4TS (01598 763342).** Within the Exmoor National Park, easily accessible on a good road, The Old Rectory is tucked away peacefully on the edge of Challacombe. A glance at the map of North Devon will show how excellently the house is placed, either for touring the spectacular coastline or for walking on Exmoor. Superbly furnished bedrooms, with tea/coffee making equipment, washbasins and heating. Ample bathroom, toilet, shower facilities. Comfortable dining room, lounge with colour TV. Bed and Breakfast from £18 per night, from £120 per week. No VAT charge. Further particulars on request.

**BARNSTAPLE near. Mrs J. Ley, West Barton, Alverdiscott, Near Barnstaple EX31 3PT (01271 858230).** Our family-run working farm of 250 acres situated in a small rural village between Barnstaple and Torrington on the B3232. Ideal base for your holiday within easy reach of Exmoor or visiting our rugged coastline of many sandy beaches. Also Dartington Glass, RHS Rosemoor Gardens, Clovelly and many other beauty spots. West Barton farmhouse is situated beside the B3232 with panoramic views of the beautiful North Devon countryside. Children welcome with reductions. Comfortable accommodation with family room, twin beds, single and double rooms available. Visitors' own lounge with colour TV. Dining room. Good farmhouse cooking including a variety of our own produce when available. Basic Food Hygiene Certificate. Regret no pets. Bed and Breakfast from £16; Evening Meal optional. Weekly terms on request.

**BIDEFORD. The Mount, Northdown Road, Bideford EX39 3LP (01237 473748).** A warm welcome awaits you at The Mount in the historic riverside town of Bideford. This small, interesting Georgian building is full of character and charm and is set in its own semi-walled garden, with a beautiful Copper Beech, making it a peaceful haven so close to the town. Within minutes easy walking, you can be in the centre of the Old Town, with its narrow streets, quay, medieval bridge and park. The Mount is also an ideal centre for exploring the coast, countryside, towns and villages of north Devon. The quiet, restful bedrooms, (single, double, twin and family) have hot and cold water and all are en suite. Tea and coffee making facilities are available. All rooms have TV. Non-smoking. Golfing breaks - discounted Green fees. **ETC/AA** ◆◆◆◆.

---

# FREE or REDUCED RATE entry to Holiday Visits and Attractions — see our READERS' OFFER VOUCHERS on pages 43-60

**BIDEFORD. Mrs Chris Leonard, Lane Mill Farm, Woolfardisworthy, Bideford EX39 5PZ (01237 431254).** Lane Mill Farm is situated three miles off the A39, south of Clovelly and three-quarters-of-a-mile from Woolfardisworthy village. Bed and Breakfast accommodation is offered at nightly or weekly rates. Evening meals are available at our own restaurant and inn, The Manor, in the village. The spacious farmhouse offers double and family bedrooms each with shower en suite; TV, tea/coffee making facilities are available. Guests have their own lounge/diner with colour TV and use of the indoor heated swimming pool. There are many local places of interest to visit including Dartington Glass, Rosemoor Gardens, The Milky Way, Big Sheep, The Tarka Trail and coastal walks. Bed and Breakfast from £18.

**BIDEFORD. Sunset Hotel, Landcross, Bideford EX39 5JA (01237 472962).** SOMEWHERE SPECIAL in North Devon. Small country hotel in quiet peaceful location, overlooking spectacular scenery in an area of outstanding natural beauty, one-and-a-half-miles from Bideford town. Beautifully decorated and spotlessly clean. Highly recommended quality accommodation. All en suite with colour TV, tea/coffee facilities. Superb cooking, everything homemade wth all fresh produce. Vegetarians and special needs catered for. Excellent reputation. Book with confidence in a NON-SMOKING ESTABLISHMENT. Licensed. Private parking. Bed and Breakfast £27 to £30; Bed, Breakfast and Evening Meal £39 to £43 daily, £235 to £240 weekly. **Mr and Mrs C.M. Lamb**, resident proprietors since 1971. **AA/ETC ♦♦♦.**

**BIDEFORD QUAY. Geoff and Sue Boundy, Tantons Hotel, New Road, Bideford EX39 2HR (01237 473317; Fax: 01237 473387).** At the heart of historic Bideford, Tantons Hotel is privately owned and managed, guaranteed personal and friendly service. Recently refurbished, over 50 single, double or twin bedrooms feature private bathrooms, colour TV, radio alarm clock, hairdryer and beverage making facilities. Bedrooms are light and airy with modern decor and bedware. Tantons Hotel has a relaxed, comfortable country-house feeling, enhanced by the salvaged wood beams and original architecture. The restaurant offers a quality à la carte menu whilst the Stable Bar offers a wide range of beverages, including real ale, outstanding bar meals and frequent live entertainment. A lift serves all floors.

*See also Colour Display Advertisement*

**BIGBURY-ON-SEA. Mrs Carol Walsh, Folly Foot, Challaborough, Bigbury-on-Sea, Kingsbridge TQ7 4JB (01548 810036).** A warm welcome awaits you at "Folly Foot", a modern bungalow 50 metres from a sandy beach and the South West Way coastal footpath. Golf course two miles. The towns of Salcombe, Totnes, Modbury and Kingsbridge are within easy reach. One double en suite, one family en suite, one double and one single with WC. Large separate bathroom. All bedrooms have TV, clock radio, tea/coffee facilities and central heating. Hearty breakfast, vegetarians welcome. Partially heated swimming pool. Children over eight years preferred. Sorry no smoking. Bed and Breakfast from £20 per night, reduced rates for children under 12 years and longer stays. Brochure available.

**BOVEY TRACEY. The Palk Arms Inn, Hennock, Bovey Tracey TQ13 9QS (01626 836584).** The Palk Arms is a traditional country pub with log fires, real ales, darts, bar billiards and other pub games. Bar meals available during the week and restaurant open from Friday night to Sunday night – bookings preferred. The pub is inside the Dartmoor National Park with fishing on three 70-acre lakes a mile away and also bird-watching/walks. Three bedrooms available (one with a four-poster), ideal for weekends and short stays. Sitting room also available for residents. Exeter 13 miles, Torquay eight. We welcome pets and smokers. Fishing licences and equipment available. Newton Abbot Races three miles and nearest beach seven miles at Teignmouth. Guided tours of Dartmoor available.

**Devon** **143**

**BRAUNTON. Mrs Roselyn Bradford, "St. Merryn", Higher Park Road, Braunton EX33 2LG (01271 813805).** Set in beautiful, sheltered garden of approximately one acre, with many peaceful sun traps to sit and relax. Ros extends a warm welcome to her guests. Rooms (£20 per person) include single, double and family rooms, all with central heating, colour TV and tea/coffee facilities. All rooms either en suite or with private bathrooms. Dinner (£12) may be served indoors or out. Guests may bring own wine. Guest lounge with books, games, colour TV/video, patio door access to garden. Swimming pool, fish ponds, hens, thatched summerhouse, barbecue facilities plus excellent parking. Please send for brochure.

**BUCKFASTLEIGH. Suzanne Lewis and Graham Rice, Kilbury Manor Farm, Colston Road, Buckfastleigh TQ11 0LN (01364 644079; Fax: 01364 644059).** This 18th century farmhouse is in a peaceful setting in the Dart Valley, an ideal base for touring Dartmoor and the South Hams Peninsula. Local interests including wildlife parks, animal sanctuaries, steam trains and good beaches. Bedrooms are attractive and comfortable with TV, tea/coffee making facilities; en suite available and a separate bath/shower room. Family suite also available. Six acre grounds with orchard and trout pond. English and continental breakfast, picnic lunches are provided. Suzanne delights in preparing delicious home cooked food, including vegetarian, using mostly our own garden produce. Our hospitality will make your stay enjoyable and memorable. Pay phone. Brochure on request. Bed and Breakfast from £22 per person per night, Evening Meal from £11. **ETC ♦♦♦♦.**
e-mail: accommodation@kilbury.co.uk
website: www.kilbury.co.uk

**BUCKFASTLEIGH. Mrs Rosie Palmer, Wellpark Farm, Dean Prior, Buckfastleigh TQ11 0LY (01364 643775).** Set on the edge of Dartmoor near Buckfast Abbey. A warm and friendly welcome is extended to all our guests. Very comfortable rooms available with colour TV, tea/coffee facilities and clock radio. Private bathroom facilities. Relaxing lounge with log fire and colour TV. Delicious farmhouse breakfasts are served. Enclosed garden with slide and swings. Excellent local 11th century inn is well worth a visit. Bed and Breakfast from £18 to £20. Reductions for children and weekly bookings. **ETC ♦♦♦♦**
*SILVER AWARD*

**BUDLEIGH SALTERTON AREA. David and Belinda Price, Greenacre, Couches Lane, Woodbury, Near Budleigh Salterton EX5 1HL (01395 233574).** Secluded guest house surrounded by countryside and stream, only four miles from the sea and five miles from the cathedral city of Exeter. The village centre is only a few minutes' walk away, boasting a Bistro (specialising in fish dishes), two pubs, a Post Office and two antique shops. An old fashioned welcome awaits you in this friendly family home. The comfortable bedrooms - two on the ground floor - all have either en suite or private facilities, colour TV and beverage tray. Well behaved pets and children are welcome. Plenty of car parking. Bed and Breakfast from £16 per person. Brochure available.

**CHAGFORD. Mrs Elizabeth Law, Lawn House, Mill Street, Chagford TQ13 8AW (01647 433329).** On the edge of Dartmoor within the National Park, Chagford is a beautiful unspoilt former stannary town dating back to the Middle Ages. In the centre of Chagford, overlooking the bowling green, stands Lawn House, a small but elegant 18th century Listed thatched house providing an ideal base for walking expeditions onto the moor. Lawn House offers friendly, comfortable, en suite Bed and Breakfast accommodation in very attractive spacious rooms, fabulous views, tea/coffee making facilities; TV lounge. Open all year round. Prices are from £20 per person. Discounts are available for stays of five nights and over. Packed lunches available.

**CHUDLEIGH. Jill Shears, Glen Cottage, Rock Road, Chudleigh TQ13 0JJ (01626 852209).** 17th century thatched cottage idyllically set in secluded garden, with stream surrounded by woods. Adjoining a beauty spot with rocks, caves and waterfall. A haven for wildlife and birds; Kingfishers and buzzards are a common sight. Outdoor swimming pool. Central for touring the moors or sea. Bed and Breakfast from £18. Tea/coffee all rooms.

**CLOVELLY. Mrs D. Vanstone, The Old Smithy, Sierra Hill, Clovelly, Bideford EX39 5ST (01237 431202).** The Old Smithy is a 16th century cottage and converted forge, situated one mile from the sea and the unspoilt picturesque village of Clovelly. Open all year except Christmas. Three family or double rooms, all with colour TV and tea/coffee making facilities. Children welcome. Large car park. This is an excellent base for touring Exmoor, Dartmoor and Cornwall. Also beautiful coastal walks on the South West Way. Bed and Breakfast from £16.50 standard, £19.50 en suite. Reductions for children in family room.

**COLEBROOKE. Pearl Hockridge, The Oyster, Colebrooke, Crediton EX17 5JQ (01363 84576).** The Oyster is a modern bungalow in the pretty, peaceful village of Colebrooke in the heart of Mid Devon. There is a spacious garden for children to play around or sit on the patio. Comfortable accommodation with tea/coffee making facilities, with TV in bedroom and lounge. Bedrooms en suite or with private bathroom – two double and one twin. Walking distance to the New Inn, Coleford, a lovely 13th century free house. Dartmoor and Exmoor are only a short drive away. Central heating. Open all year. Ample parking. Terms from £16 per person for Bed and Breakfast. Children and pets welcome. Smoking accepted. To find us take the Barnstaple road out of Crediton, turn left after one-and-a-half miles at sign for Colebrooke and Coleford. In Coleford village turn left at the crossroads, then take the left hand turning before the church, the Oyster is the second on the right.

**COOMBE MARTIN. Stephen and Claudia Moore, Channel Vista, Woodlands, Coombe Martin, North Devon EX34 0AT (01271 883514).** To the west of the village some 300 metres from the sea, beach and shops stands Channel Vista. A late Victorian residence tastefully modernised with all six guest rooms with en suite facilities, colour TV, clock radios, hairdryers and hospitality trays with tea and coffee making facilities. Relaxing lounge with colour TV/Sky, licensed conservatory bar with books and games. Choice of English and Continental breakfasts. Dine by candlelight, our dinner menus offer fresh local produce cooked by our 'chef'. Short Breaks available, reductions for children over 8 years. Non-smoking. Private parking. Bed and Breakfast from £20 per person. Brochure available. **ETC ♦♦♦**
e-mail: channelvista@freeuk.com

**CREDITON. Mrs Janet Bradford, Oaklands, Black Dog, Crediton EX17 4QJ (01884 860645).** Janet and Ivor warmly welcome you to enjoy a relaxing stay, long or short, in peaceful surroundings with lovely views and countryside walks. Large comfortable bedrooms with en suite, tea/coffee making facilities, colour TV and central heating. Large guest lounge with Sky TV and open fire in winter. Large garden with surrounding 20 acres of farmland where guests are free to wander. Walking distance of the 17th century Black Dog Inn pub/restaurant. Oaklands is situated between Dartmoor and Exmoor, ideal for touring all parts of Devon. Bed and Breakfast from £18. Reductions for children. Open all year.

**CROYDE BAY. Paul and Faith Davis, Moorsands, 34 Moor Lane, Croyde Bay EX33 1NP (01271 890781).** Following our first year's success, we look forward to meeting more new faces amongst the familiar this year. We have six en suite bedrooms, double, single, twin or family, some with stunning views over grazing horses to Croyde Burrows, the beach, sea and beyond. All rooms have a generous basket of beverages, central heating, clock radio and colour TV. Short walks to beach, village, and various local facilities help make Moorsands ideal for many holiday pursuits or for simply absorbing our warm welcome, relaxing atmosphere and Faith's delicious breakfasts. Car park, guests' lounge and cot/high chair available. Non smoking. Regret no pets. Bed and Breakfast from £20 to £26 per person per night. **ETC** ◆◆◆

---

**CULLOMPTON. Mr and Mrs T. Coleman, Town Tenement Farm, Clyst Hydon, Cullompton EX15 2NB (01884 277230).** A recommended Bed and Breakfast stop in 16th century farmhouse in quiet village, four miles from M5 Junction 28. Guests are accommodated in one double and one family room with bathroom and one double en suite with kitchen (ground floor). All rooms have tea making facilities. The guests' lounge has inglenook fireplace, exposed beams and panelled screen and is comfortably furnished. A farmhouse breakfast is served and a home cooked evening meal can be provided or guests may visit the "Five Bells" in the village. Bed and Breakfast from £16. Reduced rates for children, cots available. Open all year

---

**CULLOMPTON. Mrs Sylvia Baker, Wishay Farm, Trinity, Cullompton EX15 1PE (Tel/Fax: 01884 33223). Working farm.** Wishay Farm is a 200 acre working farm with a recently modernised Grade II Listed farmhouse with some interesting features. It is situated in a quiet and peaceful area with scenic views, yet is central for touring the many attractions Devon has to offer. Comfortable and spacious accommodation in family room with en suite bathroom, double room with washbasin and private bathroom, both with colour TV, fridge, tea/coffee making facilities. Central heating, log fire when cold. Children welcome, cot and high chair available. Bed and Breakfast from £16. Reduced rates for children. **ETC** ◆◆◆

---

**DARTMOUTH. Rhoda West, Little Weeke House, Weeke Hill, Dartmouth TQ6 0JT (01803 832380; Fax: 01803 832342).** Enjoy a warm welcome at this luxurious Bed and Breakfast set in peaceful surroundings close to the South-West Coastal Path and only one mile from the centre of Dartmouth. In summer months you can relax on the balcony, enjoying uninterrupted views across the garden to the neighbouring countryside whilst in the cooler months you can take in the same view from the comfort of the lounge by an open log fire. Superb views and peaceful location. All bedrooms en suite with colour TV, tea and coffee making facilities and hairdryer. Two-bedroom family suite with video player. Dogs welcome. Private parking. Drying room and secure indoor bicycle/fishing tackle storage. Beach one-and-a half miles. Please contact for brochure or reservations.
e-mail: RJWesty@aol.com

---

**FHG**

Visit the FHG website
## www.holidayguides.com
for details of the wide choice of accommodation
featured in the full range of FHG titles

## The Bel Alp House
*Haytor, South Devon TQ13 9XX*
**Tel: 01364 661217**
**Fax: 01364 661292**

AA ★★★

*A South Devon Jewel in the magnificent setting of Dartmoor*

This small, unique and friendly Country Hotel retains the atmosphere of a large family home, where the aim is to offer guests a high standard of comfort, good food and hospitality in magnificent and peaceful surroundings. Nestling into the hillside at 900 feet on the south eastern edge of Dartmoor, the house enjoys one of England's most spectacular settings looking out over Dartmoor to the sea some 20 miles away.

Furnished and decorated with the emphasis on quiet, restful colours, the bedrooms offer en suite bathrooms, TV, direct-dial telephones and tea/coffee making facilities. The elegant Drawing Room, with its wide bay window, has glorious views and a large selection of books on local history ; there is a small, well-stocked residents' bar and a comfortable Sitting Room. In the Dining Room, a carefully balanced table d'hôte menu is offered each evening, and can be accompanied by wine.

Dartmoor National Park is a wonderful place to explore by car, on foot or on horseback, with each season bringing its own magical beauty. Bel Alp House is ideally situated only 10 minutes from the A38.

---

## BED & BREAKFAST                SELF CATERING

*English Tourism Council*
*GUEST ACCOMMODATION*

*Dartmoor Tourist Association*

## POLTIMORE
*RAMSLEY, SOUTH ZEAL, OKEHAMPTON, DEVON. EX20 2PD.*
*TELEPHONE (01837) 840209 • FAX: 01837 849032.*

*Pretty thatched guest house, five miles from Okehampton and in a quiet position just outside the moorland village of South Zeal. Comfortable fully centrally heated en suite bedrooms, all with CTV and tea/coffee tray. Charming olde worlde beamed lounge, panelled dining room. Small pets welcome. A stay at Poltimore makes an ideal base for touring Dartmoor and the surrounding area. There is ample car parking in the guest house grounds. Write or telephone for our colour brochure giving tariff and holiday breaks. Situated on the old A30. Self-catering accommodation also available.*

### DELIGHTFULLY SITUATED IN THE DARTMOOR NATIONAL PARK WITH DIRECT ACCESS TO THE MOOR

---

**DITTISHAM. Mr & Mrs H.S. Treseder, The White House, Manor Street, Dittisham TQ6 0EX (Tel & Fax: 01803 722355).** Hugh and Jill look forward to welcoming you to The White House, an 18th century traditional stone-built village house overlooking the beautiful River Dart in the South Hams area of Devon. The centre of the village is a pleasant stroll away and Dartmouth is only three miles, with Totnes only eight miles away. Ideally situated for sailing, walking, bird-watching and visiting nearby historic towns. Accommodation consists of two double bedrooms (one with king-size and en suite, the other with private bathroom) and one twin en suite. All bedrooms are situated on the first floor and have hairdryer, TV and tea/coffee facilities. Guest sitting/breakfast room and garden terrace. Special diets catered for, if notified in advance. No smoking. No pets. Bed and Breakfast from £30 single, £55 double. 10% discount available for seven nights or more booked in advance.

**Devon** **147**

**EAST PRAWLE. Mrs Linda Tucker, Welle House, East Prawle, Kingsbridge, Devon TQ7 2BU (01548 511531). Working farm.** Welle House is part of a working mixed farm situated in the most southerly point of Devon's beautiful, unspoilt coastline. The house is in a quiet location with ample safe parking, a large garden with plenty of grass for games and views towards the village of East Prawle and the sea. All rooms (two double, one twin and one family) have en suite facilities and central heating. Access at all times and guests' lounge with colour TV and log fire. Help yourself to tea and coffee at any time. Flexible meal times. Children most welcome. Regret, no pets. Good pubs within easy walking distance. Bed and Breakfast from £15.

**EXETER. Mrs Dudley, Culm Vale Guest House, Stoke Canon, Exeter EX5 4EG (Tel & Fax: 01392 841615; Mobile: 07974 707296).** A fine old country house of great charm and character, giving the best of both worlds as we are only three miles to the north of the Cathedral city of Exeter, with its antique shops, yet situated in the heart of Devon's beautiful countryside on the edge of the pretty village of Stoke Canon. An ideal touring centre. Our spacious comfortable Bed and Breakfast accommodation includes full English breakfast, colour TV, tea/coffee facilities, washbasin and razor point in all rooms, some with bathrooms en suite. Full central heating. Our lovely gardens boast a beautiful swimming pool and there is ample free parking. Bed and Breakfast £15 to £25 per person per night according to room and season. Credit cards accepted.

**EXETER. Janet Bragg, Marianne Pool Farm, Clyst St. George, Exeter EX3 0NZ (01392 874939).** Situated in peaceful rural location two miles from M5 Junction 30, and midway between the seaside town of Exmouth and the historic city of Exeter. This thatched Devon Longhouse offers an en suite family/double room, a twin-bedded room and a single room with shared bathroom, all rooms have tea/coffee making facilities. There is a comfortable lounge with colour TV and a dining room in which a full English Breakfast is served. Large lawned garden, ideal for children. Car essential. Open March to November. Bed and Breakfast from £17 to £20 per person.

**EXETER. Mrs Heather Glanvill, Holbrook Farm, Clyst Honiton, Exeter EX5 2HR (Tel & Fax: 01392 367000).** Our dairy farm is pleasantly situated in a quiet location one mile between the Sidmouth A3052 and A30. The spacious en suite rooms are furnished to a high standard with TV and hot drinks facilities, enjoying beautiful views. Guests have their own key and entrance, access unrestricted. Treat yourself to our freshly prepared breakfast using local produce, separate tables. The historic city of Exeter, spectacular East Devon coastline and Dartmoor are close at hand. At the end of your day relax and enjoy one of our tasty suppers or visit one of the excellent pubs nearby. Bed and Breakfast £19 to £21. **ETC/AA** ◆◆◆◆.
e-mail: heatherglanvill@holbrookfarm.co.uk
website: www.holbrookfarm.co.uk

**EXETER. Mrs Gillian Howard, Ebford Court, Ebford, Exeter EX3 0RA (01392 875353; Fax: 01392 876776).** 15th century thatched farmhouse set in quiet surroundings yet only five minutes from Junction 30, M5. The house stands in pleasant gardens and is one mile from the attractive Exe Estuary. The coast and moors are a short drive away and it is an ideal centre for touring and birdwatching. The two double bedrooms have washbasins and tea/coffee facilities; sitting/dining room with colour TV. Non smoking accommodation. Open all year. Ample parking. Bed and Breakfast from £17 per night; £110 weekly.

**EXETER. Joyce Dicker, Moor Farm, Dunsford, Exeter EX6 7DP (01647 24292). Working farm.** At the end of M5 at A30 carry on until Woodleigh Junction, turn off into village of Cheriton Bishop, turn left at the Old Thatch public house, signposted Dunsford - you will find our farm two and-a-half miles on the left. The farmhouse is quietly situated on the edge of Dartmoor, in the area where "Down To Earth" was filmed. The guests have their own wing of the farmhouse, ideal for all ages. Good quality food is served. One double room, one family room, each with tea/coffee facilities. Open March-October. **ETC ◆**

**EXETER. Mrs Sally Glanvill, Rydon Farm, Woodbury, Exeter EX5 1LB (Tel & Fax: 01395 232341).** Come, relax and enjoy yourself in our lovely 16th century Devon Longhouse. We offer a warm and friendly family welcome at this peaceful dairy farm. Ideally situated for exploring the coast, moors and the historic city of Exeter. Only 10 minutes' drive from the coast. Inglenook fireplace and oak beams. All bedrooms have private or en suite bathrooms, central heating, hairdryers and tea/coffee making facilities; one room with romantic four-poster. A tradtional farmhouse breakfast is served with free-range eggs and there are several excellent pubs and restaurants close by. Pets by arrangement. Open all year. Bed and Breakfast from £24 to £27. **ETC/AA ◆◆◆◆**

**HIGHAMPTON. Mrs Gillian M. Bowden, Higher Odham, Highampton, Beaworthy EX21 5LX (01409 231324).** A dairy/beef 150 acres working farm, stream and open moorland. Watch milking, go for walks. Red brick farmhouse situated down a quiet country road off the A3072 between Holsworthy and Hatherleigh market towns. One mile to village shop, Post Office and village pub serving good food. Ideally situated for touring coast, Dartmoor and Exmoor. Fishing in many local ponds, near Tarka Trail for walking, cycling. Diningroom, lounge with open log fireplace, colour TV. Good views of Dartmoor. Large lawns with two ornamental ponds. Sorry no smoking or pets. One double en suite, one family with shower and washbasin, one twin with adjacent bathroom, separate WC. All with tea/coffee making facilities and TV. Bed and Full English Breakfast from £16 to £18.

*See also Colour Display Advertisement*

**HOLSWORTHY. Pat and Phil Jennings, Leworthy Farmhouse, Lower Leworthy, Pyworthy, Holsworthy EX22 6SJ (01409 259469).** A charming Georgian farmhouse nestling in an unspoilt backwater, with lawns, orchard, meadow, fishing lake. A genuinely warm, friendly and discreet peaceful haven. Beautifully prepared en suite guest rooms, ample fresh milk, quality teas, pretty china and bed linen. Chintzy curtains, luxury carpets. Peaceful lounge (no TV), ticking of chiming clocks, sparkling old china, Victoriana. Big comfy old sofas, books, games, puzzles. Also spacious diningroom. Breakfast traditional farmhouse, or prunes, porridge, fresh fruit, yoghurt, free range eggs, kippers, black pudding. Nearby spectacular north Cornish coast (20 minutes), good walking, fishing, cycling. Quiet pastoral enjoyment. Non-smoking. No pets.

**HOLSWORTHY near. Mrs S. Plummer, Long Cross House, Black Torrington, Near Holsworthy EX21 5QG (01409 231219).** Long Cross House is situated at the edge of the delightful village of Black Torrington, midway between the market towns of Holsworthy and Hatherleigh in rural North Devon. The centrally heated rooms in this south facing family house are en suite and have TV and tea/coffee making facilities. Evening meal can be provided by arrangement. Long Cross is an ideal place from which to explore North Devon and Cornwall, with such places as Clovelly, Bude and Dartmoor all within easy reach. Children, dogs and horses welcome. Bed and Breakfast from £17.50 per person.

**HONITON. Pamela Boyland, Barn Park Farm, Stockland Hill, Near Stockland, Honiton EX14 9JA (Tel & Fax: 01404 861297; Freephone 0800 328 2605). Working farm.** Working dairy farm situated one-and-a-half miles off the A30/A303 Junction, road sign marked Axminster/Stockland. Within reach of many beauty spots. Coast nine miles. Traditional farmhouse breakfast using eggs from our free-range hens. Barn Park Farm has en suite/private bathrooms. All bedrooms have beverage trays (TV on request). A homely atmosphere in a character farmhouse awaits you here. Open all year except Christmas Day. TV lounge, quiet sittingroom. Ground floor bedroom by arrangement. Bed and Breakfast from £16; Evening Meal from £9. No smoking in the house please. **ETC** ◆◆◆
website: www.stockland.cx

**HONITON. Mrs June Tucker, Yard Farm, Upottery, Honiton EX14 9QP (01404 861680).** A most attractively situated working farm. The house is a very old traditional Devon farmhouse located just three miles east of Honiton and enjoying a superb outlook across the Otter Valley. Enjoy a stroll down by the River Otter which runs through the farmland. Try a spot of trout fishing. Children will love to make friends with our two horses. Lovely seaside resorts 12 miles, swimming pool three miles. Traditional English breakfast, colour TV, washbasin, heating, tea/coffee facilities in all rooms. Bed and Breakfast £16. Reductions for children.

**HONITON. Jon and Ann Stockwell, The Old Vicarage, Yarcombe, Honiton, EX14 9BD (Tel & Fax: 01404 861594).** Surrounded by spectacular countryside, this imposing period house provides an excellent holiday base for rural pursuits, gardens, exhibitions, antiques, crafts, cream teas, dining out etc. Centrally located for north and south coasts - a welcome break on the 'Channel to Channel' walk. Spacious accommodation with distant views. Two double bedrooms. One twin bedroom. Guest lounge, television lounge and elegant diningroom. Large garden and studio. Ample parking. Sorry - no pets. Non-smoking. Prices from £19.50 per person.
e-mail: jonannstockwell@aol.com

*See also Colour Display Advertisement*

**ILFRACOMBE. Varley House, Chambercombe Park, Ilfracombe EX34 9QW (01271 863927; Fax: 01271 879299)** Built at the turn of the century for returning officers from the Boer War, Varley generates a feeling of warmth and relaxation, combined with an enviable position overlooking Hillsborough Nature Reserve. Winding paths lead to the Harbour and several secluded coves. Our attractive, spacious, fully en suite, non-smoking bedrooms all have colour TV, central heating, generous beverage tray, hairdryers, clock-radio-alarms and lots of thoughtful extras. Superb food, beautiful surroundings and that special friendly atmosphere so essential to a relaxing holiday. Cosy separate bar. Car Park. Children over five years of age. Dogs by arrangement. WE WANT YOU TO WANT TO RETURN. Bed and Breakfast from £24 per person. Weekly from £160 per person. Dinner available £12. **ETC/AA** ◆◆◆◆.
e-mail: info@varleyhouse.co.uk
website: www.varleyhouse.co.uk

---

Please mention *Bed and Breakfast Stops* when making enquiries about accommodation featured in these pages.

David and Marianna invite you to relax, smoke-free in the comfort of their elegant, lovingly restored period Victorian house, near lovely Bicclescombe Park in Ilfracombe, on Devon's romantic Atlantic Coast. We offer delightful spacious, individually designed, en suite bedrooms. We also have a reputation for scrumptious homemade fare. Private car park.

**"Lyncott"**
**56 St Brannock's Road,**
**Ilfracombe, North Devon EX34 8EQ**
**Tel/Fax: 01271 862425**
website: www.s-h-systems.co.uk/hotels/lyncott.html

## LYNCOTT GUEST HOUSE

*Relax in elegant smoke-free surroundings*

See also Colour Advertisement

ETC ♦♦♦♦

**ILFRACOMBE. Linda & Peter Wileman, Combe Lodge Hotel, Chambercombe Park Road, Ilfracombe EX34 9QW (01271 864518; Fax: 01271 867628).** Situated on the edge of Ilfracombe offering you a quiet and relaxing stay. We are a small eight bedroomed private hotel, most bedrooms with en suite facilities, all with colour TV, tea/coffee making facilities. Close to Exmoor and within walking distance of the shops, theatre and harbour. We are opposite the public indoor heated swimming pool. Licensed. Non-smoking. Full central heating throughout. Car park. Open all year except Christmas. Bed and Breakfast from £17; Bed, Breakfast and Evening Meal from £26. Special rates out of season. Please phone for details.

See also Colour Display Advertisement

**ILFRACOMBE. Geoff and Sharon Burkinshaw, Wentworth House, 2 Belmont Road, Ilfracombe EX34 8DR (Tel & Fax: 01271 863048).** Wentworth House, a friendly family-run private hotel built as a gentleman's residence in 1857, standing in lovely gardens only a stone's throw from the town and minutes from the sea, harbour and Torrs Walks. En suite rooms with colour TV and tea/coffee making facilities. Family rooms sleeping up to four persons. Home-cooked food with packed lunches on request. Spacious bar/lounge. Secure storage for bicycles etc. Private parking in grounds. Open all year . Bed & Breakfast from £17. Bed, Breakfast and Evening Meal from £23.50. Stay a few days or a week, we will make your visit a pleasant one.

**ILFRACOMBE. The Towers Hotel, Chambercombe Park, Ilfracombe EX34 9QN (01271 862809; Fax: 01271 879442).** The Towers is a ETC three diamond rated magnificent Victorian hotel set in its own grounds with its own car park. The hotel has tremendous views over the harbour, coast and Hillsborough Nature Reserve. From the hotel there are meandering paths to secluded coves and to beautiful Ilfracombe. Our mostly en suite rooms are well appointed with the usual extras, plus a few more. There is a residents' lounge and bar where you can just relax and admire the views. Eat our real Devon home cooking in our dining room over a glass of wine. For everyone's comfort, ours is a non-smoking hotel, as we want you to enjoy that special holiday and wish to visit us over and over again. **ETC ♦♦♦.**
e-mail: info@thetowers.co.uk
website: www.thetowers.co.uk

*Please mention Bed & Breakfast Stops when writing to enquire about accommodation*

**Devon** **151**

**ILFRACOMBE. The Cairn House Hotel, 43 St. Brannocks Road, Ilfracombe EX34 8EH.** Comfortable family-run hotel set in its own grounds overlooking Bigglescombe Park. The hotel is spacious and fully centrally heated, all bedrooms are en suite with colour TV, tea/coffee making facilities and clock radio. There is a quiet bar/lounge to relax in where pre-dinner drinks and later evening drinks can be enjoyed in a relaxed atmosphere. Guests compliment us on our food, there is a wide choice every day, good home cooking, imaginative and appetising. Any day arrival, any number of days, please telephone **Jane** or **Len** on **01271 863911** for details.

**INSTOW. Mr M. Prowse, The Anchorage Hotel, The Quay, Instow, North Devon EX39 4HX (01271 860655/860475; Fax: 01271 860767).** Number one for golf in the West Country. All rooms en suite. Superb dining and bar. Groups and associations most welcome. Luxury two-bedroomed flat also available for self-catering or using hotel facilities. Proprietors both ex-international golfers. Concessionary green fees at eight superb courses including: Royal North Devon, St. Mellion, Saunton, Bowood Park, Bude and Ilfracombe. Tailor-made itineraries.

**IVYBRIDGE near. Mrs Susan Winzer, "The Bungalow", Higher Coarsewell Farm, Ugborough, Near Ivybridge PL21 0HP (01548 821560). Working farm.** Higher Coarsewell Farm is part of a traditional family-run dairy farm situated in the heart of the peaceful South Hams countryside, near Dartmoor and local unspoilt sandy beaches. It is a very spacious bungalow with beautiful garden and meadow views. One double room with bathroom en suite and one en suite family room. Guest lounge/diningroom. Good home-cooked food, full English breakfast served. Children welcome – cot, high chair and babysitting available. Bed and Breakfast from £16 daily; optional Evening Meal extra. Open all year. A3121 turn-off from the main A38 Exeter to Plymouth road.

**KINGSBRIDGE. Anne Rossiter, Burton Farm, Galmpton, Kingsbridge TQ7 3EY (01548 561210). Working farm, join in.** Working farm in South Huish Valley, one mile from the fishing village of Hope Cove, three miles from famous sailing haunt of Salcombe. Walking, beaches, sailing, windsurfing, bathing, diving, fishing, horse-riding - facilities for all in this area. We have a dairy herd and two flocks of pedigree sheep. Guests are welcome to take part in farm activities when appropriate. Traditional farmhouse cooking and home produce. Four-course Dinner, Bed and Breakfast. Access to rooms at all times. Tea/coffee making facilities and TV in rooms, all of which are en-suite. Games room. Non-smoking. Open all year, except Christmas. Warm welcome assured. Functions catered for. Self-catering cottages also available. Dogs by arrangement. Details and terms on request. Bed and Breakfast from £24 to £30 per person.

**KINGSBRIDGE. Mrs M. Darke, Coleridge Farm, Chillington, Kingsbridge TQ7 2JG (01548 580274).** Coleridge Farm is a 600 acre working farm situated half-a-mile from Chillington village, midway between Kingsbridge and Dartmouth. Many safe and beautiful beaches are within easy reach, the nearest being Slapton Sands and Slapton Ley just two miles away. Plymouth, Torquay and the Dartmoor National Park are only an hour's drive. Visitors are assured of comfortable accommodation in a choice of one double and one twin-bedded rooms; private shower; toilet; shaver points and tea/coffee making facilities. Spacious lounge with TV. A variety of eating establishments in the locality will ensure a good value evening meal. Children welcome. Small dogs by arrangement. Terms on request.

**KINGSBRIDGE. Mrs Angela Foale, Higher Kellaton Farm, Kellaton, Kingsbridge TQ7 2ES (Tel & Fax 01548 511514 ). Working farm.** Smell the fresh sea air, and enjoy the delicious Aga-cooked breakfast in the comfort of this lovely old farmhouse. Nestled in a valley, our farm with friendly animals welcomes you. Spacious, well-furnished rooms, en suite, colour TVs, tea/coffee making facilities, own lounge, central heating and log fires. Flexible meal times. Attractive walled garden. Safe car parking. Situated between Kingsbridge and Dartmouth. Visit Salcombe by ferry. One-and-a-half miles to the lost village of Hallsands and Lanacombe Beach. Beautiful, peaceful, unspoilt coastline with many sandy beaches, paths, wild flowers and wildlife. Ramblers' haven. Good pubs and wet-weather family attractions. Open Easter to October. Non-smoking. Bed and Breakfast from £16.50. **ETC** ♦♦♦ 
e-mail: higherkellatonfarm@agriplus.net
website: www.welcometo/higherkellaton

**KINGSBRIDGE. Mr N. Alen, Ashleigh House, Ashleigh Road, Kingsbridge TQ7 1HB (01548 852893).** Situated on the edge of the town off the A381 Salcombe road, this relaxed and friendly guesthouse is an ideal base for touring the South Hams whilst having all the amenities of Kingsbridge within easy walking distance. All the comfortable, neatly decorated bedrooms are en suite with colour TV and hot beverage tray. In addition to a small bar, guest lounge and sun lounge, enjoyable freshly prepared, home-cooked meals are offered in the pleasant south-facing diningroom. Private car park. Credit cards accepted. Open all year round. **ETC/AA** ♦♦♦ 
e-mail: reception@ashleigh-house.co.uk
website: www.ashleigh-house.co.uk

**KINGSBRIDGE near. Mrs Margaret Newsham, Marsh Mills, Aveton Gifford, Near Kingsbridge TQ7 4JW (Tel & Fax: 01548 550549).** Former Mill House, overlooking the River Avon, with gardens, mill leat and duck pond. Small farm with friendly animals. Peaceful and secluded, just off A379. Kingsbridge four miles, Plymouth 17 miles, Bigbury Bay and Bantham beaches nearby, or enjoy a walk along our unspoilt river estuary. Salcombe seven miles, Dartmoor eight miles. A warm welcome awaits our guests, who have access to the house at any time. One double, one double/twin en suite. All rooms have washbasin, tea/coffee making facilities, room heaters and TV. Guest bathroom, WC; lounge/diningroom with colour TV. Car essential, ample parking. Bed and Breakfast from £18 per person. SAE for brochure, or telephone/fax. 
e-mail: Newsham@Marshmills.co.uk
website: www.Marshmills.co.uk

**LYNMOUTH. Tricia and Alan Francis, Glenville House, 2 Tors Road, Lynmouth EX35 6ET (01598 752202).** Idyllic riverside setting for a relaxing and romantic break. Delightful Victorian house built in local stone and full of character and charm at the entrance to the Watersmeet Valley. Picturesque village, harbour and unique cliff railway nestled amidst wooded valleys. This beautiful area where Exmoor meets the sea with its breathtaking scenery, magnificent walks and spectacular coastline to the heather-clad moorland is a haven of peace and tranquility for walkers and country lovers - a special paradise. Tastefully decorated bedrooms, pretty en suites. Elegant lounge overlooking river. Enjoy a four course breakfast in our attractive diningroom. Non-smoking. Licensed. Bed and Breakfast from £21 per person per night. **AA** ♦♦♦♦

---

*When making enquiries or bookings,
a stamped addressed envelope is always appreciated*

**Devon** 153

**LYNMOUTH. Mrs J. Parker, Tregonwell Riverside Guest House, 1 Tors Road, Lynmouth, Exmoor National Park EX35 6ET (01598 753369).** Truly paradise? Award-winning, outstandingly elegant Victorian (former Sea Captain's) riverside home is snuggled into the sunny side of tranquil Lynmouth's deep wooded valleys, alongside beaches, waterfalls, cascades, England's highest cliff tops and enchanting harbour, all steeped in history! A wonderful walking area, where Exmoor meets the sea. Exceptionally dramatic scenery around our Olde Worlde smugglers' village. Wordsworth, Shelley and Coleridge all kept returning here. An all year resort, each season unveiling its own spectacle. Pretty bedrooms, luxury en suites with breathtaking views. Guests' drawing room with open log fires in cooler seasons. Garage, parking. Bed and Breakfast from £22. Come as a resident then return again as a friend!

**LYNTON. Mrs V. A. Ashby, Rodwell, 21 Lee Road, Lynton EX35 6BP (01598 753324).** Rodwell is a small, friendly guest house, situated in the most level part of Lynton, facing south with lovely views of the surrounding hills and close to all amenities. Many beautiful walks start at our door and the famous Valley of Rocks and the unique cliff-railway to Lynmouth are a short walk away. Comfortable lounge with colour TV, double and twin bedrooms, all en suite, all with colour TV and tea/coffee making facilities. Non-smoking. Parking. Bed and Breakfast from £18, optional Two-course Dinner £10. **ETC** ◆◆◆

**LYNTON. South View Guest House, 23 Lee Road, Lynton EX35 6BP (01598 752289).** South View is a small friendly guest house in the heart of the picturesque Exmoor village of Lynton. Open all year, our aim is to provide a comfortable base from which to explore this beautiful coastal region. We have five rooms, all fully en suite with colour TV, tea/coffee making facilities, hair dryer, alarm clock and individually controlled heating. We serve a full breakfast with a choice of menu. Our comfortable guests' lounge is always open. Private parking is available at the rear. Overnight guests welcome. Bed and Breakfast from £15 to £20 per person per night. **ETC** ◆◆◆

**LYNTON. Pine Lodge, Lynway, Lynton EX35 6AX (01598 753230).** Built at the turn of the century Pine Lodge is set in landscaped gardens within a quiet conservation area, overlooking the Watersmeet Estate on the West Lyn Valley, ideally situated for exploring Exmoor and the spectacular North Devon Coast, but only a few minutes' walk to the village of Lynton. Here you can take a ride on the famous Victorian water-operated Cliff Railway to Lynmouth and the sea. We have comfortable, bright, en suite rooms, also ground floor accommodation and a large comfortable lounge to sit and relax in. All rooms have colour TV and tea/coffee making facilities. Optional evening meal. Ample level parking. Bed and Breakfast from £17 to £23 depending on season. Non smoking. **ETC** ◆◆◆◆
e-mail: Pine1Lodge@aol.com
website: www.pinelodgehotel.com

**LYNTON. Jane and Terry Woolnough, Croft House Hotel, Lydiate Lane, Lynton EX35 6HE (Tel & Fax: 01598 752391).** A delightful period hotel in England's Little Switzerland, offering pretty non smoking rooms, en suite, some with four-poster bed. All rooms with TV, hair dryers and tea/coffee making facilities. Home cooked meals served by candlelight; vegetarians catered for. Fully licensed with bar. Attractive walled patio garden in which to relax and enjoy your evening drink. All major credit cards accepted. Please contact Jane or Terry Woolnough for brochure. Prices from £18. **ETC** ◆◆◆◆
website: www.SmoothHound.co.uk/hotels/crofthou.html

**LYNTON. Kingford House, Longmead, Lynton EX35 6DQ (01598 752361).** If you are looking for a holiday where you can relax as if you were at home then come and stay at Kingford, situated within Exmoor National Park close to the Valley of Rocks, famous for its wild goats and spectacular coastline views. All rooms are furnished and decorated to a high standard and have colour television, beverage tray, clock radio and hair dryer. Double rooms are en suite and single rooms have private facilities. Private parking. Guest lounge has books and games for your enjoyment. Bed and Breakfast from £19.50 per person. Dinner optional £12.50 . We are a non-smoking hotel. **ETC ♦♦♦♦.**
website: www.kingfordhouse.co.uk

**NEWTON FERRERS, Near Plymouth. Pat and John Urry, "Barnicott", The Green, Parsonage Road, Newton Ferrers, River Yealm, Plymouth PL8 1AS (01752 872843).** 16th century thatched cottage situated in an Area of Outstanding Natural Beauty on a river valley. Facilities nearby for sailing, rowing, fishing, south Devon Heritage coastal path walks, short drives to beaches, Dartmoor National Park and historic Plymouth departure point of the Pilgrim Fathers. Accommodation comprises two double, one twin bedrooms, all with shaving points, heating, colour TV, washbasin, hospitality tray and rural views. Guests' bathroom. Full English breakfast or menu to suit. Three local inns and a Bistro serving Evening Meals all within walking distance. Private parking. Bed and Breakfast from £17 single; £28 double.

**NEWTON POPPLEFORD. Robin and Kate Wheelhouse, Southern Cross Guest House, High Street, Newton Poppleford EX10 0DU (01395 568439).** This historic 14th century thatched cottage, internationally famous for its Devonshire cream teas and home cooking, is ideally situated in Devonshire countryside, three miles from Sidmouth, close to enchanting bays and fishing villages of smuggling fame. We have many beautiful walks on our doorstep. Golf, riding, fishing and the West Point Centre are nearby. Exeter Airport only five minutes away. Meals may be enjoyed in our historic tea rooms or in our beautiful garden setting. En suite rooms with TV, tea and coffee facilities are available. Bed and Breakfast from £16.50 per person. Kate and Robin extend a warm welcome to visitors both old and new.

**NORTH TAWTON. Nick and Amanda Waldron, Kayden House Hotel, High Street, North Tawton EX20 2HF (01837 82242).** A character building in the heart of an historic market town. Located in the centre of Devon, we are ideally situated for exploring the real Devon. Easy reach of South Devon or North Cornwall coasts. We offer a comfortable, relaxing lounge and a bar for residents and diners only. Bar meals or à la carte menu available to suit all palates. All bedrooms are en suite and offer tea/coffee making facilities and colour TV. Family-run, Nick and Amanda look forward to welcoming you and hope your stay with us will be a memorable one. **ETC ♦♦♦.**

**OKEHAMPTON. Mrs Rosemary Ward, Parsonage Farm, Iddesleigh EX19 8SN (01837 810318).** A warm welcome awaits you in our period farmhouse, home of the famous parson Jack Russell, situated approximately one mile from the picturesque village of Iddesleigh and three miles from the market town of Hatherleigh. The Tarka Trail passes through our farmyard, with fishing available on the farm boundary. An ideal base from which to explore Dartmoor, Exmoor and coastlines. Accommodation consists of one family room and one double room, both en suite with tea/coffee making facilities and colour TV. Bed and Breakfast from £20 per person per night. Open Easter to October. No smoking or pets. Reductions for children. **ETC ♦♦♦♦** *SILVER AWARD.*

**Devon** **155**

**OTTERY ST MARY. Mrs Forth, Fluxton Farm Hotel, Ottery St. Mary, Devon EX11 1RJ (Tel 01404 812818)** Cat lovers' paradise in charming 16th century farmhouse set in beautiful Otter Valley with two acre gardens including stream, trout pond and garden railway. Only four miles from beach at Sidmouth. Beamed candle-lit diningroom; two lounges with colour TV, one non-smoking. Log fires, central heating. Teasmaid in all rooms, which are en suite with colour TV. Good home cooking our speciality, using all local fresh produce, superbly cooked. Dogs welcome free of charge. Lovely touring and walking country. Peace and quiet. All mod cons. Parking. Licensed. Open Christmas. Terms: Bed and Breakfast £23 per person per day; Dinner, Bed and Breakfast £30 per person per day. Proprietors : Mr and Mrs E. A. Forth. **AA** Listed

**PAIGNTON. Freda Dwane and Steve Bamford, Clifton Hotel, 9-10 Kernou Road, Paignton TQ4 6BA (Tel & Fax: 01803 556545).** A friendly, licensed, no-smoking hotel in an ideal level location just off the sea front and close to shops, rail and coach stations. All rooms en suite with TV and beverages. Superb evening meals available. A perfect spot to leave the car and explore on foot or by public transport South Devon, Dartmoor etc. Welcome Host and Commitment to Quality Award Holders. Open Easter to October. Bed and Breakfast from £20 per person. Spring Breaks available.
website: www.Clifton-at-Paignton.com

**PAIGNTON. Mr and Mrs Banks, Amber House Hotel, 6 Roundham Road, Paignton TQ4 6EZ (01803 558372).** Family-run licensed Hotel. Colour TVs and tea/coffee making facilities in all rooms. En suite facilities and ground floor rooms. Private telephones and clock radios in most rooms. Good food, highly recommended. Large car park. Whirlpool spa bath. Spacious suntrap garden and patio. Park close by for doggy walks. A warm welcome assured to pets and their families. Write or telephone now for further details.

**PLYMOUTH. Poppy's, 4 Alfred Street, The Hoe, Plymouth PL1 2RP (Tel & Fax: 01752 670452).** Poppy's is a quiet family-run business situated close to the seafront, Barbican, Theatre, City Centre and Channel Ferry. Rooms are en suite, very clean and tastefully decorated. All rooms have colour TV, central heating, tea/coffee making facilities and access with own entrance key. Private parking available. Full English Breakfast, Continental Breakfast for early ferry passengers (6.30am). Whatever your reason for visiting Plymouth you will be sure of a warm welcome from hosts Barry and Susan who run Poppy's together.
website: www.SmoothHound.co.uk/hotels/poppys.html

**PLYMOUTH. The Dudley Hotel, 42 Sutherland Road, Mutley, Plymouth PL4 6BN (01752 668322; Fax: 01752 673763).** The Dudley is a charming Victorian Hotel with an enviable reputation for good home cooked food and a high standard of cleanliness and comfort. Situated in a pleasant residential area close to the railway station, city centre and University, and not far from Plymouth Hoe, The Barbican and the Ferryport. Superb en suite rooms. Centrally heated throughout. All rooms with colour TV and complimentary beverage trays. Excellent Full English and Vegetarian breakfasts. Early breakfasts for ferry passengers. Evening Meal by arrangement. Secure car parking facilities. Children welcome (family rooms). For a brochure write, fax or phone. **ETC/AA** ◆◆◆◆.

**SEATON. Tony and Jane Hill, Beaumont, Castle Hill, Seaton, Devon EX12 2QW (01297 20832).** Spacious and gracious Victorian, seafront guesthouse in a quiet East Devon town in an Area of Outstanding Natural Beauty. Shopping, restaurants and leisure facilities nearby. Unrivalled views over Lyme Bay and Beer Cliffs. Half-mile promenade just yards away. All five rooms en suite with TV, tea and coffee making facilities. Parking available. Bed and Breakfast from £23 per person per night. Special weekly rate. Pre-booked Evening Meal £15. A warm welcome is assured.

**SIDMOUTH. Berwick Guest House, Salcombe Road, Sidmouth EX10 8PX (01395 513621).** Attractive 19th century house conveniently situated to all amenities. Short level walk to charming town and unspoilt seafront. Close to Coastal Path and riverside parkland. Rooms en suite with TV and tea/coffee making facilities. Comfortable lounge with TV. Parking. Mid-week bookings taken. Open March till October. Sorry, no pets or smoking. Terms from £18. Further details from: Rosemary Tingley and Tony Silverside. **ETC ♦♦♦**, *MEMBERS OF SIDMOUTH & DISTRICT HOTEL AND CATERERS ASSOCIATION.*

**SIDMOUTH. Bramley Lodge Guest House, Vicarage Road, Sidmouth EX10 8UQ. (01395 515710).** A family owned and run guest house, in a town house only half-a-mile level walk to the High Street and sea front. Relax in the residents' garden, backing on to the River Sid and The Byres Parkland. Enjoy breakfast in our dining room before exploring Sidmouth and East Devon's attractions. Seven comfortable bedrooms; single, double and family rooms, each with hot drinks facilities and TV; some with en suite facilities. Optional home-cooked evening meals. Private parking at rear. Restricted smoking. Bed and Breakfast from £18 to £25 per person. Child reductions. For further information ring Linda and David on 01395 515710.
e-mail: haslam@bramleylodge.fs.net.co.uk

**SIDMOUTH. Mrs Betty Everson, Ambleside, 82 Winslade Road, Sidmouth EX10 9EZ (01395 514423).** Ambleside is set in one-third of an acre of ground, approximately 12 minutes from the sea-front. All rooms have TV, tea/coffee making facilities and private bathroom, en suite available. Personal attention guaranteed. Freedom to come and go as you please. Parking available at rear of property. Vegetarians catered for. Pets considered. Please phone or write for further information.

*See also Colour Display Advertisement* **SIDMOUTH. Mrs B. Smith, Willow Bridge, Milford Road, Sidmouth EX10 8DR (Tel & Fax: 01395 513599).** Over the years the Willow Bridge has earned an enviable reputation for good food, comfort and a happy atmosphere. Occupying an excellent position in a picturesque riverside setting yet only five minutes level walk from the Regency town and beautiful esplanade. Sidmouth has two beaches which are especially safe for bathing, sailing or fishing and the town offers a great variety of other activities including golf, tennis and swimming, with many wonderful gardens to visit. The bedrooms are all en suite, except for one which has private bathroom with own key. All rooms have shaver point, hairdryer, colour TV, clock radio and tea/coffee making facilities. Guest lounge with TV, daily papers, magazines and books. Diningroom with individual tables and licensed bar overlooking our award-winning garden. The meals are prepared personally by the resident proprietors from fresh local produce, and we have a restaurant licence with a good selection of fine wines, beers and spirits. Car park. Full Fire Certificate. Non smoking. **ETC ♦♦♦♦**.

**Devon** **157**

**SIDMOUTH. Gerry and Kate Corr, Glendevon Hotel, Cotmaton Road, Sidmouth EX10 8QX (Tel & Fax: 01395 514028).** Stylish Victorian house which has been beautifully adapted to hotel use. Situated on the edge of Bickwell Valley in a quiet location yet only a few minutes walk from the town centre, esplanade, golf club, theatre, Connaught Gardens and Jacob's Ladder Beach. Excellent base for exploring Dartmoor, picturesque villages and the cathedral City of Exeter. Comfortable en suite rooms with colour TV, tea/coffee making facilities and central heating. A spacious, tastefully decorated lounge offers guests the opportunity of a quiet read, friendly conversation or a drink (we have a residential licence). Excellent home cooking. Non smoking policy throughout. Open all year. **AA** ♦♦♦♦.

**SIDMOUTH. Mrs Betty S. Sage, Pinn Barton, Peak Hill, Sidmouth EX10 0NN (Tel & Fax: 01395 514004).** A 330-acre farm set peacefully just off the coastal road, two miles from Sidmouth and close to the village of Otterton. Safe beaches and lovely cliff walks. Pinn Barton has been highly recommended, and offers a warm welcome in comfortable surroundings with good farmhouse breakfast. All bedrooms have bathrooms en-suite; colour TV; central heating; free hot drinks facilities; electric blankets. Children very welcome. Reductions for children sharing parents' room. Open all year. Bed and Breakfast including bedtime drink from £20 to £22. Own keys provided for access at all times. **ETC** ♦♦♦♦
website: www.SmoothHound.co.uk/hotels/pinn.html

**SIDMOUTH. Peter and Gail Bradnam, Ryton Guest House, 54 Winslade Road, Sidmouth EX10 9EX (01395 513981; Fax: 01395 519210).** Attractive and comfortable double-fronted town house. Situated on a quiet road with a sunny private garden and car park. A few minutes from National Trust walkway to the timeless town centre and level seafront walk. Bright, clean, en suite bedrooms. Family, single or double rooms available. Excellent full English breakfast and warm welcome. Terms from £20. Children and pets welcome. Winter and summer breaks. Please phone or write for a brochure. **AA** ♦♦♦.

**SLAPTON. Jane and Bryan Ashby, Start House, Start, Slapton, Kingsbridge TQ7 2QD (01548 580254).** Spacious and comfortable, Start House is situated in a quiet hamlet, one mile from Slapton. All the bedrooms overlook a beautiful valley running south-east to Slapton Ley and the sea. The delicious breakfasts, traditional or vegetarian, are cooked to order using local produce. Evening meals are available by arrangement. We are an ideal base for walkers and wildlife enthusiasts, and garden lovers will find much of interest in our large garden. Open all year for Bed and Breakfast from £22, we also have a self-catering flat for two people. Non-smokers only. Full details on request .**ETC** ♦♦♦

**SOUTH MOLTON near. Messrs H. J. Milton, Partridge Arms Farm, Yeo Mill, West Anstey, Near South Molton EX36 3NU (01398 341217; Fax: 01398 341569).** Now a working farm of over 200 acres, four miles west of Dulverton, "Partridge Arms Farm" was once a coaching inn and has been in the same family since 1906. Genuine hospitality and traditional farmhouse fare await you. Comfortable accommodation in double, twin and single rooms, some of which have en suite facilities. There is also an original four-poster bedroom. Children welcome. Animals by arrangement. Residential licence. Open all year. Fishing and riding available nearby. Bed and Breakfast from £21.00 to £26.50; Evening Meal from £10.00. *FARM HOLIDAY GUIDE DIPLOMA WINNER.*

**TEIGNMOUTH. Thornhill Hotel, Sea Front, Teignmouth TQ14 8TA (01626 773460).** An elegant and immaculate 10-bedroomed licensed Georgian hotel. Convenient parking; level quiet location on seafront close to all amenities. En suite rooms; colour TV. Non-smoking. Superb food. Large comfortable lounge; ground floor bedroom. Teignmouth has a long, level promenade, beautiful flowers and 'Den Lawns; safe sandy beach, cliff walks, bowling, tennis, golf, fishing, sailing, theatre, shops. Good public transport. Ideal base for exploring country villages, Dartmoor, seaside resorts, cities of Exeter and Plymouth. Come to Thornhill and enjoy yourselves. Bed and Breakfast £25, Half Board £36.50; reductions for three or more nights.
website: www.english-riviera.co.uk/hotels/thornhill/index.htm

**TEIGNMOUTH. Mrs Wasilewska, Lyme Bay House Hotel, Seafront, Teignmouth TQ14 8SZ (01626 772953).** Situated right on the sea front, near to rail and coach stations and shops. Teignmouth is a popular holiday resort with a long sandy beach, quaint shops to browse in, pier and children's entertainments. En suite available. Lift – no steps. Bed and Breakfast from £18. Pets welcome.

**TEIGNMOUTH. Dianne and David Loach, Coombe Bank Hotel, Landscore Road, Teignmouth TQ14 9JL (01626 772369; Fax: 01626 774159).** Coombe Bank House, set in its own grounds, offers a warm, friendly atmosphere with exceptional thought for comfort. Ground and first floor bright, spacious en suite rooms, all with colour TV, tea/coffee making facilities and radio/alarm. Central heating. Elegant candlelit restaurant offering a table d'hôte menu. Cosy, intimate bar. Wheelchair access. Garden with ample car parking. Views of the River Teign. Pets welcome by prior arrangement. Open all year. Prices range from £19.50 to £24 per person per night including Full English Breakfast. Brochure on request.
website: www.coombebankhotel.co.uk

**TEIGN VALLEY. S. and G. Harrison-Crawford, Silver Birches, Teign Valley, Trusham, Newton Abbot TQ13 0NJ (01626 852172).** A warm welcome awaits you at Silver Birches, a comfortable bungalow at the edge of Dartmoor. A secluded, relaxing spot with two acre garden running down to the river. Only two miles from A38 on B3193. Exeter 14 miles, sea 12 miles. Car advisable. Ample parking. Excellent pubs and restaurants nearby. Good centre for fishing, bird-watching, forest walks, golf, riding; 70 yards salmon/trout fishing free to residents. Centrally heated guest accommodation with separate entrance. Two double-bedded rooms, one twin-bedded room, all with own bath/shower, toilet. Guest lounge with colour TV. Diningroom, sun lounge overlooking river. Sorry, no children under eight. Terms include tea on arrival. Bed and full English Breakfast from £25 per person nightly, £168 per person weekly. Evening Meal optional. Open all year. Self-catering caravans also available from £135.

---

**FREE or REDUCED RATE entry to Holiday Visits and Attractions — see our READERS' OFFER VOUCHERS on pages 43-60**

**TIVERTON. Colin and Christine Cook, Higher Western Restaurant, Oakford, Tiverton EX16 9JE (01398 341210).** Licensed small country restaurant with en suite accommodation set in three-quarters of an acre. On the B3227 Taunton/Barnstaple holiday route, three miles west of Oakford, in an Area of Outstanding Natural Beauty. A relaxing base for touring Exmoor and the North Devon coast. Excellent food, cooked to order, specialising in imaginative menus using local and own produce, complemented by a carefully chosen wine list. We offer quality accommodation to those seeking peace and quiet. One twin-bedded and two double rooms, all en suite. Children welcome. Car essential, ample parking. Open all year round. Terms: Bed and Breakfast from £20 per night; three course luncheon £6.95. *"THE GOOD RESTAURANT GUIDE".*

**TIVERTON near. Robbie and Carol Latchem, The Old Post Office B&B, Bickleigh Heritage Village, Near Tiverton EX16 8RH (01884 855731; Fax: 07000 783845).** Timeless and enchanting 'Olde' world thatched village, renowned for its scenic beauty. Situated between Tiverton and Exeter, ideal touring base for moors and coast. We offer superb en suite accommodation or private bathroom, tea/coffee making facilities, Sky TV, good value, service, high standards of hygiene, towels, hair dryer, shampoo and soap. Excellent quality of food/cooking. Visit Bickleigh Castle, Castle Tea Rooms and Garden Centre, Bickleigh Railway and Museum, local riverside pubs and restaurants. Open all year. Families welcome. How to find us:- Off junction 27-M5 Motorway, take A396 Link Road to Tiverton, follow signs for Bickleigh to Bickleigh Village.

**TORQUAY. Mrs B. Hurren, Treander Guest House, 10 Morgan Avenue, Torquay TQ2 5RS (01803 296906).** "Service with a smile!" Come and enjoy a first class informal holiday at a clean, comfortable establishment, which is in a superb position for beaches and amenities. Central for a whole range of activities. Some rooms have a sea view. Colour TV, central heating, washbasin and tea making facilities in each room. Car park. Own key, with access at all times. Excellent home cooking. Children and pets welcome. Bed and Breakfast from £15.50; optional Evening Meal. Good reductions for children. *HOTEL ASSOCIATION "RECOMMENDED".*

**TORQUAY. Mr T. Hoverd, Green Park Licensed Hotel, 25 Morgan Avenue, Torquay TQ2 5RR (01803 293618).** GREEN PARK is a small independent licensed hotel situated in a quiet road just 300 yards from the town centre and shops, leading onto Fleet Walk, Torquay's new shopping centre, and then down to the harbour and sea front. Green Park offers our guests en suite rooms, colour TV, tea/coffee facilities, off-road car parking, large TV lounge, comfortable diningroom and bar. Full central heating. Open all year including Christmas and New Year. Bed and Breakfast from £15. Telephone Lorna or Tony for brochure. **ETC ◆◆◆**

**TORQUAY. Mrs R. Wilkinson, Deane Thatch Accommodation, Stoke-in-Teignhead, Near Torquay TQ12 4QU (Tel & Fax: 01626 873724).** A charming thatched Devonshire cob cottage, and thatched cob linhay. Situated in a secluded rural spot enjoying uninterrupted views of farmland with an atmosphere of total tranquillity. Half-a-mile from the village of Stoke-in-Teignhead and just one mile from the sea. Ideally situated for Torquay (the English Riviera) and Dartmoor National Park. All rooms have colour TV, private bathroom, shower or bidet and tea/coffee making facilities; king-size bed in linhay. Children welcome, reduced rates and babysitting available. Open all year. Bed and Breakfast from £20, discounts for weekly rate. Brittany Ferries recommended. **ETC ◆◆◆** *COMMENDED*
e-mail: deanethatch@hotmail.com
website: www.ukchoice.net/17/deanethatch.htm
website: http://.come.to/deanethatch

### HEATHCLIFF HOTEL
16 Newton Road, Torquay, Devon TQ2 5BZ
### Telephone: 01803 211580
e-mail: hhhtorquay@btclick.com
website: http://home.btclick.com/hhhtorquay/home.htm

This former vicarage is now a superbly appointed hotel equipped for today yet retaining its Victorian charm. All the bedrooms have full en suite facilities, colour TV and drink making facilities. The elegant licensed bar boasts an extensive menu and unlike many hotels, the car park has sufficient space to accommodate all vehicles to eliminate roadside parking. Torquay's main beach, High Street shops, entertainment and restaurants are all nearby and with full English breakfast included, it is easy to see why guests return time after time.

Tariff for B&B ranges between £15 and £21.50 pp. Family rooms from £49 per night. So, be it main holiday, touring or business, make the Heathcliff your 1st choice.

| VISITORS | BOOK |
|---|---|
| Rich & Elaine | Best in Devon |
| Mr & Mrs T | Excellent! |
| The S Family | 1st Class |
| Mac & June | Fantastic Hosts |

**Heathcliff** HOUSE · HOTEL

## Silverlands Hotel
27 Newton Road, Torquay TQ2 5DB
Telephone: 01803 292013

Situated on a main route to town and beach (approximately half-a-mile). Superb family-run guest house. Eleven superior rooms furnished and decorated to a high standard, mostly en suite. Relaxed and homely atmosphere. TV, hot and cold wash facilities, tea and coffee making, full central heating available in all rooms. Ample car parking. Full English breakfast. Open all year. From £14 to £20 per person.

**ETC COMMENDED.**

See also Colour Display Advertisement

**TOTNES. John and Caroline Tipper, The Hungry Horse Restaurant and B & B Accommodation, Harbertonford, TQ9 7TA (01803 732441; Fax: 01803 732780).** John and Caroline invite you to share with them the calm and comfortable surrounding of this lovely timeless building on the banks of the River Harbourne. It has long been noted for its tranquil atmosphere, and whether you stay for a few hours enjoying a relaxed dinner in the restaurant and convivial drinks in the snug bar, or stay a few days in our bed and breakfast accommodation, you are sure to unwind under the magic spell of its calming influence and charm. The restaurant offers some of the best food in the area - only fresh local produce is used. Write or call for our brochure. **ETC ♦♦♦♦**.

**Devon** 161

# BRADDON HALL HOTEL

TORQUAY HOTELS
& CATERERS ASSOCIATION

**70 Braddons Hill Road East, Torquay TQ1 1HF**
**Telephone/Fax: 01803 293908**
**E-mail: braddonhall@tinyworld.co.uk**
**Website: www.braddonhall.co.uk**
**Proprietors: Peter and Carol White**

This delightful personally run hotel is situated in a peaceful yet convenient position, only a few minutes from the harbour, shopping centre, beaches and entertainments.

★ All rooms are en suite, individual in character and tastefully decorated

★ All have remote control colour TVs and tea/coffee making facilities

★ Romantic four-poster bed available for that special occasion

★ Full central heating for those early and late breaks

★ Discounts for the over 55's on weekly bookings out of season

★ Friendly relaxed atmosphere

★ Parking

★ Bed and breakfast per person per night from £16 low season to £20 high season

*Please write or telephone for our brochure and book with confidence.*

See also Colour Display Advertisement

**TOTNES. Mrs Jeannie Allnutt, The Old Forge at Totnes, Seymour Place, Totnes TQ9 5AY (01803 862174).** A charming 600-year-old stone building, delightfully converted from blacksmith and wheelwright workshops and coach houses. Traditional working forge, complete with blacksmith's prison cell. We have our own bit of "rural England" close to the town centre. Very close to the River Dart steamer quay, shops and station (also steam train rides). Ideally situated for touring most of Devon – including Dartmoor and Torbay coasts. A day trip from Exeter, Plymouth and Cornwall. May to September – Elizabethan costume markets on Tuesdays in Summer. Double, twin and family rooms with all en suite. Ground floor rooms suitable for most disabled guests. All rooms have colour TV, telephones, beverage trays (fresh milk), colour co-ordinated Continental bedding, central heating. Licensed lounge and patio. No smoking indoors. Conservatory style leisure lounge with whirlpool spa. Parking, walled gardens. Excellent choice of breakfast menu including vegetarian and special diets. Children welcome but sorry, no pets. Bed and Breakfast from £26 to £36 per person (en suite). Cottage suite for two to six persons also available, suitable for disabled visitors. **ETC** ♦♦♦♦, *AA SELECTED (QQQQ) AWARD.*

*As seen on BBC TV's Holiday Programme*

**UMBERLEIGH. Tony and Myra Pring, The Gables, On The Bridge, Umberleigh EX37 9AB (01769 560461).** We offer friendly personal service here at The Gables, which is situated facing the River Taw, where salmon and sea trout fishing can be arranged. You will find us ideally placed for the beautiful Exmoor National Park, Darlington Glass, Lynton and Lynmouth and the sandy beaches of Woolacombe. The Barnstaple to Exeter railway line is within easy access for those who do not wish to drive. The accommodation is in three en suite rooms, one twin, one double and one single, all with central heating and tea/coffee making facilities. There is a quiet lounge and a TV lounge. Maps with three circular walks available from tea rooms. Private parking. Sorry, no children under age of 14. Open all year. Bed and Breakfast from £19.50 to £22.50.

**WINKLEIGH. Jill and Ivor Davidson, Pixton Cottage, Iddesleigh, Winkleigh EX19 8BR (01837 811003).** A warm and comfortable welcome awaits you at this traditional thatched Devon cob farmhouse with its oak beams and creaky floors. Set amidst the tranquillity of the rolling Devonshire Dales, convenient for Dartmoor, Exmoor and the spectacular North Devon cliffs and beaches. Dogs welcome. Good fishing on the Taw/Torridge. Well positioned for the Tarka Trail. Excellent local pubs for local real ales and good value food. Pixton is ideal at any time of the year for visitors wishing to slow down and recharge their batteries! Bed and Breakfast from £17.50 single and £16 double.

*See also Colour Display Advertisement*

**WOOLACOMBE. Sunnymeade Country House Hotel, West Down EX34 8NT (01271 863668).** Small, friendly, family-run country hotel. Close to Woolacombe's Blue Flag beach and Exmoor. Many local activities eg: golf, horse riding, surfing, cycling, walking and clay pigeon shooting. Award-winning home cooked food using local Devon produce. Special diets can be accommodated. Licensed bar. Two ground floor rooms. Large enclosed gardens and secure car park. **ETC** ♦♦♦
website: www.sunnymeade.co.uk

---

*When making enquiries or bookings, a stamped addressed envelope is always appreciated*

# DORSET

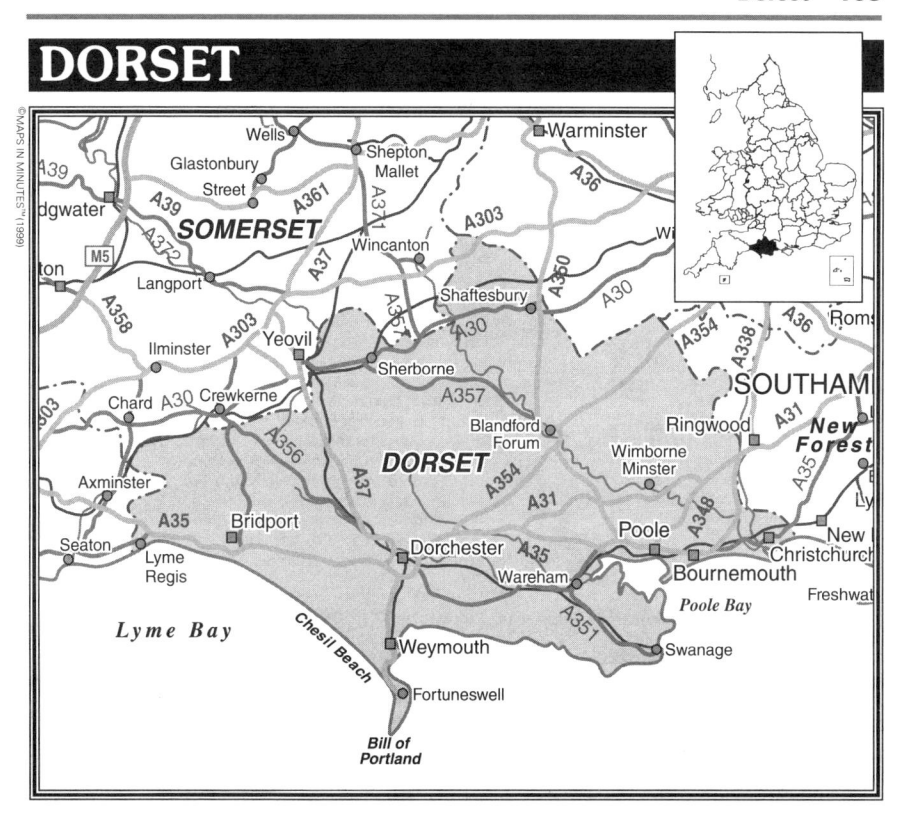

**ABBOTSBURY. Mrs Maureen Adams, Corfe Gate House, Coryates, Portesham, Nr Abbotsbury, Weymouth DT3 4HW (01305 871483; Fax: 01305 264024).** Coryates is a small hamlet set in the beautiful Waddon Valley 'off the beaten track', but within easy driving distance of Weymouth, Dorchester and Bridport. Close to the ancient village of Abbotsbury. A warm welcome awaits you in our country home - a Victorian house of character, tastefully decorated and furnished. Every comfort is provided. We have en suite twin, double and family rooms, which are spacious and comfortable. All centrally heated and equipped with hospitality tray and TV. Breakfast is served in our galleried dininghall. Corfe Gate House is the perfect location to explore the spectacular coastline and scenery of West Dorset. **ETC** ♦♦♦♦
e-mail: maureenadams@corfegatehouse.co.uk 
website: www.corfegatehouse.co.uk

**BEAMINSTER. Mrs Margaret Barrett, 49 Chantry Lane, Newtown, Beaminster DT8 3ER (01308 863565).** Beaminster is an attractive small town lying in the beautiful rolling countryside of West Dorset, seven miles from the coast. This property is situated in a peaceful location adjoining fields, but within walking distance of the town with its restaurants, inns and shops. Bedrooms have private bathroom and tea and coffee making facilities. Visitors have exclusive use of a large and sunny sitting/dinning room with colour TV and also a private terrace and garden. Full English breakfast is served. Open all year. Totally non-smoking. Please telephone or write for a brochure.

**164    Dorset**

**BEAMINSTER. Caroline and Vincent Pielesz, The Walnuts, 2 Prout Bridge, Beaminster DT8 3AY (01308 862211).** The property is very well situated in this medieval town in the heart of the beautiful Hardy countryside. Just off the main square with private parking and short walk to local inns, restaurants and tasteful little shops. Ideal for the person who enjoys coastal walks, exploring the countryside and visiting large country houses and gardens. The house has been very tastefully refurbished with en suite rooms, tea and coffee making facilities, all the comforts of home. Bed and full English breakfast from £24 per person. Totally non-smoking. **ETC ♦♦♦♦** *SILVER AWARD*

**BEAMINSTER (4 miles). Mrs Pauline Wallbridge, Watermeadow House, Bridge Farm, Hooke, Beaminster DT8 3PD (Tel & Fax: 01308 862619).** Watermeadow House is a large stone built Georgian-style country house set in a tiny West Dorset village amidst acres of beautiful countryside. Hooke is 10 miles from the sea and approximately 13 miles from Dorchester and Yeovil. Bridge Farm is a 280 acre dairy farm. The accommodation consists of one large family/twin room with en suite shower room and one double room with washbasin and own bathroom next to bedroom. Both rooms have tea/coffee making facilities and colour TV. A generous English breakfast is served in a beautiful sun lounge. Perfect for those seeking peace and quiet and friendly, personal service. Bed and Breakfast from £20. Children from £10. Recommmended by 'Which?' Good Bed & Breakfast Guide.

**BLANDFORD. The Anvil Hotel/Inn, Pimperne, Blandford DT11 8UQ (01258 453431/480182).** A long, low thatched building set in a tiny village deep in the Dorset countryside two miles from Blandford - what could be more English? And that is what visitors to the Anvil will find - a typical old English hostelry offering good, old-fashioned English hospitality. A full mouthwatering à la carte menu with delicious desserts available in the charming beamed restaurant with log fire, and a wide selection of specials in the attractive, fully licensed bar. All bedrooms have private facilities. Ample parking. Pets welcome. £120 for two persons for two nights Bed and Breakfast or £75 per night double room and £50 per night single room. Dogs £2.50 per night. **ETC ★★**, *GOOD FOOD PUB GUIDE, LES ROUTIERS SILVER KEY AWARD & HOUSEKEEPING CASSEROLE AWARD.*

**BLANDFORD. Mrs M. Jones, Cashmoor House, Cashmoor, Blandford DT11 8DN (01725 552339; Fax: 01725 552291).** Cashmoor House is a charming 17th-19th century cottage with a well-tended cottage-style garden and is enhanced by an ancient and sweetly scented wisteria. The five bedrooms are attractively decorated and furnished to give a friendly farmhouse ambience. It is situated in the rolling countryside of the Cranborne Chase and offers a wealth of good walking, cycling, touring and birdwatching opportunities. The coast is only 30 minutes, drive away and there are a number of National Trust properties and other visitor attractions easily accessible. There are good pubs and restaurants within walking distance or a short drive away.

**BLANDFORD near. Mrs J. K. Langley, Bartley House, Upper Street, Child Okeford, near Blandford DT11 8EF (01258 860420).** Bartley House is situated in the centre of this lovely Dorset backwater. Originally built as a Temperance Hall during Victoria's reign it later became the village Co-op shop, and then a private residence. Renovated and modernised to a very high standard of comfort by the present owners, it offers a diningroom, sittingroom with TV, two family rooms, one double and one twin. Three rooms have en suite showers, two have en suite WC, all have vanity units, central heating and tea and coffee making facilities. Within easy reach of Bournemouth, Poole, Weymouth and the Blackmore Vale, this is luxury accommodation at reasonable cost. Car parking space.

**Dorset** **165**

## Amitié Guest House

- Open All Year
- All Rooms En-Suite with TV, Tea/Coffee, Radio Alarm, etc
- Individually Controlled Central Heating
- Daily Chamber Service
- Full English or Continental Breakfast
- Private Car Parking
- Automobile Association 4 Diamond Approved & Member of Bournemouth Private Hotel & Guest House Association

**AA**

E-mail: B&B@amitie.co.uk   Web: www.amitie.co.uk

**Jenny & Paul**   1247 Christchurch Road, Bournemouth, Dorset BH7 6BP

☎ **0 1 2 0 2   4 2 7   2 5 5**

---

**BOURNEMOUTH. Cherry View Hotel, 66 Alum Chine Road, Bournemouth BH4 8DZ (01202 760910).** Family-run hotel, ideally situated between shops and beaches. 11 en suite rooms with TV, radio, tea-making facilities and central heating. Non-smoking rooms available. Excellent food, choice of menu. Residents' bar. Private parking. Bed and Breakfast £24 daily; weekly terms from £155 per person (based on two sharing). Room only and evening meal available. Christmas and New Year programme. Colour brochure available. Visit our website. **ETC ♦♦♦**.
e-mail: cherryview@bournemouth-net.co.uk
website: users.bournemouth-net.co.uk/~d5435/cherryview.html

**BOURNEMOUTH. Alan Sibthorpe, Denewood Hotel, 40 Sea Road, Bournemouth BH5 1BQ (01202 394493; Fax: 01202 391155).** Warm friendly-run hotel in central location, just 500 yards from the beach and close to the shops, good parking. Single, twin, double and family rooms available. All rooms en suite. Residential and Restaurant licence. TV, tea/coffee and biscuits in rooms. Health salon and spa on site. Open all year. Children and pets welcome. Bed and Breakfast from £17 to £24. Special weekly rates available and short break discounts. Please check out our website. **ETC ♦♦♦**.
website: www.denewood.co.uk

**BOURNEMOUTH. Gervis Court Hotel, 38 Gervis Road, East Cliff, Bournemouth BH1 3DH (Tel & Fax: 01202 556871).** Gervis Court is a detached Victorian villa set in its own grounds, yet it is only a few minutes' walk to the town centre. The clean sandy beach, B.I.C., shops, attractions and clubs being so close allows you to leave your car in our car park. All rooms are en suite with TV and kettles. Prices start from £20 per person depending on availability and season. For more information please look us up on our website.
e-mail: enquiries@gerviscourthotel.co.uk
website: www.gerviscourthotel.co.uk

**BOURNEMOUTH. Westcotes House Hotel, 9 Southbourne Overcliff Drive, Bournemouth BH6 3TE (01202 428512).** Comfortable private Edwardian house with stylish accommodation for the non-smoker. Situated on the cliff top with panoramic views of the bay, miles of sandy beach lie below with access by a zigzag path or cliff lift. Local shops, cafes and pubs are a short level walk away. All rooms are en suite with showers and have TV and tea/coffee facilities. Pleasant diningroom with home cooking a speciality. Private car park for peace of mind. Access at all times with own key. Whatever time of year, whether a few days or a longer stay, a warm welcome awaits you at Westcotes. Bed and Breakfast from £21 per person.

**Dorset**

**BOURNEMOUTH. Freshfields Hotel, 55 Christchurch Road, Bournemouth BH1 3PA (01202 394023).** Small licensed hotel, just a short walk to sandy beach through Boscombe Chine. Close to town and all Bournemouth's attractions, shops and theatres. Golf, tennis, putting and bowling are all nearby. All rooms have colour TV and tea/coffee, most are en suite. Access at all times with own keys. Front car park. BARGAIN BREAKS SEPTEMBER TO JUNE. Bed and Breakfast from £16. Reductions for Senior Citizens.

**BOURNEMOUTH. The Haven Hotel, 16 St Swithun's Road South, East Cliff, Bournemouth BH1 3RQ (01202 556071).** Quiet, friendly, family-run hotel. Near beach, shops, rail/coach stations, bingo club, tennis, bowling and town centre. Colour television, tea/coffee facilities in all bedrooms; most en suite. Car park. Children over five years welcome. No stag or hen groups. Bed and Breakfast from £18 to £26 per person per night; weekly from £110 to £160. For non-smokers.

**BOURNEMOUTH. Tony and Veronica Bulpitt, Sun Haven Guest House, 39 Southern Road, Southbourne, Bournemouth BH6 3SS (01202 427560).** The Sun Haven is in a superb position being only 150 yards from the cliff top, near the cliff lift and zigzag path to a beautiful sandy beach which is regularly awarded the European Blue Flag for superior water quality. Southbourne shopping area with its variety of cafes and restaurants is only a few minutes' walk away. A short drive or bus ride takes you to Bournemouth centre or Christchurch. All day access to rooms. All bedrooms have colour TV, shaver point, shaver point, washbasin, tea/coffee making facilities and central heating. En suite available. Bed and Breakfast from £17 per person per night. A friendly welcome awaits you.

**BOURNEMOUTH. Kath and Dennis Mackie, St. Antoine, 2 Guildhill Road, Southbourne, Bournemouth BH6 3EY (01202 433043).** Friendly family Guest House four minutes from Blue Flag beach and close to river walks, boating, tennis, bowls and golf. We have two family en suite rooms, two doubles, two twin and one single, all with washbasins, power points and tea/coffee facilities. Off-street parking for five cars. We are on the bus route for Christchurch and Bournemouth centres. Vegetarians, vegans welcome, with option of evening meal on request. Bed and breakfast from £18-£20 per person; Half Board from £25-£27 daily, from £150-£162 weekly. Member of Hotel and Guest House Association.
e-mail: kathden@kathden.fsnet.co.uk

**BOURNEMOUTH. Mr S. Goodwin, Cransley Hotel, 11 Knyveton Road, East Cliff, Bournemouth BH1 3QG (01202 290067).** A licensed hotel for non-smokers. This comfortable, elegant Edwardian house set in a quiet tree lined avenue in the East Cliff area of Bournemouth is situated in its own attractive grounds. Close to the heart of Bournemouth and a short stroll from the beach, the hotel is conveniently placed for all major road and rail links. Rooms are en suite with colour television and hospitality tray. Open all year. Bed and Breakfast from £22. Car park. Ground floor accommodation for the less mobile guest. Evening Meals available. **ETC/AA** ◆◆◆
e-mail: cransley@netmatters.co.uk
website: www.cransley.co.uk

**BOURNEMOUTH. Mrs S. Barling, Mayfield Private Hotel, 46 Frances Road, Knyveton Gardens, Bournemouth BH1 3SA (Tel & Fax: 01202 551839).** Sandra and Mike Barling make your comfort, food, relaxation their concern, offering a high standard of catering and comfort. Ideally situated overlooking Knyveton Gardens with bowls, petanque, tennis and sensory garden. Handy for sea, shops, shows, rail and coach stations. Residential licence. All rooms have en suite, colour TV, teamaking, central heating, hairdryer and trouser press. Own keys. Parking, evening refreshments. Bed and Breakfast from £18 to £22 daily. Bed and Beakfast and Evening Dinner from £115 to £148 weekly per person. Bargain Breaks October/April. **ETC** ◆◆◆◆
website: www.may-field.co.uk

**BOURNEMOUTH. Sid and Linda Griffith, Blakes Reach Hotel, 37 Southern Road, Bournemouth BH6 3SS (01202 426097).** A warm welcome awaits you at this small, family-run guest house featuring en suite rooms. Situated about 200 yards level walk to either Southbourne's shops or to the cliff top reaching sandy beaches by either path or lift. Bournemouth town centre and Littledown all-weather leisure complex both within 10-15 minutes' car journey. Bed and Breakfast from £16.

**BOURNEMOUTH. Ann and Barrie Towner, Southernhay Hotel, 42 Alum Chine Road, Westbourne, Bournemouth BH4 8DX (Tel & Fax: 01202 761251).** The Southernhay Hotel provides warm, friendly, high standard accommodation with a large car park. All rooms have colour TV, tea/coffee making facilities, hairdryer and radio alarm clock. The hotel is ideally situated at the head of Alum Chine (a wooded ravine) leading down to the sea and miles of safe sandy beaches. The Bournemouth International Centre, cinemas, theatres, restaurants, clubs and pubs are all within easy reach; minutes by car or the frequent bus service. Seven bedrooms, five en suite. Open all year. Bed and Breakfast from £18 to £25 per adult per night. **ETC** ◆◆◆
e-mail: southernhay@cix.co.uk

**BOURNEMOUTH. Sandy Beach Hotel, Southbourne Overcliff Drive, Southbourne, Bournemouth BH6 3QB (Tel/Fax: 01202 424385).** Family-run hotel with panoramic sea view over Bournemouth Bay. Easy access to safe, sandy, award-winning beach. Close to shops and buses. Near Bournemouth. Ideal base for touring New Forest and Dorset. All rooms en suite. Colour TV, tea/coffee facilities. Pleasant dining room with separate tables. Licensed bar. Scrumptious home cooking complements high standards of cleanliness and comfort. TV lounge. Central heating. Large car park. Access to hotel at all times. Ground floor rooms and all bedrooms non-smoking. For brochure please write or phone resident proprietors Bryan and Caroline Channing, Adrian and Alison Homa. Bed and Breakfast from £20 per night. Evening Meal optional. Special weekly rates. Christmas programme. **ETC** ★★
e-mail: sandybeach@bournemouth.co.uk
website: www.sandy-beach.co.uk

---

# FREE or REDUCED RATE entry to Holiday Visits and Attractions — see our READERS' OFFER VOUCHERS on pages 43-60

**BRIDPORT. Mrs Sally Long, Old Dairy House, Walditch, Bridport DT6 4LB (01308 458021).** Relax in an Area of Outstanding Natural Beauty, one mile from Bridport town centre. One twin, one double (non smoking) bedrooms. Tea/coffee facilities. Guests' shared bathroom, also downstairs shower/cloakroom. Central heating throughout. Guests' TV lounge with open log fire. Hearty full English breakfast with home-made preserves. Gardens abundant with birds and wildlife. Off-road parking. Rural and coastal walks. Real tennis within short walk; 18 hole golf course two miles. Good selection of restaurants and pubs nearby. Open all year for adults only. You will find an informal, friendly atmosphere and warm welcome.

**BRIDPORT. Mrs D.P. Read, The Old Station, Powerstock, Bridport DT6 3ST (01308 485301).** Peacefully situated deep in the glorious Dorset countryside, one mile south east of Powerstock, in two-and-a-half acres of garden, this former railway station enjoys beautiful views. Conveniently situated for drives into neighbouring counties; many rural walks; can be reached by public transport. Two double bedrooms, one single, all with washbasins and tea-making facilities; bathroom, three toilets; central heating. Daytime access. Off road parking; tennis, fun golf. Hearty English breakfast prettily served (vegetarian breakfast by previous arrangement). Open March through October, from £16. Badger watching possible most evenings from house. SAE, please, for details. Sorry no children or pets. No smoking.

**BRIDPORT. Neptune Cottage, 107 South Street, Bridport DT6 3PA (Tel & Fax: 01308 420907).** George and Elizabeth Davies welcome you to Neptune Cottage, a charming 18th century Grade II listed house close to the centre of Bridport, coastal walks, spectacular scenery and only a mile from the sea. We provide a high standard of bed and breakfast in large, tastefully decorated bed sitting room accommodation with easy chairs, full en suite, TV, radio and a well stocked beverage tray. A choice of either English or Continental breakfast is available. Bridport is an ancient market town, world famous for its rope and net making. This part of Dorset is rich in dramatic countryside, small villages where time seems to have stood still, mouth watering local dishes, but perhaps above all, friendly people who have time to talk. Bed and Breakfast from £18.
**ETC ♦♦♦**
e-mail: winniedog@talk21.com
website: www.neptunecottage.co.uk

**CERNE ABBAS. Mrs V.I. Willis, "Lampert's Cottage", Sydling St. Nicholas, Cerne Abbas DT2 9NU (01300 341659; Fax: 01300 341699).** Bed and Breakfast in unique 16th century thatched cottage in unspoilt village. The cottage has fields around and is bounded, front and back, by chalk streams. Accommodation consists of three prettily furnished double bedrooms with dormer windows, set under the eaves, and breakfast is served in the diningroom which has an enormous inglenook fireplace and original beams. The village, situated in countryside made famous by Thomas Hardy in his novels, is an excellent touring centre and beaches are 30 minutes' drive away. West Dorset is ideal walking country with footpaths over chalk hills and through hidden valleys, perfect for those wishing peace and quiet. Open all year. Terms on request.

---

*Please mention **Bed and Breakfast Stops** when making enquiries about accommodation featured in these pages.*

## MARSHWOOD MANOR

ETC ♦♦♦♦
**Near Bridport, Near Charmouth, Dorset DT6 5NS**
**Tel: (01308) 868442**
*Website: www.marshwoodmanor.co.uk*
Five tastefully furnished en suite rooms.
Close to Charmouth and Lyme Regis, Bed and Breakfast with Evening Meal on request.
Speciality Home Cooking.
**AA LISTED**
Weekly or Short Breaks available
*Brochure on request.*

See also Colour Display Advertisement

---

**CHARMOUTH. Ann and Andy Gorfin, Kingfishers, Newlands Bridge, Charmouth DT6 6QZ (01297 560232).** Come to Kingfishers and relax on your large sunny balcony overlooking the river and garden. Set in beautiful surroundings on the banks of the River Char, Kingfishers offers a secluded setting yet it is only a short stroll to the beach and village amenities. Ann and Andy can assure you of a warm welcome, great food and a friendly atmosphere. From £20 per night we offer a full selection of breakfasts including vegetarian. All rooms are en suite or with private bathroom, balcony, drink making facilities, colour TV and central heating. Home-baked food and clotted cream teas available throughout the day in our lovely Garden Room or outside in the garden. Free access and ample parking. Children and pets welcome.

---

**COMPTON ABBAS. Tim and Lucy Kerridge, The Old Forge, Compton Abbas, Shaftesbury SP7 0NQ (Tel & Fax: 01747 811881).** Charming 18th century converted wheelwrights with magnificent views to National Trust downland. Ideal for relaxing, walking, wildlife, etc. Choose either Bed and Breakfast in pretty en suite bedrooms (one family, one double and one single), Victorian iron beds and antique furniture, all with colour TV and tea/coffee trays or self-catering (sleeping three) in fully restored wheelwrights cottage. A traditional farmhouse breakfast is served using local organic produce. Guests have their own private sitting/dining room, garden and two acres of meadow to explore. Traditional log burning stove during colder months, we offer a warm welcome all year round. Bed and Breakfast from £22.50. **ETC ★★★★, AA ♦♦♦♦**
e-mail: theoldforge@hotmail.com
website: www.SmoothHound.co.uk/

---

**DORCHESTER. Mrs Martine Tree, The Old Rectory, Winterbourne Steepleton, Dorchester DT2 9LG (01305 889468; Fax: 01305 889737).** Built in 1850 on one acre of land situated in a quiet hamlet. The grounds have croquet lawns, putting green, children's swing. The outstanding natural surroundings offer country walks giving superb views of the valley. The four guest rooms are all individually furnished to a high standard, each with en suite facilities and containing a welcome basket filled with toiletry items you may have forgotten. No smoking. Breakfast is a delight, enjoyed in The Garden Room with views of the beautiful little courtyard. Private dining facilities are available on request for celebration dinners with Cordon Bleu cuisine. Special diets. Alternatively local pubs and a large selection of restaurants both in Dorchester (six miles) and Weymouth (eight miles) are available. Many activities for all can be enjoyed in Thomas Hardy country. French spoken. Open all year except Christmas. Bed and Breakfast from £22 per person. Brochure available. **ETC ♦♦♦♦**
e-mail: trees@eurobell.co.uk
web site: www.trees.eurobell.co.uk

**DORCHESTER. Mrs Marian Tomblin, Lower Lewell Farmhouse, West Stafford, Dorchester DT2 8AP (01305 267169).** This old, historic house, originally a farmhouse, is situated in the Frome Valley, four miles east of Dorchester in the heart of Hardy country. It is two miles from his birthplace and is reputed to be the Talbothays Dairy in his famous novel "Tess of the d'Urbervilles". Situated as it is in quiet countryside yet so near the county town, it makes an ideal base from which to explore Dorset. There are two double bedrooms and one family bedroom, all with washbasin and tea/coffee making facilities. Visitors' lounge with colour TV. Car essential, ample parking. Terms from £20. Open January to December.

**DORCHESTER near. Michael and Jane Deller, Churchview Guest House, Winterbourne Abbas, Near Dorchester DT2 9LS (Tel & Fax:01305 889296).** Our 17th century Guest House, noted for warm hospitality and delicious breakfasts and evening meals, makes an ideal base for touring beautiful West Dorset. Our character bedrooms are all comfortable and well appointed. Meals, served in our beautiful diningroom, feature local produce, with relaxation provided by two attractive lounges and licensed bar. Your hosts Jane and Michael Deller are pleased to give every assistance with local information to ensure a memorable stay. NON SMOKING. Terms: Dinner, Bed and Breakfast £36 to £44; Bed and Breakfast £22 to £32. Please call for further details. **ETC/AA** ◆◆◆.
e-mail: stay@churchview.co.uk
web site: www.churchview.co.uk

**FERNDOWN. Mrs C. Husher, Studland House, 3 Avon Road, West Moors, Ferndown BH22 0EG (01202 873776).** An attractive Victorian house with lovely garden. Friendly, comfortable, quiet location close to New Forest, Wimborne and Ringwood. Convenient for Poole and Bournemouth. One double and one twin room with tea/coffee making facilities and central heating. Lounge with TV. Off-road parking. Bed and full English Breakfast from £19 per person per night.
e-mail: billhusher@waitrose.com

**FURZEHILL. Mrs King, Stocks Farm, Furzehill, Wimborne BH21 4HT (Tel & Fax: 01202 888697).** Stocks Farm is a family-run farm and nursery situated in peaceful countryside just one-and-half miles from the lovely country town of Wimborne Minster, off the B3078. Surrounded by lovely Dorset countryside and pretty villages; coastline, beaches and New Forest within easy reach. Bed and Breakfast accommodation consists of one double en suite bedroom and one twin bedroom with private bathroom, both on ground level. Disabled guests are very welcome. Tea and coffee making facilities in both rooms. All accommodation is non-smoking. Situated in secluded garden with patio for guests to enjoy breakfast outside. Local pubs and restaurants offer varied menus. Bed and Breakfast from £19 to £20 per person per night.

**HINTON ST MARY. Sally Sofield, Old Port Office Guest House, Hinton St Mary, Sturminster Newton DT10 1NG (01258 472366; Fax: 01258 472173).** Comfortable and homely guest house, convenient for exploring the beautiful varied scenery of unspoilt Dorset. Guests' lounge with games, TV, maps and books. Car park. Large garden backing onto fields. Footpaths and River Stour, (good fishing) nearby. Village has quaint thatched houses, church, Manor House and a traditional sociable Dorset village pub. No one goes hungry here, with good traditional home cooked fayre, using local produce where possible. We do our best to provide a warm welcome, good value and a friendly place to stay. Bed and Breakfast from £19 to £25; Evening Meal (optional) £10. Cottage (sleeping three) also available. Brochure on request. **ETC** ◆◆◆◆.

**Dorset** **171**

**LILLINGTON. Mrs M. E. G. Messenger, Ash House, Lillington, Sherborne DT9 6QX (01935 812490).** Ash House is spacious, surrounded by farmland, with delightful views all round. Although so rural and peaceful it is only three miles south of the picturesque town of Sherborne, with its Abbey and other historic buildings. Easy access to Dorchester in one direction and Yeovil in the other. One double or family room (extra bed available) with washbasin, and one twin room with washbasin. Two toilets, bathroom, shower room. Ample parking. Lounge, conservatory, TV, garden. Full English Breakfast and a friendly welcome. Pets by arrangement. Bed and Breakfast £15. Rates reduced for children. South from Sherborne – A352 Dorchester Road

**LULWORTH COVE. John and Jenny Aldridge, The Orchard, West Road, West Lulworth, Wareham BH20 5RY (01929 400592).** Comfortable home offering accommodation in central yet quiet off-main road position in old vicarage orchard. Two double rooms and one twin/super king (with balcony). All have en suite shower rooms, beverage trays and colour TVs. Parking in spacious walled garden with mature fruit trees, lawns and garden furniture for guest use. Generous English, vegetarian and vegan breakfasts using home produced eggs etc when possible. 10 minute stroll from Lulworth Cove. Coast path for other beaches, Durdle Door and Fossil Forest nearby. Central for South Dorset Coast. Bed and Breakfast from £17.50 per person per night. Discounts vary with season; please phone John or Jenny for more details. Open all year except Christmas to New Year.
**e-mail: theorchard@ic24.net**

**LULWORTH COVE. Mrs Jan Ravensdale, Elads-Nevar, West Road, West Lulworth, Near Wareham BH20 5RZ (01929 400467).** The house is set in the beautiful village of West Lulworth, half-a-mile from Lulworth Cove. The rooms are large enough for a family and all have tea/coffee making facilities and colour TV. West Lulworth is central for many towns and beaches; Weymouth 14, Swanage 18, Poole 23 miles, and there are many places of interest to visit. Reduced rates for Senior Citizens out of season and children sharing with adults; also weekly bookings. Open all year. Central heating. Bed and Breakfast from £15 per person per night. Vegetarians and vegans catered for.

**LULWORTH COVE. Val and Barry Burrill, Graybank Bed and Breakfast, Main Road, West Lulworth BH20 5RL (01929 400256).** Graybank is a Victorian house built in Purbeck Stone and located in beautiful, quiet country just five minutes stroll from Lulworth Cove and the South West Coastal Path. All rooms have tea/coffee making facilities, colour TV and wash hand basin. Full breakfast menu. Good choice of cafes and restaurants including a 16th century pub all within easy walking distance. Access at all times. Children aged four and above welcome. Fire Certificate held. Parking. Bed and Breakfast from £17. Special rates for short or long breaks and also off-peak times. Open Febuary to November. Telephone Val or Barry for a brochure. **ETC** ◆◆◆

**LYME REGIS. Mrs L. Brown, Providence House, Lyme Road, Uplyme DT7 3TH (01297 445704).** Comfortable accommodation in 200-year-old character house, close to fly fishing lakes, on the edge of historic Lyme Regis. 25 minutes' walk from the sea. Ideal for artists, fossil hunting, walking etc. Easy access by road. Axminster five miles with main line connection to Waterloo. Accommodation comprises one single, one double, one double en suite; all with TV and tea/coffee making facilities. Full English Breakfast and vegetarian option. Rooms available from £16 to £21 per person per night.

**LYME REGIS. Mr Britain, Lydwell House, Lyme Road, Uplyme, Lyme Regis DT7 3TJ (01297 443522).** Situated close to the famous fossil beach at Lyme Regis, Lydwell Guest House offers a high standard of Bed and Breakfast accommodation at most affordable prices. This is a picturesque early Victorian house in its old sweeping garden featuring a folly and pond. Car parking available. The atmosphere is both warm and friendly and the standard of food served is of the highest order. All of the letting rooms are comfortable and spacious and have televisions, telephones and are all en suite. Children are welcome. Open all year. Bed and Breakfast from £23. **ETC** ◆◆◆

## Buckland Farm

Situated in quiet and unspoilt surroundings with gardens and grounds of five acres which are ideal for guests to relax or stroll in; about three miles from the lovely coastal resort of Lyme Regis and Charmouth. A warm welcome awaits you. Accommodation mainly on the ground floor. Two family bedrooms, one double en suite shower and one twin bedded room, all with TV, washbasin, tea/coffee making facilites. Bathroom, shower in bath, separate WC. Lounge with colour TV, video and log fire. Dining area with separate tables. A good English farmhouse breakfast served, a real home from home plus our very friendly dog. Friendly pub within two minutes walk for evening meals. Payphone. No smoking. Bed and Breakfast from £15. Send SAE for further details. Self catering caravan and chalet Bungalow available. Sheila and David Taylor.

*Raymonds Hill, Near Axminster EX13 5SZ*
*Tel/Fax: 01297 33222 or E-mail: sheilataylor@bucklandfarm.fsnet.co.uk*

**LYME REGIS. Coverdale Guesthouse, Woodmead Road, Lyme Regis DT7 3AB (01297 442882).** Spacious non-smoking guesthouse situated in a residential area of Lyme Regis a short walk from the sea, town, pubs and restaurants. Fine views over Woodland Trust's land to rear and sea to front. Comfortable well furnished bedrooms (double, twin, triple and single) with colour TV, tea making and excellent en suite facilities. Attractive diningroom overlooking patio and cottage garden. Access to house all day. Private parking. Ideal base for exploring countryside and unspoilt scenic coastline on foot or by car. Walkers welcome. South Coast Path/Wessex Ridgeway nearby. Fossil hunting and boat trips available. Bed and Breakfast £23 to £35. Brochure available. **AA ♦♦♦♦**

**LYME REGIS. Mrs S. Powell, Green Lane Farm, Rousdon, Lyme Regis DT7 3XW (01297 443235).** Come visit our working family farm, situated off the A3052, three miles from Lyme Regis and four miles from Seaton. A quiet location with lovely countryside views. We have one double and one twin/family room, both with washbasins, tea and coffee making, hairdryers, remote-control TV, heating and fresh towels daily. We have two guest bathrooms, guest lounge and large garden and patio. A big farmhouse breakfast and a big welcome awaits. All day access and reduced rates for children and weekly bookings. Pets by arrangement. We are a non-smoking establishment and special diets can be catered for. Bed and Breakfast from £15 to £18.

**MARNHULL. Robin and Sarah Hood, The Old Bank, Burton Street, Marnhull, Sturminster Newton DT10 1PH (Tel & Fax: 01258 821019).** The Old Bank is a comfortable, friendly 18th century house in the centre of an attractive Dorset village. The house and barns are of local stone, set around an attractive courtyard, leading to a pretty cottage garden. Set on a hill overlooking the beautiful Blackmore Vale, Marnhull is an excellent centre from which to explore Thomas Hardy country. Many other places of interest, including Stourhead, Longleat, National Trust houses and gardens. Open fires and breakfast in the farmhouse kitchen make this a friendly and relaxed place to stay. Two double, one twin, one family bedrooms; shared bathroom and shower room. £20 per person per night.

**POOLE. Mrs Stephenson, Holly Hedge Farm, Bulbury Lane, Lytchett Matravers, Poole BH16 6EP (01929 459688).** Built in 1892, Holly Hedge Farm is situated next to Bulbury Woods Golf Course, set in 11 acres of wood and grassland adjacent to lake. We are just 15 minutes away from the Purbecks, the beach and the forest. The area is ideal for walking or cycling and Poole Quay and Harbour are also nearby. Accommodation comprises two double/family rooms, one twin and one single, all with en suite showers, colour TV, tea/coffee making facilities, radio alarms and central heating. Open all year round for summer or winter breaks. Full English or Continental breakfast served. Single available from £25 to £30, Double from £42 per night.

**POOLE. Margaret and Len Justice, Peacehaven, 282 Sopwith Crescent, Merley, Wimborne BH21 1XL (01202 880281).** A warm welcome awaits you at Peacehaven, set in gardens of roses and shrubs where you can enjoy our fish pond and aviary. All of our rooms are on the ground floor and have tea/coffee making facilities and colour TV. Each morning Len serves a good, hearty English breakfast to start the day. Buses go by the door to Poole, Wimborne and Bournemouth. We are in easy reach of Sandbanks, Bournemouth's beaches, the New Forest, Wimborne Minster, sporting venues and places of historic interest. Children welcome. Sorry, no pets. Bed and Breakfast from £17.50; Evening Meals (by arrangement) £10. No smoking. **ETC ♦♦**

**SHERBORNE. David, Hazel, Mary and Gerry Wilding, White Horse Farm, Middlemarsh, Sherborne DT9 5QN (01963 210222).** Set in beautiful Hardy countryside, we offer a warm welcome in comfortable surroundings, with a hearty farmhouse breakfast. The property is surrounded by three acres of paddock and garden with a duck pond. We lie between the historic towns of Sherborne, Dorchester and Cerne Abbas and are situated next door to an inn serving good food and local ales. Delightful coastal attractions are some 30-40 minutes' drive away. All rooms have en suite showers, colour TV, central heating and tea/coffee making facilities. There is also a private conservatory/lounge and dining room. Ample parking. Bed and Breakfast from £20. Self-catering cottages also available. **ETC** *LISTED*
e-mail: enquiries@whitehorsefarm.co.uk
website: www.whitehorsefarm.co.uk

**SHERBORNE. Mrs E. Kingman, Stowell Farm, Stowell, Near Sherborne DT9 4PE (01963 370200).** A 15th century former Manor House that has retained some lovely historical features. Now a farmhouse on a family-run dairy and beef farm. It is in a beautiful rural location yet only five miles from the A303, two miles from A30 and two hours by train from London. An ideal place to relax and unwind, enjoy traditional home baking and a warm friendly atmosphere. Close to the abbey town of Sherborne, National Trust Properties and many other places of interest to suit all people. Accommodation – one double room, one twin room, guest bathroom, and lounge with colour TV and log fires. From £18 per person per night, reductions for children under 10 years and weekly stays. Evening Meal by arrangement.

**SHERBORNE. Mrs Helen Knight, Longbar, Level Lane, Charlton Horethorne, Sherborne DT9 4NN (01963 220266).** Longbar is an attractively furnished modern detached house, set in large secluded gardens backing onto farmland, in village centre, three miles from the A303 and A30. Within easy reach of the historic abbey and castle town of Sherborne, Sparkford Motor Museum, Street Village, Glastonbury, Yeovilton, Longleat, Stourhead Gardens, Dorchester and the coast. Suitable for cycling and walking. Centrally heated accommodation with relaxed family atmosphere, hearty English Breakfasts and home-made preserves. One family/double, one twin and one single rooms, all with beverage-making facilities, colour TV. Guests' bathroom, large open plan lounge with colour TV and log fire. Ample parking. Well behaved pets accepted. Excellent local pubs and restaurants. Bed and Breakfast from £17 per person; reductions for children. Evening Meals by arrangement. **ETC ♦♦♦**
e-mail: longbar@tinyworld.co.uk

*Please mention Bed & Breakfast Stops when writing to enquire about accommodation*

**SHERBORNE. Robin and Wendy Dann, Heartsease Cottage, North Street, Bradford Abbas, Sherborne DT9 6SA (Tel & Fax: 01935 475480).** "Heartsease" describes our cottage better than any brochure could. A 250 year old local honey-coloured stone and slate cottage with huge stone conservatory looking over an idyllic garden in an ancient and quiet Dorset village lane. Unlike many B&Bs we offer choices for breakfast and dinner, please call for a sample menu. Themed bedrooms - "Victoria", "Farmhouse" and "Napier" with either en suite shower room or own luxury bathroom. We live in a cottage across the private little drive with off-road parking. Guests' own sittingrooms. From £23 per person per night; one mile from A30, ideal for touring. Open all year. We look forward to seeing you at Heartsease Cottage. **ETC ♦♦♦♦♦** *AND SILVER AWARD.*
e-mail: heartsease@talk21.com

**SHILLINGSTONE. Mrs Rosie Watts, Pennhills Farm, Sandy Lane, off Lanchards Lane, Shillingstone, Blandford DT11 0TF (01258 860491).** Pennhills Farmhouse, set in 100 acres of unspoiled countryside, is situated one mile from the village of Shillingstone in the heart of Blackmore Vale, an ideal for a peaceful retreat, short break or holiday. It offers spacious comfortable accommodation for all ages. Children welcome, pets by arrangement. One downstairs bedroom. All rooms have en suite, TV and tea/coffee making facilities, complemented by traditional English breakfast with home produced bacon and sausages. Bed and breakfast from £18 per person. Good meals available locally. Vegetarians catered for. Brochure sent on request. A warm and friendly welcome is assured by your host Rosie Watts.

**SIXPENNY HANDLEY. Mrs Ann Inglis, Town Farm Bungalow, Sixpenny Handley, Near Salisbury SP5 5NT (Tel & Fax: 01725 552319).** Guests receive a warm welcome at this pretty property in a quiet location off the beaten track, yet within easy reach of the south coast and such tourist attractions as Stonehenge and Salisbury cathedral. Situated in Cranborne Chase, an area popular with walkers, there are magnificent country views across three counties. Bedrooms are clean and comfortable and in addition to the smart sitting room, opening onto the garden, there is a dining room where tea and coffee is available and hearty breakfasts are served at one big table. Bed and Breakfast from £17.50. Children welcome. Pets by arrangement. **AA** *QQ*.

**STURMINSTER MARSHALL. Heather Jewitt, 'Melrose', 16 Charborough Way, Sturminster Marshall, Wimborne BH21 4DH (01258 858359).** 'Melrose' is situated in a pretty village with a nearby golf course. Convenient for Poole, Bournemouth, Wimborne and Blandford, this is an excellent base from which to explore Dorset's beautiful countryside and the New Forest, with many delightful villages and river valleys. Sumptuous breakfasts, the warmest of welcomes and first class accommodation greet you in this pretty Stourside village. An executive home-from-home. All bedrooms are tastefully decorated and furnished to a high standard of comfort. A double bedroom with en suite is available with excellent views over the garden and countryside. Bed and Breakfast from £20 per person per night. Open all year.

**STURMINSTER NEWTON. Mrs J. Miller, Lower Fifehead Farm, Fifehead St. Quinton, Sturminster Newton DT10 2AP (01258 817335).** Come and stay with us on our 400 acre dairy farm. Our lovely Listed 17th century farmhouse with interesting mullion windows is pictured and mentioned in Dorset Books. We have three bedrooms - one double en suite, one double and one twin, each with private bathroom, own sitting room, TV and large garden. Tea and coffee making. No evening meals but we can recommend the local places. We also have a self-contained one bedroom flat with en suite bathroom, private sitting room as well as a self-catering annexe sleeping four/five. Bed and Breakfast from £20 per person. Three-day breaks from £55 per person. Right in the heart of the Blackmore Vale and "Hardy" country; lovely walks, fishing and riding can be arranged. **ETC ♦♦♦**

**SWANAGE. Janet Foran, Sandhaven Guest House, 5 Ulwell Road, Swanage BH19 1LE (01929 422322).** You can be sure of a warm welcome with good home-cooking whenever you stay at Sandhaven. We wish to make sure your stay is as relaxing and enjoyable as possible. All bedrooms are en suite, non-smoking and equipped with tea and coffee making facilities; all have colour TV. There is a residents' lounge, diningroom and conservatory for your comfort. The Purbeck Hills are visible from the guest house, as is the beach, which is only 100 metres away. Sandhaven is open all year except Christmas and Bed and Breakfast is available from £18.50 to £25.00.

**TOLPUDDLE. Paul Wright, Tolpuddle Hall, Tolpuddle, Near Dorchester DT2 7EW (01305 848986).** An historic house in village centre in an area of outstanding natural beauty, not far from the coast. Convenient for Bournemouth, Poole, Dorchester, Weymouth, Isle of Purbeck and many small market towns and villages. Centre for local interests e.g., bird-watching, walking, local history, Thomas Hardy, the Tolpuddle Martyrs, etc. Two double, one twin, one family and two single bedrooms. Full English breakfast. Tea/coffee making, TV sitting room. Pets welcome except high season. From £17.50 per person. Weekly rate available. Open all year.

**WAREHAM. Mrs Axford, Sunnyleigh, Hyde, Wareham BH20 7NT (01929 471822).** Mary offers her guests a friendly welcome to her bungalow with a cup of tea. Situated in the quiet hamlet of Hyde, five miles west of Wareham, adjacent to East Dorset Golf Club; follow the sign from Wareham and we are the first bungalow past the golf club on the right. It is an ideal base for visiting Swanage, Poole and Bovington Tank Museum, with many interesting coastal walks, including Lulworth Cove. Accommodation consists of three double bedrooms (one with twin beds), all with tea/coffee facilities, central heating. Bathroom and separate shower room; two toilets. Visitors' lounge with colour TV and log fires in winter. Open all the year except Christmas. Car essential, ample parking. Bed and Breakfast from £17; Room only £10. No smoking.

**WEYMOUTH. Chris and Samantha Wilson, Hotel Kinley, 98 The Esplanade, Weymouth DT4 7AT (01305 782264).** Welcome to The Hotel Kinley, a friendly, comfortable hotel centrally situated on Weymouth's beautiful Georgian seafront. We offer spacious en suite rooms all equipped with courtesy tray, colour TV, radio alarm clock, hairdryer and shaver point. Non smoking, sea view and balcony rooms available. Book a space in our on-site garage and relax in the knowledge that your car is securely locked up overnight. We offer superb home cooking with a wide choice for breakfast and dinner. Open all year. Short breaks available. We look forward to meeting you.
**e-mail: hotelkinley@hotmail.com**

**WEYMOUTH. Clare Harvey, Florian, 59 Abbotsbury Road, Weymouth DT4 0AQ (01305 773836; Fax: 01305 750160 ).** The Florian Guest House offers a relaxed, friendly atmosphere, great food and high standards. Breakfast can include prize-winning sausages, smoked fish and fresh fruit, and dinner menus change daily. All of our seven bedrooms are en suite or have private facilities, with colour TVs and drink making facilities. We have a car park, and are a ten minute walk to the town, beach and harbour, even closer to Radipole Nature Reserve. We are non-smoking, except in the large gardens with seating and water features. Bed and Breakfast from £17 to £26, credit cards accepted. Brochure available. **ETC** ◆◆◆

*When making enquiries or bookings, a stamped addressed envelope is always appreciated*

**WIMBORNE. Martin and Ann Oliver, 'Moor Allerton', Holtwood, Wimborne BH21 7DU (Tel & Fax: 01258 840845).** A warm Christian welcome awaits you in our peaceful home on National Trust land in glorious countryside. Secluded, yet close to Wimborne Minster, Ringwood and the New Forest, 25 minutes to Poole and the Blue Flag beaches of Bournemouth. One double, one twin and a single room, with private baths; extra bed available. TV, tea/coffee making, huge varied breakfasts. Excellent meals close by. Log fires in winter, refreshments on arrival. Terms from £19 per person per night; reduction for four days or more. Ask for our brochure.
e-mail: martinoliver1@talk21.com

**WINFRITH NEWBURGH. R. W. and J. A. Canaven, Wynards Farm, Winfrith Newburgh DT2 8DQ (01305 852660; Fax: 01305 854094).** Wynards Farm is situated on the edge of Winfrith Newburgh, set in 11 acres in an elevated position with uninterrupted views of the open countryside, close to Lulworth Cove, with direct access to footpath and bridleway. All bedrooms are en suite with own entrances, comfortably furnished with televison and tea making facilities. Three pubs locally all serving good food. Two double rooms and one twin room, ample safe parking. Open April to October. From £20 per person.
e-mail: canaven@hotmail.com

# DURHAM

**CORNFORTH. Mrs D. Slack, Ash House, 24 The Green, Cornforth DL17 9JH (01740 654654).** Built mid 19th Century, Ash House is a beautifully appointed period home combining a delicate mixture of homeliness and Victorian flair. Elegant rooms, individually and tastefully decorated, combining antique furnishings, beautiful fabrics, carved four posters and modern fittings. Spacious and graceful, filled with character, Ash House offers a warm welcome to both the road-weary traveller and those wishing merely to unwind in the quiet elegance of this charming home on quiet village green. Private parking. 10 minutes Historic Durham City, and adjacent A1 (M) motorway. Well placed between York and Edinburgh. Excellent value.

**DURHAM. Mrs J. Dartnall, Idsley House, 4 Green Lane, Spennymoor DL16 6HD (01388 814237; Fax: 01740 650888).** A large Victorian detached house situated in a quiet residential area close to the A167/A688 junction just eight minutes from Durham City. Direct route to Beamish, Metro Centre and the Dales. All rooms are spacious and well furnished. Double, twin and family bedrooms are all en suite and have colour TV and welcome tray. Full English or vegetarian breakfast is served in a pleasant conservatory overlooking a mature garden. Large guest lounge to relax. Safe parking on premises. Prices for a twin or double room £48. Evening meal. Open all year except Christmas. Visa, Mastercard, Switch, Delta cards all accepted. **ETC ♦♦♦♦**.

## Glendale

Bed and Breakfast in beautiful spacious house; three double rooms en suite, TV, tea making facilities. Separate dining and sitting rooms. No smoking, no children and no pets. Personal attention. We are situated in superb open countryside close to the village of Cotherstone. Splendid all round views, superb gardens and bedding displays, very large water feature with specimen fish. Our area is famous for Hannah of Yorkshire, High Force, Bowes Museum and breathtaking scenery for walking. Durham and Beamish 45 minutes. £36 per double room. A warm welcome awaits. Brochure on request. *WHICH? Good Bed and Breakfast Guide*, recommended by *Country Walking* magazine. **ETC** ♦♦♦ [Highly Commended]

**Mrs M. Rabbitts, Glendale, Cotherstone, Barnard Castle DL12 9UH. Tel: 01833 650384**

---

**SALTBURN-BY-SEA. Mrs Bull, Westerlands Guesthouse, 27 East Parade, Skelton, Saltburn-by-Sea (01287 650690).** This guest house is situated alongside Cleveland Way. It is a quiet, large, modern detached house with beautiful views of sea and countryside. An ideal base for touring Yorkshire Moors and the East Coast resorts, and there is a golf course nearby. Plenty of parking space. Bed and Breakfast £16 with packed lunches and flasks prepared and snack meals on request; Evening Meals by arrangement. Special meals available. Northumberland Tourist Board registered. Reduced rates for children and small reduction for Senior Citizens. Pets welcome free. Private bathrooms and/or showers. Teasmaid and TV in all bedrooms. Open March till end September.

[See also Colour Display Advertisement]

**SPENNYMOOR. John and Jean Thompson, Highview Country House, Kirk Merrington, Near Spennymoor DL16 7JT (01388 811006).** Standing in one acre of gardens, in open and rolling countryside, pace and tranquillity awaits. Private and safe parking, situated on the edge of a delightful village with all amenities. Good access from A1M and a springboard for the North of England with Durham City only 12 minutes away. Our spacious ground floor rooms are all en suite and furnished to a high standard with colour TV and hospitality tray. Residents, lounge with open balcony and views for miles. Open log fires are a feature of the dining room with fresh fruit and a full English breakfast (grilled). Bed and Breakfast rates from £23 per person per night; (reduced rates for children). Also three-bedroomed apartment also available. Please ring for brochure. **ETC** ♦♦♦.
e-mail: highviewhouse@genie.co.uk

**STANLEY. Mrs P. Gibson, Bushblades Farm, Harperley, Stanley DH9 9UA (01207 232722).** Ideal stop-over when travelling north or south. Only 10 minutes from A1M Chester-le-Street. Durham City 20 minutes, Beamish Museum two miles, Metro Centre 15 minutes, Hadrian's Wall and Northumberland coast under an hour. Comfortable Georgian farmhouse set in large garden. Twin ground-floor en suite room plus two double first floor bedrooms. All rooms have tea/coffee making facilities, colour TV and easy chairs. Ample parking. Children over 12 years welcome. Sorry, no pets. Bed and Breakfast from £17 to £19.50 per person per night, single £20 to £25. Self catering accommodation also available. Leave A1(M) at Chester-le-Street for Stanley on the A693, then Consett half-a-mile after Stanley. Follow signs for Harperley, farm on right half-a-mile from crossroads. Bed and Breakfast from £17 to £19.50. **ETC** ♦♦♦

---

## FHG

Visit the FHG website
**www.holidayguides.com**
for details of the wide choice of accommodation featured in the full range of FHG titles

# ESSEX

**BRAINTREE. Mrs A. Butler, Brook Farm, Wethersfield, Braintree CM7 4BX (01371 850284).** Beautiful Listed farmhouse, parts dating back to 13th century, on a 100-acre mixed farm set on the edge of a picturesque village. Essex can offer many picturesque places to visit and the Suffolk villages of Long Melford, Lavenham and Dedham, as well as Constable Country, are all within easy reach. Warm, spacious and comfortable rooms, guests' lounge, safe parking. Thirty minutes from Stansted Airport. Camping also available. Open all year. Prices from £20 per person in double, twin or family rooms; from £25 single. **ETC** ◆◆◆.

**COLCHESTER. Mrs Wendy Anderson, The Old Manse, 15 Roman Road, Colchester CO1 1UR (01206 545154).** This spacious Victorian family home is situated in a quiet square beside the Castle Park. Only three minutes' walk from bus/coach station or through the Park to town centre. We promise a warm welcome and a friendly, informal atmosphere. All rooms have central heating, TV and tea/coffee making facilities. Ground floor double room has private facilities; two twin-bedded rooms on first floor, one en suite. Full, varied English Breakfast. Bed and Breakfast from £30 single, £42 double. Only 30 minutes' drive from Harwich and Felixstowe. Within easy reach of Constable country and one hour's train journey from London. Sorry, no smoking.

**KELVEDON. Mr and Mrs R. Bunting, Highfields Farm, Kelvedon CO5 9BJ (Tel & Fax: 01376 570334).** Highfields Farm is set in a quiet area on a 700 acre arable working farm. This makes a peaceful overnight stop on the way to Harwich or a base to visit historic Colchester and Constable country. Convenient for Harwich, Felixstowe and Stansted Airport. Easy access to A12 and main line trains to London. The accommodation comprises one twin room with private bathroom, one twin room en suite and one double en suite, all with TV and tea/coffee making facilities. Residents' lounge. Good English Breakfast is served in the oak beamed diningroom. Ample parking. Bed and Breakfast from £22 single to £44 twin or double. **ETC** ◆◆◆

**PELDON. Yvonne Romain Accommodation, Sunnyside, Colchester Road, Peldon, Colchester CO5 7QP (01206 735945; Fax: 01206 735946).** Peldon is a small village near the historic towns of Colchester (six miles) and West Mersea (three miles) with its boating activities; near to the picturesque Blackwater and Dedham Vale areas. Harwich is just 25 miles away. Sunnyside is a spacious family home set in half an acre. Private parking for all cars, garaging possible. The historic free public house "The Peldon Rose" is about 300 yards away. Local attractions include nature reserves, walking, water activities and various gardens (including Beth Chatto's). Yvonne enjoys quilting and other 'needle' skills and Peter likes computers. Children and pets may be accommodated. Prices from £18.50.
e-mail: yvonne@romain.co.uk

# RETREAT GUEST HOUSE ◆◆◆

*Arrive as a guest - leave as a friend*

12 Canewdon Road, Westcliff-on-Sea,
Essex SS0 7NE
Mr & Mrs Bartholomew
Tel: 01702 348217/337413; Fax: 01702 391179

Close to Cliffs Pavilion, Palace Theatre, Westcliff station and near to the sea front leading to Southend's main attractions and shopping centre.
Most rooms en suite. Some on ground floor.
● All remote -controlled colour TV ● Some rooms with video ● Tea/Coffee making facilities ● Choice of English Breakfast ● Private secure parking.
Quality accommodation competitively priced. Open all year, in excellent location, for business, pleasure and group bookings. Bed and Breakfast from £25 per person.

e-mail: retreatguesthouse.co.uk@tinyworld.co.uk   website: www.retreatguesthouse.co.uk

**Gloucestershire** 179

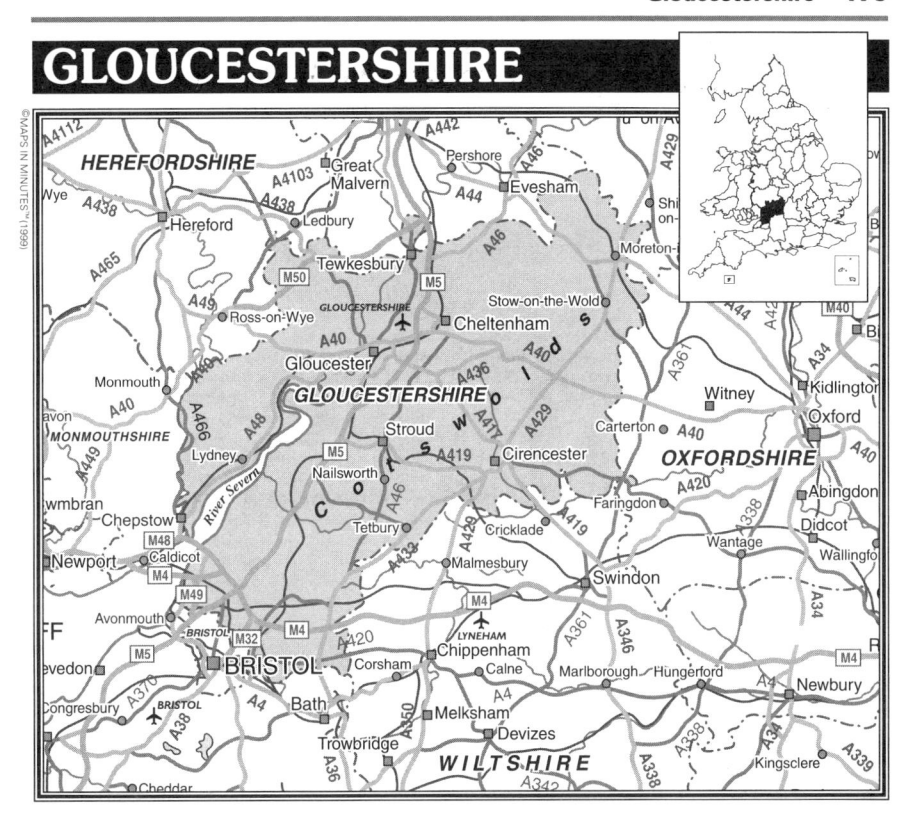

# GLOUCESTERSHIRE

**BATH near. Mrs Lynn Hooper, Greenway Farm, Bath Road, Wick, Near Bristol BS30 5RL (01179 373201).** Greenway is a small working beef farm with a large early Georgian house, just a few yards off the A420 leading to Lansdown, Bath and four miles from Exit 18 on the M4. We are overlooking/adjacent to Tracy Park Golf Course. All rooms have tea/coffee making facilities, colour TV, central heating; some en suite. We also have a spacious garden with Koi pond and are surrounded by beautiful country scenery. Bath four miles, Bristol six miles. Sorry, no pets. Terms from £21 per person.

**BATH near. Mrs Pam Wilmott, Pool Farm, Wick, Bristol BS30 5RL (0117 937 2284). Working farm, join in.** Welcome to our 350 year old Grade II Listed farmhouse on a working dairy farm. On A420 between Bath and Bristol and a few miles from Exit 18 of M4. We are on the edge of the village, overlooking fields, but within easy reach of pub, shops and golf club. We offer traditional Bed and Breakfast in one family and one twin room with tea/coffee facilities; TV lounge. Central heating. Ample parking. Open all year except Christmas. Terms £18 to £22

# 180　Gloucestershire

**BIRDLIP. Mrs P.M. Carter, Beechmount, Birdlip GL4 8JH (Tel & Fax: 01452 862262).** Good central base for touring Cotswolds, conveniently situated for many interesting places and picturesque views with lovely walks, Beechmount is in the centre of Birdlip village, convenient for Post Office/village shop. Front door key is provided so that guests may come and go freely. Bedrooms are equipped to a high standard. all having washbasins; some en suite facilities; bathroom. separate shower, shaver point; toilet. Children welcome at reduced rates; cot and high chair provided. Pets allowed by arrangement. Parking space. Open January to December. Bed and Breakfast from £16 per person; Evening Meal by prior arrangement using home produce when available. Choice of menu for breakfast. Small, family-run guest house. Highly recommended and with competitive rates.
**ETC ♦♦♦**

**BRISTOL. Thornbury Golf Lodge, Bristol Road, Thornbury, Bristol BS35 3XL (01454 281144; Fax: 01454 281177).** Five miles A38 north from junctions M4/M5 at Almondsbury. Thornbury Golf Lodge has 11 well appointed spacious bedrooms, single or twin, all with en suite. Conference facilities available. 36 holes and floodlit driving range. Full clubhouse facilities. Package deals. Terms from £39.50 per room per night. Send for brochure to: **Thornbury Golf Centre, Bristol Road, Thornbury, Bristol BS35 3XL.**

**BRISTOL. Mrs Marilyn Collins, Box Hedge Farm, Coalpit Heath, Bristol BS36 2UW (01454 250786).** Box Hedge Farm is set in 200 acres of beautiful rural countryside on the edge of the Cotswolds. Local to M4/M5, central for Bristol and Bath and the many tourist attractions in this area. An ideal stopping point for the South West and Wales. We offer a warm, friendly atmosphere with traditional farmhouse cooking. All bedrooms have colour TV and tea/coffee making facilities. Bed and Breakfast from £20 single standard, £29 single en suite, £35 double standard, £46 double en suite. Family rooms - prices on application. Dinner £8.50. All prices include VAT.

**CHELTENHAM. Mr John Sparrey, Parkview, 4 Pittville Crescent, Cheltenham GL52 2QZ (01242 575567).** We offer accommodation in Cheltenham's nicest area but only ten minutes' walk from the centre. The bedrooms are large and airy and have TV, tea, coffee and provide views onto Pittville Park. This fine Regency house is inspected annually by the Tourist Authority which gives a classification of "Commended" The RAC and "Which?" Bed and Breakfast Guide also inspect. Cheltenham is famous for horse racing and festivals of music and literature while nearby Prestbury is the most haunted village in England. The Cotswold villages stand in the surrounding hills while Stratford is one hour's drive. Tours can be arranged. Pets welcome. Bed and Breakfast from £20.
e-mail: jospa@tr250.freeserve.co.uk

**CHELTENHAM. Dove House, 128 Cheltenham Road, Bishops Cleeve, Cheltenham GL52 4LZ (01242 679452/679600; Fax: 01242 679600).** Dove House is situated on the outskirts of Cheltenham, close to the Racecourse and is ideal as a base for touring/walking the Cotswolds, Forest of Dean, Tewkesbury, Evesham. Golf courses and private fishing lakes close by. All rooms are furnished to a high standard and have central heating, colour TV and tea/coffee making facilities. Ample parking and garden for guests' use. Bed and Breakfast from £18 per person per night; en suite available. Open all year

# Gloucestershire 181

**CHELTENHAM. Mrs C. J. Christensen, Beechworth Lawn Hotel, 133 Hales Road, Cheltenham GL52 6ST (01242 522583; Fax: 01242 574800).** Renowned for its warm welcome, personal service and very comfortable accommodation, the Beechworth Lawn Hotel is situated close to Cheltenham town centre and within easy reach of the major routes A40, M5 and M4. It makes an ideal base for exploring the beautiful Cotswold region, including Broadway, Stratford-on-Avon and the Georgian City of Bath. Children welcome. Pets by arrangement. Bed and Breakfast from £25 per person. **ETC/AA** ◆◆◆◆ 
e-mail: beechworth.lawn@dial.pipex.com
website: www.beechworthlawnhotel.co.uk

*See also Colour Display Advertisement* **CHELTENHAM. Clive and Anna Rooke, Frogfurlong Cottage, Down Hatherley GL2 9QE (01452 730430).** Frogfurlong Cottage is situated in the green belt area within the triangle formed by Gloucester, Cheltenham and Tewkesbury. Originally two cottages, built in 1805 but recently modernised and extended, it stands on its own, back from the road and surrounded by fields. There is an indoor heated swimming pool which guests may use mornings and evenings, at their own risk. Accommodation consists of "The Pool Room" - a double bedded room with en suite bathroom with jacuzzi and direct access to pool, or "The Garden Room" - a twin/king size room with en suite shower bathroom. Ideally placed for visiting Gloucester and Cheltenham with Bristol, Bath, Stratford-upon-Avon and Oxford all within easy reach. Non-smoking. Sorry, no pets. Evening meals by prior arrangement. Terms from £24 per person per night (Pool Room) and £22 per person per night (Garden Room) includes full breakfast. Evening Meals from £14.50 for three courses and coffee.

**CHELTENHAM. Sandra and David Tompkins, Wishmoor House, 147 Hales Road, Cheltenham GL52 6TD (01242 238504; Fax: 01242 226090).** Wishmoor House is a late Victorian residence, tastefully refurbished to retain its original charm and character. Situated on the eastern side of Cheltenham town, just a walk from the shopping centre, Racecourse and Pittville Park. Conveniently situated at the base of the Cotswold Hills, it makes an ideal location for touring the Wye Valley, Malvern Hills, Royal Forest of Dean and the Cotswold villages. The scenic towns of Hereford, Stratford-on-Avon and Bath are also conveniently situated for day visits. At Wishmoor you will find a warm and friendly welcome from your hosts, who aim to provide a relaxed but efficient atmosphere so that you may enjoy your stay to the full. We have eleven bedrooms, mostly en suite. All have colour TV, hospitality tray, central heating and lashings of hot water. Quiet guest lounge and private off road parking. Bed and Breakfast from £27.50 per person. Family rooms and evening meals available. **ETC** ◆◆◆◆ *SILVER AWARD.*

**CHELTENHAM near. Fossebridge Inn, Fossebridge, Near Cheltenham GL54 3JS (0800 074 1387; Fax:01285 720793).** Diners here are spoiled for choice by the variety of delicious home-cooked fare offered. The Bridge Restaurant and Bar both present imaginative menus based on the finest local produce, and a comprehensive bar snack menu with daily changing specials caters for lighter appetites or diners with limited time to spare. With origins as a coaching inn in Tudor times, the Fossebridge is most delightfully situated, with beautiful lawned gardens leading down to the River Coln. If the charm of the Cotswolds proves irresistible, individually styled bedrooms, some with lake and garden views, provide comfortable overnight accommodation. Children and pets welcome. Reductions for children. **AA** ★★ *AND ROSETTE.*
e-mail: fossebridgeinn@compuserve.com 
website: www.fpb.net.fossebridge

*Please mention this guide when writing to enquire about accommodation*

# Gloucestershire

**CHIPPING CAMPDEN. Mrs C. Hutsby, Holly House, Ebrington, Chipping Campden GL55 6NL (01386 593213; Fax: 01386 593181).** Holly House is set in the centre of the picturesque thatched Cotswold village of Ebrington. Ideally situated for touring the Cotswolds and Shakespeare's country. Two miles Chipping Campden and Hidcote Gardens, five miles Broadway, 11 miles Stratford-upon-Avon, 19 miles Warwick. Double, twin and family rooms available, all beautifully appointed with en suite facilities, TV and tea and coffee. Laundry facility available. Private parking. Lovely garden room at guests' disposal. Village pub serves meals. Bike hire available locally. Directions: from Chipping Campden take B4035 towards Shipston on Stour, after half-a-mile turn left to Ebrington, we are in the centre of the village. Prices from £21 to £24 per person. Child reductions. Non-smoking. **AA ◆◆◆◆** 
e-mail: hutsby@talk21.com
website: www.stratford-upon-avon.co.uk/hollyhouse.htm

**CHIPPING CAMPDEN. Mrs Gené Jeffrey, Brymbo, Honeybourne Lane, Mickleton, Chipping Campden, Glos. GL55 6PU (01386 438890; Fax: 01386 438113).**

COTSWOLD COUNTRY BED AND BREAKFAST

A warm and welcoming farm building conversion with large garden in beautiful Cotswold countryside, ideal for walking and touring. Close to Stratford-upon-Avon, Broadway, Chipping Campden and with easy access to Oxford and Cheltenham. All rooms are on the ground floor, with full central-heating. The comfortable bedrooms all have colour television and tea/coffee making facilities. Sitting room with open log fire. Breakfast room. Children and dogs welcome. Parking. Maps and guides to borrow. Sample menus from local hostelries for your information. Home-made preserves a speciality. FREE countryside tour of area offered to three-night guests. Rooms: two double, two twin, one family. Bathrooms three en suite, two shared. Bed and Breakfast per person from £18.00, en suite £21.00. Brochure available. **ETC ◆◆◆◆**. 
e-mail: enquiries@brymbo.com
website: www.brymbo.com

**COTSWOLDS. Mrs Alison Coldrick, Hill Barn, Clapton Road, Bourton-on-the-Water GL54 2LF (01451 810472).** In the midst of beautiful rolling pastures yet only five minutes' drive from the picturesque village of Bourton-on-the-Water, this 17th century converted barn offers high standard en suite accommodation, tea/coffee making facilities and TV in all rooms, with a choice of breakfast from £20 per person. Beautiful views. Ample parking. Lovely walks directly from the property. Open all year. Sorry, no smoking or pets. Ideally situated for exploring the Cotswolds, Gloucestershire, Oxfordshire and Warwickshire.

**DIDMARTON. Mrs M.T. Sayers, The Old Rectory, Didmarton GL9 1DS (01454 238233; Fax: 01454 238909).** Small and comfortable, this former Rectory, with a pleasant walled garden, is set in an attractive little south Cotswold village on the A433. It has a very friendly informal atmosphere and is an ideal base for touring the Cotswolds, Severn Vale, North Wiltshire and Bath area, or as we are close to M4/5 is a convenient overnight stop. Westonbirt Arboretum is five minutes away and the antiques centre of Tetbury is less than 10. Three double/twin rooms with colour TV, hairdryer, en suite or private bathroom. Central heating. Guests' sittingroom. Ample parking. Food available within walking distance. Terms: Double room £48. Single occupancy £30 to £35. **ETC ◆◆◆◆** *GOLD AWARD*.

---

**When making enquiries please mention FHG Publications**

## Gloucestershire

**DURSLEY. Burrows Court, Nibley Green, North Nibley, Dursley GL11 6AZ (Tel & Fax: 01453 546230).** This 18th century mill is idyllically set in an acre of garden surrounded by open country with beautiful views of the Cotswolds. Decorated and furnished in the country style. The house has six bedrooms, all with private bathroom, colour TV, beverage facilities and radio. Other facilities include two lounges, one with residents' bar; central heating. There is a good choice of restaurants and pubs nearby. Children over five years welcome. Bed and breakfast from £20 to £25 per person. Close to M5 motorway between Junctions 13 and 14. **ETC ◆◆◆ RAC** *HIGHLY ACCLAIMED.*

**DURSLEY near. Mrs Catherine Bevan, Hodgecombe Farm, Uley, Near Dursley GL11 5AN (Tel & Fax: 01453 860365).** Situated in the lower Cotswolds, Hodgecombe Farm lies in a quiet valley between Uley and Coaley, tucked under the Uley Bury Roman Fort with spectaular views across open countryside to the River Severn and beyond. The Cotswold Way winds lazily past Hodgecombe Farm and visitors find this the perfect place to relax in unspoilt surroundings. Three double rooms, one en suite, are comfortably furnished with armchairs, tea/coffee making facilities, clock-radio and central heating. Bed and Breakfast from £17 to £21 per person; Evening Meal £9.50. Sorry no smokers, animals or under five-year-olds. Open March to October. **AA ◆◆◆◆**

**DURSLEY near. Rose & Crown Inn Nympsfield, Stonehouse GL10 3TZ (01453 860240; Fax: 01453 86900).** Three-hundred-year-old Cotswold Stone coaching inn situated in centre of quiet, friendly, unspoilt village, half-a-mile from Cotswold Way; with easy access to M5/M4. Ideal base for touring, walking, cycling and gliding in the Cotswolds. Accommodation includes centrally heated, spacious, en-suite family and double rooms. Evening meals are optional and can be selected from a comprehensive bar menu. Bed and Breakfast from £30 per night. Open all year. All credit/debit cards accepted. **AA, RAC,** *RELAIS ROUTIERS LISTED.*

**DYMOCK. Sally Wood-Robinson, The White House, Dymock GL18 2AQ (01531 890516).** 17th century former farmhouse situated in the picturesque village of Dymock, four miles from the market towns of Ledbury and Newent. An ideal base for exploring the Malverns, Forest of Dean, the Wye Valley and the historic cathedral cities of Gloucester, Worcester, Hereford and the Spa town of Cheltenham. Accommodation comprises two double rooms (one of which is suitable for use as a family room), with a bathroom for the sole use of guests. There is a comfortable living/diningroom with inglenook fireplace, TV and tea/coffee making facilities. Families and children very welcome. Full English or Continental breakfast served. Terms £17 per person per night (£20 for single occupancy). Reduced rates available for longer stays.

---

## PUBLISHER'S NOTE

While every effort is made to ensure accuracy, we regret that FHG Publications cannot accept responsibility for errors, omissions or misrepresentations in our entries or any consequences thereof. Prices in particular should be checked because we go to press early. We will follow up complaints but cannot act as arbiters or agents for either party.

## Gloucestershire

**FRAMPTON-ON-SEVERN. Archway House, The Green, Frampton-on-Severn GL2 7DY (01452 740752; Fax: 01452 741629).** Archway House stands at the far end of the Village Green at Frampton-on-Severn. The house was built in around 1780 and retains some of its original features. Guests are accommodated on the first floor. There is a choice of a double or twin-bedded rooms. All have tea and coffee making facilities, hair dryer, television and radio alam clock. A bathroom can be booked in advance for private use at a small supplement. However, a twin room, with private shower room, is available on the ground floor, in an annexe adjoining the main house. The annexe, which has three bedrooms is also available as a a self-catering holiday let. Bed and Breakfast from £25. Non-smoking. **ETC ♦♦♦♦**.

*See also Colour Display Advertisement*

**GLOUCESTER. Penny and Peter Stevens, Edgewood House, Churcham, Gloucester GL2 8AA (01452 750232).** Family-run country guest house set in two acres of lovely gardens. Ideal for visiting Forest of Dean, Wye Valley, Cotswolds and Malverns. Close to RSPB Reserve and viewpoint for Severn Bore Tidal Wave. Spacious, centrally heated double, family and twin rooms tastefully furnished with comfortable beds and colour televisions. Most rooms are en suite and have tea/coffee making facilities. Spacious dining room and lounge. Ample parking. Generous cooked breakfasts. Several excellent eating places nearby. Bed and Breakfast from £22 to £25 per person. Children over ten years welcome with reductions if sharing with two adults. Sorry no smoking or pets. Open all year. Recommended by the "Which?" guide. **AA ♦♦♦♦**

*See also Colour Display Advertisement*

**GLOUCESTER. Mrs Ellie Wiltshire, Woodgreen Farm, Bulley, Churcham, Gloucester GL2 8BJ (01452 790292; Fax: 01452 790107).** A 300-year-old homely farmhouse which has recently been refurbished to a high standard. Situated in a peaceful countryside location ideal for exploring Gloucester, Forest of Dean, Wye Valley and the Cotswolds on foot, bike or car. We offer three attractive, comfortable bedrooms each with en suite bathroom, tea and coffee making facilities and colour television. Full central heating, open fires, a cosy guest sittingroom and a large garden which guests can use. Secure off-road parking for cars and bikes. You are assured of an excellent breakfast. We also offer traditional home cooked evening meals from a varied menu. Bed and Breakfast from £19 per person. Open all year. Sorry, no smoking or pets. We promise you a comfortable, warm, friendly atmosphere from which to enjoy your holiday. **ETC ♦♦♦♦**
e-mail: woodgreen_farm@hotmail.com
website: www.fweb.org.uk/woodgreenfarm

**GLOUCESTER near. S.J. Barnfield, Kilmorie Smallholding, Gloucester Road, Corse, Staunton, Near Gloucester GL19 3RQ (Tel & Fax: 01452 840224).** Quality all ground floor accommodation. Kilmorie is Grade II Listed (c1848) within conservation area in a lovely part of Gloucestershire. Deceptively spacious yet cosy, tastefully furnished: double, twin, family or single bedrooms all with tea tray, colour TV, radio, mostly en suite. Very comfortable guests' lounge; traditional home cooking is served in the separate diningroom overlooking large garden where there are seats to relax, watch our free range hens (who provide excellent eggs for breakfast!) or the wild birds and butterflies which we encourage to visit. Perhaps walk waymarked farmland footpaths which start here. Children may "help" with our child's pony, pygmy goats whose tiny pretty kids arrive in spring, and hens. Rural yet ideally situated to visit Cotswolds, Royal Forest of Dean, Wye Valley and Malvern Hills. Children over five years welcome. Three-course Evening Dinner, Bed and Breakfast from £24; Bed and full English Breakfast from £16. Ample parking. **ETC ♦♦♦**
e-mail: kilmorie.bb@freeuk.com

---

Terms quoted in this publication may be subject to increase if rises in costs necessitate

**LECHLADE near. Mrs Elizabeth Reay, Apple Tree House, Buscot, Near Faringdon SN7 8DA (01367 252592).** 17th century listed house situated in small interesting National Trust Village, two miles from Lechlade and four miles from Faringdon on the A417. River Thames five minutes' walk through village to Buscot Lock and weirs. Ideal touring centre for the Cotswolds, Upper Thames, Oxford, etc. Good fishing, walking and cycling area. Access at all times to the three guest bedrooms, all of which have washbasin, razor point, tea/coffee making facilities and central heating when necessary. En-suite room available. Residents' TV lounge with log fire in winter. Bed and Breakfast from £26 per person per night, when sharing bathroom, £38 double. Private facilities available to all rooms if required. Choice of many restaurants, etc., within a five-mile radius of Buscot. I look forward to welcoming you to Apple Tree House. **ETC ◆◆◆** 
e-mail: emreay@aol.com

**LECHLADE ON THAMES. Mr and Mrs J. Titchener, Cambrai Lodge, Oak Street, Lechdale on Thames GL7 3AY (01367 253173; Mobile: 07860 150467).** Situated in an attractive village on the River Thames this family-run guest house is only eight miles from Burford and 12 miles from Swindon. Ideal base for touring the Cotswolds with Kemscott Manor and Buscot House and Gardens nearby. We are close to the river and guests can make use of our lovely garden. One family, two double (en suite), one twin (en suite) and two single rooms available. One room has a Victorian four-poster bed and one room is on the ground floor. Breakfast is served in our airy conservatory overlooking the garden. Non-smoking. Pets by arrangement. Open all year. Bed and Breakfast from £27 to £40 single; £40 to £55 double. A warm and friendly welcome is assured at Cambrai Lodge. **ETC ◆◆◆◆** *SILVER AWARD.*

**LYDNEY. Marion Allen, "Woodcroft", Lower Meend, St. Briavels, Lydney GL15 6RW (01594 530083).** Woodcroft is a secluded house set in a five acre smallholding on the side of the Wye Valley near Tintern. A peaceful spot surrounded by woods and lovely walking country, including the Offa's Dyke Path half-a-mile away. We have three en suite rooms - two family and one twin, the latter having wheelchair access and therefore suitable for disabled guests. Each has tea and coffee making facilities. There is a guest lounge and breakfast is served at a time of your choice and includes our own free range eggs; home made bread and home made jams and marmalade. Bed and Breakfast £18. Brochure available. Non-smoking establishment.

**MINCHINHAMPTON, near Stroud. Mrs Margaret Helm, Hunters Lodge, Dr Brown's Road, Minchinhampton Common, Near Stroud GL6 9BT (01453 883588; Fax: 01453 731449).** Hunters Lodge is a beautiful stone-built Cotswold country house set in a large secluded garden adjoining 600 acres of National Trust common land at Minchinhampton. Accommodation available - one double room en suite; two twin/double bedded rooms both with private bathrooms. All have tea/coffee making facilities, central heating and colour TV and are furnished and decorated to a high standard. Private lounge with TV and a delightful conservatory. Car essential, ample parking space. Ideal centre for touring the Cotswolds - Bath, Cheltenham, and Cirencester, with many delightful pubs and hotels in the area for meals. You are sure of a warm welcome, comfort, and help in planning excursions to local places of interest. Bed and Breakfast from £22 per person. Non-smokers. Children over 10. No dogs. SAE please for details, or telephone. **AA ◆◆◆◆◆.**

---

# FREE or REDUCED RATE entry to Holiday Visits and Attractions — see our READERS' OFFER VOUCHERS on pages 43-60

# Gloucestershire

**MORETON-IN-MARSH. Stanley and Susan Woolston, Farriers Cottage, 44 Todenham, Near Moreton-in-Marsh GL56 9PF (01608 652664; Fax: 01608 652668).** Midway between Moreton and Shipston-on-Stour, off the Fosse Way, Todenham is ideally placed for exploring the Cotswolds. Hidcote and Kiftsgate Gardens are close at hand and Stratford-upon-Avon, Oxford and Cheltenham only a short journey away. Set in the heart of the village, this carefully restored Cotswold stone cottage, with beams and inglenook, has full central heating and offers en suite shower-room, TV and tea/coffee making facilities. Ample parking. Excellent meals at the nearby Farriers Arms. Sorry, no pets and no smoking – just a warm welcome and generous English breakfast. Bed and Breakfast from £35 per room. **RAC** ◆◆◆
e-mail: susanannwoolston@aol.com

**NAILSWORTH. Mrs Lesley Williams-Allen, The Laurels at Inchbrook, Nailsworth GL5 5HA (Tel & Fax: 01453 834021).** A lovely rambling house, part cottage-style and part Georgian. The emphasis is on relaxation and friendly hospitality. All six rooms are en suite and include family, twin and double rooms, each with colour TV and tea making facilities. There is a ground floor room suitable for disabled guests. We have a panelled study/reading room with piano, and a beamed lounge with snooker table and board games. In our licensed dining room we serve excellent breakfasts and home cooked dinners. The secluded streamside garden backs onto fields and offers a swimnming pool and the opportunity to observe wildlife. We are ideally situated for touring all parts of the Cotswolds and West Country, surrounded by a wealth of beautiful countryside and all kinds of activities. Children and pets welcome. Non-smoking. Bed and Breakfast from £21 per person; Dinner by arrangement. Brochure on request. Self catering cottage also available. **RAC** *ACCLAIMED*.

**NEWLAND. Ann Edwards, Rookery Farmhouse, Newland GL16 8NJ (01594 832432).** Converted 300-year-old stables on the edge of the lovely 13th century village of Newland overlooking a stream with ducks and surrounded by fields and woods. Newland is situated in the beautiful and unspoilt Forest of Dean. Ideal walking and fishing country with stables, cycle paths and golf courses nearby. Spacious en suite rooms with bath and shower, colour TV and tea/coffee making facilities. Bed and Breakfast from £20 per person. Dogs welcome by prior arrangement. Self catering cottages also available. **ETC** ◆◆◆.

**STONEHOUSE. Mrs D.A. Hodge, Merton Lodge, 8 Ebley Road, Stonehouse GL10 2LQ (01453 822018).** A former gentleman's residence situated about three miles from Stroudwater interchange on the M5 (Junction 13), on B4008 (keep going on old road) just outside Stonehouse towards Stroud. Opposite side to Wyevale Garden Centre, 300 yards from the Cotswold Way. Full central heating and washbasins in all bedrooms; one en-suite. Only cotton or linen sheets used. Two bathrooms with showers. Large sittingroom with panoramic views of Selsey Common. Well placed for Cotswold villages, Wildfowl Trust, Berkeley Castle, Westonbirt Arboretum, Bath/Bristol, Cheltenham and Gloucester ski slope and Forest of Dean. Satisfaction guaranteed. Excellent cuisine. Carvery/pub 200 yards away. Bed and Breakfast from £19 per person, en suite from £21 per person. Children half price Friendly welcome. Sorry, no smoking or dogs. **ETC** ◆◆

**STOW-ON-THE-WOLD. Robert and Dawn Smith, Corsham Field Farmhouse, Bledington Road, Stow-on-the-Wold GL54 1JH (01451 831750).** Homely farmhouse with traditional features and breathtaking views, one mile from Stow-on-the-Wold. Ideally situated for exploring all the picturesque Cotswold villages such as Broadway, Bourton-on-the-Water, Upper and Lower Slaughter, Chipping Campden, Snowshill, etc. Also central point for places of interest such as Blenheim Palace, Cotswold Wildlife Park, Stratford and many stately homes and castles in the area. Twin, double and family rooms available, most with en suite facilities. Other rooms have washbasin, TV and tea/coffee making equipment. Pets and children welcome. Bed and full English Breakfast from £17 to £23 per person. Good pub food five minutes' walk away. **ETC/AA** ◆◆◆.

## Gloucestershire 187

**STOW-ON-THE-WOLD. Mr Brian Sykes, Woodlands, Upper Swell, Stow-on-the-Wold GL54 1EW (01451 832346)..** Situated in a hamlet on the outskirts of the town this mellow stone house has pretty gardens and superb views of the countryside. Bedrooms are well equipped and comfortable. Accommodation comprises three double, one twin and one single, all en suite. The diningroom is used as a small sitting area during the evening. The Skyes family are very friendly and attentive hosts. Bed and Breakfast from £26 to £28. Reduced rates for children. Pets welcome. **ETC/AA** ◆◆◆◆ *SELECTED. HEART OF ENGLAND TOURIST BOARD.*

**STOW-ON-THE-WOLD. Mrs F.J. Adams, Aston House, Broadwell, Moreton-In-Marsh GL56 0TJ (01451 830475).** Aston House is a chalet bungalow overlooking fields in the peaceful village of Broadwell, one-and-a-half miles from Stow-on-the-Wold. It is centrally situated for all the Cotswold villages, while Blenheim Palace, Warwick Castle, Oxford, Stratford-upon-Avon, Cheltenham, Cirencester and Gloucester are within easy reach. Accommodation comprises a twin-bedded and a double/twin room, both en suite on the first floor, and a double room with private bathroom on the ground floor. All rooms have tea/coffee making facilities, radio, colour TV hairdryer and electric blankets for the colder nights. Bedtime drinks and biscuits are provided. Guests and children over ten years, are welcomed to our home from February to November. No smoking. Car essential, parking. Pub within walking distance. Bed and good English breakfast from £22 to £24 per person daily; weekly from £155 per person.**ETC** ◆◆◆◆
e-mail: fja@netcomuk.co.uk 
website: www.netcomuk.co.uk/~nmfa/aston_house.html

**STOW-ON-THE-WOLD. Graham and Helen Keyte, The Limes, Evesham Road, Stow-on-the-Wold GL54 1EN (01451 830034/831056).** The centre of the Cotswolds. Large attractive garden with ornamental pond and waterfall overlooking fields. Only four minutes' walking distance to town centre. Central for places to visit like Stratford-upon-Avon, Burford, Cheltenham, Oxford, Broadway, Evesham, Chipping Campden, etc, all within 20 miles radius. Good sized bedrooms; one four-poster, four rooms en-suite, all with colour TV, hair dryer and tea/coffee making facilities; TV lounge; diningroom. Cot, high chair. Established for over 22 years, we have many guests returning each year, even from abroad, and are well recommended. Many guests book for one or two nights then stay for a week. Bed and Breakfast from £20 to £25 per person per night. Central heating. Car park. Open all year except Christmas. Children and pets welcome. **AA** ◆◆◆, **RAC** *LISTED.*

**STOW-ON-THE-WOLD. Mrs S. Davis, Fairview Farmhouse, Bledington Road, Stow-on-the-Wold, Cheltenham GL54 1JH (Tel and Fax: 01451 830279).** You are assured of a warm welcome at Fairview Farmhouse situated one mile from Stow-on-the-Wold on a quiet B road with outstanding panoramic views of the surrounding Cotswold Hills. Ideal base for touring the pretty villages of Bourton-on-the-Water, The Slaughters, Broadway, Chipping Campden, also famous Stratford etc. The cosy bedrooms are furnished to a high standard with a king-size four-poster de luxe for that special occasion; all are en suite with colour TV and tea/coffee making equipment. Lounge and additional lounge area with books, maps, etc. Central heating. Ample parking. Open all year. Prices from £45 to £55 (two people sharing). **ETC** ◆◆◆ *SILVER AWARD*

**STOW-ON-THE-WOLD. The Golden Ball Inn, Lower Swell, Near Stow-on-The-Wold, Cheltenham GL54 1LF (01451 830247).** Delightful 17th century inn of warm Cotswold stone, offering good home cooked food, real ales and a welcoming friendly atmosphere. Situated on the beautiful "Donnington Way" (details on request). All rooms en suite. From £22.50 per person per night. We look forward to welcoming you.

## 188  Gloucestershire

*The Ragged Cott Inn* is a beautiful 17th Century Cotswold Coaching Inn set in attractive gardens high on top of Minchinhampton Common which forms part of 600 acres of National Trust land some two miles from Gatcombe Park and Minchinhampton Golf Club, which has two 18 hole courses and where the Inn's guests enjoy preferential green fees. The Historic Inn serves numerous real ales as well as the more well known brands and offers a choice of 75 malt whiskies from its traditional beamed bars, with its open fires and exposed Cotswold stone walls. It offers succulent home cooked food complete with fresh vegetables and locally supplied free range meat. There is a non-smoking restaurant if preferred. The ten superb double or twin en-suite bedrooms make the Inn the perfect base to explore the Cotswolds and is a haven for lovers of country pursuits. Dogs and horses are welcome (but please advise beforehand). Located virtually central between Stratford and Bath with Cheltenham just 15 miles away and Cirencester ten miles, there are just too many places and things of interest to list here. The Ragged Cot Inn is recommended in a range of guides including the Millennium Edition of the Good Pub Guide and the Good Beer Guide and is Three Crowns commended by the English Tourist Board. **The Ragged Cott Inn, Cirencester Road, Hyde, Near Stroud, Gloucestershire GL6 8PE Tel: 01453 884623 • Fax: 01453 731166 • website: http://home.btclick.com/ragged.cot**

| See also Colour Advertisement |

**STROUD. Monica, Iain and Niall McRiner, Glenfinlas, 5 Castle Villas, Castle Street, Stroud GL5 2HP (01453 759256).** Share our home in the English Cotswolds, at the heart of five valleys. Enjoy the warm friendly atmosphere in this family home, an early Victorian stone villa, situated in a secluded part of Stroud. One twin bedded room with private facilities, with additional single room available on request. Non smoking. Continental or English breakfast. Relax in the garden or conservatory, stroll down to the centre of Stroud and browse around the shops, or enjoy a coffee in one of the numerous cafes. Stroud is surrounded by beautiful countryside and is ideally placed for visiting many interesting and varied places. The area is ideally suited for cycling and walking. Also available: golfing, gliding, hot air ballooning and horse riding. Bed and Breakfast from £20 per person. Brochure available.
e-mail: glenfinlas.com@virgin.net

| See also Colour Display Advertisement |

**STROUD near. Mrs Caroline Garrett, Lamfield, Rodborough Common, Stroud GL5 5DA (01453 873452).** Delightful Cotswold stone house altered over the years from a row of cottages dating back to 1757. Situated 500ft above sea level bordering National Trust Common land two miles south east of Stroud between A46 and A419, we enjoy superb views across the valley. Lamfield offers one room with a double bed and one with twin beds. Both with washbasin. Shared bathroom. Sittingroom for guests (TV on request). Set in three-quarters of an acre of secluded garden. Ample off-road parking. Excellent pubs locally for evening meals. Bed and Breakfast from £35 per room for two sharing. Come and share my home for a night or two.

**TEWKESBURY. Caroline and Keith Page, Corner Cottage, Stow Road, Alderton, Tewkesbury GL20 8NH (01242 620630).** National Grid Ref: SO 997 327. Corner Cottage was originally a pair of farm cottages now a family home standing in two acres. The en suite rooms are decorated in cottage style and have views over surrounding countryside. Your hosts have extensive local knowledge and will help you plan your trips. The Cotswolds are nearby with the towns of Cheltenham, Broadway, Winchcombe and Stratford-upon-Avon within easy driving distance. The M5, Junction 9, is less than five miles away giving access to North and South. The house is easy to find with plenty of parking. **ETC ♦♦♦**.
e-mail: cornercottagebb@talk21.com

**When making enquiries please mention FHG Publications**

**WINCHCOMBE. Mick and Sally Simmonds, Gower House, 16 North Street, Winchcombe GL54 5LH (01242 602616).** A warm welcome awaits you at this 17th century town house situated close to the town centre of Winchcombe, a small picturesque country town on the Cotswold Way. It is an ideal base for ramblers, cyclists and motorists to explore the beautiful Cotswold countryside. The three comfortable bedrooms (one double with private bathroom, two twin/double en-suite) all have TV, radio, tea/coffee making facilities, full central heating. There is a TV lounge and a large secluded garden available for guests' use. Off road car park with two garages. Children welcome but sorry, no pets. Bed and Breakfast from £21 per person.

*See also Colour Display Advertisement*

**WINCHCOMBE. The Plaisterers Arms, Abbey Terrace, Winchcombe, Near Cheltenham GL54 5LL (Tel & Fax: 01242 602358).** Set in the heart of historic Winchcombe (the capital of Mercia in the Middle Ages), and close to Sudeley Castle, the Plaisterers Arms is an unusual split-level Cotswold stone inn with oak-beamed ceilings and a wonderful traditional atmosphere. The inn serves a veried selection of hand-pulled real ales and a wide range of meals, including delicious home-made pies, daily specials and a traditional roast lunch on Sundays. Upstairs are five well-appointed and attractively decorated en suite bedrooms, all with colour television and tea/coffee making facilities. At the rear is a large beer garden with attractive patios which overflow with spectacular floral displays during spring and summer.

**WINCHCOMBE near. Mr and Mrs Bloom, The Homestead, Smithy Lane, Greet, Near Winchcombe GL54 5BP (01242 603808).** The Homestead is a 16th century period country house, built in Cotswold stone and standing in one acre of lovely gardens, with commanding views of the Cotswold Hills. It is situated just one mile from the Anglo-Saxon village of Winchcombe and Sudeley Castle, and within easy reach of many Cotswold villages and Stratford-upon-Avon. There are several pubs and a restaurant nearby for evening meals. We have two double rooms, one with en-suite facilities, one family room ensuite and one twin room with washbasin. All rooms have exposed beams and lovely views. Tea making facilities in rooms. Bed and Breakfast from £20 to £25. Private parking for cars.

**WOODCHESTER. Mrs Wendy Swait, Inschdene, Atcombe Road, South Woodchester, Stroud GL5 5EW (01453 873254).** Inschdene is a comfortable family house with magnificent views across the valley, set in an acre of garden near the centre of a quiet village. A double room with private bathroom and a twin-bedded room are available, both being spacious with washbasin and tea/coffee making facilities. Colour TV available in the rooms. Woodchester is an attractive village with excellent local pubs renowned for their food, and all within easy walking distance. An ideal centre for the Cotswolds and close to Slimbridge, Berkeley Castle and Westonbirt Arboretum and more, including Badminton and Gatcombe Horse Trials. Guests are requested not to smoke in the house. Bed and Breakfast from £15 per person.

---

# FREE or REDUCED RATE entry to Holiday Visits and Attractions — see our READERS' OFFER VOUCHERS on pages 43-60

# HAMPSHIRE

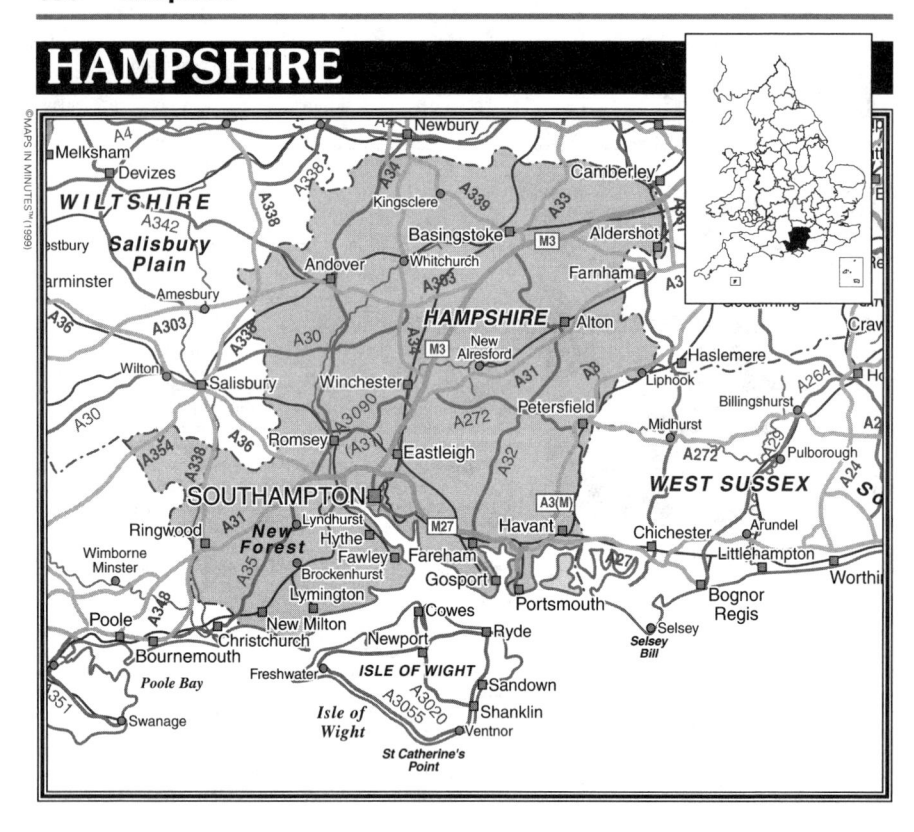

**BURLEY. Mrs Gina Russell, Charlwood, Longmead Road, Burley BH24 4BY (01425 403242).** Charlwood is situated on the edge of Burley, a picturesque little village in the midst of the New Forest. An ideal walking and touring base, Bournemouth and Southampton only 16 miles away and Isle of Wight ferry 12 miles. Riding and golf are nearby. The bedrooms, one double, one twin, have washbasin, colour TV and tea/coffee makiing facilities. Central heating throughout. The friendly family home stands in its own attractive grounds on a no-through forest road offering visitors a peaceful "away from it all" break. A full traditional English Breakfast is served. Pets welcome. No smoking. Open January to November. Bed and Breakfast from £22. **ETC** ♦♦♦♦

**CADNAM (NEW FOREST). Simon and Elaine Wright, Bushfriers, Winsor Road, Winsor, Southampton SO40 2HF (023 8081 2552).** Bushfriers is situated in the peaceful farming village of Winsor within the unique location of the New Forest Heritage Area. Our individual character cottage offers a comfortable double bedroom with countryside views and private bathroom with an adjoining sitting/single bedroom. One extra double bedroom is available if required. Tea/coffee making facilities in both rooms. Guests may enjoy the TV/sitting room with log fire in winter and our delightful secluded garden. Our highly rated breakfasts are freshly prepared from local farm produce with home-made breads and preserves. Bed and Breakfast from £20 per person per night. 17th century village pub four minutes' walk away serving excellent good value food.

**EASTLEIGH. Pat and Colin Morris, Twyford Lodge Guest House, 104-106 Twyford Road, Eastleigh SO50 4HN (023 8061 2245).** Twyford Lodge Guest House is conveniently situated for Eastleigh town centre, Southampton Airport and M3/M27 motorways. Car park. Comfortable rooms. Good English Breakfast and a friendly atmosphere are always on offer. Southampton with its shopping and shipping is a 20 minute drive away as is historic Winchester. Bournemouth/Portsmouth and the New Forest are easily reached in less than an hour. Bed & Breakfast from £20.

## Langley Village Restaurant
**Lepe Road, Langley, Near Beaulieu, Southampton SO45 1XR**
**Tel/Fax: 023 8089 1667; Mobile: 07989 781616**

A friendly family atmosphere will greet you in this large detached property on the edge of the beautiful New Forest. Ample off-road parking. Each day begins with a hearty full English breakfast. Accommodation comprises one twin, one double and two single rooms, all tastefully decorated and having washbasins, central heating, colour TV and tea-making facilities. A restaurant is attached offering meals all day. Conveniently situated for golf, fishing, horse riding and walking. Close to Exbury Gardens, Lepe Country Park and Beaulieu Motor Museum. Open all year. Bed and Breakfast from £20.00. Special diets catered for by arrangement.

**website: www.langley-hampshire.co.uk**

---

**FAREHAM. Ian and Sarah Pike, Bembridge House, 32 Osborn Road, Fareham PO16 7DS (Tel & Fax: 01329 317050).** You will be warmly welcomed to this elegant family home in a delightful Victorian house set in the conservation area of the town centre. Within a quarter of a mile there are many pleasant places to dine; Italian, Indian, French, Chinese cuisine or good British food restaurants and some excellent local pubs. A variety of character rooms is available all with colour television, coffee and tea making facilities and welcome tray. Comfortable beds with crisp cotton bed-linen. There is ample off road private parking. Our five-course breakfast is sumptuous! Single rooms from £39 to £51, double or twin rooms from £44 to £58. Credit cards accepted. Self-contained flat also available. **RAC ♦♦♦♦** *SPARKLING DIAMOND AWARD.* 
e-mail: ian@bembridgehouse.freeserve.co.uk
website: http://joinme.net/bembridge

---

**HOOK. Mr Field, Oaklea Guest House, London Road, Hook, Near Basingstoke RG27 9LA (01256 762673).** Oaklea is a fine Vistorian house one mile from Junction 5 of M3. Ideally placed for the West Country with easy access to Southampton, Reading, London, Guildford also Heathrow and Gatwick Airports. Accommodation offered in single, double and family rooms, some en suite with TV. Guest lounge. Homely atmosphere. Bed and Breakfast from £28 (single) to £48 (double/twin) including VAT. Licensed. **AA** *LISTED.* 
e-mail: oaklea@bun.com

---

**HYTHE, near Southampton. David and Marion Robinson, Four Seasons Hotel, Hamilton Road, Hythe, Southampton SO45 3PD (023 8084 5151 or 023 8084 6285).** A warm welcome is extended to guests staying in this friendly, family run hotel. Situated on the edge of the New Forest close to Beaulieu and Exbury it is ideal for touring. The picturesque market town of Hythe with its pubs and restaurants is one-and-a-half miles distant. Here is an attractive Marina and a regular ferry service to Southampton and the Isle of Wight. Golf, horse riding, wind surfing and other sports are available within five miles. Bedrooms have colour TVs and tea/coffee making facilities; en suite facilities available. Highly praised for its standard of good home cooking, there is also a licensed bar, attractive garden and ample parking. Bed and Breakfast from £22.50.

---

## FREE or REDUCED RATE entry to Holiday Visits and Attractions — see our READERS' OFFER VOUCHERS on pages 43-60

**"Dolphins"** is a very comfortable and homely Victorian cottage in a quiet location, Central Lymington, offering warm hospitality and the highest standard of accommodation. Single, twin, double and family rooms all with colour TV and tea/coffee making facilities; king-size or twin en suite available. Spacious and very comfortable sittingroom with open log fire (in winter) and colour satellite TV. Choice of breakfast; traditional home-cooked evening meals optional. Excellent position, just a few minutes' walk from railway/bus/coach stations, ferry and Sea, restaurants and town centre. Beautiful Forest walks and excellent cycle rides (mountain bikes with hats and maps provided). Inclusive in the price is the use of leisure club facilities, beach chalet and mountain bikes. Also walking distance of Marinas and beautiful Nature Reserve. Access/Visa/Mastercard accepted. Please write or telephone for brochure. B&B from £18pppn; children half price.

Jane & Mike Finch, "Dolphins", 6 Emsworth Road, Lymington SO41 9BL
Tel: 01590 676108/0958 727536; Fax: 01590 688275

**LYMINGTON. Durlston House, Gosport Street, Lymington SO41 9EG (01590 676908/677364).** Durlston House combines high standards of comfort and hospitality with a warm relaxed atmosphere. All our bedrooms are en suite and equipped to a high quality level, with remote control TVs and tea/coffee making facilities as standard features. There is also a comfortable, quiet residents' lounge where you may relax at any time of the day. Acclaimed by the RAC as " An excellent quality establishment, excellent furnishings and first class en suites. Spotlessly clean everywhere! Congratulations!" Private car park. Bed and Breakfast £17.50 to £25 per person per night. **ETC** ♦♦♦♦, **RAC** *ACCLAIMED,* **AA** *QQQQ SELECTED..*

*See also Colour Display Advertisement*

**LYMINGTON. Mrs R. Sque, Harts Lodge, 242 Everton Road, Lymington SO41 0HE (01590 645902).** Bungalow (non-smoking) set in three acres. Large garden with small lake and an abundance of birdlife. Quiet location. Three miles west of Lymington. Friendly welcome and high standard of accommodation comprising double, twin and family en suite rooms. Each with tea and coffee making facilities and colour TV. Delicious four-course English breakfast. The sea and the forest are five minutes away by car. Horse riding, fishing and golf are nearby. The village pub serving excellent home-made meals is a half- mile away. Children and pets welcome. Bed and Breakfast from £21 per person. **AA** ♦♦♦♦

*See also Colour Display Advertisement*

**LYMINGTON. Our Bench, Lodge Road, Lymington SO41 8HH (Tel & Fax: 01590 673141).** A warm welcome awaits you in this non-smoking and no children award-winning home. This quiet bungalow is situated between the New Forest and the coast. All rooms are en suite with colour television, tea/coffee making facilities; a four-course breakfast and optional evening meals are served in the diningroom. An indoor heated pool, jacuzzi and sauna within the grounds for your enjoyment, and mountain bikes available for hire. National Accessibility Scheme 3. Tariff from £22 per person. **ETC** ♦♦♦♦ *GOLD AWARD, ENGLAND FOR EXCELLENCE WINNER, FHG DIPLOMA WINNER.*
e-mail: enquiries@ourbench.co.uk
website: www.ourbench.co.uk

# FHG PUBLICATIONS LIMITED
publish a large range of well-known accommodation guides. We will be happy to send you details or you can use the order form at the back of this book.

**LYNDHURST. Penny Farthing Hotel, Romsey Road, Lyndhurst SO43 7AA (023 802 84422; Fax: 023 802 84488).** The Penny Farthing is a cheerful small Hotel ideally situated in Lyndhurst village centre, the capital of "The New Forest". The Hotel offers en suite single, double, twin and family rooms with direct-dial telephone, tea/coffee tray, colour TV and clock radio. We also have some neighbouring cottages available as Hotel annexe rooms or on a self-catering basis. These have been totally refitted, much with "Laura Ashley" decor, and offer quieter, more exclusive accommodation. The hotel has a licensed bar, private car park and bicycle store. Lyndhurst has a charming variety of shops resturants, pubs and bistros and "The New Forest Information Centre and Museum". All major credit cards accepted. **AA/RAC/ETC ♦♦♦♦.** 
website: www.pennyfarthinghotel.co.uk

**LYNDHURST (NEW FOREST). Lyndhurst House, 35 Romsey Road, Lyndhurst SO43 7AR (023 8028 2230).** Detached house built in the early 1900's. Situated just two minutes' walk from village centre and open forest. Run by owners Christine and Brian Wood, offering comfortable, friendly accommodation, tastefully furnished and operating a non-smoking policy. Accommodation comprises of double, twin and family rooms, some with four-poster bed. All rooms en suite with colour TV, tea/coffee making facilities, hairdryer and radio alarm. All rooms have central heating. We serve a hearty full English or vegetarian breakfast. Children over the age of ten most welcome. A locked cycle store and off-street parking are available to our guests. Bed and Breakfast from £22 per person per night. **ETC/RAC ♦♦♦♦** *SILVER AWARD*. 
e-mail: bcjwood@lynhouse.freeserve.co.uk
website: www.newforest.demon.co.uk/lynho.html

**MILFORD-ON-SEA (NEW FOREST). Carolyn and Roy Plummer, Ha' Penny House, 16 Whitby Road, Milford-on-Sea, Lymington SO41 0ND (01590 641210; Fax: 01590 641219).** Ha' Penny House is a delightful character house with a warm, friendly atmosphere. Set in a quiet area of the unspoilt village of Milford-on-Sea and just a few minutes' walk to both sea and village, it is ideally situated for visiting the New Forest, Bournemouth, Salisbury and the Isle of Wight. The comfortable bedrooms are all en suite and beautifully decorated, with TV, hospitality tray and many extra touches. Four course, multi-choice breakfast. Large sunny diningroom and cosy guest lounge. Attractive gardens and summer house. Ample private parking. Two double, one twin, one single. Non-smoking. Bed and Breakfast from £21. Self-catering apartment also available. Open all year. **ETC ♦♦♦♦.** 
website: www.SmoothHound.co.uk/hotels/hapenny.html

**NEW FOREST. Mrs J. Pearce, "St. Ursula", 30 Hobart Road, New Milton BH25 6EG (01425 613515).** Large detached family home offering every comfort in a friendly relaxed atmosphere. Off Old Milton Road, New Milton. Ideal base for visiting New Forest with its ponies and beautiful walks; Salisbury, Bournemouth easily accessible. Sea one mile. Leisure centre with swimming pool etc, town centre and mainline railway to London minutes away. Twin (en suite), double, family, single rooms, all with handbasin, TV and tea-making facilities. High standards maintained throughout; excellent beds. Two bathrooms/showers, four toilets. Downstairs twin bedroom suitable for disabled persons. Children and pets welcome. Cot etc., available. Pretty garden with barbecue which guests are welcome to use. Lounge with large colour TV. Two diningrooms. Smoke detectors installed. Full central heating. Open all year. Bed and Breakfast from £20. **ETC ♦♦♦,** *NATIONAL ACCESSIBLE SCHEME 3.*

---

Please mention ***Bed and Breakfast Stops*** when making enquiries about accommodation featured in these pages.

## Hampshire

**NEW FOREST. Mrs Sandra Hocking, Southernwood, Plaitford Common, Salisbury Road, Near Romsey SO51 6EE (01794 323255 or 322577).** Modern country family home, surrounded by farmland, on the edge of the New Forest. Two double, one family and one twin bedrooms. Full English breakfast. Cots and high chairs available for babies. Four miles from M27 off A36. Salisbury, Southampton 11 miles, Stonehenge 17 miles. Portsmouth half an hour. Winchester 14 miles, Romsey five miles. Within easy reach of Continental ferries. Large garden. Ample parking. Lounge area for guests. TV. Tea/coffee always available. Horse riding, golf, fishing, swimming, walking in New Forest 10 minutes. Local inns for good food. Bed and Breakfast from £15. Open all year..

**NEW FOREST (Fritham). John and Penny Hankinson, Fritham Farm, Fritham, Lyndhurst SO43 7HH (Tel & Fax: 023 8081 2333).** Lovely farmhouse on working farm in the heart of the New Forest. Dating from the 18th century, all bedrooms have en suite facilities and provision for tea/coffee making. There is a large comfortable lounge with TV and log fire. Fritham is in a particularly beautiful part of the New Forest, still largely undiscovered and with a wealth of wildlife. It is a wonderful base for walking, riding, cycling and touring. No smoking. Children 10 years and over welcome. Come and enjoy peace and quiet in this lovely corner of England. Bed and Breakfast £20 to £22. **ETC/AA** ♦♦♦♦

**NEW MILTON. Mariette and Trevor Jelley, Holmsley Road, Wooton, New Milton, Hants BH25 5TR (01425 629506; Mobile: 07773 527626)** This graciously decorated New Forest cottage is presented by myself, Mariette and my husband Trevor, whose home-cooked breakfasts are a veritable joy, served in the conservatory overlooking the garden. Our cottage is located in the heart of the New Forest where you can enjoy all the verdant tranquil beauty and step back in time as you traverse the leafy glades. Take care to observe the spectacular wildlife in their natural environment. There are many local pubs and restaurants which will happily welcome your pet. For pets and families alike we offer a warm and friendly welcome. All en suite rooms, tea/coffee making facilities, TV, towels and toiletries. **AA** ♦♦♦♦

**PETERSFIELD. Mrs Mary Bray, Nursted Farm, Buriton, Petersfield GU31 5RW (01730 264278). Working farm.** This late 17th century farmhouse, with its large garden, is open to guests throughout most of the year. Located quarter-of-a-mile west of the B2146 Petersfield to Chichester road, one-and-a-half-miles south of Petersfield, the house makes an ideal base for touring the scenic Hampshire and West Sussex countryside. Queen Elizabeth Country Park two miles adjoining picturesque village of Buriton at the western end of South Downs Way. Accommodation consists of three twin-bedded rooms (two with washbasin), two bathrooms/toilets; sittingroom/breakfast room. Full central heating. Children welcome, cot provided. Sorry, no pets. Car essential, ample parking adjoining the house. Non-smoking. Bed and Breakfast only from £18 per adult, reductions for children under 12 years. Open all year except Christmas, March and April.

---

Visit the **FHG** website
# www.holidayguides.com
for details of the wide choice of accommodation featured in the full range of FHG titles

**Hampshire** **195**

**PORTSMOUTH. Graham and Sandra Tubb, "Hamilton House", 95 Victoria Road North, Southsea, Portsmouth PO5 1PS (Tel & Fax: 023 928 23502).** Delightful Victorian townhouse B&B, centrally located five minutes by car from Continental and Isle of Wight ferry terminals, M27/A27, stations, city centres, university, sea-front, historic ships/museums and all the tourist attractions that Portsmouth, and its resort of Southsea, has to offer. Bright, modern, centrally heated rooms with remote control colour TV, hairdryer, clock, cooler fan and generous tea/coffee making facilities. Some rooms have en suite facilities. Ideal touring base for southern England. Full English, vegetarian and continental breakfasts are served from 6.15am (for early travellers) in the lovely Spanish-style diningroom. Nightly/weekly stays welcome all year. Bed and Breakfast £20 to £21 per person nightly in standard rooms and £22 to £24 per person in en suite rooms. **ETC/AA** ◆◆◆◆ 
e-mail: sandra@hamiltonhouse.co.uk    website: www.resort-guide.co.uk/portsmouth/hamilton

**RINGWOOD (NEW FOREST). Joan and Brian Peck, Old Stacks, 154 Hightown Road, Ringwood BH24 1NP (TeL & Fax: 01425 473840).** Joan and Brian warmly welcome you to Old Stacks, their delightful spacious bungalow where home from home hospitality awaits. The twin en suite room with its own garden entrance and patio and the double room with its large private bathroom adjoining have colour TV and tea and coffee facilities and are both attractively decorated and comfortable. Relaxation awaits in their lovely garden and cosy log fires warm the lounge in winter. A country inn is conveniently close by and Ringwood with its weekly Wednesday market and many excellent restaurants and pubs is a mile away. Explore the beautiful New Forest and walk along Bournemouth's sandy beaches, 15 minutes' drive by car. An ideal centre for your holiday. For non-smokers only. Bed and Breakfast from £20 per person. **ETC/AA** ◆◆◆◆
e-mail: oldstacksbandb@aol.com

**RINGWOOD (New Forest). Margaret and Steve Willis, 1 Hiltom Road, Ringwood BH24 1PW (01425 461274).** A warm and friendly welcome awaits you in our quiet old modernised cottage. Comfortable accommodation in two double rooms and one single room, all en suite. TV and tea/coffee making facilities in each room. Good English Breakfast. Comfortable lounge for residents' use. Garden smoking only. Ample parking. Sorry, no children under 12 years or pets. We are centrally situated for forest and sea. Ideal for fishing, horse riding, walking, golf and bird watching etc. Terms from £17 per person. Open all year. **ETC** ◆◆◆

**ROMSEY/NEW FOREST. Mrs J. Hayter, Woodlands, Bunny Lane, Sherfield English, Romsey SO51 6FT (01794 884840).** Woodlands is a small family-run guest house close to the New Forest and situated in a quiet country lane. Our bedrooms – double, twin and family en suite – overlook dairy fields and have washbasin, colour TV and tea/coffee making facilities. Guests' lounge. Close to the Isle of Wight ferry, Southampton, Salisbury, Winchester, Romsey, Florence Nightingale Country, Broadlands, Hillier Arboretum. Hearty breakfast and home-cooked evening meals available. Local village pubs. Roy and Jenny offer a warm welcome to all guests. Bowlers Bed and Breakfast from £15 per person. Evening Meal from £5. Weekly bookings also. Open all year.

**ROPLEY. David and Sue Lloyd-Evans, Thickets, Swelling Hill, Ropley, Alresford SO24 0DA (01962 772467).** This spacious country house, surrounded by a two acre garden, has fine views across the Hampshire countryside. There are two comfortable twin bedded rooms with private bath or shower room. Tea/coffee making facilities available. Guests' sitting room with TV. Full English Breakfast. Local attractions include Jane Austen's House, ten minutes by car; Winchester, with its fine cathedral, is 20 minutes away and Salisbury, Chichester and the New Forest are all within easy reach. Heathrow Airport is one hour away. Several good pubs in the area. Restricted smoking. Children welcome from the age of 10 years. Regret, no pets. Open all year, except Christmas and New Year. Bed and Breakfast from £22.

## Hampshire

**SOUTHAMPTON. Mrs Rose Pell, Verulam House, 181 Wilton Road, Shirley, Southampton SO1 5HY (023 8077 3293 or 07790 537729).** Rose and Dick warmly welcome guests to their comfortable, warm, roomy Edwardian establishment, in a nice residential area. Good cuisine. One double or family, one twin, one single bedrooms all with TV and tea/coffee making facilities; two bathrooms - plenty of hot water. Car parking space. Five minutes by car to historic Southampton city noted for its parks; railway station 10 minutes. Airport, Cross Channel ferries and Isle of Wight within easy reach and not far from M27, M3, Portsmouth, Winchester, Bournemouth, New Forest and coast. Bed and Breakfast from £19 per person; Evening Meal from £8 per person. Bed and Breakfast £120 weekly. Non-smokers only.

**STOCKBRIDGE. Mr and Mrs A.P. Hooper, Carbery Guest House, Stockbridge SO20 6EZ (01264 810771).** Ann and Philip Hooper welcome you to Carbery Guest House situated on the A30, just outside the village of Stockbridge, overlooking the famous trout fishing River Test. This fine old Georgian House has one acre of landscaped gardens, with swimming pool. Stonehenge and numerous places of interest nearby; sporting and recreational facilities close at hand. Accommodation includes double, twin, family and single rooms, available with private facilities. Centrally heated with colour TV, tea and coffee making equipment, hair dryers, radio alarms. Cots, high chairs. Car essential, parking. Open January to December for Evening Dinner, Bed and Breakfast or Bed and Breakfast only. Terms on application. ETC ♦♦♦, RAC/AA

**WINCHESTER. Mrs S. Buchanan, "Acacia", 44 Kilham Lane, Winchester SO22 5PT (01962 852259; 07801 537703 Mobile).** First class Tourist Board inspected accommodation in a peaceful location on the edge of the countryside, yet only a five minute drive from Winchester city centre. Excellent and easy access to road and rail communications to many tourist areas, all within one hour including London (by rail), Portsmouth, the New Forest, Salisbury, Stonehenge, etc. The accommodation consists of one double and two twin bedrooms, all of which have en suite or private bathroom and tea/coffee making facilities. Charming sitting room with satellite TV. Excellent choice of breakfast. Non-smokers only. Off street parking. Leave Winchester by the Romsey road, Kilham Lane is right at the second set of traffic lights. "Acacia" is 200 metres on the right. Bed and Breakfast from £22 per person. ETC/AA ♦♦♦♦.

**WINCHESTER. Lang House, 27 Chilbolton Avenue, Winchester SO22 5HE (Tel & Fax: 01962 860620).** Winchester is one of the most beautiful cities in Britain and somewhere that demands exploration. Good accommodation is a must, and that is to be found at Lang House. Built at the beginning of the 20th century it has all the graciousness of buildings of that time. You will be warm in winter and enjoy the cool airy rooms in summer. Ample parking in the grounds and the house overlooks the Royal Winchester Golf Course. All bedrooms have en suite facilities and are comfortable and well furnished with colour TV and tea/coffee making facilities. You can be assured of a warm and friendly welcome and Winchester has a plethora of good eateries. Single from £36, double from £48.

**WINCHESTER. Richard and Susan Pell, "The Lilacs", 1 Harestock Close, off Andover Road North, Winchester SO22 6NP (Tel & Fax: 01962 884122).** This attractive Georgian-style family home offers comfortable, clean and friendly accommodation, together with excellent home cooking, including home-made preserves. Situated on the outskirts of Winchester off the B3420, close to beautiful countryside, yet only one-and-a-half-miles from the city centre, which is convenient for all the attractions in the area. One twin-bedded room and one double/family room, both with tea/coffee making facilities, TV and central heating. Ironing facilities. Full English Breakfast is served. Non-smokers please. Open all year. Bed and Breakfast from £18. Reductions for children and long stays. From Winchester, on Andover Road North (B3420), take left turn after Mountbatten Court, and before Harestock Road.
e-mail: richard@rbpell.freeserve.co.uk

# HEREFORDSHIRE

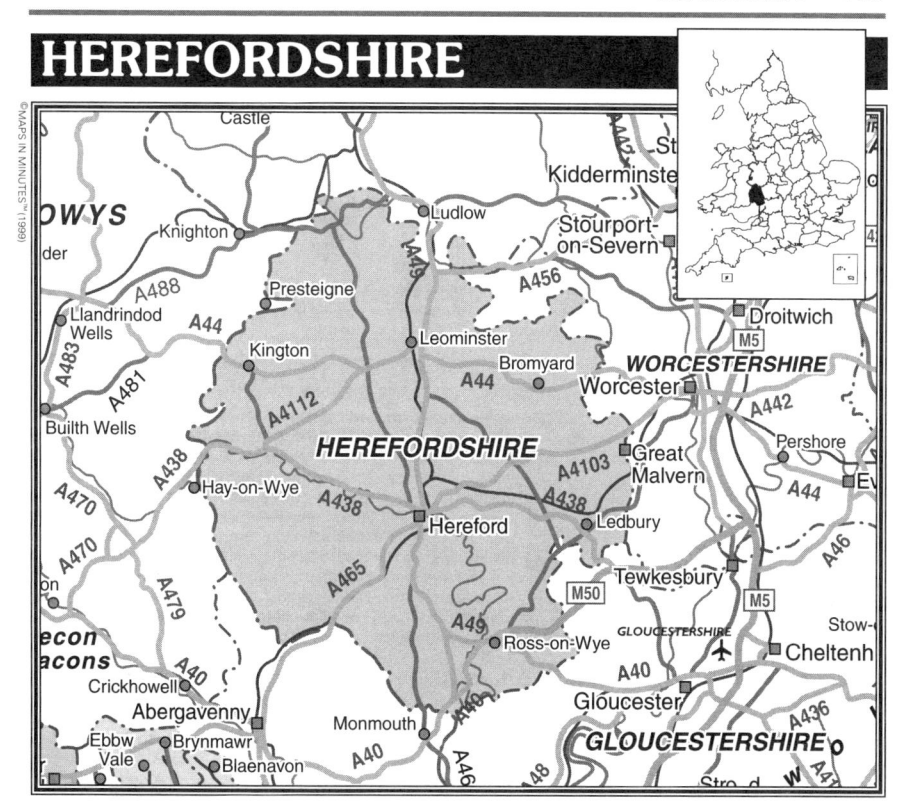

**See also Colour Display Advertisement**

**GOLDEN VALLEY. Mrs Joyce Powell, The Old Vicarage, Vowchurch, Hereford HR2 0QD (Tel & Fax: 01981 550357).** Warm hospitality guaranteed in this Victorian house of character, once the home of Lewis Carroll's brother. Ideal for walking/cycling through rich agricultural land, by historic churches and castles, near the Black Mountains (Welsh Border) and Offa's Dyke Path. Visit Hay-on-Wye, world famous town of books, or Hereford's Mappa Mundi. Golf course five minutes away. Enjoy our attractively presented quality breakfasts after restful nights in individually decorated rooms single, double, family, twin, (en suites/private bathrooms) from £21 per person; refreshment trays, fresh fruit and flowers await you. Home-made breads and preserves. Delightful candlelit dinners from £14 (also vegetarian and special diets) may be ordered in advance. Award Winners of the Flavours of Herefordshire. Delicious dishes from the best ingredients are presented with pride - local and home grown a premium. Non-smoking. Small celebratory groups most welcome. **ETC** ♦♦♦♦ *SILVER AWARD*.
website: www.golden-valley.co.uk/vicarage

**HEREFORD. Heron House, Canon Pyon Road, Portway, Burghill, Hereford HR4 8NG (01432 761111; Fax: 01432 760603).** Heron House, with its panoramic views of the Malvern Hills, provides friendly and spacious Bed and Breakfast services. Facilities include en suite, family room, vanity units, colour TV, tea making equipment, breakfast room/lounge with stone fireplace and real log fire. Situated four miles north of Hereford in a rural location, this is an ideal base for walking, fishing, golf, cycling and bird-watching. Business facilities available on site. Secure off-road parking. Non smoking. Bed and full English Breakfast from £17.50 per person per night. Evening meal by arrangement. **ETC** ♦♦♦
e-mail: bb.hereford@tesco.net

## FELTON HOUSE
Felton, Near Hereford HR1 3PH Tel/Fax: (01432) 820366
website: www.herefordshirebandb.co.uk
website: www.smoothhound.co.uk/hotels/felton.html

Marjorie and Brian Roby offer guests, children and pets a very warm welcome to their home, a country house of immense character set in beautiful tranquil gardens in the heart of unspoilt rural England. Relax with refreshments in the library, drawing room or garden room. Taste excellent evening meals at local inns. Sleep in an antique four-poster or brass bed and awake refreshed to enjoy, in a superb Victorian dining room, the breakfast you have selected from a wide choice of traditional and vegetarian dishes. Felton House is 20 mins by car from Hereford, Leominster, Bromyard and Ledbury off A417 between A49 and A465. Non- smoking. Children and pets welcome. **Tourist Board Highly Commended.**

*Bed & Breakfast £23 per person with en suite or private bathroom.    ETC/AA* ◆◆◆ *Silver Award*

**HEREFORD. Diana and Colin Sinclair, Holly House Farm, Allensmore, Hereford HR2 9BH (01432 277294;Fax: 01432 261285; mobile: 07885 830223).** Spacious luxury farmhouse and over 10 acres of land with horses, situated in beautiful and peaceful open countryside. Bedrooms en suite or with private bathroom, central heating, TV and tea/coffee making facilities. We are only five miles south-west of Hereford city centre. Ideal base for Welsh Borders, market towns, Black Mountains, Brecon and Malvern Hills and the Wye Valley. We have a happy family atmosphere and pets are welcome. Brochure on request. From £20 per person per night and with our delicious English Breakfast you will be fit for the whole day!
e-mail: hollyhousefarm@aol.com

**HEREFORD. David Jones, Sink Green Farm, Rotherwas, Hereford HR2 6LE (01432 870223). Working farm.** Warm and friendly atmosphere awaits your arrival at this 16th century farmhouse, on the banks of the River Wye. Three miles south of the cathedral city of Hereford, with Ross-on-Wye, Leominster, Ledbury, Malvern and the Black Mountains within easy reach. All rooms en suite, tea/coffee making facilities and colour TV. One room with four-poster, family room by arrangement. Guests' own lounge. Pets by arrangement. Bed and Breakfast from £20 per person. **AA** QQQQ.

**HEREFORD. Peter Agate, Hedley Lodge, Belmont Abbey, Hereford HR2 9RZ (01432 277475; Fax: 01432 277597).** Superbly located on the edge of historic Hereford, Hedley Lodge is only two miles from the city centre and is an ideal base for those travelling on business or leisure. There are 17 excellently appointed twin or double bedrooms each with en suite bathroom or shower, remote-control TV, international shaving points, direct dial telephone/private extension and tea/coffee making facilities. The elegant restaurant offers an extensive choice of dishes, together with a range of wines to suit every taste. There is also a good choice of conference and seminar suites which can cater for 200 people. Local attractions include Hereford Cathedral and Hay-on-Wye with its many bookshops and annual music festival. Terms £29.50 to £31.50 single, £24.50 to £26.50 double/twin. Special rates available.
e-mail: Procoffice@aol.com        website: belmontabbey.org.uk/hedley.shtml 

## FREE or REDUCED RATE entry to Holiday Visits and Attractions — see our READERS' OFFER VOUCHERS on pages 43-60

**KIMBOLTON. Mrs Jean Franks, The Fieldhouse Farm, Kimbolton, Near Leominster HR6 0EP (01568 614789) Working farm.** A warm friendly welcome awaits you on our working family farm three miles from the attractive market town of Leominster, and 11 miles from the historic town of Ludlow. We offer excellent accommodation in peaceful surroundings, with truly magnificent views. The comfortable and spacious bedrooms have tea/coffee making facilities. Private bathroom available. There is an attractive guests' sitting/dining room with oak beams and inglenook fireplace. Home cooking is a speciality and delicious breakfasts are served by Mrs Franks, a former Home Economics teacher; Evening Meals on request. Personal attention and high standards are assured. Bed and Breakfast from £19 to £22 per person. **ETC** ◆◆◆.

**LEDBURY. Mrs S. W. Born, The Coach House, Putley, near Ledbury HR8 2QP (Tel & Fax: 01531 670684).** The Coach House is an 18th century coaching stable set in gorgeous Herefordshire. It lies six miles west of historic Ledbury in the old village of Putley amongst orchards and woodlands. The spectacular Wye Valley National Footpath is only five miles away, browse the "Black and White Trail" or play golf on the many nearby courses. The accommodation comprises double, twin and single rooms all en suite. TV, tea/coffee making facilities are provided in each room. A hearty, full English breakfast is served in the stable diningroom. Self-catering also available. Tariffs are £17.50 per person double and twin, £25 single.
e-mail: wendyborn@putley-coachhouse.co.uk
website: www.putley-coachhouse.co.uk

*See also Colour Display Advertisement*

**LEDBURY. Jan and Mike Williams, The Leadon House Hotel, Ross Road, Ledbury HR8 2LP (01531 631199; Fax: 01531 631476).** A graceful Edwardian country house set in a tranquil corner of 'England's most rural county'. Recently refurbished in period style with comfortable, well equipped en suite bedrooms, elegant lounge bar and diningroom serving high quality home cooked food. One mile distant, nesting in the scenic approaches to the Malvern Hills, lies the picturesque and historic market town of Ledbury, renowned for its many well preserved black and white buildings. Equidistant from the cathedral cities of Gloucester, Hereford and Worcester, an ideal base from which to explore the nearby Malvern Hills, Wye Valley and Herefordshire's famous black and white villages. Smoking restricted to bar. Special diets by arrangement. Children welcome. Regret no pets. Bed and Breakfast from £25. **ETC** ★★
e-mail: leadon.house@amserve.net

**LEDBURY. Mrs Julia Powell-Tuck, Pridewood, Ashperton, Ledbury HR8 2SF (01531 670416)** . **Working farm**. Pridewood is a working farm, mainly arable and hops. The farmhouse is full of character and has two large rooms for guests, one double en suite and one twin with private shower room. We offer a snooker room, tennis court and a well-stocked coarse fishing lake. The farmhouse is set in a spacious walled garden. We are ideally situated for touring the Cotswolds, Malverns, Wye Valley and Welsh borders. Pets and children are most welcome. Prices start from £18 to £27 per person per night. **ETC** ◆◆◆

**LEOMINSTER. Chesfield B&B, 112 South Street, Leominster HR6 8JF (01568 613204).** Georgian house five minutes' walk from town centre. We offer a warm friendly welcome. Most bedrooms (twin, double and family) are en suite; all have TV and tea/coffee making facilities. This is a very convenient centre for exploring Wales and the Wye Valley. Bed and Breakfast from £18 single, from £32 double/twin room. **ETC** ◆◆◆

**LEOMINSTER. Mrs J. S. Connop, Broome Farm, Pembridge, Leominster HR6 9JY (01544 388324).
Working farm, join in.** A comfortable 17th century farmhouse situated in beautiful rural Herefordshire midway between the picturesque Black and White villages of Pembridge and Eardisland, seven miles from the market town of Kington; Leominster six miles. An excellent stopping-off place on a journey to Wales or South Coast. Two double and two twin-bedded rooms; two bathrooms, toilet; sittingroom and diningroom. Cot, babysitting and reduced rates for children. Pets permitted but not encouraged. Car essential, ample parking. Open all year. Bed and Breakfast from £16 per night including bedtime drink.

**LONGTOWN. Mrs I. Pritchard, Olchon Cottage Farm, Longtown, Hereford HR2 0NS (Tel & Fax: 01873 860233).. Working farm.** Small working farm. An ideal location for a peaceful holiday in lovely walking country close to Offa's Dyke Path and Welsh Border. The farmhouse is noted for its good, wholesome, home produced food and many guests return to enjoy the homely, relaxing atmosphere. Magnificent views and many places of interest to visit. Accommodation comprises two family bedrooms (also used as singles/doubles) both en suite with colour TV, radio, hairdryer and tea/coffee facilities. Guests sitting room and dining room with separate tables. Towels provided. Reductions for children under 10 years; cot, high chair and babysitting offered. Open all year except Christmas. Bed, Breakfast and Evening Meal or Bed and Breakfast from £20. Car essential, parking. Terms on application with stamp for brochure, please. Luxury six berth caravan also available to let. ETC ◆◆◆ *WELCOME HOST AWARD.*
website: www.golden-valley.co.uk/olchon

**MANSEL LACY. Margaret Price, Thatched Cottage, Mansel Lacy HR4 7HQ (01981 590332).** We look forward to welcoming you to our home in the lovely, peaceful village of Mansel Lacy. Situated in the country, within easy distance of historic Hereford, Hay on Wye, Ludlow and local amenities. We offer our visitors a double or twin room, bathroom with shower and a downstairs sittingroom with TV. Bed and Breakfast £15 per person. Children welcome.

**MONNINGTON-ON-WYE. Clare and Edward Pearson Gregory, Dairy House Farm, Monnington-on-Wye HR4 7NL (01981 500143).** A superbly appointed farmhouse situated down a long drive off the A438 between Hereford and Hay-on-Wye. On a working farm, this large, luxury farmhouse is close to the river and Wye Valley walk. Lovely bedrooms with wonderful views of the farm and surrounding countryside. One double bedroom en suite and one twin bedroom with private bathroom and power shower, both rooms furnished to a very high standard with TV, and tea/coffee facilities. Pets by arrangement only. Guest will enjoy a happy family atmosphere and a traditional hearty breakfast cooked on the Aga. A wonderful spot to relax and explore the Welsh Borders, Black Mountains, Hay-on-Wye (Town of Books), Mappa Mundi, Ludlow and Black and White Villages. Fishing, canoeing and riding can be arranged. Bed and Breakfast from £18 per person. Evening meals by prior arrangement.

**ROSS-ON-WYE. Mrs H. Smith, Old Kilns, Howle Hill, Ross-on-Wye HR9 5SP (Tel & Fax 01989 562051).** A high quality bed and breakfast establishment in picturesque, quiet village location. Centrally heated, private parking. Easy walking distance to village inn where home-cooked meals are served. Some rooms with super king-size bed plus en suite shower, toilet; also brass king-size four-poster bed with private bathroom and jacuzzi. Colour TV and tea/coffee making facilities in bedrooms. Lounge with log fire. Full English breakfast. Central for touring Cotswolds, Malvern, Stratford-upon-Avon, Wye Valley and Royal Forest of Dean. Open all year. Bed and Breakfast from £15 per person. Children and pets welcome (high chair, cots and babysitting service provided). Please telephone for free brochure. Self-catering cottages also available sleeping 2–14 with four-poster beds and jacuzzi.

*When making enquiries or bookings,
a stamped addressed envelope is always appreciated*

**ROSS-ON-WYE. Mrs Mary Savidge, Wharton Farm, Weston under Penyard, Ross-on-Wye HR9 5SX (01989 750255).** Situated on the edge of the Royal Forest of Dean and the Wye Valley, this is an arable farm. Part 16th and 18th century farmhouse. Four miles from Ross-on-Wye, just off the A40, 14 miles from Gloucester. Easily accessible from the M50/M5 motorway, also South Wales and the M4 motorway. Excellent accommodation comprises two double rooms - one en suite, one with private bathroom and shared separate toilet, one twin room with en suite shower room and shared separate toilet. All rooms have colour TV and tea/coffee making facilities. Children by arrangement. Bed and Breakfast from £20. Ideal base for walking, cycling or touring. **ETC** ◆◆◆

# HERTFORDSHIRE

**HEMEL HEMPSTEAD. Alexandra Guest House, 40/42 Alexandra Road, Hemel Hempstead HP2 5BP (01442 242897; Fax: 01442 211829).** Situated near Hemel Hempstead old town centre, close to the historic High Street, and only five minutes from the new shopping centre. Hemel Hempstead is well served by motorways, 30 minutes' drive from Heathrow, 30 minutes by train to London Euston. There is a great emphasis placed on creating a pleasant, homely atmosphere to make you welcome. Accommodation consists of single, double/twin and triple bedrooms and are all equipped with TV and tea/coffee facilities. Rooms for smokers available. Full English or Continental breakfast available. Lift. Terms from £29.50 single, £40.00 double, £42.00 twin, and £60.00 triple. En suite available.
**e-mail: alexhous@aol.com**

**RICKMANSWORTH. Mrs Elizabeth Childerhouse, Tall Trees, 6 Swallow Close, Nightingale Road, Rickmansworth WD3 2DZ (01923 720069).** Large detached house situated in a quiet cul-de-sac with the centre of Rickmansworth only a short walk away. It is a small picturesque old town where there are many places to eat. We are five minutes' walk from the Underground station, half-an-hour to central London. Full breakfast served with homemade bread and preserves. Vegetarians and coeliacs catered for. Tea and coffee making facilities in rooms. Off-street parking. Convenient for M25 and Watford. No pets. This is a non-smoking household. Bed and Breakfast from £22..

# FHG

PLEASE MENTION THIS GUIDE WHEN YOU WRITE
OR PHONE TO ENQUIRE ABOUT ACCOMMODATION

IF YOU ARE WRITING, A STAMPED, ADDRESSED
ENVELOPE IS ALWAYS APPRECIATED

# ISLE OF WIGHT

**FRESHWATER. Kathy and Jim Chettle, Brookside Forge Hotel, Brookside Road, Freshwater PO40 9ER (01983 754644).** A substantial detached property recently converted and extended to meet the hotel requirements of today. Ideally located for the beautiful West Wight countryside and the three coastal bays of Freshwater, Colwell and Totland. All bedrooms are en suite and have colour TV, tea/coffee making facilities and hair dryers. Lounge has colour TV and is available at all times. We serve an excellent standard of cuisine and enjoy an enviable reputation on the Island. Terraced lawns with sun chairs and patio provide a peaceful haven after your day's activities. Bed and Breakfast from £22 per night; Bed, Breakfast and three-course Evening Meal from £34 per night. Brochure available. Ferry arranged. **ETC** ◆◆◆.

**RYDE. Mr David D. Wood, Seaward Guest House, 14/16 George Street, Ryde PO33 2EW (Tel & Fax: 01983 563168; freepnone: 0800 915 2966; mobile: 0787 929 6979).** Seaward is a friendly, family-run, 200-year-old guest house. All rooms have colour TV, tea/coffee making facilities, washbasin and razor point. Some en suite rooms available. Telephone, hair dryer and ironing facilities available for guest's use. Courtesy car for collection from ferries. An excellent base from which to tour the island, with bus, train stations and ferry/hovercraft terminals, as well as shops and sea front within three minutes' walk. Open all year. Special rates for Senior Citizens. Full English, Continental or vegetarian breakfast. Bed and Breakfast from £15. **ETC** ◆◆.
e-mail: seaward@fsbdial.co.uk

**SHANKLIN. Mrs L. Miller, Westbourne Guest House, 23 Queens Road, PO37 6AW (01983 862360).** We are conveniently situated just five minutes' walk from the town centre, Shanklin Old Village, the theatre, cliff walk to Sandown and the lift to the beach. Most rooms have en suite shower rooms and all have colour TV and tea/coffee making facilities. Reductions for children. Open all year. Bookings 'any day to any day'.

**SHANKLIN. Pete and Barbara Tubbs, Hazelwood Hotel, 14 Clarence Road, Shanklin PO37 7BH (Tel & Fax: 01983 862824).** Guests of all ages can enjoy the freedom of our family-run hotel, with its home from home atmosphere and great value for money. Good home cooking with a choice of menu at dinner, served in our lovely diningroom. All rooms are en suite and have a TV. Family suites are available. Tea/coffee making facilities are provided at no extra cost and we are fully centrally heated. Large TV lounge. Hazelwood is set in spacious grounds, in a quiet tree-lined road close to the sea, station, shops and the famous cliff path. Parking. Two nights Bed and Breakfast from £50 to £54, with reductions for children and over 55's. All major credit cards accepted. After leaving the ferry, follow signs for Shanklin; take the A3055 into Shanklin and take a right off Arthurs Hill. **ETC** ◆◆◆
e-mail: barbara.tubbs@thehazelwood.free-online.co.uk

---

**FHG** Visit the FHG website
**www.holidayguides.com**
for details of the wide choice of accommodation
featured in the full range of FHG titles

## Frenchman's Cove Country Hotel ETC/AA ♦♦♦

Our delightful family-run country hotel is set amongst National Trust downland, not far from the Needles and safe sandy beaches. Ideal for ramblers, birdwatchers, cyclists and those who enjoy the countryside. We have almost an acre of grounds with outdoor play equipment. Cots and high chairs are available. All rooms are en suite, all with colour TV and tea/coffee making facilities. Guests can relax in the cosy bar or in the attractive lounge. Also available is the Coach House, a delightfully appointed apartment (ETC ♛♛♛♛) for two adults and two children. Please contact Sue or Chris Boatfield for details.

**Alum Bay Old Road, Totland, Isle of Wight PO39 0HZ Tel: 01983 752227; Fax: 01983 755125**

---

# FHG

Other specialised
## FHG PUBLICATIONS

Published annually: Please add 50p postage (UK only) when ordering from the publishers

- Recommended COUNTRY HOTELS OF BRITAIN    £4.99

- Recommended WAYSIDE & COUNTRY INNS OF BRITAIN    £4.99

- PETS WELCOME!    £5.99

- B&B IN BRITAIN    £3.99

- THE GOLF GUIDE Where to Play / Where to Stay    £9.99

### FHG PUBLICATIONS LTD
### Abbey Mill Business Centre,
### Seedhill, Paisley,
### Renfrewshire
### PA1 1TJ

Tel: 0141-887 0428
Fax: 0141-889 7204
E-mail: fhg@ipcmedia.com
website: www.holidayguides.com

# KENT

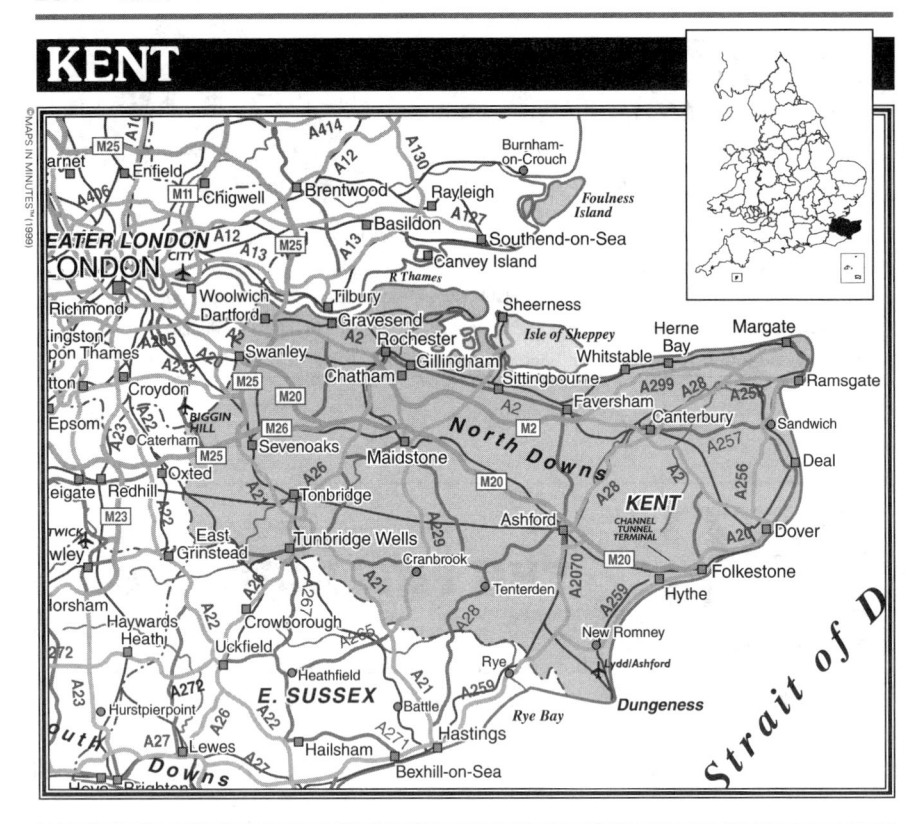

## WARREN COTTAGE HOTEL & RESTAURANT
### 136 The Street, Willesborough, Ashford, Kent TN24 0NB

A cosy atmosphere awaits you at this 17th century hotel and restaurant, set in 2.5 acres. Near M20 Junction 10 and minutes from Ashford International Station, Channel Tunnel, Dover and Folkestone.

One single, three double, one twin and one family bedroom, all en suite, with colour TV. Our delightful oak beamed restaurant offers a daily menu of fresh, home made food. Ideal location for small weddings and private parties. Large car park. All major credit cards accepted.

*For more information telephone:*

**01233 621905/632929 or fax: 01233 623400**

e-mail: general@warrencottage.co.uk • website: www.warrencottage.co.uk

| Double/Twin room: from £50.00 |
| Single room: from £39.90 |
| Family room: from £60.00 |

**ASHFORD. Bernard & Else Broad, The Coach House, Oakmead Farm, Bethersden TN26 3DU (Tel & Fax: 01233 820583)** Comfortable family home, set well back from road in five acres of gardens and paddocks. Breakfast of your choice served in the dining room or conservatory, also used as a sitting room for guests. One mile from village - central for ferries, Tunnel (Dover 40 minutes), Eurostar (15 minutes), Canterbury, Leeds Castle, Sissinghurst and all tourist attractions. Dutch spoken. One twin en suite, two double en suite/private bathroom £19 per person per night. **ETC** ♦♦♦.

**ASHFORD. Mrs Janet Feakins, Old Farm House, Soakham Farm, Whitehill, Bilting, Ashford TN25 4HB (01233 813509).** Soakham is a working farm situated on the North Downs Way between Boughton Aluph and Chilham and adjoining Challock Forest. It is ideally located both for walking and visiting many places in the South East area. Canterbury and Ashford are ten miles and five miles respectively. The farmhouse was originally a Hall House and Grade II Listed with much exposed woodwork. It offers the following accommodation; two double rooms including one with a four-poster bed and a twin-bedded room. Prices are from £16 per person for Bed and Breakfast. Ample parking is available, and we are open all year around.

**ASHFORD near. Pam and Arthur Mills, Cloverlea, Bethersden, Ashford TN26 3DU (01233 820353; mobile: 07711 739690).** A warm welcome awaits in a spacious country bungalow in a lovely peaceful location. Breakfast is served in a new sun-room overlooking the large garden, fields and woods. Ideal for Ashford International Station (10 minutes), Folkestone, Eurotunnel (half-an-hour), visiting Canterbury, Rye, Sissinghurst and Leeds Castles, and many gardens of interest. Superb accommodation in two twin rooms, both en suite (family). Both have colour TV, tea/coffee making facilities, hair dryer, radio and biscuits. Central heating. Excellent breakfasts, home produced bread and eggs. Ample safe parking. Good pub food three-quarters of a mile. Bed and Breakfast from £19. Reductions for three days or more. Non-smoking. **ETC** ♦♦♦

**BIDDENDEN, Bettmans Oast, Hareplain Road, Biddenden, Ashford TN27 8LJ (Tel & Fax: 01580 291463).** A warm welcome is assured at this Grade II Listed oast house and converted barn. Set in 10 acres of lovely Kent countryside. Bettmans Oast is close to Sissinghurst Castle and Gardens and is convenient for visiting Leeds Castle, Scotney Castle and Great Dixter Gardens. The Three Chimneys Country Inn is within walking distance. The towns of Ashford, Canterbury, Rye and Dover are within easy driving distance. London is just over an hour away by train. All rooms have colour TV/video and coffee/tea making facilities. Guests have the use of a comfortable lounge with log fires in winter. Terms from £25 per person. **AA/ETC** ♦♦♦♦ *SILVER AWARD.*

*See also Colour Display Advertisement*

**CANTERBURY. The White House, 6 St. Peter's Lane, Canterbury CT1 2BP (01227 761836).** A gracious Regency townhouse in an ideal location within the old city walls. We are situated in a quiet lane, yet adjacent to the Marlowe Theatre and the High Street, and only five minutes walk from the Cathedral, all attractions and the bus/rail stations. Nearby is a delightful mix of shops, restaurants and parks. Our nine spacious bedrooms are all en suite with colour television and tea/coffee trays. We provide an excellent English breakfast, but cater happily for vegetarian and special diets by arrangement. The MacDonald family will do its best to make your stay comfortable and enjoyable. Open all year. Bed and Breakfast from £45 to £55 for twin/double, £55 to £70 for family room and £30 single.

**CANTERBURY. Mr and Mrs R. Linch, Upper Ansdore, Duckpit Lane, Petham, Canterbury CT4 5QB (01227 700672; Fax: 01227 700840).** Beautiful secluded Listed Tudor farmhouse with various livestock, situated in an elevated position with far-reaching views of the wooded countryside of the North Downs. The property overlooks a Kent Trust Nature Reserve, is five miles south of the cathedral city of Canterbury and only 30 minutes' drive to the ports of Dover and Folkestone. The accommodation comprises one family, three double and one twin-bedded rooms. All have shower and WC en suite and tea-making facilities. Dining/sitting room, heavily beamed with large inglenook. Pets welcome. Car essential. Bed and full English Breakfast from £21 per person. Credit cards accepted. **AA** *QQQ.*

**CANTERBURY. Maria and Alistair Wilson, Chaucer Lodge Guest House, 62 New Dover Road, Canterbury CT1 3DT (01227 459141).** A highly recommended friendly guest house which is elegantly decorated and immaculately clean. Fully double glazed and centrally heated. Secure parking. Seven bedrooms en suite, including family rooms, with colour TV, tea/coffee making facilities, radio/alarm and hair dryer. Open all year round. 10 minutes' walk to city centre, cathedral, bus and rail stations. Hospital and cricket ground only five minutes' walk. Ideal base for touring Kent and for trips to the Continent. Bed and Breakfast from £19 per person.

**CANTERBURY. Mrs Prudence Latham, Tenterden House, The Street, Boughton, Faversham ME13 9BL (01227 751593).** Stay in one of the en suite bedrooms (one double, one twin) in this delightful gardener's cottage and stroll through the shrubbery to the 16th century diningroom, in the main house, for a traditional English breakfast, beneath the Dragon Beam. Close to Canterbury, Whitstable and the Channel Ports. It makes an ideal base for exploring Kent, then walk to one of the historic inns in the village for your evening meal. Tea/coffee making facilities. Off-road parking. Open all year. Bed and Breakfast from £20.

**CANTERBURY. Mrs Lewana Castle, Great Field Farm, Misling Lane, Stelling Minnis, Canterbury CT4 6DE (01227 709223).** Situated in beautiful countryside, our spacious farmhouse is about eight miles from Canterbury and Folkestone, 12 miles from Dover and Ashford. We are a working farm with some livestock, including friendly ponies and chickens. We provide a friendly and high standard of accommodation with full central heating and double glazing, traditional breakfasts cooked on the Aga, courtesy tray and colour TV in each of our suites/bedrooms. Our annexe suite has private staircase, lounge, kitchen, double bedroom and bathroom, also available for self-catering holidays. Our cottage suite has its own entrance stairs, lounge, bathroom and twin bedded room. Our large double/family bedroom has en suite bathroom with airbath. There is ample off road parking and good pub food nearby. Bed and Breakfast from £18 per person, reductions for children. Non-smoking establishment.

*See also Colour Display Advertisement*  **CANTERBURY. Mrs Joan Hill, Renville Oast, Bridge, Canterbury CT4 5AD (01227 830215).** Renville Oast is a 150 year old building previously used for drying hops for the brewery trade. It is situated in beautiful Kentish countryside only two miles from the cathedral city of Canterbury; 10 miles from the coast and one-and-a-half-hour's drive from London. Many interesting castles, historic houses, gardens and Howletts Wildlife Park within easy reach. All rooms are comfortably furnished, with tea making facilities. One family room en suite, one double en suite and one twin-bedded room with private bathroom. TV lounge for guests. Ample parking space. Friendly welcome. Excellent pub food nearby. Bed and Breakfast from £22.50 per person.

# FHG PUBLICATIONS

**FHG** publish a large range of well-known accommodation guides. We will be happy to send you details or you can use the order form at the back of this book.

# BLERIOT'S
### 47 Park Avenue, Dover, Kent CT16 1HE Tel: (01304) 211394

A Victorian Residence set in a tree lined avenue, in the lee of Dover Castle. Within easy reach of trains, bus station, town centre, Hoverport and docks. Channel Tunnel approximately 10 minutes' drive. Off road parking. We specialise in one night 'Stop-Overs' and Mini-Breaks. Single, Double, Twin and Family rooms with full en suite. All rooms have colour TV, tea and coffee making facilities and are fully centrally heated. Full English breakfast served from 7.00 am. Reduced rates for room only. Open all year.

**Rates: Bed and Breakfast: £18.00 to £23.00 per person per night.**
**Mini-Breaks January to April and October to December £18.00 per person per night.**
MASTERCARD & VISA ACCEPTED • *AA* inspected

---

*See also Colour Display Advertisement*

**DOVER. Lyn and Chris Heynen, Chrislyn's Guest House, 15 Park Avenue, Dover CT16 1ES (01304 202302; Fax: 01304 203317).** A warm welcome awaits you at Chrislyn's Victorian Guest House, internationally renowned for its hospitality and cleanliness. Full English breakfast, or vegetarian on request. Two family, two twin and one double rooms available. All rooms have washbasin, some have shower, all have colour TV, tea/coffee making facilities, radio/alarm and hairdryer. Central heating throughout. Situated in quiet residential part of the town, only five minutes' drive from the docks and five minutes' walk from the town centre, castle and parks. French and Dutch spoken by Chris. Children welcome. Regret, no pets. Bed and Breakfast from £16.
**ETC** ♦♦♦

**DOVER. Mike and Margi Brunt, Whitmore Guest House, 261 Folkestone Road, Dover CT17 9LL (01304 203080; Fax: 01304 240110).** You will be made very welcome at this friendly Victorian guest house. Conveniently situated for the ferries, Hoverport, cruise terminal, trains and buses and just ten minutes from the Channel Tunnel. We have double, twin, single and family rooms and en suite facilities are available. All rooms have colour TV, complimentary tea/coffee, hairdryers, alarm clocks and are double glazed and have central heating. Our guests enjoy a total non-smoking policy. Children are made welcome. Our substantial full English breakfast is served from 6.30am. Car park at rear of premises. All major credit cards accepted. Rates per person for Bed and Breakfast: £16 to £25. Children under 12 half price. **ETC/RAC** ♦♦♦ *RAC SPARKLING DIAMOND AWARD.* 
e-mail: whitmoredover@aol.com
website: www.SmoothHound.co.uk/hotels/whitmore.html

*See also Colour Display Advertisement*

**DOVER. Annette and Keith McPherson, Penny Farthing Guest House, 109 Maison Dieu Road, Dover CT16 1RT (01304 205563; Fax: 01304 204439).** Spacious and comfortable Victorian Guest House privately owned, minutes away from ferries, hoverport, trains and Tunnel. Ideally situated for restaurants, banks, shops and all other amenities. We cater for both overnight and short term stays offering a high standard at reasonable prices. All of our rooms feature en suite or with private shower, colour TV, tea/coffee making facilities. Guests have a wide choice of breakfasts, provision is made for early departures. Quotes for family rooms or 'room only' are available on request. Parking space available on the forecourt. **RAC/AA** ♦♦♦, *MEMBER OF THE WHITE CLIFFS OF DOVER HOTEL & GUEST HOUSE GROUP*

---

*Please mention Bed & Breakfast Stops when writing to enquire about accommodation*

**FOLKESTONE. Mr and Mrs R. Shorland, Wycliffe Hotel, 63 Bouverie Road West, Folkestone CT20 2RN (Tel & Fax: 01303 252186).** However long, or short, your stay, a warm welcome is guaranteed at our friendly, family hotel offering clean, comfortable and affordable accommodation. We are based centrally and are close to all amenities. Our menu is interesting and varied, and guests have their own keys for freedom of access at all times. If you are travelling to or from the Continent we can offer an ideal stopover as we are conveniently situated just a short distance from the Channel Tunnel/Seacat terminals, and Folkestone is an easy drive from the port of Dover. Off-street parking. Pets and children welcome. All major credit cards, francs and deutschmarks accepted. Bed and Breakfast from £17.50, Evening Meal £9.00. Discount for four or more nights. Please write or call for our brochure.
**e-mail: shorland@wycliffehotel.freeserve.co.uk**
**website: www.visitus.co.uk/bnbhtm/wycliffe.htm**

**FOLKESTONE. Mrs L. Dowsett, Sunny Lodge Guest House, 85 Cheriton Road, Folkestone CT20 2QL (01303 251498; Fax: 01303 258267).** Mrs Linda Dowsett welcomes you to her comfortable family-run guest house and lovely garden. Home-made English breakfast and Continental. Coffee/tea making facilities and colour TV in each room. Private car park. Five minutes town centre and Seacat to Boulogne, two minutes Folkestone Central railway station, 10 minutes Channel Tunnel, 20 minutes to Dover for France and Belgium. Bed and Breakfast from £18. Children welcome. Early starters and late arrivals catered for. Own keys.
**e-mail: linda.dowsett@btclick.com**
**website: www.SmoothHound.co.uk/hotels/sunnyl/html**

*See also Colour Display Advertisement*

**FOLKESTONE/ASHFORD. Duncan and Alison Taylor, Bolden's Wood, Fiddling Lane, Stowting, Near Ashford TN25 6AP (Tel & Fax: 01303 812011).** Between Ashford/Folkestone. Friendly atmosphere on a working smallholding set in unspoilt countryside. Modern centrally heated accommodation built for traditional comforts. Non-smoking throughout. One double, one twin, two single rooms. Log burning stove in TV lounge. Full English breakfast. Evening meals by arrangement. Country pub nearby. Children love the old-fashioned farmyard, the free range chickens and friendly sheep and cattle. Our paddocks, ponds, stream and small wood invite relaxation. Nearby, our private secluded woodland and downland allow quiet visitors to observe bird life, rabbits, foxes, badgers and occasionally deer. To round off your stay you could even book a short sightseeing or fishing trip on our Folkestone fishing boat! Easy access to Channel Tunnel and Ferry Ports. Bed and Breakfast £17.50 per person.

**FOLKESTONE/DOVER. Dianne & Tony Hughes, Bramble Hill Cottage, Meggetts Lane, West Hougham, Near Dover CT15 7BS (01303 253180).** At Bramble Hill Cottage, a friendly welcome is assured. Cottage bedrooms with en suite and coffee/tea making facilities. Full English breakfast served in delightful cottage-beamed dining room with TV. Local pubs and restaurants close by. Set in beautiful gardens with stables and paddocks with views across to Dover Castle. Surrounded by country walks and bridle-ways. City of Canterbury is 20 minutes' drive away and only two minutes to cliff tops with views to France. The ferry ports of Dover and Folkestone and the Channel Tunnel terminal are only 12 minutes' drive away. Bed and Breakfast from £17 per person per night. No smoking.

---

Terms quoted in this publication may be subject to increase if rises in costs necessitate

# Kent 209

**See also Colour Display Advertisement** HAWKHURST. **Susan Woodard, Southgate, Little Fowlers, Rye Road, Hawkhurst, Near Cranbrook TN18 5DA (Tel & Fax: 01580 752526).** Stay in our Listed 300-year-old former Dower House on the Kent/Sussex borders. Historic Hawkhurst, once famous for smuggling, is near Sissinghurst, Rye, Bodiam, Batemans, Scotney, Tunbridge Wells, Battle, Hever and coast. Folkestone approximately half-an-hour's drive. All en suite bedrooms – four-poster, double/twin/triple furnished with antiques and all have magnificent views, TV, tea/coffee facilities. Relax in our one-acre gardens. Choice of breakfast in our flower-filled original Victorian conservatory. Guests' sitting room. Excellent village restaurant and inn a few minutes' walk. Helpful and friendly family. Non-smoking. Bed and Breakfast from £25–£30 (based on two sharing). **AA** ◆◆◆◆.
e-mail: Susan.Woodard@southgate.uk.net
website: www.southgate.uk.net/

HEADCORN. **Mrs Dorothy Burbridge, Waterkant Guest House, Moat Road, Headcorn, Ashford TN27 9NT (01622 890154).** Waterkant is a small guest house situated in the tranquil setting of olde worlde charm of Wealdon Village. A warm and friendly welcome is assured and the relaxed and informal atmosphere is complemented by fine cuisine, excellent service and comfortable surroundings. Bedrooms have private or en suite bathrooms, four-poster beds, tea/coffee making facilities, colour TV and are centrally heated and double glazed. Lounge with colour TV. The beautifully landscaped secluded garden bounded by a stream provides a large pond, summerhouse for visitors' use and ample parking. Fast trains to London and a wealth of historic places to visit nearby. Open all year. Visitors return year after year. Bed and Breakfast from £18, with reduced rates for children, Senior Citizens, mid-week and winter season bookings. Participants in ETC's Quality Assurance schemes.

MAIDSTONE. **Mrs Clifford, Langley Oast, Langley Park, Langley, Maidstone ME17 3NQ (01622 863523).** Langley Oast was built in 1873 as part of Langley Park Farm, which was owned at that time by "Fremlins", the local brewery. The farm was a working farm until 1985 when the farm buildings were sold for conversion to homes. Langley Park, as it is now known, forms a secluded hamlet of about twelve homes, a quarter of a mile from the main road, the A274, about two miles from the centre of Maidstone and two miles from Leeds Castle. The Oast is set in the heart of Kentish countryside with fields as far as the eye can see, with a lake at the bottom of the nearest field. Maidstone is the county town of Kent and an ideal touring base for London or to visit the many tourist attractions in Kent. Or as a 'Stop Over' to or from the Continent, we are only 35 minutes from Folkestone and Dover. The Oast has been luxuriously converted by its present owners, Peter and Margaret Clifford. Bedrooms are either in the large Roundel rooms (24 ft across), one with jacuzzi en suite, or in twin rooms with Half Tester Canopies. Peter and Margaret look forward to welcoming you and will do everything in their power to ensure that your stay will be a happy and enjoyable one. Single room from £25. **AA** ◆◆◆◆, *MEMBER SOUTH EAST ENGLAND TOURIST BOARD.*

MAIDSTONE. **Mrs Diane Leat, Bramley Knowle Farm, Eastwood Road, Ulcombe, Maidstone ME17 1ET (01622 858878; Fax: 01622 851121).** A warm welcome awaits you at our modern farmhouse built in the style of a Kentish Barn. Set in 45 acres of peaceful Kentish countryside, yet only ten minutes drive from M20 Junction 8. Evening Meals within walking distance. Ideal location for visiting Leeds Castle, Sissinghurst Gardens, Canterbury and Rye. Three-quarters of an hour's drive from Channel Ports. London one hour by train. Accommodation consists of one double en suite, one double and one single sharing guests-only bathroom. TV and tea/coffee making facilities in all bedrooms. Dining/sitting room with TV and video. Non smoking. Children over three welcome. Bed and Breakfast from £20.00 per person. **ETC** ◆◆◆.

**MAIDSTONE. Mrs Jane Bence, Roydon Hall, Seven Mile Lane, East Peckham TN12 5NH (01622 812121; Fax: 01622 813959).** Roydon Hall is a 16th Century Tudor Manor set in 11 acres of woodland, terraces and gardens, and graced by magnificent views of the Weald of Kent. Nearby are landmarks of historical interest and walkers are well placed for the Greensands Way, a long distance footpath. Perfect for exploring the beautiful houses and gardens of Kent and Sussex and the historic towns of Tunbridge Wells, Canterbury, and hastings. Prices range from £21-£46 per night for a single, £33-£55 for a twin/double with Continental breakfast. Organic vegetarian evening meals available. One hour's drive from Central London and Ports of Dover and Folkestone and 50 minutes by rail from Charing Cross. Very peaceful!

**MARGATE. Malvern Hotel, 29 Eastern Esplanade, Cliftonville, Margate CT9 2HL (Tel & Fax: 01843 290192).** NON-SMOKING dining room. Open all year. Small seafront private hotel. Unrestricted parking opposite. Bedrooms have television and tea/coffee making facilities, most en suite. Bed and Breakfast (choice of menu). Double/Twin bedroom £40-£45 per night; Family and Single room price on request. Ideally situated within easy reach of Dover, Folkestone (Channel Tunnel) and Canterbury. Short Breaks and overnight stops (mention *B&B Stops* when booking). Switch, Visa, Mastercard telephone bookings accepted. Most credit cards (not Amex/Diners). NO VAT. **e-mail: malvern-accom@supanet.com**

**NEW ROMNEY. Warren Lodge Motel, Dymchurch Road, New Romney TN28 8UE (01797 362138).** Set in the grounds of the Cafe Bistro, the Warren Lodge Motel was built to provide comfortable and flexible accommodation offering high standards and a friendly atmosphere. Situated in the heart of the historic Romney Marsh, we are ideally placed to explored the Garden of England or the many local places of interest. The Channel Tunnel is the gateway to Europe and is only 20 minutes away; we are a good base for a day trip or to start your European holiday. All our rooms are spacious and have en suite facilities; each is fully heated and tastefully decorated, and all rooms are at ground level and open to the garden area. Room service available and overnight laundry service. Ample free parking.

**PLUCKLEY. Mrs Veronica Johnson, Yew Tree Cottage, Pluckley, Ashford TN27 0QT (01233 8405470).** Fifteenth century Kentish Hall House with a wealth of beams hiding within a Georgian exterior in attractive village location overlooking the Weald of Kent. Excellent for exploring the varied scenery and many places of interest in the 'Garden of England'. Within easy reach of Channel Tunnel, Port of Dover and coast. Many footpaths, including Greensand Way. Several good pubs locally serving a range of excellent food. Two spacious double/family rooms with private bathroom or shower room. Tea and coffee making facilities. Off-road parking. Sorry, no smoking or pets. Bed and Breakfast from £18.50. Open 1st April to 2nd October.

**SITTINGBOURNE/LYNSTED. David Bage, Forge Cottage, Lynsted, Sittingbourne ME9 0RH (01795 521273; ).** 17th century property in the pretty village of Lynsted on the North Downs, an ideal touring centre and within easy reach of the Isle of Thanet, seaside towns and the Weald of Kent. Many exposed timbers throughout and there is an inglenook fireplace in the visitors' TV lounge. Accommodation comprises one twin-bedded room, one double and one family room and two bathrooms. For the comfort of our guests and the safety of the building a strict no smoking rule applies. Children over 10 years and pets welcome. Good English breakfast; other breakfasts, beverages, evening sandwiches and packed lunches available. Bed and Breakfast from £16.
**website: www.s-h-systems.co.uk/hotels/forge.html**

**TENTERDEN/BIDDENDEN. Mrs Susan Twort, Heron Cottage, Biddenden, Ashford TN27 8HH (01580 291358).** Peacefully situated in own grounds of six acres amidst acres of arable farmland, boasting many wild animals and birds, a stream and pond for coarse fishing. Within easy reach of Leeds Castle and many National Trust Properties including Sissinghurst Castle. You can choose between three tastefully furnished rooms with en suite and TV, or two rooms with separate bathroom. All rooms are centrally heated and have tea/coffee making facilities. There is a residents' lounge with log fire. Evening meals by arrangement. Bed and Breakfast from £17.50 to £25 per person per night.

**TONBRIDGE near. Mrs L. Tubbs, Dunsmore, Hadlow Park, Hadlow, Near Tonbridge TN11 0HX (01732 850611).** Hadlow is a small village situated on the A26 between Tonbridge and Maidstone. The M25, M26 and M20 are just a few miles away, making Hadlow a convenient `stop-over' point for Continental trips or a base for visiting the many places of interest that abound in Kent. The accommodation has its own entrance to a large ground floor twin bedded/sittingroom, shower and WC. Additional children's beds available. Colour TV and tea-making facilities. Doors lead onto own patio with views of Downs. Easy parking. No smoking. Bed and Breakfast from £20 per person per night. Very peaceful.

**TUNBRIDGE WELLS. Mrs Field, Cheviots, Cousley Wood, Wadhurst TN5 6HD (Tel & Fax: 01892 782952).** Cheviots is a comfortable modern guesthouse in the beautiful Weald. A completely non-smoking establishment. Double, twin and single rooms available (some en suite). All have colour TV and tea/coffee facilities. Excellent home cooking with full English breakfast and optional evening meals. Separate guests' lounge without television, but with an open fire on chilly evenings. Extensive two acre garden. Games room with full sized snooker table and table tennis. Close to Hever and Leeds Castles and many National Trust properties incuding Sissinghurst and Chartwell. London is conveniently reached by a one hour train journey and we are one hour's drive from Gatwick and Dover. Off road parking available. Children welcome. Bed and Breakfast from £20 to £30 per night, including bedtime drink. Evening meal from £12 to £15.

**WINGHAM. The Dog Inn, Canterbury Road, Wingham CT3 1AB (01227 720339).** Colin and Vivienne McIntyre welcome you to their 13th century village inn situated in the old picturesque village of Wingham, five miles east of historic Canterbury on the A257. Sit and enjoy the fine ales, lagers and wines in our cosy, beamed pub with crackling log fire in winter or in our beer garden in summer. We serve food seven days a week in our restaurant, comprising separate smoking and non-smoking areas. Six en suite letting rooms provide quaint accommodation with TV and tea/coffee making facilities. Full English breakfast is served in our conservatory. We look forward to seeing you.

---

# FREE or REDUCED RATE entry to Holiday Visits and Attractions — see our READERS' OFFER VOUCHERS on pages 43-60

# LANCASHIRE

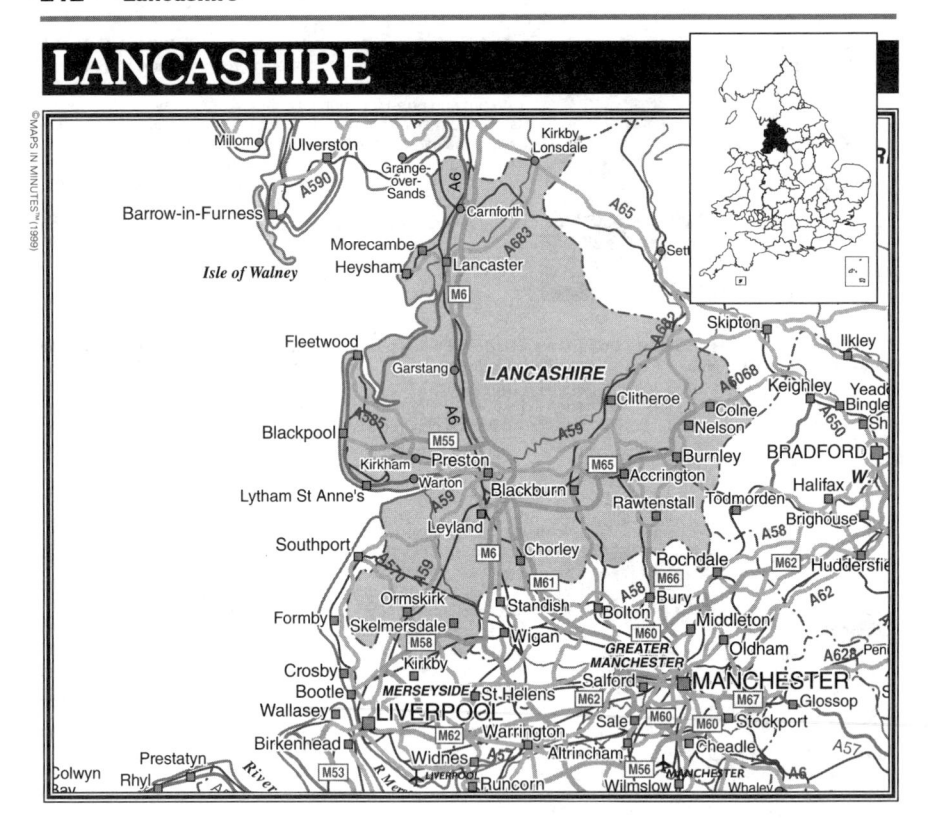

**BLACKBURN near. The Brown Leaves Country Hotel, Longsight Road, Copster Green, Near Blackburn BB1 9EU (01254 249523; Fax: 01254 245240).** Conveniently situated on the A59 about halfway between Preston and Clitheroe, five miles from Junction 31 on the M6 in the beautiful Ribble Valley. All rooms ground floor, have en suite facilities, TV, tea-making and hairdryer. Guests lounge and bar lounge. Car parking facilities. Pets by arrangement. Member of Les Routiers, Winner of 1998 Casserole Award and 1998 Housekeeping Award. All credit cards welcome.

**BLACKPOOL. Elsie and Ron Platt, Sunnyside and Holmesdale Guest House, 25-27 High Street, North Shore, Blackpool FY1 2BN (01253 623781).** Two minutes from North Station, five minutes from Promenade, all shows and amenities. Colour TV lounge. Full central heating. No smoking. Late keys. Children welcome; high chairs and cots available. Reductions for children sharing. Senior Citizens' reductions May and June, always welcome. Special diets catered for, good food and warm friendly atmosphere awaits you. Bed and Breakfast from £18; extra for optional Evening Meal. Morning tea available. Overnight guests welcome. Small parties catered for.

## Mark and Claire Smith,
### 50 Dean Street, Blackpool FY4 1BP
### Tel: 01253 349195 Fax: 01253 344330

An historic detached house surrounded by its own award winning gardens in the heart of Blackpool; one minute from the sea and The Pleasure Beach. Free car parking. All bedrooms are non-smoking and fully en suite with all usual facilities and more! Four-poster beds available. Open all year for Bed and Breakfast from £25. Licensed restaurant. Private outside jacuzzi in Japanese style garden leading from large conservatory where smoking is permitted.

*Blackpool Tourism Award 1998/99*
*NWTB B&B of the Year 1998/9*
*RAC Small Hotel of the Year 1998/9*

See also Colour Display Advertisement

*The Award-winning*
## Old Coach House

ETC ♦♦♦♦♦ *Silver Award*

---

**BLACKPOOL. Proprietress: Mrs Yvonne Anne Duckworth, "Kelvin Private Hotel", 98 Reads Avenue, Blackpool FY1 4JJ (01253 620293).** Welcome to our comfortable small hotel. Centrally situated between sea and Stanley Park, Lake District, Scotland, North Wales and Yorkshire. TV lounge; plenty of good food. Bed and English Breakfast; Evening Dinner optional; light snacks. Tea/coffee making facilities all bedrooms. Ground floor bedroom. Overnight, Short Break and period stays welcome. Open most of the year. Car park. Bed and Breakfast from £14 per person according to season. Reduced rates for children and Senior Citizens. Weekly rates competitive. Now in our 13th year! SAE for brochure.

---

**BLACKPOOL. Brabyns Hotel, Shaftesbury Avenue, Blackpool FY2 9QQ (01253 354263).** The Brabyns Hotel, is a well maintained private hotel. Situated just off Queens Promenade, close to the cliffs in the quiet North Shore area of Blackpool, but still conveniently placed for visiting the famous Blackpool attractions i.e. Tower, Pleasure Beach, live shows, night clubs and the famous Blackpool Illuminations. Within a 10 mile radius of the hotel is a choice of nine golf courses, including the renowned Royal Lytham St. Annes. An ideal base for touring the rural Fylde coast, English Lakes and Yorkshire Dales. Comfortable, friendly hotel with 25 tastefully decorated bedrooms all with en suite facilities, direct-dial telephones, hairdryers, tea/coffee making facilities, colour TV, Sky TV. Licensed. Free car parking and open all year. **ETC/AA/RAC ★★**

---

**BLACKPOOL (NORTH SHORE). Barbara and Steve Hornby, The Birchley Hotel, 64 Holmfield Road, Blackpool FY2 9RT (01253 354174).** The Birchley is situated in a pleasant, select North Shore area adjacent to Queens Promenade. Open most of the year and totally non-smoking. Seven bedrooms, all with shower, en suite facilities, tea and coffee tray, colour TV and central heating, lovely lounge with separate tables and a small licensed bar for residents' use. Full English breakfast with optional evening dinner offering choice of menu, excellent food and generous portions. Bed and Breakfast from £17 to £20 per person per night. Full weeks (seven nights) £110 per person. Bed, Breakfast and Evening Dinner from £24 to £26 per person per night. Single nights £1.50 supplement per person. Full weeks (seven nights) £150 per person.

---

*When making enquiries or bookings, a stamped addressed envelope is always appreciated*

**214    Lancashire**

**See also Colour Display Advertisement**

**BLACKPOOL. Castlemere Hotel, 13 Shaftesbury Avenue, North Shore, Blackpool FY2 9QQ (01253 352430; Fax: 01253 350116).** The Castlemere is a licensed family-run hotel. The resident proprietors Dave and Sue Hayward have been running the Castlemere for the past 11 years and have established an excellent clientele. The hotel is situated in the very pleasant North Shore area of Blackpool, adjacent to the delightful Queens Promenade with its lovely views across the Irish Sea. The busy town centre, bus and train stations are convenient and a range of entertainment opportunities for all ages and tastes are within an easy walk or short tram ride, including a casino and golf course. Blackpool is ideally situated for visiting the dales, Lake District, Bronte Country and the Fylde Coast. Easy accesses to M55. All rooms are en suite with central heating, colour TV, alarm clock radio, hairdryer and tea/coffee making facilities. Ironing facilities are also available. The Castlemere has a cosy bar, where evening snacks are available. Evening dinner is optional. Open all year. Car park. All major credit cards accepted. Terms from £22 per person Bed and Breakfast  **AA ♦♦♦** *FHG DIPLOMA WINNER.*
e-mail: bookings@hotelcastlemere.co.uk
website: www.hotelcastlemere.co.uk

**CARNFORTH. Mrs Melanie Smith, Capernwray House, Capernwray, Carnforth LA6 1AE (Tel & Fax: 01524 732363).** Situated in the Lower Lunesdale Valley on the North Lancashire and Cumbria borders (M6 Junction 35, off B6254) where the peace and solitude of the countryside are yours to enjoy. The house is beautifully furnished to ensure a delightful and comfortable stay for the non-smoking guest. Centrally heated en suite bedrooms with tea/coffee facilities, TV, shoe cleaning, clock radio and hair dryer. Panoramic views can be enjoyed over the Cumbrian or Pennine Hills. Superb location in eighteen acres of rolling countryside, ideal for the coast, Lakes, Dales, Lancaster bird reserves, historic houses, steam railways or a break en-route London-Scotland. Spacious lounge. Ample parking. Sorry, no pets. Children welcome. Bed and Breakfast from £21 single, £45 double en suite and £46 twin en suite; Dinner £10. Open all year. Brochure available. Also small select touring caravan park. All major credit cards accepted. **ETC ♦♦♦♦** *SILVER AWARD, FHG DIPLOMA WINNER.* 
e-mail: thesmiths@capernwrayhouse.com
website: www.capernwrayhouse.com

**CHORLEY. Mrs Val Hilton, Jepsons Farm, Moor Road, Anglezarke, Chorley PR6 9DQ (01257 481691).** Jepsons Farm, formerly a 17th century inn, is a stone built farmhouse with oak beams and wood burning stoves and is situated in Anglezarke, next to Rivington in the West Pennine Moors. Non-working farm apart from horses. It boasts excellent views and is surrounded by beautiful countryside for all outdoor activities including riding, walking, climbing, abseiling, cycling and fishing or simply relaxing. Good food assured and bedrooms have colour TV and tea/coffee trays; en suite facilities. Accommodation for horses in spacious looseboxes; bridleways in abundance for all riding requirements. Places of interest include Wigan Pier, Martin Mere, Astley Hall, Camelot and coastal resorts of Blackpool and Southport. Bed and Breakfast from £20; Evening Meal from £7.50. Reductions for children. Special rates for longer stays.

**CLITHEROE near. Mrs Marje Adderley, Rose Cottage, Longsight Road (A59), Clayton-le-Dale, Ribble Valley BB1 9EX (01254 813223; Fax: 01254 813831).** A warm welcome awaits at our picturesque cottage situated at the gateway to the Ribble Valley, five miles from M6 and M65 on A59. Excellent night-stop travelling to and from Scotland, easy access to Yorkshire Dales, Lake District and Blackpool. Full English breakfast included in price; Single occupancy from £23. Double £19 per person. Three night break to include Sunday night shared occupancy £52 per person, two-night weekend breaks £35 per person shared occupancy. Comfortable well equipped rooms offering tea/coffee, TV and Sky, radio alarm, heated towel rail, hair dryer, shoe cleaning, smoke detectors; all have private facilities. Phone for our brochure. Nearby Ribbleway, cycling, walking, fishing. Trace your family at Records Office, Preston. Major credit cards accepted.
e-mail: bbrose.cott@talk21.co.uk 
website: www.SmoothHound.co.uk/hotels/rosecott.html

**Lancashire** 215

**CLITHEROE near. Mr Frank Hargreaves, Mitton Green Barn, Church Lane, Great Mitton BB7 9PJ (01254 826673).** Mitton Green Barn offers luxury accommodation with panoramic views over open countryside. Double and twin en suite. Double with separate bathroom. Tea and coffee making facilities. TV lounge. Non smoking. Only 10 minutes' drive from the historic town of Clitheroe and 20 minutes from Blackburn, Burnley and other local towns. Within easy reach of the Yorkshire Dales and the Lake District. Bed and Breakfast from £22 per person including full cooked English Breakfast. Open throughout except Christmas and New Year. 'A warm and friendly welcome awaits you.'

**LANCASTER. Roy and Helen Domville, Three Gables, Chapel Lane, Galgate, Lancaster LA2 0PN (01524 752222).** A large detached bungalow, three miles south of Lancaster and 400 yards from Lancaster University. Access from M6 Junction 33 and A6 in Galgate village. Two double bedrooms each with shower, toilet, colour TV and tea/coffee making facilities. One bedroom also has a private TV lounge. Open all year with full central heating. A cot and high chair are available. Spacious parking. A good location for visiting Blackpool, Morecambe, the Lake District and Yorkshire Dales. You will be sure of a friendly welcome and a homely atmosphere. Sorry, no pets. Non-smokers only please. Bed and Breakfast £15 per person.

**LYTHAM-ST-ANNES. Mr Anthony Duggan, New England Inn, 314 Clifton Drive North, St Annes-on-Sea FY8 2DB (Tel & Fax: 01253 722355).** The New England Inn in Lytham-St-Annes is a family-run hotel with a friendly atmosphere in a central position for easy access and just a few minutes' stroll to the promenade, shops, entertainment and casino. With Royal Lytham Golf Course close by we offer luxuriously spacious accommodation with all the facilities you would expect of a first class hotel. It is ideal for couples and families alike. We are open all year round. Parking available. Ten large en suite bedrooms, all with queen sized beds; colour TV; coffee/tea making facilities; trouser press; telephone and hair dryer. Prices from £25 per person; Evening Meal from £6.95. **AA ★★** 67%

**LYTHAM ST. ANNES. Harcourt Hotel, 21 Richmond Road, St. Annes on Sea, Lytham St. Annes FY8 1PE (01253 722299).** Small 10 bedroomed private Hotel. Perfectly situated adjacent to town centre and 200 yards from sandy beach and Promenade. Open all year with central heating. One mile from Blackpool. Tea making facilities in all rooms. Colour TV in some bedrooms. En suite rooms available. Twin bedded and double rooms, family rooms. Free car park. Licensed. Friendly personal service from **Sue and Andy Royle**. Bed and Breakfast from £17; en suite from £19. Long and short stays available. Special reductions for Senior Citizens on weekly terms. Child reductions for up to 14 year olds, under five years FREE.

**MANCHESTER. Margaret and Bernard Satterthwaite, The Albany Hotel, 21 Albany Road, Chorlton-cum-Hardy, Manchester M21 0AY (0161-881 6774; Fax: 0161-862 9405).** The Albany Hotel, having undergone a major refurbishment, offers luxurious and elegant period accommodation with all the comforts of a modern de luxe hotel, plus the personal attention of the owners. Facilities include Erica's restuarant, licensed bar, games room and full conference facilities. A choice of single (from £39.50 per room), double (from £59.50 per room) or family rooms, all with shower or en suite bathroom, direct-dial telephone, colour TV, hairdryer, radio and tea/coffee. Conveniently located being only 10 minutes from the City and Airport, five minutes from Manchester United, L.C.C.C., Salford Quays, Trafford Park, Trafford shopping centre and Universities. Directions - just off the (A5145) Wilbraham Road, approximately one mile from Metrolink, junction 7 M60 from M61, M6 north and M62 east and west. Two miles M56 from M6 south. Brochure and tariff on request. **ETC/AA/RAC ★★**. *LES ROUTIERS*

## Lancashire

**MORECAMBE. Mrs R. Holdsworth, Broadwater Hotel, 356 Marine Road, East Promenade, Morecambe LA4 5AQ (01524 411333).** The Broadwater is a small friendly hotel, situated on the select East Promenade with glorious views of Morecambe Bay and Lakeland Mountains. Only five minutes walk from the town centre, shops and amusements. We offer every comfort and the very best of foods varied and plentiful with choice of menu. All rooms en suite with heating, colour TV and tea making facilities. A perfect base for touring, the Broadwater is only 45 minutes' drive away from Blackpool, Yorkshire Dales and Lake District, and 10 minutes from the historic city of Lancaster. Open all year. Dinner available. Bed and Breakfast from £17.

**PILLING. Beryl and Peter Richardson, Bell Farm, Bradshaw Lane, Scronkey, Pilling, Preston PR3 6SN (01253 790324).** Beryl and Peter welcome you to their 18th century farmhouse situated in the quiet village of Pilling, which lies between the Ribble and Lune Estuaries. The area has many public footpaths and is ideal for cycling. From the farm there is easy access to Blackpool, Lancaster, the Forest of Bowland and the Lake District. Accommodation consists of one family room, one double and one twin; all rooms en suite. Tea and coffee making facilities. Lounge and dining room. All centrally heated. Children and pets welcome. Full English Breakfast is served. Open all year, except Christmas and New Year. Bed and Breakfast from £20.00.

**ROCHDALE/BURY. Mrs Jane Neave, Leaches Farm, Ashworth Valley, Bamford, Rochdale OL11 5UN (01706 641116/7 or 224307).** Hill farm in the "Forgotten Valley", with magnificent views of the Roch, Irwell and Mersey river valleys; West Yorkshire, Lancashire and Derbyshire hills, Cheshire Plain, Jodrell Bank Telescope, Welsh mountains. At night there are the panoramic twinkling lights of Greater Manchester. Accommodation features oak beams, 18-inch walls, log fires and central heating. Unique rural wildlife in the heart of industrial East Lancashire. Three miles from M62 and M66, 30 miles from Manchester Airport. Ideal for holiday or business visitors. Bed and Breakfast from £22 single, £40 double.

**SOUTHPORT. Rosedale Hotel, 11 Talbot Street, Southport PR8 1HP (Freephone: 0800 0738 133; Fax: 01704 530604).** One of Southport's most centrally situated hotels, ideally placed for the beach, parks, entertainment, golf courses and the famous Lord Street. The perfect location whether you are on holiday or on business. Resident proprietors Joan and Alan Beer make every effort to ensure that all their guests have a happy and comfortable stay. Full central heating and private parking. All rooms have tea/coffee making facilities and colour TV with satellite link. Residents' bar and separate TV lounge. A lovely secluded rear garden is available for guests' enjoyment. Children welcome. Sorry no pets. Bed and Breakfast from £24. **ETC** ◆◆◆

**SOUTHPORT. The Sidbrook Private Hotel, 14 Talbot Street, Southport PR8 1HP (01704 530608).** Glyn and Penny, resident proprietors, welcome you to The Sidbrook, situated in the town centre yet in a quiet area. Close to the Tourist Information Centre and railway station with many of the country's top golf courses in the area. All our bedrooms are en suite and have remote control colour TV, clock radio, hairdryer, hospitality tray and toiletries. For that special occasion there is a four-poster room. Our attractive dining room has separate tables and cosy atmosphere - enjoy your three-course breakfast. Comfortable lounge/bar. With our secluded garden, free parking and access at all times, your stay can be as active or as relaxed as you want it to be. **ETC/AA** ◆◆◆
e-mail: sidbrookhotel@tesco.net

#  LEICESTERSHIRE including Rutland

**BELTON-IN-RUTLAND, Near Uppingham. The Old Rectory, Belton-in-Rutland, Oakham LE15 9LE (01572 717279; Fax: 01572 717343).** Victorian country house and guest annexe in charming village overlooking Eyebrook valley and rolling Rutland countryside. Comfortable and varied selection of rooms, mostly en suite, with direct outside access. Prices from £16 to £30 per person per night including breakfast. Small farm environment (horses and sheep) with excellent farmhouse breakfast. Public house 100 yards. Lots to see and do: Rutland Water, castles, stately homes, country parks, forestry and Barnsdale Gardens. Non-smoking. Self catering also available. **RAC ◆◆◆**
e-mail: bb@stablemate.demon.co.uk

**CALDECOTT near Corby. Peter and Penny Walton, The Old Plough, 41 Main Street, Caldecott, Near Corby, Rutland LE16 8RS (Tel & Fax: 01536 772031).** A stone built former Coaching Inn/Ale House of great charm and character and still named "The Old Plough". Just one mile from Rockingham Castle. Two good food pubs within 200 yards. All our rooms have recently been created with en suite bathrooms, individual entrances leading from the gardens and secure parking. Colour TV, tea/coffee making facilities, refrigerator. Close to Eyebrook Reservoir, Rutland Water, Kirby Hall and Deene Park. Single room £23, Double room £42. New for 2001 - self-catering apartments in the Coach House for longer breaks. A warm welcome is assured, just phone for details.

**LOUGHBOROUGH. Ms R.C. Howard, De Montfort Hotel, 88 Leicester Road, Loughborough LE11 2AQ (01509 216061; Fax: 01509 233667).** A charming Victorian building decorated in style. Nine bedrooms, all with tea/coffee making facilities and colour TV. Conveniently situated for Steam Trust, Bell Foundry, University and Airport and five minutes' walk from the town centre. We have a bar and TV lounge with satellite channels. Evening meals available. Single from £28; twin from £38; double from £40; family room from £50. Three-night weekend rates. All major credit cards accepted. A warm welcome guaranteed. Please phone for brochure. **ETC/AA/RAC ◆◆◆**

**LOUGHBOROUGH. Keith and Emily Indge, The Highbury Guest House, 146 Leicester Road, Loughborough LE11 2AQ (01509 230545; Fax: 01509 233086).** The Highbury was built in 1922. A conversion was made during the last eight years from a private home to its present use. The house is set back from the road, has double glazing and is surrounded by a well-developed and cared for private garden which is frequently used in warm weather for sun bathing. The entrance hall is spacious. It is lightened by a leaded stained glass window at the top of the staircase. Recently an extension has been added to the diningroom space. This leads into the conservatory type sittingroom. Watch satellite TV. A large secluded car park is situated at the back of the house. Most bedrooms are fully en suite. All rooms offer remote-control TV, tea/coffee making facilities and wash-hand basin. Located half-a-mile from Loughborough town centre.

---

Terms quoted in this publication may be subject to increase if rises in costs necessitate

# Leicestershire

**LOUGHBOROUGH. L. & K. Charwat, Charnwood Lodge, 136 Leicester Road, Loughborough LE11 2AQ (01509 211120; Fax 01509 211121).** Charnwood Lodge is a quality Bed and Breakfast which is tastefully decorated throughout. It has superior en suite rooms, colour TV/satellite, tea/coffee facilities, its own car park, quiet surroundings and private gardens with conservatory. We have single, twin/double, family and four-poster bedrooms. Available on request (free of charge) cot, high chair, ironing board and hair dryer. We are close to all local amenities within the Charnwood area. East Midlands airport is eight miles, Derby 18 miles, Donington Park nine miles, Nottingham 15 miles, Leicester 12 miles. We hope you enjoy your stay with us, and will recommend us to your friends. Rates from £30 to £57 per night. Now licensed. We accept Visa, Access, Mastercard and Eurocard.
**website: www.charnwoodlodge.com**

**MEDBOURNE. Mrs J.A. Wainwright, Homestead House, 5 Ashley Road, Medbourne, Market Harborough LE16 8DL (01858 565724; Fax: 01858 565324).** Open all year for Bed and Breakfast, Homestead House is situated in an elevated position overlooking the Welland Valley on the outskirts of Medbourne, a picturesque village dating back to Roman times, with a meandering brook running through the centre. Surrounded by open countryside, the village has two public houses, post office/shop, etc. Local places of interest include Foxton Locks on Grand Union Canal, Rockingham Castle, Rutland Water (sailing, fishing, windsurfing), Eyebrook Reservoir (fishing, bird watching), Naseby Battlefield, various houses and halls, gliding, riding, nature trails and many delightful picnic spots. Accommodation comprises three twin-bedded rooms, all en-suite and having TVs, telephones and tea/coffee making facilities; sittingroom, diningroom. Children welcome. Central heating. Car not essential, although there is parking for four cars. Bed and Breakfast from £19.75 to £25.00. Evening Meal available. Reductions for children. **ETC** ◆◆◆◆

**MELTON MOWBRAY Mrs Linda Lomas, Shoby Lodge Farm, Shoby, Melton Mowbray LE14 3PF (01664 812156).** Set in attractive gardens, Shoby Lodge is a spacious, comfortable, tastefully furnished farmhouse. Enjoy an Aga-cooked breakfast and beautiful views of the surrounding countryside. Accommodation comprises two double en suite rooms and one double room with private bathroom. All rooms have tea and coffee making facilities and TV. Close to the market town of Melton Mowbray and ideally situated for Leicester and Nottingham. Coarse fishing available on the farm. Terms from £18 per person. **ETC** ◆◆◆◆

**MELTON MOWBRAY. Mr R. S. Whittard, Elms Farm, Long Clawson, Melton Mowbray LE14 4NG (01664 822395; Fax: 01664 823399).** Welcome to our 18th century farmhouse in the beautiful vale of Belvoir! Situated between M1 and A1, six miles north of Melton Mowbray, 25 minutes drive from Leicester, Nottingham, Grantham, and Loughborough. Local attractions include Belvoir, Stamford, Burghley House and Belton House. Enjoy delicious home cooking and attractive, comfortable accommodation with full central heating. One double/family room and one single room; separate diningroom and lounge with colour TV. Also our self-contained cottage is now available for Bed and Breakfast or weekly self-catering. Bed and breakfast from £18 per adult; cottage Bed and Breakfast from £42 per couple; Dinner by arrangement from £9. Open all year except Christmas. No smoking in the house please.
**e-mail: elmsfarm@whittard.net**

---

*Please mention Bed & Breakfast Stops when writing to enquire about accommodation*

**MELTON MOWBRAY (four miles). Mrs Brenda Bailey, Church Cottage, Main Street, Holwell, Melton Mowbray LE14 4SZ (01664 444255).** Church Cottage, an 18th century Listed building, is situated next to Holwell's 13th century church in the heart of the Leicestershire countryside. This is an excellent location for walkers and lovers of the rural scene. The high standard accommodation offers an en suite double room and one twin bedroom, plus own colour TV, radio and tea-making facilities. Guests also have private use of lounge and summerhouse. Full central heating. Children welcome. Bed and Breakfast from £20 per person. Non-smoking.

# LINCOLNSHIRE

**BENNIWORTH. Kay Olivant, Skirbeck Farm, Panton Road, Benniworth LN3 6JN (01507 313682; Fax: 01507 313692).** Enjoy a stay on a working farm whilst visiting the beautiful Lincolnshire Wolds. The peaceful location is surrounded by good walking country including the Viking Way. It is 16 miles east of the cathedral City of Lincoln and only a few miles from the interesting market towns of Louth, Norcastle and Market Rasen. The east coast and South Yorkshire (via the Humber Bridge), all within easy touring distance. The farm has its own coarse and fly fishing lakes and over four miles of natural lakes. Local attractions include Benniworth Springs off-road driving track, Hemswell antiques, Market Rasen Races and Cadwell racing circuit. The farmhouse is comfortably furnished, has central heating and log fires. All bedrooms have colour TV, Teasmaid, and own bathroom. Sun lounge overlooking secluded garden. Children welcome. Non-smokers please. Self-catering cottages also available.

*See also Colour Display Advertisement*

**CLEETHORPES. Mr D. Turner, Clee House, 31/33 Clee Road, Cleethorpes DN35 8AD (Tel & Fax: 01472 200850).** Clee House is a magnificent Edwardian property that stands in its own grounds just a few minutes' walk from the sea front and many other attractions of Cleethorpes. We have 10 bedrooms, mostly en suite with tea/coffee making facilities, one with private bathroom; direct dial telephones and satellite TV. Some rooms have wheelchair access. Disabled facilities available. On site parking. All major credit cards accepted. Open all year round. **ETC/AA ♦♦♦♦**
e-mail: cleehouse@pobox.com
website: www.cleehouse.com

# FHG PUBLICATIONS

**FHG** publish a large range of well-known accommodation guides. We will be happy to send you details or you can use the order form at the back of this book.

## Lincolnshire

**GRANTHAM. Mrs Helen Porter, Stonepit Farmhouse, Swinstead Road, Corby Glen, Grantham NG33 4NU (Tel & Fax: 01476 550614).** A picturesque stone house in a quiet corner, on the edge of the village of Corby Glen. Four miles from the A1 trunk road, between Grantham and Stamford. Three minutes' walk to pub/restaurant. Large courtyard and lovely garden with views over rolling countryside. Separate guest wing with TV lounge/breakfast room. Ground floor rooms are one single and one twin-bedded room each with washbasin, shared bathroom and one first floor double en suite bedroom, radio/alarm, hair dryer. Central heating. Beverages available in the lounge. Full English Breakfast. Ample parking. Non-smoking. Price from £20 per person per night. **ETC** ◆◆◆

**HOLBEACH. Mrs M Biggadike, Cackle Hill House, Cackle Hill Lane, Holbeach PE12 8BS (01406 426721; Fax: 01406 424659).** A warm and friendly welcome awaits you at our comfortable home set in a rural position. We are ideally situated for many attractions in Lincolnshire, Norfolk and Cambridgeshire. Two twin and one double rooms are available, all of which are tastefully furnished, have either en suite or private facilities and hospitality trays. There is an attractive guests' lounge with colour TV. Bed and Breakfast from £20. **RAC** ◆◆◆ *SPARKLING DIAMOND AWARD.*

**HORNCASTLE. Mrs C.E. Harrison, Baumber Park, Baumber, Near Horncastle LN9 5NE (01507 578235; Fax: 01507 578417).** Spacious elegant farmhouse of character in quiet parkland setting on a mixed farm. Large gardens, wildlife pond and grass tennis court. Fine bedrooms with lovely views, period furniture and log fires. Central in the county and close to the Lincolnshire Wolds, this rolling countryside is little known and quite unspoilt. Bridleways and lanes ideal for walking, cycling or riding: stabling for horses available. Two championship golf courses at nearby Woodhall Spa. Well located for historic Lincoln, interesting market towns and many antique shops. Single, double en suite and twin with private bathroom. Bed and Breakfast from £20. A warm welcome awaits. **ETC** ◆◆◆◆

**LANGTON-BY-WRAGBY. Miss Jessie Skellern, Lea Holme, Langton-by-Wragby, Market Rasen LN3 5PZ (01673 858339).** Ground floor accommodation in comfortable, chalet-type house set in own half-acre peaceful garden. All amenities. Central for touring Wolds, coast, fens, historic Lincoln etc. So much to discover in this county with wonderful skies and room to breathe. Attractive market towns, Louth, Horncastle (famed for antiques), Boston, Spilsby, Alford, Woodhall Spa (noted for golf). Accommodation offered in two double bedrooms (can be let as single), with washbasins; bathroom, toilet adjoining; lounge with colour TV always available to guests, separate diningroom. Drinks provided. Children welcome at reduced rates. Pets welcome (no charge). Car almost essential, parking. Basically room and breakfast, but limited number of evening meals may be available. Numerous eating places nearby. Bed and Breakfast from £20 per person. Open all year.

---

**FHG**

Visit the FHG website
## www.holidayguides.com
for details of the wide choice of accommodation
featured in the full range of FHG titles

**Lincolnshire** 221

**LINCOLN. Dave Barnes, Ridgeways Guest House, 243 Burton Road, Lincoln LN1 3UB (Tel & Fax: 01522 546878).** Ridgeways is an attractive detached guest house with a private car park and pleasant gardens for guests' use. Situated in uphill Lincoln within easy walking distance of the historic heart of Lincoln Cathedral, castle and Lawn Conference Centre. En suite twin, double and family rooms available, all with colour TV, tea/coffee trays, hair dryers; a ground floor room is available for disabled guests. Centrally heated throughout and a non-smoking rule applies for your safety and comfort. Vegetarians are catered for. Bed and Breakfast from £20 to £30. Credit cards accepted. Further information available on request. **ETC** ♦♦♦

**LINCOLN. Edward King House, The Old Palace, Lincoln LN2 1PU (01522 528778; Fax: 01522 527308).** A former palace of the Bishops of Lincoln, Edward King House offers Bed and Breakfast accommodation in a friendly and informal atmosphere. It is in a wonderful setting at the heart of historic uphill Lincoln, next to the Cathedral and Old Palace and overlooking the modern city with views over many miles to the west and south. Single and twin-bedded rooms (non-smoking) are all centrally heated and have washbasins and tea/coffee making facilities. Prices from £19 single, £37 twin with Continental breakfast (full breakfast £2 extra per person). **AA** ♦♦

**LINCOLN. South Park Guest House, 11 South Park, Lincoln LN5 8EN (01522 528243; Fax: 01522 524603).** A warm welcome is offered at this fine Victorian detached house, lovingly restored to preserve its character and charm and yet also providing quality guest house accommodation. Situated in a leafy suburb on the south side of historic Lincoln overlooking the south common and golf course, only a short walk to shops, restaurants, pubs, city centre and tourist attractions. All rooms en suite with a choice of baths or showers, tea and coffee making facilities and colour TV in all rooms, some with cable TV. Private parking with security lighting.

**LOUTH. Sarah J. Doe, The Priory Hotel, Eastgate, Louth LN11 9AJ (01507 602930; Fax: 01507 609767).** The Priory is a Grade II Listed building dating from 1818. With its stunning Victorian-Gothic style architecture, set in beautiful tranquil surroundings, it is the ideal location for those seeking a relaxing break – business or social. The hotel is set in three acres with mature trees, a lake with a fountain, old folly and a ruined mausoleum. 12 en suite bedrooms, recently refurbished. Restaurant, Cafe Bar, conference room, marquee facilities, wedding receptions, private parties, weekend breaks, French, Anglo cuisine, car parking. Our friendly and caring staff are just as impressive as the setting. Please telephone for further information.
website: www.theprioryhotel.com

# FREE or REDUCED RATE entry to Holiday Visits and Attractions – see our READERS' OFFER VOUCHERS on pages 43-60

**NORTH HYKEHAM. Mrs J. Henry, Loudor Hotel, 37 Newark Road, North Hykeham, Lincoln LN6 8RB (01522 680333; Fax: 01522 680403).** A comfortable family run hotel, situated just three miles from the city centre of Lincoln, on the A1434 just off the A46. We offer a friendly welcome to all guests. All rooms are ensuite with TV, tea/coffee making facilities, direct-dial telephones, licensed bar and ample parking. Single £34 per night Bed and Breakfast, Double/Twin £45, Family £50 with a discount for two nights at weekend or five nights including weekend. **AA ★★**.
e-mail: theloudorhotel@yahoo.co.uk
website: www.loudorhotel.co.uk

**PETERBOROUGH. Mrs S. M. Hanna, Courtyard Cottage, 2 West End, Langtoft, Peterborough, Cambridgeshire PE6 9LS (Tel & Fax: 01778 348354).** A warm, sincere welcome greets you to our delightful tastefully renovated 18th century stone cottage. We are situated in a small village just 50 yards off A15 at the Langtoft crossroads. We are ideally sited for visiting Peterborough, Stamford, Spalding, Bourne, Sleaford and Lincoln. Our home is maintained to high standards, has double glazing, central heating and we offer a hearty breakfast. Guests accommodated in twin and double room en suite or family suite; rooms have colour TV, tea making facilities and hair dryer. Evening meals (from £7.00) available. Bed and Breakfast from £22.50 per person per night based on two sharing. Open all year. Non-smoking. Full details on request. **ETC ♦♦♦♦**.
e-mail: david_tinegate@ic24.net

**SKEGNESS. The Chatsworth Hotel, 16 North Parade, Skegness PE25 2UB (01754 764177; Fax: 01754 761173).** Centrally situated in a premier sea front position, The Chatsworth is no more than a few minutes walk away from all the major attractions, including Natureland Marine Life Centre, bowling greens, Bottoms Amusement Park, the newly refurbished Embassy Centre and Theatre, Skegness Pier and of course the beach. The railway and coach stations are just 15 minutes walk away, although taxis are plentiful. We have limited space for cars, but there is a large car park just across the road. All our rooms are fully en suite, with either bath or shower, with colour TV and tea/coffee making facilities. We have four sea-view premier rooms, two with balcony, plus two sea view single sooms, both with balcony. Bed and Breakfast includes a traditional English breakfast, and with Dinner a four-course meal with tea or coffee. Lunches, snacks and sandwiches available in our non-smoking restaurant, bar, lounge or even on the patio (weather permitting).
e-mail: Altipper@aol.com
website: www.Chatsworthskegness.co.uk

**SPALDING. Chris Cave, Sycamore Farm, 6 Station Road, Gedney Hill, Spalding PE12 0NP (Tel & Fax: 01406 330445; Mobile: 07889 147001).** Exploring East Anglia? Why not spend a while in the "Land of the Big Sky"? A warm and comfortable welcome awaits you at this 150-year-old home, which is on the B1166, in the small Lincolnshire village of Gedney Hill. Your exclusive accommodation includes lounge with TV, diningroom, and shower/bathroom. Only a stone's throw away is a 'real' village shop, bakery, post office, and pubs with local 'flavour'. Flying, gliding, golf and fishing are also available. Bed and Breakfast £25 per adult per night. Sited within the grounds of the farmhouse is a fully serviced eight-berth static caravan. Hard or grass standings for caravans or tents are also available.
e-mail: sycamore.farm@virgin.net
website: www.bedandbreakfast.freeserve.co.uk

---

Terms quoted in this publication may be subject to increase if rises in costs necessitate

## Bed & Breakfast at No. 19 West Street, ETC ♦♦♦♦

**Kings Cliffe, Near Stamford, Peterborough PE8 6XP   Telephone 01780 470365**

A beautifully restored 500-year-old listed stone house, reputedly one of King John's Hunting Lodges, situated in the heart of the stone village of Kings Cliffe on the edge of Rockingham Forest. Both the double and twin rooms have their own private bathrooms, and there is colour TV and a welcome tray in each. In the summer breakfast can be served on the terrace overlooking a beautiful walled garden. Off street parking is behind secure gates. Within 10 miles there are seven stately homes including Burghley House famous for the Horse Trials, Rutland Water, and the beautiful old towns of Stamford and Oundle. Imaginative evening meals are available on request and prices range from £12 to £18. Open all year. Non smokers are much appreciated.

*Bed and breakfast from £20 per person.*

---

**THORPE FENDYKES. Mrs S. Evans, Willow Farm, Thorpe Fendykes, Wainfleet, Skegness PE24 4QH. (01754 830316).** In the heart of the Lincolnshire Fens, Willow farm is a working smallholding with free range hens, goats, horses and ponies. Situated in a peaceful hamlet with abundant wildlife, ideal for a quiet retreat – yet only 15 minutes from the Skegness coast, shops, amusements and beaches. Bed and Breakfast is provided in comfortable en suite rooms at £28 per room per night (suppers and sandwiches can be provided in the evening on request). Rooms have tea and coffee making facilities and a colour TV and are accessible to disabled guests. Friendly hosts! Ring for brochure.

**WOODHALL SPA. Mrs Claire Brennan, Claremont Guest House, 9-11 Witham Road, Woodhall Spa x LN10 6RW (01526352000).** Homely Bed and Breakfast in a traditional, unspoilt Victorian guest house in the centre of Woodhall Spa, Lincolnshire's unique resort. Off-street parking. Good food close by. Excellent centre for touring, walking and cycling. En suite rooms. Golf locally. Parking. Tea and coffee making facilities and TV in rooms. Special rates for short breaks. Prices from £15 per person. **ETC ♦♦, AA** QQ

**WOODHALL SPA. Barbara and Tony Hodgkinson, Kirkstead Old Mill Cottage, Tattershall Road, Woodhall Spa LN10 6UQ (01526 353637).** A warm welcome awaits you at this peaceful, sunny, detached non-smoking house, which is set beside the River Witham on the outskirts of Woodhall Spa, a village which is noted for its 'old world' charm, park with open-air heated swimming pool, Kinema in the woods and championship golf course. A new garden, three-acre wild garden, rowing boat, riverbank walks and membership of a local leisure club are also yours to enjoy, plus seasonal coarse fishing. There are numerous pubs and restaurants locally, or you are welcome to bring back a takeaway. We have a telephone, e-mail, fridge, iron and hairdryer for guests to use, and our three guest bedrooms (one en suite) each has a TV, clock radio and hot drinks tray. A video, piano and open fire help to make the lounge a relaxing area. From £18 per person, a cooked typical English breakfast is served or you can choose a lighter, healthy option.
website: www.woodhallspa.org

---

**PLEASE SEND A STAMPED ADDRESSED ENVELOPE WITH ENQUIRIES**

# NORFOLK

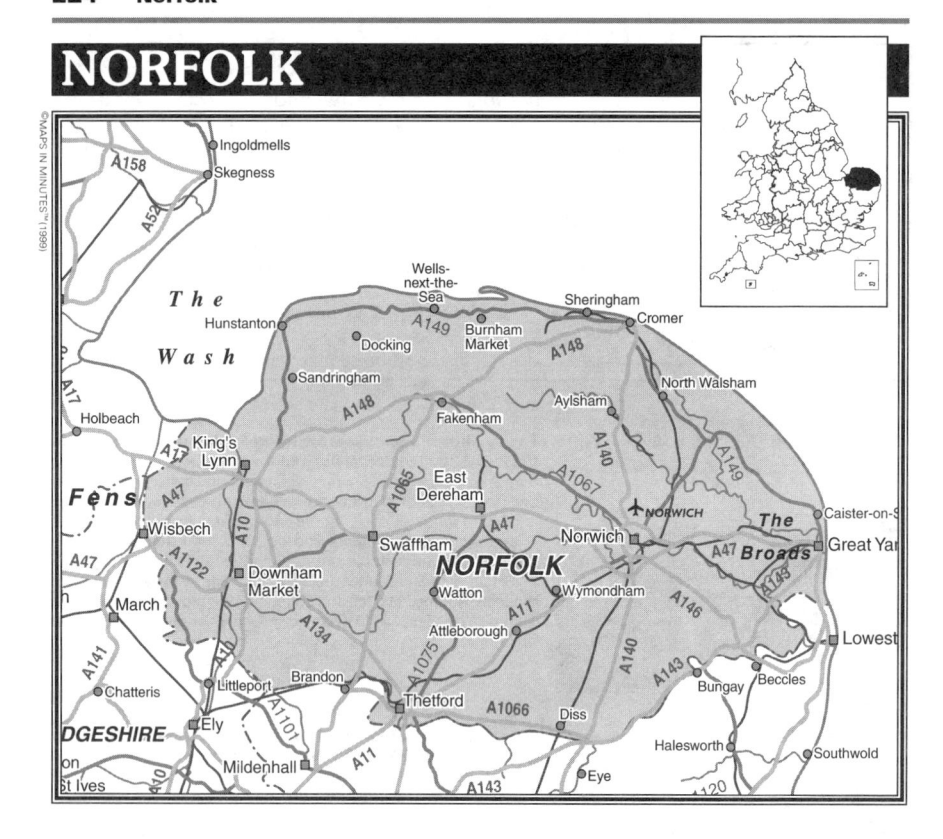

**ACLE. East Norwich Inn, Old Road, Acle, Norwich NR13 3QN (01493 751112).** Acle is midway between Great Yarmouth and Norwich. We are ideally situated for visiting all Heritage, National Trust and holiday attractions. The inn is situated on a quiet residential road and has a full 'on' licence with a good local bar trade. All our rooms are situated well away from the bar area and comprise two twin rooms, four double rooms and three family rooms, all have en suite bathrooms, colour TV with Sky and tea/coffee making facilities. Bed and Breakfast from £17.50 per person per night. Three-night break prices available. Ample car parking.

**ALDBOROUGH near. The Grange, Harmers Lane, Thurgarton, Near Aldborough NR11 7PF (01263 761588).** A fine Victorian country house, former rectory, situated in secluded grounds of two acres offering peace and tranquillity in warm, friendly and comfortable surroundings. Close to Cromer and the coast and central for all the North Norfolk attractions and National Trust properties. The accommodation comprises two spacious double/twin bedrooms with tea and coffee making facilities and private shower/bathrooms. A large guests' diningroom and lounge with colour TV. Double bed and full English breakfast from £20 to £25 per person per night. Evening meals on request. Two night Short Breaks including evening meals at reduced rates. Private parking. Non-smoking. No pets. Open May to November. Further information on request.

**ATTLEBOROUGH. Mr Beales, Hill House Farm, Deopham Road, Great Ellingham, Attleborough NR17 1AQ (01953 453113).** A working farm in quiet rural setting situated within easy reach of all local attractions. We offer our guests a warm welcome, children welcome, pets by arrangement only. Attractions include Banham Zoo, world famous Butterfly Gardens, Snetterton Racing Circuit and fishing lakes are close by; seaside resorts and Norfolk Broads are approximately 40 miles distant. Comfortable rooms with washbasins, tea/coffee facilities and colour TV. Ample parking. Open all year. Awarded Good Food Hygiene Certificate. Terms from £19 per person per night. Reduction for children up to 10 years.

**AYLSHAM. Mr and Mrs Parry, The Old Bank House, 3 Norwich Road, Aylsham NR11 6BN (01263 733843 or 708606).** A warm homely, historic atmosphere greets you in this lovely Queen Anne house. Formerly Aylsham's private bank, the rooms are spacious and welcoming, with central heating, TV, tea/coffee making facilities and radio alarms. En suite available. Homely guest lounge, lovely diningroom and cellar/games room with sauna, table tennis and darts. Access to rooms all day, private courtyard parking. Hearty breakfasts. Freshly prepared evening meals available by arrangement. Central for coast, Broads and Norwich, Blickling Hall two miles, Weavers Way and National Trust walks nearby. Children welcome, pets by arrangement. Tariff: £22 per person per night double, single £25. Whole house available for self-catering (★★★★) sleeping ten from £295. *"WHICH?' GUIDE RECOMMENDED*, **AA** *QQQQQ PREMIER SELECTED 1997/98.*
e-mail: bankhouse.beechwood@talk21.com
website: www.broadland.com/oldbankhouse

**AYLSHAM. The Old Pump House, Holman Road, Aylsham, Norwich NR11 6BY (01263 733789).** This comfortable 1750's house, facing the thatched pump a minute from Aylsham's church and historic marketplace, has six bedrooms, four en suite, with colour TV and tea/coffee facilities. English Breakfast with free-range eggs and local produce (or vegetarian breakfast) is served in the pine-shuttered sitting room overlooking the peaceful garden. Aylsham is central for Norwich, the coast, the Broads, National Trust houses, steam railways and unspoilt countryside. Well behaved children are very welcome. Bed and Breakfast from £18 to £27.50 Dinner by prior arrangement from October to May. Non-smoking. Off road parking for six cars. **ETC** ◆◆◆◆

**AYLSHAM. Tim and Janet Bower, Old Mill House, Cawston Road, Aylsham NR11 6NB (Tel & Fax: 01263 732118).** Old Mill House is a converted 19th century granary attached to a magnificent disused windmill. There is ample parking and guests are welcome to enjoy the pretty terrace and peaceful gardens. We have one double room and one twin room, each with washbasin and sharing a private bathroom. Both rooms have TV, radio and tea/coffee making facilities. Norwich, the Broads and the north Norfolk coast are all only 10 miles. We are on Marriots Way cycle trail and only half-a-mile from Weavers Way footpath. Warm welcome guaranteed all year. Bed and Breakfast from £16 to £20 per person Self-catering accommodation also available in The Windmill, please telephone for details.

# FREE or REDUCED RATE entry to Holiday Visits and Attractions — see our READERS' OFFER VOUCHERS on pages 43-60

## Norfolk

**BECCLES near. Mrs Rachel Clarke, Shrublands Farm, Burgh St. Peter, Near Beccles, Suffolk NR34 0BB (Tel & Fax: 01502 677241).** This attractive homely farmhouse offers a warm and friendly welcome and is peacefully situated in the Waveney Valley on the Norfolk/Suffolk border, surrounded by one acre of garden and lawns. The River Waveney flows through the 550 acres of mixed working farmland; opportunities for bird-watching. Ideal base for touring Norfolk and Suffolk; Beccles, Lowestoft, Great Yarmouth and Norwich are all within easy reach. The house has two double rooms with en suite facilities and one twin-bedded room with private bathroom, shower room and toilet. All have satellite colour TV and tea/coffee making facilities; diningroom, lounge with colour TV. Non-smoking rooms. Tennis court available. Swimming pool and food at River Centre nearby. Children over five years welcome at reduced rates. No pets. Car essential - ample parking. Open all year, except Christmas. Bed and Breakfast from £20 per person, reductions for longer stays. SAE please. **ETC** ◆◆◆◆.

**BINHAM. Mrs Brown, Abbot Farm, Walsingham Road, Binham NR21 0AW (01328 830519; Mobile: 07808 847582; Fax: 01328 830519).** Liz and Alan Brown offer a warm welcome to their Norfolk brick bungalow set in 150 acres of arable land, close to Little Walsingham and the north Norfolk coastline. Breakfasts are taken in the sunny conservatory, comfortable accommodation is found in the attractive loft conversion. Accommodation consists of one double and one twin bedroom, both en suite; colour TV and tea/coffee making facilities. No smoking. Terms from £16.
**ETC/AA** ◆◆◆

**CROMER. Morag and Tony Jackson, Birch House, 34 Cabbell Road, Cromer NR27 9HX (01263 512521).** Birch House is ideally situated for those who require a pleasant and relaxed holiday. The bedrooms are comfortably furnished, with tea and coffee making facilities, TV with satellite channels, washbasins, (en suite available) and electric shaver point. Cleanliness is the keynote of the house and every attention is paid to detail. The sunny lounge is tastefully furnished for the comfort of our guests. The diningroom has separate tables where you may enjoy meals of high quality prepared in the strictest hygienic conditions. We are situated within reach of all amenities. All efforts are made to make our guests feel welcome. Our aim is to provide genuine value for money, and in doing so continue the high reputation of Birch House. Non-smoking. Bed and Breakfast from £18 - £21 per person; three nights from £51. **ETC** ◆◆◆

---

*The* **FHG**
# GOLF GUIDE
*Where to Play Where to Stay*
## 2001

Available from most bookshops, the 2001 edition of **THE GOLF GUIDE** covers details of every UK golf course – well over 2500 entries – for holiday or business golf. Hundreds of hotel entries offer convenient accommodation, accompanying details of the courses – the 'pro', par score, length etc.

*In association with 'Golf Monthly' and including the Ryder Cup Report as well as Holiday Golf in Ireland, France, Portugal, Spain, The USA, South Africa and Thailand.*

**£9.99 from bookshops or £10.50 including postage (UK only) from FHG Publications, Abbey Mill Business Centre, Paisley PA1 ITJ**

**Norfolk** **227**

**DEREHAM. Mrs Jeanne Partridge, Shilling Stone, Church Road, Old Beetley NR20 4AB (01362 861099).** A friendly welcome awaits you in our comfortable family home with full central heating and parking. Situated on the edge of the village of Beetley (B1146), next to the church and set in its own extensive grounds with an informal garden. Double, twin and single rooms available all en suite, with colour TV, tea/coffee. Residents' lounge, diningroom. Pets welcome. The area's small market towns are a short drive away. Ideal base for touring East Anglia, Norwich, Sandringham, Broads, Gressing Hall Rural Life Museum, National Trust properties; golf and fishing nearby. Open all year. Non-smoking. Bed and full English Breakfast from £18. Reduced rates for children. **ETC ♦♦♦**.

**DEREHAM. Hill House, 26 Market Place, Dereham NR19 2AP (01362 699699).** Relax in the comfort of an elegant town centre location period residence with comfortable rooms and charming gardens. All bedrooms en suite, with colour TV, radio and tea/coffee making facilities; one four-poster. Full English breakfast; vegetarians and special diets welcomed. Ample off-road parking, secure cycle unit; laundry and drying facilities. Ideal touring base, situated in the heart of Norfolk with Norwich, the coast and Broads,Gressenhall, historic and other attractions a short drive away. Ground floor room for those with walking difficulty. More rooms planned for 2001. No smoking, no children under 16. Bed and Breakfast from £25.

**DEREHAM. David and Annie Bartlett, Bartles Lodge, Church Street, Elsing, Dereham NR20 3EA (01362 637177).** If you would like a peaceful tranquil stay in the heart of Norfolk's most beautiful countryside yet only a short drive to some of England's finest sandy beaches, then Bartles Lodge could be the place for you, with all rooms tastefully decorated in country style, with full en suite facilities, TVs, tea/coffee making facilities, etc. Overlooking 12 acres of landscaped meadows with its own private fishing lakes. The local village inn is within 100 metres and has a restaurant which serves "pub grub". Bed and Breakfast from £20. Why not telephone David and Annie so that we can tell you about our lovely home.

**DEREHAM. Mrs Pam Gray, Sycamore House, Yaxham Road, Mattishall NR20 3PE (01362 858213).** A guesthouse offering friendly, personal service, ideal for overnight stops and short breaks. Quiet rural location in central Norfolk within easy reach of Norwich, the Broads, beaches, country houses, etc. All rooms with colour TV, washbasins, tea/coffee making facilities. Separate WC and shower for guests' use. Traditional home cooking with fruit and vegetables from the garden in season. Early breakfasts if required, served with a smile. Village pub within walking distance. Ample off road parking. We regret no pets. Bed and Breakfast from £16.50; three-course Evening Meal £9.50.

# FHG

PLEASE MENTION THIS GUIDE WHEN YOU WRITE

OR PHONE TO ENQUIRE ABOUT ACCOMMODATION

IF YOU ARE WRITING, A STAMPED, ADDRESSED

ENVELOPE IS ALWAYS APPRECIATED

## THE HALF MOON INN
### Rushall, Near Diss, Norfolk IP21 4QD
### Tel & Fax: 01379 740793

This 16th century coaching inn offers a warm welcome to business guests and holidaymakers alike. Seven bedrooms are in modern chalet-style accommodation, and the remainder are in the inn which has a wealth of exposed beams. Bedrooms have colour television, central heating and tea and coffee making facilities. An excellent selection of home-cooked meals are available and reservations may be made in the conservatory dining area. The bar offers a range of real ales and a good value wine list is available. The friendly atmosphere, reasonably priced accommodation and delightful rural location combine to make this an excellent base for visiting East Anglia. *South Norfolk Council Gold Award Winner 98/99/2000.*

10 BEDROOMS, 8 WITH PRIVATE BATHROOM; FREE HOUSE WITH REAL ALE; HISTORIC INTEREST; CHILDREN WELCOME; BAR MEALS; NON-SMOKING AREAS; HARLESTON 3 MILES.

---

**DISS. Strenneth, Airfield Road, Fersfield, Diss IP22 2BP (01379 688182; Fax: 01379 688260)** Strenneth is a well established, family-run business situated in unspoiled countryside just a short drive from Bressingham Gardens and the picturesque market town of Diss. Offering first-class accommodation the original 17th century building has been carefully renovated to a high standard with a wealth of exposed beams and a newer single storey courtyard wing. There is ample off-road parking and plenty of nice walks nearby. All seven bedrooms, including a four-poster and an executive, are tastefully arranged with period furniture and distinctive beds, each having remote-control colour TV, hospitality tray, central heating and full en suite facilities. The establishment is smoke-free and the guest house has a log fire on cold winter evenings. There is an extensive breakfast menu using local produce. Ideal touring base. Pets most welcome at no extra charge – outside kennels with runs if required. Hair and beauty salon now open. Bed and breakfast from £25. **ETC** ♦♦♦♦
e-mail: ken@strenneth.co.uk
website: www.strenneth.co.uk

---

**DISS. Mrs April Pulford, Tanglewood, Clarke Close, Palgrave, Diss IP22 1BE (01379 640302; Mobile: 07779 741797).** Tanglewood is a comfortable modern house in a pretty village complete with duck ponds with Bressingham Gardens and Steam Museum nearby. It is an ideal touring base for Norwich, Norfolk Broads, Sandringham, Norfolk/Suffolk coastline and Bury St Edmunds. One double and one twin, luxurious private bathroom, guests' lounge/diningroom with colour TV, ample parking and spacious, peaceful garden adjoining woodland. We are renowned for excellent breakfasts using local produce. Warm welcome assured. Bed & Breakfast is £19 for one night, £52 for three nights. Reduced prices for children, no single supplement, evening meals by arrangement. Non-smoking.

---

**DOWNHAM MARKET. Crosskeys Riverside Hotel, Bridge Street, Hilgay, Near Downham Market PE38 0LD (01366 387777).** Country hotel beside River Wissey in converted 17th century buildings. Renovations have retained the original character with oak beams and inglenook fireplace complemented by a rustic bar. All bedrooms have en suite bathrooms, colour TV, coffee/tea making facilities; three rooms with four-poster beds. Two ground floor rooms. Ideally suited for touring Norfolk and Cambridgeshire Fens. Free fishing from the hotel frontage. Pets most welcome. Bed and Breakfast from £25. **ETC** ♦♦♦

---

*Please mention Bed & Breakfast Stops when writing to enquire about accommodation*

**GREAT YARMOUTH. Mrs E. Dack, `Dacona', 120 Wellesley Road, Great Yarmouth NR30 2AP (01493 856863 or 855305).** Homely guest house with own keys and access at all times. Centrally situated, it is only two/three minutes from the seafront and five minutes from shopping centre. Every amenity provided - tea making facilities in all rooms, comfortable accommodation and an ideal location. Bed and Breakfast terms from £13 to £14 nightly. Small parties (up to 24) welcomed. Children catered for (half-price rates). Dogs accepted on enquiry.

**GREAT YARMOUTH. Mr and Mrs Junker, Anglia House Hotel, 56 Wellesley Road, Great Yarmouth NR30 1EX (01493 844395).** This comfortable private hotel is pleasantly situated adjacent to the sea front and near the coach station, just three minutes from pier and town centre. A warm and friendly welcome awaits you. Our reputation and good name have been built on service, a friendly atmosphere and fine food with a choice of menu. Radio, colour TV and tea making facilities in all bedrooms. Most rooms en suite. Own front door keys with access to rooms at all times. Licensed bar. Children welcome. Bed and Breakfast from £13; Bed, Breakfast and Evening Meal from £99 weekly. Open all year. For a happy holiday please send SAE or telephone. **RAC** *LISTED.*

**HARLESTON. Mrs June E. Holden, Weston House Farm, Mendham, Harleston IP20 0PB (01986 782206; Fax: 01986 782414).** Peacefully located 17th century Grade II Listed farmhouse on a 300 acre mixed farm just outside village of Mendham in the heart of the Waveney Valley. Within easy reach of Suffolk heritage coast, Norfolk Broads, historic city of Norwich and nearby Otter Sanctuary. Comfortable, spacious accommodation comprises two double and one twin bedded rooms, all with en suite facilities, TV, hostess tray, clock-radio and shaver point. Guest lounge with colour TV, games, books and piano. Attractive diningroom overlooking large garden. Adequate parking space. Non-smoking. Bed and Breakfast £27 single, £45 double. Discounts for longer stays. **ETC/AA** ◆◆◆.

**HEMSBY. Mrs Margaret Lake, Old Station House, North Road, Hemsby, Near Great Yarmouth NR29 4EZ (01493 732022).** This large country house, set in the village of Hemsby, is only half-a-mile from golden beaches and is ideally situated for touring the Norfolk Broads and National Trust properties. The lovely accommodation comprises lounge with colour TV; separate diningroom; three double bedrooms and one family room, all with vanity unit and washbasin. Separate toilet and bathroom. Free tea making facilities. Full central heating. Bed and Breakfast from £17.50 per person per night. Open all year except Christmas. Telephone or send SAE for further details. Non-smoking. *"WHICH?" MAGAZINE RECOMMENDED.*

---

Visit the **FHG** website
**www.holidayguides.com**
for details of the wide choice of accommodation featured in the full range of FHG titles

**HINGHAM. Ann and Jeremy Peirson, 23 Market Place, Hingham NR9 4AF (01953 850398).** Hingham is close to 100 miles of coastline, all within 25 to 40 miles. Ideally placed for Sandringham, Wymondham Abbey, Norwich, etc., the Broads are less than an hour's drive away and Hingham is equidistant (seven miles) from Watton, Dereham and Wymondham. Grade II Listed, No. 23 dates from Tudor times, and is heavily beamed. Accessed via own front door, the accommodation consists of a dedicated (24-hour) livingroom with inglenook fireplace - an open wood-fire is very welcoming. The downstairs bedroom is en suite, with a wash room annexed and substantial power shower adjacent. The rooms are light and airy, surprising considering the age of the property. Upstairs are two further bedrooms, one with a double bed and the other with twin beds suitable for children. Guests are invited to use the garden. Provided are:- fridge, microwave, toaster, tea/coffee making facilities, fruit, full English Breakfast (vegetarians catered for). Also large TV and video (PAL). No pets, and non-smoking. Private parking. Single from £25 and double from £35. We prefer to let to one family/party at a time to ensure the amenities are private. All year round bookings welcomed. See more on our website. Tourist Board Commended in 1992.
e-mail: j.j.peirson@btinternet.com
website: www.btinternet.com/~j.j.peirson.bb1.htm

**HOLME-NEXT-THE-SEA. Mary & Robbie Burton, Meadow Springs, 15 Eastgate Road, Holme-next-the-Sea PE36 6LL (01485 525279).** Peacefully located in large, well stocked gardens. Meadow Springs offers quality accommodation. Motel-style rooms open onto west-facing patio, ideal for that early evening relaxing drink! Modern, attractively furnished rooms – one double, one twin – both with en suite bathrooms, CTV, radio and tea/coffee making facilities. Sunny breakfast room for exclusive use of guests. The pretty village of Holme is in a designated Area of Outstanding Natural Beauty. There are sandy beaches, nature reserves and championship golf courses nearby. Peddars Way long distance footpath also ends here. Close by are the Royal House of Sandringham, Holkham Hall and Norfolk Lavender. The traditional seaside resort of Hunstanton is just three miles away. £24 to £26 per person per night.

**HOLT. Mrs Lynda-Lee Mack, Hempstead Hall, Holt NR25 6TN (01263 712224). Working farm.** Enjoy a relaxing holiday with a friendly atmosphere in our 19th century flint farmhouse, beautifully set on a 300 acre arable farm with ducks, donkeys and large gardens. Close to the north Norfolk coast and its many attractions. Take a ride on the steam train or a boat trip to Blakeney Point Seal Sanctuary. There is a five mile circular walk through our conservation award-winning farm to Holt Country Park. Large en suite family room, double with private bathroom. Colour TV, tea/coffee facilities. Large lounge with log burning stove. Non-smoking. Sorry, no pets indoors. Bed and Breakfast from £20 per person. Children's reductions. Member of Farm Holiday Bureau. **ETC** ◆◆◆.
website: www.broadland.com/hempsteadhall

**HORSEY CORNER. The Old Chapel, Horsey Corner NR29 4EH (01493 393498).** Tranquil and traditional English Bed and Breakfast. A short stroll from both the wide sandy beach and Horsey Mere, part of the Broads National Park. Our non-smoking accommodation offers three ground floor en suite rooms, all with colour TV and tea/coffee making facilities. Ideal for bird/seal watchers, walkers, nature lovers and those seeking a peaceful environment. The Old Chapel is centrally heated throughout and you can be assured of a warm welcome. A unique location combining beach and Broads. Prices from £18 to £22 per person sharing double/twin room including breakfast. Please phone Peter and Margaret Glibbery for illustrated brochure and reservations. **ETC** ◆◆◆◆

---

Please mention *Bed and Breakfast Stops* when making enquiries about accommodation featured in these pages.

## WHITE HOUSE FARM
Knapton, Norfolk NR28 0RX
Colin & Fiona Goodhead   Tel/Fax: 01263 721344
E-mail: GOODHEAD@whfarm.swinternet.co.uk

Enjoy a taste of country living at White House Farm, our Grade II Listed farmhouse. Whether walking along the nearby sandy beaches or just relaxing in our peaceful gardens, you can certainly get away from it all. The quiet village location combines the historic character of a traditional flint and brick home with the modern touches you need to relax (en-suite facilities, four-poster bed, log fires). Our full English breakfast includes homemade bread and jams and Fiona will be delighted to cook your evening meals, by arrangement. Bed and Breakfast £17-£24. Self-catering cottages also available. We want you to enjoy and remember your visit; please telephone to discuss your booking or to obtain our brochure. AA♦♦♦♦

---

**KING'S LYNN. The Stuart House Hotel, 35 Goodwins Road, King's Lynn PE30 5QX (01553 772169; Fax: 01553 774788).** An elegant Victorian Hotel, quietly situated in its own grounds, just a few minutes' walk from the centre of this historic market town and port of King's Lynn. All bedrooms (some four-poster) have en suite facilities, colour TV with satellite channels, refreshment tray and direct-dial telephone. Superb à la carte restaurant. Cosy bar with real ales and varied bar meals. Quiet garden. Private parking. Bed and Breakfast from £29. Open all year. Special breaks available. **ETC/AA ★★**, *CAMRA "GOOD BEER GUIDE" LISTED.* 
e-mail: stuarthousehotel@btinternet.com
website: www.stuart-house-hotel.co.uk

*See also Colour Display Advertisement*

**KING'S LYNN. Mrs M. Howard, Jubilee Lodge, Station Road, Docking, King's Lynn PE31 8LS (Tel & Fax: 01485 518473).** Jubilee Lodge offers high standard bed and breakfast accommodation. All bedrooms en suite with colour TV. These complement the comfortable residents' lounge and the unique diningroom. Choice of English or Continental breakfasts. Packed lunches are also available on request. Good food and a friendly welcome is assured. Many local eating places offer varied menus for evening meals. The house is situated only four miles from a glorious, sandy beach, convenient for golf, sailing, walking, bird-watching. Close to Sandringham and other places of historic interest. Smoke and pet free establishment. Bed and Breakfast £17.50 per person per night. **ETC ♦♦♦** 
e-mail: marjoriehoward@hotmail.com

**KING'S LYNN. Mrs Bastone, Maranatha/Havana Guest House, 115/117 Gaywood Road, King's Lynn PE30 2PU (01553 774596/772331; Fax: 01553 763747).** Large completely re-decorated and appointed guest house. Single, double, twin and family rooms, many en suite. Close to town, Sandringham and the coast on bus route; five minutes to railway. Children and pets welcome. Open all year. Reasonable prices. **AA ♦♦♦**

---

# FREE or REDUCED RATE entry to Holiday Visits and Attractions — see our READERS' OFFER VOUCHERS on pages 43-60

# Norfolk

**LODDON near. Mrs Joan Thompson, Church Barn, Sisland NR14 6EE (Tel & Fax: 01508 520320).** You will be guaranteed a warm welcome in this traditional oak framed Norfolk Barn, converted to provide comfortable accommodation of a high standard. Set in idyllic rural countryside, yet within easy access of Norwich (10 miles), the Norfolk coast, the Broads, boat hire in Loddon and local market towns. The large bedrooms have either en suite or private bathrooms and all have colour TV and tea/coffee making facilities. The food is of a superb standard as the owner is a professional caterer and diets can be catered for. Bed and Breakfast from £20. Dinner available from £10. Children welcome.

**MATTISHALL, near Dereham. Mrs Betty Jewson, Ivy House Farm, Welgate, Mattishall, Dereham NR20 3PL (01362 850208). Working farm.** This architecturally interesting house dates from the Cromwellian period with a strong Jacobean influence and a later Georgian facade. Situated in 17 acres in the village of Mattishall, four miles from East Dereham, 12 from Norwich and within easy reach of the Coast and Norfolk Broads. Guests are accommodated in one double and two twin-bedded rooms; bathroom and toilet; guests' own dining and drawing room. We provide a full English Breakfast, a four course Evening Meal if required, and packed lunches. Bed and Breakfast from £15, Evening Meal from £8. Reductions for children. Pets welcome. Brochure available.

**NORWICH. Mr Brian and Mrs Diane Curtis, Rosedale Guest House, 145 Earlham Road, Norwich NR2 3RG (01603 453743; Fax: 01603 259887).** Friendly, family-run Victorian Guest House pleasantly situated within short walking distance of city centre and University, on the B1108. All rooms have colour TV, tea/coffee making facilities and own keys for your convenience. A full English breakfast is served in the diningroom and vegetarians are made very welcome. There are several good eating places nearby and once you have parked your car you can relax and enjoy Norwich. The Norfolk Broads are just seven miles away and the coast 20 miles. Full central heating. Bed and Breakfast from £18 per person. Completely no smoking. All major credit cards accepted. **ETC ♦♦**.
e-mail: drcbac@aol.com

**NORWICH. Freda and Ken Hawes, Oakbrook, Frith Way, Great Moulton, Norwich NR15 2HE (01379 677359).** Visitors book: "Very friendly, nothing too much trouble", "The best breakfast in a long time". Former village school, 13 miles south of Norwich. Locally country walks, fishing, gliding, swimming, leisure centre, Banham Zoo and Bressingham Steam Museum and Gardens. Children and pets welcome. Full laundry facilities. Nearby village pub serves excellent food. Specialist facilities for the disabled. Come and try our Norfolk hospitality. Three bedrooms, one single, one twin/double, one family. Two with private w.c. en suite. Three public bathrooms. Bed and Breakfast from £16.50 single, twin/double from £33, family from £41. Winter Breaks: 1st October - 1st April; one night £19, two nights £35, three nights £48 per person. Any extra nights £16 per person.
website: www.norfolkbroads.com/oakbrook/

**NORWICH. Mrs M.A. Hemmant, Poplar Farm, Sisland, Loddon, Norwich NR14 6EF (01508 520706). Working farm.** This 400 acre working farm is situated one mile off the A146, approximately nine miles south east of Norwich, close to Beccles, Bungay, Diss and Wymondham. An ideal spot for the Broads and the delightful and varied Norfolk coast. We have a Charolais X herd of cows, with calves born March-June. The River Chet runs through the farm. Accommodation comprises double, twin and family rooms, bathroom, TV sittingroom/diningroom. Central heating. Tennis court. Children welcome. A peaceful, rural setting. Car essential. Open all year for Bed and Breakfast. Terms from £17 per person per night.

## Norfolk

**Earlham Guest House,** 147 Earlham Road, Norwich, Norfolk NR2 3RG    *Nearest Road B1108*

ETC ◆◆◆◆    AA ◆◆◆◆

Susan and Derek Wright extend a warm welcome to their elegant late Victorian residence, ideally situated five minutes from the southern bypass on the B1108, close to historic Norwich and the university. Seven well-appointed and tastefully decorated rooms (all non-smoking), provide comfort with modern facilities including colour TV, hospitality tray and full central heating. English or vegetarian breakfasts, cooked to order, are served in the pretty breakfast room. Residents' Lounge. Patio garden. Local parking.

**Susan and Derek Wright**
**Tel & Fax: 01603 454169**
e-mail: earlhamgh@hotmail.com

AMEX • MASTERCARD • VISA

*B&B from £20 – £23, two single, three twin, two double, three family rooms, most en suite. Non-smoking. Children over eight years welcome. Sorry no pets. Open all year except Christmas and New Year.*

---

**RACKHEATH. Julie Simpson, Barn Court, Back Lane, Rackheath NR13 6NN (Tel & Fax: 01603 782536).** Friendly and spacious accommodation in a traditional Norfolk Barn conversion built around a courtyard. Situated five miles from the historic city of Norwich and two miles from the heart of the Norfolk Broads at Wroxham. Our accommodation consists of one double en suite room with a four-poster and two double/twin rooms. All rooms have colour TV and facilities for making tea/coffee. We are within walking distance of a very good Norfolk pub which serves reasonably priced meals. Packed lunches and dinners are available on request. Children are very welcome. Bed and Breakfast from £18 to £21. **ETC ◆◆◆**

**RACKHEATH. Mr and Mrs R. Lebbell, Manor Barn House, Back Lane, Rackheath, Norwich NR13 6NN (01603 783543).** 17th century converted barn with a wealth of exposed beams. A family home with lovely gardens in quiet surroundings, situated just off A1151. Very convenient for Norwich (five miles), and two miles from Wroxham, heart of Broadland. Accommodation includes twin/double rooms with central heating, tea/coffee facilities, TV and own bathroom. Separate lounge area with colour TV. We are 100 yards from traditional old Norfolk pub, "The Green Man", where it is possible to eat very well and inexpensively. Open all year for Bed and Breakfast from £21 to £29 single, £42 to £48 double. **ETC ◆◆◆◆**

**SHERINGHAM. Mrs Pat Pearce, The Birches, 27 Holway Road, Sheringham NR26 8HW (01263 823550).** Small guest house conveniently situated for town and sea front. Ideal centre for touring North Norfolk. Accommodation comprises one double and one twin bedded room, both with luxury bathrooms, tea/coffee making equipment and colour TV. Full central heating. Open Easter to October. Bed and Breakfast, one night £25 per person, two nights break £40 per person. No children under 12 years. No pets. NON-SMOKING ESTABLISHMENT. Member of the North Norfolk Hotel and Guest House Association. **AA ◆◆◆◆**.

**SHERINGHAM. Pinecones, 70 Cromer Road, Sheringham NR26 8RT (Tel & Fax: 01263 824955).** Sheringham is an attractive little seaside town with a nice traditional character. Excellent beaches, impressive cliffs and a surrounding landscape of hills, woods and heaths, along with historic houses and England's best bird-watching, make this corner of north Norfolk a great area to explore by foot, cycle or car. At Pinecones we have private parking, a sheltered garden to relax in, and a guest lounge with lots of books and videos. All our three rooms are en suite with colour TV, video player, and tea/coffee making tray. We have route-plans and maps for the best of the local walks, and cycles or tandems you can take out free of charge. Bed and Breakfast is £19-£24 per person per night, £114-£132 per week. **ETC◆◆◆◆**.

## Norfolk

**SWAFFHAM. Mrs Green, "Paget", Lynn Road, Narborough, King's Lynn PE32 1TE (01760 337734).** Private house offering Bed and Breakfast. Lounge available, log fire. TV in bedrooms. Ample parking. Pleasant local river, lakes and rural walks. Various water sports and horse riding nearby. Situated between the old market town of Swaffham and King's Lynn. Trout and coarse fishing lakes nearby. Pets welcome. Bed and Breakfast £16 per person. SAE please.

**SWAFFHAM (Barton Bendish). Carole, Roger and Lucie Gransden, Spread Eagle Country Inn, Church Road, Barton Bendish, near Swaffham PE33 9DP (01366 347295; Mobile: 07808 906201; Fax: 01366 347995).** This TRUE Country Inn, run personally by the Gransden Family for the past seven years stands in the centre of a quiet picturesque old village in a large well-stocked garden with customer seating. Barton Bendish lies south of RAF Marham off the A1122 with Swaffham and Downham just six miles away. Mainline stations at Downham, Cambridge half-an-hour by train, King's Lynn and beyond, Sandringham and the unspoilt Norfolk Coast are a 30 minutes' drive away. Well furnished bedrooms with all facilities – TV and tea, etc. Double en suite £45 per room. Twins - bathroom very close £35 per room. Prices include a Continental breakfast, however cooked is available at an extra charge. Two non-smoking restaurants, serving excellent home cooked food, with the bar serving Real Ales and other drinks. Log fire in bar. Gardens in summer. Open all year. Dogs and well-behaved children' by arrangement. 
e-mail: luciegransden@btinternet.com
website: www.countryinns.co.uk

**THURSFORD. Mrs Sylvia Brangwyn, The Heathers, Hindringham Road, Thursford, Fakenham NR21 0BL (01328 878352).** Very quiet country location ideal for touring, walking and visiting stately homes (ie., Sandringham, Holkham Hall, Blickling and Felbrigg), bird watching at Cley, Titchwell and Blakeney Point; Walsingham Shrine four miles. There is one ground floor double room with one twin and one double on first floor; all rooms have private en suite with shaver point, colour TV and tea/coffee making facilities. Full central heating. Christmas and New Year Breaks. Car is essential; ample parking facilities. Bed and Breakfast from £19 to £21 per person per night for two people sharing; optional Evening Meals by prior arrangement.

**THURSFORD. John and Jenny Duncan, Mulberry Cottage, Green Farm Lane, Thursford Green, Fakenham NR21 0BX (01328 878968).** We are situated six miles from Holt and three miles from Walsingham. The sandy beaches of the North Norfolk coast lie within easy reach. Plenty of walks for the energetic. Accommodation comprises double and twin-bedded rooms (one on ground floor), both are en suite and have TV and tea and coffee making facilities. Log fire in winter to relax by. Wide choice of breakfast. Ample parking. We regret our home is not suitable for children or pets and we would ask guests to kindly refrain from smoking. Bed and Breakfast from £23 per person per night.10% discount for stays of four or more nights. **ETC ♦♦♦♦**

**WATTON. Mrs Sue Baldwin, The Croft, 69 Hills Road, Saham Toney, Watton, Thetford IP25 7EW (01953 881372).** An attractive Victorian farmhouse covered in Virginia creeper and set in large well tended gardens. Working farm situated on the edge of Breckland two miles north of the small town of Watton. Central position makes this an ideal base to explore Norfolk: Norwich, King's Lynn, Sandringham, Bury St. Edmunds and the coast are all within 30 miles. Non-smoking guests are accommodated in one double room en suite and one twin bedroom. Bed and Breakfast from £20. Ample parking. Sorry, no pets.

**WELLS-NEXT-THE-SEA. Mrs Dorothy MacCallum, Machrimore, Burnt Street, Wells-next-the-Sea NR23 1HS (01328 711653).** A warm welcome awaits you at this attractive barn conversion. Set in quarter-of-an-acre in quiet location close to the shops and picturesque harbour of Wells. En suite guest bedrooms at ground floor level overlook their own patio and garden area. Ample car parking. Sorry no smoking in the bedrooms. Ideal for the bird watching sanctuaries at Cley, Salthouse and Titchwell. Close to Sandringham, Holkham and the Shrines at Walsingham. Prices from £22 to £24 daily; £140 to £155 weekly. 10% reduction three nights or more. **ETC** ◆◆◆◆

*See also Colour Display Advertisement*

**WELLS-NEXT-THE-SEA. Oyster Cottage B&B, 20 High Street, Wells-next-the-Sea NR23 1EP (01328 711997).** Located in the old High Street, this Grade II Listed building is of historic interest. Offering bed and breakfast from mid-January to mid-December, it makes an ideal retreat for families, couples and friends. There are en suite rooms with TV and tea/coffee making; amenities include central heating, laundry service, baby equipment, room service and cycle storage. A wide breakfast menu is available, including traditional English, Continental, vegetarian and other specialist diets.
**website: www.oyster-cottage.co.uk**

**WOODTON. Mrs J. Read, George's House, The Nurseries, Woodton, Near Bungay NR35 2LZ (01508 482214; Fax: 01508 482778).** A charming 17th century cottage with a six acre free-range egg unit and working forge/ blacksmith's showroom, situated in the centre of the village, just off the main Norwich to Bungay road. Wonderful holiday area, ideal for touring Norfolk and Suffolk. Within 10 miles is historic Norwich, with its castle, cathedral, theatre and excellent shops. Coast 18 miles. Guest accommodation comprises three double bedrooms with washbasins. Bathroom, shower, toilet, dining room, lounge/TV, sun room. Ample parking. Bed and Breakfast £18 per person per night. Excellent pub meals available 100 yards.
**website: www.rossmag.com/georges/**

**WROXHAM. Wroxham Park Lodge, 142 Norwich Road, Wroxham NR12 8SA (01603 782991).** Friendly Bed and Breakfast in an elegant Victorian house, situated in Wroxham 'Capital of Norfolk Broads'. Ideal for touring, day boats and boat trips on the beautiful Broads, fishing, steam railways, National Trust Houses, Wroxham Barns. Near north Norfolk coast, Great Yarmouth and Norwich. Good local restaurants and pubs. Guests arriving by train will be met. Open all year. All rooms en suite, tea/coffee making facilities, colour TV. Conservatory, garden, car park, ground floor room, central heating and public telephone. Pets by arrangement. Bed and Breakfast from £20 per person. Ring for brochure. **ETC** ◆◆◆◆.

---

# FHG

### Visit the FHG website
## www.holidayguides.com
for details of the wide choice of accommodation
featured in the full range of FHG titles

# NORTHAMPTONSHIRE

**BRACKLEY. Mrs Field, The Thatches, Whitfield, Brackley NN13 5TQ (01280 850358).** Situated in quiet village overlooking beautiful countryside, well appointed, comfortable rooms with tea and coffee making facilities and television. Full English breakfast with local free range produce when available. One double and two twin rooms. Within immediate area for Silverstone Rally School and Racing Circuit, Towcester Racecourse and Stowe Gardens (NT). Close to Oxford and Cotswolds. Bed and Breakfast from £17.50 per person per night. Non-smokers please. **ETC** ◆◆◆

# NORTHUMBERLAND

**ALLENDALE. Mrs Eileen Ross Finn, Thornley House, Allendale NE47 9NH (01434 683255).** Beautiful country house in spacious grounds surrounded by field and woodland, one mile out of Allendale, 10 miles south of Hexham, near Hadrian's Wall. Two large beautifully furnished lounges, one with TV, one with Steinway Grand Piano; three bedrooms all with private facilities, tea makers, radios and home-made biscuits. Marvellous walking country where you don't see anybody. Conducted walks sometimes available. Riding school, golf course nearby. Home baking. Bring your own wine. Packed lunches, vegetarians catered for. Christmas Breaks. Ample parking. Bed and Breakfast from £19.50. Dinner £11. Bed and Breakfast weekly from £120. A no smoking house. **ETC** ◆◆◆◆
e-mail: e.finn@ukonline.co.uk

*See also Colour Display Advertisement*

**ALNMOUTH. Janice Edwards, Westlea, 29 Riverside Road, Alnmouth NE66 2SD (01665 830730)** We invite you to relax in the warm, friendly atmosphere of "Westlea" situated at the side of the Aln Estuary. We have an established reputation for providing a high standard of care and hospitality. Guests start the day with a hearty breakfast of numerous choices and in the evening a varied and appetising four-course traditional meal is prepared using local produce. All bedrooms are bright, comfortable and en suite with colour TVs, hot drinks facilities, central heating and electric blankets. Two bedrooms on the ground floor. Large visitors' lounge and diningroom overlooking the estuary. Ideal for exploring castles, Farne Islands, Holy Island, Hadrian's Wall. Fishing, golf, pony trekking, etc within easy reach. Private parking. Bed and Breakfast from £20; Bed, Breakfast and Evening Meal from £32. Numerous Hospitality awards. **ETC** ◆◆◆

# Northumberland 237

**See also Colour Display Advertisement** **ALNWICK. K. and B. Jones, Charlton House, 2 Aydon Gardens, South Road, Alnwick NE66 2NT (01665 605185).** Charlton House is a very special guest house, where our guests are always welcomed in a friendly, relaxed atmosphere. All rooms are beautifully decorated, some with original fireplaces and patchwork quilts. All bedrooms have private facilities, hospitality trays and colour TV. There is also a comfortable guest lounge. Choose from Traditional English, vegetarian or Continental breakfasts. 'Lion Heart Award' for the most popular small guest house in the Alnwick district and recommended by 'Which?' in their 'Good Bed and Breakfast' Guide. Private and off-street parking. Tariff from £20 per person per night. (includes Breakfast). We think you will remember Charlton House fondly, long after your stay has ended. **ETC ◆◆◆◆**

**ALNWICK. Mrs Ann Bowden, Roseworth, Alnmouth Road, Alnwick NE66 2PR (01665 603911).** A warm Northumbrian welcome awaits you at Roseworth, set in a beautiful situation covered in Virginia creeper and roses. You can enjoy sitting in our large prize-winning garden. Roseworth is a very clean and comfortable house which is very tastefully decorated to the highest standards. Two en suite rooms, and one with private facilities. All bedrooms have tea trays, colour TV and double glazed windows. Comfortable lounge. Each morning Ann serves a good hearty Northumbrian breakfast to start the day. Alnwick is a good touring area with good, clean beaches four miles to the east and 17 miles north west to the Cheviot Hills. Many castles and good country walks available. Bed and Breakfast from £20. Please telephone for further details. Recommended by "WHICH?" Good Bed and Breakfast Guide. **ETC ◆◆◆◆**

**ALNWICK. Mrs B. Sutherland, Rock Midstead Organic Farm, Rock Midstead, Alnwick NE66 2TH (01665 579225; Fax: 01665 579326).** Enjoy a relaxing stay on our peaceful organic dairy farm. Comfortable farmhouse has guests' own lounge and choice of two double/twin bedrooms with en suite or private bathrooms. Tea/coffee making facilities in every room, with colour TV and radio. Delicious breakfasts and evening meals using produce from the farm and fresh baked bread every day. Located five miles from the market town of Alnwick, the farm is convenient for the A1 and within easy reach of the Northumbrian coast, Cheviot Hills, Northumberland National Park, and many castles, historic sites and golf courses. Children welcome, dogs by arrangement. Sorry, no smoking. Bed and Breakfast from £18. **ETC ◆◆◆**
e-mail: ian@rockmidstead.freeserve.co.uk

**ALNWICK. Mrs B. Gaines, Crosshills House, 40 Blakelaw Road, Alnwick NE66 1BA (01665 602518).** Come and join us at Crosshills for your stay in historic Northumberland. A friendly guest house situated in a quiet area near golf course and only a short walk into town. We have two double rooms and one twin room, all en suite and having colour TV and tea/coffee making facilities. Twin room has balcony with a beautiful view of coast and countryside. Sorry, no dogs. Bed and Breakfast from £21 per person. Parking available. **ETC ◆◆◆◆**.

**ALNWICK. The Hotspur Hotel, Bondgate Without, Alnwick NE66 1PR (01665 510101; Fax: 01665 605033).** Originally a coaching inn, the Hotspur is located in the town centre, within walking distance of Alnwick Castle, the seat of the Duke of Northumberland. Set between sandy beaches and rolling moorland, it is surrounded by numerous places of interest, including many fine golf courses. The hotel offers a friendly welcome, comfortable en suite bedrooms, a high standard of food and fine ales. Non-smoking accommodation available. Children welcome, reductions when sharing with adults. please telephone for brochure. **AA/RAC ★★**, *LES ROUTIERS*.

**BERWICK-UPON-TWEED. Harberton Guest House, 181 Main Street, Spittal, Berwick-upon-Tweed TD15 1RP (01289 308813).** Harberton is a Victorian villa situated one-and-a-half miles from the walled town of Berwick-upon-Tweed, convenient for the A1. The house has full central heating, and bedrooms have colour TV and tea-making facilities. Fully licensed bar for residents; à la carte dinner served each evening. There are designated areas for smokers. Pleasant garden with direct access to promenade and beach. Bed and Breakfast from £17.50 standard, from £20 en suite. **ETC** ♦♦♦
e-mail: maurw@zetnet.co.uk
website: www.harberton.com

**BERWICK-UPON-TWEED. Mrs Anne Tait, Dervaig Guest House, 1 North Road, Berwick-upon-Tweed TD15 1PW (Tel & Fax: 01289 307378).** Beautiful Victorian guest house tastefully furnished and centrally heated. Large walled garden and fish pond for guests' use. Two minutes from railway station, five minutes from town centre. Full English breakfast served, vegetarians catered for. Private parking. Cot and high chair available. Small dogs welcome. Open all year. Bed and Breakfast from £20 per person. **ETC/AA** ♦♦♦♦.

**BERWICK-UPON-TWEED. Mrs Margo Newington-Bridges, High Steads, Lowick TD15 2QE (Tel & Fax: 01289 388689).** High Steads is a Georgian farmhouse some four miles from the A1, close to Holy Island and Berwick-upon-Tweed. We are an ideal base from which to explore the many castles, coastline and Cheviot Hills. Close by there is fishing, horse riding, shooting, golf and beautiful walking country. We have two en suite rooms, one double, one twin and guests' sittingroom. Our house is non-smoking except in the summer house. Ample courtyard parking. Extensive grounds with magnificent views and croquet on the lawn. Well behaved dogs welcome. Varied and interesting breakfasts including Eggs Benedict and Gentleman's Victorian Omelette. Bed and Breakfast from £22.50 per person per night. **ETC/AA**♦♦♦♦.
e-mail: highstead@aol.com

**CORBRIDGE. Mrs M. J. Matthews, The Hayes, Newcastle Road, Corbridge NE45 5LP (01434 632010).** Large spacious, stone-built country house set in seven acres of gardens and woodland on the edge of this historic village, and with easy nearby access to the A69 and A1M. All rooms with tea/coffee facilities and TV; most en suite. Stair lift available. Well-furnished throughout. Plenty of car parking. Bed and Breakfast from £20 with reductions for children. Self-catering cottages also available (3 Keys Commended). Brochure on request. **ETC** ♦♦
e-mail: MJCT@mmatthews.fsbusiness.co.uk

**HADRIAN'S WALL. Mrs Lesley Armstrong, Carrsgate East, Bardon Mill, Hexham NE47 7EX (01434 344376; Fax: 01434 344011).** A comfortable 17th century home. Large lounge with real fire, relaxed surroundings and great views, a retreat from the hustle and bustle of everyday life. Two double en suite rooms with TV, tea/coffee making facilities, hairdryer and clock-radio. Two miles from Hadrian's Wall and settlements. Ideal base for exploring Northumberland. Walks, beautiful countryside, Newcastle, Carlisle, Lake District and many historic attractions within one hour's drive. Bus stops outside, train three miles, ample parking. No children or pets, no smoking establishment. Open February to November. Bed and Breakfast from £23 to £27. Please visit our website for pictures and more information or call for brochure. **ETC** ♦♦♦
e-mail: lesley@carrsgate-east.com
website: www.carrsgate-east.com

**HADRIAN'S WALL. Hadrian Lodge, North Road, Above Haydon Bridge, Hadrian's Wall NE47 6NF (01434 688688; Fax: 01434 684867).** Hadrian Lodge is in a beautiful rural location overlooking lakes and set in 18 acres of open pasture bordered by pine forests. This quality conversion of a stone-built hunting/fishing lodge offers comfortable, well furnished bed and breakfast and self-catering accommodation. Hadrian Lodge provides a friendly social atmosphere with single, twin double and family rooms (en suite available). Situated two miles from Hadrian's Wall and close to Roman forts of Vindolanda and Housesteads, it provides the ideal base from which to explore the beauty and the history of the Northumberland National Park. A licensed bar and all-day tea room host a varied menu of delicious home cooked food. There is ample parking, a private trout lake and a warm welcome. Bed and Breakfast from £19.50. Ring or write for brochure. 
e-mail: hadrianlodge@hadrianswall.co.uk   website: www.hadrianswall.co.uk

**HALTWHISTLE. Mrs K. McNulty, Saughy Rigg Farm. Twice Brewed, Haltwhistle NE49 9PT (01434 344120)** A warm welcome awaits you at our beautifully converted farm buildings complex situated in the Northumberland National Park close to Hadrian's Wall and central for touring the Scottish Borders and the Lake District with Newcastle only 35 miles away. Fishing, walking and bird-watching are only a few of the local attractions for your enjoyment. Stabling is available on the farm. We offer comfortable accommodation of the highest standard comprising one twin room and one family room (sleeps five). Rooms are en suite and include tea/coffee making facilities. Read a book, watch television or just relax in our cosy guests' lounge. Short Breaks available. Children and pets are most welcome. Bed and Breakfast £15 per person. Evening Meal optional. **ETC ♦♦♦**

**HEXHAM. Mrs Eileen Mitchell, Thistlerigg Farm, High Warden, Hexham NE46 4SR (Tel & Fax: 01434 602041).** Thistlerigg is a 650 acre working farm, set on a hill with spectacular views in all directions. It is not far from Hadrian's Wall and overlooks the North and South Tyne Meetings. Bed and Breakfast terms are from £16 per person. **ETC ♦♦♦**

**HEXHAM, The Dale Hotel, Market Place, Allendale NE47 9BD (01434 683212/01207 235354).** Situated in the traditional Dales village of Allendale Town in south west Northumberland – one of the most beautiful, unspoilt areas of the country and popular for walking, cycling and touring by car with many places of interest including Hadrian's Wall within easy reach. A 30 bedroom hotel offers comfortable accommodation in a friendly atmosphere with licensed bar, sauna, pool table, darts. Golf course nearby, horse riding available, lock up for cycles. Full English Breakfast Buffet also Evening Meals and Packed Lunches available

**HEXHAM. Mrs E. Courage, Rye Hill Farm, Slaley, Hexham NE47 0AH (01434 673259; Fax: 01434 673608).** This is a 300-year-old stone farmhouse set in its own 30 acres of rural Tynedale. Rye Hill Farm offers you the freedom to enjoy the pleasures of Northumberland throughout the year while living comfortably in the pleasant family atmosphere of a cosy farmhouse adapted especially to receive holidaymakers. Family, double and single rooms, all with colour TV, hot-beverage facilities and bathrooms en suite. Full English Breakfast, three-course Evening Meal (optional); table licence. There is even room for your caravan if you prefer not to live in. Well-mannered children and pets are more than welcome. Terms for Bed and Breakfast from £20; Evening Meal from £12. Major credit cards accepted. Brochure available. **ETC ♦♦♦♦**

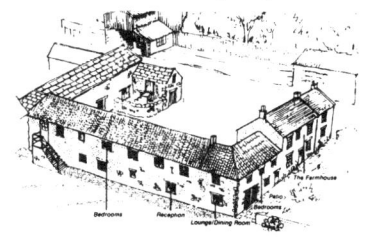

---

*Please mention Bed and Breakfast Stops when writing to enquire about accommodation*

This traditional country cottage is set in beautiful terraced gardens with a stream and is only five minutes' walk to the village, castle, river walks and sandy beaches. The accommodation is comfortably furnished and includes two double rooms and one family room. All on ground floor with washbasin, shaver point, colour TV, tea/coffee making facilities and heating; en suite available. Residents' lounge. Warkworth makes an ideal base from which to explore rural Northumberland and the Borders with their unspoilt beauty and historic interest. Children welcome, reduced rates. Non-smoking. Private parking. Colour brochure available. Bed and Breakfast from £18.50. Open all year.

*ETC* ♦♦♦♦

**BECK 'N' CALL** Birling West Cottage,
Warkworth NE65 0XS Tel: 01665 711653
e-mail: beck-n-call@lineone.net
website: www.beck-n-call.co.uk

See also Colour Display Advertisement

---

**HEXHAM. Mrs Ruby Keenleyside, Struthers Farm, Catton, Allendale, Hexham NE47 9LP (01434 683580).** Struthers Farm offers a warm welcome in the heart of England, with many splendid local walks from the farm itself. Panoramic views. Situated in an area of outstanding beauty. Double/twin rooms, en suite, central heating. Good farmhouse cooking. Ample safe parking. Come and share our home and enjoy beautiful countryside. Children welcome, pets by prior arrangement. Open all year. Bed and Breakfast from £20; Evening Meal from £10. Farm Holiday Bureau Member.

---

**WARKWORTH. John and Edith Howliston, North Cottage, Birling, Warkworth NE65 0XS (01665 711263).** Situated on the outskirts of the historic coastal village of Warkworth, we are an ideal base from which to explore Northumberland with its superb beaches and castles. We have four comfortable, well furnished no-smoking rooms – two double and one twin-bedded rooms en suite, and one single with washbasin; all have colour TV. All bedrooms have hospitality trays, central heating and electric overblankets and all are on ground floor. There is of course a bathroom with shower, and a sittingroom with cheery gas fire and colour TV. A full breakfast is served in the diningroom and afternoon tea is served (free of charge) with home-made cakes/biscuits. Large well kept garden and water garden. Warkworth has its own castle, river, golf course and beautiful sandy beaches. Bed and Breakfast from £20 per person per night. Weekly rates from £137 per person.
**ETC** ♦♦♦♦

---

The **FHG**
**GOLF GUIDE**
*Where to Play Where to Stay*
**2001**

Available from most bookshops, the 2001 edition of
**THE GOLF GUIDE** covers details of every UK golf course – well over 2500 entries – for holiday or business golf. Hundreds of hotel entries offer convenient accommodation, accompanying details of the courses – the 'pro', par score, length etc.

*In association with 'Golf Monthly' and including the Ryder Cup Report as well as Holiday Golf in Ireland, France, Portugal, Spain, The USA, South Africa and Thailand.*

**£9.99 from bookshops or £10.50 including postage (UK only) from FHG Publications,
Abbey Mill Business Centre, Paisley PA1 ITJ**

# NOTTINGHAMSHIRE

**BURTON JOYCE. Mrs V. Baker, Willow House, 12 Willow Wong, Burton Joyce, Nottingham NG14 5FD (0115 931 2070).** A large period house (1857) in quiet village location yet only four miles from city. Attractive, interesting accommodation with authentic Victorian ambience. Bright, clean rooms with tea/coffee facilities, TVs. Walking distance of beautiful stretch of River Trent (fishing). Ideally situated for Holme Pierrepont International Watersports Centre; golf course; National Ice Centre; Trent Bridge (cricket); Sherwood Forest (Robin Hood Centre) and the unspoiled historic town of Southwell with its Minster and Racecourse. Good local eating. Evening Meal by arrangement. Private parking. From £17.50 per person per night. Reduced rates for children. Please phone first for directions.

**EDWINSTOWE. (near Mansfield). Robin Hood Farmhouse B&B, Rufford Road, Edwinstowe NG21 9JA (Tel & Fax: 01623 824367).** Traditional Olde English farmhouse in Robin Hood's village in the middle of Sherwood Forest. We are in close proximity of Clumber and Rufford Country Parks and adjacent to Center Parcs and South Forest Leisure Complex. Easy access to Nottingham and Lincoln. The farmhouse which is set in extensive gardens is open and centrally heated all year round. Accommodation comprises double/family and twin room, colour TV, tea/coffee making facilities in all rooms. Tariff from £17.50 per person per night. Reductions for children and extra nights. Pets and special requirements available on request. Ample secure parking.
e-mail: robinhoodfarm@aol.com

**FARNSFIELD. Ken and Margaret Berry, Lockwell House, Lockwell Hill, Old Rufford Road, Farnsfield, Newark NG22 8JG (01623 883067).** Set in 25 acres with 10 acres of woodland and situated on the edge of Sherwood Forest near Rufford Park on the A614, we are within easy reach of Nottingham, Newark, Mansfield, Worksop and all local country parks and tourist attractions. Small family-run Bed and Breakfast offering friendly service and comfort. All bedrooms are en suite and have tea/coffee making facilities, TV. Full English Breakfast. Ample car parking. Good pubs and restaurants nearby. Brochure available. Rates from £20.

**MANSFIELD. Mrs L. Palmer, Boon Hills Farm, Nether Langwith, Mansfield NG20 9JQ (01623 743862).** This is a stone-built farmhouse, standing 300 yards back from A632 on edge of village. It is on a 155-acre mixed farm with dogs, cats, goats, chicks, calves. Situated on the edge of Sherwood Forest, six miles from Visitors' Centre, eight miles from M1, 10 miles from A1. Chatsworth House, Newstead Abbey, Hardwick Hall and Creswell Crags all within easy reach. Two double and one twin-bedded room; bathroom; toilet; fitted carpets throughout. Open fires. Background central heating for comfort all year round. Large sittingroom/diningroom with colour TV. Children welcome, cot and babysitting. No Pets. Car essential - parking. Bed and Breakfast from £17 per night, which includes bedtime drink. Evening Meal available nearby. Non-smokers only. Rates reduced for children. Open March to October inclusive.

---

*Readers are requested to mention this guidebook when seeking accommodation (and please enclose a stamped addressed envelope).*

**NOTTINGHAM. Peter and Josephine Howat, Andrews Private Hotel, 310 Queens Road, Beeston, Nottingham NG9 1JA (Tel & Fax: 0115 925 4902).** Everything at Andrews Hotel is done with a view to making your stay enjoyable and relaxing. Renowned for its good food, friendly atmosphere and a sense of home-from-home. All rooms have colour TV, tea/coffee and washbasins, some are en suite. We are within easy reach of the Derbyshire Dales and Robin Hood country. We are situated on the west side of Nottingham, 10 minutes from the city centre. Also close by is Nottingham Tennis Centre and University. Prices start at £21 basic single, and £16 per person for a twin bedded room including breakfast. **ETC ♦♦♦. RAC** *LISTED.*

**NOTTINGHAM/CLIFTON VILLAGE. Alan and Jane Haymes, Camellia House, 76 Village Road, Clifton Village, Nottingham NG11 8NE (0115 9211653).** A quiet picturesque village only three miles from city centre, backing onto the River Trent with riverside wooded walks. Our new traditionally built house in mature setting is double glazed, has central heating and private parking. We offer double, twin and single rooms with colour TV and tea/coffee making facilities. Continental breakfast consisting of fruit juice, cereals, grapefruit, prunes, yoghurt, toast, jams, marmalade, warm rolls, cheeses, tea and coffee. Our rates are from £17.50 per night. We aim to provide a warm welcoming atmosphere at all times.

**SUTTON-IN-ASHFIELD. Mr P. Jordon, Dalestorth Guest House, Skegby Lane, Skegby, Sutton-in-Ashfield NG17 3DH (01623 551110).** Dalestorth Guest House is an 18th century Georgian family home converted in the 19th century to become a school for young ladies of the local gentry and a boarding school until the 1930s. In 1976 it was bought by the present owners and has been modernised and converted into a comfortable, clean and pleasant guest house serving the areas of Mansfield and Sutton-in-Ashfield, offering overnight accommodation of Bed and Breakfast or longer stays to businessmen, holidaymakers or friends and relations visiting the area. Please send for further information.

# FOR THE MUTUAL GUIDANCE OF GUEST AND HOST

Every year literally thousands of holidays, short breaks and overnight stops are arranged through our guides, the vast majority without any problems at all. In a handful of cases, however, difficulties do arise about bookings, which often could have been prevented from the outset.

It is important to remember that when accommodation has been booked, both parties – guests and hosts – have entered into a form of contract. We hope that the following points will provide helpful guidance.

**GUESTS:** When enquiring about accommodation, be as precise as possible. Give exact dates, numbers in your party and the ages of any children. State the number and type of rooms wanted and also what catering you require – bed and breakfast, full board etc. Make sure that the position about evening meals is clear – and about pets, reductions for children or any other special points.

Read our reviews carefully to ensure that the proprietors you are going to contact can supply what you want. Ask for a letter confirming all arrangements, if possible.

If you have to cancel, do so as soon as possible. Proprietors do have the right to retain deposits and under certain circumstances to charge for cancelled holidays if adequate notice is not given and they cannot re-let the accommodation.

**HOSTS:** Give details about your facilities and about any special conditions. Explain your deposit system clearly and arrangements for cancellations, charges etc. and whether or not your terms include VAT.

If for any reason you are unable to fulfil an agreed booking without adequate notice, you may be under an obligation to arrange suitable alternative accommodation or to make some form of compensation.

*While every effort is made to ensure accuracy, we regret that FHG Publications cannot accept responsibility for errors, omissions or misrepresentations in our entries or any consequences thereof.*

*Prices in particular should be checked because we go to press early. We will follow up complaints but cannot act as arbiters or agents for either party.*

# OXFORDSHIRE

**BANBURY. Mrs Rosemary Cannon, High Acres Farm, Great Bourton, Banbury OX17 1RL (Tel & Fax: 01295 750217).** New Farmhouse situated on edge of village off A423 Southam Road, three miles north of Banbury overlooking the beautiful Cherwell Valley. Ideally situated for touring Cotswolds, Stratford, Warwick, Oxford, Blenheim Palace. Pub in village serving evening meals Tuesdays to Saturdays. Very comfortable accommodation comprising one twin room, one family room (one double and one single bed). Tea/coffee making facilities, hair dryers; central heating; shower room with electric shower; guests' sittingroom with colour TV. All rooms fully carpeted. Non-smoking. Parking. Bed and Breakfast from £18. Child under 10 sharing family room £10. Sorry, no pets. A warm welcome awaits you.

**BANBURY. Mr Searle, Grafton Lodge Private Guest House, 63 Oxford Road, Banbury OX16 9HJ (01295 257000).** Grafton Lodge Private Guest House is fully centrally heated and the rooms are spacious with en suite facilities benefiting from colour TV and tea/coffee making facilities. The diningroom has a most unique Pantell wooden carved ceiling with extravagant plaster backed inset lighting, a leaded glass chandelier and leaded and stained glass windows to the ground floor. All facilities have softened water for the best care of residents. If you are looking for a quiet restful place to stay, with excellent breakfasts and with full car parking at the rear of the premises, then this is the place to go.

**BANBURY. Mrs E.J. Lee, The Mill Barn, Lower Tadmarton, Banbury OX15 5SU (01295 780349).** Tadmarton is a small village three miles south-west of Banbury. The Mill, no longer working, was originally water-powered and the stream lies adjacent to the house. The Mill Barn has been tastefully converted, retaining many beams and exposed stone walls and with all the amenities a modern house can offer. Two spacious en suite bedrooms, one downstairs, are available to guests in this comfortable family house. Base yourself here and visit Stratford, Oxford, Woodstock and the Cotswolds, knowing you are never further than an hour's drive away. Open all year round for Bed and Breakfast from £20. Reductions for children. Weekly terms available.

**BLADON near. Tom and Carol Ellis, Wynford House, 79 Main Road, Long Hanborough OX8 8JX (01993 881402; Fax: 01993 883661).** Wynford House is situated in the village of Long Hanborough a mile from the Bladon burial place of Sir Winston Churchill, three miles from Woodstock and Blenheim Palace. Oxford is twelve miles away and the Cotswolds are close by. Comfortable non-smoking accommodation. Family or double en suite, double and twin rooms with colour TV, tea/coffee making facilities. Pubs serving good food within walking distance. Bed and Breakfast from £20.

**BRAILES. Mrs M. Cripps, Agdon Farm, Brailes, Banbury OX15 5JJ (Tel & Fax: 01608 685226). Working farm.** A warm welcome awaits all our guests. Our comfortable Cotswold stone farmhouse is set in 500 acres of mixed farming, in an unspoilt part of the countryside. Two miles from B4035, five miles from A422. Within walking distance of Compton Wynyates, in close driving range of the Cotswolds, Warwick, 10 miles Stratford-upon-Avon and Banbury Cross. Many local village pubs. Accommodation with TV room, separate diningroom, guests' bathroom, pleasant bedrooms with tea/coffee facilities. Central heating. Evening Meals available.

**244   Oxfordshire**

**FARINGDON (Oxon). Mr D. Barnard, Bowling Green Farm, Stanford Road, Faringdon, Oxfordshire SN7 8EZ (01367 240229; Fax: 01367 242568).** Attractive 18th century period farmhouse offering 21st century comfort, situated in the Vale of White Horse, just one mile south of Faringdon on the A417. Easy access to the M4 Exit 13 for Heathrow Airport. An ideal place to stay for a day or longer. This is a working farm of cattle and horse breeding, poultry and ducks. Large twin-bedded/family room (en suite) on ground floor. All bedrooms have colour TV, tea/coffee making facilities and full central heating throughout. Ideal area for riding, golf, fishing and walking the Ridgeway. Interesting places to visit include Oxford, Bath, Windsor, Burford, Henley-on-Thames, Blenheim Palace and the Cotswolds. Open all year. Member of Farm Holiday Bureau. **ETC** ♦♦♦
website: www.bowling-green-farm.co.uk

**FARINGDON. Mrs Pat Hoddinott, Ashen Copse Farm, Coleshill, Faringdon SN6 7PU (01367 240175; Fax: 01367 241418). Working farm.** Perfect place to tour or relax. Our 650 acre National Trust farm is set in wonderful, peaceful countryside, teeming with wildlife. The quiet, comfortable accommodation is a great centre for walking or visiting Cotswolds, Vale of the White Horse, Oxford, Bath, Stratford and all little places in between! So much to see and do. Facilities locally for fishing, golfing, riding, boating and swimming. Many places to eat out nearby. Open all year. One family en suite, one twin and one single bedroom. Bed and Breakfast from £22 to £25. Reduction for children sharing. No smoking please. **ETC** ♦♦♦
e-mail: pat@hodd.demon.co.uk
website: www.hodd.demon.co.uk

**FREELAND. Mrs B. B. Taphouse, Wrestlers Mead, 35 Wroslyn Road, Freeland, Witney OX8 8HJ (Tel & Fax: 01993 882003).** A warm welcome awaits you at the home of the Taphouses. We are conveniently situated for Blenheim Palace (10 minutes), Oxford (20 minutes), and the Cotswolds (25 minutes). Accommodation comprises one en suite double/twin and one single room with washbasin on the ground floor. One first floor triple room also en suite. All rooms have tea/coffee making facilities. The double and triple rooms have colour TV. There is a large garden for guests' use. Parking. Visa and Mastercard accepted. Bed and Breakfast from £21.

**HENLEY-ON-THAMES. Mrs Liz Roach, The Old Bakery, Skirmett, Near Henley-on-Thames RG9 6TD (01491 638309).** This welcoming family house is situated on the site of an old bakery, seven miles from Henley-on-Thames and Marlow; half-an-hour from Heathrow and Oxford; one hour from London. It is in the Hambleden Valley in the beautiful Chilterns, with many excellent pubs selling good food. Excellent village pub in Skirmett within easy walking distance. Two double rooms with TV, one twin-bedded and two single rooms; two bathrooms. Open all year. Parking for five cars (car essential). Children and pets welcome. Bed and Breakfast from £25 to £30 single; £45 to £50 double.

**LONG HANBOROUGH. Miss M. Warwick, The Close Guest House, Witney Road, Long Hanborough OX8 8HF (01993 882485).** We offer comfortable accommodation in house set in own grounds of one-and-a-half acres. Two family rooms, one double room; all are en suite and have colour TV and tea/coffee making facilities. Lounge. Full central heating. Use of garden and car parking for eight cars. Close to Woodstock, Oxford and the Cotswolds. Babysitting. Open all year except Christmas. Bed and Breakfast from £15.

**MINSTER LOVELL. Mrs Katherine Brown, Hill Grove Farm, Crawley Road, Minster Lovell OX8 5NA (01993 703120; Fax: 01993 700528).** Hill Grove is a mixed family-run 300 acre working farm situated in an attractive rural setting overlooking the Windrush Valley. Ideally positioned for driving to Oxford, Blenheim Palace, Witney (Farm Museum) and Burford (renowned as the Gateway to the Cotswolds and for its splendid Wildlife Park.). New golf course one mile. Hearty breakfasts. One double/private shower, one twin/double en suite. Children welcome. Open all year except Christmas. Bed and Breakfast from £22 per person per night for double/private shower; £24 per person per night for double or twin en suite. Non-smoking. **ETC ◆◆◆◆**.

**OXFORD. Mr Stratford, The Bungalow, Cherwell Farm, Mill Lane, Old Marston, Oxford OX3 0QF (01865 557171).** Modern bungalow on five acres set in countryside but only three miles from the city centre. Offering comfortable accommodation and serving traditional breakfast. Colour TV, tea/coffee facilities in all rooms. Private parking. Non-smoking. Not on bus route. Bed and Breakfast from £22 to £24 per person. **ETC ◆◆◆**

**OXFORD. Mr and Mrs L. Price, Arden Lodge, 34 Sunderland Avenue (off Banbury Road), Oxford OX2 8DX (01865 552076; 07702 068697).** Modern detached house in select part of Oxford, within easy reach of Oxford Centre. Excellent position for Blenheim Palace and for touring Cotswolds, Stratford, Warwick etc. Close to river, parks, country inns and golf course. Easy access to London. All rooms have tea/coffee making and private facilities. Parking. Bed and Breakfast from £24 per person per night.

**OXFORD. Mr Afzal, Westminster Guest House, 350 Iffley Road, Oxford OX4 4AU (01865 250924).** Situated 1.4 miles from Oxford city centre, offering pleasant, clean and friendly accommodation Two double, two single and one twin bedrooms, all with tea/coffee facilities (twin room en suite). TV lounge. Central heating. Children over seven years welcome. Open all year. Car parking available. Bed and Breakfast accommodation from £22 single, £38 double, £42 twin/family.

**OXFORD. John and Gaynor Dean, Pembroke House, 379 Woodstock Road, Oxford OX2 8AA (01865 310782; Fax: 01865 310649).** Pembroke House is situated in one of the most beautiful approach roads into Oxford. This imposing family house has recently been refurbished to a very high standard. All rooms have central heating, tea/coffee making facilities and TV with video. The spacious bedrooms offer the perfect place to relax at the end of the day. One Master double, en suite bedroom, one guest double, en suite, one guest double with private luxury bathroom. Off street parking available. Sorry no smoking. Bed and Breakfast from £25 per person sharing. **ETC ◆◆◆◆**
e-mail: john@gcpipkins.freeserve.co.uk
website: www.oxfordcity.co.uk/accom/pembroke

**OXFORD. Diana and Richard Mitchell, Highfield West, 188 Cumnor Hill, Oxford OX2 9PJ (01865 863007).** Welcome to our comfortable home, which is in a quiet residential area on the western outskirts of Oxford – on a bus route to the centre of Oxford, we are near to the ring road and to Cumnor village where two attractive inns serve meals. Blenheim Palace is nearby – London, Stratford-on-Avon, Bath and the Cotswolds are within comfortable travelling distance. Our well-appointed rooms have central heating, colour TV and refreshment trays. The family, double and twin rooms are en suite, the two single rooms share a bathroom. Our large outdoor pool is heated in season. Non-smoking. Vegetarians welcome. **ETC ◆◆◆**
e-mail: highfieldwest@email.msn.com

---

*Please mention BED & BREAKFAST STOPS when writing to enquire about accommodation*

## Oxfordshire

**SOULDERN. Toddy and Clive Hamilton-Gould, Tower Fields, Tusmore Road, Near Souldern, Bicester OX27 7HY (01869 346554; Fax: 01869 345157).** Tower Fields is in an unspoilt elevated position with outstanding views, situated half-a-mile from the village of Souldern. A recently renovated farmhouse and barn provide comfortable en suite bedrooms on the ground floor, all with colour TV and tea/coffee making facilities. This is a working smallholding where you will see rare breeds of cattle, sheep, poultry and pigs. Full English breakfast using home produce is available. Stabling and garaging available on request. Non-smoking. Disabled guests accommodated. Three miles Junction 10 M40. Ideally situated Cotswolds, Silverstone, Birmingham, Oxford. Bed and Breakfast from £25. Full details on request. **ETC ♦♦♦**
e-mail: **hgould@strayduck.com**

**TACKLEY. June and George Collier, 55 Nethercote Road, Tackley, Kidlington OX5 3AT (01869 331255; mobile: 07990 338225; Fax: 01869 331670).** We welcome you and your family, you and your dog, you and your horse! Ground floor accommodation - twin or double room, and an excellent breakfast. We are an ideal base for touring, walking and riding, or a refreshing change for an overnight business trip. Central for Oxford, the Cotswolds, Stratford-upon-Avon, Blenheim Palace and Woodstock. Tackley is an exceptional village with a regular train and bus service, and local hostelries serving excellent food. Dogs and horses made especially welcome. Bed and Breakfast from £25.

**TETSWORTH, near THAME. Mrs Julia Tanner, Little Acre, Tetsworth, Thame, Oxford OX9 7AT (01844 281423).** Charming country retreat with pretty landscaped gardens and waterfall. Quiet location but only two miles from J6 M40. Near Chilterns, Oxford, Cotswolds, Heathrow Airport. Comfy beds, hearty breakfasts, 'olde worlde' style dining room. Open all year with friendly, relaxed atmosphere. En suite rooms; ground floor bedrooms. Tea/coffee making facilities and TV in rooms. Pets welcome. Highly recommended by previous guests. Bed and Breakfast from £18.

**WITNEY. Mrs Elizabeth Simpson, Field View, Wood Green, Witney OX8 6DE (01993 705485; Mobile: 07768 614347).** Witney is famous for blankets, made here for over 300 years. Our house was built in 1959, of Cotswold stone. Set in two acres and situated on picturesque Wood Green, with football and cricket pitches to the rear, yet only 10 minutes' walk from the centre of this lively, bustling market town. An ideal touring centre for Oxford University (12 miles), Blenheim Palace (eight miles), Cotswold Wildlife Park (eight miles) and country walks. Ample parking. Three delightful en suite bedrooms with central heating, tea/coffee making facilities and colour TV. Non-smoking. A peaceful setting and a warm, friendly atmosphere await you. Bed and full English Breakfast from £23.50. **ETC ♦♦♦♦** *SILVER AWARD.*
e-mail: **jsimpson@netcomuk.co.uk**
website: **www.netcomuk.co.uk/~kearse/index.html**

**WOODSTOCK. The Leather Bottel, East End, North Leigh, Near Witney OX8 6PY (01993 882174).** Joe and Nena Purcell invite you to The Leather Bottel guest house situated in the quiet hamlet of East End near North Leigh, convenient for Blenheim Palace, Woodstock, Roman Villa, Oxford and the Cotswolds. Breathtaking countryside walks. Two double en suite bedrooms, one family room with own bathroom, one single bedroom, all with colour TV and tea/coffee making facilities. Bed and Breakfast £30 per night for single room, from £40 for double. Children welcome. Open all year. Directions: follow signs to Roman Villa off A4095. **ETC ♦♦♦**

## Oxfordshire

**WOODSTOCK. Mrs Mandy Buck, Elbie House, East End, North Leigh, Near Witney OX8 6PZ (01993 880166).** Lovely 16th century home recently converted from an Inn. Two luxurious, flexible and spacious en suite rooms offer our guests relaxed and private accommodation, one with four-poster bed. English or Continental/vegetarian breakfasts served in rooms. Ground floor accommodation allows easy access for less able visitors. Large well stocked and lovingly cared for garden with security lit parking. Superb location for visiting Blenhein Palace, Oxford and touring the Cotswolds. A warm and friendly welcome awaits you. Children over seven welcome. From £22.50 per person. Single occupancy from £30. **ETC** ♦♦♦♦
e-mail: elbiehouse@freeserve.co.uk

**WOODSTOCK. Mrs Kay Bradford, Hamilton House, 43 Hill Rise, Old Woodstock OX20 1AB (Tel & Fax: 01993 812206; Mobile: 07778 705568).** Highly recommended Bed and Breakfast establishment with parking, overlooking Blenheim Park, Blenheim Palace and the town centre with good selection of restaurants, pubs and shops within walking distance. Accommodation offered - one twin-bedded room and two double rooms, all en suite with colour TV and tea making facilities. Pleasant diningroom. Excellent selection of Continental and full English breakfast. Comfortable and relaxed atmosphere with informative and very hospitable hostess. Ideal base for Blenheim Palace, Bladon, the Cotswolds, Stratford-upon-Avon, Oxford and major airports. Access off A44 northern end of Woodstock, 200 yards from Rose and Crown pub. Children and pets welcome. Bed and Breakfast from £20 per person, based on two people sharing.
website: www.SmoothHound.co.uk/hotels/hamiltonh.html

*See also Colour Display Advertisement*

**WOODSTOCK. Gorselands Hall, Boddington Lane, North Leigh, Witney OX8 6PU (01993 882292; Fax: 01993 883629).** Lovely old Cotswold stone farmhouse with oak beams and flagstone floor in delightful rural setting. Large secluded garden, grass tennis court and croquet lawn. Ideal for Blenheim Palace, the Cotswolds and Oxford. Roman villa close by. Good walking country. Comfortable, attractively furnished bedrooms with views of the garden or the surrounding countryside. All rooms are en suite with colour TV and tea/coffee making facilities. Non smoking. Lounge with snooker table for residents' use. A choice of excellent pubs within easy reach. Bed and Breakfast from £22.50. Winter discounts available. **ETC** ♦♦♦.
e-mail: hamilton@gorselandshall.com
website: www.gorselandshall.com

---

# FREE or REDUCED RATE entry to Holiday Visits and Attractions – see our READERS' OFFER VOUCHERS on pages 43-60

---

# FHG PUBLICATIONS

publish a large range of well-known accommodation guides. We will be happy to send you details or you can use the order form at the back of this book.

# SHROPSHIRE

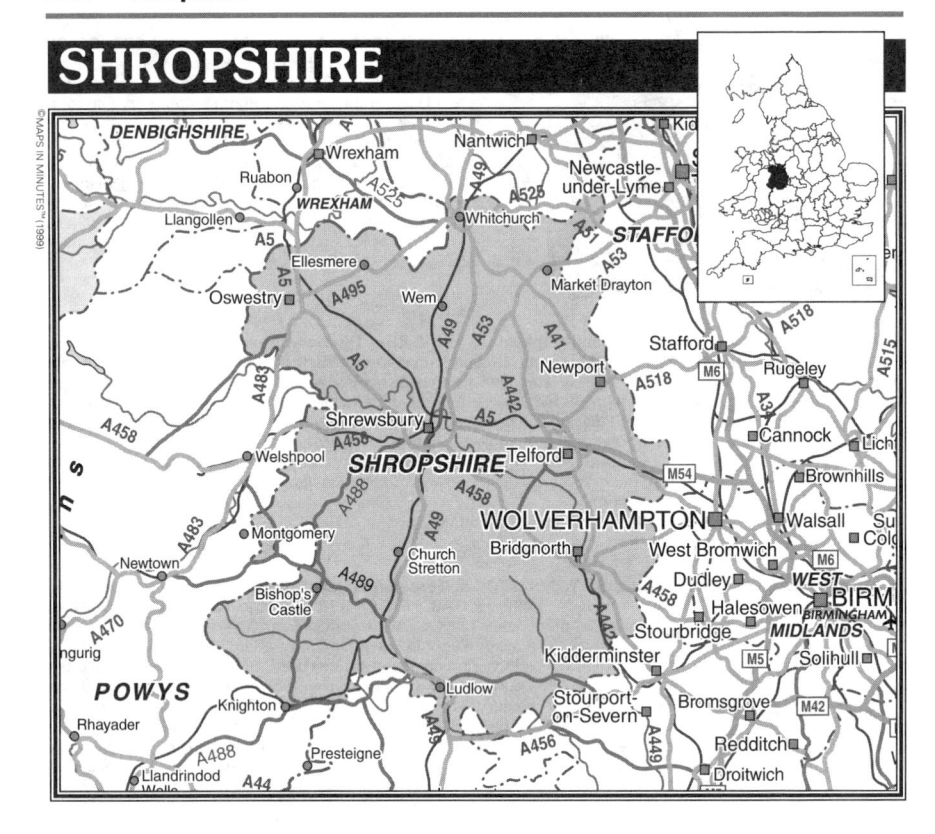

**BISHOP'S CASTLE. Mrs Ann Williams, Shuttocks Wood, Norbury, Bishop's Castle SY9 5EA (01588 650433; Fax: 01588 650492).** Shuttocks Wood is a Scandinavian house in woodland setting situated within easy travelling distance of the Long Mynd and Stiperstone Hills. Accommodation consists of one double and two twin-bedded rooms, all en suite and with tea/coffee facilities and colour TV. Good walks and horse riding nearby and a badger set just 20 yards from the door! Ample parking. Non-smoking establishment. Children over 12 years welcome. Sorry, no pets. Open all year. Bed and Breakfast from £22 per person per night. Credit cards accepted.

**BRIDGNORTH. Jutta and Alan Ward, Linley Crest, Linley Brook, Near Bridgnorth WV16 4SZ (Tel & Fax: 01746 765527).** Very convenient for the medieval towns of Shrewsbury, Bridgnorth and Much Wenlock; Ludlow, Ironbridge and the dramatic landscape of the Long Mynd. We offer three generous double rooms with TV, beverage tray, hairdryer – two of which have a shower en suite, guest-controlled heating and easy access; additionally, one has a private conservatory. The third bedroom has a private bathroom. Delicious English breakfast provided and special diets catered for. Winners of the Bridgnorth District Council Healthy Eating Gold Award since 1999. Open all year; off road parking; drying facilities. No smoking, no pets, no cards. Children very welcome. From £20 per person per night. Wir sprechen Deutsch – Herzlich willkommen! Warm welcome assured. **ETC ♦♦♦♦** *SILVER AWARD.*
**e-mail: linleycrest@easicom.com**

# Shropshire 249

**BUCKNELL. Mrs Christine Price, The Hall, Bucknell SY7 0AA (Tel & Fax: 01547 530249).** You are assured of a warm welcome at The Hall, which is a Georgian farmhouse with spacious accommodation. The house and gardens are set in a secluded part of a small South Shropshire village, an ideal area for touring the Welsh Borderland. Offa's Dyke is on the doorstep and the historic towns of Shrewsbury, Hereford, Ludlow and Ironbridge are within easy reach as are the Church Stretton Hills and Wenlock Edge. Accommodation - one triple room with private bathroom, one twin en-suite. Both have tea-making facilities and TV. Guest lounge. Ample parking. Bed and Breakfast from £20 – £22; Evening Meal £11. SAE, please, for details. **ETC** ♦♦♦.
e-mail: hall@ukworld.net
website: www.ukworld.net/hall

*See also Colour Display Advertisement*

**CHURCH STRETTON. Willowfield Country Guest House, Lower Wood, All Stretton, Church Stretton (01694 751471).** Quiet and idyllic, in its own grounds with beautiful rural views. An interesting house from Elizabethan to Edwardian, all bedrooms en suite with posture sprung beds, settee, TV and beverages. Guest lounge with open fire. Elizabethan diningroom, individual tables, candlelit dinners. Delicious home cooking, home grown and local produce. Ideal central location for days out, visiting the many places of interest. Licensed. Non-smoking. No pets. Philip and Jane Secrett offer you a warm and friendly welcome to enjoy their hospitality. All is revealed in our colour brochure. **ETC** ♦♦♦♦♦ *GOLD AWARD*, **AA** ♦♦♦♦♦ *PREMIER COLLECTION*.

**CHURCH STRETTON. Mrs Lyn Bloor, Malt House Farm, Lower Wood, Church Stretton SY6 6LF (01694 751379).** Olde worlde beamed farmhouse situated amidst spectacular scenery on the lower slopes of the Long Mynd hills. We are a working farm producing beef cattle and sheep. One double and one twin bedrooms, both with en suite bathrooms, colour TV, hairdryer and tea tray. Good farmhouse cooking is served in the diningroom. Private guests' sittingroom. Non-smoking. Regret no children or pets. Bed and Breakfast from £18.50 per person per night; Evening Meal from £15 per person. Now fully licensed.

**CHURCH STRETTON. Mrs Mary Jones, Acton Scott Farm, Acton Scott, Church Stretton SY6 6QN (01694 781260; Fax: 0870-129 4591).** Lovely 17th century farmhouse in peaceful village amidst the beautiful hills of South Shropshire, an area of outstanding natural beauty. The house is full of character and the rooms, which are all heated, are comfortable and spacious with en suite or private bathroom and beverage making facilities. Colour TV lounge. We are a working farm, centrally situated for visiting Ironbridge, Shrewsbury and Ludlow, each being easily reached within half-an-hour. Visitors' touring and walking information available. No smoking. Bed and full English Breakfast from £19 per person. Weekly rate £130 per person. Farm Holiday Bureau member. **ETC** ♦♦♦

**CHURCH STRETTON. Mrs J. Brereton, Brereton's Farm, Woolston, Church Stretton SY6 6QD (Tel & Fax: 01694 781201). Working farm.** Peace, tranquillity and unforgettable views of rambling countryside (including working of sheep dogs) can be enjoyed from extensive gardens surrounding our elegant red brick farmhouse; an ideal base for visiting Ludlow, Ironbridge, Shrewsbury and Powis Castle, or walk onto the Long Mynd from our working farm. Twin and two double bedrooms (one with pine four-poster), all en suite, with tea making facilities and fresh milk. Residents' lounge with log burner. Hearty English Breakfast. Bed and Breakfast from £20, Evening Meal £13. **ETC** ♦♦♦.
e-mail: jbrereton@crosswinds.net

## Shropshire

**CLEOBURY MORTIMER near. Mrs Carole Morrison, Clod Hall, Milson, Cleobury Mortimer DY14 OBJ (01584 781421).** Clod Hall is a comfortable, well-appointed centrally heated house surrounded by fields and woods and situated on a good road between the pretty towns of Cleobury Mortimer and Tenbury Wells, within easy reach of Ludlow. Guests will enjoy beautiful views over farmland with the Clee Hills in the distance. Accommodation comprises one double room, one single room with a spacious bathroom and a shower cubicle. There is a private diningroom for guests. The bedrooms are provided with tea/coffee making facilities and TV. Children and non-smokers welcome, also small house-trained dogs if requested. Eighteen acres of garden and field are open to guests. Prices start at £17 per person for Bed and Breakfast.

CLOD HALL, MILSON,

**CLUN. Mrs Angela McHale, Sun Inn, 10 High Street, Clun SY7 8JB (01588 640559).** The XVth century Sun Inn serves excellent home-cooked food and real ales. Six en suite bedrooms, three of which are at ground level. Private parking. Situated on the "Shropshire Way", Clun is an ideal base for exploring Offa's Dyke, South Shropshire and the Welsh Marches, with the beautiful towns of Ludlow, Montgomery and Shrewsbury all near by. Listed in the Good Pub and Good Food Guides and Roger Protz, 'Britain's Best 500 Pubs". **ETC** ♦♦♦.

**CLUN. Mrs M. Jones, Llanhedric, Clun, Craven Arms SY7 8NG (01588 640203). Working farm.** Put your feet up and relax on the recliners as the beauty of the garden, the trickle of the pond, and the views of Clun and its surrounding hills provide solace from the stress of modern day life. Receive a warm welcome to this traditional oak-beamed farmhouse, set back from the working farm. Three bedrooms, double en suite; tea/coffee facilities and good home cooking. Visitors' lounge with inglenook fireplace; separate dining room. Walks, historic sites and attractions all close. Non-smoking household. Regret no dogs in house. Open April to October. Bed and Breakfast from £18; Bed, Breakfast and Evening Meal from £28. Reductions for children. **ETC** ♦♦♦

**CRAVEN ARMS. Mrs Thirza Watkins, Broadward Hall, Clungunford, Craven Arms SY7 0QA (01547 530357). Working farm.** Broadward Hall is a mixed working farm set in the beautiful Clun Valley, nine miles west of historic Ludlow and eight miles east of Clun. The house is an 18/19th century castellated rebuild of an early 12th century residence. The area is ideal for walking and bird-watching. Ironbridge Museums, Central Wales and Severn Valley Railways, National Trust Houses, Border castles and hillforts are all nearby. Two rods available for fly fishing. Two twin rooms (one with washbasin) and one double room are available. Two guest bathrooms, one with shower. Smoking restrictions. £17 per person, £16 for three or more nights. Open Easter (or April 1st) to October.

**CRAVEN ARMS. Stokesay Castle Coaching Inn, School Road, Craven Arms (01588 672304; Fax: 01588 673877).** Shropshire has a special magic which, once experienced, casts a lasting spell. Rich in undulating farmland and dotted with quiet market towns, the county has, in the past, taken a leading role in often violent struggles across its border with Wales typified by Stokesay Castle, a perfectly preserved 13th century fortified manor house from which this little gem of an hotel takes its name. The present owners lost no time in enhancing the inn's reputation for excellent, well presented food with a positive flair for traditional home cooking by bringing in first class, well-trained staff with a special gift of making visitors feel welcome. To discover the secret allure of the area, acquaintance with this friendly retreat is strongly recommended. First-rate accommodation is available in rooms with en suite facilities, satellite television and tea and coffee-makers.

---

*Please mention **Bed and Breakfast Stops** when making enquiries about accommodation featured in these pages.*

**DORRINGTON. Ron and Jenny Repath, Meadowlands, Lodge Lane, Frodesley, Dorrington SY5 7HD (01694 731350).** Former farmhouse attractively decorated, set in eight acres of gardens, paddocks and woodland. Quiet location in a delightful hamlet seven miles south of Shrewsbury. The guest house lies on a no-through road to a forested hill rising to 1000ft. Meadowlands features panoramic views over open countryside to the Stretton Hills. Guest accommodation includes en suite facilities and every bedroom has a colour TV, drink-making facilities and a silent fridge. Guests' lounge with maps and guides for loan. Drinks on arrival. Central heating. Plenty of parking space. Strictly no smoking. Bed and Breakfast from £18; Evening Meal from £10 by arrangement. Brochure available. **ETC** ♦♦♦

**IRONBRIDGE** see also entries under **BRIDGNORTH**

**IRONBRIDGE/TELFORD. John and Diana Dell, The Old Church Guest House, Park Avenue, Madeley, Telford TF7 5AB (Tel & Fax: 01952 583745).** Built in 1874 as a church, it has been carefully converted to a home of comfort and character. Situated in the area of the Industrial Revolution, the Old Church is a short walk from Blists Hill Victorian town and within easy reach of all the historic museum sites of the Ironbridge Gorge. A short drive and you can visit the Severn Valley Railway, Cosford Aerospace Museum, historic towns, priories and castles. Alternatively within ten minutes you can be in the heart of Telford's shopping or business areas, at the exhibition/conference/sports centres, or enjoying the many entertainments available. All rooms are on the ground floor and are equipped with clock-radio, colour TV and tea/coffee making facilities. Hairdryers and irons available if required. En suite available. Bed and Breakfast from £36 per room. **ETC** ♦♦♦♦ *SILVER AWARD*.

**LUDLOW. Mr and Mrs R. Cecil-Jones, Henwick House, Gravel Hill, Ludlow SY8 1QU (01584 873338).** A warm and friendly welcome awaits you in this privately owned former coach house Bed and Breakfast. Delightful en suite rooms, TV, tea/coffee making facilities, comfortable beds and good traditional English Breakfast. Private parking. Situated approximately half-a-mile from the castle and shops and local inns. One double room, one twin, both en suite and one twin room with single bathroom. Terms from £20 to £22 per person.

**LUDLOW. M.A. and E. Purnell, Ravenscourt Manor, Woofferton, Ludlow SY8 4AL (01584 711905).** Ravenscourt is a superb, newly renovated Tudor Manor set in two acres of lovely gardens. Beautifully furnished and equipped bedrooms. Wonderful area for walking or touring. Two miles from Ludlow, famous for its restaurants and architecture, eight miles from Leominster, famous for antiques, and 15 miles from Hereford and Worcester with their historic cathedrals. Close to National Trust properties and only 40 minutes from Ironbridge and Stratford. Excellent home cooked food, dinner available. All rooms are en suite with remote-control colour TV, tea/coffee facilities and central heating. Bed and Breakfast from £25 per person; two nights Dinner, Bed and Breakfast £85 per person. Warm welcome assured. Also self-catering cottages available. **ETC** ♦♦♦♦ *GOLD AWARD*.

**LUDLOW. Number Twenty Eight, Lower Broad Street, Ludlow SY8 1PQ (Reservations: 0800 081 5000).** A very warm welcome awaits you at this guest house which comprises several Listed houses in this delightful, ancient street. The accommodation is entirely en suite, each individually furnished to the highest standards for total comfort and relaxation. Nowadays we have more Michelin restaurants within walking distance that one can shake a knife and fork at! Details from **Patricia and Philip Ross**. **ETC** ♦♦♦♦♦ *GOLD AWARD*
e-mail: ross@no28.co.uk
website: www.no28.co.uk

**LYDBURY NORTH. Mr and Mrs R. Evans, "Brunslow", Lydbury North SY7 8AD (01588 680244). Working farm, join in.** "Brunslow" is a beautiful Georgian style farmhouse, centrally heated throughout, ideal for walking and for those who enjoy the peace and quiet of unspoiled countryside. The house is set in large gardens with lovely views in all directions and the farm produces mainly milk; pigs, poultry and calves are reared and "feeding time" is very popular with younger guests. One double, one single and two family rooms, all having washbasin and tea/coffee making facilities. Central heating throughout. Bathroom, toilets; separate sittingroom and diningroom; colour TV, high chair and babysitting available. Open all year, except Christmas, for Bed and Breakfast from £18; Evening Dinner £8 if required. SAE please for terms. Packed lunches available. Car essential, parking.

**MARKET DRAYTON. Mrs Moira Roberts, Willow House, Shrewsbury Road, Tern Hill, Market Drayton TF9 3PX (Tel & Fax: 01630 638326).** Modern farmhouse overlooking open countryside. Two spacious twin rooms with en suite, one double room with private bathroom, guests lounge/TV room. Central heating. All rooms have tea/coffee trays. Large car park and garden. Homely atmosphere. Many inns and restaurants nearby. Places of interest include Hodnet Hall Gardens, Wollerton Gardens, Hawkstone Follies, Dorothy Clive Garden and Bridgemere Garden World. Convenient for visiting Chester, Nantwich, the Potteries, Shrewsbury, Telford and Ironbridge. Prices per night per room for bed and full English breakfast - single en suite from £25, double with private bathroom from £46 and twin en suite from £46. Reductions for three nights or more.

**MINSTERLEY. Paul Costello, Cricklewood Cottage, Plox Green, Minsterley, Shrewsbury SY5 0HT (01743 791229).** A delightful 18th century cottage at the foot of the Stiperstones Hills, retaining its original character with exposed beams, inglenook fireplace and traditional furnishings. The bedrooms are fully en suite with lovely views of the Shropshire countryside. Breakfast is served in the sun room, looking out to the hills, with an attractive choice of dishes. Especially inviting is the pretty cottage garden where guests can wander amongst many old-fashioned and unusual plants and stroll alongside the trout stream. Excellent restaurants/inns nearby - full details supplied to guests. Ideal for visiting Shrewsbury and Ironbridge. Private parking. Non smoking. Bed and Breakfast from £23.50. Call for brochure. **ETC** ♦♦♦♦

See also Colour Display Advertisement **NEWPORT. Mrs Green, Peartree Farmhouse, Farm Grove, Newport TF10 7PX (01952 811193).** Charming farmhouse set in picturesque gardens, enjoying the best of both worlds on the very edge of historic market town yet in country setting. Immaculate modern accommodation, non-smoking environment, TV lounge. All rooms satellite TV, tea/coffee making facilities, controllable central heating, mostly en suite. Ample private parking. Very convenient for Telford, Ironbridge etc. Bed and Breakfast from £25 per person.

---

# FREE or REDUCED RATE entry to Holiday Visits and Attractions — see our READERS' OFFER VOUCHERS on pages 43-60

**Shropshire** 253

**OSWESTRY. Mrs Margaret Jones, Ashfield Farm House, Maesbury, Near Oswestry SY10 8JH (Tel & Fax: 01691 653589; mobile: 07989 477414).** Scented roses and scarlet creepers ramble and lacy wisterias cover this delightful 16th century coach house and Georgian farmhouse, one mile from Oswestry, A5 and A483 amidst an English/Welsh border mix. Very pretty, cosy yet spacious en suite rooms (one has luxury private bath/shower room), all fully equipped with TV, payphone, hostess tray, etc., plus great Welsh mountain views. "Olde Worlde" dining and sittingrooms, log fires, ample books and games. Many original features throughout. Five minutes walk to canalside inn, good food and boat hire. Beautiful area overflowing with castles, lakes, mountains and woodlands. Chester, Llangollen, Shrewsbury 20-30 minute drive. North Wales and South Shropshire on your doorstep. Bed and Breakfast from £19.75 per person per night. Short Breaks available. Please telephone for brochure. **ETC ♦♦♦♦** *SILVER AWARD.*
website: www.ashfieldfarmhouse.co.uk

**OSWESTRY near. Mrs Jill Plunkett, Rhoswiel Lodge, Weston Rhyn, Near Oswestry SY10 7TG (01691 777609).** Victorian country house in delightful gardens beside the Shropshire Union/Llangollen Canal. We are easy to find - just 400 yards from the A5. A convenient place to stop overnight or better still as a centre to explore the Welsh hills, forests, lakes and castles to the west or the verdant, rural quietness of North Shropshire to the east. We enjoy where we live and would be disappointed should you not enjoy our area and our home - at a price of course! Bed and Breakfast from £17 to £22 per person. Double room is en suite and twin room has its own separate facilities.

**SHREWSBURY. Anton Guest House, 1 Canon Street, Monkmoor, Shrewsbury SY2 5HG (01743 359275).** The Anton Guest House is an attractive corner-positioned Victorian house which stands on a main road just 10 minutes' stroll from both Shrewsbury town centre and the 10th century Abbey church. Family owned and run, offering a very friendly welcome to guests. Very tastefully decorated with each of the three bedrooms warm and comfortable (house has double glazing) and with tea/coffee making facilities and TVs. Breakfast is wholesome and delicious. The world famous Brother Cadfael books by the late Ellis Peters (now serialised for TV) are set in the area and visitors may be interested in retracing the intrepid monk's steps in the Brother Cadfael Walks. Open all year. Smoking banned throughout. Children welcome. No pets. **ETC ♦♦♦♦**
e-mail: antonhouse@supanet.com
website: www.antonhouse.supanet.com

**SHREWSBURY. E.W. and J.A. Bottomley, Lythwood Hall, Bayston Hill, Shrewsbury SY3 0AD (0707 874747; Fax: 01743 874747).** Quality Bed and Breakfast accommodation in a comfortable, spacious Georgian house. Enjoy the peaceful rural surroundings, our beautiful gardens or the log fire in winter. Relax in the guests' lounge, visit our spotted horses or walk on the Shropshire Way. We are centrally placed for guests to tour Shropshire and the Welsh Borders. The medieval town of Shrewsbury is just three miles away and we offer a collection service from the railway station. There is easy access to all main routes, e.g. A5, A49, M54, M6. We are open all year. Kennel and run available for dogs. Bed and Breakfast £19.50, Evening meal £10. Home-grown produce, vegetarians welcome.

---

Terms quoted in this publication may be subject to increase if rises in costs necessitate

## Shropshire

**SHREWSBURY. The Stiperstones Guest House, 18 Coton Cresent, Coton Hill, Shrewsbury SY1 2NZ (01743 246720/350303; Fax: 01743 350303).** The Stiperstones is situated in a quiet residential area only 10 minutes' pleasant walk from the town centre. Off road car parking is available. A location map is available on request. Our six guest bedrooms are very comfortable, spacious, and light. Each bedroom is attractively decorated, tastefully furnished and has its own character. All rooms have hospitality tray, colour teletext TV, and direct dial telephone. There is a well presented guest lounge. A high standard of cleanliness is offered throughout. We offer traditional English, Continental-style, and vegetarian breakfasts. Eggs are free-range. All major credit and debit cards are accepted. **ETC/AA ◆◆◆** 
e-mail:stiperston@aol.com
website: www.go2.co.uk/stiperstones

**SHREWSBURY. Mrs Janet Jones, Grove Farm, Preston Brockhurst, Shrewsbury SY4 5QA (01939 220223).** This lovely 17th century farmhouse with a beautiful view, offers warmth and comfort to all guests. It is set in a little village on the A49, seven miles north of Shrewsbury. The house has a large lounge and dining room with fires and colour TV; four lovely bedrooms (one double/family, one twin both with showers en suite, one double, one single both with washbasins) with easy chairs and tea/coffee trays. Guests' bathroom. Central heating throughout. Visitors are welcomed with tea and home-made cakes, and there is always a variety of delicious food offered for breakfast. Sorry, no smoking. No pets. Bed and Breakfast from £20 to £35. We look forward to welcoming you to our home. Reduced rates for children in family room. Short breaks and weekly terms available. **AA ◆◆◆◆**

**SHREWSBURY near. Mrs Gwen Frost, Oakfields, Baschurch Road, Myddle, Shrewsbury SY4 3RX (01939 290823).** Visiting Shropshire? Why not enjoy the warm welcome and home-from-home atmosphere at Oakfields, which is in a quiet, idyllic setting located in the picturesque village of Myddle made famous by Gough's "History of Myddle" written in 1700. All ground floor bedrooms, each tastefully decorated and equipped with colour TV, tea-making facilities, washbasin, hairdryer and shaver point; cot and high chair also available; guests' TV lounge. Central heating throughout. Large and pleasant garden for guests to enjoy. 15 minutes from Shrewsbury and Hawkstone Park and convenient for Ironbridge, Wales, Chester, etc. Golf and riding nearby. Extensive car park. Non-smoking. Bed and Breakfast from £18. Nearest main road A528, also straight road from A5. **ETC ◆◆◆**

**TELFORD. Mrs Hazel Miller, The Old Rectory, Stirchley Village, Telford TF3 1DY (Tel & Fax: 01952 596308).** The Old Rectory, which dates from 1734, is set in an acre of quiet, secluded gardens and is adjacent to the Telford Town Park. It is one-and-a-half miles from the town centre, Racquet Centre and Exhibition Centre. All of the bedrooms at the Old Rectory have either en suite facilities or private bathrooms, TV, clock radio, tea/coffee making facilities and central heating. One ground floor bedroom is suitable for wheelchair users (Category 1). The sitting room has a log fire, TV and video. A full English breakfast is served in the dining room which has a beamed ceiling and inglenook fireplace. We do ask guests not to smoke in the house please. Bed and Breakfast from £21 per person. **ETC ◆◆◆◆**

---

**FHG**

Visit the FHG website
**www.holidayguides.com**
for details of the wide choice of accommodation
featured in the full range of FHG titles

**TELFORD. Mrs Mary Jones, Red House Farm, Longdon-on-Tern, Wellington, Telford TF6 6LE (01952 770245).** Red House Farm is a late Victorian farmhouse in the small village of Longdon-on-Tern, noted for its aqueduct, built by Thomas Telford in 1796. Two double bedrooms have private facilities, one family room has its own separate bathroom. All rooms are large and comfortable. Excellent breakfast. Farm easily located, leave M54 Junction 6, follow A442, take B5063. Central for historic Shrewsbury, Ironbridge Gorge museums or modern Telford. Several local eating places. Open all year. Families most welcome, reductions for children. Pets also welcome. Bed and Breakfast from £18. 
e-mail: rhf@virtual-shropshire.co.uk
websites: www.goto.co.uk/redhouse
www.virtual-shropshire.co.uk/red-house-farm

**WELSH/SHROPSHIRE BORDER. Mrs Hibbert, Corner House Farm, The Cadney, Bettisfield, Near Whitchurch SY13 2LD (01948 710572).** Smallholding in idyllic surroundings, peacefully situated with lovely walks. Easy access to Mid Wales and North Wales coastal resorts and within easy reach of Chester, Shrewsbury and Whitchurch. One single, one twin or family suite with bathroom. Rates start at £16 per person; Evening Meal on request. Open all year except Christmas.

**WEM, near Shrewsbury. Mrs B. Barnes, Foxleigh House, Foxleigh Drive, Wem SY4 5BP (01939 233528).** This elegant period country house of immense character is ideally placed for touring Roman Chester, Ironbridge and Wedgwood, where museums and visitor centres are plentiful. Moreover, it is within easy reach of the mountains of Snowdonia and National Trust castles and houses, and the Hawkstone Park Follies are nearby. Quietly situated, yet convenient for Wem station (Shrewsbury 12 minutes), Foxleigh is near to swimming pool, tennis club and sports centre, and has its own croquet lawn. Accommodation comprises one large twin-bedded room with private bathroom and one family suite with three rooms and private bathroom (sleeps five/six) both with colour TV and tea/coffee facilities. Hairdryer and iron available. Both dining room and drawing room are beautifully appointed with classic period furniture - ideal for evening relaxtion. Traditional English or Continental breakfast. Parking. Dinner by arrangement from £11.50. Many good pubs and restaurants locally. From £20 to £23 per night. Brochure from Mrs Barnes. **AA** *QQQQ. "WHICH?" MAGAZINE.*

# PLEASE NOTE

All the information in this book is given in good faith in the belief that it is correct. However, the publishers cannot guarantee the facts given in these pages, neither are they responsible for changes in policy, ownership or terms that may take place after the date of going to press. Readers should always satisfy themselves that the facilities they require are available and that the terms, if quoted, still apply.

**WHITCHURCH. Miss J. Gregory, Ash Hall, Ash Magna, Whitchurch SY13 4DL (01948 663151).**
An early 18th-century house in the small North Shropshire village of Ash Magna. One-and-a-half miles from the A41 with easy access to Chester, Crewe, Shrewsbury, Wrexham, Llangollen: all 20 miles or less. Medium sized mixed farm with pedigree Friesians. The farmhouse has oak panelling in several rooms with a large oak staircase as a particular feature. Accommodation in two bedrooms, one with en suite bathroom. Children are welcome and rates are reduced. Open all year. **ETC** ♦♦

**WHITCHURCH. Mrs Mayer, Wood Farm, Old Wood Houses, Whitchurch SY13 4EJ (01948 871224).**
Charming 16th century farmhouse in a traditional courtyard setting on working dairy farm in peaceful countryside. Unwind in the guests' lounge in front of an inglenook fireplace after sightseeing as we are central to Chester, Ironbridge, Shrewsbury and the Potteries. Spacious beamed bedrooms (one with traditional brass bed) and welcome baskets. Ground floor room available. All facilities. One-and-a-half-miles off A41. Good food and drinking pub within walking distance. Business visitors welcome. Bed and Breakfast from £19 to £25. **ETC** ♦♦♦
*SILVER AWARD.*

# FHG

Other specialised

# FHG PUBLICATIONS

Published annually: Please add 50p postage (UK only) when ordering from the publishers

- Recommended COUNTRY HOTELS OF BRITAIN   £4.99
- Recommended WAYSIDE & COUNTRY INNS OF BRITAIN   £4.99
- PETS WELCOME!   £5.99
- B&B IN BRITAIN   £3.99
- THE GOLF GUIDE Where to Play / Where to Stay   £9.99

**FHG PUBLICATIONS LTD**
Abbey Mill Business Centre,
Seedhill, Paisley, Renfrewshire PA1 1TJ

Tel: 0141-887 0428 • Fax: 0141-889 7204
e-mail: fhg@ipcmedia.com • website: www.holidayguides.com

# SOMERSET

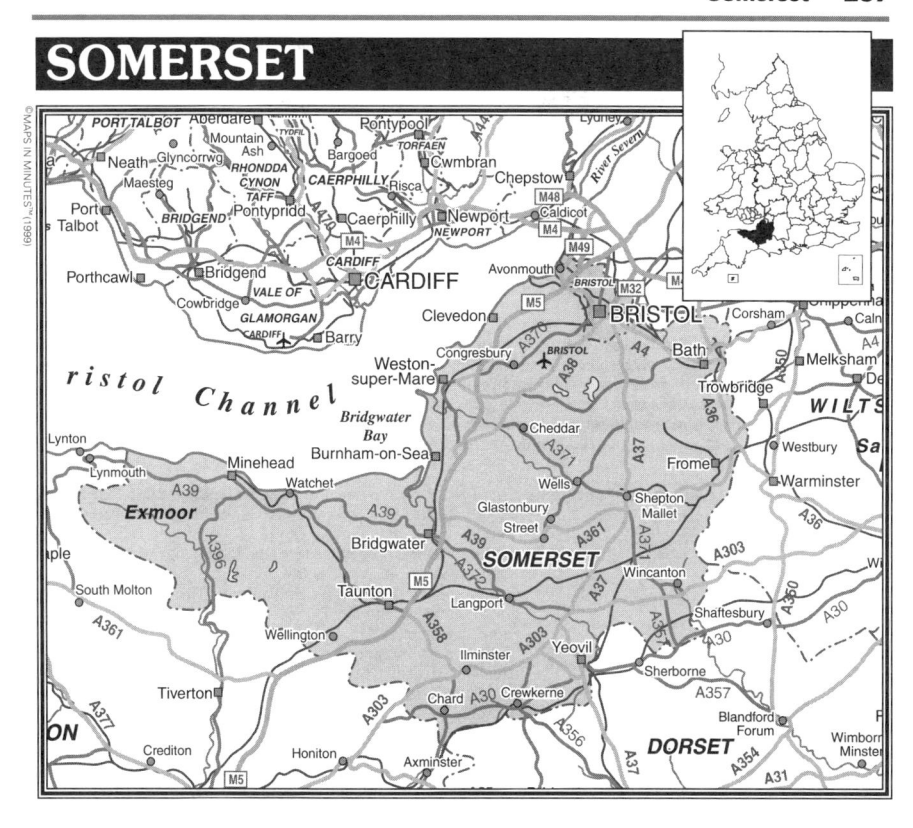

**ALLERFORD. Jean and Ian Hamilton, Fern Cottage, Allerford, Near Porlock, Exmoor TA24 8HN (Tel & Fax: 01643 862215)** Large 16th century traditional Exmoor cottage in a tiny National Trust Village sitting in the lush wood-fringed Vale of Porlock with spectacular coastal and moorland scenery. Walks start on the doorstep. Much acclaimed for our contemporary English/bistro style dinner served around our large table in an informal "dinner party style" or depending on numbers a more intimate setting. Comprehensive cellar. Private parking. Non-smoking. Credit cards accepted. Bed and Breakfast £29 per person per night, Dinner £13.75. The Exmoor Break: three nights Dinner Bed and Breakfast £122 per person. Brochure. **ETC ◆◆◆◆.**
website: www.exmoortourism.org/ferncottage.htm 
www.SmoothHound.co.uk/hotels/ferncott.html

**ASHBRITTLE. Mrs Ann Heard, Lower Westcott Farm, Ashbrittle, Near Wellington TA21 0HZ (01398 361296).** On Devon/Somerset border, 230 acre family farm with Friesian herd, sheep, poultry and horses. Ideal for walking, touring Exmoor, Quantocks, both coasts and many National Trust properties. Pleasant farmhouse, tastefully modernised but with olde worlde charm, inglenook fireplaces and antique furniture. Set in large gardens with lawns and flower beds in peaceful scenic countryside. Two family bedrooms with private facilities and tea/coffee making; large lounge, separate dining room. Offering guests every comfort, noted for relaxed, friendly atmosphere and good home cooking. Bed and Breakfast from £18; Dinner £10 per person. Reductions for children. Brochure available. **ETC ◆◆◆**

## Somerset

**BATH. Mrs June E. A. Coward, Box Road Gardens, Box Road, Bathford, Bath BA1 7LR (01225 852071).** Homely, comfortable country house in two acres, situated on A4 road three miles east of Bath City Centre. Easy access to M4, local beauty spots. Accommodation in twin, double and family rooms with central heating, vanity units, tea/coffee making facilities; TV. Some with shower en suite. Ample parking and good local "pub food". Open all year for Bed and Breakfast from £17 per person. This is a non-smoking house. Sorry, no pets. Phone June on **01225 852071** for further details.

**BATH. Mrs D. Strong, Wellsway Guest House, 51 Wellsway, Bath BA2 4RS (01225 423434).** A comfortable Edwardian house with all bedrooms centrally heated; washbasin and colour television in the rooms. On bus route with buses to and from the city centre every few minutes or an eight minute walk down the hill. Alexandra Park, with magnificent views of the city, is five minutes' walk. Bath is ideal for a short or long holiday with many attractions in and around the city; Longleat, Wells and Bristol are all nearby. Parking available. Bed and Breakfast from £15, with a pot of tea to welcome you on arrival. **ETC** ◆◆.

**BATH. Jenny and David Nixon, Footman's Cottage, High Street, Wellow, Bath BA2 8QQ (Tel & Fax: 01225 837024).** A warm welcome awaits you at this delightful 18th century cottage in the centre of the conservation village of Wellow. We are three miles from the Bath Park and Ride, close to Longleat, Wells, etc. Wellow Trekking Centre is close by and we are surrounded by excellent walking country. Three pretty bedrooms are available, each with TV, radio and beverage trays. Our twin room is en suite, whilst the double and single rooms share a bathroom. Homemade bread and preserves are served with an excellent breakfast. Special diets are catered for with prior notice. Good pub food is available nearby. Bed and Breakfast from £20 per person per night. Please call or write for a copy of our brochure.

**BATH. Mrs Judith Goddard, Cherry Tree Villa, 7 Newbridge Hill, Bath BA1 3PW (01225 331671).** Friendly Victorian home approximately one mile from centre of Bath, at the start of the A431. Very frequent bus service, or for those who enjoy walking, a stroll through Victoria Park will take you comfortably into the city. Bright comfortable bedrooms, all with washbasin, colour TV and tea/coffee making facilities. Full central heating and off-street parking. Bed and full English Breakfast from £18 per person per night. Children welcome. From city centre take main A4 Upper Bristol road, at Weston Pub take A431 and Cherry Tree Villa lies on the left hand side. Winner of an FHG Diploma awarded by readers. **ETC** ◆◆◆

**BATH. Michael and Carole Bryson, Walton Villa, 3 Newbridge Hill, Bath BA1 3PW (01225 482792; Fax: 01225 313093).** Our immaculate Victorian family-run B&B offers non-smoking accommodation in a relaxed and friendly atmosphere. Just a short bus journey or 25 minute stroll to town centre, via the beautiful gardens of the Royal Victoria Park. Our three en suite bedrooms are delightfully decorated and furnished for your comfort, with colour TV, hairdryer and hospitality tray. Enjoy a delicious Full English or Continental breakfast served in our gracious diningroom. Sorry, no children or pets. Off street parking. Bed and Breakfast from £22.50. **ETC** ◆◆◆

**BATH. The Old Malt House Hotel, Radford, Timsbury, Near Bath BA3 1QF (01761 470106; Fax 01761 472726).** Between Bath and Wells in beautiful country surroundings, ideally situated for visiting many places of interest. A relaxing comfortable hotel, built in 1835 as a brewery malt house, now a hotel of character with interesting paintings, furnishings, etc., and with log fires in the colder months. Car park, gardens and lawns. Owned/managed by the same family for over 20 years. All 12 bedrooms (including two on the ground floor) have private facilities, colour TV, telephone and beverage tray. Extensive menus. Restaurant and bar meals served every evening. Full licence, wide choice including draught Bass. Bed and Breakfast from £30 to £39; Dinner, Bed and Breakfast from £44 to £56. **ETC/AA** ★★.
e-mail: hotel@oldmalthouse.co.uk
website: www.oldmalthouse.co.uk

**When making enquiries please mention FHG Publications**

**Somerset** 259

## The Gainsborough Hotel
Weston Lane Bath - Avon - BA1 4AB
Telephone (01225) 311380. Fax.(01225)447411

A very spacious and comfortable country house style bed and breakfast hotel, situated in our own grounds with nice views, near the Botanical Gardens, municipal golf course and centre. The Abbey, Roman Baths, Pump Room and shops are a very pleasant walk through Victoria Park. The Hotel provides a warm and relaxing informal atmosphere for our guests, as well as a large attractive residents' lounge overlooking the hotel's lawns. All our 17 individual and tastefully furnished bedrooms are en suite with colour and satellite TV, direct-dial telephones, hairdryers and complimentary beverage facilities. A delicious five course breakfast is served each day. We also have a small friendly bar, two sun terraces and private car park.

Singles: £45 to £59 high season.
Doubles/Twins: £58 to £90 high season.
(All room rates include English Breakfast and V.A.T.) **AA**

*See also Colour Display Advertisement*     **RAC**     ◆◆◆◆

---

**BATH. Mrs Luzia Heard, Watergardens, 131 Yarnbrook Road, West Ashton, Trowbridge BA14 6AF (01225 752045; Fax: 01225 719427).** Friendly Bed and Breakfast set in half an acre of grounds, your ideal solution when visiting the Bath area of Britain. All rooms are en suite and fitted with televisions and tea/coffee making facilities. The Longs Arms, a 'Hungry Horse' pub, is just a five minute walk away; famous for their big plate meals. Also The Royal Oak is a five minute drive away and has an excellent chef. Bath, Stonehenge, Longleat, Lacock, Avebury, Stourhead, Salisbury and Wells can all be reached within 10-50 minutes. **AA** ◆◆◆.
**e-mail: lucy@heard28.freeserve.co.uk**
**website: www.s-h-systems.co.uk/hotels/water2.html**

**BATH. Mrs Chrissie Besley, The Old Red House, 37 Newbridge Road, Bath BA1 3HE (01225 330464; Fax: 01225 331661).** Welcome to our romantic Victorian "Gingerbread" house which is colourful, comfortable and warm; full of unexpected touches and intriguing little curiosities. The leaded and stained glass windows are now double glazed to ensure a peaceful night's stay. Each bedroom is individually furnished with canopied or king-size bed, colour TV, complimentary beverages, radio alarm clock, hairdryer and either en suite shower or private bathroom. Generous four-course breakfasts are served. Waffles, pancakes or kippers are just a few alternatives to our famous hearty English grill. Dinner is available at the local riverside pub, just a short stroll away. We are non-smoking and have private parking. Prices range from £20 to £33 per person in double rooms.
**e-mail: oldredhouse@amserve.net**

**BATH. Mrs Margaret Gentle, Ellsworth, Fosseway, Midsomer Norton, Bath BA3 4AU (01761 412305).** Situated on the A367 Bath/Wells/Exeter Road, Ellsworth is eight miles from Bath and within easy reach of Bristol, Wells, Glastonbury, Cheddar and the heart of the West Country. The house is surrounded by an attractive garden, with plenty of garden furniture for relaxing. Ample parking space. There are three double/family rooms and one single room, all with colour TV, shaver points, electric kettle for early morning tea or coffee. One with en suite bathroom. TV lounge. Central heating throughout. Non smoking. Good English Breakfast served. Open all year. Bed and Breakfast from £25. Reductions for children under 12.

**BATH. Irene and John Snook, Cornerways Cottage, Longcross, Zeals BA12 6LL (Tel & Fax: 01747 840477).** Cornerways is an 18th century cottage offering a high standard of accommodation with a lovely cottage feel, complemented by excellent breakfasts in the old dining room. Situated just off A303 this is an ideal place to stay for touring, with Stonehenge, Salisbury, Bath, Longleat and Stourhead all being within easy travelling distance. Riding, walking, fishing and golf are all available locally. Single room form £25 to £30, double/twin (for two) from £38 to £42.**ETC** ◆◆◆◆
**e-mail: cornerways.cottage@btinternet.com**
**website: www.SmoothHound.co.uk/hotels/cornerwa.html**

**BATH. Mrs M. A. Cooper, Flaxley Villa, 9 New Bridge Hill, Bath BA1 3PW (01225 313237).** Follow A4 through Bath to Queen Square, take top left-hand exit and follow one mile to Sportsman Pub, take right hand lights A431. Flaxley Villa is a comfortable Victorian house five minutes from town centre. All rooms with colour TV, also showers and tea/coffee making facilities. En suite room available. Parking. Full English Breakfast. Terms from £22.00 per person per night.

**BATH. Mrs K.M. Addison, Bailbrook Lodge, 35/37 London Road West, Bath BA1 7HZ (01225 859090; Fax: 01225 852299).** Bailbrook Lodge is a splendid Georgian hotel and with a warm welcome assured it makes an excellent base to tour the area. Its 12 bedrooms are elegantly furnished, all offering en-suite bathrooms or showers, TV, coffee and tea making facilities; some with antique four-poster beds. Dining room and bar. Situated just off the A4 London road, Bailbrook Lodge is just one-and-a-half miles from Bath city centre and has ample car parking facilities. It is 100 yards from the A46 which leads to Junction 18 of the M4 and is also close to the beautiful villages of Castle Combe and Lacock. Price per person including full English breakfast is from £25 to £40. **ETC/AA** ♦♦♦
e-mail: hotel@bailbrooklodge.demon.co.uk

**BATH. Jan and Bryan Wotley, The Albany Guest House, 24 Crescent Gardens, Bath BA1 2NB (01225 313339).** A warm welcome awaits you at our Victorian home, ideally placed to enjoy the delights of Bath – just five minutes' level walk from the city centre, Roman Baths, Abbey, etc. Our four attractively decorated bedrooms are equipped with colour TV, tea/coffee making facilities, washbasins and central heating. Enjoy a traditional English breakfast or try our delicious homemade vegetarian sausages! We happily cater for special dietary needs with prior notification. Many of our guests return again and again to enjoy the personal and unpretentious service we offer. Private parking. Non-smoking. Bed and Breakfast from £17 per person..

**BECKINGTON, Near Bath. Mrs Barbara Keevil, Eden Vale Farm, Mill Lane, Beckington, Near Bath BA3 6SN (01373 830371).** Eden Vale Farm nestles down in a valley by the River Frome. Enjoying a picturesque location, this old watermill offers a selection of rooms including en suite facilities, complemented by an excellent choice of full English or Continental breakfasts. Beckington is an ideal centre for visiting Bath, Longleat, Cheddar, Salisbury, Stourhead and many National Trust Houses including Lacock Village. Only a ten minute walk to the village pub, three-quarters of a mile of river fishing. Local golf courses and lovely walks. Very friendly animals. Dogs welcome. Please phone or write for more information. Open all year. **ETC** ♦♦♦

See also Colour Display Advertisement

**BREAN. Mrs Helen Perrett, The Old Rectory, Church Road, Brean, Burnham on-Sea TA8 2SF (01278 751447; Fax: 01278 751800).** A friendly welcome awaits you at The Old Rectory, situated next to the village church, within a five minute walk of five miles of golden sandy beach. Comfortable ground floor rooms available with en suite facilities. All rooms have colour TV and tea/coffee making facilities. Large walled gardens, with children's play area. Private car park. Golf and swimming 10 minutes' walk. Horse riding one mile. Hair and Beauty Salon 75 yards. Restaurants nearby. An ideal base from which to explore local places of interest such as Cheddar Caves, Wookey Hole, Secret World, Animal Farm, fishing and many more.

**BREAN SANDS. Mrs H. Davies or Miss M. Brown, Martins Hill Farm House, Red Road, Berrow, Brean Sands TA8 2RW (01278 751230/751726).** Quiet country farmhouse overlooking open countryside and Brean Golf Course (Burnham and Berrow Golf Course one mile). One mile from Brean Sands, horseriding and leisure park. Local attractions include animal farm, Secret World and model car racing to name but a few. We are only a short driving distance from Burnham on Sea and Weston-super-Mare which both have some very nice restaurants. All rooms have a colour TV and tea and coffee making facilities. Sorry no smoking. All rooms are from £20 per person including breakfast, children sharing half price.

**BRIDGWATER. Richard and Carol Wright, Model Farm, Perry Green, Wembdon, Near Bridgwater TA5 2BA (01278 433999).** Model Farm is a licensed country house situated in a peaceful rural setting, close to the North Somerset/Devon coast, Quantock Hills and county towns. Ideally located for both leisure and business guests, the property is a 17th century farmhouse (non-working) with an imposing Victorian frontage. Spacious comfortable bedrooms with en suite shower facilities and a range of hot beverages provided. By arrangement a set three-course evening meal is available, guests being joined by the owners, around a refectory table. A warm and friendly atmosphere awaits all who visit. Bed and Breakfast £25 to £35 per person per night. No smoking throughout. **ETC/AA ♦♦♦♦**.
e-mail: Rmodelfarm@aol.com

**BRIDGWATER. Mrs M. Tingey, Greinton House, Greinton TA7 9BW (01458 210307; Mobile: 0798 9032463).** Greinton is on the A361 between Taunton and Glastonbury where Clarks renowned factory shop village is located. The house is a beautiful Listed former rectory (dating back to the 16th century) with panelling and galleried hall, situated on the southern slopes of the Polden Hills, overlooking Sedgemoor. Accommodation can be arranged to suit individual requirements. There are two bathrooms, one luxury en suite and a shower room. All bedrooms have tea/coffee making facilities and TV. Three sitting rooms. Ample parking. There is a hard tennis court and croquet lawn. The premises are not suitable for young children and no pets are allowed in the house. Non-smokers only. In winter there is oil-fired central heating and log fires. Open all year for Bed and Breakfast from £25 nightly.

**BRIDGWATER. Jim and Edith Pumfrey, Phoenicia, 31 Liney Road, Westonzoyland TA7 0EU (01278 691385)** A warm and genuine welcome awaits you at 'Phoenicia'. Quietly located at the edge of the village, this is an ideal base from which to explore the Somerset countryside and is also within easy reach of the coastal resorts. Golf and fishing nearby. Close to local pubs and restaurants. Accommodation comprises one double room and one twin room (interconnecting), ideal for families. Private shower and toilet. Guests' private lounge with CTV and tea/coffee making facilities. Ideal to relax in at the end of the day. Central heating. Ample off-road parking. Non-smoking. No children under 10 years. No pets. Directions: close to Junction 23 M5. Take A372 from Bridgwater at Westonzoyland through village past St Marys Church and turn off A372 after approximately 2000 yards into Liney Road. Open Easter to end November.

**BRISTOL. Mrs P. Hurley, Oakfield Hotel, 52/54 Oakfield Road, Clifton, Bristol BS8 2BG (0117 9735556; Fax: 0117 9744141).** Friendly, family-run since 1946. The Oakfield Hotel is near the University, Bristol Zoo, Clifton Suspension Bridge, Queens Road and Whiteladies Road shops. All rooms have washing facilities, tea/coffee making and televisions. Bathrooms are shared (we have 27 rooms and eight bathrooms). On-site car parking limited. Separate television lounge and reading lounge. **RAC & AA** *LISTED*.

**BRISTOL. Downs View Guest House, 38 Upper Belgrave Road, Clifton, Bristol BS8 2XN (0117 9737046; Fax: 0117 9738169)** A well established, family-run Victorian guest house situated on the edge of Durdham Downs. All rooms have panoramic views over the city or the Downs. We are one-and-a-half miles north of the city centre, just off Whiteladies Road where there are plenty of restaurants, shops and buses. We are within walking distance of Bristol Zoo and Clifton Suspension Bridge. All rooms have tea/coffee making facilities, washbasin, colour TV and central heating. There are seven en suite rooms. We offer a varied menu including traditional English breakfast. Bed and Breakfast from £30. **ETC/RAC ♦♦♦**

**BRISTOL. Mrs Griffin, Stoneycroft House, Stock Lane, Langford, Bristol BS18 7EX (01934 852624).** Stoneycroft House is situated in the Wrington Valley, set in 20 acres of farmland, close to the Mendip Hills and only 10 minutes from Bristol Airport. Superb four-poster/family room with en suite, twin room with en suite and double room with adjacent bathroom. All rooms have colour TV, tea/coffee making facilities and excellent views. Enjoy your choice of breakfast in the beamed dining room with its Minster stone fireplace. Unlimited parking. Nearby attractions are the Cheddar Gorge, Wells Cathedral and the historic cities of Bath and Bristol. Sporting facilities and seaside nearby. Open all year. Brochure available. Self Catering Cottages Available.

**BRISTOL. Mrs Colin Smart, Leigh Farm, Pensford, Near Bristol, BS39 4BA (Tel & Fax: 01761 490281)** Close to Bath, Bristol, Cheddar, Mendip Hills. Carp and Tench fishing close to the farmhouse Large, comfy, stone built farmhouse with lawns. Twin, single, family, double room, most en suite; cot and high chair available. Guests' private lounge with night storage heating and open log fires in cold weather. Breakfast choice. Tea/coffee facilities, hair dryer. Floodlit car park. Sorry, no pets. Bed and Breakfast from £23. Also self-catering accommodation available (one, two or three bedroomed) £150 to £400 weekly (♛♛ Approved).

**BURNHAM-ON-SEA. Mrs F. Alexander, Priors Mead, 23 Rectory Road, Burnham-on-Sea TA8 2BZ (Tel & Fax: 01278 782116; Mobile: 07990 595585).** Peter and Fizz welcome guests to enjoy their enchanting Edwardian home set in half-an-acre of beautiful gardens with weeping willows, croquet and swimming pool. All three rooms have either twin or king-size beds, en suite/private facilities, washbasins, hospitality trays, colour TVs, etc. Peaceful location, walk to the sea, town, golf and tennis clubs. Ideal touring base for Bristol, Bath, Wells, Glastonbury, Wookey Hole, Cheddar and Dunster. A no-smoking home. Parking. Easy access to Junction 22 M5 for Wales, Devon and Cornwall. Bed and Breakfast from £17 to £18. Reductions for three nights. **ETC ♦♦♦** *"WHICH?" RECOMMENDED.*
e-mail: priorsmead@aol.com
website: www.SmoothHound.co.uk/hotels/priors.html

**CHEDDAR. Market Cross Hotel, Church Street, Cheddar BS27 3RA (01934 742264; Fax: 01934 741411).** This privately owned, licensed Regency hotel is situated in the village of Cheddar, five minutes' walk from the famous Gorge, caves and Mendip Hills, making it an ideal centre for rambling, riding, caving, fishing, sightseeing. Wells, Glastonbury, Bath and Bristol are all within easy reach; the seaside is only 10 miles away. Seven bedrooms, some family, some en suite, are all centrally heated to ensure a comfortable stay. Log fires burn in the lounge during colder periods. A choice of excellent fresh home-cooked food and a desire to please ensures our guests a happy stay at moderate prices. Bed and Breakfast from £21.50 to £30.00. Open all year. Excellent self-catering apartments also available in adjacent Georgian house. **ETC/AA ♦♦♦**

---

**When making enquiries please mention Bed & Breakfast Stops**

# Brinsea Green Farm

Brinsea Green is a Period farmhouse surrounded by open countryside. Set in 500 acres of farmland, it has easy access from the M5, (J21), A38 and Bristol Airport. Close to the Mendip Hill, the historic towns of Bath, Bristol and Wells, plus the wonders of Cheddar Gorge and Wookey Hole. Beautifully furnished en suite/shower bedrooms offer lovely views, comfortable beds, complimentary hot drinks and biscuits, radio, alarm, toiletries, sewing kit and hairdryer for your convenience. Both guest lounge (with TV) and dining room have inglenook fireplaces providing a warm, home from home atmosphere. Choose from our wide range of books and enjoy real peace and tranquillity. Early booking recommended.

**Mrs Delia Edwards, Brinsea Green Farm
Brinsea Lane, Congresbury, Near Bristol BSl9 5JN
Tel: (01934) 852278**

# The Cottage
## Fordgate, Bridgwater, Somerset TA7 0AP
### Tel: 01278 691908
*Beverley & Victor Jenkins*

A charming country cottage set in two acres of garden in an area of outstanding natural beauty and special interest, close to rivers and canal where birds and wildlife flourish.

A centre for the famous Somerset Levels and all of this historic county.

We offer you privacy, comfort and tranquillity, staying in king-size antique four-poster or twin-bedded en suite rooms with TV and heating. Easy access with all rooms at ground level opening directly onto the gardens.

Evening Meals available by arrangement. English country cooking at its best, using our own fresh vegetables, fruit, honey and free-range eggs.

Bed and Breakfast £21pp per night

Easy access Junction 24 M5. Ample secure parking.
No smoking in house please. A delightful place to stay especially for that short break. Phone or write for brochure and map.

HIGHLY RECOMMENDED

**Open all year.**
E-mail: Jenkins@thecottage.fsnet.co.uk

**Somerset**

**See also Colour Display Advertisement**

**CHEDDAR. Mrs Caroline Rymell, The Poacher's Table, Cliff Street, Cheddar BS27 3PT (01934 742271).** A friendly and warm welcome to all at our family-run guest house and licensed restaurant built in the 17th century and featuring many exposed oak beams. Situated at the foot of Cheddar Gorge within walking distance of caves and gorge, ideally placed to visit the many local places of interest including Bath, Wells, Glastonbury and Bristol. Three double en suite bedrooms and one twin standard bedroom, all have colour TV and tea/coffee making facilities. Bed and full English Breakfast from £18 per person per night. Evening Meal also available in our candlelit restaurant.

**CHURCHILL (Bristol near). Ms Susan Lewis, The Mendip Gate Guest House, Bristol Road (A38), Churchill BS25 5NL (01934 852333; Fax: 01934 852001).** Easy to find on A38 four miles south of Bristol airport. Handy hostelries for tasty Evening Meals and comfortable rooms for a convenient overnight stop on longer journeys. Or take time to wander round historic cities like Wells, Bristol, or Bath, or hike over the beautiful Mendip Hills pausing in one of the stone taverns to sample local Cheddar cheese, Somerset cider and draught ales. Children welcome. En suite singles from £27.50; doubles/twins from £36. 
e-mail: sarahvowles@mendipgate.freeserve.co.uk

**CREWKERNE. Mrs Catherine Bacon, Honeydown Farm, Seaborough Hill, Crewkerne TA18 8PL (Tel & Fax: 01460 72665).** We are a working dairy farm on the Somerset/Dorset border, one and a half miles from Crewkerne, with panoramic views. National Trust properties, private gardens and numerous other places of interest are within easy reach, and the coast is only 14 miles away. Golfing, fishing, riding, walking and cycling all available locally. Centrally heated accommodation comprises one twin and two double rooms, all with washbasins, tea/coffee trays and clock/radio. Enjoy the patio and garden or relax in the guest lounge with books, stereo or television. Non smoking. Bed and Breakfast from £18 per person per night. Brochure available. 
e-mail: cb@honeydown.freeserve.co.uk
website: www.honeydown.freeserve.co.uk

**DULVERTON. Mrs Gill Summers, Higher Langridge Farm, Exbridge, Dulverton TA22 9RR (01398 323999).** This 17th century farmhouse is on a working farm on the southern edge of Exmoor National Park four miles from Dulverton (two-and-a-half miles off A396 at Exebridge). From guests' own dining/sitting room with wood-burner and inglenook fireplace, guests may observe red deer while breakfasting on eggs from the farm's own speckledy hens, local sausages and bacon, Devon Quince honey and homemade marmalade. Dinner and light suppers available if ordered. Spacious bedrooms (one en suite) with traditional furnishings and good country views, all around is rural peace and quiet. Open all year. AA ♦♦♦♦ 
e-mail: info@langridgefarm.co.uk
website: www.langridgefarm.co.uk

**EAST LAMBROOK. Liz Applegate, Penryn, Southhay, East Lambrook, South Petherton TA13 5HQ (01460 241358).** A peaceful, rural setting - our bungalow is in an acre of garden surrounded by cider orchards. Stay two miles north of A303 to explore Somerset or break your journey to the West Country. Discover National Trust properties, beautiful gardens, The Levels, Hamstone villages, Dorset coast; fascinating towns - Wells, Sherborne, Glastonbury, Taunton and find much more. One twin bedroom, colour TV, en suite with bath and separate shower. Your sitting/dining room opens onto the garden. Bed and Breakfast £20 per person. Three course evening meal using local produce £8. Diets catered for. Weekly rates available. Non smoking. Open April to October. Ask for brochure. **ETC** ♦♦♦♦. 
e-mail: pjandea@tesco.net

**Somerset** **265**

## THE EXMOOR WHITE HORSE INN
**Exford, West Somerset TA24 7PY**
**Tel: 01643 831229   Fax: 01643 831246**
e-mail:exmoorwhitehorse@demon.co.uk
Managers: Peter and Linda Hendrie

**INN:** Situated in the delightful Exmoor village of Exford, overlooking the River Exe and surrounded by high moorland on almost every side, this family-run 16th Century Inn is an ideal spot for that well- earned break. The public rooms are full of character with beams, log fires (Oct-April) and Exmoor stone throughout. There are 26 bedrooms, all of which have en suite facilities, colour TV, teamaking and central heating, and are furnished in keeping with the character of the Inn.

**RESTAURANT:** A variety of dishes to excite the palate served, including lobster, seafood platters, local venison and fish, whilst the bar has an extensive snack menu, with home made pies, local dishes and is renowned for its carvery. The menus change regularly with daily specials available.

**NEARBY:** Excellent walking country with a selection of circular walks from the Inn, plus many other local walks available. The village is also noted for its excellent riding facilities. Hunting, fishing and shooting can be arranged upon request. Open all year. Mini Breaks a speciality.

See also Colour Display Advertisement

## HIGHERCOMBE FARM

Relax and enjoy our special hospitality on a 450 acre working farm (including 100 acres of woodland), in an outstanding, peaceful, situation on **Exmoor**. Off the beaten track yet only four miles from Dulverton. We are an ideal base for exploring coast and moor. There is an abundance of wildlife on the farm including wild red deer. We are happy to take you on a farm tour. The farmhouse enjoys spectacular views, central heating, large visitors' lounge and log fires. Pretty rooms with generous en suite bathrooms.

Delicious farmhouse cooking, fresh produce, home-made marmalade, etc. Bed and Breakfast from £19.50, Dinner, Bed and Breakfast from £34. Private, well equipped self-catering wing of farmhouse also available.

**Abigail Humphrey, Highercombe Farm,**
**Dulverton, Exmoor TA22 9PT   Telephone/Fax: 01398 323616**
**E-mail: abigail@highercombe.demon.co.uk**
**Website: www.highercombe.demon.co.uk**

ETC ♦♦♦♦ Silver Award          ETC ★★★

*See also Colour Advertisement*

**EXFORD. Exmoor House Hotel and Restaurant, Exford TA24 7PY (01643 831304).** Small, family-run Bed and Breakfast hotel overlooking the village green in the beautiful village of Exford and situated in the heart of the Exmoor National Park. Exford is an excellent base from which to enjoy riding, fishing, game shooting or just to explore the delights of the Moor. All our bedrooms have tea/coffee making facilities, colour TV, clock radios and offer en suite or private facilities. Children and pets welcome. There is a reading/residents' lounge. Please write or phone for our brochure.

See also Colour Display Advertisement

**EXMOOR. Mrs Blackshaw, North Down Farm, Pyncombe Lane, Wiveliscombe, Taunton TA4 2BL (Tel & Fax: 01984 623730).** In tranquil, secluded surroundings on the Somerset/Devon Border. Traditional working farm set in 100 acres of natural beauty with panoramic views of over 40 miles. M5 motorway seven miles and Taunton ten miles. All rooms tastefully furnished to high standard include en suite, TV, and tea/coffee facilities. Family room, double or single available. Dining room and lounge with log fires for our guests' comfort; central heating and double glazed. Drying facilities. Delicious home produced food a speciality. Fishing, golf, horse riding and country sports nearby. Dogs welcome. Bed and Breakfast from £20 per person, generous discounts on seven or more nights stay. North Down Break: three nights Bed and Breakfast and Evening Meal £80 per person. **ETC ♦♦♦.**

**PLEASE SEND A STAMPED ADDRESSED ENVELOPE WITH ENQUIRIES**

**GLASTONBURY. Mrs D. P. Atkinson, Court Lodge, Butleigh, Glastonbury BA6 8SA (01458 850575).** A warm welcome awaits at attractive, modernised 1850 Lodge with homely atmosphere. Set in picturesque garden on the edge of Butleigh, three miles from historic Glastonbury. Only a five minute walk to pub in village which serves lovely meals. Accommodation in one double, one twin and two single bedrooms; constant hot water, central heating. Bathroom adjacent to bedrooms. TV lounge. Tea/coffee served. Bed and Breakfast from £15.50; Evening Meal by arrangement. Children welcome at reduced rates. **AA** and **RAC** *RECOMMENDED*.

**GLASTONBURY. Mrs J.M. Gillam, Wood Lane House, Butleigh, Glastonbury BA6 8TG (01458 850354).** Charming old AA Listed house with lovely views over open countryside and woods. Quiet yet not isolated and only 200 yards from excellent village "local". Ideal touring centre for Cheddar, Wells, Bath and many beauty spots and only 20 miles from coast. Attractions include Butterfly Farm, Fleet Air Arm Museum, Rural Life Museum, cheese making, steam engines and many places of historic interest. Accommodation comprises three double rooms with well equipped en suite facilities, tea/coffee and TV. Comfortable and warm sitting/dining room. Open all year round except Christmas and New Year. Car essential. Parking. Bed and Breakfast from £20. Half price for children.

**GLASTONBURY near. Mrs M.A. Bell, New House Farm, Burtle Road, Westhay, Near Glastonbury BA6 9TT (01458 860238; Fax: 01458 860568).** Working dairy farm, situated on the Somerset Levels. Large Victorian Farmhouse offering comfortable accommodation, central for touring Wells, Cheddar, Bath, Burnham-on-Sea etc. Accommodation comprises one family room and two double room, each with en suite facilities, colour TV, tea/coffee facilities, hair dryer, clock radio, etc; lounge with colour TV, separate diningroom and conservatory. Central heating throughout. Ample parking and warm welcome assured. Bed and full English Breakfast from £23; Evening Meal £13. Self catering also available. Directions: near Peat Moor Visitor Centre which is signposted from A39 and B3151. **ETC ♦♦♦♦** *SILVER AWARD*.
e-mail: newhousefarm@farmersweekly.net

**GLASTONBURY near. Mrs M. White, Barrow Farm, North Wootton, Near Glastonbury BA4 4HL (01749 890245). Working farm.** Barrow is a dairy farm of 146 acres. The house is 15th century and of much character, situated between Wells, Glastonbury and Shepton Mallet. It makes an excellent touring centre for visiting Somerset's beauty spots and historic places, for example, Cheddar, Bath, Wookey Hole and Longleat. Guest accommodation consists of two double rooms, one family room, one single room and one twin-bedded room, each with washbasin, TV and tea/coffee making facilities. Bathroom, two toilets; two lounges, one with colour TV; diningroom with separate tables. Guests can enjoy farmhouse fare in generous variety, home baking a speciality. Bed and Breakfast, with optional four-course Dinner available. Car essential; ample parking. Children welcome; cot and babysitting available. Open all year except Christmas. Sorry, no pets. Bed and Breakfast from £14 to £17; Dinner £10. This farm accommodation is **AA** *QQQ LISTED.*

---

# FREE or REDUCED RATE entry to Holiday Visits and Attractions — see our READERS' OFFER VOUCHERS on pages 43-60

**Quiet Corner Farm, Henstridge, Near Sherborne, Somerset BA8 0RA (Tel/Fax: 01963 363045)**
Lovely old stone farmhouse and barns, some converted to self-catering cottages sleeping two/three, set in five acres beautiful garden and orchards with sheep and miniature Shetland ponies. The village, 'twixt Shaftesbury and Sherborne, has super pubs, two restaurants, shops and post office. Marvellous centre for touring Somerset, Dorset and Wiltshire with host of National Trust and other houses and gardens. Golf and fishing nearby. The spacious farmhouse is most comfortable with central heating throughout. Bedrooms with washbasins and tea making facilities; one en suite. Safe car parking. Payphone. Bed and Breakfast from £21. Reductions for children under 12 years. SAE, or telephone, for brochure. Special offer: Three days for price of two (subject to availability) October 1st to end April except Public Holidays. Recommended by "Which?" Good Bed & Breakfast Guide. ETC ◆◆◆◆
e-mail: quietcorner.thompson@virgin.net

**HIGHBRIDGE. Mrs L. Sinclair, Sandacre, 75 Old Burnham Road, Highbridge TA9 3JG (Tel & Fax: 01278 781221).** Sandacre is a 175-year-old house with beamed ceilings, situated just off the A38, one mile from J22 M5 and one mile from the seaside at Burnham-on-Sea. The detached house in a quiet area provides large comfortable rooms, each with colour TV, washbasins and tea/coffee making facilities. Ample off-road parking. Non-smoking. **ETC ◆◆◆**.
e-mail: lynne.peter@highbridge62.fsnet.co.uk

**ILMINSTER. Mrs G. Phillips, `Hermitage', 29 Station Road, Ilminster TA19 9BE (01460 53028).** Enjoy the friendly atmosphere of a lovely Listed 17th century house with beams and inglenook. Four-poster beds. Two acres of delightful gardens, woods and hills beyond. Twin or double rooms with washbasin; en suite available. Lounge with log fire and colour TV. Tea or coffee with home-made biscuits on arrival. Full English breakfast. Traditional inns nearby for evening meals. Ideal touring centre for Quantock Hills, Wells, Glastonbury, Lyme Regis and many picturesque villages. Several National Trust properties, gardens and historic house within a few miles. Ten miles from M5, one mile from A303. Bed and Breakfast from £17. **ETC ◆◆◆**

**MARK. Mrs B. M. Puddy, Laurel Farm, Mark Causeway, Near HighbridgeTA9 4PZ (01278 641216; Fax: 01278 641447).** Laurel Farm is on the Wells to Burnham-on-Sea B3139 road; M5 Junction 22 two miles; 12 miles from the cathedral city of Wells, five miles from Burnham-on-Sea. Ideal for overnight or short breaks to tour our lovely area. Nicely furnished and decorated, with a large well kept lawn and flower garden at the back. Doubles, singles and family rooms available. All en suite with tea/coffee facilities. Large sitting room, colour TV. Central heating, electric blanket and log fires for cooler evenings. **ETC ◆◆**

**MONTACUTE. Paterson and Sue Weir, Slipper Cottage, 41 Bishopston, Montacute TA15 6UX (01935 823073; mobile: 07966 368544).** A friendly welcome awaits you at this charming 17th century cottage, in one of Somerset's prettiest villages. Montacute House, excellent pubs and restaurants just around the corner. Tintinhull House Gardens, Barrington Court, Stourhead, Lytes Cary, Wells Cathedral, Sherborne Abbey, Glastonbury Abbey and Lyme Regis not far away. Four golf courses within ten miles. Accommodation consists of one double and one twin bedded room, both with vanity basin, shaver point, colour T.V, central heating and tea/coffee making facilities.Terms from £38 to £40 per room, per night including breakfast. Single occupancy £26 to £40. Sorry, no pets, no smoking. Open all year except Christmas and New Year. **RAC ◆◆◆**
e-mail: sue.weir@totalise.co.uk
website: www.slippercottage.co.uk

**NORTH CADBURY. Mr & Mrs J Wade, Ashlea House, High Street, North Cadbury BA22 7DP (01963 440891)** Ashlea House is situated in a quiet Camelot village with Post Office, Church and Inn. Four miles from Castle Cary Station, Paddington/Penzance Bristol/Weymouth lines. Courier service arranged. An ideal centre for walkers having four major trails and cycle route. Cadbury Arthurian Centre, Haynes Classic Car and Fleet Air Arm Museums, Glastonbury Tor and Abbey with the coastal resorts of Bournemouth and Weymouth nearby. Accommodation consists of one twin en suite room and one double room with private facilities, radio/alarm clock, remote control TV and beverage tray. Highly commended service, facilities and cuisine. Brochure on request. **ETC ♦♦♦♦.** 
e-mail: ashlea@btinternet.com
website: www.ashlea.btinternet.com.uk

**PORLOCK. Margery and Henry Dyer, West Porlock House, West Porlock, Near Minehead TA24 8NX (01643 862880).** Imposing country house in Exmoor National Park on the wooded slopes of West Porlock commanding exceptional sea views of Porlock Bay and countryside. Set in five acres of beautiful woodland gardens unique for its variety and size of unusual trees and shrubs and offering a haven of rural tranquillity. The house has large spacious rooms with fine and beautiful furnishings throughout. Two double, two twin and one family bedrooms, all with en suite or private bathrooms, TV, tea/coffee making facilities, radio-alarm clock and shaver point. Licensed. Non-smoking. Private car park. Bed and Breakfast from £25 to £27 per person. Credit Cards accepted. **ETC ♦♦♦♦**

**PORLOCK. Mrs A.J. Richards, Ash Farm, Porlock, Near Minehead TA24 8JN (01643 862414).** Ash Farm is situated two miles off the main Porlock to Lynmouth road (A39) and overlooks the sea. It is two-and-a-half miles from Porlock Weir, and eleven from Minehead and Lynmouth. Only 10 minutes to the tiny church of "Culbon", and Coleridge is reputed to have used the farmhouse which is 200 to 300 years old. The house has double, single and family bedrooms, all with washbasins; toilet; large sittingroom and diningroom. Open from Easter to October. Oare Church, Valley of Rocks, County Gate, Horner Valley and Dunkery Beacon are all within easy reach. Bed and Breakfast from £16 which includes bedtime drink. SAE please

See also Colour Display Advertisement

**PORLOCK. Mr and Mrs Growden, Burley Cottage Guest House, Parsons Street, Porlock, Exmoor National Park TA24 8QJ (01643 862563).** Ideal base for visiting Exmoor and to see the beautiful countryside. Private guest lounge; en suite facilities; radio, TV, tea and coffee making facilities in each room; full central heating. Packed meals on request. Non-smoking. Car parking. Please telephone or write for a brochure or the booking of a room.

---

# FREE or REDUCED RATE entry to Holiday Visits and Attractions — see our READERS' OFFER VOUCHERS on pages 43-60

# Somerset 269

**QUANTOCK HILLS. Mrs M. Morse, Stowey Tea Rooms, Nether Stowey, Bridgwater TA5 1LN (01278 733686; Fax: 01278 733022).** These charming "olde worlde" tea rooms are set in the heart of this delightful village at the foot of the Quantocks. We offer comfortable accommodation with en-suite, TV and tea/coffee making facilities. The village has three pubs, farm shop and Coleridge Museum. Ideal base for exploring the Quantock Hills and Exmoor. Non-smoking. Off road parking. Bed and Breakfast £35 per double room. Just off A39 between Bridgwater and Minehead.

**QUANTOCK HILLS. Susan Lilienthal, Parsonage Farm, Over Stowey, Bridgwater TA5 1HA (01278 733237; Fax: 01278 733511).** Traditional 17th century farmhouse and organic smallholding in quiet location in Quantock Hills with delightful walled gardens; orchard; and walks to explore. Delicious meals are prepared using the farm's produce - fresh eggs, home-made breads and jams - and served before an open fire. Three double bedrooms include colour TV and tea/coffee facilities, en suite available. Guests are invited to enjoy the gardens or relax in the log-fired sitting room. Spacious and welcoming, this is an ideal base for rambling and exploring the Quantock Hills, Exmoor, North Somerset Coast, as well as Glastonbury and Wells. No smoking. Bed and full Breakfast from £20, reductions for children. Optional Evening Meal £15.

**SHEPTON MALLET. Mr and Mrs J. Grattan, Park Farm House, Forum Lane, Bowlish, Shepton Mallet BA4 5JL (01749 343673; Fax: 01749 345279).** A 17th century house formerly a working farm situated in a conservation area. The accommodation comprises one twin-bedded room (bathroom en suite) and a suite of a double bedroom and a twin bedroom with private bathroom. There is ample discreet car parking. Conveniently situated close to the ancient Cathedral City of Wells (four miles), Cheddar Gorge and caves, Clarks village at Street and Longleat within 12 miles. The Georgian city of Bath, and Bristol, are only 18 miles away. Shepton Mallet has good restaurants, many local pubs and easy access to the scenic Mendip Hills. Bed and Breakfast from £17.50 per person per night: no single person supplement.

**TAUNTON. Mrs J. Greenway, Woodlands Farm, Bathealton, Near Taunton TA4 2AH (01984 623271). Working farm.** A warm, relaxed atmosphere, delicious food and comfortable accommodation are only some of the hallmarks of this cosy farmhouse which welcomes guests from June to September, Ideal for touring Somerset, Devon, Exmoor and the coast, there is also ample opportunity for simply relaxing on the farm or enjoying some carp fishing. Children welcomed at reduced rates. Family room en suite, one double and one twin room available. Also available self-catering wing sleeping five. Bed and Breakfast, including bedtime drink and tea making facilities, from £16 to £18 daily.

**TAUNTON. Mr and Mrs P.J. Painter, Blorenge House, 57 Staplegrove Road, Taunton TA1 1DG (Tel & Fax: 01823 283005).** Spacious Victorian residence set in large gardens with a swimming pool and large car park. Situated just five minutes' walking distance from Taunton town centre, railway, bus station and Records Office. 23 comfortable bedrooms with washbasin, central heating, colour TV and tea making facilities. Five of the bedrooms have traditional four-poster beds, ideal for weekends away and honeymoon couples. Family and twin rooms are available. The majority of rooms have en suite facilities. Large diningroom traditionally furnished; full English breakfast/ Continental breakfast included in the price. Evening Meals available on request. Please send for our colour brochure. **ETC** ◆◆◆, **AA** *QQQ RECOMMENDED.*
website: www.blorengehouse.co.uk

**TAUNTON. Anne and Bill Slipper, The Old Mill, Bishop's Hull, Taunton TA1 5AB (Tel & Fax: 01823 289732).** Relax and enjoy the hospitality in this Grade II Listed former Corn Mill, situated on the edge of a conservation village just two miles from Taunton. We have two lovely double bedrooms, The Mill Room with en suite facilities overlooking the weir pool, and The Cottage Suite with its own private bathroom, again with views over the river. Both rooms are centrally heated, with TV, generous beverage tray and thoughtful extras. Guests have their own lounge and dining area overlooking the river, where breakfast may be taken from our extensive breakfast menu amidst machinery of a bygone era. We are a non-smoking establishment. **ETC ♦♦♦♦♦** *SILVER AWARD*
e-mail: slipperoldmill@talk21.com

**TAUNTON. Ian and Jill Read, Brookfield House, 16 Wellington Road, Taunton TA1 4EQ (Tel & Fax: 01823 272786).** Enjoy our charming comfortable Grade II Listed early Victorian residence with a friendly family atmosphere. All accommodation is en suite, centrally heated, with colour TV, and tea/coffee making facilities. We have a ground floor room available, ample parking and bicycle storage. Ideally situated five minutes' walk to town centre, Musgrove Park Hospital, Somerset College of Art & Technology and coach station. We are also convenient to Vivary Park, the cricket ground and racecourse. **AA ♦♦♦.**

**TAUNTON. Tom and Rowena Kirk, Yallands Farmhouse, Staplegrove, Taunton TA2 6PZ (01823 278979; Fax: 0870 284 9194).** A delightful 16th century Listed farmhouse which has become an oasis of "Old England" as the town has expanded over the former farmland. Quietly situated one-and-a-half miles north-west of the town centre. Guests are assured of a warm welcome and individual attention. The en suite bedrooms are comfortable, well furnished and attractive with colour TV and tea/coffee making facilities. Ground floor single room available. Special diets catered for. Ideally situated between the Quantock and Blackdown Hills, with many places of interest within easy reach. Pub within easy walking distance. Ample parking. Open all year. Short Breaks available. Brochure and tariff available. **ETC ♦♦♦♦**
e-mail: mail@yallands.co.uk

**TAUNTON. Christine M. Haynes, Hall Farm Guest House, Stogumber, Taunton TA4 3TQ (01984 656321).** Hall Farm is situated on a working farm in the centre of Stogumber Village, surrounded by the Quantocks and Exmoor. Within easy reach of the sea, Minehead, Blue Anchor, Watchet and St. Audries Bay. Accommodation for 12 to 14 guests. The bedrooms are comfortable and have en suite facilities. The catering is under the personal supervision of the proprietress, whose concern it is to make your holiday a happy one. Dogs are welcome if kept well under control. Good parking. Breakfast at 9am with Evening Dinner at 6.30pm. Traditional Sunday lunches at 1pm. **ETC ♦♦♦.**

---

# FHG
Visit the FHG website
# www.holidayguides.com
for details of the wide choice of accommodation featured in the full range of FHG titles

**TAUNTON near. Mrs Pam Parry, Pear Tree Cottage, Stapley Churchstanton, Taunton TA3 7QA (Tel & Fax: 01823 601224).** An old thatched country cottage halfway between Taunton and Honiton, set in the idyllic Blackdown Hills, designated an Area of Outstanding Natural Beauty. Picturesque countryside laced with winding lanes full of natural flora and fauna. Wildlife abounds. Three-quarters of an acre traditional cottage garden leading off to two-and-a-half acres of meadow garden planted with specimen trees. Central for north/south coasts of Somerset, Dorset and Devon. Exmoor, Dartmoor, Bristol, Bath, etc within little more than an hour's drive. Many gardens and National Trust properties encompassed in a day's outing. Double/single and family suite with own facilities, TV, tea/coffee. Conservatory/Garden Room. Dining/sitting room. Evening Meals available. Open all year.
e-mail: colvin.parry@virgin.net

---

**THEALE. Gill and Vern Clark, Yew Tree Farm, Theale, Near Wedmore BS28 4SN (01934 712475).** A lovely large 17th century farmhouse with a very friendly atmosphere - near to Wookey Hole, Cheddar, Wells and golf courses, with the cities of Bath and Bristol near by. Weston and Brean are also a short distance away. Idyllic walks are close at hand as well as the Somerset Levels and bird sanctuaries. There are three large super bedrooms, two double and one twin. Own lounge with colour TV, as well as coffee and tea making facilities. Complimentary pot of tea or coffee on arrival. Tuesday to Friday three-course dinner on request. From £16 per person per night. Large car park.

---

*See also Colour Display Advertisement*

**WASHFORD. Mrs Sarah Richmond, Hungerford Farm, Washford, Watchet TA23 0JZ (01984 640285).** Hungerford Farm is a comfortable 13th century farmhouse on a 350 acre mixed farm, three-quarters of a mile from the West Somerset Steam Railway. Situated in beautiful countryside on the edge of the Brendon Hills and Exmoor National Park. Within easy reach of the North Devon coast, two-and-a-half miles from the Bristol Channel and Quantock Hills. Marvellous country for walking, riding, and fishing on the reservoirs. Family room and twin-bedded room, both with colour TV; own bathroom, shower, toilet. Own lounge with TV and open fire. Children welcome at reduced rates, cot and high chair. Sorry, no pets. Bed and Breakfast from £17. Evening drink included. Open February to November.
e-mail: sarah.richmond@virgin.net

---

**WATCHET. Susan and Roger Vincent, Wyndham House, 4 Sea View Terrace, Watchet TA23 0DF (Tel & Fax: 01984 631881).** Our Grade II Listed Georgian home overlooks Watchet Harbour and the new marina, with views across the Bristol Channel to Wales. The extensive gardens border the West Somerset (steam) Railway. The house has an elegant dining room and well furnished bedrooms with either an en suite shower room or washbasin, TV, comfortable chairs, and tea-making facilities and home-made biscuits. Watchet is an interesting and historic town, which makes an ideal base for exploring The Quantocks, Exmoor and the North Devon coast. Come and discover a well kept secret! Children and pets by arrangement. No smoking. Ample parking. Bed and Breakfast from £20.
e-mail: rhv@dialstart.net

---

**WELLS. Mrs Sheila Stott, Lana, Hollow Farm, The Hollow, Westbury-sub-Mendip, Near Wells BA5 1HH (01749 870635).** Modern farmhouse accommodation on working farm. Gently elevated site offering beautiful views over the moors and Somerset Levels, Glastonbury Tor in the distance and the Mendip Hills behind. En suite rooms including fridge, hairdryer, tea/coffee facilities, shaver point, colour TV and central heating. Attractively furnished and comfortable. Breakfast room - sole use of guests, breakfasts served at separate tables in the farmhouse style room. Full English breakfast and a varied menu. Browse through the tourist information and relax in comfort. Non-smoking. Two double rooms, one twin room, all en suite with shower facilities. Prices from £20 per person per night, £14 children under 12 years old. Reduced rates for three nights or more.

## Somerset

**See also Colour Display Advertisement**

**WELLS. Mr & Mrs Betton-Foster, Infield House, 36 Portway, Wells BA5 2BN (01749 670989; Fax: 01749 679093).** Victorian townhouse beautifully restored with period decor and portraits. A short walk to the city centre, Cathedral and Bishop's Palace. Short drive to Cheddar, Wookey Hole, Glastonbury and 40 minutes to Bath. Wonderful walks on Mendip Hills. Double or twin bedrooms, all en suite with colour TV and tea/coffee making facilities. Evening meals on request. Bed and full English/ Vegetarian/Continental breakfasts £21 to £24.50 per person per night. **AA** ◆◆◆◆.

**WESTON-SUPER-MARE. Mr and Mrs H. Wallington, Braeside Hotel, 2 Victoria Park, Weston-super-Mare BS23 2HZ (Tel & Fax: 01934 626642).** Delightful family-run hotel, ideally situated near sandy beach; shops and park are close by. All our nine bedrooms have bath/shower and toilet en suite, colour TV and coffee/tea making facilities and are tastefully decorated, creating just the right atmosphere in which to relax after a busy day. Some rooms with sea views. Unrestricted on-street parking. Good base for exploring Mendip and Quantock Hills, Exmoor, etc. Directions: with sea on left, take first right after Winter Gardens, then first left into Lower Church Road, Victoria Park is the cul-de-sac on the right after the left hand bend. **ETC/AA** ◆◆◆◆
e-mail: braeside@tesco.net

**See also Colour Display Advertisement**

**WESTON-SUPER-MARE. Mrs Margaret Holt, Moorlands, Hutton. Weston-Super-Mare BS24 9QH (Tel & Fax: 01934 812283).** Enjoy fine food and warm hospitality at this impressive late Georgian house set in landscaped gardens below the slopes of the Western Mendips. A wonderful touring centre, perfectly placed for visits to beaches, sites of special interest and historic buildings. Families with children particularly welcome; reduced terms and pony rides. Full central heating, open fire in comfortable lounge. Licensed. Open all year. Bed and Breakfast from £19 per person. **ETC** ◆◆◆.

**See also Colour Display Advertisement**

**WESTONZOYLAND. John and Liz Knight, Staddlestones, 3 Standards Road, Westonzoyland TA7 0EL (01278 691179; Fax: 01278 691333).** Relax in the spacious comfort of our elegant Georgian-converted 17th century farmhouse. Centrally located in the historic village of Westonzoyland, close to Junction 23 of the M5 motorway, Staddletones provides an ideal base for exploring Somerset. The area is renowned for walking, fishing, cycling and wildlife and also has excellent golf courses. Double or twin rooms with en suite facilities or private bathroom, and tea/coffee making facilities. Guest sitting room with inglenook fireplace, TV and video. Large secluded garden with pond. Good local pubs/restaurants for evening meals. Business facilities available. Open all year. Private parking. Full central heating. Please note that we have a no-smoking policy at Staddletones and regrettably cannot accept small children or pets. **ETC** ◆◆◆◆ *SILVER AWARD.*
e-mail: staddlestones@euphony.net
website: www.guide2britain.co.uk/where2stay/staddlestones

---

# FHG

Visit the FHG website
## www.holidayguides.com
for details of the wide choice of accommodation
featured in the full range of FHG titles

**Somerset** 273

## West Hay Farm

Situated within the beautiful Wrington Vale, nicely secluded at the end of a track yet close to all amenities and overlooking breathtaking views of the Mendip hills. Less than 10 minutes from Bristol Airport, with Bath, Bristol, the seaside resort of Weston-super-Mare and Cheddar not far away. Double and twin en suite rooms, all have TV and hot drinks facilities. Ground floor rooms also available. Enjoy breakfast overlooking the beautiful Mendip Hills whilst relaxing in a friendly and informal atmosphere – it has been described as the best B&B ever. Excellent food served at the local pub just five minutes away. Prices from £38 per night per couple. Special weekend and mid-week breaks available.

*Mrs Louise Hemmens, West Hay Farm, West Hay Road, Wrington BS18 7NR*
*Tel: 01934 863549   Mobile: 07970 025027*

**See also Colour Display Advertisement**

**YEOVIL. White Horse Inn, 10 St Michael's Avenue, Yeovil BA21 4LB (01935 476471; Fax: 01935 476480).** This popular local inn has newly refurbished en suite rooms. It is situated within easy walking distance of the town centre and local amenities. Guests are assured of home-cooked inn food in comfortable surroundings, and the day starts with a full English breakfast. Open all year. Three bedrooms, all with shower and toilet. Children welcome. Bar meals, real ale. Taunton 21 miles.

**YEOVIL. Beverly White, Jessops, Chilthorne Domer, Yeovil BA22 8RY (01935 841097).** A warm and friendly welcome to this 'home away from home' Bed and Breakfast set in open countryside for a peaceful stay. TV, tea and coffee in all rooms. Large, quiet bedrooms, one en suite with four-poster bed. Full central heating. Hearty English breakfast. Yeovil town just five minutes' drive away and a short walk to the local pub. Terms from £20 to £25 per person

**YEOVIL. Mrs Undine Reder, Merry Moles Bed and Breakfast, Primrose Hill, East Coker BA22 9NJ (01935 862302; Fax: 01935 862043).** Lovely walking country on Dorset and Somerset border. Peace and quiet with lovely views and special atmosphere. Yeovil is only seven minutes away with plenty of good local pubs. Bath, Exmoor and Thomas Hardy country nearby. Accommodation consists of two double and two single bedrooms with washbasin. Separate bath/shower and separate toilet. Drying facilities. Safe parking. We have foxes, badgers and deer who visit every night, as well as excellent wild birds plus our own water fowl collection. Sorry, no pets. Bed and Breakfast from £22 per person.
**e-mail: reder@tinyworld.co.uk**

---

## FHG PUBLICATIONS LIMITED
publish a large range of well-known accommodation guides.
We will be happy to send you details or you can use the
order form at the back of this book.

# STAFFORDSHIRE

**ALTON. Jean and John Simpson, Gancy Croft, Gallows Green, Alton ST10 4BN (01538 702177).** Enjoy Bed and Breakfast in this idyllic country cottage situated on B5032 between Ashbourne and Cheadle. Single, twin and family accommodation with central heating, colour televisions and tea/coffee facilities. Dining area and bathroom adjacent. Cot and high chair available. Ideal centre for Alton Towers, Uttoxeter Races, Peak District, Potteries Towns, walking/touring/golfing breaks. Secure private parking with transport to/from local rail stations etc. if required. Excellent Evening Meals at local pubs within easy walking distance in Alton Village. Open all year from £17.50 per person per night.

*See also Colour Display Advertisement*

**BUTTERTON, near Newcastle. Ms. Sarah Jealouse, Butterton House, Park Road, Butterton, Newcastle-under-Lyme ST5 4DZ (01782 619085).** Situated one-and-a-half miles from Junction 15 on the M6, in beautiful gardens and countryside with a tennis court and croquet lawn. Ideal for visiting pottery factory shops, Alton Towers, Chester and the Peak District, etc. Large comfortable en suite rooms. Voted "Best B&B in England" by Country Rover Brochure guests. Great English Breakfast - vegetarians catered for. Directions:- after leaving M6 at J15 turn right three times. We are first house on the right down the small winding country lane. **ETC ♦♦♦**.
e-mail: sjtoast@aol.com
website: www.touristnetuk/wm/butterton.com

**ECCLESHALL. Mrs Sue Pimble, Cobblers Cottage, Kerry Lane, Eccleshall ST21 6EJ (Tel & Fax: 01785 850116).** A five minute walk from the centre of historic Eccleshall and just past the 12th century church is Cobbler's Cottage, in a quiet lane within the conservation area. We offer two bedrooms: one double and one twin/family, both en suite with colour TV, tea/coffee making facilities and central heating. Eccleshall has seven pubs, five with restaurants for your evening meal. Ideally situated for the Potteries, Wedgwood, Ironbridge, Alton Towers and other attractions. Children and pets welcome. Non-smoking. Bed and Breakfast from £18 per person per night; £27 for single occupancy. Reduction for children sharing. M6 J14 is 10 minutes away, J15 is 15 minutes. **ETC ♦♦♦♦**
e-mail: cobblerscottage@tinyonline.co.uk

**ECCLESHALL. M. Hiscoe-James, Offley Grove Farm, Adbaston, Eccleshall ST20 0QB (01785 280205).** You'll consider this a good find! Quality accommodation and excellent breakfasts. Small traditional mixed farm surrounded by beautiful countryside. The house is tastefully furnished and provides all home comforts. En suite rooms available. Whether you are planning to book here for a break in your journey, stay for a weekend or take your holidays here, you will find something to suit all tastes among the many local attractions. Situated on the Staffordshire/Shropshire borders we are convenient for Alton Towers, Stoke-on-Trent, Ironbridge, etc. Just 15 minutes from M6 and M54; midway between Eccleshall and Newport, four miles from the A519. Reductions for children. Play area for small children. Open all year. Bed and Breakfast (all en suite) from £20. Reductions for children. Many guests return. Self-catering cottages available. Brochure on request. **AA/RAC ♦♦♦**
e-mail: accomm@offleygrovefarm.freeserve.co.uk
website: www.offleygrovefarm.freeserve.co.uk

**Staffordshire** 275

**ECCLESHALL. Mrs Helen Bonsall, Slindon House Farm, Slindon, Eccleshall ST21 6LX (01782 791237).** Slindon House Farm is a working dairy, arable and sheep farm. The house is set in a large attractive garden and offers excellent accommodation, comfortable, spacious and well equipped rooms. We are easy to find, situated on the A519, located between Junctions 14 and 15 of the M6, ideal for an overnight break or a longer stay to visit such local attractions as the Potteries, County Showground, Bridgemere, Stapeley Water Gardens, Telford and Ironbridge. There is a good selection of local places to eat. Regret no pets. **ETC/AA** ◆◆◆◆.
e-mail: bonsallslindonhouse@supanet.com

**LEEK. Mr Griffiths, Prospect House Guest House, 334 Cheadle Road, Cheddleton, Leek ST13 7BW (01782 550639).** Charming 19th Century converted Coach House. Beamed en suite rooms in a courtyard setting with independent access. All rooms have colour TV, hospitality tray, hairdryer, iron etc. There are two lounges, one overlooking the cottage garden, together with a children's play area. Delightful country and canal side walks. Close to Peak District National Park, Alton Towers, the historic market town of Leek and the Potteries. The Churnet Valley and Cheddleton Steam Railway are within easy walking distance. Open all year. Ample parking. French and German spoken. Ground floor rooms available. Bed and Breakfast from £21. Child discounts available. **ETC** ◆◆◆◆
e-mail: prospect@talk21.com
website: www.touristnetuk/wm/prospect/index.htm

**NEWCASTLE-UNDER-LYME. Mary Hugh, The Old Hall, Poolside, Madeley, Near Crewe CW3 9DX (01782 750209).** Civic Trust Award. English Heritage Grade II Starred Listed family-owned timbered house of great character and historic interest. Built in 1647 as shown on front of the house "Walke knave what lookest at?" Situated in large attractive gardens with ornamental pool, tennis court and croquet lawn for visitors' use. Excellent accommodation; one room en suite; all with tea and coffee facilities, TV and central heating. Situated on A525, close to the Potteries and two of the largest garden centres in Europe - Bridgemere and Stapeley. Children over ten welcome at reduced rates. Bed and Breakfast from £25. Dinner £15; all meals by arrangement. Open all year.

**STOKE-ON-TRENT. Mr and Mrs J. Little, Lee House Farm, Leek Road, Waterhouses, Stoke-on-Trent ST10 3HW (01538 308439).** Josie and Jim Little welcome you to their charming 18th century farmhouse in the heart of Waterhouses, a village with many amenities set in the Peak District National Park. The house is tastefully furnished and retains many of its original features. Ample off-road parking is available. All rooms are en suite and centrally heated. The non-smoking bedrooms are equipped with TV and drinks facilities. Waterhouses is an ideal centre for visiting the Derbyshire Dales, Staffordshire Moorlands, Alton Towers and the Potteries. Bed and Breakfast from £20 per person. **HETB** ◆◆◆◆

*Please mention **Bed and Breakfast Stops** when making enquiries about accommodation featured in these pages.*

# SUFFOLK

**BOXFORD. Mrs Janet Havard-Davies, Cox Hill House, Boxford, Sudbury CO10 5JG (01787 210449).** Cox Hill House is a delightful Suffolk country house situated on the top of Cox Hill overlooking the old wool village of Boxford with its Anglo Saxon church and Elizabethan Grammar School. Nearby are the market towns of Sudbury (15 minutes), Hadleigh (10 minutes) and the picturesque village of Kersey (eight minutes). Within easy reach of Colchester, Ipswich, Harwich, Felixstowe, Dedham and Flatford Mill (Constable country), Cambridge and Lavenham. The accommodation comprises two twin-bedded rooms with en suite bathroom and one double bedded room with own facilities. Ample parking. Golf at Stoke-by-Nayland Golf Club by prior arrangement. Bed and Breakfast £30 single, £40-£48 double. No smoking. **AA ♦♦♦♦**.
e-mail: coxhillhouse@hotmail.com

**BURY ST. EDMUNDS. John Kemp, Gifford's Hall, Hartest, Near Bury St. Edmunds IP29 4EX (01284 830464; Fax: 01284 830229).** Gifford's Hall is a vineyard and small country living set in some of Suffolk's most beautiful and tranquil surroundings, midway between Bury, Lavenham and Sudbury. It is a listed Georgian farmhouse with large comfortable rooms including two twin and one double with en suite bathrooms. Guests have the use of the large drawing/TV/games room and breakfast is usually taken in the conservatory. You will be welcome to explore our 33 acres which includes 12 acres of vines and a winery, wild flower meadows grazed by rare breed sheep, pigs and pure breed free range hens, an acre rose garden, sweet peas and chrysanthemums, an organic vegetable garden and even a shop and tea room where you can enjoy a cream tea or taste the wines. Bed and Breakfast £44 double, £46 and £50 twin. Brochures on request.

**CLARE. Jean and Alastair Tuffill, "Cobbles", 26 Nethergate Street, Clare, Near Sudbury CO10 8NP (01787 277539; Fax: 01787 278252).** Situated in one of the loveliest parts of East Anglia, a friendly welcome awaits you at Cobbles - this Grade II listed beamed house dates back to the 14th century. Clare is an historic market town and the area abounds in history and ancient buildings, with many antique shops and places of interest to visit. The house is within easy walking distance of the ancient castle and country park, and the town centre with pubs and restaurants which provide excellent food. Accommodation is provided in one twin and one single bedroom in the house with bathroom. Within the pretty walled garden is the charming beamed twin-bedded en suite cottage with private access. All rooms have central heating, colour TV, handbasins and tea/coffee making facilities. Bed and Breakfast from £24 per person per night. Easy parking. We are strictly non-smoking.

**CLARE. Mrs Debra Bowles, Ship Stores, 22 Callis Street, Clare, Sudbury CO10 8DX (01787 277834).** Situated in the delightful small town of Clare, Ship Stores comprises a small village store, tea room and five-bedroomed guest house. All rooms are en suite with colour TV and tea and coffee making facilities. A comfortable guests' lounge is available with TV and video (free video hire from shop). As well as being recommended in the "Which?" Guide we are proud of our Tourist Board grading. Ideally situated for Constable country, Cambridge and Bury St. Edmunds. Children welcome. Sorry, no pets. Bed and Breakfast from £21.50 per person; Evening Meal from £9.50 per person. **ETC/AA ♦♦♦**
e-mail: shipclare@aol.com
website: www.ship-stores.co.uk

---

**PLEASE SEND A STAMPED ADDRESSED ENVELOPE WITH ENQUIRIES**

**Suffolk** 277

**FRAMLINGHAM. Mrs Jennie Mann, Fiddlers Hall, Cransford, Near Framlingham, Woodbridge IP13 9PQ (01728 663729). Working farm, join in.** Signposted on B1119, Fiddlers Hall is a 14th century, moated, oak-beamed farmhouse set in a beautiful and secluded position. It is two miles from Framlingham Castle, 20 minutes' drive from Aldeburgh, Snape Maltings, Woodbridge and Southwold. A Grade II Listed building, it has lots of history and character. The bedrooms are spacious; one has en suite shower room, the other has a private bathroom. Use of lounge and colour TV. Plenty of parking space. Lots of farm animals kept. Traditional farmhouse cooking. Bed and Breakfast terms from £22.

**FRAMLINGHAM. Mrs C. Jones, Bantry, Chapel Road, Saxtead, Woodbridge IP13 9RB (01728 685578).** Bantry is situated in the picturesque village of Saxtead close to the historic castle town of Framlingham. Saxtead is best known for its working windmill beside the village green. Bantry is set in half an acre of gardens overlooking open countryside and three-quarters-of-a-mile along Tannington Road on right-hand side from Saxtead Windmill. We offer you accommodation in one of three purpose-built self-contained apartments, separate from the house. For secluded comfort each comprises an en suite bedroom leading through to its own private lounge/diningroom with TV and drink-making facilities. Bed and Breakfast from £19.50 per person. Non-smoking.
website: www.sleepysuffolk.co.uk

**FRAMLINGHAM. Brian and Phyllis Collett, Shimmens Pightle, Dennington Road, Framlingham, Woodbridge IP13 9JT (01728 724036).** Shimmens Pightle is situated in an acre of landscaped garden, surrounded by farmland, within a mile of the centre of Framlingham, with its famous castle and church. Ideally situated for the Heritage Coast, Snape Maltings, local vineyards, riding, etc. Cycles can be hired locally. Many good local eating places. Double and twin bedded rooms, with washbasins, on ground floor. Comfortable lounge with TV overlooking garden. Morning tea and evening drinks offered. Sorry, no pets or smoking indoors. Bed and traditional English Breakfast using local cured bacon and home made marmalade, from £21 per person, reduced weekly rates. Vegetarians also happily catered for. SAE please. Open Mid-March to November.

**HADLEIGH. Mrs Jan Cattell, Badgers, Rands Road, Lower Layham, Ipswich IP7 5RW (01473 823396).** Quiet country location ideal for walking, cycling and touring Suffolk with golf courses nearby. Comfortable centrally heated bedrooms, one twin and one single, colour TV, radio and tea/coffee making facilities. Both rooms are en suite. Harwich and Felixstowe are within easy reach. No smoking. Parking. Bed and Breakfast from £22. **ETC ♦♦♦♦**.
e-mail: catbadgers@aol.com

**IPSWICH. Mrs Rosanna Steward, High View, Back Lane, Washbrook, Ipswich IP8 3JA (01473 730494).** A comfortable modernised Edwardian house set in a large secluded garden located four miles south of Ipswich the county town of Suffolk. Ideally situated to explore the Suffolk heritage coast and countryside, we are within easy reach of "Constable Country", Lavenham, Kersey, the historic market town of Bury St. Edmunds plus many other picturesque locations. There is a maze of public footpaths in and around the village providing a good variety of walks through woodland and open countryside. Twin and double bedrooms; guests' bathroom with shower and toilet, lounge with TV. Good pub meals available in the village. Double and Twin £20 and Single £22 per person per night. **ETC ♦♦♦♦**

**LOWESTOFT. Doreen and Vince Moran, Kensington House, 22A Pakefield Road, South Lowestoft NR33 0HS (01502 538618).** Kensington House is a family-run, very comfortable guest house, situated in Britain's most easterly point and only 100 yards from the award winning beach. The property is facing well-kept colourful gardens offering bowling greens, tennis courts, boating lake, aviary and tea rooms. We are within easy reach of the town centre, railway and bus stations, wildlife parks, The Broads and Great Yarmouth. All bedrooms have colour TV with tea/coffee making facilities and a full English breakfast is served. Bed and Breakfast from £13.50 to £15.00 per person per day, children over five welcome at reduced rates. Weekly discounts available.

**SUDBURY. The Perseverance Hotel, Station Road, Long Melford, Sudbury CO10 9HN (01787 375862).** Situated on the edge of the village, at the end of a country walk made from the old rail line from Sudbury to Long Melford. Just five minutes from the market town of Sudbury, surrounded by places of interest such as Lavenham and Kersey, and good towns for shopping such as Colchester, Bury St Edmunds and Ipswich. Also en suite family unit sleeping up to four adults with TV and tea making facilities. There are three en suite chalets (two twin and one double), all with TV and tea/coffee making facilities. Prices are £25 per person per night including breakfast, £30 per night for single occupancy. Children under 14 years at £10 per night.

**WENHASTON. Mrs Margaret Plues, The Compasses Inn, The Street, Wenhaston IP19 9EF (01502 478319).** Feel at home in this friendly little inn, hidden just off the A12 near Southwold. The village has many lovely footpaths and commons, with Suffolk's Heritage Coast and RSPB Minsmere just a few minutes away. We have three comfortable bedrooms (two en suite) with colour TV and tea/coffee facilities, and serve late, leisurely breakfasts (as large as you like!). Our evening bistro offers fresh local fish, steaks etc with Mediterranean, Mexican and other specials on request. Bar, car park, garden and stair lift can be used by guests. Well-behaved dogs most welcome. No children. Bed and Breakfast from £15 per person. Leaflet on request.

# SURREY

**FARNHAM. Mariners Hotel, Millbridge, Frensham, Farnham GU10 3DJ (01252 792050; Fax: 01252 792649).** Within easy reach of Gatwick and Heathrow Airports and ideally placed for visits to London, this well-organised hotel has a tranquil situation by the River Wey. Guests of all ages are warmly welcomed and for parents there are baby sitting and listening arrangements and a useful laundry and ironing service. Bedrooms are spacious and provided with a private bathroom, colour television, direct-dial telephone and tea and coffee-making facilities. For disabled guests, there is easy access to ground-floor rooms which overlook well-kept gardens. Dining here presents an interesting choice in a bistro-style restaurant with a range of Italian dishes as well as an extensive buffet and à la carte menu. Food is also served in the cosy lounge bar. **ETC** ◆◆◆.

**GATWICK. Carole and Adrian Grinsted, The Lawn Guest House, 30 Massetts Road, Horley RH6 7DE (01293 775751; Fax: 01293 821803).** The Lawn, a totally non-smoking establishment, is a lovely Victorian house in a pleasant garden, two minutes from the centre of Horley and one-and-a-half miles from Gatwick. All rooms are en suite with colour TV, hairdryers, tea/coffee/chocolate trays and direct dial telephones. Horley, with its restaurants, shops and pubs is 150 yards away. The mainline railway station (300yards) has services to London (Victoria 40 minutes) and Brighton (45 minutes). The Lawn is ideal for those 'overnighting' before or after a flight from Gatwick Airport. On site holiday parking by arrangement. Bed and Breakfast from £22.50 per person in a twin/double. **ETC/AA/RAC** ◆◆◆◆. *ETC SILVER AWARD, RAC SPARKLING DIAMOND*
e-mail: info@lawnguesthouse.co.uk
website: www.lawnguesthouse.co.uk

**HAMPTON COURT. Mrs S. Mayho, 85 Bedster Gardens, East Molesey KT8 9TB (020 8979 8857 / 5655).** Set in a peaceful location close to the river offering one twin and one single room with guest bathroom, large comfortable sittingroom with TV and study. Only five minutes from Hampton Court Palace and mainline station (Wimbledon, Waterloo 25 minutes). Convenient for Sandown and Kempton Park racecourses, Kew, Wisley, Windsor, Royal Parks and National Trust Houses and Gardens. Close to Heathrow and M25 for Gatwick. Traditional or Continental breakfast. Tea and coffee available. Easy parking. Children and pets welcome. Reasonable terms.

**Surrey** **279**

**LINGFIELD. Mrs Vanessa Manwill, Stantons Hall Farm, Eastbourne Road, Blindley Heath, Lingfield RH7 6LG (01342 832401).** Stantons Hall Farm is an 18th century farmhouse, set in 18 acres of farmland and adjacent to Blindley Heath Common. Family, double and single rooms, most with WC, shower and wash-hand basins en suite. Separate bathroom. All rooms have colour TV, tea/coffee facilities and are centrally heated. There are plenty of parking spaces. We are conveniently situated within easy reach of M25 (London Orbital), Gatwick Airport (car parking for travellers) and Lingfield Park racecourse. Enjoy a traditional English breakfast in our large farmhouse kitchen. Bed and Breakfast from £23 per person, reductions for children sharing. Cot and high chair available. Well behaved dogs welcome by prior arrangement.

**LINGFIELD. Mrs Vivienne Bundy, Oaklands, Felcourt, Lingfield RH7 6NF (01342 834705).** Oaklands is a spacious country house of considerable charm dating from the 17th century. It is set in its own grounds of one acre, about one mile from the small town of Lingfield, and three miles from East Grinstead, both with rail connections to London. It is convenient for Gatwick Airport and ideal as a stop-over or as a base to visit the many places of interest in south-east England. Dover and the Channel Ports are two hours' drive away whilst London and Brighton are about one hour distant. One en suite room; one double and one single bedrooms, with washbasins; two bathrooms, two toilets; sittingroom; diningroom. Cot, high chair, babysitting and reduced rates for children. Gas central heating. Open all year. Parking. Bed and Breakfast from £22. Evening Meal by arrangement.

**OXTED. Pinehurst Grange Guest House, East Hill (A25), Oxted RH8 9AE (01883 716413).** Victorian ex-farmhouse offers one double, one twin and one single bedroom. All with washbasin, tea/coffee making facilities, colour TV; residents' dining room. Private parking. Close to all local amenities. Only 20 minutes' drive from Gatwick Airport and seven minutes' walk to the station with good trains to London/Croydon. Also close to local bus and taxi service. There are many famous historic houses nearby including "Chartwell", "Knole", "Hever Castle", and "Penshurst Place". Very handy for Lingfield Park racecourse. WALKERS NOTE: only one mile from North Downs Way. No smoking.

**REDHILL. Mrs Trozado, Lynwood Guest House, 50 London Road, Redhill RH1 1LN (01737 766894).** Gatwick Airport 12 minutes by train or car; London 35 minutes by train. Six minutes' walk to Redhill Station and town centre. Comfortable rooms with en suite facilities, colour TV and tea/coffee facilities. Car park. English Breakfast. **AA** *QQQ*.

**WALTON-ON-THAMES. Mrs Joan Spiteri, Beechtree Lodge, 7 Rydens Avenue, Walton-on-Thames KT12 3JB (01932 242738; Fax: 01932 886667).** A comfortable Edwardian home situated in a quiet avenue, plenty of parking. Minutes from local shops and restaurants; station 10 minutes' walk, Waterloo 25 minutes. Easy access by bus to Heathrow and handy for Hampton Court, Chessington World of Adventure, Thorpe Park, Kempton and Sandown Exhibition Centres, Brooklands Aero/Motor Museum and glorious countryside. All rooms warm and comfortable with washbasins; colour TV, tea/coffee. Families catered for and business people welcome. French, Italian and Greek spoken. Coach trips can be booked. Bed and Breakfast from £18; family rates available. Sorry, no smoking. **ETC** ◆◆◆
e-mail:fredspiteri@yahoo.co.uk

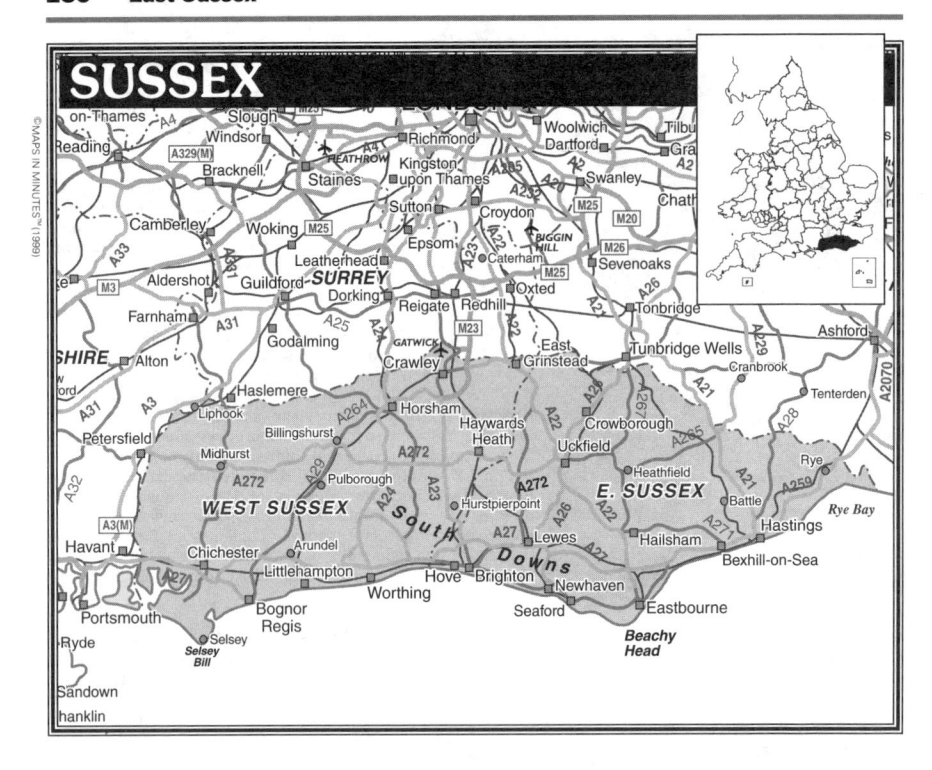

# EAST SUSSEX

**BRIGHTON. "Brighton" Marina House Hotel, 8 Charlotte Street, Brighton BN2 1AG (00 44 (0)1273 605349; Fax: 00 44 (0)1273 679484).** As a premier Bed and Breakfast, we enjoy a pivotal postition located just off the seafront and walking distance from all major attractions. Luxuriously appointed rooms are fully equipped offering en suite facility. In the Breakfast Room, we are committed to creating the ultimate breakfast experience, offering various breakfast times. We cater for vegans, vegetarians, Continental and if you enjoy the 'English cooked' breakfast, we have the full works. Our speciality is romantic rooms. Children welcome. Prices from £15 to £45 per person per night. **ETC/AA/RAC ♦♦♦**
e-mail: rooms@jungs.co.uk
website: www.s-h-systems.co.uk/hotels/brightma

**BRIGHTON. Mrs M.A. Daughtery, Ma'on Hotel, 26 Upper Rock Gardens, Brighton BN2 1QE (01273 694400).** This completely non-smoking Grade II Listed building is run by proprietors who are waiting with a warm and friendly welcome. Our standard of food has been highly commended by many guests who return year after year. Two minutes from the sea and within easy reach of conference and main town centres, 30 minutes from airport. All nine bedrooms are furnished to a high standard and have colour TV, hospitality tray, radio alarm clock and hairdryer; most en suite. A lounge with colour TV is available for guests' convenience. Diningroom. Full central heating. Access to rooms at all times. NO CHILDREN. Terms from £28. Brochure on request with SAE.

**BURGESS HILL. Mr. Mundy, The Homestead, Homestead Lane, Valebridge Road. Burgess Hill RH15 0RQ (Tel & Fax: 01444 246899; Mobile: 07808 567241).** Tranquil, country setting in seven-and-a-half acres, at end of private lane. Home also to a variety of wildlife, including foxes, badgers, squirrels, rabbits, the occasional deer and our own free range hens. Close to Wivelsfield station with frequent trains to Gatwick, London, Brighton, Lewes and Eastbourne. Centrally situated for Glyndebourne, South Downs Way, numerous NT locations, gardens, Bluebell Railway and the Lavender Line. Opportunities for walking, fishing and golf. All rooms en suite and fully equipped. Wheelchair access to ground-floor bedrooms. Extensive breakfast menu, vegetarian option available. Strictly non-smoking. Children over 12 welcome. Unlimited parking. Bed and Breakfast from £22.50 - £25 per night. **AA/ETC ♦♦♦♦**.
e-mail: homestead@burgess-hill.co.uk
website: www.burgess-hill.co.uk

**BURWASH. Mrs E. Sirrell, Woodlands Farm, Burwash, Etchingham TN19 7LA (Tel & Fax: 01435 882794). Working farm, join in.** Woodlands Farm stands one-third-of-a mile off the road, surrounded by fields and woods. This peaceful and beautifully modernised 16th century farmhouse offers comfortable and friendly accommodation. Sitting/dining room; two bathrooms, one en suite, double or twin-bedded rooms (one has four poster bed) together with excellent farm fresh food. This is a farm of 108 acres with mixed animals, and is situated within easy reach of 20 or more places of interest to visit and half-an-hour from the coast. Open all year. Central heating. Literature provided to help guests. Children welcome. Dogs allowed if sleeping in owner's car. Parking. Evening Meal optional. Bed and Breakfast from £20 to £23 per person per night. Telephone or SAE, please. **AA** QQ.
e-mail: liz_sir@lineone.net

**EASTBOURNE. Alfriston Hotel, 16 Lushington Road, Eastbourne BN21 4LL (01323 725640).** Trevor and Brenda Gomersall welcome you to the Alfriston Hotel, a friendly, comfortable, family-run hotel in the centre of Eastbourne. Most bedrooms are en suite and all are non-smoking with colour TV and tea/coffee making facilities. Full English breakfasts are served with free-range eggs cooked to your requirements. Vegetarians welcome. Home-cooked evening dinners are available if booked, but there are also plenty of eating places nearby. We are close to the shopping centre and railway station, while the sea front, theatres and Devonshire Park are less than half-a-mile away. Bed and Breakfast from £19 to £21. Open March to October. Sorry, no pets. **ETC ♦♦♦**
e-mail: alfristonhotel@fsbdial.co.uk

**EASTBOURNE Tony and Trish Callaghan, Far End Private Hotel, 139 Royal Parade, Eastbourne BN22 7LH (01323 725666).** From the moment you arrive you are assured of a warm welcome and real "home from home" atmosphere. Our bedrooms are tastefully decorated and have colour TV, central heating and tea/coffee making facilities. Most have sea views. Residents have use of the garden as well as their own lounge. Enjoy freshly prepared traditional home cooking, with vegetarian and special diets catered for. We are adjacent to the popular Princes Park with boating lake, lawns and pitch 'n' putt, and close by you can enjoy sailing, yachting, fishing, bowling, tennis and swimming. We are within easy reach of Beachy Head, the South Downs and Newhaven. We will be delighted to provide information on local attractions and services and do our best to make your stay as memorable and pleasant as possible – right up to the time you leave. Bed and Breakfast from £18; Evening Meal available. Low season short breaks. Please call or write for our colour brochure.

---

Terms quoted in this publication may be subject to increase if rises in costs necessitate

**East Sussex**

**EASTBOURNE. The Cherry Tree Hotel, 15 Silverdale Road, Eastbourne BN20 7AJ (01323 722406; Fax: 01323 648838).** Award winning small, non-smoking, family-run hotel. Converted from an Edwardian residence it retains all its original charm, elegance and character. In a quiet residential area close to the sea front, theatres and downlands, the area benefits from unrestricted parking. All rooms are en suite and have colour TV, radio, hospitality tray and direct dial telephones. Noted for its excellent traditional English cuisine and is licensed to residents. Open February to December, offering the highest standard of facilities and service which you would expect from a Four Diamond Silver Award Hotel. Bed and Breakfast from £26.00, Dinner, Bed and Breakfast from £38.50. Special Breaks and weekly terms on request. **ETC** ♦♦♦♦ *SILVER AWARD*.
e-mail: anncherrytree@aol.com
website: www.eastbourne.org/cherrytree-hotel

**HAILSHAM near. David and Jill Hook, Longleys Farm Cottage, Harebeating Lane, Hailsham BN27 1ER (Tel & Fax: 01323 841227).** Situated in quiet private country lane one mile north of the market town of Hailsham with its excellent amenities including modern sports centre and leisure pool, surrounded by footpaths across open farmland. Ideal for country lovers. Dogs and children welcome. The coast at Eastbourne, South Downs, Ashdown Forest and 1066 country are all within easy access. The non-smoking accommodation comprises one twin room, double room en suite; family room en suite and tea/coffee making facilities. Bed and Breakfast from £18. Reductions for children.

*See also Colour Display Advertisement*

**HARTFIELD. Bolebroke Castle, Hartfield TN7 4JJ (01892 770061; Fax: 01892 771041).** Henry VIII hunting lodge is set in a stunningly beautiful location on a 30 acre estate away from main roads and noise. There are two lakes, woodlands and views to the Ashdown Forest where you will find Pooh Bridge. The castle has antique furniture, original beamed ceilings and the second largest fireplace in England. Four-poster suite. Colour TV. Tea/coffee facilities. Bed and Breakfast and self-catering available. Tunbridge Wells five miles. Eastbourne and Brighton 30 miles. Telephone for brochure. **ETC** ♦♦♦.

**HASTINGS. Peter Mann, Grand Hotel, Grand Parade, St. Leonards, Hastings TN38 0DD (Tel & Fax: 01424 428510).** Seafront family-run hotel, half-a-mile west of Hastings Pier. Spacious lounge, licensed bar, central heating. All bedrooms have colour TV, radio/room-call/baby-listening and some rooms have en suite facilities. Free access at all times. Unrestricted/disabled parking. Non-smoking restaurant. In the heart of 1066 country close to Battle Abbey, Bodiam and Hever Castles, Kipling's Bateman and historic Cinque Ports plus Hastings Castle Caves, Sealife Aquarium, local golf courses and leisure centres. Open all year. Bed and Breakfast from £14; Evening Meal from £8. Children welcome, half price when sharing room. SAE for further information. **ETC** ♦♦♦.

**HASTINGS. Mrs Afroditi G. Wall, Beechwood Hotel, 59 Baldslow Road, Hastings TN34 2EY (01424 420078).** Beechwood is an original Victorian villa and this atmosphere has been retained in the 12 bedrooms and the public rooms. It is a large family run guesthouse with full central heating, lounge, large south facing garden and unrivalled views of Alexandra Park. Situated in quiet surroundings, adjacent to good bus routes or 15 minute walk to town centre, seafront or station. Off the A2101 and is ideal for touring south east England. On and off road parking. TV and tea/coffee making facilities on request, fully licensed. Open all year. Private facilities and family rooms available. Bed and English Breakfast from £15, Dinner £9. Bargain Breaks. Resident Proprietor: Afroditi G. Wall MHCIMA MRSH. **ETC** ♦♦♦

*When making enquiries or bookings, a stamped addressed envelope is always appreciated*

East Sussex  283

# Cleavers Lyng Country Hotel

For excellent home cooking in traditional English style, comfort and informality, this small, family-run hotel in the heart of rural East Sussex is well recommended. Peacefully set in beautiful landscaped gardens extending to 1.5 acres featuring an ornamental rockpool. Adjacent to Herstmonceux Castle West Gate, the house dates from 1577 as its oak beams and inglenook fireplace bear witness. This is an ideal retreat for a quiet sojourn away from urban clamour. The castles at Pevensey, Scotney, Bodiam and Hever are all within easy reach, as are Battle Abbey, Kipling's House, Batemans, Michelham Priory and the seaside resorts of Eastbourne, Bexhill and Hastings. The bedrooms are fully en suite, and all have central heating and tea/coffee making facilities, colour TV and direct dial telephones. On the ground floor there is an oak-beamed restaurant with a fully licensed lounge bar, cosy residents' lounge with television, and an outer hall with telephone and cloakrooms. Peace, tranquillity and a warm welcome await you. Special Attraction: Badger Watch. Room Rate from £30 pp, sharing Double/Twin rooms. No single rooms available, however, at certain times of the year, we offer a reduced single occupancy rate for double/twin bedroom.

**Church Road, Herstmonceux, East Sussex BN27 1QJ**
**Tel: (01323) 833131    Fax: (01323) 833617**

| See also Colour Display Advertisement |

**HASTINGS. Pat and Tim Lowe, Bell Cottage, Vinehall, Robertsbridge TN32 5JN (01580 881164; Fax: 01580 880519).** 16th century converted Inn full of charm and character with inglenooks and beams throughout. Guests are assured of a warm welcome and may sit in our lovely garden. Breakfast is full English complemented with homemade preserves. We are situated in 1066 country close to Battle, Rye and Hastings; Canterbury, Brighton and Sissinghurst Gardens are within easy driving distance. We are nine miles from Hastings, on the A21, between Whatlington and Robertsbridge. The accommodation consists of one double bedroom with private bathroom, one twin with private bathroom plus one twin en suite, all with colour TV and tea and coffee facilities. Rates from £40 to £45 per room (two sharing). Brochure on request. All rooms No Smoking. ETC ♦♦♦♦ *BED AND BREAKFAST OF THE YEAR 1997.* 
e-mail: patricia.lowe@tesco.net     website: www.bellcottage.co.uk

**HASTINGS. Mr and Mrs R. Steele, Amberlene Guest House, 12 Cambridge Gardens, Hastings TN34 1EH (01424 439447).** Hastings town centre, two minutes' walk from the beach, shops, entertainments, rail/bus stations and central car park. Single, double, twin and family rooms; some with en suite. Very clean, comfortable, well carpeted and decorated. All with central heating, colour TV, washbasins, power and shaver points. Guests have their own front door keys and access to rooms and facilities at all times. Bed and full four-course English Breakfast £14 to £20 per night (room only, £2 less), half price for children sharing. All prices include tea/coffee and biscuits in your room. Baby cots free. No extra charges. Sorry, no pets. Also holiday flats available nearby. ETC ♦♦♦

**HEATHFIELD. Mrs Angela Wardell, Yew Tree Cottage, Street End Lane, Broad Oak, Heathfield TN21 8SA (01435 864053).** Yew Tree Cottage dates back to 1750 and has been extensively modernised. Situated one mile east of Heathfield off the A265 and having glorious views over the Rother Valley. Close to the Sussex/Kent border making an ideal touring centre. South Coast and the historic towns of Battle, Rye and Hastings together with many other places of interest within easy reach; Dover two hours, Ashford one hour's drive. Many attractive eating houses in the vicinity. Accommodation comprises two double rooms (one with twin bed option) and one single. Tea-making facilities and TV. No pets. Ample parking. Open all year. Log fires. A warm welcome. Bed and Breakfast £18.50 per person.

**RYE. Mrs Wanda Bosher, The Old Vicarage at Rye Harbour, Rye TN31 7TT (01797 222088).** Enjoy quality bed and breakfast of the highest standard in our former Victorian vicarage. Very quietly situated, with original features, open fires, linen and lace, antique furniture and oil paintings – be transported back to the genteel pace and ambience of times past. Breakfasts are taken in the elegant diningroom and with fresh local produce, it is certainly a meal to remember. During the winter a crackling log fire adds to the pleasure. Monica Edwards, the well-known children's author, lived here once – one can imagine her planning her tales of intrigue and adventure in Westling Harbour (Rye Harbour). Excellent walking, bird-watching and private parking. Less than an hour from Channel ports and Tunnel, and offering a perfect base for exploring many local towns, historic houses and gardens. Bed and Breakfast from £18.50 to £25.50. AA ★★★

**East Sussex**

**See also Colour Display Advertisement** **RYE. Mrs J.P. Hadfield, Jeake's House, Mermaid Street, Rye TN31 7ET (01797 222828).** Dating from 1689, Jeake's House stands on one of the most beautiful cobbled streets in Rye's medieval town centre. Each stylishly restored bedroom with brass, mahogany or four-poster bed combines traditional elegance and luxury with every modern comfort. 12 rooms, 10 with private bathrooms; honeymoon suite. A roaring fire greets you on cold mornings in the elegant galleried chapel, which is now the dining room. Choosing either a traditional or vegetarian breakfast, the soft chamber music, airy setting and unhurried atmosphere will provide the perfect start to any day. There is a comfortable sitting room and bar with books and pictures lining the walls. Private car park nearby. **ETC/AA/RAC** ◆◆◆◆◆, *SILVER AWARD, AA PREMIER SELECTION AWARD, GOOD HOTEL GUIDE CÉSAR AWARD.*
e-mail: jeakeshouse@btinternet.com
website: www.jeakeshouse.com

**RYE. Mrs Heather Coote, "Busti", Barnetts Hill, Peasmarsh, Rye TN31 6YJ (Tel & Fax: 01797 230408).** Comfortable and clean accommodation in detached house on the edge of the rural village of Peasmarsh. Ideally located for touring both East Sussex and Kent and for visiting Bodiam Castle, the historic town of Rye, Great Dixter, Sissinghurst, Battle Abbey and many other seasonal attractions; lake fishing locally. Guest lounge/dining room with TV. Guests' shower/toilet. Bedrooms have tea/coffee making facilities. Central heating throughout. Hairdryer available. Friendly service and tourist advice provided. Full English breakfast or alternative. Ample off road parking. No smoking in the house. Member of Rye and District Hotels and Caterers Association. Bed and Breakfast from £17.50. **ETC** ◆◆◆.

**RYE. Rita Cox, Four Seasons, 96 Udimore Road, Rye TN31 7DY (01797 224305).** Four Seasons is situated on Cadborough Cliff with spectacular views across the south facing garden to the Brede Valley, Rye and the sea. We offer excellent B&B in our attractive house which is decorated to reflect the changing seasons. Centrally heated rooms are en suite or have private facilities and have TV and hot drinks tray. Breakfasts are full English or vegetarian, with home-made preserves and local produce. Evening Meals on request. Four Seasons is a short walk from the town centre and has private parking. It is an excellent centre for touring East Sussex and Kent, and is convenient for the Channel Ports and Tunnel. Rates are from £18 per person with special winter bargain breaks mid-November to February. Brochure on request.

**RYE. Geoff and Gillian Woods, The Strand House, Winchelsea, Near Rye TN36 4JT (01797 226276; Fax 01797 224806).** Nestling beneath the cliff of the ancient medieval town of Winchelsea lies the 15th century Strand House. Full of atmosphere with oak beams and inglenook fireplaces, but with the comfort of en suite facilities, central heating, colour TV and beverage tray. Romantic four-poster bedroom available. A lounge with log fires in winter leads onto a pretty garden for your enjoyment in summer. A residents' bar, payphone, and ample parking in the grounds make your visit relaxed and enjoyable. An ideal place to stay while you explore the many places of interest within easy reach. Tariff from £24 to £34 per person. Visa/Mastercard/Eurocard accepted. **ETC** ◆◆◆◆, *AA QQQQ SELECTED, RAC SPARKLING DIAMOND AWARD*
e-mail: strandhouse@winchelsea98.fsnet.co.uk

**FREE or REDUCED RATE entry to Holiday Visits and Attractions — see our READERS' OFFER VOUCHERS on pages 43-60**

**RYE near. Alison and Alan Richards, Kimbley Cottage, Main Street, Peasmarsh, Rye TN31 6UL (01797 230514).** Friendly country house with views from all aspects. Historic Rye five minutes' drive, beaches 15 minutes. Ample off-road parking. Ideal base for visiting Kent and Sussex. Two large double rooms with shower, toilet, washbasin en suite; smaller double with en suite bathroom. All rooms have colour TV, radio alarm, refreshment tray, hairdryer and central heating. Generous traditional English breakfast, vegetarian or Continental on request. Non-smoking house. Good pubs/restaurants nearby in village. On A268 three miles from Rye, in the direction of London. Bed and Breakfast from £21 per person per night. **ETC** ◆◆◆
e-mail: kimbley@clara.co.uk

**SEAFORD. Christine & Michael Nott, Avondale Hotel, Avondale Road, Seaford BN25 1RJ (01323 890008; Fax: 01323 490598).** A delightful family-run Hotel, within walking distance of beaches, restaurants, shops, station and buses. The Seacat Ferry service to Dieppe and the Seven Sisters Country Park are close by. All bedrooms (mostly en suite) have a remote-control teletext colour TV, radio, call/baby listening, tea and coffee making facilities and central heating. Delicious breakfasts from a varied menu are served in the spacious diningroom. Cot and highchair available. Stair lift together with disabled access. No smoking policy. Bed and Breakfast from £20 to £25 per person per night. Easy parking. Open all year. Major credit cards accepted. **AA** ◆◆◆◆
website: www.avondalehotel.co.uk

**WINCHELSEA. Mrs Wendy Hysted, Orchard Spot, Icklesham, Winchelsea TN36 4AS (01424 814681).** A very private detached room in a garden setting with own patio and ample parking. Freedom to come and go as you please. Picturesque area, near to the historic towns of Winchelsea, Rye and Battle. Good walking and cycling and within close proximity of many seaside resorts. Many good local pubs serving a vast variety of excellent food. Twin bedded non-smoking room, with colour TV, tea/coffee making facilities and private en suite. Friendly atmosphere and a good English breakfast is served. Bed and Breakfast from £18. Open April to October. Home-made cakes available.

# WEST SUSSEX

**ARUNDEL. Mrs Victoria Chambers, Mango Wine Bar and Brasserie, 63 High Street, Arundel BN18 9AT (01903 883029; Fax: 01903 889933).** Situated in the heart of Arundel opposite the famous 12th century castle, Mango has four quality letting rooms above its lively wine bar and brasserie. All rooms have en suite showers, TV and refreshments. Mango is central to Arundel's host of antique shops and art galleries with all the local attractions including the wildlife parks, river, cricket ground and cathedral all within walking distance. Arundel forms an ideal base for exploring the South Coast beaches and picturesque Downland villages of Sussex.

**West Sussex**

**ARUNDEL. Mrs Vicki Richards, Woodacre, Arundel Road, Fontwell, Arundel BN18 0SD (01243 814301).** Woodacre offers bed and breakfast in a traditional family home with accommodation for up to 10-12 guests. The house is set in a beautiful garden surrounded by woodland. We are well positioned for Chichester, Arundel, Goodwood and the seaside and easily accessible from the A27. Our rooms are clean and spacious and two are on the ground floor. We serve a full English breakfast in our conservatory or diningroom overlooking the garden. Evening meals are available by arrangment. Plenty of parking space. Everyone is very welcome. Bed and Breakfast from £20 per person. Evening Meal from £15. Credit cards accepted. Pets welcome. **ETC** ♦♦♦♦
e-mail: wacrebb@aol.com
website: www.woodacre.co.uk

**ARUNDEL near. Peter and Sarah Fuente, Mill Lane House, Slindon, Arundel BN18 0RP (01243 814440).** Magnificent views to the coast. 17th century house with three acres of grounds, in pretty National Trust village on South Downs. Direct access to many miles of footpaths including South Downs Way; superb bird-watching locally, at coastal harbours and Amberley Brooks. Easy reach Arundel Castle, Goodwood, Chichester with Roman Palace, Cathedral and Festival Theatre. Sandy beach six miles. Pubs within easy walking distance. Rooms en suite and with TV; central heating and log fires in winter. One mile Junction A27/A29. Bed and Breakfast (double/twin room) £22.50 per person per night. Single occupancy and family rooms on request. Weekly terms available.

**ARUNDEL near. Mrs Jocelyne Newman, Pindara, Lyminater BN17 7QF (01903 882628).** Charming country house with modern comfort, warm welcome, lovely garden, open air swimming pool. Three pretty bedrooms, two double (one en suite) and one twin-bedded; all have washbasins, colour TV, radio, tea/coffee trays, hairdryers. Generous healthy breakfasts, delicious home cooking. Arundel is two miles northwards, the coast three miles south and we can direct you to stately homes, small villages, bird sanctuaries, South Downs walks, castles and cathedrals! Pindars is on the A284, turning off the A27 one mile east of Arundel, house on left one mile further. Non-smoking. Children over 10 years welcome. Bed and Breakfast from £17 per person. Evening meals can be provided. Full details on request. **ETC** ♦♦♦♦.

**BOGNOR REGIS. Deborah S. Collinson, The Old Priory, 80 North Bersted Street, Bognor Regis PO22 9AQ (01243 863580; Fax: 01243 826597).** A charming 17th century Priory restored to its former glory with a blend of historic charm. Situated in a picturesque rural village close to Bognor Regis, Chichester, Arundel, Goodwood, Fontwell and within easy access of Portsmouth, Brighton, Continental ferry port and all major commuting routes. Facilities include superb en suite rooms equipped to 4 star standard, four-poster water bed with jacuzzi bath, secluded outdoor swimming pool, Cordon Bleu cuisine, homemade bread and jams, residential licence, open all year. Tariff: single £30, doubles from £25 to £30 inclusive of full English Breakfast. **AA/ETC** ♦♦♦ *SILVER AWARD*.
e-mail: old.priory@mcmail.com
website: www.old.priory.mcmail.com

---

# FHG PUBLICATIONS

**FHG** publish a large range of well-known accommodation guides. We will be happy to send you details or you can use the order form at the back of this book.

---

**PLEASE SEND A STAMPED ADDRESSED ENVELOPE WITH ENQUIRIES**

## West Sussex

ETC ♦♦♦
### WATERHALL COUNTRY HOUSE
RAC ♦♦♦

Prestwood Lane, Ifield Wood, Near Crawley, West Sussex RH11 0LA Tel: 01293 520002
Fax: 01293 539905 e-mail: info@waterhall.co.uk

Surrounded by open countryside and yet only five minutes from Gatwick Airport, Waterhall Country House is an ideal place for an overnight stay. The house is attractively decorated and furnished and we provide a warm and friendly welcome to all our guests. We have a variety of rooms – all with en suite bath or shower, remote control colour TV and tea making facilities. There is an attractive guest lounge, and breakfast is served in the luxury dining room. Children are welcome. Holiday parking available.

*Double/twin £45; Single £35; Family from £55*
*Prices are per room and include full English or Continental Breakfast*

See also Colour Display Advertisement

**GATWICK. Armani Guesthouse, Gatwick (01293 511938; Mobile: 07973 897676; Fax: 01293 425172).** Are you flying to and from Gatwick Airport? Need somewhere clean, a comfortable and convenient place to stay? We are only 12 minutes away from Gatwick Airport. We cater for travellers and business people. All types of rooms with private facilities available all year round at reasonable rates. Please contact: **Mr Gino Patanian, "Terricon", Ifield Green, Ifield, Crawley RH11 0NU** e-mail: bookings@ArmaniGuestHouses.com

**HENFIELD. Mrs J. Forbes, Little Oreham Farm, off Horne Lane, Near Woodsmill, Henfield BN5 9SB (01273 492931).** Delightful old Sussex farmhouse situated in rural position down lane, adjacent to footpaths and nature reserve. One mile from Henfield village, eight miles from Brighton, convenient for Gatwick and Hickstead. Excellent base for visiting many gardens and places of interest in the area. The farmhouse is a Listed building of great character; oak-beamed sittingroom with inglenook fireplace (log fires), and a pretty diningroom. Three comfortable attractive bedrooms with en suite shower/bath; WC; colour TV; tea making facilities. Central heating throughout. Lovely garden with views of the Downs. Situated off Horne Lane, one minute from Woodsmill Countryside Centre. Winner of Kellog's award: "Best Bed and Breakfast" in the South East. You will enjoy a friendly welcome and pleasant holiday. Sorry, no children under 10. Bed and Breakfast from £20 per person. Evening Meals by arrangement. Non- smoking. Open all year.

See also Colour Display Advertisement

**HENFIELD. Mrs J.A. Pound, The Squirrels, Albourne Road, Woodmancote, Henfield BN5 9BH (01273 492761).** The Squirrels is a country house with lovely large garden set in a secluded area convenient for south coast and downland touring. Brighton and Gatwick 20 minutes. Good food at pub five minutes' walk. One family, one double, one twin and one single rooms, all with colour TV, washbasin, central heating and tea/coffee making facilities. Ample parking space. A warm welcome awaits you. Open all year. Directions: from London take M25, M23, A23 towards Brighton, then B2118 to Albourne. Turn right onto B2116 Albourne/Henfield Road - Squirrels is approximately one-and-a-half miles on left. Bed and Breakfast £20.

**PETWORTH. Phyl Folkes, "Drifters", Duncton, Petworth GU28 0JZ (01798 342706).** Welcome to a quiet, friendly, comfortable house overlooking countryside. One double en suite, two twin and one single rooms. Duncton is three miles from Petworth on the A285 Chichester Road, South Downs Way close by and many interesting places to visit. Petworth House and Gardens, Roman Villa, Chichester Cathedral and Theatre, Goodwood House and racecourse, Weald and Downland Museum and many more. TV and tea/coffee making facilities in all rooms. Sorry no young children. Non- smoking. Bed and Breakfast from £20 to £25 per person.

## SAXONHURST
### Mr and Mrs R. V. Hutty,
### North Bank, Hassocks BN6 8JG
### Tel: 01273 846604; Fax: 01273 843722

Situated on a quiet private road, yet only three minutes from the station (London 1 hour, Brighton 15 mins), Saxonhurst is a Victorian house, comfortably furnished with many antiques. Mrs Hutty serves freshly prepared 4-course dinners in the elegant dining room, where you are welcome to bring your own wine. Sample menus available on request. A substantial farmhouse breakfast is served and picnic lunches are available. Situated at the foot of the South Downs, Saxonhurst is an ideal base for visiting the sights and countryside of both East and West Sussex. We will do all we can to ensure a pleasant stay.

**Bed & Breakfast: £22.00**     **Dinner, Bed & Breakfast: £35.00**

---

**STEYNING. Mrs A. Shapland, Wappingthorn Farmhouse, Horsham Road, Steyning BN44 3AA (01903 813236). Working farm.** Delightful traditional farmhouse with oak-beamed lounge, open log fire and pretty dining room. Situated in rural position viewing "South Downs", four miles from seaside, seven miles Worthing, 12 miles Brighton, Gatwick and Hickstead convenient. Comfortable, attractive, spacious bedrooms with en suite shower/bath; WC; colour TV; tea/coffee making facilities. Lovely garden with heated swimming pool. Many footpaths surround the farm and old market town. Bed and Breakfast from £20. Evening meal and picnic baskets available. Children welcome. Babysitting possible. There is also a converted barn with two self-contained cottages. Fully equipped, sleeps two/four, from £126 per week. Short breaks available. Open all year.
**website: www.wappingthorn.demon.co.uk**

**STORRINGTON/PULBOROUGH. Mrs M. Smith, Willow Tree Cottage, Washington Road, Storrington RH20 4AF (01903 740835).** Family-run B&B situated at the foot of South Downs Way surrounded by fields and horses. Large off-road parking area. Twin or double rooms, all en suite with colour TV, tea making facilities. Centrally heated. Full choice English breakfast. Ideally situated for walking holidays (Grid Ref: 104134); Arundel Castle 10 minutes by car, Parham House five minutes. Worthing 15 minutes, Storrington village 15 minutes' walk with good choice of restaurants and pubs. Open all year except Christmas Day and Boxing Day. Non-smoking. Terms from £20 per person. Reduced rates for three or more nights. Brochure available.

---

# PLEASE NOTE

All the information in this book is given in good faith in the belief that it is correct. However, the publishers cannot guarantee the facts given in these pages, neither are they responsible for changes in policy, ownership or terms that may take place after the date of going to press. Readers should always satisfy themselves that the facilities they require are available and that the terms, if quoted, still apply.

# WARWICKSHIRE

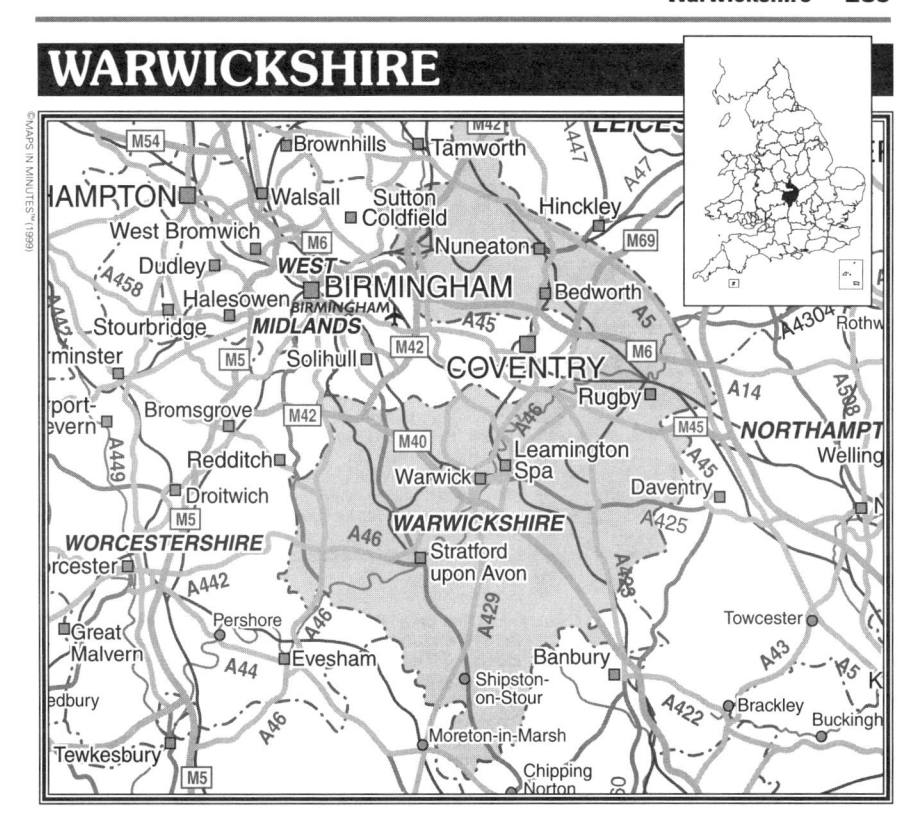

**ALCESTER. Mrs Margaret Kember, Orchard Lawns, Wixford, Alcester B49 6DA (01789 772668).** A warm welcome awaits you at our charming centrally heated house of character set in delightful gardens, in a pretty village seven miles from Stratford-upon-Avon, and two miles from Alcester. Situated on the Heart of England Way, Orchard Lawns is ideally located for touring the Cotswolds and Shakespeare Country or visiting Warwick Castle, Ragley Hall and the NEC. The comfortable accommodation comprises double en suite bedroom, twin-bedded and single rooms with washbasin and guest bathroom. All rooms have colour TV, tea/coffee making facilities and hairdryer. Bed and full English or vegetarian Breakfast from £20 per person. Visa accepted. Totally non-smoking establishment. **ETC ♦♦♦♦** *SILVER AWARD.*

*See also Colour Display Advertisement*

**ALCESTER. The Globe Hotel and Licensed Restaurant, 54 Birmingham Road, Alcester B49 5EG (Tel & Fax: 01789 763287).** Situated in the historic market town of Alcester with its many timber framed buildings, some dating from as early as the 16th century. The Globe Hotel offers the best in hospitality, luxury, accommodation and outstanding cuisine and service. All central heated bedrooms are en suite with colour TV and hospitality trays. Our conservatory lounge-bar provides a perfect atmosphere to relax. Local to Ragley Hall and Caughton Court., we are ideally placed for Stratford-upon-Avon (seven miles), historic Warwick, motorway networks M40/M42, NEC/Airport 30 minutes and touring the Cotswolds with many places of interest and beauty. Colour brochure available. Open all year. Ground floor room, disabled access. Bed and Breakfast rates from £25 to £30, single from £35. *ETC GRADING APPLIED FOR.*

## Warwickshire

**ALCESTER. John and Margaret Canning, Glebe Farm, Exhall, Alcester BA9 6EA (Tel & Fax: 01789 772202).** Shakespeare named our village "Dodging Exhall" and it has somehow "dodged" the passing of time, so if you want a true taste of rural England, come and relax in our quaint old farmhouse - parts of it dating from Tudor times - with its log fires, four-poster bed and country hospitality. One double, one twin and two single rooms, all with tea/coffee trays, electric blankets. Smoking in lounge. Payphone. Laundry. Children and pets welcome. Ample parking. Bed and Breakfast from £20 to £25. Open all year except Christmas and New Year.

*See also Colour Display Advertisement*

**BANBURY/WARMINGTON. Lady Cockcroft, The Old Rectory, Warmington, Banbury OX17 1BU (01295 690531; Fax: 01295 690526).** Charming Georgian Grade II listed old rectory, jutting out on to the Green in the beautiful and peaceful village of Warmington. Convenient for Blenheim Palace, the Cotswolds, Oxford, Stratford, Silverstone, Warwick Castle and the Fairport Convention! Also many fine gardens, including Brook Cottage, nearby. Three spacious, well-furnished bedrooms available, with oak-panelled drawingroom in which to relax. Good restaurants close to hand, as well as The Plough in the village itself. Bed and Breakfast from £25 to £35.
e-mail: sirwhcockcroft@clara.co.uk

**COVENTRY near. Mrs Sandra Evans, Camp Farm, Hob Lane, Balsall Common, Near Coventry CV7 7GX (01676 533804).** Camp Farm is a farmhouse 150 to 200 years old. It is modernised but still retains its old world character. Nestling in the heart of England in Shakespeare country, within easy reach of Stratford-upon-Avon, Warwick, Kenilworth, Coventry with its famous Cathedral, and the National Exhibition Centre, also the National Agricultural Centre, Stoneleigh. Camp Farm offers a warm homely atmosphere and good English food, service and comfortable beds. The house is carpeted throughout. Diningroom and lounge with colour TV. Three double rooms or three single rooms, all with washbasins. All terms quoted by letter or telephone. **ETC ◆◆◆**.

**FENNY COMPTON. Mrs C.L. Fielder, Willow Cottage, Brook Street, Fenny Compton, Southam CV47 2YH (01295 770429).** A warm welcome awaits you in the centre of this attractive village near the Oxfordshire/ Northamptonshire borders. Character cottage with delightful garden and terrace in rural situation. Easy access to the Cotswolds and Shakespeare country and, for the businessman, to the NEC, Warwick, Leamington and Banbury. Very tasteful twin-bedded and single accommodation with own washing facilities, colour TV and radio. Family atmosphere. Dinner by previous arrangement from £10; Bed and Breakfast from £18.

**KENILWORTH. Trudi and Ken Wheat, The Hollyhurst Guest House, 47 Priory Road, Kenilworth, CV8 1LL (01926 853882; Fax: 01926 855211).** A comfortable Victorian guest house close to the town centre and a pleasant stroll from Kenilworth Castle. A bustling town with excellent restaurants, located in the heart of the Warwickshire countryside, Kenilworth is well connected by road and convenient for the NEC, NAC and the University of Warwick. You'll find the Hollyhurst perfect as a business base or holiday stopover. In either case we offer real hospitality and home comforts in our seven bedroom, fully licensed guest house. Three rooms are en suite and we have private parking for up to nine vehicles. Non-smoking. No pets. Bed and Breakfast from £20 per person. **AA ◆◆◆**
e-mail: admin@hollyhurstguesthouse.co.uk
e-mail: kenwheat@compuserve.com

**LIGHTHORNE, near Warwick. Mrs J. Stanton, Redlands Farm, Banbury Road, Lighthorne, Near Warwick CV35 0AH (01926 651241).** A beautifully restored 15th century farmhouse built of local stone, the Old Farmhouse is set in two acres of garden with its own swimming pool, well away from the main road, yet within easy travelling distance of Stratford and Warwick; two miles Junction 12 M40. Handy for the Cotswolds. Guest accommodation in one double (with bathroom), one single and one family bedrooms, all with tea making facilities; bathroom, beamed lounge with TV, dining room. Rooms are centrally heated and the farmhouse also has open fires. Bed and Breakfast from £18.00. Children welcome, facilities available and reduced rates. No pets. A car is recommended to make the most of your stay. **AA** *QQQ*.

**PILLERTON HERSEY. Mrs Carolyn Howard, Docker's Barn Farm, Oxhill Bridle Road, Pillerton Hersey, Warwick CV35 0QB (01926 640475; Fax: 01926 641747).** Idyllically situated 18th century stone barn conversion surrounded by its own land, handy for Warwick, Stratford-upon-Avon, Cotswolds, NAC, NEC, Heritage Motor centre and six miles from Junction 12 M40. The house is full of character with antiques and interesting collections. The warm, attractive en suite bedrooms have tea/coffee trays and colour TV, and the four-poster suite has its own front door. Wildlife abounds and lovely walks lead from the barn, and we keep a few sheep, horses and poultry. If you are looking for total peace with friendly attentive service from £20 per person, Docker's Barn is for you. No smoking establishment. **AA** *QQQ*.

**SHIPSTON-ON-STOUR. Mrs Posy McDonald, Brook House, Stourton, Shipston-on-Stour CV36 5HQ (01608 686281).** A most attractive house furnished with antiques, situated just off the A34 on the edge of a North Cotswold village in an area of outstanding beauty. Double room en suite (with adjoining room for families), overlooking garden; double room with private bathroom. There is a lovely guests' sitting room with log fire and TV. Ideally situated for visiting Stratford-on-Avon, Warwick, Oxford and North Cotswolds. Highly renowned food in village pub or Evening Meal provided if booked in advance. The visitors' book confirms the very warm welcome and lovely peaceful house! Bed and Breakfast from £20, special family rates.
e-mail: graememcdonald@msn.com

**STRATFORD-UPON-AVON. Mrs Austin, Hunter's Moon Guest House, 150 Alcester Road, Stratford-upon-Avon CV37 9DR (01789 292888; Fax: 01789 204101).** Stratfordians Rosemary and David Austin, welcome you to Shakespeare's town to enjoy your visit at our family-run guest house, which is situated on the A422, five miles from the M40 motorway link, half-a-mile from the town centre and close to Anne Hathaway's Cottage and other Shakespearean properties. All bedrooms have en suite facilities, colour TV, hairdryer, tea/coffee making facilities; singles, doubles, twin and family rooms. An excellent English or vegetarian breakfast is served. Private car parking. Please ring for reservations. Arthur Frommer Recommended 2001, Welcome Host Award. **AA** ◆◆◆
e-mail: thehuntersmoon@ntlworld.com

**STRATFORD-UPON-AVON. Arrandale, 208 Evesham Road, Stratford-upon-Avon CV37 9AS (01789 267112).** A friendly, double glazed, centrally heated guest house run by Hazel and Arthur Mellor. Situated on the town end of the A439/B439 Evesham/Bidford Road, 10 minutes' walking distance to the Royal Shakespeare Theatre, and the Shakespearean properties. We offer for your comfort a double/twin en suite, a double en suite, and a double with shower. Pets are welcome to stay in the rooms. £18 per person en suite; £15.50 with shower. Three course evening meal £6.50; weekly terms from £105 to £120. Special short breaks available. Closed Christmas, Boxing Day and New Year's Eve. Major credit cards accepted.

**See also Colour Display Advertisement** STRATFORD-UPON-AVON. **Ms Diana Tallis, Linhill, 35 Evesham Place, Stratford-upon-Avon CV37 6HT (01789 292879; Fax: 01789 299691).** Linhill is a comfortable Victorian Guest House run by a friendly young family. It is situated only five minutes' walk from Stratford's town centre with its wide choice of fine restaurants and world famous Royal Shakespeare Theatre. Every bedroom at Linhill has central heating, colour TV, tea/coffee making facilities and washbasin. En suite facilities are also available, as are packed lunches and evening meals. Bicycle hire and babysitting facilities if desired. Leave the children with us and re-discover the delight of a candlelit dinner in one of Stratford's inviting restaurants. Bed and Breakfast from £16 to £30; Evening Meal from £6.50 to £8. Reduced rates for Senior Citizens. **HETB** ◆◆◆.
e-mail: linhill@bigwig.net
website: www.linhillguesthouse.co.uk

STRATFORD-UPON-AVON. **Nando's Guest House, 18/20 Evesham Place, Stratford-upon-Avon CV37 6HT (Tel & Fax: 01789 204907).** A warm welcome awaits you at Nando's where we pride ourselves on a high standard of cleanliness, good home cooking and a friendly atmosphere. Nando's is Two Diamond rated and a member of "Best Bed and Breakfast in the World" Association. It is ideally located only five minutes' walking distance from the town centre and famous Royal Shakespeare Theatre. It is also conveniently placed for the Cotswolds, Warwick Castle, Blenheim Palace and the National Exhibition Centre. Nando's has 21 rooms, 17 of which are en suite and four of these are located on the ground floor. All rooms are centrally heated, double glazed and have colour TV and tea/coffee making facilities. Private parking is available. Room charges (including full English breakfast and VAT) start from £16 per person. Visa/Mastercard, Amex welcome. **ETC** ◆◆

STRATFORD-UPON-AVON. **Susan and Derek Learmount, Green Haven Guest House, 217 Evesham Road, Stratford-upon-Avon CV37 9AS (01789 297874).** A cosy and prettily refurbished Guest House, centrally heated with colour TV, courtesy trays and many thoughtful extras. Within easy walking distance of the Town Centre, and easily accessible to historic Warwick and the beautiful Cotswolds. Our bedrooms are all en suite, two family rooms with extra large showers and plenty of hot water. Our competitive rates include a delicious English, vegetarian/vegan or Continental breakfast. Private parking and payphone for guests. **ETC** ◆◆◆
e-mail: susanlearmount@green-haven.co.uk
e-mail: information@green-haven.co.uk
website: www.green-haven.co.uk

STRATFORD-UPON-AVON. **Janet and Keith Cornwell, "Midway", 182 Evesham Road, Stratford-upon-Avon CV37 9BS (01789 204154).** Relax, enjoy Stratford's attractions and surrounding area with us. Clean, centrally heated rooms - three double, all en suite, with colour TV, clock radio, tea/coffee making facilities, tastefully and comfortably furnished. Superb English breakfast. Pleasant diningroom with separate tables. Keys provided, access at all times. Park your car on our forecourt and take a 10/15 minute walk to town centre, theatres, Anne Hathaway's Cottage or race course. Personal friendly service. Map and information on attractions provided in rooms. Fans in bedrooms during summer. Full Fire Certificate held. Open all year. Sorry no dogs. **ETC** ◆◆◆

# FHG
## Visit the FHG website
### www.holidayguides.com
for details of the wide choice of accommodation featured in the full range of FHG titles

## Penryn Guest House
**126 ALCESTER ROAD • STRATFORD-UPON-AVON CV37 9DP**
*Telephone: (01789) 293718 • Fax: (01789) 266077*
*E-mail: penrynhouse@btinternet.com*
*Website: www.stratford-upon-avon.co.uk/penryn.htm*

Penryn Guest house is personally run by Andrew and Gill Carr, who provide a comfortable and friendly environment. All bedrooms en suite with colour TV, hairdryer and tea/coffee making facilities. Situated one mile from town centre, convenient for all major Shakespearean attractions, with Warwick Castle and Cotswolds villages within easy reach. Private car park. Full English or Continental breakfast served. All major credit cards accepted.

**RAC : ETC ◆◆◆◆**

**STRICTLY NON SMOKING**

See also colour advertisement

---

**STRATFORD-UPON-AVON. Mrs Julia Downie, Holly Tree Cottage, Birmingham Road, Pathlow, Stratford-upon-Avon CV37 0ES (Tel & Fax: 01789 204461).** Period cottage dating back to the 17th century, with beams, antiques, tasteful furnishings and friendly atmosphere. Large picturesque gardens with extensive views over the countryside. Situated three miles north of Stratford towards Henley-in-Arden on A3400, convenient for overnight stops or longer stays, and ideal for theatre visits. Excellent base for touring Shakespeare country, Heart of England, Cotswolds, Warwick Castle and Blenheim Palace. Well situated for National Exhibition Centre. Double, twin and family accommodation with en suite and private facilities; colour TV and tea/coffee making facilities in all rooms. Full English Breakfast. Restaurant and pub meals nearby. Bed and Breakfast from £24. Telephone for information.

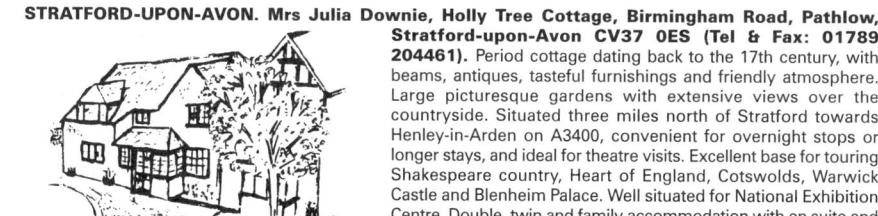

**STRATFORD-UPON-AVON. Mrs M. Turney, Cadle Pool Farm, The Ridgeway, Stratford-upon-Avon CV37 9RE (01789 292494). Working farm.** Situated in picturesque grounds, this charming oak-panelled and beamed family home is situated two miles from Stratford-upon-Avon. The Royal Shakespeare Theatre is only eight minutes away by car. Ideal touring centre for Warwick, Kenilworth, Oxford and the Cotswolds. Accommodation comprises one family, one double room both with en suite bathroom and TV, and another double bedroom with private bathroom. All have tea/coffee making facilities. There is an antique oak dining room and guest lounge. The gardens and ornamental pool are particularly attractive, with peacocks and ducks roaming freely. Children over ten years welcome. Rates per person with en suite £26, without £24.

**STRATFORD-UPON-AVON. Mrs Karen Cauvin, Penshurst Guest House, 34 Evesham Place, Stratford-upon-Avon CV37 6HT (01789 205259; Fax: 01789 295322)..** You'll get an exceptionally warm welcome at this prettily refurbished, totally non-smoking Victorian townhouse, five minutes' walk from the centre of town. Attention to detail is obvious and the proprietors, Karen and Yannick will go out of their way to make you feel at home. You'd like a lie-in while on holiday? No problem!! Delicious English or Continental breakfasts are served from 7.00 right up until 10.30 in the morning. Rooms have been individually decorated and are well-equipped with many little extras apart from the usual TV and beverages. Home-cooked evening meals by arrangement. Brochure available on request. Excellent value for money is obtained at Penshurst with prices ranging from £16 to £23 per person. **ETC ◆◆◆**

---

*When making enquiries or bookings, a stamped addressed envelope is always appreciated*

## Warwickshire

**STRATFORD-UPON-AVON. Highcroft, Banbury Road, Stratford-upon-Avon CV37 7NF (01789 296293).** Highcroft visitors are assured of a warm welcome and an informal atmosphere, only two miles from Stratford on A422 in two acres of gardens surrounded by open countryside. We have two large rooms, double/family, adjacent to house with own access and suitable for disabled guests; one double in main house with the benefit of its own stairs. Both rooms enjoy en suite facilities, central heating, colour TV and tea/coffee making facilities. Excellent country pubs nearby for eating out. Ideally situated for Cotswolds, Stratford, Warwick. Terms from £42 double room; discounts for children. Telephone for more details. **ETC/AA** ◆◆◆

**STRATFORD-UPON-AVON. Mrs A. Cross, Lemarquand, 186 Evesham Road, Stratford-upon-Avon CV37 9BS (01789 204164).** Small homely accommodation, highly recommended, friendly atmosphere and personal attention. Providing full English Breakfast and comfortable beds. All rooms centrally heated, with washbasins, some with private shower; tea/coffee making facilities and pleasant views. Separate tables in dining room. Parking on own private forecourt of house. Close to town centre, theatres, leisure centre, river and local places of interest including Shakespeare's birthplace and Anne Hathaway's Cottage; Warwick Castle and Cotswold villages are easily accessible and there are numerous golf courses for the golfing enthusiast. Local inns provide good food. Open all year. Non-smoking.

**STRATFORD-UPON-AVON. Moonlight Bed and Breakfast, 144 Alcester Road, Stratford-upon-Avon CV37 9DR (01789 298213).** Small family guesthouse near the town centre, offering comfortable accommodation at reasonable prices. One single, one double, one twin and one triple rooms available, most en suite with colour TV. Guest bathroom. Tea/coffee making facilities, full central heating and hairdryers in all rooms. Within walking distance of Stratford-upon-Avon town centre and close to Ann Hathaway's Cottage and railway station. Children welcome. Private parking. Bed and Breakfast from £15 to £18 (single); £30 to £36 (double).

### MOONLIGHT
### Bed & Breakfast

**STRATFORD-UPON-AVON. Hampton Lodge, 38 Shipston Road, Stratford-upon-Avon CV37 7LP (Tel & Fax: 01789 299374).** Situated just five minutes' walk from the historic centre of Stratford-upon-Avon, you will receive the warmest welcome at Hampton Lodge, the perfect base for exploring Shakespeare Country and the north Cotswolds. The seven spacious rooms are individually decorated benefiting from en suite facilities, direct dial telephone, colour television, tea and coffee trays and hair dryers. Off-street parking is also available. Home-cooked, traditional dinner is served in the conservatory at 6.30pm with earlier pre-theatre dinners available on request. For details of current special offers, more information and pictures please visit our website . **ETC/RAC** ◆◆◆, *RAC DINING AWARD, WARM WELCOME, SPARKLING DIAMOND.*
e-mail: hamptonlodge@aol.com
website: www.hamptonlodge.co.uk

---

**PUBLISHER'S NOTE:** While every effort is made to ensure accuracy, we regret that FHG Publications cannot accept responsibility for errors, omissions or misrepresentations in our entries or any consequences thereof. Prices in particular should be checked because we go to press early. We will follow up complaints but cannot act as arbiters or agents for either party.

**STRATFORD-UPON-AVON near. Mrs Joan James, Whitchurch Farm, Wimpstone, Near Stratford-upon-Avon CV37 8NS (01789 450275). Working farm.** This large Georgian farmhouse is set in parklike surroundings, four-and-a-half miles from Stratford-upon-Avon, on the edge of the Cotswolds and ideal for a touring holiday. It is open to guests all year with central heating. The accommodation is in one twin room and two double rooms, all en suite with tea/coffee making facilities; bathroom, toilet, shower room; sittingroom, diningroom. Children are welcome; there is a cot and babysitting is offered. Sorry, no pets. A car is essential and there is parking space. Good farmhouse English breakfast served. Evening Meal. Reduced rates for children. Bed and Breakfast from £19 per person nightly; optional Evening Meal £12.

**TANWORTH IN ARDEN. Monica and Brian Palser, Mungunyah, Poolhead Lane, Tanworth in Arden, Near Solihull B94 5EH (01564 742437).** Monica and Brian Palser welcome you to their attractive home set in the peaceful Warwickshire countryside overlooking a golf course on the outskirts of the pretty village of Tanworth in Arden. It is centrally located for the National Exhibition Centre and major tourist attractions (Stratford-upon-Avon, Warwick Castle, National Trust Houses, etc) being only five minutes' drive from M42 Junction 3. They offer two twin-bedded rooms (one with washbasin), guests' private bathroom and sittingroom with TV. Tea/coffee making facilities plus hospitality tray on arrival and evening drink are included. Ample parking. Non-smokers please. Bed and Breakfast from £22 per person. Twin occupancy.

**WARWICK. Mrs Elizabeth Draisey, Forth House, 44 High Street, Warwick CV34 4AX (01926 401512; Fax: 01926 490809).** Our rambling Georgian family home within the old town walls of Warwick provides two luxurious, peaceful guest suites hidden away at the back of the house. One family sized ground floor suite opens onto the garden, while the other overlooks it. Both are en suite with private sitting and dining rooms. TV, fridge, telephone, hot and cold drink facilities. Ideally situated for holidays or business. Stratford, Oxford, Birmingham and Cotswold villages within easy reach. Breakfasts, full English or Continental, at times agreed with our guests. Private parking. Junction 15 of M40 only two miles away.
**e-mail: info@forthhouseuk.co.uk**
**website: www.forthhouseuk.co.uk**

**WARWICK. Mr and Mrs D. Clapp, The Croft, Haseley Knob, Warwick CV35 7NL (Tel & Fax: 01926 484447).** Join David and Pat and share the friendly family atmosphere, the picturesque rural surroundings, home cooking and very comfortable accommodation. Bedrooms, most en-suite, have colour TV, tea/coffee making equipment. Ground floor en-suite bedrooms available. Bed and Full English Breakfast from £23 per person sharing a double/twin room. Centrally located for touring Warwick (Castle), Stratford (Shakespeare), Coventry (Cathedral), and Birmingham. Also ideal for the businessman visiting the National Exhibition Centre or Birmingham Airport, both about 15 minutes. No smoking inside. Ample parking. Mobile home available, also caravan park. Large gardens. Open all year. French spoken. **ETC ♦♦♦♦, RAC** *ACCLAIMED.*

**WARWICK. Mrs D.E. Bromilow, Woodside, Langley Road, Claverdon, Warwick CV35 8PJ (01926 842446; Fax: 01926 843697).** Woodside Guest House offers its guests something very special. Situated amidst acres of gardens and privately owned conservation woodland, it is perfect for families and those wishing to get away from traffic, yet is only 15 minutes from Warwick and Stratford-upon-Avon. Each of the large bedrooms have garden and woodland views and are comfortably and individually furnished providing tea and coffee making facilities (two en suite and one private). Claverdon Village only five minutes away has a choice of pubs offering evening meals, alternatively dinner can be arranged at Woodside. Pets and children welcome. Open all year. Bed and Breakfast from £23. Reductions for children.

# WEST MIDLANDS

## Boxtrees Farm
**Stratford Road, Hockley Heath, Solihull B94 6EA**
**Telephone: 01564 782039 • Fax: 01564 784661**

Boxtrees Farm is on the A3400, just one mile from Junction 4 of the M42 and is within easy reach of Birmingham International Airport/NEC/Rail link (10 minutes) and Stratford-upon-Avon (20 minutes). The 18th century farmhouse has all the comforts of modern living whilst retaining its traditional features. The delightful farm courtyard has a 12 unit craft centre and coffee shop-bistro. Tastefully converted large twin bedded, family and double rooms available. All rooms are en suite with TV and tea/coffee making facilities. Bed and Breakfast from £45 per room per night. 
E-mail: b&b@boxtrees.co.uk  Website: www.boxtrees.co.uk

**BIRMINGHAM. Ian and Angela Kerr, Awentsbury Hotel, 21 Serpentine Road, Selly Park, Birmingham B29 7HU (0121-472 1258).** A Victorian country house set in its own large garden. Close to buses, trains, Birmingham University, BBC Pebble Mill, Queen Elizabeth and Selly Oak Hospitals, and only two miles from the city centre. All rooms have colour TV, telephone, tea/coffee making facilities, washbasin and central heating. Some rooms en suite, some with showers. TV lounge. Ample car parking. Open all year. Pets and children welcome. Reductions for children. Terms from £33 single room, from £48 twin room, inclusive of breakfast and VAT; Evening Meals if required. Light supper or bedtime drink at small charge. **AA** and **RAC** *LISTED*

# WILTSHIRE

**CHIPPENHAM. Mrs Margaret Read, Oakfield Farm, Easton Piercy Lane, Yatton Keynell, Chippenham, SN14 6JU (01249 782355; Fax: 01249 783458).** Welcome to our Cotswold stone farmhouse, situated in open countryside, on our working livestock farm. One en suite double/family room, one double and one twin room, all with hospitality tray and colour TV. Non-smoking throughout. Enjoy a good hearty breakfast before exploring beautiful countryside with idylic villages and National Trust properties. Also within easy reach of Bath, Stonehenge, Castle Combe, Lacock and the Cotswolds. Ample private parking and large garden to relax in. £20 to £22.50 per person per night. ETC ♦♦♦♦

**CHIPPENHAM. Jeffrey and Victoria Lippiatt, Manor Farm, Alderton, Chippenham SN14 6NL (Tel & Fax: 01666 840271). Working farm.** Manor Farm is a beautiful 17th century farmhouse which may be found nestling near the church in picturesque Alderton. Home to the Lippiatt family, the house offers warmth and comfort coupled with high standards. The lovely bedrooms are spacious and well equipped, with delightful views. The farm is only four miles from junction 17 and 18 of the M4. Bath, Malmesbury, Badminton and Castle Combe are all a short drive away. We have a selection of super English country pubs nearby. Bed and Breakfast from £30 per person. One twin, two double rooms, all en suite. Restricted smoking. Children from 12. Pets by arrangement. Non-smoking accommodation available. Open all year except Christmas and New Year. **AA** *QQQQQ PREMIER SELECTED.*

# Wiltshire

**CHIPPENHAM near. Mrs Diana Barker, Manor Farm, Sopworth, Near Chippenham SN14 6PR (01454 238676). Working farm, join in.** Manor Farm is a working mixed farm on the Beaufort estate near Badminton. The Jacobean farmhouse was updated in Georgian and Victorian times. It is very quietly situated in lovely countryside yet near many places of interest: Malmesbury, Tetbury and South Cotswolds, Berkeley Castle, Bristol, Bath, Castle Combe, Lacock Abbey, Avebury. Ideal overnight stop for travellers to South West. Junction 18, M4 six miles and close to Fosse Way and M5. Spacious comfortable rooms with heating and en suite available. Lounge/diningroom with open fires in winter. Personal attention and a warm welcome. Bed and Breakfast from £12 to £25 per person.
e-mail: manor.farm@virgin.net

**DEVIZES. Jill and Robin Myerscough, Heathcote House, The Green, Devizes SN10 5AA (01380 725080).** Heathcote House is a Georgian House dated 1786 and is the family home of Jill and Robin Myerscough The house is situated in the market town of Devizes and overlooks the Green. Devizes Leisure Centre is only a minute's walk away, with tennis, squash courts, swimming pool etc. Accommodation is available in two double/family rooms and one twin, all en suite. Terms: double £45, single £25. **ETC** ◆◆◆

**DEVIZES. Littleton Lodge, Littleton Panell (A360), West Lavington, Devizes SN10 4ES (01380 813131; Fax: 01380 816969).** Superb Victorian family house set in one acre of private grounds, in pretty conservation village only five minutes' drive from historic Devizes. All rooms en suite with beverage tray, TV and radio/alarms. Choice of scrumptious breakfast. Excellent meals are available at two pubs within five minutes' walk. Stonehenge is only 15 minutes' drive and Littleton Lodge is an ideal base to explore the Wiltshire White Horses, prehistoric Avebury, Georgian Bath (30 minutes), Salisbury (30 minutes) and the "Pride and Prejudice" village of Lacock, as well as numerous country houses and gardens. Private parking. Mastercard, Visa. Single room from £25, Double room from £40. **ETC/AA** ◆◆◆◆.
e-mail: stay@littletonlodge.co.uk
website: www.littletonlodge.co.uk

**LANDFORD. Mr and Mrs Westlake, Springfields, Lyndhurst Road, Landford, Salisbury SP5 2AS (01794 390093).** Situated on the edge of the New Forest Springfields is a large house offering an ideal touring location. Salisbury with its famous cathedral is just 10 miles away whilst Southampton, Lyndhurst, Beaulieu and the coast are all within easy reach. The New Forest starts within a few minutes' walk. Watch out for all the animals! Horse riding, golf, pretty pubs serving home made food, walking all close by. Springfields offers two double rooms and one single each able to accommodate an extra bed for accompanying children and with colour TV, radio and tea/coffee making facilities. Payphone. Garden. Off road parking. Non-smoking. Bed and Breakfast from £18 per person per night. **AA** ◆◆◆◆

**MALMESBURY. Mrs Susan Barnes, Lovett Farm, Little Somerford, Near Malmesbury SN15 5BP (Tel & Fax: 01666 823268; mobile:07808 858612). Working farm.** Enjoy traditional hospitality at our delightful farmhouse just three miles from the historic town of Malmesbury with its wonderful Norman abbey and gardens and central for Cotswolds, Bath, Stratford, Avebury and Stonehenge. Two attractive en suite bedrooms with delightful views, each with tea/coffee making facilities, colour TV and radio. Delicious full English breakfast served in our cosy dining room/lounge. Central heating throughout. Bed and Breakfast from £23. Non-smoking accommodation. Open all year. Farm Holiday Bureau Member. **ETC/AA** ◆◆◆◆.
e-mail: lovetts_farm@hotmail.com

# Wiltshire

**MALMESBURY. Ann and Martin Shewry-Fitzgerald, Manby's Farm, Oaksey, Malmesbury SN16 9SA (01666 577399; Fax: 01666 577241).** Our new farmhouse, situated within stunning countryside on the Wiltshire/Gloucestershire border, close to the Cotswold Water Park. We offer luxury accommodation from where you can either stay and enjoy the peace and quiet or plan a visit to one of the many places of interest such as Malmesbury, Castle Combe, Oxford, Stratford-upon-Avon, Stonehenge, Longleat and many more. Our farmhouse has central heating and snooker room with indoor swimming pool adjacent. Guest accommodation consists of three double bedrooms (all en suite), twin bedrooms, family room, ground floor and first-floor rooms also available.. Each room has tea/coffee making facilities, radio and colour TV. A log fire and Inglenook will ensure our winter guests are kept warm. Three course dinner and packed lunches are available by arrangement. Come and enjoy a comfortable bed and hearty English breakfast from £20 per person per night, with discounts for more than three nights. Visa and Access accepted. **ETC/AA ♦♦♦♦**. 
e-mail: manbys@oaksey.junglelink.co.uk
website: www.cotswoldbandb.com

**MELKSHAM. Mrs Linda Bailey, The Old Manor, 48 Spa Road, Melksham SN12 7NY (01225 793803; mobile: 07703 388158).** The Old Manor is a lovely 1900 Victorian house set in three-quarters of an acre of lawned garden with a central willow tree. A very quiet spot yet only five minutes' walk to the centre of Melksham, an old Wiltshire market town, and 10 miles from the historic city of Bath. Featuring elegant decor throughout, a marble hallway and a diningroom with separate tables. All rooms have tea and coffee making facilities and colour TV. Child-sitting service available free of charge. Ample off-street parking. Very easy going hosts and friendly service at all times. Large English breakfast for the big appetite. Highly recommended by previous guests. 
e-mail: lin@herhomepc.co.uk

**MERE. Mrs Jean Smith, The Beeches, Chetcombe Road, Mere BA12 6AU (01747 860687).** A comfortable, old Toll House with interesting carved stairway and gallery, standing in beautiful garden at entrance to early English village. Centrally situated for Bath, Wells, Salisbury, Bournemouth, New Forest and Sherborne. In close proximity to the famous Stourhead Gardens and Longleat House and Wildlife Park. We have two double and family rooms. The house is furnished to a very high standard, is centrally heated with TV, tea/coffee making facilities, washbasin and shaver point in all rooms, one room having en suite shower, another room en suite bath and bidet. Large lounge. Large enclosed car park. Open all year. Bed and Breakfast from £19. Reductions for children. **ETC ♦♦♦**

**SALISBURY. Mrs Suzi Lanham, Newton Farmhouse, Southampton Road, Whiteparish, Salisbury SP5 2QL (01794 884416).** This historic Listed 16th century farmhouse on the borders of the New Forest was formerly part of the Trafalgar Estate and is situated eight miles south of Salisbury, convenient for Stonehenge, Romsey, Winchester, Portsmouth and Bournemouth. All rooms have pretty, en suite facilities and are delightfully decorated, six with genuine period four-poster beds. The beamed diningroom houses a collection of Nelson memorabilia and antiques and has flagstone floors and an inglenook fireplace with an original brick built bread oven. The superb English breakfast is complemented by fresh fruits, home made breads, preserves and free-range eggs. Dinner is available by arrangement, using home grown kitchen garden produce wherever possible. A swimming pool is idyllically set in the extensive, well stocked gardens and children are most welcome in this non-smoking establishment. **AA/ETC ♦♦♦♦♦** *SILVER AWARD. THREE EGGCUPS, ONE LADLE.*
e-mail: reservations@newtonfarmhouse.co.uk 
website: www.newtonfarmhouse.co.uk

---

*Please mention Bed & Breakfast Stops when writing to enquire about accommodation*

**Wiltshire** **299**

**SALISBURY. Audrey Jerram, Chicklade Lodge, Chicklade, Hindon, Salisbury SP3 5SU (01747 820389).** Ideally situated for exploring this interesting area - Salisbury, Stonehenge, Shaftesbury, Stourhead, Longleat, Bath, Wells, Glastonbury, etc. This is a 19th century house of character set amidst lovely countryside. Charming twin-bedded rooms with washbasins, shaver points and tea/coffee making facilities. Pets welcome. Open all year. Painting Holidays are also available, full details on request. Ample parking space. Location: A303 nearby, about 28 miles west of Andover. Going through Chicklade turn right at the small cross road (signposted Hindon on left). Bed and Breakfast from £20; optional Evening Meal. Non-smoking.

**SALISBURY. Mrs Sue Combes, Manor Farm, Burcombe, Salisbury SP2 0EJ (01722 742177; Fax: 01722 744600). Working farm.** An attractive stone-built farmhouse with a lovely walled garden, set in a quiet village amid downland and water meadows, five miles west of Salisbury. The two bedrooms are very comfortable with en suite facilities, TV, tea trays and clock-radios. Large lounge and access to garden. This is an ideal location for Salisbury, Wilton and Stonehenge and easy access to many places of historic interest and gardens. For those seeking peace this is an idyllic place to stay with various walks and the local pub only a five minute stroll. Children welcome. Bed and Breakfast from £22 to £23. **ETC** ◆◆◆

**SALISBURY. Dawn and Alan Curnow, Hayburn Wyke Guest House, 72 Castle Road, Salisbury SP1 3RL (Tel & Fax: 01722 412627).** Hayburn Wyke is a Victorian house, situated adjacent to Victoria Park, and a ten minute riverside walk from the city centre. Salisbury and surrounding area has many places of interest to visit, including Salisbury Cathedral, Old Sarum, Wilton House and Stonehenge. Most bedrooms have en suite facilities, all have washbasin, television, and tea/coffee making equipment. Children are welcome at reduced rates. Sorry, no pets (guide dogs an exception). Private car parking for guests. Open all year. Bed and full English Breakfast from £19. Credit cards and Switch accepted. **AA/RAC** ◆◆◆
e-mail: hayburn.wyke@tinyonline.co.uk

**SWINDON. County View Guest House, 31/33 County Road, Swindon SN1 2EG (01793 610434/618387; Fax: 01189 394100).** This Victorian property is situated on the main road and is only five minutes' walk from town centre, coach and rail stations and only five minutes' drive from Junction 15 and 16 M4. It is ideally placed for business and leisure visits to Swindon and Wiltshire area. All rooms have tea/coffee making facilities and TV. En suite and shower rooms. Private parking. Evening meals. It is like home from home. Children and pets accepted by arrangement. Cot and high chair available. Ground floor bedrooms. Bed and Breakfast single room from £18, twin room from £30 per night. Pilgrims Progress Commendation.

**FREE or REDUCED RATE entry to Holiday Visits and Attractions — see our READERS' OFFER VOUCHERS on pages 43-60**

# WORCESTERSHIRE

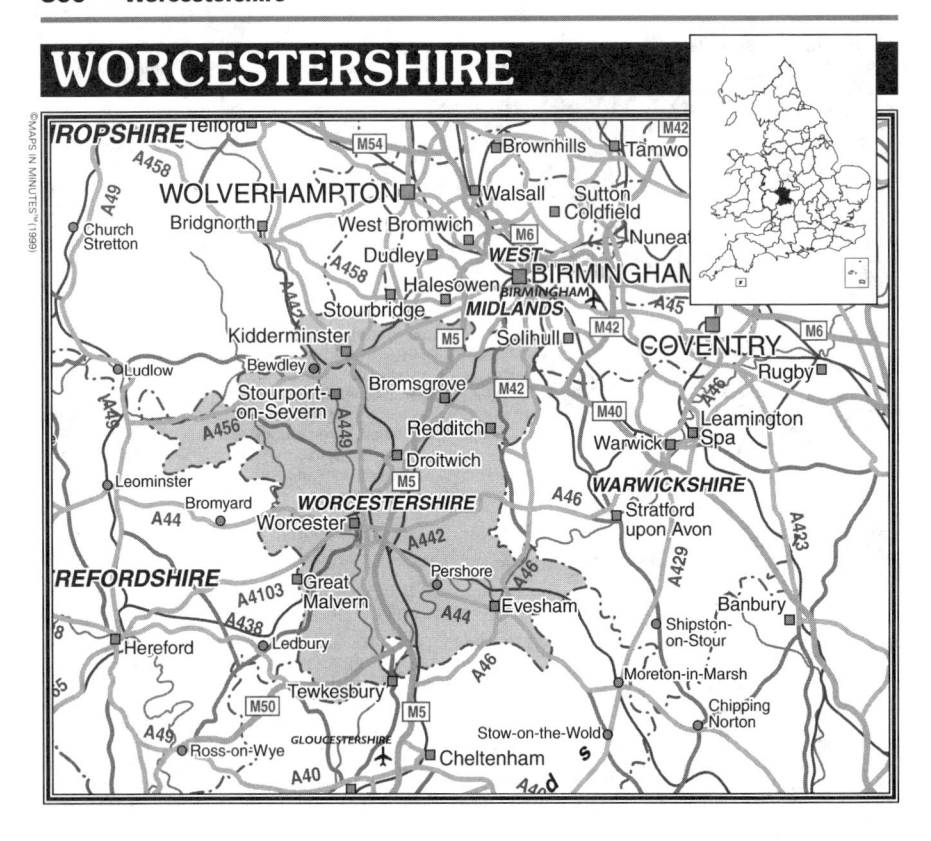

**BEWDLEY. Fleur Nightingale, Bank House, 14 Lower Park, Bewdley DY12 2DP (01299 402652)** Situated in the older part of the Georgian town of Bewdley, Bank House offers spacious bedrooms and a warm homely atmosphere from which to explore the delights of this unique area. Closely situated to the town centre with its fine architecture, antique shops, pubs and restaurants, leading on to Thomas Telford's bridge over the River Severn, through to the Severn Valley Railway. Almost adjoining Bank House is the Worcestershire Way giving easy access to a number of walks around the Wyre Forest. We are renowed for our generous breakfasts. Bed and Breakfast from £20 per person. **ETC** ◆◆◆

**DROITWICH. Mrs Salli Harrison, Middleton Grange, Salwarpe, Droitwich Spa WR9 0AH (01905 451678; Fax: 01905 453978).** Enjoy high quality accommodation and hospitality in this traditional 18th century country house surrounded by peaceful and picturesque gardens. All rooms have en suite/private facilities with colour TV, generous beverage tray, hairdryer, radio alarm and more. Excellent breakfast. Wedding nights catered for. Children welcome. Babysitting service. Dogs by arrangement. Superbly situated for exploring the Heart of England. Stratford-upon-Avon, Warwick, Cotswolds, Birmingham and Wales all with one hour. M5 motorway six minutes. Many traditional eating establishments close by. Single from £25, double from £45. **ETC** ◆◆◆◆. 
e-mail: salli@middletongrange.demon.co.uk
website: www.middletongrange.demon.co.uk

**Worcestershire** 301

**GREAT MALVERN. Mrs F. W. Coates, Mill House, 16 Clarence Road, Great Malvern WR14 3EH (01684 562345).** Originally a 13th century Water Mill at the foot of the beautiful Malvern Hills. Situated in tranquil grounds with croquet lawns and hill views. A few minutes' walk from the town centre or Great Malvern Station. Malvern is ideal for touring the Cotswolds, Severn and Wye Valleys and Welsh Marches. Comfortable accommodation with full central heating, washbasin and tea/coffee making facilities in all bedrooms (one en suite double, one double with shower, one twin). One en suite shower room, two separate WCs. Parking within grounds. NO SMOKING! No pets or children. Bed and English Breakfast from £22. Advance bookings only.

**GREAT MALVERN. Mr and Mrs Mobbs, Elm Bank, 52 Worcester Road, Great Malvern WR14 4AB (01684 566051).** Richard and Helen Mobbs welcome you to Elm Bank. We have six large, comfortable bedrooms, all non-smoking, all with central heating, complimentary tea/coffee making facilities, colour TV, and either en suite or private bathrooms. English breakfast menu. Elm Bank dates back to 1840 and is a Grade II Listed building which has retained many original features. Traditional log-burning stoves during the colder months, but we offer a warm welcome all year round. Licensed. Close to a number of excellent golf courses. Bed and Breakfast from £20 per person.

**MALVERN near. Ann and Brian Porter, Croft Guest House, Bransford, Worcester WR6 5JD (01886 832227; Fax: 01886 830037).** 16th-18th century part black and white cottage-style country house situated in the River Teme Valley, four miles from Worcester and Malvern. Croft House is central for visiting numerous attractions in Worcester, Hereford, Severn Valley and surrounding countryside. There is fishing close by and an 18-hole golf course opposite. Facilities include three en suite rooms (two double, one family) and two double rooms with washbasins, hospitality trays; TV in all bedrooms. Double glazing, central heating, residential licence and home-cooked dinners. There is a TV lounge, sauna and large jacuzzi for guests' use. A cot and baby listening service are provided. Bed and Breakfast from £21 to £29 single, £39 - £50 double. Festive Christmas and New Year Breaks available. **ETC** ◆◆

*See also Colour Display Advertisement*

**MALVERN near. Mrs P. Diplock, Hidelow House, Acton Green, Acton Beauchamp WR6 5AH (01886 884547; Fax: 01886 884060).** Lovely small stone country house amongst peaceful pastureland on the Herefordshire/Worcestershire borders. Central for many places of historic interest, walking and golf. Tastefully refurbished en suite rooms, magnificent residents' lounge with grand piano, log fires on cooler days; sun terrace overlooking extensive gardens, fishpool, waterfall and stunning open views across unspoilt Herefordshire countryside. Suite with four-poster bed. Disabled persons' accommodation in adjoining adapted cottage. Home cooked evening meals by arrangement. Personal transport service. Self catering cottages nearby in converted stone and timber hop and tithe barns. **ETC** ◆◆◆◆ *SILVER AWARD*.
e-mail: fhg@hidelow.co.uk
website: www.hidelow.co.uk

# FHG PUBLICATIONS

publish a large range of well-known accommodation guides. We will be happy to send you details or you can use the order form at the back of this book.

## Worcestershire

**MALVERN WELLS. Mrs J.L. Morris, Brickbarns Farm, Hanley Road, Malvern Wells WR14 4HY (016845 61775). Working farm.** Brickbarns, a 200-year-old mixed farm, is situated two miles from Great Malvern at the foot of the Malvern Hills, 300 yards from the bus service and one-and-a-half miles from the train. The house, which is 300 years old, commands excellent views of the Malvern Hills and guests are accommodated in one double, one single and one family bedrooms with washbasins; two bathrooms, shower room, two toilets; sitting room and dining room. Children welcome and cot and babysitting offered. Central heating. Car essential, parking. Open Easter to October for Bed and Breakfast from £16 nightly per person. Reductions for children and Senior Citizens. Birmingham 40 miles, Hereford 20, Gloucester 17, Stratford 35 and the Wye Valley is just 30 miles.

**OMBERSLEY. Mrs M. Peters, Tytchney, Boreley, Ombersley WR9 0HZ (01905 620185).** 16th Century black-and-white medieval Hall House in peaceful country lane. Views over Severn Valley to Malvern Hills. Quaint olde worlde cottage atmosphere. Inglenook log fires and beams. Within easy reach of Worcester, Malvern, Bewdley. Two-and-a-half miles Ombersley, a picturesque black-and-white village with pubs and restaurants, local shop, bakery and Post Office. Nearby attractions: Worcester Cathedral, Royal Worcester Porcelain, Commandery Civil War Museum, Severn Valley Railway, Witley Court (English Heritage), Hanbury Hall (NT), Bewdley Safari Park, Coughton Court (Guy Fawkes), Elgar's Birthplace, Webb's Garden Centre. Double, family and single rooms; cot available. Bed and Breakfast from £17.

**WORCESTER. "St. Helen's", Green Hill, London Road, Worcester WR5 2AA (01905 354035).** A particularly handsome Grade II Listed period residence with exceptional and spacious family accommodation. Set within partly walled gardens of approximately one third of an acre in a conservation area, close to town centre, Royal Worcester Porcelain factory and Commandery, rivers and canals. TV lounge. Tea facilities. Car parking. Airport collection/return. Prices from £20 single, £30 double, £40 family room.

---

# FHG

PLEASE MENTION THIS GUIDE WHEN YOU WRITE
OR PHONE TO ENQUIRE ABOUT ACCOMMODATION

IF YOU ARE WRITING, A STAMPED, ADDRESSED
ENVELOPE IS ALWAYS APPRECIATED

# YORKSHIRE

Visit the FHG website
**www.holidayguides.com**
for details of the wide choice of accommodation
featured in the full range of FHG titles

# EAST YORKSHIRE

**BRIDLINGTON. Christine and Peter Young, The White Rose, 123 Cardigan Road, Bridlington YO15 3LP (01262 673245).** We are a small hotel situated in a quiet residential area close to the South Beach and within walking distance of the Spa and Harbour. We offer comfortable accommodation with most bedrooms en suite with colour TV, hospitality tray and gas heating. We have a non-smoking bedroom and dining room. We offer choice of menus at all meals; choice of early or late evening dinner. Open all year including Christmas. Bed and Breakfast from £20 per person. Weekend winter breaks with two nights bed and breakfast and candle-lit meal on Saturday £82 per couple; mid-week winter breaks of four nights Monday to Friday bed and breakfast, one adult pays full price £80, second adult pays £48 when sharing double/twin room. Available October to February inclusive, except during Christmas and New Year. **ETC ♦♦♦**

**BRIDLINGTON. John and Helen Gallagher, Rosebery House, 1 Belle Vue, Tennyson Avenue, Bridlington YO15 2ET (01262 670336; Fax: 01262 608381).** Grade II Listed Georgian house with character. It has a long sunny garden and superb views of the gardens and sea. Amenities are close by making it an ideal centre for walking, bird-watching, golfing, wind and sailboarding or touring the historic, rolling Wolds. A high standard of comfort, friendliness and satisfaction guaranteed. All rooms are en suite, centrally heated, have colour TV and tea/coffee facilities. Vegetarians are most welcome. Open all year except Christmas and New Year. Bed and Breakfast from £18.50 per person.

**DRIFFIELD. Mrs Katrina Gray, The Wold Cottage, Wold Newton, Driffield YO25 3HL (Tel & Fax: 01262 470696).** The Wold Cottage is a spacious Georgian farmhouse, set in its own grounds. We can offer you peace and tranquillity with views of new and mature woodlands and continuous Wold Land. So come and relax and forget the pressures of everyday life, stroll around and observe the wildlife and history, or explore the wonders of the East Coast, York and Moors. We have a twin, double, and four-poster room with air spa bath, all en suite and tastefully furnished and decorated. There are beverage making facilities in each room. We pride ourselves on our cleanliness and do not allow any smoking or pets in the house. A warm friendly, family atmosphere awaits you. Bed and Breakfast £22 to £30 per person per night. Evening Meal £14. **ETC/AA ♦♦♦♦♦** *SILVER AWARD*

---

*PLEASE MENTION THIS GUIDE WHEN YOU WRITE*

*OR PHONE TO ENQUIRE ABOUT ACCOMMODATION.*

*IF YOU ARE WRITING, A STAMPED,*

*ADDRESSED ENVELOPE IS ALWAYS APPRECIATED.*

# NORTH YORKSHIRE

Beadale Cottage is 200 years old and situated in Ampleforth, on the southern slopes of the Hambleton Hills within the National Park, and on the edge of the North York Moors (Herriot and Heartbeat country). We have one double bedroom en suite, one double bedroom with private bathroom and two singles with shared bathroom. All rooms are equipped with heating, washbasins and tea/coffee making facilities. Guests have their own sitting/dining room with TV and video. Large garden. Good places to eat locally. In fact, everything you need for a relaxing break! Bed and Breakfast from £18 to £20 per person. Discount for longer stays.

## Beadale Cottage
West End, Ampleforth, North Yorkshire YO62 4DX
**Tel: 01439 788383**

e-mail: bb1103@swiftlink.pnc-uk.net
website: www.swiftlink.pnc-uk.net/bb/1103.htm

**ASKRIGG. Mrs B. Percival, Milton House, Askrigg, Leyburn DL8 3HJ (01969 650217).** Askrigg is situated in the heart of Wensleydale and is within easy reach of many interesting places – Aysgarth Falls, Hardraw Falls, Bolton Castle. Askrigg is one of the loveliest villages in the dale. This is an ideal area for touring or walking. Milton House is a lovely spacious house with all the comforts of home, beautifully furnished and decor to match. All bedrooms are en suite with colour TV and tea/coffee making facilities. Visitors' lounge, diningroom. Central heating. Private parking. Milton House is open all year for Bed and Breakfast. Good pub food nearby. You are sure of a friendly welcome and a homely atmosphere. Please write or phone Mrs Beryl Percival for details and brochure. **ETC** ◆◆◆

**BALDERSBY, Near Thirsk. The Barn,** A warm welcome awaits you in a rural Yorkshire village. Perfect stopover for the Dales, Moors; England/Scotland touring, being one-and-a-half miles from A1. Well-appointed non-smoking accommodation offering twin and small double rooms with en suite facilities. Central heating throughout; cosy sittingroom with TV. We provide a substantial English or Continental breakfast, which includes Sylvia's homemade preserves. Ideal for walkers, anglers (advice available), photographers, etc. Tour "Heartbeat" and Herriot country; visit the Herriot Museum in nearby Thirsk (five miles); not forgetting Ripon and its historic cathedral (five miles). Over 10's welcome. Bed and Breakfast £26 single; £20 per person for two sharing on one night, £19 per person for two or more nights. **ETC** ◆◆◆ Contact : **Mrs Sylvia Thain, Nemur, Baldersby, Thirsk YO7 4PE (01765 640561; mobile: 07785 746015; Fax 01765 609399).**
e-mail: s.thaine@zoom.co.uk

**BEDALE. Mrs M. Keighley, Southfield, 96 South End, Bedale DL8 2DS (01677 423510).** This is a quiet country town only five minutes from A1, so is ideal for breaking journey from South to Scotland. With the Dales immediate and the Lakes only one hour away, it is a good base for touring. Area attractions include Fountains Abbey, Ripon Cathedral, Harewood House, Bolton Castle, Lightwater Valley (as on TV) and many more. Two 18-hole golf courses and swimming, to keep husband and children happy. Free off-road parking for four/five cars. Two double en suite bedrooms, one twin and one single both with washbasins and tea/coffee making facilities and sittingroom. SAE please. Now open all year. Established 1977. *"WHICH?"* AND **AA** *RECOMMENDED.*

## North Yorkshire

**BEDALE. Mrs Jo Howells, The White Rose Hotel, Bedale Road, Leeming Bar, Northallerton DL7 9AY (01677 422707/424941; Fax: 01677 425123).** Family-run, 18 bedroom private hotel situated in village on A684, half-a-mile from A1 motorway. Warm, friendly atmosphere. Ideal base for touring North York Moors, Dales and coastal resorts. All bedrooms have en suite bathrooms, colour TV, radio, telephone, trouser press and tea/coffee making facilities. Fully licensed; restaurant. Bed and Breakfast from £24 per person, some budget rooms available. Pets welcome. Please write or telephone for further details. **ETC/RAC ★★**

**BEDALE. Mrs Valerie Anderson, Ainderby Myers Farm, Near Hackforth, Bedale DL8 1PF (01609 748668/748424).** Historic manor house set amidst moors and dales with orgins going back to the 10th century. Terrific atmosphere. Once farmed by the monks of Jervaulx Abbey. Sheep, crops, pastures and a stream. Walk the fields and discover the wildlife. Visit castles and abbeys. Excellent base for walkers. Pony trekking and fishing by arrangement. Children welcome. Traditional Yorkshire breakfasts. Local village inn. Picnic facilities. Private bathrooms available. Open all year. Bed and Breakfast from £20; Evening Meal from £10. **ETC ♦♦**

**BEDALE. Bobbies XVIIth Century Cottage, Aiskew, Bedale DL8 1DD (01677 423385).** Charming beamed cottage with inglenook fireplace, surrounded by old cottage gardens. Situated on A684 midway between Bedale and A1. Easy walking distance to the old market town of Bedale and a good base for exploring Herriot's Yorkshire Dales and Moors. Numerous historic attractions can be reached easily by car and Lightwater Valley Theme Park is approximately 15 minutes' drive away. Pretty rooms - one double and two twin, have washbasin, colour TV, tea/coffee making facilities, razor point and central heating. Personal, friendly welcome and Full English Breakfast included making good value at prices from £17 per person per night. Open all year – this is our 22nd year!

**BEDALE. David and Thea Smith, Waterside, Glenaire, Crakehall, Bedale DL8 1HS (01677 422908).** A warm and friendly welcome awaits you at Waterside where you can relax and enjoy the mature one acre gardens running down to the trout stream. As a holiday centre it is ideal for exploring by car or on foot the glories of the Yorkshire Dales and Moors ..."The Gateway to Herriot Country"... Bed and Breakfast with private facilities £22 per person; reductions for longer stays. Room only from £17 (two sharing). Full details on request. Central heating, TV, tea and coffee facilities, radio in all rooms. No smoking.

**BEDALE. Mrs D. Hodgson, Little Holtby, Leeming Bar, Northallerton DL7 9LH (01609 748762).** A period farmhouse with beautiful views at the gateway to the Yorkshire Dales, within easy distance of many places of great interest, just 100 yards off the A1 between Bedale and Richmond. Little Holtby has been restored and furnished to a high standard whilst still retaining its original character; polished wood floors, open fires and original beams in many of the rooms. All bedrooms have colour TV, tea/coffee making facilities and are centrally heated. One double bedroom (en suite), two twin-bedded rooms with washbasins. Bed and Breakfast from £20.00; Evening Meal available..
e-mail: littleholtby@yahoo.co.uk

---

Terms quoted in this publication may be subject to increase if rises in costs necessitate

**COVERDALE. Mrs Julie A. Clarke, Middle Farm, Woodale, Leyburn DL8 4TY (01969 640271).** Middle Farm is a peacfully situated traditional Dales farmhouse, with adjoining stable block for guests accommodation. Situated on the unclassified road linking Wensleydale and Wharfedale. Ideal place to escape the 'madding crowd'. Good base for walking and touring any of the Dales' many beauty spots. Noted for excellent home cooking, offering Bed and Breakfast with optional Dinner. Two double and one twin-bedded rooms all en suite. Separate lounge, dining room. Guests' privacy assured. Pets and children welcome. Ample private off-road parking. Open all year round. Brochure available on request.
e-mail: middlefarm@talk21.com

**COVERDALE. Mrs Caroline Harrison, Hill Top Farm, West Scrafton, Coverdale DL8 4RU (Tel & Fax: 01969 640663). Working farm, join in.** A warm and comfortable welcome is guaranteed at Hill Top. Relax and unwind in the peace and tranquillity, surrounded by panoramic views. West Scrafton is a hamlet, in the heart of the Yorkshire Dales National Park, hugging the hillside between the moors and the deep green valley of Coverdale. It is just three miles from the historic town of Middleham and within easy access of the A1. Tea/coffee facilities, welcome pack, lounge with colour TV, central heating, log fires, clothes drying facilities, fishing. Ideal area for walking. Livery and grazing available. Bed and Breakfast from £20. Please call for our brochure.

**DANBY. Jack and Mary Lowson, Sycamore House, Danby, Whitby YO21 2NW (01287 660125; Fax: 01287 669122).** "Make yourselves at home" is our house rule at Sycamore. We provide all that is necessary for your comfort, be it an 'overnight' or longer stay. Residents' lounge with TV. Bedrooms with TV and tea/coffee making facilities. Stunning views from all rooms — with a choice of family, double, twin or single. Good walking and touring area, ideally placed for Heartbeat and Herriot country. Whitby, Scarborough, Middlesbrough, Pickering, York, Durham, Beamish and Hartlepool are all within easy reach. Too many places of interest to visit in just one week!. Bed and Breakfast from £20, weekly terms available. Optional Evening Meal £12. Reductions for children. Pets by arrangement. Please contact us for our brochure. **ETC** ♦♦♦
e-mail: sycamore.danby@btinternet.com

**EASINGWOLD. Mrs Lorna Huxtable, Dimple Wells, Thormanby, Easingwold YO61 4NL (Tel & Fax: 01845 501068).** Our secluded country house lies betwixt the Yorkshire Moors and Dales, set within gardens and grounds extending to six-and-a-half acres with two large ponds containing fish and wildlife. Bedrooms have en suite shower rooms, colour TV, tea/coffee tray. The guest lounge houses a collection of paperbacks, available for your enjoyment, but please leave them when you go. Aga cooked breakfasts and homebaked bread starts the day. Visit Thirsk and see 'The World of James Herriot'. York is 20 minutes away - see York Minster, the National Railway Museum, or spend the evening "Ghost Walking". We have so much to offer, come and see for yourself. No smoking. Bed and Breakfast from £25 per person per night. **ETC** ♦♦♦♦

---

**FHG**

Visit the FHG website
# www.holidayguides.com
for details of the wide choice of accommodation
featured in the full range of FHG titles

**EASINGWOLD. Mrs Rachel Ritchie, The Old Rectory, Thormanby, Easingwold, York YO61 4NN (01845 501417).** A warm welcome awaits you at this interesting Listed Georgian rectory built in 1737 and furnished with many antiques including a four-poster bed. Three comfortable and very spacious bedrooms, two en suite, with tea/coffee making facilities; charming lounge with colour TV and open fire. Separate diningroom. Large mature garden. An excellent base for touring the Moors, Dales and York. This is the centre of "James Herriot" country with many historic houses and abbeys to visit in the area. Thormanby is a small village between Easingwold and Thirsk. Historic York is 17 miles away. Many delightful inns and restaurants serving good food locally. Bed and Breakfast from £13, reductions for children under 12 years. Reduced weekly rates. Ample parking. SAE for brochure or telephone. Open all the year.

**EASINGWOLD. Mrs Christine Kirman, The Old Vicarage, Market Place, Easingwold YO6 3AL (01347 821015; Fax: 01347 823465).** This 18th century house sits in a corner of this quiet Georgian market town just off the A19 halfway between York and Thirsk. It provides an excellent touring centre for York, the Dales and the moors. The centrally heated "no smoking" accommodation comprises two twin and two double bedrooms, all enjoying en suite facilities, colour TV, radio alarm and beverage tray. A large sitting room is available solely for guests and the private grounds include a croquet lawn and walled rose garden. Tea and Yorkshire biscuits await you on arrival. Bed and Breakfast from £27.50 per person per night. **ETC ♦♦♦♦** *SILVER AWARD*
e-mail: kirman@oldvic-easingwold.freeserve.co.uk

**FILEY. Mr Len Morris & Ms Cheryl Sluder, Sea Brink Hotel, 3 The Beach, Filey YO14 9LA (01723 513257; Fax: 01723 514139).** Licensed, traditional seafront hotel with coffee shop/restaurant overlooking panoramic Filey Bay with delightful en suite rooms, many with breathtaking sea views; all with central heating, colour TV, clock/radio/direct-dial phone and hot beverage tray. Excellent food in a convivial atmosphere. No matter what the weather, come and relax in a peaceful seaside town or enjoy the many outdoor pursuits. Join Lenny nightly for drinks and a laugh! Ideal touring base. Children and pets welcome when accompanied by well-behaved adult! Bed and Breakfast from £26. Open February - December. **ETC ★★**
e-mail: seabrink@supanet.com
website: www.seabrink.co.uk

**GOATHLAND. Christine Chippindale, Barnet House Guest House, Goathland, Whitby YO22 5NG (01947 896201).** Situated in large garden on edge of delightful village of Goathland with magnificent views of the surrounding moors. Overlooking North York Moors Railway and Goathland Station. Ideal centre for walking, touring moors, dales and coast. Warm comfortable accommodation, friendly atmosphere, excellent food, lounge with colour TV. Triple, double, twin and single rooms, some en suite. All with washbasins, razor points, heating and tea/coffee facilities. Reductions for children (minimum six years). Non smoking. Parking in grounds. Open from March to November for Bed and Breakfast from £20, Evening Meal, Bed and Breakfast from £29.50. Brochure on request. **ETC ♦♦♦**.

**HARROGATE. Mrs Judy Barker, Brimham Guest House, Silverdale Close, Darley, Harrogate HG3 2PQ (01423 780948).** The family-run guest house is situated in the centre of Darley, a quiet village in unspoilt Nidderdale. All rooms en suite and centrally heated with tea/coffee making facilities and views across the Dales. Full English breakfast served between 7am and 9am in the dining room; a TV lounge/conservatory is available for your relaxation. Off street parking. Central for visits to Harrogate, York, Skipton and Ripon, or just enjoying drives through the Dales and Moors where you will take in dramatic hillsides, green hills, picturesque villages, castles and abbeys. Children welcome. Bed and Breakfast from £17.50 per person per night (double room) to £25 (single room), reductions for three nights or more. Yorkshire in Bloom Winner 1999. **ETC ♦♦♦♦**

**North Yorkshire** 309

**HARROGATE. Mr Derek and Mrs Carol Vinter, Spring Lodge, 22 Spring Mount, Harrogate HG1 2HX (01423 506036).** Attractive Edwardian guest house situated in a quiet cul-de-sac, yet close to all the amenities of Harrogate, Britain's floral spa town, with its elegant and outstanding architecture and gardens, antique shops and restaurants. Ideal tourist base for visiting the Dales and North York Moors, historic York and bustling Leeds. Children welcome, cot and high chair provided. All year round a warm welcome awaits you from the resident proprietors. Short breaks available. Accommodation comprises four double rooms, one triple/family and one single. En suite rooms available. Coffee and tea making facilities in all rooms. Residential licence. We are a non-smoking guesthouse. Bed and Breakfast from £19. **ETC** ◆◆◆

**HARROGATE. Mrs E. Gourlay, Glenayr, 19 Franklin Mount, Harrogate HG1 5EJ (01423 504259).** Whether you visit Harrogate for business or pleasure you won't find a warmer welcome or enjoy genuine hospitality anywhere to match the comfortable Victorian home of Elizabeth Gourlay who treats her guests as invited friends. Harrogate's elegant town centre is a leisurely five minute' walk and the International Conference and Exhibition Centre a mere 200 yards from the hotel. Six light and pleasantly furnished bedrooms with en suite bathroom offer home from home comfort. You can savour a traditional and substantial English breakfast. Brochure available. **AA** *QQQ.*

**HARROGATE. Scotia House Hotel, 66 Kings Road, Harrogate HG1 5JR (01423 504361; Fax 01423 526578).** Award-winning licensed hotel five minutes' walk from town centre. Scotia House offers guests a relaxing atmosphere and can happily cater for people with special dietary needs. Whether here for business or pleasure, on your own or with the whole family, you can be sure of a comfortable and enjoyable stay. En suite bedrooms with colour TV, hospitality tray, telephone. Central heating throughout. On site parking. Pets welcome. **ETC** ◆◆◆,.**AA and RAC** ★
e-mail: info@scotiahotel.harrogate.net
website: www.scotiahotel.harrogate.net

**HARROGATE. Gillmore Hotel, 98 Kings Road, Harrogate HG1 5HH (01423 507122; Fax: 01423 563223).** A family-run hotel, ideally positioned within easy walking distance of the Conference Centre and Exhibition Complex, with the shops, cafes, theatres, cinemas and all the many amenities of Harrogate town centre very close at hand. 20 bedrooms comprising doubles, twins, singles– some en suite and all with colour TV, shaver points, hairdrying points and tea/coffee making facilities. Family rooms available. Access at all times. Comfortable TV lounge; licensed bar; spacious dining room. Private car park. Pets welcome by arrangement. Open all year. A warm welcome and friendly atmosphere await all guests. Please send for our brochure and tariff.
e-mail: gillmoregh@aol.com

**HARROGATE. Mrs C.E. Nelson, Nidderdale Lodge Farm, Fellbeck, Pateley Bridge, Harrogate HG3 5DR (01423 711677). Working farm.** Homely, comfortable, Christian accommodation. Spacious stone built bungalow in beautiful Nidderdale which is very central for touring the Yorkshire Dales; Pateley Bridge two miles, Harrogate 14 miles, Ripon nine miles. Museums, rocks, caves, fishing, bird watching, beautiful quiet walks, etc all nearby. En suite rooms (one twin, two double), TV. Private lounge. Tea making facilities available. Choice of breakfast. Evening meals available one mile away. Ample parking space on this working farm. Open Easter to end of October. **ETC** ◆◆◆

**HARROGATE. Mrs Alison Harrison, Garden Cottage, Moor Park, Norwood Lane, Beckwithshaw, Harrogate HG3 1QN (01423 530197).** Set in secluded woodland grounds, three miles west of Harrogate with pastoral views. One luxury twin en suite and one family en suite ground floor apartments with private patio. Also single room with private bathroom. Purpose built from converted pottery to high standard. Comfy beds, electric blankets, TV, beverage trays, gas and convector heating. Roomy non-slip power showers, large windows, own entrance. Breakfast in Listed cottage diningroom. Pub in village and good dining places within five minutes. A good base for touring and walking. Harrogate is 10 minutes' drive, York, Leeds and Dales 25 minutes. Reasonably disabled friendly. Open all year. Bed and Breakfast from £22.50 per person. A warm welcome assured. **ETC** ♦♦♦♦

**HARROGATE. Charles and Gill Richardson, The Coppice, 9 Studley Road, Harrogate HG1 5JU (01423 569626; Fax: 01423 569005).** A high standard of comfortable accommodation awaits you at The Coppice, with a reputation for excellent food and a warm friendly welcome. All rooms en suite with telephones. Quietly located off Kings Road, five minutes' walk from the elegant shops and gardens of the town centre. Just three minutes' walk from the Conference Centre. Ideal location to explore the natural beauty of the Yorkshire Dales. Midway stop Edinburgh–London. Free Yorkshire touring map - ask for details. Bed and Breakfast £26 single, £44 double, family from £54; Evening Meal £15. **ETC** ♦♦♦
e-mail: coppice@harrogate.com
website: www.harrogate.com/coppice

**HARROGATE. Pauline and Robert McKay, Parnas Hotel, 98 Franklin Road, Harrogate HG1 5EN (Tel & Fax: 01423 564493).** A family-run licensed, spacious 10 bedroomed Hotel where a friendly atmosphere is our priority plus comfort and a hearty breakfast. An easy walk to town and conference centre. Single, double, twin or family rooms, all en suite. All have TV and tea/coffee facilities. Harrogate is a sophisticated Spa Town with beautiful buildings and exclusive shops. Take an evening stroll to beautiful Valley Gardens and then enjoy a drink in the hotel. Ideal base for touring – York 19 miles, Leeds Royal Armoury 17 miles, and near Dales. Ample parking. Prices from £24 per person. Children's rates available. Brochure on request.

**HARROGATE. Mrs A. Wood, Field House, Clint, Near Harrogate HG3 3DS (01423 770638).** Field House with its beautiful large gardens is situated five miles from Harrogate commanding lovely views over the Nidd Valley. Ideal for exploring the Dales and Moors with ancient abbeys, castles and country houses. The market towns of Skipton, Ripon and Knaresborough and the historic city of York are all within easy reach. Accommodation is in one twin and one double room with private bathroom. Private sittingroom with TV, etc. Open all year. Car essential - private parking. Bed and Breakfast from £18 with Evening Meals readily available. A warm welcome guaranteed in a peaceful friendly atmosphere. Telephone or SAE, please, for further details.
e-mail: annwoodclint@lineone.net

**HARROGATE. Mrs Joan Smith, Dalriada, Cabin Lane, Dacre Banks, Harrogate HG3 4EE (01423 780512; mobile: 0771 280 5383).** Homely hospitality awaits you at Dalriada, situated on a country lane in a small Nidderdale village four miles from Pateley Bridge and nine miles from Harrogate, famous for its beautiful gardens. Fountains Abbey, Ripley Castle, Newby Hall and Harewood House are just some of the nearby attractions. A very good centre for touring the Yorkshire Dales and excellent walking country (on Nidderdale Way). Comfortable rooms - one double, one twin with washbasins and tea making facilities, one en suite single and TV lounge. Ample private parking. Good home cooking and inns nearby. Bed and Breakfast from £18. Open all year. **ETC** ♦♦

**HARROGATE. Anne and Bob Joyner, Anro Guest House, 90 King's Road, Harrogate HG1 5JX (01423 503087; Fax: 01423 561719).** "Comfortable and friendly!", "Excellent!", "Enjoyed every visit!", "Great!", "Clean, friendly great breakfast!"- just a few of the testimonials that visitors have written in our book on leaving. Situated in a tree-lined avenue in a central position close to all amenities, Conference and Exhibition Centre two minutes' walk, Valley Gardens, town, bus and rail stations near by. Our house is fully centrally heated with thermostats on all radiators, all rooms recently refurbished. Tea/coffee making facilities, colour TV, hairdryers and complimentary items in all rooms. Some rooms en suite. Home cooking. Four-course dinner plus tea or coffee upon request. Ideal centre for touring Dales/Herriot country. Bed and Breakfast from £23, Dinner £14. Well recommended. **AA/ETC ◆◆◆.** 
e-mail: info@theanro.harrogate.net
website: www.theanro.harrogate.net

**HARROGATE. Peter Thompson, The Delaine Hotel, 17 Ripon Road, Harrogate HG1 2JL (01423 567974; Fax: 01423 561723).** Welcome to the Delaine Hotel, set in its own beautiful award-winning gardens and only minutes from the centre of Harrogate. We offer our guests a warm welcome, and take pride in ensuring that you have a pleasant and enjoyable stay in a homely atmosphere. Our en suite bedrooms are beautifully decorated and all have colour TV, tea and coffee making facilities, hairdryer and direct-dial telephone. We also have a private car park. The Delaine is personally run by Peter Thompson, ex Preston, Liverpool, Bolton and English International footballer and wife Debbie. We hope you enjoy your stay with us. **ETC/AA ◆◆◆.**

**HELMSLEY. Mrs C Swift, Stilworth House, 1 Church Street, Helmsley YO6 5AD (01439 771072).** Helmsley is beautifully situated for touring the North York Moors National Park, East Coast, York, "Herriot" and "Heartbeat" country. There is a wealth of footpaths and bridleways to explore. Stilworth House overlooks the All Saints Church to the front and Helmsley Castle to the rear. A warm welcome awaits you in the comfortable relaxed atmosphere of this elegant Georgian town house just off the market square. Highly recommended for good food. All rooms are en suite, with tea/coffee making facilities, colour TV, radio alarms, hairdryer, central heating. Private gardens and car park. Bed and Breakfast from £20 per person per night. Please telephone, or write, for colour brochure. As recommended by the "Which?" Good B&B Guide. **ETC ◆◆◆.**

**HELMSLEY. Mrs J. Milburn, Barn Close Farm, Rievaulx, Helmsley YO6 5LH (01439 798321). Working farm.** Farming family offer homely accommodation on mixed farm in beautiful surroundings near Rievaulx Abbey. Ideal for touring, pony trekking; good walking terrain! Home-made bread, own home-produced meat, poultry, free range eggs - in fact Mrs Milburn's excellent cooking was praised in "Daily Telegraph". En suite double and one family bedrooms; bathroom; toilets; sittingroom and diningroom. Children are welcome, cot, high chair and babysitting available. Open all year round. Open log fires. Storage heaters in bedrooms. Car essential – parking. Bed and Breakfast from £20 to £25; Dinner £12. Reduced rates for children under 10 sharing parents' room. Pets by arrangement. Farm Holiday Bureau Member.

*When making enquiries or bookings, a stamped addressed envelope is always appreciated*

**INGLETON. Susan and Peter Ring, Ferncliffe Guest House, Ingleton, via Carnforth, North Yorkshire LA6 3HJ (015242 42405).** A spacious late Victorian detached house offering comfortable accommodation. All rooms en suite with TV and tea and coffee trays. Ferncliffe is situated on the edge of the village of Ingleton known for its waterfalls, glens and walks. It serves as an ideal location to visit the Yorkshire Dales and the Lake District. Bed and Breakfast £23 per person per night. Longer stay and weekly rates available. Brochure and tariff on request. Ring or write for full details. **ETC** ◆◆◆◆
e-mail: ferncliffe@hotmail.com

**INGLETON. Mrs Mollie Bell, "Langber Country Guest House", Ingleton, Via Carnforth LA6 3DT (015242 41587).** Ingleton, "Beauty Spot of the North" in the Three Peaks/Dales National Park area. Renowned for waterfalls, glens, underground caves, magnificent scenery, and Ingleboro' Mountain (2,373 feet), an excellent centre for touring Lakes, Dales and coast. Golf, fishing, swimming, bowls, and tennis in vicinity; pony trekking a few miles away. Guests are warmly welcomed to "Langber", a detached country guest house with beautiful views and 82 acres of gardens, terrace and fields. Lambs and sheep kept. Ample parking space available. Three family, three double/twin and one single bedrooms, all with washbasins and razor points, some en suite. Bathroom and two toilets. Sunny comfortable lounge and separate diningroom. Central heating; fire precautions. Babysitting offered. Open all year except Christmas and New Year. Fire Certificate granted Highly recommended. Bed and Breakfast from £17.50; Bed, Breakfast and Evening Meal from £24.50. Reductions for children under 13 sharing with two parents.

**INGLETON. Mrs Nancy Lund, Gatehouse Farm, Far Westhouse, Ingleton LA6 3NR (015242 41458/41307).** Bryan and Nancy invite you to their farm which they run with their son who lives at Lund Holme (next door). You are welcome to wander round and look at the cows, calves and sheep or stroll in the quiet country lanes and enjoy the wild flowers. Gatehouse, situated in the Yorkshire Dales National Park, is in an elevated position with beautiful views over open countryside; it was built in 1740 and retains the original oak beams. Double or twin rooms (families welcome), all with private facilities and tea/coffee trays; guests' diningroom and lounge with colour TV. M6 turnoff 34, 15 miles, one-and-a-half miles west of Ingleton, just off A65. Bed and Breakfast from £20; Evening Meal available.

**LEEDS near. Mrs Jean A. Tomlinson, Wheelgate Guest House, 7 Kirkgate, Sherburn-in-Elmet, Near Leeds LS25 6BH (01977 682231).** Wheelgate Guest House is set in the attractive village of Sherburn-in-Elmet, only 20 minutes' drive from York, Selby or Leeds. Easy access to M62 and M1 motorways and an ideal stop when travelling north/south. Sherburn is easily accessible, only three miles off the A1 on the B1222 road. The house is olde worlde, set in attractive gardens; central heating throughout; guests' lounge; some en suite rooms; washbasins, tea/coffee making facilities, colour TV in all rooms. Superb home cooking; Evening Meals and packed lunches available. Private car park. CCTV. Children and pets welcome. Open all year. Licensed. Terms on request. **ETC** ◆◆◆.

**MALHAM (Yorkshire Dales National Park). Peter and Vera Sharp, Miresfield Farm, Skipton BD23 4DA (01729 830414).** Miresfield is situated on the edge of the village of Malham in the Yorkshire Dales National Park. An ideal centre for exploring the Dales or for visiting the City of York, Settle and Skipton. Within walking distance is Malham Cove, Gordale Scar with its spectacular waterfalls, and Malham Moor with the famous Field Centre and home of Charles Kingsley's "Water Babies". Miresfield is set in a well-kept garden and offers accommodation in six double rooms, six twin and two large family rooms, most en suite. There are two well furnished lounges with TV, one has open fire. Good, old-fashioned farmhouse cooking is served in the large, beamed diningroom.

# North Yorkshire 313

**MALTON. Mrs Ann Hopkinson, The Brow, 25 York Road, Malton YO17 0AX (01653 693402).** The Brow is a large house with beautiful views. It was the home of the Walker family who owned the oldest of the five breweries for which Malton was famous. Captain Walker of Whitby (to whom Captain Cook was apprenticed) was a member of the same Walker family. A visit to The Brow should not be missed. A warm welcome awaits you here with TV and tea/coffee making facilities in all rooms. Children welcome, reduced rates. Bed and Breakfast from £25 to £30 per person per night.

**OTLEY. Mrs C. Beaumont, Paddock Hill, Norwood, Otley LS21 2QU (01943 465977).** Converted farmhouse on B6451 south of Bland Hill. Open fires, lovely views, in the heart of the countryside. Within easy reach of Herriot, Bronte and Emmerdale country and with attractive market towns around – Skipton, Knaresborough, Otley and Ripon. Walking, bird-watching and fishing on the nearby reservoirs. Residents' lounge with TV. Comfortable bedrooms. Non-smoking accommodation available. Children welcome. Pets by arrangement. Bed and Breakfast £15, en suite £22. **ETC** ♦♦

**PICKERING. Mrs Sandra M. Pickering, "Nabgate", Wilton Road, Thornton-le-Dale, Pickering YO18 7QP (01751 474279; Mobile: 07703 804859).** Situated at the eastern end of this beautiful village "Nabgate" was built at the turn of the century. Accommodation comprises two double and one twin rooms, all en suite, all with TV, tea making facilities, shaver point. Central heating. Diningroom and lounge for guests' use. Keys provided for access at all times. Car park. Children and pets welcome. Thornton Dale has three pubs all providing meals, also cafes, fish and chip shop and bistro. Situated in the North York Moors National Park it is an ideal base for East Coast, Steam Railway, Flamingoland, Castle Howard, York and "Heartbeat" village. Open all year. Bed and Breakfast from £18. Welcome Host and Hygiene Certificate held. **ETC** ♦♦♦♦

**PICKERING. Mrs Ella Bowes, Banavie, Roxby Road, Thornton-le-Dale, Pickering YO18 7SX (01751 474616).** Banavie is a large stone built semi-detached house set in Thornton-le-Dale, one of the prettiest villages in Yorkshire with a stream flowing through the centre. Situated in an attractive part of the village off the main road, it is ideal for touring coast, moors, Castle Howard, Flamingo Park, Eden Camp, North Yorkshire Moors Railway and "Heartbeat" country. A real Yorkshire breakfast is served by Mrs Bowes herself which provides a good start to the day. One family en suite bedroom and two double en suite, all with shaver point, colour TV and tea-making facilities. Diningroom. Lounge with TV, central heating. Children and pets welcome; cot, highchair, babysitting. Own door keys. Car park. Open all year. Bed and Breakfast (including tea and biscuits at bedtime) from £18. SAE, please. Thornton-le-Dale has three pubs, two restaurants and fish and chip shop for meals. Cycle shed. Welcome Host, Hygiene Certificate held. **ETC** ♦♦♦
e-mail: ella@banavie.fsbusiness.co.uk 
website: www.SmoothHound.co.uk/hotels/banavie.html

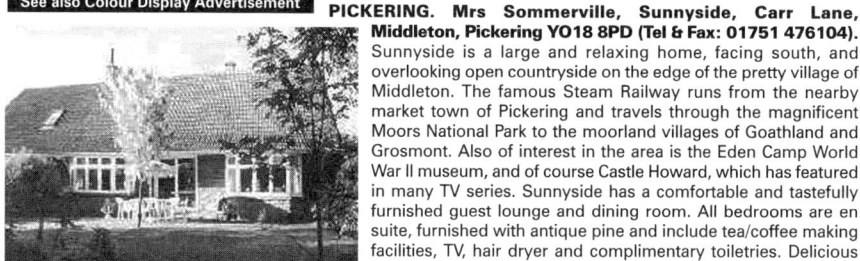

**See also Colour Display Advertisement**

**PICKERING. Mrs Sommerville, Sunnyside, Carr Lane, Middleton, Pickering YO18 8PD (Tel & Fax: 01751 476104).** Sunnyside is a large and relaxing home, facing south, and overlooking open countryside on the edge of the pretty village of Middleton. The famous Steam Railway runs from the nearby market town of Pickering and travels through the magnificent Moors National Park to the moorland villages of Goathland and Grosmont. Also of interest in the area is the Eden Camp World War II museum, and of course Castle Howard, which has featured in many TV series. Sunnyside has a comfortable and tastefully furnished guest lounge and dining room. All bedrooms are en suite, furnished with antique pine and include tea/coffee making facilities, TV, hair dryer and complimentary toiletries. Delicious imaginative breakfasts. Double single and family rooms, some ground floor rooms. Private parking. Gardens for guests' use. Evening dinner can be provided if required. Bed and Breakfast from £26 to £28 single, from £46 to £48 double. **ETC** ♦♦♦♦
website: www.SmoothHound.co.uk/hotels/sunny.html

# 314  North Yorkshire

**PICKERING. Mr Gardner, The Old Manse, 19 Middleton Road, Pickering YO18 8AL (01751 476484).** This Edwardian House with on-site car parking, garden and orchard is only four minutes' walk from the North York Moors railway station and town centre. All rooms are en suite and we enjoy an excellent reputation for our breakfasts, evening meals and packed lunches. The Ryedale towns of Malton, Norton, Helmsley and Kirkbymoorside all have street markets. Whitby, Scarborough and Filey and many coastal villages offer interesting alternatives. The moors and the forest are a few miles away and provide pleasure and leisure for thousands. You will find friendly hospitality throughout your stay with us. The Manse is open all year.

**PICKERING. The Blacksmiths Arms, Aislaby, Pickering YO18 8PE (01751 472182).** The Blacksmiths Arms is a former 17th century blacksmith's, now an excellent restaurant with en suite bedrooms. The old forge is in the bar with log fires. We offer good food and a friendly relaxed atmosphere in our beamed restaurant and comfortable lounge. A large car park is to the side. All rooms have tea/coffee making facilities, television, central heating, clock radio and hair dryer. Situated two miles from Pickering, close to North York Moors Railway, Castle Howard and the North York Moors and ideally based for East Coast and York. Open all year. Pets welcome. Bed and Breakfast from £20.

**PICKERING. Mrs J. Hornsby, Grindale House and Cottages, 123/124 Eastgate, Pickering YO18 7DW (01751 476636).** As hosts of Grindale House we welcome you to our beautiful home. Accommodation consists of double, twin or family rooms, comfortably furnished and beautifully decorated, some with en suite or private facilities. There are many attractions for you to enjoy in Pickering including Castle Howard, Eden Camp (genuine prisoner of war camp), Flamingo Land theme park, with York, Scarborough and Whitby being only miles away. Prices from £20 per person per night. Self-catering cottage also available. **ETC** ◆◆◆◆

**RAVENSCAR. Mrs S. Gregson, Smuggler's Rock Country Guest House, Ravenscar YO13 0ER (01723 870044).** Smuggler's Rock is a stone built Georgian house between Whitby and Scarborough, with panoramic views over surrounding North Yorkshire National Park and sea. The house has a homely and relaxed atmosphere. Home cooking is served in our old world diningroom, and there is a beautiful open-beamed lounge. All bedrooms have en suite facilities and TV. We have a residential licence and our own car park. This is an ideal country holiday area, with many picturesque seaside villages on the Heritage Coast, and beautiful Dales just a few miles inland. Reasonable prices; please send for brochure. Also two self catering cottages available. **ETC** ◆◆◆
website: www.smugglersrock.co.uk

**REETH. Richard and Rebecca Keyse, Hackney House, Reeth, Richmond DL11 6TW (01748 884302).** Situated amid the beauty of Swaledale and conveniently astride the coast to coast route, Reeth is a haven for the weary walker, cyclist or motorist. Principal cities and cultural attractions are within easy reach, or simply enjoy the peace and quiet to be found in the Dales and villages, which offer a wealth of leisure facilities and good restaurants. Hackney House offers comfortable accommodation for both the overnight guest or those who wish to stay longer. Ideal touring base. Accommodation comprises double, twin and single rooms, all centrally heated and double glazed, with colour TV and beverage making facilities. Some rooms en suite, guests have own lounge and diningroom. Bed and Breakfast from £17. Packed Lunches available. Private off-street parking. **ETC** ◆◆◆

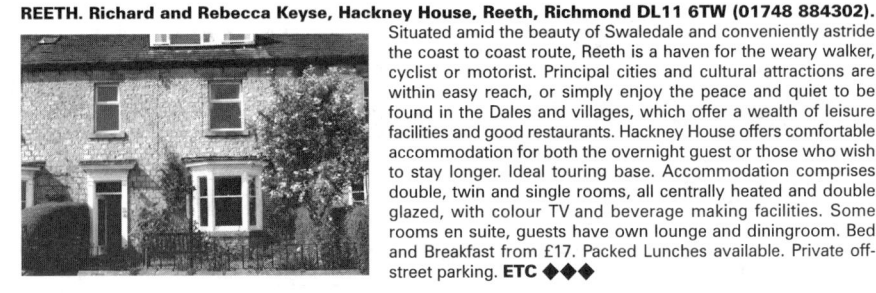

## Browson Bank Farmhouse Accommodation

A newly converted granary set in 300 acres of farmland. The accommodation consists of three very tastefully furnished double/twin rooms all en suite, tea and coffee making facilities, colour TV and central heating. A large, comfortable lounge is available to relax in. Full English breakfast served. Situated six miles West of Scotch Corner (A1). Ideal location to explore the scenic countryside of Teesdale and the Yorkshire Dales and close to the scenic towns of Barnard Castle and Richmond. Terms from £18.00 per night.

**Browson Bank Farmhouse, Browson Bank, Dalton, Richmond DL11 7HE**
**Tel: (01325) 718504 or (01325) 718246**

See also Colour Display Advertisement

---

**RICHMOND. Mrs Dorothy Wardle, Greenbank Farm, Ravensworth, Richmond DL11 7HB (01325 718334).** This 170-acre farm, both arable and livestock, is four miles west of Scotch Corner on the A66, midway between the historic towns of Richmond and Barnard Castle, and within easy reach of Teesdale, Swaledale and Wensleydale. Only an hour's drive from the Lake District. The farm is one mile outside the village of Ravensworth, with plenty of good eating places within easy reach. Guests' own lounge, diningroom; two double rooms and one en suite room, one family room. All bedrooms have washbasin, tea/coffee facilities, heating and electric blankets. Children welcome. Sorry, no pets. Car essential. Bed and Breakfast from £15. Reductions for children and Senior Citizens. Open all year except Christmas and New Year. Luxury mobile home available.

**RICHMOND. Mrs L. Brooks, Holmedale, Dalton, Richmond DL11 7HX (Tel & Fax: 01833 621236).** Holmedale is a Georgian house set in a quiet village midway between Richmond and Barnard Castle. Seven miles from Scotch Corner and ideally situated for touring Swaledale, Wensleydale and Teesdale. One double en suite and one twin with separate bathroom, both with central heating. Comfortable sittingroom with open fire when necessary. Good plain home cooking with plentiful Yorkshire helpings. Tea/coffee making facilities available. Bed and Breakfast from £18 per person; Bed, Breakfast and Evening Meal from £26, single room from £18. **ETC** ◆◆◆

See also Colour Display Advertisement

**RICHMOND. Mrs Diana Greenwood, Walburn Hall, Downholme, Richmond DL11 6AF (Tel & Fax: 01748 822152).** Walburn Hall is one of the few remaining fortified farmhouses dating from the 14th century. It has an enclosed courtyard and terraced garden. Accommodation for guests includes two double (one with four poster) and one twin bedroom all with en suite facilities. The guests' lounge and dining room have beamed ceilings and stone fireplaces with log fires as required. Your stay at Walburn Hall in the heart of the Yorkshire Dales of Swaledale and Wensleydale gives the opportunity to visit Richmond, Middleham and Bolton Castles and numerous Abbeys. York, Durham and Harrogate are one hour away. Sorry no pets. Non smoking. Bed and Breakfast from £25 per person. Open March – November. Self-catering Dales farmhouse available, sleeps seven plus cot. Brochure on request. **ETC** ◆◆◆ *SILVER AWARD.*

---

**FREE or REDUCED RATE entry to Holiday Visits and Attractions — see our READERS' OFFER VOUCHERS on pages 43-60**

**316    North Yorkshire**

**RICHMOND. Mrs S. Lawson, Stonesthrow, Dalton, Near Richmond DL11 7HS (01833 621493; Mobile: 097 706 55726).** With a welcoming fire, private garden and conservatory Stonesthrow offers you a friendly family atmosphere. Unmistakable Yorkshire hospitality from the moment you arrive - we greet you with a tea or coffee and home made cakes. Situated mid-way between the towns of Richmond and Barnard Castle, it offers you an ideal base for exploring the Yorkshire Dales, Teesdale, and York. Stonesthrow, a non-smoking Bed and Breakfast, has well appointed bedrooms with TV, tea/coffee facilities and full central heating. Off road parking. Children eight and over are welcome. Sorry no pets. **ETC** ◆◆◆

**RIPON. Mrs Dorothy Poulter, Avenue Farm, Bramley Grange, Ilton Road, Grewelthorpe, Ripon HG4 3DN (01765 658348).** Friendly and homely farmhouse accommodation at the foot of the Yorkshire Dales set in lovely countryside with beautiful scenic views and walks. Near James Herriott country. Easy reach of A1 York, Fountains Abbey and Lightwater Valley Pleasure Park. Three miles from Masham with the taste of Black Sheep Ale, eight miles from Ripon. Also golf, fishing and pony trekking nearby. Avenue Farm guarantees a warm welcome with a cup of tea on arrival and a bed time drink. TV lounge. Central heating. One double or family room, one twin or single room. Children over nine welcome. Bed and Breakfast from £14 per night.

**RIPON. Mrs S. Gordon, St. George's Court, Old Home Farm, High Grantley, Ripon HG4 3EU (01765 620618).** At beautifully situated St. George's Court sleep in our renovated cow byre and dairy. Modern comfort with old world charm. Five bedrooms - three double, one twin and one family suite, all with private bathrooms, colour TV and tea-making facilities. Each room has superb views over farmland and woods. All rooms on ground level. Peace and tranquillity are assured. We are 200 yards from any road. We have a third-of-an acre pond where wildlife and flora are encouraged to flourish. Breakfast in our 17th century farmhouse, before a log fire. Only fresh local food cooked to a very high standard. A warm and friendly welcome guaranteed. Open all year. Children and dogs welcome. Bed and Breakfast from £24. **ETC** ◆◆◆◆

**RIPON. Mrs Maggie Johnson, Mallard Grange, Aldfield, Near Fountains Abbey, Ripon HG4 3BE (01765 620242). Working farm.** Historically linked with nearby Fountains Abbey, Mallard Grange is a rambling 16th century working farm oozing character and charm in a glorious rural setting. Offering a superb level of quality and comfort, spacious rooms furnished with care and some lovely antique pieces. Four en suite bedrooms have colour TV, hairdryer, beverages and homely extras. Delicious breakfasts complemented by homemade preserves. Yorkshire Dales, historic properties, gardens, York and Harrogate within easy reach making this the perfect centre for a peaceful, relaxing stay in a Designated Area of Outstanding Natural Beauty. Open most of the year. Bed and Breakfast from £25. Brochure available. **ETC** ◆◆◆◆ *SILVER AWARD*
e-mail: mallardgrange@btinternet.com

**RIPON. Valerie Leeming, Bay Tree Farm, Aldfield, Near Fountains Abbey, Ripon HG4 3BE (Tel & Fax: 01765 620394).** As featured in "Which? B&B", this 17th century converted stone hay barn combines character with comfort in quiet hamlet. Beautiful Fountains Abbey, half-a-mile to York, Harrogate and Dales all in easy reach. Lovely circular walks from our door returning to open fires and super cooking (HE trained). All rooms en suite, central heating, beverages, TV. Kettle always on the boil. Ideal for "get togethers" or just a peaceful few days. Colour brochure. Open all year. Bed and Breakfast from £22.50; Evening Meal from £12. Children and pets welcome.

**ROBIN HOOD'S BAY. Mrs B. Reynolds, 'South View', Sledgates, Fylingthorpe, Whitby YO22 4TZ (01947 880025).** Pleasantly situated, comfortable accommodation in own garden with sea and country views. Ideal for walking and touring. Close to the moors, within easy reach of Whitby, Scarborough and many more places of interest. There are two double rooms, lounge and diningroom. Bed and Breakfast from £17, including bedtime drink. Parking spaces. Phone for further details.

**ROBIN HOOD'S BAY near. David and Angela Pattinson, Hogarth Hall, Boggle Hole Road, Near Robin Hood's Bay, Whitby YO22 4QQ (01947 880547).** Hogarth Hall is a newly built farmhouse set in 145 acres of habitat, situated at the top of the valley with wonderful views of sea, farmland, moors and sky. Experience the wonder of glorious sunrises and sunsets, June being the loveliest month for these. Bring your binoculars to study the wildlife all around. All rooms are en suite with whirlpool baths and TV. Tea/coffee making facilities available. There is a large lounge for relaxing and enjoying these views and we also have a sauna. Scarborough 15 miles, Whitby nine miles, York 40 miles, Durham 60 miles, Hornsea 50 miles. Bed and Breakfast from £35 per room. Please write, or telephone, for further details.

**ROSEDALE EAST. Maureen and John Harrison, Moordale House, Dale Head, Pickering YO18 8RH (01751 417219).** Dating back to the mid 17th century Moordale House once served the local iron ore mining community as a granary and general stores. Today after extensive refurbishment and modernisation Maureen and John offer you a visit they hope will remain in your heart and memory for years to come. Accommodation is available in one family, two double, two twin bedded rooms, all with en suite facilities. Tea/coffee making facilities. Full central heating. Separate shower room, bathroom and toilets. Guests are offered Bed and full English Breakfast, five-course Evening Dinner optional in the spacious diningroom which benefits from magnificent views over the valley. Comfortable, relaxing lounge with open fire and colour TV, also quiet lounge. A family-run licensed guest house offering good home cooking, every comfort and a happy, friendly atmosphere. Members of the Yorkshire and Humberside Tourist Board. Full Fire Certificate. Brochure and terms on request. **ETC** ◆◆◆

**SCARBOROUGH. Angela and Roland Thompson, The Old Mill Hotel, Mill Street, Off Victoria Road, Scarborough YO11 1SZ (01723 372735).** 18th century windmill. Built around the windmill is The Old Mill Hotel, comprising 12 attractively decorated en suite rooms surrounding the mill courtyard. All are tastefully furnished with tea/coffee making facilities, colour TV and central heating. Breakfast is served on the ground floor of the Mill itself. There is private parking in the courtyard. Within the Mill is the contemporary Toy Museum, tea rooms and play area for children. The mill is a few minutes' walk from the town centre, rail and bus stations. Pets welcome by arrangement. Bed and Breakfast from £21 to £25. Children aged 4 to 14 years half price. **ETC** ◆◆◆
website: www.windmill-hotel.co.uk

**SCARBOROUGH. Sue and Tony Hewitt, Harmony Country Lodge, Limestone Road, Burniston, Scarborough YO13 0DG (0800 2985840).** DISTINCTIVELY DIFFERENT. Peaceful and relaxing retreat, octagonal in design and set in two acres of private grounds with 360° panoramic views of the National Park and sea. An ideal centre for walking or touring. Two miles from Scarborough and within easy reach of Whitby, York and the beautiful North Yorkshire countryside. Tastefully decorated en suite centrally heated rooms with colour TV and all with superb views. Attractive dining room, guest lounge and relaxing conservatory. Traditional English breakfast, optional evening meal including vegetarian. Fragrant massage available. Bed and Breakfast from £20.50 to £30.00. Non smoking, licensed, private parking facilities. Personal service and warm, friendly Yorkshire hospitality. Spacious eight berth caravan also available for self-catering holidays. Children over seven years welcome. Open all year. **ETC** ◆◆◆◆
website: www.spiderweb.co.uk/Harmony

**SCARBOROUGH. Mike and Lynne Simons, The Premier Hotel, 66 Esplanade, Scarborough YO11 2UZ (01723 501062).** This lovely Victorian licensed Hotel overlooking the sea and coastline has all the warmth and hospitality of a bygone era. It is conveniently situated for all Scarborough's attractions and is near the Italian, Rose and Holbeck Gardens; also convenient for the historic city of York, North Yorkshire Moors, Whitby and many stately homes in the area. The Premier has a high reputation for its standards of food and service, specialising in traditional English cuisine using the very best local produce. Peaceful, relaxing atmosphere; lift to comfortable bedrooms, some with magnificent sea views and all with private facilities en suite, colour TV, tea tray, clock radio and hairdryer. Private car park. Pets very welcome. **AA** QQQ Recommended.

**SCARBOROUGH. Sylvia and Chris Kirk, The Terrace Hotel, 69 Westborough, Scarborough YO11 1TS (01723 374937).** A small family-run Hotel situated between North and South Bays, close to all Scarborough's many attractions and only a short walk from the town centre, rail and bus stations. Private car park. Three double bedrooms (one en suite), three family rooms (one en suite) and one single bedroom, all with colour TV and tea making facilities. Full Fire Certificate. Non-smoking accommodation available. Bed and full English Breakfast from £16. En suite facilities £3 extra per person per night. Children (sharing room with adults) under four years FREE, four to 11 years half price.

**SCARBOROUGH. Sue Batty, Wheatcroft Lodge (Non-Smoking), 156-158 Filey Road, Scarborough YO11 3AA (01723 374613).** RAC 2000 Inspection Report quotes "A great deal of care and thought has gone into maintaining the cleanliness throughout this property to the point of being pristine". Wheatcroft Lodge is situated on the southern outskirts of Scarborough and offers clean, comfortable centrally heated accommodation. Rooms, all non-smoking and en suite, have colour TV, direct dial telephone, clock-radio with alarm, hairdryer and tea/coffee making facilities. Private car park. No pets. Closed Christmas. **RAC ♦♦♦**, *WARM WELCOME AND SPARKLING DIAMOND AWARDS, ROY CASTLE GOOD AIR AWARD.*

**SCARBOROUGH. Mrs D.M. Medd, Hilford House, Crossgates, Scarborough YO12 4JU (01723 862262).** Detached country guest house, quietly situated in own grounds adjoining Scarborough – Seamer road just off A64. Near Scarborough, but handy for touring all coast and countryside of North Yorkshire. Three double, one single and one family bedrooms all with washbasins and central heating. En suite available. Bathroom, two toilets; diningroom with separate tables and guests' lounge with colour TV. Cot, high chair and babysitting available. Full Fire Certificate held. Open all year round. Personal supervision ensures complete satisfaction of guests. Non-smoking accommodation available. Own home grown fruit and vegetables served in season, also fresh Scarborough cod and local meats. Private car parking. Bed and Breakfast from £18 to £22. Reductions for children sharing.

**SKIPTON. Mrs Heather Simpson, Low Skibeden Farmhouse, Harrogate Road, Skipton BD23 6AB (07050 207787/01756 793849; Fax: 01756 793804).** Detached 16th century farmhouse in private grounds one mile east of Skipton off the A59/A65 gateway to the Dales, eg Bolton Abbey - Malham, Settle. Luxury bed and breakfast with fireside treats in the lounge. All rooms are quiet, spacious, have panoramic views, washbasins, tea facilities and electric overblankets. Central heating October to May. All guests are warmly welcomed and served tea/coffee and cakes on arrival, bedtime beverages are served from 9.30pm. Breakfast is served from 7am to 8.45am in the dining room. No smoking. No pets and no children under 12 years. Safe parking. New arrivals before 10pm. Quality and value guaranteed. Bed and Breakfast from £20 per person per night for standard room with shared hot and cold facilities, en suite from £24 per person per night; single occupancy from £25-£30, in en suite £30-£40.Two piece toilet with hot and cold facilities £22 per person per night. Farm cottage sometimes available. A deposit secures a room. Open all year. Credit Cards accepted. **AA ♦♦♦♦ ETC ★★★**, *"WELCOME HOST", "WHICH?"*
e-mail: skibhols.yorksdales@talk21.com 
website: www.yorkshirenetco.uk/accgde/lowskibeden

# North Yorkshire 319

**THIRSK. Mrs Julie Bailes, Glen Free, Holme-on-Swale, Sinderby, Near Thirsk YO7 4JE (01845 567331).** Glen Free is an old Lodge Bungalow set in a very peaceful situation, but still only one mile from A1 motorway (off the B6267 Masham/Thirsk road). Approximately seven miles from Ripon, Thirsk, Bedale. York and Harrogate 40 minutes approximately. One double room and one double with single bed with washbasin. Central heating, tea making facilities and TV. All rooms ground floor. Golf, fishing, swimming and riding available locally. Ideal for touring the Dales and Herriot country. Bed and Breakfast from £15 per person.

**THIRSK. Mrs R. Dawson, Long Acre, 86a Topcliffe Road, Sowerby, Thirsk YO7 1RY (01845 522360).** A warm welcome awaits you at Long Acre, a small family smallholding offering you a comfortable stay – just like home. Situated on the edge of Thirsk, ideal for touring the Dales/Moors. Our comfortable rooms have tea/coffee making facilities, colour TV, and washbasins; one room en suite. Relax in our lounge. Children and pets welcome. Bed and Breakfast from £16.50, optional Evening Meal. **ETC** ♦♦.

**THIRSK. Mrs S. Barker, Fourways Guest House, Town End, Thirsk YO7 1PY (01845 522601; Fax: 01845 522131).** FOURWAYS is a comfortable family home with the advantage of being only two minutes' walk from the Town Centre and James Herriot's veterinary practice. Ideal for touring North Yorkshire Moors and Yorkshire Dales. All rooms have colour TV, tea/coffee making facilities, washbasins; all rooms en suite facilities. Traditional English Breakfast with Evening Meal available if booked in advance. Licensed. Open all year. Ample parking provided. Bed and Breakfast from £19 per person with reductions for children. Evening Meal from £9.

**THIRSK. Joyce Ashbridge, Mount Grace Farm, Cold Kirby, Thirsk YO7 2HL (01845 597389; Fax: 01845 597872).** A warm welcome awaits you on working farm surrounded by beautiful open countryside with magnificent views. Ideal location for touring or exploring the many walks in the area. Luxury en suite bedrooms with tea/coffee facilities. Spacious guests' lounge with colour TV. Garden. Enjoy delicious, generous helpings of farmhouse fayre cooked in our Aga. Children from 12 years plus. No smoking. No pets. Bed and Breakfast from £25; Weekly rates available. Open all year except Christmas. **ETC** ♦♦♦♦
e-mail: joyce@mountgracefarm.com
website: www.mountgracefarm.com

**THORNTON-LE-DALE. Mrs S. Wardell, Tangalwood, Roxby Road, Thornton-le-Dale, Pickering YO18 7SX (01751 474688).** Tangalwood is a large detached family house providing a warm welcome, clean comfortable accommodation and good food. Situated in a quiet part of this picturesque village, which is in a good central position for Moors, "Heartbeat" country, coast, North York Moors Railway, Flamingo Park Zoo and forest drives, mountain biking and walking. Good facilities for meals provided in the village. Accommodation in one twin room en suite and two doubles (one with washbasin), all with tea/coffee making facilities and TV; bathroom, two toilets and washroom; diningroom; central heating. Open Easter to October for Bed and Breakfast from £15.50 each. Private car park. **ETC** ♦♦♦

♦♦♦ **Highly Commended**

**BRIDGEFOOT GUEST HOUSE**
*Chestnut Avenue, Thornton-le-Dale, Pickering
North Yorkshire YO18 7RR
Telephone 01751 474749*

Bridgefoot Guest House is situated in the village of Thornton-le-Dale, by the trout stream in a wall-enclosed garden next to the thatched cottage. Ideal touring base for the moors, east coast, countryside, forestry, and York. Centrally heated throughout, open fires in season. Family room; several double and twin-bedded rooms; ground floor double (all rooms en suite), tea and coffee facilities, shaver points, electric blankets. Colour TV. Guest lounge; dining room. Bed and Breakfast from £19.50 to £21. Car parking. Open Easter to November. Contact **Mr and Mrs B. Askin** for brochure.

**THORNTON-LE-DALE. Mrs Ella Bowes, Banavie, Roxby Road, Thornton-le-Dale, Pickering YO18 7SX (01751 474616).** Banavie is a large stone built semi-detached house set in Thornton-le-Dale, one of the prettiest villages in Yorkshire with a stream flowing through the centre. Situated in an attractive part of the village off the main road, it is ideal for touring coast, moors, Castle Howard, Flamingo Park, Eden Camp, North Yorkshire Moors Railway and "Heartbeat" country. A real Yorkshire breakfast is served by Mrs Bowes herself which provides a good start to the day. One family en suite bedroom and two double en suite, all with shaver point, colour TV and tea-making facilities. Diningroom. Lounge with TV, central heating. Children and pets welcome; cot, highchair, babysitting. Own door keys. Car park. Open all year. Bed and Breakfast (including tea and biscuits at bedtime) from £17. SAE, please. Thornton-le-Dale has three pubs, two restaurants and fish and chip shop for meals. Cycle shed. Welcome Host, Hygiene Certificate held. **ETC** ♦♦♦♦ 
e-mail: ella@banavie.fsbusiness.co.uk
website: www.SmoothHound.co.uk/hotels/banavie.html

**THRESHFIELD. Long Ashes Inn, Threshfield, Near Skipton BD23 5PN (01756 752434; Fax: 01756 752937).** You will receive a warm welcome and personal attention in this charming, traditional old Dales Inn, set in picturesque Wharfedale in the Yorkshire Dales National Park. A tranquil retreat in an idyllic setting, perfect for relaxing or as a base from which to enjoy everything the Yorkshire Dales have to offer at any time of the year. The de luxe accommodation includes en suite bathrooms, central heating, tea and coffee making facilities and TV. There is a wide range of hand-pulled ales and freshly prepared food, served in the restaurant, and in the bar, plus a heated indoor pool, sauna, squash courts, etc adjacent for use by residents. **ETC/AA** ♦♦♦♦. 
e-mail : info@longashesinn.co.uk
website: www.longashesinn.co.uk

**WENSLEYDALE. Barbara and Barrie Martin, The Old Star, West Witton, Leyburn DL8 4LU (01969 622949).** Formerly a 17th century coaching inn, now a family-run guest house. You are always welcome at the Old Star. The building still retains many original features. Comfortable lounge with oak beams and log fire. Dinner available if ordered in advance. Bedrooms mostly en suite with central heating and tea/coffee making facilities. In the heart of the Yorkshire Dales National Park we are ideally situated for walking and touring the Dales. Large car park. Open all year except Christmas. Bed and Breakfast from £17 to £20 with special breaks available. **ETC** ♦♦♦.

*When making enquiries or bookings,
a stamped addressed envelope is always appreciated*

**North Yorkshire** 321

**WHITBY. Mrs Flora Collett, Ashford Non-Smoking Guest House, 8 Royal Crescent, Whitby YO21 3EJ (01947 602138).** "Come as a Guest - Leave as a Friend". The Ashford is a family run guest house providing a relaxed, informal atmosphere and friendly service. Situated on Whitby's West Cliff, the Ashford occupies a superb position in Royal Crescent, overlooking Crescent Gardens and the sea. It is ideally situated for coastal and country walks, and makes an excellent base for exploring the North York Moors. Take a short drive inland and visit "Heartbeat Country", the North York Moors Railway, Rievaulx Abbey, Pickering and a myriad of pretty moorland villages, or take the coast road to discover the attractions of Scarborough, Bridlington and Filey. A little further afield you will find the historic city of York and Harrogate. Full central heating. Comfortable lounge. All bedrooms have en suite facilities, courtesy tray and colour TV. Good home cooking. Access at all times.

**WHITBY near. Mrs Pat Beale, Ryedale House, Coach Road, Sleights, Near Whitby YO22 5EQ (Tel & Fax: 01947 810534).** Exclusive to non-smokers, welcoming Yorkshire house of character at the foot of the moors, National Park "Heartbeat" country. Three-and-a-half-miles from Whitby. Magnificent scenery, moors, dales, picturesque harbours, cliffs, beaches, scenic railways, superb walking - its all here! Highly commended, beautifully appointed rooms with private facilities, many extras. Guest lounge; breakfast room with separate tables and views over Esk Valley. Enjoy the large south-facing terrace and landscaped gardens, relax and be waited on. Extensive traditional and vegetarian breakfast choice. In the evening local inns and restaurants - two within a short walk. Parking available, also public transport. Bed and Breakfast double £19 to £20, single £17 to £22. Minimum stay two nights. Regret, no pets or children. **ETC ♦♦♦♦**

**WHITBY near. Mrs G. Watson, The Bungalow, 63 Coach Road, Sleights, Whitby YO22 5BT (01947 810464).** Be sure of a warm Yorkshire welcome at this large, comfortable, well appointed bungalow in the picturesque village of Sleights, just three miles from historic Whitby, half-an-hour's drive from Scarborough, close to North Yorkshire Moors National Park, Moors Railway, "Heartbeat" country, River Esk for fishing and boating; bowling nearby. Superb area for walkers. We offer two double and one twin room, all large, with en suite bathrooms, colour TV and tea/coffee making equipment. Central heating. Large lounge, separate diningroom. Substantial breakfast. Large parking area. Suitable for disabled. Bed and Breakfast from £18 to £19. Open Easter to October. Car not essential, near bus route.

---

# FHG PUBLICATIONS

**FHG** publish a large range of well-known accommodation guides. We will be happy to send you details or you can use the order form at the back of this book.

---

Readers are requested to mention this guidebook
when seeking accommodation (and please enclose
a stamped addressed envelope).

**YORK. Mrs Helen Butterworth, Wellgarth House, Wetherby Road, Rufforth, York YO23 3QB (01904 738592 or 738595).** A warm welcome awaits you at Wellgarth House, ideally situated in Rufforth (B1224) three miles from York, one mile from the Ring Road (A1237) and convenient for "Park and Ride" into York City. This country guest house offers a high standard of accommodation with en suite Bed and Breakfast from £18.50. All rooms have complimentary tea/coffee making facilities, colour TV. Some rooms have four-poster bed. Excellent local pub just two minutes' walk away which serves lunches and dinners. Large private car park. Telephone or write for brochure. **ETC/AA** ◆◆◆

**YORK. Mrs Susan Viscovitch, The Manor at Acaster Malbis, Acaster Malbis, York YO2 1UL (Tel & Fax: 01904 706723).** Atmospheric Manor in rural tranquillity with our own private lake set in five-and-a-half-acres of beautiful mature grounds. Preservation orders on all trees with abundant bird life. Fish in the lake, cycle or walk, bring your own boat for river cruising. Close to racecourse and only 10 minutes' car journey from the city or take the leisurely river bus (Easter to October). Conveniently situated to take advantage of the Dales, Moors, Wolds and splendid coastline. Find us via A64 exiting for Copmanthorpe, York, Thirsk, Harrogate or Bishopthorpe (Sim Balk Lane). 10 centrally heated en suite bedrooms with direct-dial phones, hair dryers, TV, courtesy tray. Licensed. Bed and Breakfast from £28 to £40 per person per night. For details SAE or telephone. See our Colour Advertisement on the Outside Back Cover of this guide. **ETC** ◆◆◆◆
e-mail: manorhouse@selcom.co.uk
website: www.manorhse.co.uk

**YORK. Allan and Diane Ashton, The Park View, 34 Grosvenor Terrace, Bootham YO30 7AG (Tel & Fax: 01904 620437).** A warm friendly welcome awaits you at The Park View, a family-run guest house only seven minutes' walk to the beautiful historic city of York. Our rooms are tastefully decorated with en suite showers, towels, central heating, tea/coffee facilities and TV. To prepare you for the day, a full English breakfast is available. Choose from one family, two twin/double or one single rooms. Please contact Diane or Allan and we will do our best to accommodate you. Parking permit available, plus helpful information on where to go and what to see. Bed and Breakfast from £22 per person. **ETC** ◆◆◆
e-mail: park_view@talk21.com

**YORK. Mrs J.W. Harrison, Fairthorne, 356 Strensall Road, Earswick, York YO32 9SW (01904 768609; Fax: 01904 768609).** John and Joan Harrison invite you for a restful holiday in a peaceful country setting - a dormer bungalow with central heating, TV, shaver points, tea making facilities and en suite in bedrooms; TV lounge and dining room. Pleasant family atmosphere. Situated three miles north of York, within easy reach of East Coast and Yorkshire Moors and near golf course. Bus stop 50 yards if required. Bed and Breakfast from £16 per night. Reductions for children. Private car park and large garden. Open all year. **ETC** ◆◆◆

**YORK. Mr and Mrs G. Steel, Alder Carr House, York Road, Barmby Moor, York YP42 5HT (Tel & Fax: 01759 380566; Mobile: 07885 277740).** A Georgian style house in 10 acres with a large garden for guests to relax in. Rooms are spacious with good views over countryside. The nearby market town of Pocklington has a National Water Lily collection and a Gliding Club. A wide range of local restaurants and country pubs offer an excellent choice for evening meals. Within easy reach of the York 'Park and Ride', Yorkshire Coast, Moors and Wolds. Your historian hostess will be happy to share her local knowledge to help you make the most of your visit. Closed Christmas and New Year. Twin, double/family rooms, all en suite or private facilities. Children welcome. Restricted smoking.

**YORK. Ian McNabb. The Hazelwood, 24-25 Portland Street, Gillygate, York YO31 7EH (01904 626548; Fax: 01904 628032).** Luxury and elegance in the very heart of York. Situated only 400 yards from York Minster yet in an extremely quiet residential area and having its own car park, The Hazelwood is a Victorian townhouse retaining many original features where the atmosphere is friendly and informal. Our bedrooms are individually styled: they are all en suite and centrally heated and have been fitted to the highest standard using designer fabrics. We offer a wide choice of high quality breakfasts including vegetarian, ranging from traditional English to croissants and Danish pastries. Completely non-smoking. Bed and Breakfast from £32. **ETC/AA/RAC** ◆◆◆◆
e-mail: reservations@thehazelwoodyork.com
website: www.thehazelwoodyork.com

*See also Colour Display Advertisement*

**YORK. Mrs J.Y. Tree, Inglewood Guest House, 7 Clifton Green, York YO3 6LH (01904 653523).** The Inglewood Guest House has a warm and friendly atmosphere where guests will really feel at home. The bedrooms all have colour TV and some have en suite bathrooms. Open all year with central heating. Breakfast is an enjoyable experience in our pleasant diningroom with dark wooden tables and chairs. Helpful information is given on where to go and what to see. It is an ideal centre for exploring York and making day excursions to many market towns and attractive villages around York. There are many places of historic interest also to visit. Children are welcome. Sorry, no pets. A car is not essential, but there is parking. Bed and Breakfast from £17.50; reductions for children. Non-smoking.
website: www.SmoothHound.co.uk/hotels/inglewood.html

**YORK. Tree's Hotel, 8 Clifton Green, York YO3 6LH (01904 623597).** Small, elegant hotel, privately owned and managed. Attractive location overlooking Clifton Green. Just 10 minutes' walk to the city centre and York Minster. Spacious bedrooms, some with en suite bathrooms and all with colour televisions. Children welcome. Private car parking. Bed and Breakfast from £17.50. Reductions for children and Senior Citizens. Bargain Short Breaks between November and March. No smoking. **AA** and **RAC** *LISTED*. Contact: Mr D.G. Tree.
website: www.SmoothHound.co.uk/hotels/inglewood.html

**YORK. Mrs R. Foster, Brookland House, Hull Road, Dunnington, York YO19 5LW (01904 489548; mobile: 07801 496248).** Private house where a warm welcome awaits you. Beautifully appointed and spacious double rooms, one twin, one double, each with vanity unit, washbasin, shaver point and a small single room. All have hostess tray, colour TV and are double glazed. Bathroom plus additional toilet for guests' use only. Enjoy full English breakfast with homemade preserves, diningroom overlooking delightful garden. Non-smoking. Five minute walk to pub serving evening meals from 6pm. Park and ride nearby. Private parking. Within easy reach of Elvington Air Museum, Castle Howard, North Yorkshire Moors and coastal resorts. Bed and Breakfast from £16.

**YORK. Mav and Maureen Davidson, "Oaklands" Guest House, 351 Strensall Road, Old Earswick, York YO32 9SW (01904 768443).** A warm welcome awaits you at our attractive family house set in open countryside, yet only three miles from York with close access to the York ring road (A1237), A64, A1 and A19. Ideally situated for City, Coast, Dales and Moors. Our comfortable bedrooms are centrally heated with vanity unit, colour TV, razor point, tea making equipment, radio alarms and hairdryers. En suite facilities available. A more than ample full breakfast is served in a light airy diningroom. Your hosts, Maureen and Mav very much look forward to seeing you. Bed and full English Breakfast from £18. Discounts available. Open all year. No pets. Smoking in garden only. **ETC** ◆◆◆

**YORK. St Paul's Hotel, 120 Holgate Road, York YO2 4BB (01904 611514).** St Paul's is situated a short walk from the centre of the historic city of York, which has something to offer everyone, with museums, shopping, tours, restaurants and nightlife ranging from olde worlde pubs to the very latest in bars. Deep in the heart of Yorkshire, it is only a short drive to breathtaking views of the Yorkshire Moors and Dales. Situated in a pleasant residential location, we have six stylish rooms with en suite facilities, colour television and tea/coffee making facilities. We can provide twin, double or family accommodation and even have a four-poster room. Our residents' lounge offers the opportunity to meet other guests, relax and unwind. We pride ourselves on friendly and reliable service to make sure your stay with us is an enjoyable one. Bed and full English Breakfast from £25. reductions for longer stays.

**YORK. Jenny Clark, Cumbria House, 2 Vyner Street, Haxby Road, York YO31 8HS (01904 636817).** A warm and friendly welcome awaits you at Cumbria House - an elegant, tastefully decorated Victorian guest house, where comfort and quality are assured. We are convenient for the city, being only 12 minutes' walk from York's historic Minster and yet within minutes of the northern by-pass (A1237). A launderette, post office and children's park are close by. All rooms have colour TV, radio alarms and tea/coffee facilities. Most are en suite or have certain private facilities. Central heating. Fire Certificate. Guests' car park. Full English breakfast or vegetarian alternative. £18 to £22 per person. "You arrive as guests but leave as friends".
**AA** QQQ.
e-mail: clark@cumbriahouse.freeserve.co.uk

**YORK. Mont-Clare Guest House, 32 Claremont Terrace, Gillygate, York YO31 7EJ (01904 627054; Fax: 01904 651011).** Take advantage and enjoy the convenience of City Centre accommodation in a quiet location close to magnificent York Minster. A warm and friendly welcome awaits you at the Mont-Clare. All rooms are en suite, some with four-posters, tastefully decorated, with colour TV (Satellite), Radio Alarm, Direct Dial Telephone, Hairdryer, Tea/Coffee Tray, Shoe Cleaning, etc. All of York's attractions are within walking distance and we are ideally situated for the Yorkshire Dales, Moors and numerous Stately Homes. Fire and Hygiene Certificates. Cleanliness, good food, pleasant surroundings and friendliness are our priorities. Private car park with CCTV. Open all year. Reduced rates for weekly stay. Bed and Breakfast from £25 pppn.
e-mail: montclareY@aol.com
website: www.mont-clare.co.uk

**YORK. Mr Mike Cundall, Orillia House, 89 The Village, Stockton on Forest, York YO3 9UP (01904 400600).** A warm welcome awaits you at Orillia House, conveniently situated in the centre of the village, three miles north east of York, one mile from A64. The house dates back to the 17th century and has been restored to offer a high standard of comfort with modern facilities yet retaining its original charm and character. All rooms have private facilities, colour TV and tea/coffee making facilities. Our local pub provides excellent evening meals. We also have our own private car park. Bed and Breakfast from £19. Telephone for our brochure. **ETC** ◆◆◆

**YORK. Mrs Raine, Astley House, 123 Clifton, York YO30 6BL (01904 634745; Tel & Fax: 01904 621327).** Enjoy superb accommodation centrally situated only minutes away from all the historic attractions. A warm and friendly welcome awaits you at Astley House, a small family-run hotel offering excellent value for money. All rooms are en suite and tastefully equipped, some with four-poster beds, colour TV with satellite, tea/coffee tray, etc. Car park. Bed and Breakfast from £20 to £35.
e-mail: astley123@aol.com
website: www.astley123.co.uk

**YORK. Carol & Baz Oxtoby, Clifton View Guest House, 118/120 Clifton, York YO3 6BQ (01904 625047).** Family-run guest house overlooking picturesque Clifton Green. Situated on main A19 (north), leave your car in our secure car park and enjoy a short 12 minute walk into the city. We have 13 comfortable bedrooms, all non-smoking and with colour TV, tea/coffee making facilities, clock-radio alarm and hair dryer. Most have a shower cubicle and en suite available. English breakfast menu. Comfortable residents' lounge where smoking is permitted. Children and pets welcome. Bed and Breakfast from £14 to £19 per person according to room and season. **ETC** ◆◆◆

*See also Colour Display Advertisement*

**YORK. The Kismet Guest House, 147 Haxby Road, York YO31 8JZ (01904 621056).** A warm welcome awaits you at the Victorian "Kismet Guest House". Relax and enjoy your stay with Nigel and Barbara. Close to all city centre amenities and with easy access to the Yorkshire Dales and coast. Ten minute walk to the city walls, restaurants and shops. Ten minute drive to the railway station. Most rooms en suite, all centrally heated with colour TV and tea/coffee making facilities. Substantial full English breakfast is served, vegetarians catered for. Secure off-road parking is available, as is an evening meal upon request. No pets, no smoking. Open all year. Bed and Breakfast from £22.50 per person.
**e-mail: kismetGuestHouse@yahoo.com**
**website: www.kismetguesthouse.com**

**YORK. Virginia Collinson, Hall Farm, Gilling East, York YO62 4JW (01439 788314).** Come and stay with us at Hall Farm, a beautifully situated 400 acre working stock farm with extensive views over Ryedale. Completely away from all the traffic, we are half-a-mile away from the road, as you drive up to the farm you may see cows with their calves and in spring and early summer ewes with their lambs. We offer a friendly, family welcome with homemade scones on arrival. A ground floor double en suite room is available and includes hospitality tray with home-made biscuits. Sittingroom with TV and open fire on chilly evenings, diningroom with patio doors to garden, where breakfast may be served on the warmest of mornings. You will be the only guests so the breakfast time is up to you. Full English Breakfast includes home made bread and preserves with our own free range eggs. There are lots of excellent places to eat in the evenings in the historic market town of Helmsley and nearby villages. York, Castle Howard and the North York Moors within half-an-hour drive. Terms from £18 per person.

**YORK. Ray and Caroline Batten, Clarence Gardens Hotel, Haxby Road, York YO31 8JS (01904 624252; Fax: 01904 671293).** We extend a warm welcome to all our guests and aim to provide a comfortable and friendly atmosphere with careful attention to individual needs. Ideally situated 10 minutes' walk from the city centre. All our bedrooms are en suite and beautifully furnished, some with a mini-bar. A traditional 'good ole' Yorkshire breakfast is served in our diningroom. In the evening you can select from our extensive table d'hôte menu. The hotel has a spacious bar/lounge where guests can relax and enjoy a drink. A large children's park is located next to the hotel and the local swimming pool is five minutes' walk. Top class bowling greens are adjacent to the hotel. Ample parking is available. Call or write for a brochure. **ETC** ◆◆◆

---

Terms quoted in this publication may be subject to increase if rises in costs necessitate

**YORK. Mr G. Harrand, Hedley House Hotel, 3 Bootham Terrace, York YO30 7DH (01904 637404; Fax: 01904 639774).** Family-run hotel in quiet residential area within 10 minute walk of city centre. All rooms en suite, remote-control colour TV, telephone and hospitality tray. Vegetarian and special diets catered for. Off street car parking. Small/medium groups welcome. Open all year, Self-catering available next door to hotel. **ETC** ★★
e-mail: h.h@mcmail.com
website: www.hedleyhouse.com

**YORK. Mrs S. Benson, Spring Cottage, Ampleforth, York YO62 4DA (01439 788579).** Spring Cottage is a stone-built house dating back over 200 years, with ample off-street parking, large garden for guests' use and delightful views over Ryedale. We are located on the edge of the National Park and within easy reach of the North York Moors (Herriot and Heartbeat country) and the historic city of York. Accommodation comprises one family suite and one double/twin room, both with en suite facilities, colour TV, tea and coffee tray, radio, hair dryer and magazines. Guests have their own lounge with open log fire, TV, books and magazines. Breakfast includes English, Continental and Vegetarian. Children and pets are welcome. Prices from £20 per person. **ETC** ◆◆◆

**YORK. Church View, Stockton-on-the-Forest, York YO32 9UP (01904 400403; Fax: 01904 400325; Mobile: 07971 431074).** Enjoy a short stay any season in our pretty village three miles east of York. Our 200-year-old cottage offers real fires in our cosy visitors' lounge (candlelit dinner if required). Music, TV available; games room with full-size snooker table; pub over the road. There is a golf course in the village and the area is perfect for visiting the North York Moors (location of Heartbeat), Castle Howard (location of Brideshead Revisited), the East Coast, and of course, the beautiful city of York. Please ring for further information. Bed and Breakfast from £20 per person per night.

See also Colour Display Advertisement

**YORK. The Red House, Oswaldkirk, York YO62 5XY (Tel & Fax: 01439 788063).** An attractive period property located on the edge of the beautiful North Yorkshire Moor National Park. It is within easy driving distance of the London/Edinburgh A1 motorway and is situated 20 miles north of York, with easy access to the coast and the historic towns of Harrogate, Whitby and Scarborough. The Red House is close to Ampleforth Abbey and is set in three-quarters of an acre offering good en suite accommodation. The village has a 16th century coaching inn serving evening meals. There are many excellent restaurants and places of interest close by, including Castle Howard as featured in 'Brideshead Revisited' TV series. A warm welcome, log fires in the winter and home cooking guaranteed.
e-mail: d.matthias@themutual.net

**YORK. Peggy Swann, South Newlands Farm, Selby Road, Riccall, York YO4 6QR (01757 248203).** Friendliness, comfort and good traditional cooking are always on offer to our guests. The kettle's always on the boil in our kitchen, and the comfortable lounge is yours to relax in at any time. Easy access to York and the Dales and Moors. Our farm is a strawberry and plant nursery with a five-caravan site adjacent. No smoking please.

**YORK. Church Cottage, York Road, Escrick, York YO19 6EX (01904 728462; Fax: 01904 728896).** Church Cottage is a traditional country home dating from 1850. Over the years we have sympathetically extended the buildings to provide spacious and comfortable accommodation. The house is set in two acres of lawn and woodland and lies in a quiet village setting yet close to York and Selby. We have seven en suite rooms, which are furnished to the highest standard and have all modern facilities. Room rates are from £45 and all credit cards are accepted. **ETC** ◆◆◆◆
e-mail: church cottage@rgm.co.uk

**YORK, near Castle Howard. Sandie and Peter Turner, High Gaterley Farm, Near Welburn, York YO60 7HT (Tel & Fax: 01653 694636).** High Gaterley enjoys a unique position, located within the boundaries of Castle Howard's magnificent country estate. It is ideally situated for easy access to the City of York, East Coast and the North Yorkshire Moors renowned for ruined abbeys and castles. The tranquil ambience with panoramic views over the Howardian Hills make it a perfect location for a peaceful and relaxing stay in a comfortable well-appointed farmhouse with the option of fine cuisine. En suite facilities with tea and coffee in all rooms, log fire in the drawing room, TV, non-smoking, dogs by prior arrangement. Open all year. Bed and breakfast from £19. Optional evening meal and special diets by arrangement. **ETC** ◆◆◆◆
e-mail: relax@highgaterley.com
website: www.highgaterley.com

# WEST YORKSHIRE

**ILKLEY. The Roberts Family B&B, 63 Skipton Road, Ilkley LS29 9HF (01943 817542).** Pleasant detached family house with gardens and private parking. Level access to town, shops, amenities and trains to Leeds and Bradford. Two ground floor double en suite bedrooms (not suitable for wheelchairs), one upstairs twin with shared bathroom. All have tea/coffee facilities, TV, central heating and double glazing. Open all year including Christmas and New Year. Special offers available - please enquire. Only well behaved pets, kids and grans welcome. ABSOLUTELY NO SMOKING. Bed and Breakfast £20 per person. Visa/Mastercard accepted

**PONTEFRACT/WENTBRIDGE. Mrs I. Goodworth, The Corner Cafe, Wentbridge, Pontefract WF8 3JJ (01977 620316).** A sixteenth century cottage featuring oak beams and a lovely secluded garden with plenty of car parking space, set in a small village but within easy reach of main roads (a quarter-of-a-mile A1). Accommodation includes two single, one double, one twin with private bathroom and two family rooms en suite, all with washbasin, TV, tea and coffee making facilities and full central heating. Non-smoking accommodation available. Two family rooms en suite in annexe. This picturesque village has three very nice old inns and restaurants where evening meals or snacks can be obtained. Children welcome. Terms from £18. Open all year round, except Christmas.

Terms quoted in this publication may be subject to increase if rises in costs necessitate

# THE FHG DIPLOMA

## HELP IMPROVE BRITISH TOURIST STANDARDS

You are choosing holiday accommodation from our very popular FHG Publications.
Whether it be a hotel, guest house, farmhouse or self-catering accommodation, we think you will find it hospitable, comfortable and clean, and your host and hostess friendly and helpful.
Why not write and tell us about it?

As a recognition of the generally well-run and excellent holiday accommodation reviewed in our publications, we at FHG Publications Ltd. present a diploma to proprietors who receive the highest recommendation from their guests who are also readers of our Guides. If you care to write to us praising the holiday you have booked through FHG Publications Ltd. – whether this be board, self-catering accommodation, a sporting or a caravan holiday, what you say will be evaluated and the proprietors who reach our final list will be contacted.

The winning proprietor will receive an attractive framed diploma to display on his premises as recognition of a high standard of comfort, amenity and hospitality. FHG Publications Ltd. offer this diploma as a contribution towards the improvement of standards in tourist accommodation in Britain. Help your excellent host or hostess to win it!

---

## FHG DIPLOMA

We nominate ..................................................................................................................

..................................................................................................................

Because

Name ..................................................................................................................

Address..................................................................................................................

..................................................................................................................

Telephone No............................................

# SCOTLAND

# ABERDEENSHIRE, BANFF & MORAY

**ABERDEEN. Anne and Alan Dey, Kildonan Guest House, 410 Great Western Road, Aberdeen AB10 6NR (01224 316115).** Personally run, comfortable guest house on main city bus route, and very conveniently situated for touring Royal Deeside, Donside and all other areas of Grampian. All rooms are non-smoking and are equipped with tea/coffee making facilities and colour TV. Ground floor rooms available. En suite rooms. **STB ★★** *GUEST HOUSE.* **AA** *QQ,* **RAC** *LISTED.*
e-mail: dey@kildonan.fsbusiness.co.uk

**PETERHEAD. Carrick Guest House, 16 Merchant Street, Peterhead AB42 1DU (Tel & Fax: 01779 470610).** Comfortable accommodation centrally situated for all amenities. Two minutes' walk from main shopping centre, harbour and beach. All rooms en suite, colour television, hospitality tray, trouser press, hairdryer. Full central heating. Good car parking. Terms from £20 to £25 per person. **STB ★★** *GUEST HOUSE.*

**ROYAL DEESIDE. Callater Lodge Guest House, 9 Glenshee Road, Braemar AB35 5YQ (01339 741275; Fax: 01339 741345).** Braemar is a pretty award-winning village close to Balmoral Castle in beautiful Royal Deeside. Callater Lodge is a comfortable, friendly guest house in spacious grounds close to the village centre. Surrounded by superb hill country, with many of Scotland's finest mountains nearby, it is ideal for walking, cycling, climbing, touring, golf and other country holidays. Close to Glenshee Ski Centre it is also ideal for ski breaks. Licensed, lounge, drying room, parking, etc. Bed and Breakfast with en suite bathroom from £24 to £30, Dinner £15. **STB ★★★★** *GUEST HOUSE.* **AA ♦♦♦♦**. Also quiet, well-equipped self-catering cottage sleeping four adults, and chalet sleeping two also available from £190 to £330. (STB ★★★/★★★★ *SELF-CATERING).* Contact: Maria or Mike Franklin.
e-mail: mariaf@hotel-braemar.co.uk
website: www.hotel-braemar.co.uk

**STONEHAVEN. Mrs Aileen Paton, Woodside of Glasslaw, Stonehaven AB39 3XQ (01569 763799).** Modern extended bungalow set in one acre of gardens with ample safe parking. Four centrally heated en suite bedrooms with colour TV and hospitality trays. Lounge/dining room and fitted kitchen are available to guests. Accommodation is accessible for disabled guests. The guest house is situated two miles south of the seaside town of Stonehaven and close to the spectacular Dunnottar Castle. Aberdeen is 15 miles away and Stonehaven is a good base for touring Royal Deeside. Bed and Breakfast from £18 per person.

---

All the information in this book is given in good faith in the belief that it is correct. However, the publishers cannot guarantee the facts given in these pages, neither are they responsible for changes in policy, ownership or terms that may take place after the date of going to press. Readers should always satisfy themselves that the facilities they require are available and that the terms, if quoted, still apply.

# ARGYLL & BUTE

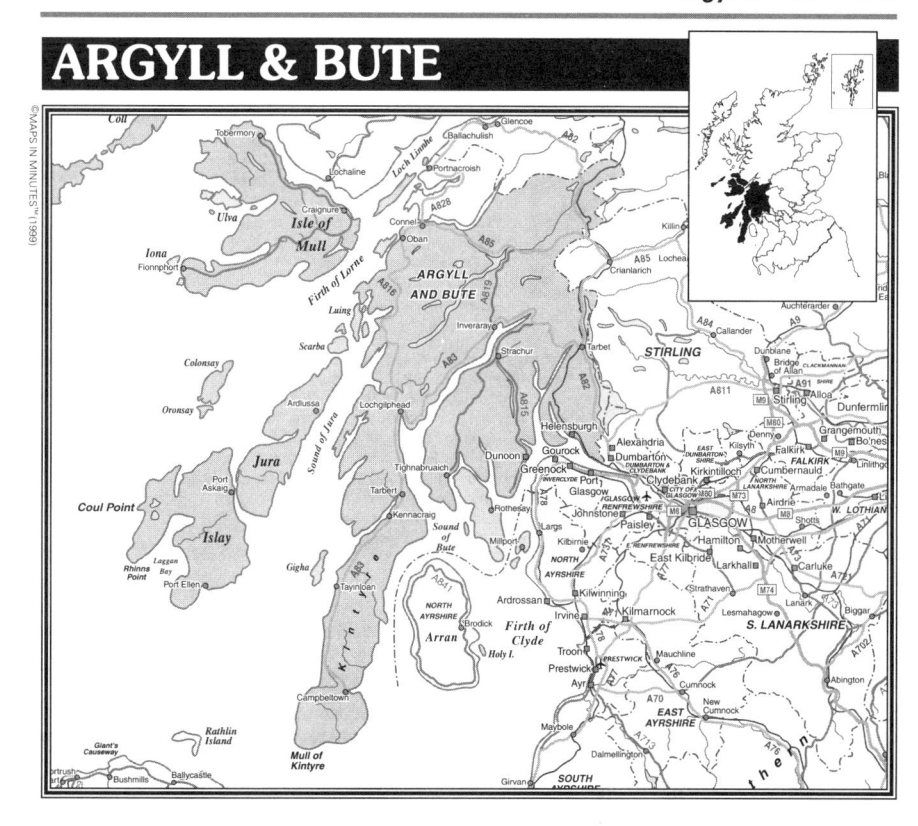

**ARROCHAR. Mary and Gordon Chandler, Rowantree Cottage, Mainstreet, Arrochar G83 7AA (Tel & Fax: 01301 702540).** A non-smoking establishment. Relax! Unwind! Enjoy the peace and spectacular views. We offer good food, breakfasts and evening meals, with special diets catered for. Bed and Breakfast from £20 to £24 per person per night. Evening meals from £10. All our rooms are en suite, with views over Loch Long and the Arrochar Alps. From our cottage you can enjoy day trips to many beautiful and historical places, including Oban, Fort William, Stirling, Edinburgh and the Trossachs. Alternatively take a cruise on Loch Lomond, only two miles away. For the more active there are many mountain and glen walks in and around Arrochar. Take advantage of our special off-season breaks - three nights for the price of two. **STB** ★★★ *GUEST HOUSE.*
e-mail: rowantreecottage@cs.com
website: www.arrochar-bb.com

**BALLACHULISH (near Glencoe). Mr and Mrs J.A. MacLeod, Lyn-Leven Guest House, Ballachulish PA39 4JW (01855 811392; Fax: 01855 811600).** Lyn-Leven, a superior award-winning licensed guest house overlooking Loch Leven, with every comfort, in the beautiful Highlands of Scotland, is situated one mile from historic Glencoe village. Four double, two twin and two family bedrooms, all rooms en suite; sittingroom and diningroom. Central heating. Excellent and varied home cooking served daily. Children welcome at reduced rates. An ideal location for touring. Fishing, walking and climbing in the vicinity. The house, open all year, is suitable for disabled guests. Car not essential but private car park provided. Dinner, Bed and Breakfast from £195 to £210 per person per week. **STB** ★★★ *GUEST HOUSE,* **AA** *QQQQ SELECTED,* **RAC** *ACCLAIMED.*

**CARRADALE. Mrs D. MacCormick, Mains Farm, Carradale, Campbeltown PA28 6QG (01583 431216). Working farm.** From April to October farmhouse accommodation is offered at Mains Farm, five minutes' walk from safe beach, forestry walks with views of Carradale Bay and Arran. Near main bus route and 15 miles from airport. Golf, sea/river fishing, pony trekking, canoeing locally. Comfortable accommodation in one double, one single, one family bedrooms; guests' sitting/diningroom with coal/log fire; bathroom, toilet. Heating in rooms according to season. Children welcome at reduced rates, cot and high chair available. Pets by prior arrangement. The house is not suitable for disabled visitors. Good home cooking and special diets catered for. Bed and Breakfast from £17.00. Tea making facilities in rooms. **STB ★★** *B&B*.

**DUNOON. Royal Marine Hotel, Marine Parade, Hunter's Quay, Dunoon PA23 8HJ (01369 705810; Fax: 01369 702329).** Beautiful Tudor-style building overlooking the Firth of Clyde. Superbly located for touring, walking, fishing, golf and the great outdoors. Three family, 13 double, 13 twin and nine single rooms, all en suite with central heating, hairdryer and telephone. Pets and children welcome, cot available. Washing and ironing facilities available. Open all year, Christmas breaks. Parking. No smoking. Terms from £30 - £38 single, £25 - £38 double/twin. **STB ★★★** *HOTEL*.
**e-mail: rmhotel@sol.co.uk**

**DUNOON. Manfred and Mary Kohls, Ashgrove Guest House, Wyndham Road, Innellan, Dunoon PA23 7SH (01369 830306; Fax: 01369 830776).** Mid 19th century house with many original features. Excellent facilities. Peaceful location, outstanding views over the Firth of Clyde, large secluded gardens. Ideal for relaxing, walking or touring. Pets welcome. Bed and Breakfast from £21. Self-catering studio flat available. Brochure. **STB ★★★** *B&B*
**e-mail: ashgrovebb@hotmail.com**

**INVERARAY. Mr R. Gayre, Minard Castle, Minard PA32 8YB (Tel & Fax: 01546 886272).** Stay in exclusive style in our 19th Century Scottish castle which stands in its own grounds in beautiful countryside beside Loch Fyne, three-quarters-of-a-mile from the A83 Inveraray to Lochgilphead road. A peaceful location for a quiet break, you can stroll in the grounds, walk by the loch, explore the woods, or use Minard Castle as your base for touring this beautiful area with its lochs, hills, gardens, castles and historic sites. Breakfast in the Morning Room and relax in the Drawing Room. The three comfortable bedrooms have colour television, tea/coffee making facilities and en suite bathrooms. No smoking in the house. Evening Meals available within five miles. Bed and Breakfast £30 to £40 per person, children half price. We offer a warm welcome in a family home. Self-Catering properties also available, £100 to £350 per week.
**e-mail: reinoldgayre@bizonline.co.uk**

---

# FHG
Visit the FHG website
## www.holidayguides.com
for details of the wide choice of accommodation featured in the full range of FHG titles

# KILLEAN FARMHOUSE

Killean Farmhouse is located just a few miles outside Inveraray. Ideally situated for walking, climbing, pony trekking or just touring. There's fishing for trout, pike or salmon and opportunities to enjoy boating, water skiing or windsurfing. The whole area is steeped in history and the town of Inveraray itself is a classic example of 18th century Scottish town planning. With all this in mind the cottages provide high quality accommodation for family holidays. All enquiries to: Mrs Semple, Killean House, Inveraray PA32 8XT. Telephone (01499) 302474.

---

**LOCHGOILHEAD. Mrs Rosemary Dolan, The Shorehouse Inn, Lochgoilhead PA24 8AJ (01301 703340).** Friendly informal Inn, fully licensed, has seven letting rooms, central heating and double glazing. There are two family, three twin, one single and one double bedrooms. Residents' lounge, a bar of unusual character and licensed restaurant. Home cooking, bar meals. Formerly the old manse on a historic site with lochside and panoramic views looking southward down Loch Goil, situated in the village on the shore. Local amenities include water sports, fishing, pony trekking, tennis, bowls, golf, swimming pool, curling in winter and a good area for hill walking. Some rooms with private facilities. Fully licensed. One hour travel time from Glasgow. Open all year round. Ideal for winter or summer breaks. Rates from £16 per person Bed and Breakfast; en suite £20 per person.

**OBAN. Mrs C. MacDonald, Bracker, Polvinister Road, Oban PA34 5TN (01631 564302; Fax: 01631 571167).** Bracker is a modern bungalow built in 1975 and extended recently to cater for visitors. We have three guest rooms two double and one twin-bedded, all en suite with TV and tea/coffee making facilities. Small TV lounge and diningroom. Private parking. The house is situated in a beautiful quiet residential area of Oban and is within walking distance of the town (approximately eight to 10 minutes) and the golf course. Friendly hospitality and comfortable accommodation. Bed and Breakfast £17 to £18. Non-smoking. **STB ★★★** *GUEST HOUSE.*

**OBAN. Mr and Mrs I. Donn, Palace Hotel, Oban PA34 5SB (01631 562294).** A small family hotel offering personal supervision situated on Oban's sea front with wonderful views over the Bay, to the Mull Hills beyond. All rooms en suite, with colour TV, tea/coffee making facilities, several non-smoking. The Palace is an ideal base for a real Highland holiday. By boat you can visit the islands of Kerrera, Coll, Tiree, Lismore, Mull and Iona, and by road Glencoe, Ben Nevis and Inveraray. Fishing, golf, horse riding, sailing, tennis and bowls all nearby. Children and pets welcome. Reductions for children. Please write or telephone for brochure. Competitive rates.

---

*Please mention Bed & Breakfast Stops when writing to enquire about accommodation*

**OBAN. Morven and Keith Wardhaugh, Kathmore Guest House, Soroba Road, Oban (01631 562104).** Located in the picturesque coastal town of Oban, Kathmore Guest House provides a superb base from which to explore and capture the breathtaking beauty of the West Highlands and Islands. Our rooms are well furnished and equipped with colour TV, tea and coffee trays, hair dryer etc. Most of the rooms are en suite. There are many beautiful places to visit: Mull of Kintyre, Glen Coe, Isle of Mull, Loch Ness and Ben Nevis, Britain's highest mountain. There are also the historic villages and islands such as Kilmartin, Easdale and Iona as well as a variety of attractions: Sea Life Centre, Rare Breeds Park and Inveraray Jail. Whatever you fancy, we are always available and happy to give you ideas on what to see and do when you come to Oban. Bed and Breakfast £14 - £22.50. **STB ★★★** *GUEST HOUSE, RUNNER-UP IN THE 1999 TOURIST BOARD FX AWARDS.*

**OBAN by. Loch Etive House, Connel Village, By Oban PA37 1PH (01631 710400; Fax: 01631 710680).** Off the A85 and just five miles from Oban, Loch Etive House, although small and unpretentious is a 'gem' of comfort, hospitality and cleanliness, created by Bob and Fran. They endeavour to help their residents make the best of their holiday whatever the weather, providing good home-cooking and a selection of wines in a friendly and convivial atmosphere. Bed and Breakfast from £18 to £27 per person per night. **STB ★★★** *GUEST HOUSE.* **RAC/AA ♦♦♦♦.**
e-mail: bob@r.cook.easynet.co.uk

**OBAN by. Mrs E. Campbell, Asknish Cottage, Arduaine, By Oban PA34 4XQ (01852 200247).** A warm welcome from Elspeth at Asknish Cottage. Arduaine, with panoramic views towards Shuna, Scarba, Luing and Jura is halfway between Oban, 18 miles to the north, and Lochgilphead to the south. Ideally placed to take advantage of the many local activities, around boat trips, dinghy and sailing boat hire, fishing and diving or visiting the main islands by ferry; this is good walking country either energetic or leisurely; horse riding or trekking. Argyll has many gardens and historic sites. There are a number of good restaurants in hotels and inns within six miles of the cottage, one within walking distance. Pets welcome. Wild garden, tame owner. Two double, one twin bedrooms, £16.50 to £17.50 per person per night.

**OBAN near. Margaret and Norman Hill, Lerags House, Lerags, By Oban PA34 4SE (01631 563381).** Situated in almost two acres of mature gardens set in the tranquil and picturesque Lerags Glen, yet only a short drive from Oban with its town facilities, shopping and ferry terminal for the Islands. Good quality accommodation, food and service at value for money prices in a warm and relaxing atmosphere. Seven spacious guest bedrooms all en suite, situated on the first floor, most with views over Loch Feochan. Guest lounge with open fire. Dinner by prior reservation with the emphasis on traditional recipes and local produce. Fully licensed. Open March to October. Bed and Breakfast from £22.50, Bed, Breakfast and Evening Meal from £35. We are a non-smoking establishment.

---

# FREE or REDUCED RATE entry to Holiday Visits and Attractions — see our READERS' OFFER VOUCHERS on pages 43-60

# AYRSHIRE & The Island of Arran

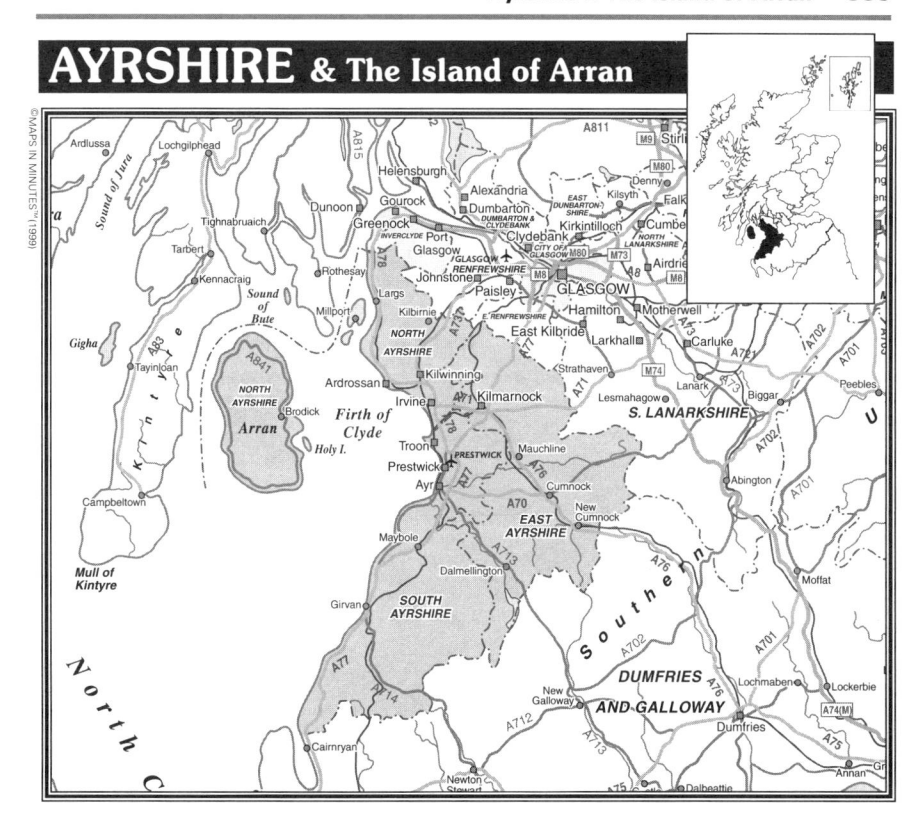

**AYR. Mrs Wilcox, Fisherton Farm, Dunure, Ayr KA7 4LF (Tel & Fax: 01292 500223).** Traditional stone-built farmhouse on working mixed farm with extensive sea views to Arran. Convenient for golf, walking and Burns Country. Also convenient for Culzean Castle and Prestwick Airport. From Ayr take A719 coast road past Haven Craig Tara; farm is five miles south of Ayr. Accommodation comprises one double and one twin en suite, ground floor bedrooms with TV and tea/coffee making facilities. Central heating throughout. Children welcome. Pets by arrangement. Please write, telephone or fax for further information. Prices from £18.50 to £20. **STB** ★★★ *B&B. WELCOME HOST.*

**AYR. Peter and Julia Clark, Eglinton Guest House, 23 Eglinton Terrace, Ayr KA7 1JJ (01292 264623).** In Welcome Host Scheme. Situated within a part of Ayr steeped in history, within a few minutes' walk of the beach, town centre and many other amenities and entertainment for which Ayr is popular. There are sea and fishing trips available from Ayr Harbour, or a cruise "Doon the Water" on the "Waverley"; golf, swimming pool, cycling, tennis, sailing, windsurfing, walking, etc all available nearby; Prestwick Airport only three miles away. We have family, double and single rooms, all with washbasins, colour TV and tea/coffee making facilities. En suite facilities and cots available on request. We are open all year round. Please send for our brochure for further information.

## 336  Ayrshire & The Island of Arran

**AYR near. Mrs Agnes Gemmell, Dunduff Farm, Dunure, Ayr KA7 4LH (01292 500225).** Welcome to Dunduff Farm where a warm friendly atmosphere awaits you. Situated just south of Ayr at the coastal village of Dunure, this family-run beef and sheep unit of 600 acres is only 15 minutes from the shore providing good walks and sea fishing and enjoying close proximity to Dunure Castle and Park. Accommodation is of a very high standard yet homely and comfortable. Bedrooms have washbasins, radio alarm, tea/coffee making facilities, central heating, TV, hair dryer and en suite facilities (the twin room has private bathroom). There is also a small farm cottage available sleeping two/four people. Bed and Breakfast from £23 per person, weekly rate £130. Cottage £230 per week. Colour brochure available. **STB ★★★★ B&B, AA/RAC ♦♦♦♦♦**

**BEITH. Mrs Jane Gillan, Shotts Farm, Beith KA15 1LB (01505 502273).** Comfortable friendly accommodation is offered on this 160 acre dairy farm situated one-and-a-half miles from the A736 Glasgow to Irvine road; well placed to visit golf courses, country parks, or leisure centre, also ideal for the ferry to Arran or Millport and for many good shopping centres all around. A high standard of cleanliness is assured by Mrs Gillan who is a first class cook holding many awards, food being served in the diningroom with its beautiful picture windows. Three comfortable bedrooms (double en suite, family and twin), all with tea-making facilities, central heating and electric blankets. Two bathrooms with shower; sittingroom with colour TV. Children welcome. Bed and Breakfast from £14. Dinner can be arranged. **STB ★★★ B&B. AA ★★★.**

**DUNLOP. Mrs W. Burns, East Langton Farm, Dunlop KA3 4DS (01560 482978).** A warm welcome in peaceful surroundings, close to all amenities. 20 minutes to Glasgow or Prestwick Airport, also 20 minutes from the coast with spectacular views overlooking the Isle of Arran, Dalry and the Kilbirnie hills, and Ben Lomond in the distance. Very quiet, peaceful countryside. One double and two twin rooms, all with private bathroom/shower, TV with Teletext, radio alarm, tea/coffee making facilities and hairdryer. Terms from £18.50 to £22.50 per person.

**KILMARNOCK. Mrs M. Howie, Hill House Farm, Grassyards Road, Kilmarnock KA3 6HG (01563 523370).** Enjoy a peaceful holiday on a working dairy farm two miles east of Kilmarnock. We offer a warm welcome with home baking for supper, choice of farmhouse breakfasts with own preserves. Three large comfortable bedrooms with lovely views over Ayrshire countryside, en suite facilities, tea/coffee, electric blankets, central heating; TV lounge, sun porch, diningroom and garden. Excellent touring base with trips to coast, Arran, Burns Country and Glasgow nearby. Easy access to A77 and numerous golf courses. Children very welcome. Bed and Breakfast from £18 (including supper). Self-catering cottages also available. **STB ★★★★ B&B.**

**KILMARNOCK near. Mrs Nancy Cuthbertson, West Tannacrieff, Fenwick, Kilmarnock KA3 6AZ (01560 600258).** A warm welcome awaits all guests to our home. West Tannacrieff is a traditional farmhouse with one double room with private facilities and a new Bed and Breakfast establishment adjoining our farmhouse opening in spring 2001. It is a working dairy farm in the peaceful Ayrshire countryside. All new rooms are en suite with colour TV, tea making facilities and all modern amenities. Large parking area and garden for you to enjoy. Situated just off the A77 so easily accessible for Glasgow, Prestwick Airport and the south. An ideal base for exploring Ayrshire's attractions and day trips to Arran or Millport, also golf and fishing. Enjoy a full Scottish breakfast made with local produce and home-baking for supper.

**Ayrshire & The Island of Arran**   337

**KILMARNOCK near. Mr and Mrs P. Gibson, Busbiehill Guest House, Knockentiber, Near Kilmarnock KA2 0DJ (01563 532985).** Situated in a rural setting almost in the centre of Ayrshire, looking westwards towards the Arran hills on the Firth of Clyde. Within easy reach of all the popular seaside towns, Burns Country, Culzean Castle. Day trips available to Loch Lomond, Edinburgh and Isle of Arran; sailings on Firth of Clyde. Also many golf courses. Kilmarnock four miles, Ayr 13, Troon 10, Irvine five miles, Ardrossan 13. Eight rooms, five bathrooms; two double rooms with own bathrooms. Tea making facilities, electric blankets. Bed and Breakfast £17. No pets.

**MAUCHLINE. Mrs J. Clark, Auchenlongford, Sorn, Mauchline KA5 6JF (01290 550761).** The farm is situated in the hills above the picturesque village of Sorn, with its Castle set on a promontory above the River Ayr, and nearby its 17th century church. It is only 19 miles east from the A74 and 20 miles inland from the town of Ayr. Accommodation can be from a choice of three attractive, furnished bedrooms and there is also a large well appointed residents' lounge. Full Scottish breakfast is served with home made jams and marmalade; traditional High Tea and/or Dinners are also available on request. Bed and Breakfast £18; Bed, Breakfast and Evening Meal £28. Brochure available.

**PINWHERRY. Mr and Mrs Tester, Drumspillan, 4 Main Street, Pinwherry KA26 0RN (01465 841693).** Mr and Mrs Tester welcome you to their B&B establishment in Pinwherry. Full central heating, tastefully furnished. One family room, one double room, both with colour TV and tea/coffee making facilities. Seven miles from Girvan, within easy reach of Ayr and Stranraer. Culzean Castle, Galloway's forests, Castle Kennedy, gardens, golf courses at Turnberry and Brunston Castle. Fishing is just a few minutes away. Parking. No smoking. Bed and Breakfast from £15.

## The Island Of Arran

**BRODICK. Mrs O' Meara, Sunnyside, Kings Cross, Brodick, Isle of Arran KA27 8RG (01770 700422).** Arran is an island renowned for its contrasting scenic beauty, hill walking and easy coastal strolls, geological faults, historic settlements, Brodick Castle and grounds with rare vegetation. Kings Cross is a small, easily accessible, off-the-beaten-track hamlet, situated at the south east corner of Arran, eight-and-a-half miles from Brodick. Sunnyside, a modern detached bungalow with spacious drive and garden, provides guests with a private entrance to a comfortably furnished double en suite room, having superb views across the Clyde. There is also a twin/single room with private facilities. Decking and a secluded sun-trap garden combine to create an ideal spot for holiday makers seeking a haven of peace and tranquillity.

**CATACOL/ARRAN. Catacol Bay Hotel, Catacol, Isle of Arran KA27 8HN (01770 830231; Fax: 01770 830350).** Escape from the pressures of mainland life, stay awhile by clear shining seas, rocky coast and breathtaking hills and mountains. Comfortable, friendly, small country house hotel where good cooking is our speciality. Extensive bar menu, meals are served from noon until 10pm. Centrally heated. Open all year. Details of Special Breaks and brochure on request. Les Routiers. Children and pets welcome.
**e-mail: davecatbay@lineone.net**
**website: www.catacol.co.uk**

# BORDERS

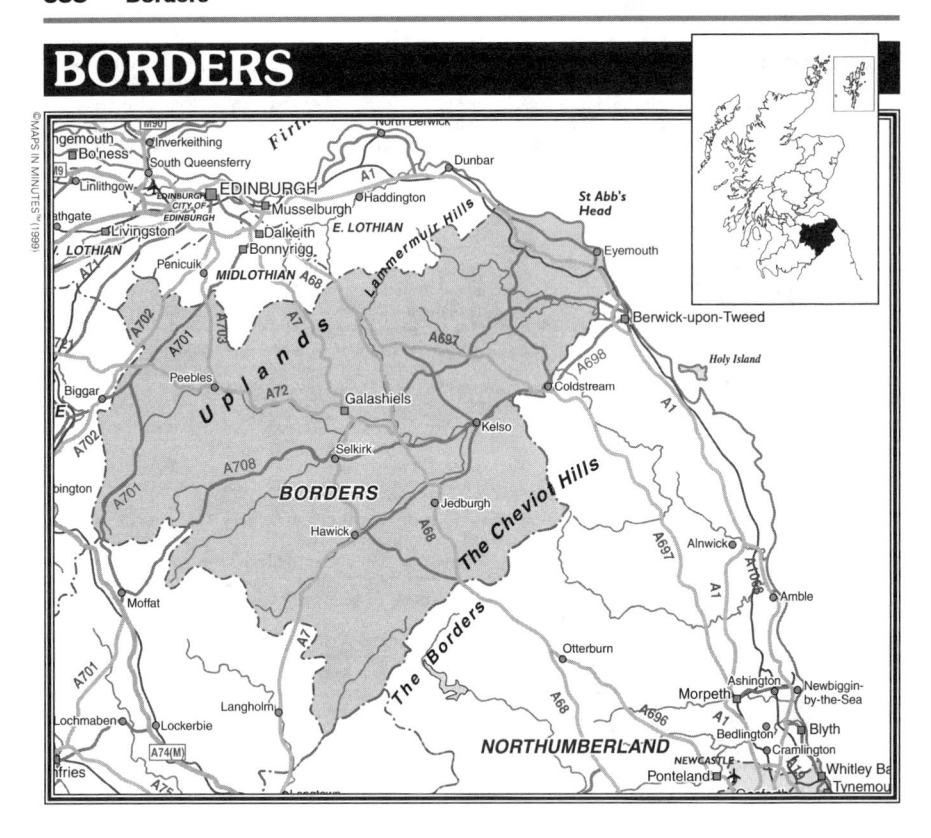

**ASHKIRK. Mrs Betty Lamont, Ashkirktown Farm, Ashkirk, Selkirk TD7 4PB (Tel & Fax: 01750 32315). Working farm.** Situated off the A7 midway between Hawick and Selkirk. Ashkirktown Farm offers a warm welcome in a peaceful and tranquil setting. Whether en route to Edinburgh or exploring the beautiful Borders area of Scotland a comfortable stay is assured. The old farmhouse has been tastefully furnished. Large private lounge with colour TV, tea/coffee making facilities. Open all year. Bed and Breakfast from £18. Reduced rates for children. Non-smoking accommodation available. **STB ★★★ B&B.**

**BIGGAR. Mrs Rosemary Harper, South Mains Farm, Biggar ML12 6HF (01899 860226). Working farm.** South Mains Farm is a working family farm, situated in an elevated position with good views, on the B7016 between Biggar and Broughton. An ideal place to take a break on a North/South journey. Edinburgh 29 miles, Peebles 11 miles. Well situated for touring the Border regions in general. A comfortable bed and excellent breakfast provided in this centrally heated and well furnished farmhouse, which has two double and one single bedrooms. Open all year. Car essential, parking. Terms £16 per night which includes light supper of home made scones, etc. If you are interested just ring, write or call in. Warm welcome assured.

# Borders

**COLDSTREAM. Mrs Jenkins, Attadale, 1 Leet Street, Coldstream TD12 4BJ (01890 883047).** Traditional house in quiet central location in Tweedside Border town. Ideal location for fishing, golf. Lovely garden; ample parking. En suite bedrooms, (one double, one family) with TV. Non-smoking. Open all year. Bed and Breakfast from £15 per person.

**DUNS. Mrs Alison Landale, Green Hope, Ellem Ford, Duns TD11 3SG (01361 890242; Fax: 01361 890295).** Situated in beautiful surroundings in the Lammermuir Hills. Perfect for relaxing, walking and visiting all Scottish Borders attractions. Next door to East Lothian and only one hour from Scotland's capital Edinburgh. Accommodation comprises the Garden Flat, sleeping two to four persons, and Green Hope Cottage which sleeps six to eight persons. Fully equipped, no TV. The perfect riverside hideaway – totally secluded. Golf course, fishing, wonderful walks and beautiful beaches within easy reach. Self-catering terms from £200 depending on season. Bed and Breakfast accommodation also available nearby. Video available. Facilities for disabled.
**e-mail: whitchesterwood@appleonline.net**

**DUNS. St. Albans, Clouds, Duns TD11 3BB (01361 883285; Fax: 01361 884534).** Recommended in "Staying Off The Beaten Track". Pleasant Georgian house with secluded south-facing garden. Magnificent views over small country town to Cheviot Hills. Excellent centre for touring. Very quiet location but only three minutes from town centre. Open all year. Colour TV, tea/coffee making facilities, towelling bath robes and hot water bottles in all bedrooms. Two double or twin rooms available, two public bathrooms. Excellent varied breakfast served in gracious surroundings. Bed and Breakfast from £19.50 to £25.00, 5% reduction for stay of three days, 10% reduction for seven days or more. Credit cards accepted (except AMEX). Service charge of 5% unless paid in full at time of booking. No children under 14 years. Directions:- Clouds is a lane running parallel to and to the North of Newtown Street where the police station and county offices are situated. Proprietor: **Mrs M. Kenworthy. STB ★★★★** *GUEST HOUSE.*
**e-mail: st_albans@email.msn.com**

**ST. ABBS. Mrs Barbara Wood, Castle Rock Guest House, Murrayfield, St. Abbs TD14 5PP (018907 71715; Fax: 018907 71520).** An attractive Victorian house situated on a wonderful cliff-top with views of the harbour and the bay from each room. The village of St. Abbs is an unspoilt village in the Border country, there is a safe sandy beach nearby and birdwatching and rambling on St. Abbs nature reserve. All rooms have en suite facilities, TV, direct dial telephone, hospitality tray, electric blanket, hairdryer and clock-radio. There is a public whirlpool bath on the mezzanine floor. Four-poster room available. Bed and Breakfast £24 per person per night; Bed, Breakfast and Evening Meal £40. Open February to October. Castle Rock is highly recommended by the STB and by "Which?" as well as various other guide books. **STB ★★★** *GUEST HOUSE*.
**e-mail: boowood@compuserve.com**

---

**FHG**

Visit the FHG website
**www.holidayguides.com**
for details of the wide choice of accommodation
featured in the full range of FHG titles

# DUMFRIES & GALLOWAY

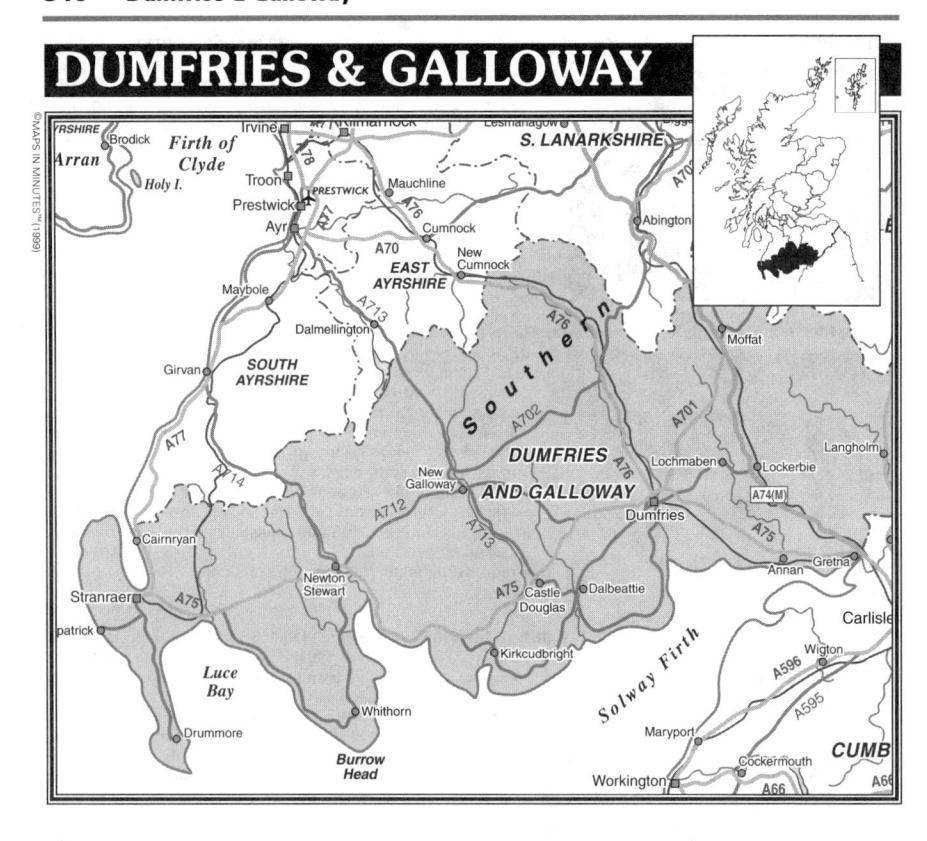

**CANONBIE. Mrs Matthews, Four Oaks, Canonbie DG14 0TF (01387 371329).** Bed and Breakfast accommodation in comfortable, peaceful family home, with open views of lovely rolling countryside and farmland. Near the village of Canonbie and the River Esk, off the A7 just north of Carlisle, providing an excellent base for touring the Borderlands. Accommodation is provided in one twin en suite, and one double en suite with bath and shower room. Cot available. Visitors' lounge with TV. Tea/coffee making facilities provided. Garden. Good parking.

*See also Colour Display Advertisement*

**CASTLE DOUGLAS. Mrs Jessie Shaw, High Park Farm, Balmaclellan, Castle Douglas DG7 3PT (Tel & Fax: 01644 420298).** Enjoy a holiday amidst beautiful scenery while staying at our comfortable farmhouse situated by Loch Ken. High Park is a family-run dairy, beef and sheep farm offering accommodation in one family room, one twin bedroom (upstairs), one double bedroom (ground floor); all have washbasins, shaver points and tea/coffee making facilities. Central heating, home baking. Comfort, cleanliness and good food guaranteed. Open Easter to October. Bed and Breakfast from £16. Brochure on request. **STB ★★** *B&B*.
e-mail: high.park@farming.co.uk

## Dumfries & Galloway

**CASTLE DOUGLAS. Margaret Wormald, Balcary Mews, Balcary Bay, Auchencairn, By Castle Douglas DG7 1QZ (01556 640276).** Balcary Mews is a spacious, well appointed residence in a superb seashore location. It is tastefully furnished throughout and has ample private parking. The comfortable guest sittingroom has picture window frontage affording panoramic views accross the bay. All guest bedrooms are beautifully co-ordinated and have magnificent sea views. We offer a comprehensive breakfast menu and home-made bread and preserves are our speciality. Balcary Mews provides an excellent base for exploring Galloway, bird watching, fishing, walking, golf etc. We are very sensitive to the individual requirements of our guests and strive to offer a friendly personal service of the highest possible standard from £22 to £26 per night. Brochure available. **STB** ★★★★ *B&B,* **AA** ◆◆◆◆

**CASTLE DOUGLAS by. Kerr and Sheila Steele, Rose Cottage Guest House, Gelston, Castle Douglas DG7 1SH (01556 502513).** Small country guest house situated in quiet village two and a half miles from Castle Douglas. We have one twin, two double (one en suite) and one single room, all situated on the ground floor. Each room has washbasin, beverage tray, shaver point and colour television. There is also a guest lounge. A car park is situated in the grounds, which are large with a stream and a waterfall bordering the property. Rose Cottage is centrally positioned for touring Galloway and is within easy reach of all major towns and attractions. (One and a half miles to Threave Gardens). Bed and Breakfast £18 - en suite facilities £2.50 extra. Evening Meal £11. Dumfries and Galloway Tourist Board Good Service Award. **STB** ★★★ *GUEST HOUSE.*

**DUMFRIES. The Maxwell Family, Southpark Guest House, Quarry Road, Locharbriggs, Dumfries DG1 1QG (Tel & Fax: 01387 711188).** Situated in one of Scotland's most beautiful and unexplored areas, an ideal base for touring, relaxing or a business stay, with easy access to all major routes and yet only five minutes from the town centre. Many leisure facilities nearby. Accommodation consists of one double and one twin, both en suite, and one family room with private adjoining facilities. Additional ground floor en suite rooms are being built for 2001. All bedrooms are well furnished, with hospitality tray, hairdryer, TV and radio alarm clock. Guest lounge with Sky TV, video and hi-fi. Terms from £19.50 per person per night en suite, £17.00 room only. Discounts for children and longer stays. **STB** ★★★ *B&B,* **AA** ◆◆◆.
e-mail: ewan@southparkhouse.co.uk
website: www.southparkhouse.co.uk

**DUMFRIES. Mr & Mrs G. Hood, Wallamhill House, Kirkton, Dumfries DG1 1SL (Tel & Fax: 01387 248249; Mobile: 07850 750150).** A charming country house, tastefully furnished, with a warm, friendly, welcoming atmosphere. The spacious en suite bedrooms - two double/family and one twin, have lovely views over garden and countryside. Beautifully appointed, each room has colour and satellite TV plus video, tea/coffee making facilities, shower and toilet and full central heating. Small leisure suite and sauna available for guests' use. Situated in peaceful countryside only three miles from Dumfries town centre with excellent shopping, swimming pool, ice bowl for curling, green bowling, fishing and golf. Hill and forest walks, birdwatching, cycling and mountain bike trails all nearby. Bed and Breakfast from £19 to £21. Please send for our brochure for further information. **STB** ★★★★ *B&B.*
e-mail: wallamhill@aol.com

---

# FREE or REDUCED RATE entry to Holiday Visits and Attractions — see our READERS' OFFER VOUCHERS on pages 43-60

**MOFFAT. Mr and Mrs W. Gray, Barnhill Springs Country Guest House, Moffat DG10 9QS (01683 220580).** Barnhill Springs is an early Victorian country mansion standing in its own grounds overlooking Upper Annandale. Situated half-a-mile from the A74/M, the house and its surroundings retain an air of remote peacefulness. Internally it has been decorated and furnished to an exceptionally high standard of comfort. Open fire in lounge. Accommodation includes family, double, twin and single rooms, some en suite. Children welcome. Pets welcome free of charge. Open all year. Bed and Breakfast from £20; Evening Meal (optional) from £14. **STB** ★★ *GUEST HOUSE.* **AA** ◆◆◆

**MOFFAT. Mrs Wells, Morlich House Licensed Guest House, Ballplay Road, Moffat DG10 9JU (01683 220589; Fax: 01683 221032).** In beautiful 'Burns Country', this superb, award-winning, Victorian country guest house is set in quiet elevated grounds overlooking the town and surrounding hills. Just five minutes' walk from town centre. Rooms are en suite with colour TV, radio alarm, tea/coffee, private bar and direct-dial telephone; four poster available. Evening meals (menu choice), licensed, private car park. Well behaved dogs welcome. Open February to November. JPC Merit Awards 1998. B&B from £20 per person, three-course evening meal from £9.50. Weekly terms available. **STB** ★★ *GUEST HOUSE.*
e-mail: morlich.house@ndirect.co.uk
website: www.morlich-house.ndirect.co.uk

**MOFFAT. Mrs Deakins, Annandale House, Moffat DG10 9SA (01683 221460).** Situated just five minutes walk from Moffat Town Centre and one mile off the M74, Annandale House is a haven of peace, surrounded by mature gardens with private parking. The three well-appointed spacious bedrooms all have central heating, tea/coffee making facilities and hairdryers. There is one en suite double with king-size bed, one twin and one family room. Well behaved pets welcome. TV lounge. Open all year. An ideal base for exploring South-West Scotland and the Scottish Borders. Bed and Breakfast from £17.50 per person per night (reduced rates for children). Non-smokers please.

**MOFFAT. Mr and Mrs Keyte, Queensberry House, 12 Beechgrove, Moffat DG10 9RS (01683 220538).** Queensberry House is a Listed Victorian town house in a quiet conservation area in Moffat. A four-star Scottish Tourist Board establishment, demonstrating the high standard of this family-run Bed and Breakfast. Accommodation comprises three double rooms, all with en suite facilities. Moffat is an attractive Borders spa town within easy reach of the beautiful Solway coast and Edinburgh. The town offers many facilities such as an attractive park, many shops, hotels and restaurants. Sporting facilities cater for golf, bowls and tennis; and the surrounding countryside is excellent for walkers. Moffat has also won the Britain in Bloom award. Bed and Breakfast from £20. **STB** ★★★★ *B&B.*
e-mail: queensberryhouse@amserve.net

---

# FHG
## Visit the FHG website
## www.holidayguides.com
for details of the wide choice of accommodation
featured in the full range of FHG titles

**Dumfries & Galloway** 343

**NEWTON STEWART. Miss K.R. Wallace, Kiloran, 6 Auchendoon Road, Newton Stewart DG8 6HD (01671 402818).** Spacious, luxury bungalow set in secluded landscaped garden, with panoramic views of Galloway Hills, in quiet area of Newton Stewart. Enjoy comfortable accommodation on one level in two double bedrooms (one twin-bedded); bathroom with shower; cloakroom with WC. Soap and towels supplied. Lounge (colour TV), dining room where good home cooking is served (menu changed daily). Central heating. Children over 10 years welcome. Dogs allowed, but not in house. Ideal centre for touring Galloway. Safe, sandy beaches 12 miles. Within easy reach of hill walking, golf, riding and trekking. Terms on request. SAE, please, for Evening Dinner, Bed and Breakfast or Bed and Breakfast only. For Auchendoon Road, turn at Dashwood Square to Princes Street, then second on right. Ample parking available. **STB ★★** *B&B*.

**PORTPATRICK. Mark & Karen Bevan, The Knowe Guest House, 1 North Crescent, Portpatrick, Stranraer DG9 8SX (Tel & Fax: 01776 810441).** Occupies a slightly elevated, picturesque position with unrestricted views over the harbour, and across the sea to Northern Ireland, from en suite guest rooms, conservatory dining room and patio. Centrally heated throughout; all rooms have tea/coffee making facilities, colour TV and shaver sockets. Packed lunches are available. Convenient free public parking. The port, situated at the foot of rocky cliffs, and surrounded by secluded bays and beaches, is the start of the Southern Upland Way and also provides excellent opportunities for angling, golf, bowls, tennis and putting. It lies eight miles south of Stranraer where the A77 and A75 converge. **STB ★★** *GUEST HOUSE*.

**WHITHORN. Barbara Fleming, Belmont, St. John Street, Whithorn, Newton Stewart DG8 8PG (01988 500890).** Belmont is ideal for a quiet relaxing holiday in a very beautiful and historically interesting part of Galloway – the Whithorn Dig is nearby. There is an attractive sitting/diningroom, colour TV is available downstairs and in bedrooms. There are two bathrooms. Various and generous meals are provided, with tea/coffee making faciltiies in all bedrooms. All guests (maximum five) are given a warm welcome and well behaved pets are allowed (two resident cats and one dog). Prices from £18 per person per night.

---

*The* **FHG**
**GOLF GUIDE**
*Where to Play Where to Stay*
**2001**

Available from most bookshops, the 2001 edition of **THE GOLF GUIDE** covers details of every UK golf course – well over 2500 entries – for holiday or business golf. Hundreds of hotel entries offer convenient accommodation, accompanying details of the courses – the 'pro', par score, length etc.

*In association with 'Golf Monthly' and including the Ryder Cup Report as well as Holiday Golf in Ireland, France, Portugal, Spain, The USA, South Africa and Thailand .*

**£9.99 from bookshops or £10.50 including postage (UK only) from FHG Publications, Abbey Mill Business Centre, Paisley PA1 ITJ**

---

**When making enquiries please mention FHG Publications**

# DUNBARTONSHIRE

**See also Colour Display Advertisement** **LOCH LOMOND. Inverbeg Inn, Inverbeg, Luss, Loch Lomond G83 8PD (01436 860678; Fax: 01436 860686).** The Inverbeg Inn stands on the banks of Scotland's most famous stretch of water, Loch Lomond, just beyond the village of Luss. Surrounded by breathtaking scenery, history and culture, and only 30 minutes from Glasgow. Bordering on Rob Roy country, and en route to the West Coast through Arrochar, and the North by Rannoch Moor, the location for touring and sightseeing is second to none. The hotel offers a choice of accommodation from comfy individuality to sheer luxury. The three suites in the Lodge are perfect for that special occasion. Eat in style in the traditional diningroom, offering fresh local produce or take a snack in the Caledonian Bar with Scottish real ale, or one of our fine range of whiskies. Open all year excluding Christmas and New Year. 18 en suite rooms. Major credit cards accepted. **STB ★★★★** *INN, WELCOME HOST,* e-mail: inverbeg@onyxnet.co.uk
website: www.scottish-selection.co.uk

**LUSS by. Mrs K. Carruthers, The Corries, Inverbeg, By Luss G83 8PD (Tel & Fax: 01436 860275).** In beautiful, easily accessible rural location, with panoramic views of Loch Lomond. Accommodation available in one twin, one double, one family rooms, all en suite. Children welcome. Ideal base for exploring the Trossachs, Rob Roy Country; Glasgow and Stirling within easy reach. Expect a very warm welcome to this family home. Bed and Breakfast from £25 single, from £20 per person in double/twin room.

# DUNDEE & ANGUS

**ARBROATH. Mrs A. Cheyne, Renmure Cottage, Friockheim, Arbroath DD11 4RZ (01674 820348).** A family-run, semi-self sufficient household where you will be welcomed as one of the family. Set on a quiet farm with spacious grounds. Ideal base for touring, golf, fishing, birdwatching, castles and Angus glens. We run only one guest bedroom, so there is lots of privacy and you will be made to feel special. Panoramic views from the conservatory dining room which is heated by a solid fuel stove and is candlelit in the evenings for romantic dinners. Bedroom is centrally heated with en suite bathroom, colour TV, tea/coffee making facilities. Bed and Breakfast from £20 per person. Evening Meals available. Home baking, home-made bread and preserves.

**BROUGHTY FERRY. Mrs M. Stafford, Abertay Guest House, 65 Monifieth Road, Broughty Ferry, Dundee DD5 2RW (01382 730381).** Abertay Guest House is situated close to Broughty Ferry's town centre with its wealth of shops, restaurants and pubs. Dundee city centre is approximately five miles away, easily reached by bus. There are many golf courses within reasonable driving distance, and the Angus countryside and glens are easily accessible. There are two family rooms, one double and two twin rooms, all en suite, and one single room with private facilities. All rooms are centrally heated, have tea/coffee making facilities and TV. Private parking is available at the rear of the house. Bed and Breakfast from £20 per person per night. **STB ★★★** *GUEST HOUSE.*

**Dundee & Angus** 345

**BROUGHTY FERRY. Mrs L. Berrie, St Helens Guest House, 25 Dalhousie Road, Broughty Ferry, Dundee DD5 2SP (Tel & Fax: 01382 774657).** A warm welcome awaits you. St Helens is a family-run establishment which provides an ideal base to discover Dundee whether on business or pleasure. A ten minute drive from Dundee is Broughty Ferry where there is a great selection of pubs and restaurants and which is only a short drive away from several golf courses including Carnoustie and St Andrews. All bedrooms en suite, colour TV, coffee and tea making facilities, hairdryer. Laundry service. Courtesy mini bus for wedding and golf parties. Bed and Breakfast £17.50 - £25 per person. **STB ★★★** *GUEST HOUSE*

**DUNDEE. Douglas and Barbara Robbie, Dunlaw House Hotel, 10 Union Terrace (off Constitution Road), Dundee DD3 6JD (Tel & Fax: 01382 221703).** We would like to welcome you to our "home" and garden, located on a quiet terrace in a conservation area of the city but only five minutes to the centre. Our reputation is based on cleanliness, personal attention and freshly prepared good home cooking; steaks a speciality. Most rooms have private facilities. Douglas specialises in golfing parties and is happy to advise and/or arrange your game or whole outing for you. If you decide to come to our hotel, we shall do our utmost to make your function, business trip or holiday a memorable one.
e-mail: dunlaw@talk21.com
website: www.vacations-in-scotland.co.uk

**EDZELL. Mrs A. McMurray, Inchcape, High Street, Edzell DD9 7TF (01356 647266).** Inchcape is situated within the lovely village of Edzell, four miles off the A90 Dundee to Aberdeen road. With the Angus glens and rivers all within easy reach we are the perfect base for walking, cycling, fishing and golfing. Edzell golf course is just across the road and 10% off green fees can be arranged. Three bedrooms all recently refurbished and all en suite. Tea/coffee making facilities, drying room available. TV lounge. Double/twin £16 per person. Single £18. **STB ★★★** *B&B*.
e-mail: inchcapebb.edzell@virgin.net

**LETHAM. Mrs J. Stewart, Woodville, Heathercroft, Guthrie Street, Letham, By Forfar DD8 2PS (01307 818090).** A warm welcome awaits you. Excellent food and accommodation. Two twin rooms are available each with wash-hand basin, tea/coffee making facilities, TV. Letham is a village set in the middle of Angus. Excellent for touring Glens of Angus, Royal Deeside and Glamis. It is also near to new Pictavia Centre. Birdwatching, walks, fishing, golf, Pictish interest. Aberdeen, St Andrews and Edinburgh are all within easy reach. Bed and Breakfast from £18 per person, Bed and Breakfast and Evening Meal from £28. Open January to December excluding Christmas and New Year.

---

# FREE or REDUCED RATE entry to Holiday Visits and Attractions — see our READERS' OFFER VOUCHERS on pages 43-60

# EDINBURGH & LOTHIANS

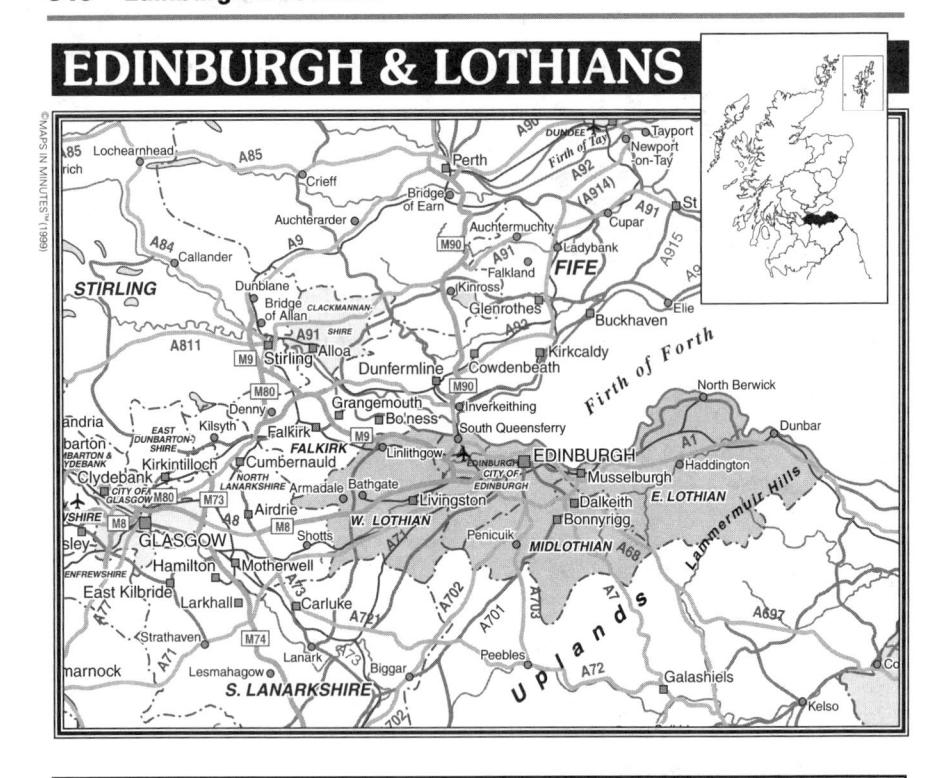

## Arthur's View Guest House

Welcome to the City of Edinburgh and to the Arthur's View Guest House, conveniently located for all major attractions including the Castle and Royal Scottish Museum.

It is owned by James and Elizabeth Woodrow, whose attention to detail ensures the warm, friendly atmosphere for which their establishments have become renowned.

*All the attractively furnished bedrooms are equipped with en suite facilities, colour television, tea/coffee hospitality tray, direct-dial telephone, hairdryer etc. There is an elegant and restful residents' lounge.*

**PRIVATE CAR PARK.**

*10 Mayfield Gardens, Edinburgh EH9 2BZ*
*Tel: 0131-667 3468 • Fax: 0131-662 4232*
*e-mail: arthursview@aol.com*

## Southdown Guest House

A warm welcome and personal service is assured at the Southdown Guest House. Conveniently situated on a main bus route in a prime residential area just ten minutes from Princes Street, The Castle, Holyrood Palace and several golf courses are within easy reach. We have several full en suite rooms available while all others have private showers. Cable/Sky TV, tea/coffee making facilities. There is a comfortable residents' lounge with colour TV. Full Scottish Breakfast with home produce our speciality. Bed and Breakfast from £17.50 (singles from £22.50). Reduced rates for families and groups. Own key access all day. Full central heating and Fire Certificate. Private car park. Cot, high chair and babysitting service available. **Mastercard/Visa accepted.**

### 20 Craigmillar Park, Edinburgh EH16 5PS
### Telephone: 0131-667 2410; Fax: 0131-667 6056
### e-mail: muriel@southdownguesthouse.fsnet.co.uk

FHG

---

**EAST CALDER. Ashcroft Farmhouse, East Calder, Near Edinburgh EH53 0ET (01506 881810; Fax: 01506 884327).** Ashcroft is a modern tastefully decorated farmhouse. Set in five acres, the farmhouse is surrounded by countryside and yet is only ten miles from Edinburgh city centre, providing the perfect setting for a peaceful break or a busy golfing, sightseeing or touring holiday. Two family, three twin and one double bedroom with four-poster bed, all with en suite facilities, remote-control colour TV and a hospitality tray with tea/coffee and shortbread. Ample parking. Special diets catered for. Completely non-smoking. Pets not allowed indoors. Bed and Breakfast from £28 per person per night. **STB** ★★★★ *GUEST HOUSE*, **AA** ♦♦♦♦♦ 
e-mail: scottashcroft7@aol.com
website: www.ashcroft-farmhouse.com

**EDINBURGH. Mr T. C. Borthwick, Belford Guest House, 13 Blacket Avenue, Edinburgh EH9 1RR (0131-667 2422; Fax: 0131-667 7508).** Belford House, lying only a short distance from the city centre, is an ideal base from which to explore Edinburgh's historic past, and rests in a quiet tree-lined avenue running between the A7 and the A701. An attractive stone Victorian terrace house, Belford House is one mile from Princes Street and close to Holyrood Park, and the Royal Commonwealth Pool. The house is only four miles from the Straiton Junction on the Edinburgh City By-Pass. An excellent bus service provides easy transport to all the attractions of the capital. Some bedrooms have en suite facilities and all are comfortably furnished with washbasins, tea/coffee hospitality tray and colour TV. An attractive dining room offers wholesome full Scottish breakfasts to prepare guests for a full day's touring in the capital. Bed and Breakfast Double/Twin en suite from £25.00, Single en suite from £35.00, Double/Twin standard £20.00, Single standard £25.00. **STB** ★★ *GUEST HOUSE.*

## ALLISON HOUSE HOTEL
15/17 Mayfield Gardens, Edinburgh EH9 2AX
Tel: 0131 6678049 • Fax: 0131 6675001
• e-mail: enquiry@allisonhousehotel.com
• website: www.allisonhousehotel.com

Personal service is assured at the Allison House Hotel where David and Anne-Marie Hinnrichs take great pride and care in the welcoming their guests receive. Situated close to the major air, road and rail links around Edinburgh yet only 10 minutes from the city centre. The hotel boasts an elegant restaurant, comfortable residents lounge with satellite TV, and 23 bedrooms all with private bathroom/shower-room offering the essentials you will need to make your stay enjoyable

AA/RAC ★  STB ★★★

*See also Colour Advertisement*

**EDINBURGH. Mr and Mrs Cecco, Villa Nina Guest House, 39 Leamington Terrace, Edinburgh EH10 4JS (Tel & Fax: 0131-229 2644).** Very comfortable Victorian terraced house situated in a quiet residential part of the City, yet only ten minutes' walk to Princes Street, the Castle, theatres, shops and major attractions. TV in all rooms. Some rooms with private showers. Full cooked breakfast. Closed Christmas and New Year. Member STB, GHA, AA. Bed and Breakfast from £16.00 per person.
**e-mail: villanina@amserve.net**

**EDINBURGH. Mrs Rhoda Mitchell, Hopetoun Guest House, 15 Mayfield Road, Edinburgh EH9 2NG (0131-667 7691; Fax 0131-466 1691).** "Which?" Good Bed and Breakfast Guide. COMPLETELY NON-SMOKING. Hopetoun is a small, friendly, family-run guest house situated close to Edinburgh University, one-and-a-half miles south of Princes Street, and with an excellent bus service to the city centre. Very comfortable accommodation is offered in a completely smoke-free environment. Having only three guest bedrooms, and now offering private facilities, the owner prides herself in ensuring personal attention to all guests in a friendly, informal atmosphere. All rooms have central heating, washbasin, colour TV and tea/coffee making facilities. Parking is also available. Bed and Breakfast from £20 to £30. Visa/Access/Delta. **STB ★★★ GUEST HOUSE.**
**e-mail: hopetoun@aol.com**
**website: members.aol.com/hopetoun**

**EDINBURGH. Mr and Mrs Derek Mowat, Dunstane House Hotel, 4 West Coates, Haymarket, Edinburgh EH12 5JQ (Tel & Fax 0131-337 6169).** A beautiful detached mansion of historic and architectural interest, set in delightful gardens. Handy for town centre, good bus service, railway station, golf courses and 15 minutes by car to airport, five minutes to Princes Street. A friendly welcome awaits you at this private, family-run hotel, open all year. Bedrooms are all newly refurbished with en suite facilities, direct-dial telephone, hairdryer, colour TV and welcome tray. Four-poster rooms available. Licensed residents' bar. Private secluded car park. Bed and Breakfast from £33.50 to £49 per person. Special winter breaks available. **STB ★★★** *HOTEL.* **AA ◆◆◆◆**

---

*When making enquiries or bookings,*
*a stamped addressed envelope is always appreciated*

## The Hotels, Guesthouse & B&B Association
### (Edinburgh and Lothians)

The Association is a group of Edinburgh Hotel and Guesthouse owners who believe that personal service and attention to the little details is so important. Within the Edinburgh section of this book you will find a selection of independent Hotels and Guesthouses, all privately owned and run, each offering you, the customer, something that is missing in so many of the larger hotels these days, *"The Personal Touch"*.

Whether you are on business or holiday, you can be sure of one thing – personal service from some of the most experienced Hotel/Guesthouse owners in Edinburgh.
For more details visit our website:
www.edinburgh-hotel-guesthouse-association.com
**SEE ALSO COLOUR ADVERTISEMENT ON INSIDE BACK COVER**

# INTERNATIONAL GUEST HOUSE

**AA ♦♦♦♦**    37 Mayfield Gardens, Edinburgh EH9 2BX    **STB ★★★★**
Tel: 0131 667 2511    Fax: 0131 667 1112    Mrs Niven
E-mail: intergh@easynet.co.uk
Internet: www.accommodation-edinburgh.com

**The International** is an attractive, stone-built Victorian terrace house conveniently situated one-and-a-half-miles south of Princes Street on the main A701 and only four miles from the Straiton junction on the Edinburgh city by-pass. Lying on the main bus route, access to the city centre is easy. **The International** has ample private parking. Visitors who require a touch of luxury a little out of the ordinary can do no better than visit **The International**. All bedrooms have en suite, direct dial telephone, colour television and tea/coffee maker facilities. The decor is outstanding with ornate plasterwork on the ceilings as fine as in 'The New Town.' Some rooms enjoy magnificent views across to the extinct volcano of Arthur's Seat. The full Scottish breakfasts served on the finest bone china are a delight.

*19th century setting with 21st century facilities!*
In Britain magazine has rated **The International** as their 'find' in all Edinburgh.

# Edinburgh & Lothians

**EDINBURGH. Mr Ian McCrae, 44 East Claremont Street, Edinburgh, EH7 4JR (Tel & Fax 0131-556 2610).** Situated in the Victorian part of Edinburgh's New Town, McCrae's is only 15 minutes' walk from the city centre giving easy access to all attractions. The comfortable accommodation comprises three twin-bedded rooms all at ground level. All rooms have en suite facilities, central heating, colour TV, radio/alarm, hairdryer and tea/coffee trays. Iron available on request. A full traditional breakfast is served using fresh local produce. Unrestricted on-street parking immediately outside. Rates from £24.50 per person per night sharing or from £27.50 for single occupation. Reductions available for long stays. Visa/Mastercard accepted. Open all year. **STB** ★★★ *B&B*.
e-mail: mccraes.bandb@lineone.net
website: http://website.lineone.net/~mccraes.bandb

**EDINBURGH. Mrs H. Donaldson, "Invermark", 60 Polwarth Terrace, Edinburgh EH11 1NJ (0131-337 1066).** "Invermark" is a Georgian semi-detached villa situated in quiet surburbs on the main bus route into the city and only five minutes by car. Edinburgh bypass – Lothianburn Junction – two miles – left Balcarres Street, right Myreside Road – Grays Loan– right into Polwarth Terrace. Edinburgh is one of Europe's most splendid cities, famous for its dramatic beauty, historic interest, extensive shopping and dining facilities. There is a park to the rear of the house. Accommodation consists of one single, one twin and one family rooms (with tea/coffee making facilities); TV lounge/diningroom; toilet; bathroom/shower. Non-smoking accommodation available. Friendly atmosphere. Children and dogs welcome. Bed and Breakfast from £20. Reductions for children.

**EDINBURGH. Alan and Angela Vidler, Rowan House, 13 Glenorchy Terrace, Edinburgh EH9 2DQ (Tel & Fax: 0131-667 2463).** Elegant Victorian home, quietly located in an attractive area of the city only 10 minutes by bus from the centre. Rooms have colour TV, tea/coffee making facilities and are mostly en suite. Children welcome at reduced rates. Convenient for Castle, Royal Mile, University, theatres and restaurants. Located just off the A701 from the south (turn left at Bright's Crescent, just off Mayfield Gardens) and close to major roads A1, A7 and A702. Unrestricted street parking. Bed and Breakfast from £23 per person. **STB/AA** ★★★ *B&B*.
e-mail: rowanhouse@hotmail.com

**EDINBURGH. Mr and Mrs Birnie, Casa Buzzo, 8 Kilmaurs Road, Edinburgh EH16 5DA (0131-667 8998).** Casa Buzzo is a Victorian style guest house, situated just ten minutes from Edinburgh city centre, in a quiet residential area serviced by a very good bus route. We are a family-run, non-smoking establishment offering accommodation in large, well-equipped bedrooms, two of which are en suite. Ample parking. Bed and Breakfast from £17 to £24 per person per night, reduced rates considered for families and groups. Open all year. **STB** ★★★ *GUEST HOUSE*.

**EDINBURGH. Mrs Saddlah, Harvest Guest House, 33 Straiton Place, Portobello, Edinburgh EH15 2BH (0131-657 3160; Fax: 0131-468 7028).** Georgian house beside Portobello Beach. Easy access to Edinburgh City Centre, close to shops, restaurants, swimming pool and A1. Parking, central heating, tea/coffee making facilities and colour TV. En suites available. £15 to £25 per night. From city centre - Princes Street, London Road, Portobello Road, Portobello High Street, Bellfield Street then to Straiton Place. From city centre bypass - A1 Edinburgh direction, look for Portobello sign, Portobello Road, Portobello High Street, Bellfield Street then to Straiton Place. **STB** ★ *GUEST HOUSE*.
e-mail: sadol@cabeinet.co.uk

## CENTRAL EDINBURGH

**AVERON GUEST HOUSE**

44 Gilmore Place
Central Edinburgh EH3 9NQ
PRIVATE CAR PARK
Comfortable Georgian Town House
Bed and Breakfast from £16
10 Minutes Walk to Castle and Princes Street
Close to International Conference Centre
*ALL CREDIT CARDS WELCOME*

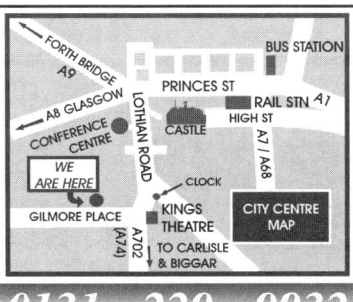

**AA** **RAC**

*0131 - 229 - 9932*

---

**EDINBURGH. Mr and Mrs McCulloch, Lorne Villa Guest House, 9 East Mayfield, Edinburgh EH9 1SD (Tel & Fax: 0131-667 7159).** The warmest of welcomes will be yours to our family run Victorian guest house, situated in a quiet street just one mile from the city centre and a short stroll from the main bus route. Traditional bed and breakfast in comfortable, well-appointed rooms tastefully decorated. Convenient for Edinburgh University, The Royal College of Surgeons and the Commonwealth Pool, also the perfect base from which to explore Edinburgh and beyond. Single, twin, double and family rooms available, each with TV, hairdryer and hospitality tray. En suite and ground floor rooms available. Choice of breakfasts. Evening meal by arrangement, special diets catered for. restricted smoking. Private parking. Payphone. Children welcome, pets by arrangement. Open all year. **STB** ★★★ *GUEST HOUSE.* 
e-mail: lornevilla@cableinet.co.uk
website: www.lornevilla.pwp.blueyonder.co.uk

**EDINBURGH. David and Angela Martin, Spylaw Bank House, 2 Spylaw Avenue, Colinton, Edinburgh EH13 0LR (0131-441 5022).** Elegant Georgian Country House built around 1790, situated within the city of Edinburgh. It has a secluded position in walled gardens close to Colinton village and three miles from the city centre. Luxuriously appointed en suite bedrooms with many personal touches. Relax in the original drawing room with its open fire and antique furnishings and take breakfast in the period dining room. Ideally situated for sightseeing in Edinburgh and touring the Borders, Fife and Perthshire. Five miles from airport, one from city by-pass. Ample parking. Frequent buses to city centre – a 15 minute journey. Bed and Breakfast from £25 per person. **STB** ★★★★ *B&B.* 
e-mail: angela@spylawbank.freeserve.co.uk
website: www.spylawbank.freeserve.co.uk

**EDINBURGH. Sonas Guest House, 3 East Mayfield, Edinburgh EH9 1SD (0131-667 2781; Fax: 0131-667 0454)** Sonas Guest House is a lovely stone terraced building, with well proportioned bright rooms all with en suite bathrooms. Warm, clean and comfortable. Sonas offers a delightful stay for your trip to Edinburgh. Just over one mile from the city centre, leave your car in our free car park and walk into town or take one of several frequent buses. Sonas is an old Gaelic word for bliss! 
e-mail: info@sonasguesthouse.com

**EDINBURGH. Mrs Maureen Sandilands, Sandilands House, 25 Queensferry Road, Edinburgh EH4 3HB (0131-332 2057; Fax 0131-315 4476).** Sandilands House is ideally located five minutes from Edinburgh's city centre by bus with its own guests' private parking. A distinctive and attractive detached bungalow in its own gardens with excellent bus service to the city centre or a short walk to the city's West End; also near to Murrayfield Stadium. Enjoy the friendly welcome and relax in the well-furnished and tastefully decorated accommodation with en suite facilities. All rooms have central heating, colour TV, hair dryer, tea/coffee making facilities, etc. Two four-poster bedrooms. Full Scottish breakfast is included. Family rooms available and discounts of 50% apply for children under 12 years sharing with adults. Open all season. Terms from £20 to £35 per person sharing for en suite double/twin room or from £35 to £50 for single occupancy. **STB ★★★★** *B&B.* 
e-mail: sandilandshouse@aol.com
website: www.guesthouse-sandilands.com

**EDINBURGH. James and Ann O'Connor, Emerald House, 3 Drum Street, Gilmerton, Edinburgh EH17 8QQ (0131 664 5918).** Family-run Victorian villa situated on bus route into city centre (15 minutes). This villa retains much of its original character and offers a warm and friendly atmosphere to all. Nearby attractions - Butterfly Farm, golf, skiing, swimming. 20 minutes from airport, 10 minutes from main national routes, Evening Meal on request. Comfortable bedrooms with good facilities, plus a good breakfast menu. We offer a first class service. Children over four years welcome. Bed and Breakfast from £20. Open all year except Christmas. **STB ★★** *GUEST HOUSE.*

**EDINBURGH. The Ivy Guest House, 7 Mayfield Gardens, Edinburgh EH9 2AX (0131-667 3411; Fax: 0131-620 1422).** Bed and Breakfast in a comfortable Victorian villa. Open all year round. Private car park. Close to city centre and all its cultural attractions with excellent public transport and taxi services available on the door step. Many local sports facilities (booking assistance available). All rooms have central heating, washbasins, colour TV and tea/coffee making facilities. Choice of en suite or standard rooms, all power showers. Public phone. Large selection of eating establishments nearby. A substantial Scottish breakfast and warm welcome is assured, courtesy of Don and Dolly Green. Terms from £18 per person per night. **STB ★★★** *GUEST HOUSE.* **AA ♦♦♦, RAC ♦♦♦♦**.
e-mail: don@ivyguesthouse.com 
website: www.ivyguesthouse.com

---

# FHG

PLEASE MENTION THIS GUIDE WHEN YOU WRITE

OR PHONE TO ENQUIRE ABOUT ACCOMMODATION

IF YOU ARE WRITING, A STAMPED, ADDRESSED

ENVELOPE IS ALWAYS APPRECIATED

**EDINBURGH. Angus Beag Guest House, 5 Windsor Street, Edinburgh EH7 5LA (0131-556 1905).** City centre Georgian guest house close to all amenities. 10 minutes Princes Street, adjacent Playhouse Theatre, and 10 minutes from railway station and airport buses. Lots of tourist attractions worth a visit e.g.: Princes Sreet., Carlton Hill, The Castle, Holyrood House, John Knox House and many more. All rooms have washbasins, shower, TV, tea/coffee facilities; one en suite. Delicious full Scottish breakfast available. Terms from £19 per person per night.

**EDINBURGH. Rothesay Hotel, 8 Rothesay Place, Edinburgh EH3 7SL (0131-225 4125; Fax: 0131-220 4350).** Within Edinburgh's Georgian New Town, situated five minutes' walk from Princes Street – Edinburgh's shopping and commercial centre. 36 rooms with private bathroom and colour TV, tea/coffee facilities. Elevator. Bar and restaurant where Traditional Scottish Breakfast is served. Children welcome. Reasonable terms, open all year. Contact Mr Fariday. **STB ★★ HOTEL. AA ★★.**
e-mail: info@rothesay.hotel.demon.co.uk
website: www.rothesay-hotel.com

**EDINBURGH. Kenvie Guest House, 16 Kilmaurs Road, Edinburgh EH16 5DA (0131-668 1964; Fax: 0131-668 1926).** A charming and comfortable Victorian town house situated in a quiet and pleasant residential part of the city, approximately one mile south of the centre and one small block from Main Road (A7) leading to the City and Bypass to all routes. Excellent bus service. We offer for your comfort, complimentary tea/coffee, central heating, colour TV and No Smoking rooms. En suite rooms available. Lovely breakfasts and lots of additional caring touches. A warm and friendly welcome is guaranteed from Richard and Dorothy.
e-mail: dorothy@kenvie.co.uk

**EDINBURGH. Hotel Ritz, 14, 16 & 18 Grosvenor Street. Edinburgh EH12 5EG (0131-337 4315; Fax: 0131-346 0597).** A warm welcome awaits you at this privately owned and managed hotel within 10 minutes' walk of Princes Street with its excellent shopping facilities on one side and the beautiful gardens overshadowed by Edinburgh Castle on the other: bus service takes visitors to the many historic places of interest in the city. There are 36 bedrooms, all with private facilities, colour TV, telephone, hair dryer, trouser press, radio and tea making facilities: four-poster beds on request. Comfortable residents' lounge and well stocked Cocktail Bar. Central heating. Brochure available.

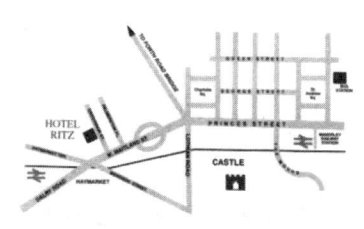

*See also Colour Display Advertisement*

**EDINBURGH. Castle Park Guest House, 75 Gilmore Place, Edinburgh EH3 9NU (0131-229 1215; Fax: 0131-229 1223).** A warm welcome awaits you at our family-run guest house, close to the King's Theatre, conference centre and city centre. Travel along the Royal Mile with Edinburgh Castle at one end and the Palace of Holyrood, the Queen's official Scottish residence, at the other. All rooms are tastefully decorated with colour TV and tea/coffee making facilities and are centrally heated throughout. Twin, single and en suite rooms available. Pleasant diningroom where guests can enjoy a hearty breakfast. Children welcome; special prices. Off street parking. Full Scottish/ Continental breakfast. Bed and Breakfast from £17.50 to £25 per person.

**EDINBURGH. Crion Guest House, 33 Minto Street, Edinburgh EH9 2BT (0131-667 2708; Fax: 0131-662 1946).** Crion Guest House is an attractive Georgian House situated in the Newington area of Edinburgh, one-and-a-quarter-miles from Princes Street. Near the Castle, Holyrood Palace, University and most attractions in the capital city. The house lies on a major bus route and is very well served by public transport. All rooms are decorated to a high standard. **STB ★★★** *GUEST HOUSE.* 
e-mail: w.cheape@gilmourhouse.freeserve.co.uk
website: www.edinburghbedbreakfast.com

**EDINBURGH. The Inverleith Hotel, 5 Inverleith Terrace, Edinburgh EH3 5NS (0131-556 2745; Fax: 0131-557 0433).** The Inverleith Hotel is a small private hotel, dating back to 1860, nestling in the quiet area of Inverleith yet only 10 minutes' away from the hub of city life. We have a residents' bar with a selection of fine wines, Scottish malt whiskies, beers and spirits. All rooms have en suite, with direct dial telephones and tea and coffee making facilities. To start your day cereals and Full Scottish Breakfast are offered in our Victorian breakfast room, on the ground floor. The hotel has a completely non-smoking policy. Credit cards accepted. Group discounts available. 
e-mail: Hotel@5Inverleith.freeserve.co.uk
website: www.inverleithhotel.co.uk

**EDINBURGH. The Afton Town House, 6 Grosvenor Crescent, Edinburgh EH12 5EP (0131-225 7033; Fax: 0131-225 7044).** Centrally located in an elegant West End crescent with private gardens opposite, a few minutes' walk from Princes Street, the International Conference Centre and a whole range of visitor attractions. The comfortable, clean and spacious bedrooms all have shower and toilet (some also have bath), tea and coffee tray, TV, direct-dial telephone, radio, hairdryer, modem point and trouser press. Amenities include public bar, TV lounge with snooker table, babysitting (by arrangement), private parking. At the Afton Town House we strive to enhance the visitor's experience through the welcome and the high level of servive we extend to all our guests. 
e-mail: afton.town.house@scotland.com

**EDINBURGH. Barony House, 4 Queens Crescent, Edinburgh EH9 2AZ (Freephone 0800 980 4806; Fax: 0131-667 6833).** This Victorian detached villa is situated in a quiet residential area just off the main road but convenient for the city centre and all major attractions. The proprietor is famous for her warm welcome and quality of service. Accommodation is in spacious, comfortable and attractively furnished rooms, all with central heating, direct-dial telephone, colour TV, hair dryers and tea/coffee making facilities. There is a choice of super king, double, twin and single bedded accommodation (some en suite). Full Scottish Breakfast. Evening Meals on request. Special diets catered for by previous arrangement. Open all year except Christmas. Bed and Breakfast from £18 per person. **STB ★★★** *GUEST HOUSE*

**EDINBURGH. Mrs Scott, Regent House Hotel, 3/5 Forth Street, Edinburgh EH1 3JX (0131-556 1616).** A small, friendly, family-run Georgian property set in the heart of the city centre, offering comfortable accommodation at very competitive rates for Bed and Breakfast. Situated only a few minutes' walk from the bus and train stations. Short and long term stays welcome. For families, groups or individuals on business or leisure, the hotel makes an ideal base to explore the beautiful city of Edinburgh. Self-catering accommodation also available.
e-mail: hotel@regenthouse.fsnet.co.uk 
website: www.regenthousehotel.co.uk

# Edinburgh & Lothians

**EDINBURGH (14 miles). Mrs Janet Burke, Patieshill Farm, Carlops, Penicuik EH26 9ND (01968 660551; Fax: 01968 661162).** This is a working hill sheep and cattle farm set in the midst of the Pentland Hills with panoramic views of the surrounding countryside yet only 20 minutes' drive from the city of Edinburgh. It is situated near the main A702 Edinburgh - Carlisle road close to the village of Carlops. Accommodation, all in separate guest wing, consists of two double and one twin-bedded rooms, all with full en suite facilities. Each room has tea/coffee making facilities, central heating and TV. This is an ideal base for many activities including fishing, golf, skiing, hill walking and pony trekking. A very warm and friendly welcome is extended to all guests. Bed and Breakfast from £20 with reductions for children. **STB** ★★★ *B&B*.

---

**GULLANE. Mrs Mary Chase, Jadini Garden, Goose Green, East Lothian EH31 2BA (01620 843343).** Comfortable family home in a delightful secluded walled garden, which guests are welcome to use. Private parking for up to eight cars. Gullane is a charming coastal village, well-known for its famous golf courses. Gullane Golf Club is just a few minutes' walk from Jadini Garden, and Muirfield is at the other end of the village. Nearby also are the beautiful sandy beaches bordered by cliffs and dunes, providing spectacular walks and seabird nature trails. Edinburgh is only 30 minutes by car. French, German and Spanish spoken. Bed and Breakfast from £20 to £30 per person.
e-mail: marychase@jadini.com
website: www.jadini.com

---

**INVERESK. 16 Carberry Road, Inveresk, Musselburgh EH21 7TN (0131-665 2107).** A lovely Victorian stone detached house situated in a quiet conservation village seven miles east of Edinburgh, overlooking fields and close to a lovely river walk and seaside with harbour. Buses from door to city, very close to sports centre with swimming pool and within easy distance of many golf courses. Spacious accommodation comprises one family room and two double rooms, all have central heating, colour TV and tea/coffee making facilities. Two large, fully equipped bathrooms adjacent. Parking in quiet side road or in garden if required by arrangement. Full cooked breakfast included from £20 per person per night; reduction for children.

---

**LINLITHGOW. Mr and Mrs R. Inglis, Thornton, Edinburgh Road, Linlithgow EH49 6AA (01506 844693; Fax: 01506 844876).** Comfortable family-run Victorian house with original features retained. Central situation in a peaceful location near the Union Canal in historic Linlithgow - only five minutes' walk from the town centre, Linlithgow Palace and railway station. This is a real home from home offering quality accommodation and friendly personal attention in a relaxing atmosphere. Open all year except Christmas and New Year. Excellent base for visiting Edinburgh, Stirling, Glasgow and central Scotland. Edinburgh Airport 10 miles. Early booking advisable. Credit Cards accepted. Terms from £22 per person. Recommended by "Which?" B&B Guide. **STB** ★★★★ *B&B*.
e-mail: inglisthornton@hotmail.com

---

**LINLITHGOW. Mrs J. Erskine, Arn House, Woodcockdale Farm, Lanark Road, Linlithgow EH49 6QE (01506 842088). Working farm, join in.** Look no further, be among one of the many guests who return to Woodcockdale - a busy dairy and sheep farm. Ideal base for touring central Scotland. The accommodation comprises two double and two family en suite rooms, one family and one twin bedded basic room. Tea/coffee making facilities, radio alarm and TV in all rooms. Children and pets welcome. Non smoking accommodation available. Situated one-and-a-half miles from Linlithgow on Lanark A706 road. Bed and Breakfast from £18 to £22 per person per night. Phone now!

**LIVINGSTON. Ms M. Easdale, 3 Cedric Rise, Dedridge East, Livingston EH54 6JR (Tel & Fax: 01506 413095).** A friendly welcome is assured. Open all year except Christmas and New Year, with central heating, a friendly welcome is assured in this New Town accommodation situated 15 miles from Edinburgh. Easy access to the motorway for visitors touring north or south. Fife, Borders, Trossachs, Loch Lomond, country parks in Lothian and Central regions, recreation park at Falkirk, all within easy driving distance. Four golf courses in the surrounding area. Accommodation comprises one twin-bedded, one single, one room with double and single beds and a triple bedded room (these rooms are located on the first and second floors). Tea/coffee making facilities and TV in all bedrooms. Bathroom with shower, two toilets; shared sitting/diningroom. Sorry, no pets. Parking nearby. No bookings from 3/12/00 to 25/2/01. Bed and Breakfast from £20.

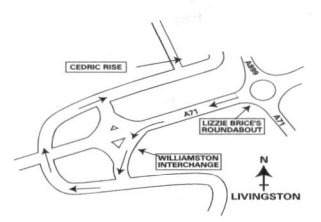

**MUSSELBURGH. Inveresk House, Inveresk Village, Musselburgh EH21 7UA (0131-665 5855; Fax: 0131-665 0578).** Historic Mansion house and award-winning Bed & Breakfast. Family-run "home from home". Situated in three acres of garden and woodland. Built on the site of a Roman settlement from 150 AD, the remains of a bathhouse can be found hidden in the garden. Three comfortable en suite rooms. Original art and antiques adorn the house. Edinburgh's Princes Street seven miles from Inveresk House. Good bus routes. Families welcome. Off street parking. Telephone first. Price from £35 per person. Family room £100 to £120.
e-mail: chute.inveresk@btinternet.com

**PATHHEAD. Mrs Anne Gordon, "Fairshiels", Blackshiels, Pathhead EH37 5SX (01875 833665).** We are situated on the A68, three miles south of Pathhead at the picturesque village of Fala. The house is an 18th century coaching inn (Listed building). All bedrooms have washbasins and tea/coffee making facilities; one is en suite. The rooms are comfortably furnished. We are within easy reach of Edinburgh and the Scottish Borders. A warm welcome is extended to all our guests - our aim is to make your stay a pleasant one. Cost is from £16 per person; children two years to 12 years £9.00, under two years FREE.

**SOUTH QUEENSFERRY. Calmyn and Gordon Lamb, Priory Lodge, 8 The Loan, South Queensferry, EH30 9NS (Tel & Fax: 0131-331 4345).** This comfortable family guest house is tastefully furnished to a high standard providing guests with a homely and relaxed atmosphere. Two double/twin, one four-poster, one family and one twin room. Each room has a remote-control colour television and hospitality tray, as well as its own private shower and toilet; fresh towels are provided daily. A tasteful hearty Scottish breakfast is served to you in our diningroom where you will enjoy our ancient Scottish theme. Separate television lounge for visitors. Private off-street parking. Non-smoking. Sorry no pets.

---

# FREE or REDUCED RATE entry to Holiday Visits and Attractions — see our READERS' OFFER VOUCHERS on pages 43-60

**Fife** 357

# FIFE

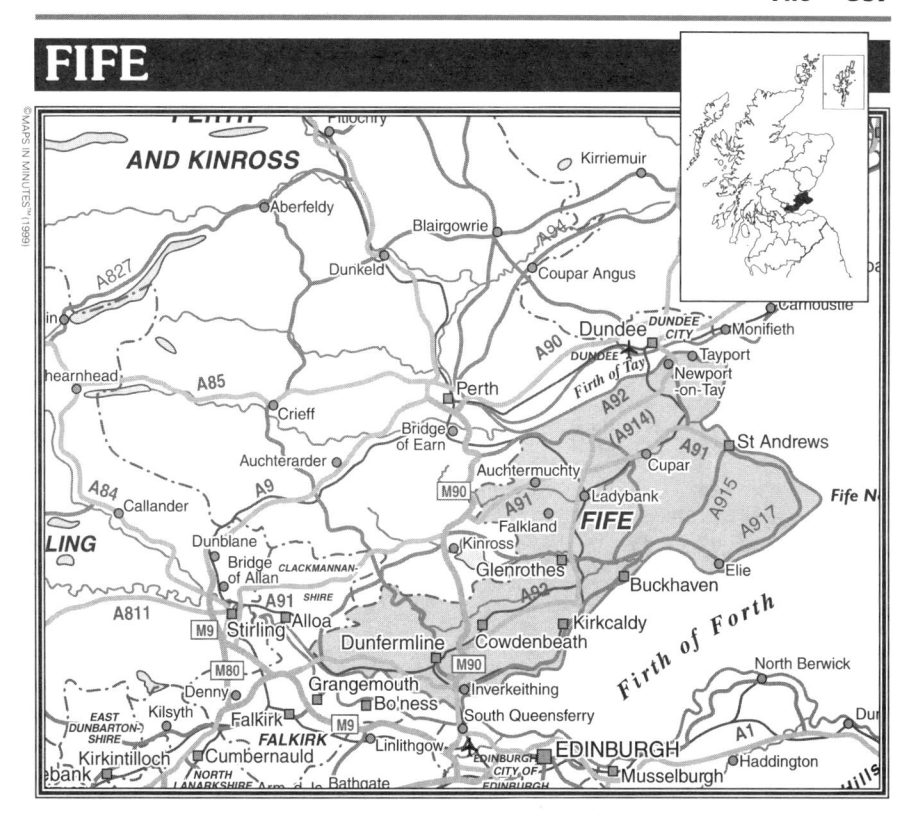

**COALTOWN OF WEMYSS. The Earl David Hotel, Main Street, Coaltown of Wemyss KY1 4NN (01592 654938).** The Earl David stands on the outskirts of the village. Built in 1911, it was named after David, Second Earl of Wemyss. The hotel is family-run by the Andersons and their first priority is the satisfaction and comfort of their guests. All rooms have en suite/private bathrooms, colour TV and tea-making facilities. There is a friendly bar where lunches and snacks are available and a restaurant catering for all tastes. As well as being central for all of Scotland – Edinburgh 45 minutes and the beautiful scenery of the Highlands two hours – Fife is world-famous for golf. 35 courses can be reached from the hotel within 45 minutes. Bed and Breakfast from £25.

**COWDENBEATH, Struan Bank Hotel, 74 Perth Road, Cowdenbeath KY4 9BG (01383 511057).** Family-run hotel situated in the town centre and convenient for the railway station. An excellent touring centre, ideal for golfers. There are two single, five double/twin and two family bedrooms, six of which are en suite. Full licence. Bed and Breakfast from £24 per person single, £20 per person twin. Evening meals available. Parking. Children and pets welcome. Further information on request from Hilary and Derek Hutton. **STB ★★** *GUEST HOUSE.*

**CUPAR (Near St. Andrews). Mrs M. Chrisp, Scotstarvit Farm, By Cupar KY15 5PA (Tel & Fax: 01334 653591).** Just off the A916, nestled by the 16th century ancient monument of Scotstarvit Tower and National Trust places of interest, our traditional stockrearing farm is five minutes from the market town of Cupar and the historic village of Ceres, with St Andrews only ten minutes' drive away. Explore the quaint, bustling fishing villages of the East Neuk of Fife after a fifteen minute drive. The cities of Edinburgh, Glasgow, Perth, Dundee and Aberdeen are all within easy reach for a day trip. Scotstarvit is a peaceful, unspoilt scenic spot giving you the best of both worlds by being in an enviable central location for all leisure activities and entertainment including the numerous golf courses on our doorstep, or you may enjoy the relaxing, peaceful atmosphere and wonderful panoramic scenery in our comfortable characteristic farmhouse, where you will enjoy a hearty breakfast. Open April to October. From £16 per night. Delightful self-catering cottage also available - prices from £140 to £300 per week (**STB ★★★** *SELF-CATERING*).
e-mail: chrisp.scotstarvit@uk.gateway.net

**DUNFERMLINE. St. Margaret's Hotel, 1 Canmore Street, Dunfermline KY12 7NU (01383 722501).** Situated next to Dunfermline Abbey in the old town centre, this elegant hotel is enriched with historical tradition and offers an enchanting atmosphere. All bedrooms are en suite and offer direct-dial telephone, remote control colour TV, hairdryer, trouser press, tea and coffee making facilities. In addition our honeymoon suite offers an attractive lounge area. We have our own Cloisters à la carte Restaurant and Cocktail Bar, Cafe Lounge Bar and adjoining nightclub. All enquiries welcome.

**DUNFERMLINE. Mr Alan Morrison, Jacobean Hotel, Halbeath Road, Dunfermline KY11 4LF (01383 732152).** The Jacobean is a small family-run hotel on the eastern outskirts of Dunfermline. It is situated less than half-a-mile away from Junction 3 of the M90. The hotel is set in a quiet, secluded spot with adequate parking for up to 20 cars. The eight twin rooms (one double, seven twin - all en suite) are tastefully decorated and comfortably furnished. Each has a TV, tea/coffee making facilities and a small desk for those who require to work in the comfort of their room. Bed and Breakfast from £24 per person per night (double/twin) to £30 per night (single). Discounts for longer stays.

**FALKLAND. Mrs C. Wilson, The Red House, Freuchie, Falkland KY15 7EZ (01337 857555).** Built in 1736, this traditional house is situated in a lovely village in the rural heart of the Kingdom. Less than one hour's drive from Edinburgh, Stirling and Pitlochry and a stone's throw from St. Andrews, Perth and Dundee. Golfers love it here - over 50 courses within a 30 mile radius including Ladybank, Carnoustie and the Old Course. National Trust properties, especially Falkland Palace, convenient, as are clean beaches, sports facilities, entertainment, crafts and shops. Start your day with a wholesome breakfast served in the conservatory overlooking our beautiful mature gardens. Come and savour Scottish hospitality at its best.

**KIRKCALDY. Mrs A. Crawford, Crawford Hall, 2 Kinghorn Road, Kirkcaldy KY1 1SU (01592 262658).** Crawford Hall is a large rambling old house over 100 years old and was once the local vicarage. Spacious rooms and some sea views. Teasmaid and colour TV in all rooms. Guests have use of hairdryer and iron on request. Pay phone. Ample private parking. Lovely walled gardens. Five minutes' walk to town centre. Handy for golf course, cinema, theatre and ice rinks. Kirkcaldy also boasts two beautiful parks. Evening meal by arrangement. Double and twin rooms £18 per person, Single room £20 per person.

**KIRKCALDY. Mr James Dickson, Bennochy Bank, 26A Carlyle Road, Kirkcaldy KY1 1DB (01592 200733).** This privately run B&B, with private off road parking, enjoys a central location which is close to rail and bus stations, museum, theatre, all local amenities and entertainment centre. The house has been totally refurbished and upgraded. A warm welcome awaits along with colour TV, tea and coffee making facilities, washbasins and centrally heated rooms. En suite is available along with separate toilet and shower room. **STB ★★★** *B&B*.

**LEVEN. Mrs MacDonald, Dunclutha Guest House, 16 Victoria Road, Leven KY8 4EX (01333 425515; Fax: 01333 422311).** This quiet Victorian former rectory provides the ideal location for touring. Ideal base for golf enthusiasts, within easy reach of 26 golf courses and only 14 miles from St. Andrews. 40 minutes from Edinburgh Airport, Perth and 30-35 minutes from Dundee. Facilities include three en suite rooms - one double, one twin, one family (sleeps three to four), one family (sleeps three) with private bathroom. Colour TV and tea/coffee facilities in all rooms, cot available. Visitors' lounge with TV. Most credit cards accepted. Open all year. Terms from £25 per person per night. Non-smoking. **STB ★★★** *GUEST HOUSE*
e-mail: pam.leven@dunclutha-accomm.demon.co.uk
website: www.dunclutha-accomm.demon.co.uk

**LEVEN By. Mrs Audrey Hamilton, Duniface Farm, By Leven KY8 5RH (Tel & Fax: 01333 350272).** **Working farm.** Spacious, peaceful Victorian farmhouse with lovely gardens, situated on A915, is ideally placed for exploring historic Fife, playing numerous golf courses and visiting the endless places of interest within the county and surrounding area. There is a wide variety of both indoor and outdoor activities nearby and a choice of many excellent eating houses. St Andrews, Dundee, Perth and Edinburgh are within 20 to 40 minutes' drive. Rooms are comfortably furnished with tea/coffee making facilities and colour TV. A warm welcome and relaxed atmosphere assured. Rates from £15 - £17 per person. Open all year.
e-mail: audreymhamilton@tinyworld.co.uk

**NORTH QUEENSFERRY. Dalwhinnie, East Bay, North Queensferry KY11 1JX (Tel & Fax: 01383 410547).** Modern bungalow dramatically situated on the waterfront with panoramic views down the Forth from the lounge. Easy access to Edinburgh – 20 minutes by car or train. Accommodation available in single, twin and double rooms, with en suite facilities, TV, radio, hairdryer and tea/coffee making facilities. Children welcome; reduced rates. Special diets can be catered for. Bed and Breakfast from £20 per person per night. **STB ★★★** *B&B*

---

**NOTE**

All the information in this book is given in good faith in the belief that it is correct. However, the publishers cannot guarantee the facts given in these pages, neither are they responsible for changes in policy, ownership or terms that may take place after the date of going to press. Readers should always satisfy themselves that the facilities they require are available and that the terms, if quoted, still apply.

## Newton of Nydie Farmhouse Bed & Breakfast

A working Scottish farm situated in the Kingdom of Fife. Three miles from St Andrews, ideally situated for Perth, Edinburgh and Dundee, not forgetting the picturesque fishing villages of East Fife. St Andrews boasts several golf courses including the famous Old & Royal Ancient clubhouses. Beautiful sandy beaches with Blue Flag awards and historic castles. This area also boasts one of the driest and sunniest climates in the UK. A warm welcome awaits all who stay.

*Self-catering bungalow sleeps 6, in rural position on the farm, see brochure for details.*

Sam and Doreen Wood, Newton of Nydie, Strathkinness, St Andrews, Fife KY16 9SL
Tel: 01334 850204  e-mail: nydiefarmhouse@talk21.com

STB ★★★

*See also Colour Advertisement*

**ST. ANDREWS. Mrs Duncan, Spinkstown Farmhouse, St. Andrews KY16 8PN (01334 473475).** Only two miles from St. Andrews on the picturesque A917 coast road to Crail, Spinkstown is a uniquely designed farmhouse with views of the sea and surrounding countryside. Bright and spacious, it is furnished to a high standard. Accommodation consists of double and twin rooms, all are en suite and have tea/coffee making facilities; diningroom and lounge with colour TV. Substantial farmhouse breakfast to set you up for the day, evening meals by arrangement only. The famous Old Course, historic St. Andrews and several National Trust properties are all within easy reach, as well as swimming, tennis, putting, bowls, horse riding, country parks, nature reserves, beaches and coastal walks. Plenty of parking available. Bed and Breakfast from £20; Evening Meal £12. **STB ★★★★** *B&B.* **AA ♦♦♦♦**.
e-mail: anne-duncan@lineone.net

*See also Colour Display Advertisement*

**TAYPORT. Mrs M. Forgan, B&B, 23 Castle Street, Tayport DD6 9AE (Tel & Fax: 01382 552682).** A warm, friendly welcome awaits you at this family run Bed and Breakfast. Five minutes' drive from Dundee, 15 minutes' drive to St Andrews. Good bus service. Near many local attractions and surrounded by golf courses. An ideal touring base - one hour's drive from Edinburgh, two hours to Inverness. Cyclists and walkers welcome. Situated on the River Tay only one minute walk from the picturesque harbour and a short walk to Tentsmuir Forest and four miles of sandy beach - ideal for birdwatchers and walkers. Five minutes' drive to Kinshaldy Riding Stables. Good traditional home cooked Scottish Breakfast. Special diets catered for. Evening Meals on request. Children free when sharing with adults. Discounts available for longer stays. Smoking outside only please. Accommodation consists of two twin, one double, all with wash-hand-basin, tea making facilities, colour TV and video. Bed and Breakfast from £15 to £19 per person. **STB ★★★** *B&B, WELCOME HOST, SCOTLAND'S BEST.*
website: www.forgan.ukf.net/

---

Visit the **FHG** website
# www.holidayguides.com
for details of the wide choice of accommodation featured in the full range of FHG titles

---

Terms quoted in this publication may be subject to increase if rises in costs necessitate

# GLASGOW & DISTRICT

*14 Belhaven Terrace,*
*Glasgow. G12 0TG*

■ ■ ■ ■

Tel: 0141-337 3377
Fax: 0141-400 3378

*e-mail: admin@the-terrace.fsnet.co.uk*

## THE TERRACE HOUSE

The Terrace House is situated in the heart of Glasgow's celebrated West End; minutes walk from the world famous Botanical Gardens.

A five minute walk finds you in fashionable Byres Road, with its wide variety of bars, restaurants and shops. As you will discover the West End has much to offer in the way of culture, entertainment and shopping and our hotel is the ideal base. The City Centre is also easily accessed within minutes via the City's Underground system or the well-connected bus links.

The family-run Terrace House was built between 1864-69, originally for one of the Tobacco Barons. It boasts fine period features, such as ornate cornices, wall friezes and grand entrance columns. The building has been refurbished to give the present 8 en suite bedrooms. All rooms have colour satellite T.V., fridge, tea/coffee making facilities and trouser/skirt press. Please ask about our Self-Catering Apartments..

Our rates are **£45 single, £29 per person Twin and Double (based on two sharing) and £25 per-person (based on three or more sharing)** including Continental breakfast and VAT. Please ask for any other seasonal and family rates. Prices quoted are per person per night.

Why not view our hotel on the internet!, you can find us on the web at:
**www.the-terrace.fs.net.co.uk**

*We thank you for your interest and hope to be of future service.*

**AA ♦♦♦♦**

---

**GLASGOW. Mrs P. Wells, "Avenue End" B&B, 21 West Avenue, Stepps, Glasgow G33 6ES (Tel & Fax: 0141-779 1990).** Stepps village is situated north-east of Glasgow just off the A80. This self-built family home nestles down a quiet leafy lane offering the ideal location for an overnight stay or touring base with the main routes to Edinburgh, Stirling and the North on our doorstep. Easy commuting to Loch Lomond, the Trossachs or Clyde Valley. M8 exit 12 from the south, or A80 Cumbernauld Road from the north. Glasgow only ten minutes away, Glasgow Airport 12 miles. Ample parking. All rooms offer colour TV, compliments tray and en suite or private facilities. Home from Home - warm welcome assured! All from £20 per person per night. **STB ★★★** *B&B*.
e-mail: **avenueEnd@aol.com**

---

# FHG

PLEASE MENTION THIS GUIDE WHEN YOU WRITE
OR PHONE TO ENQUIRE ABOUT ACCOMMODATION

IF YOU ARE WRITING, A STAMPED, ADDRESSED
ENVELOPE IS ALWAYS APPRECIATED

# HIGHLANDS

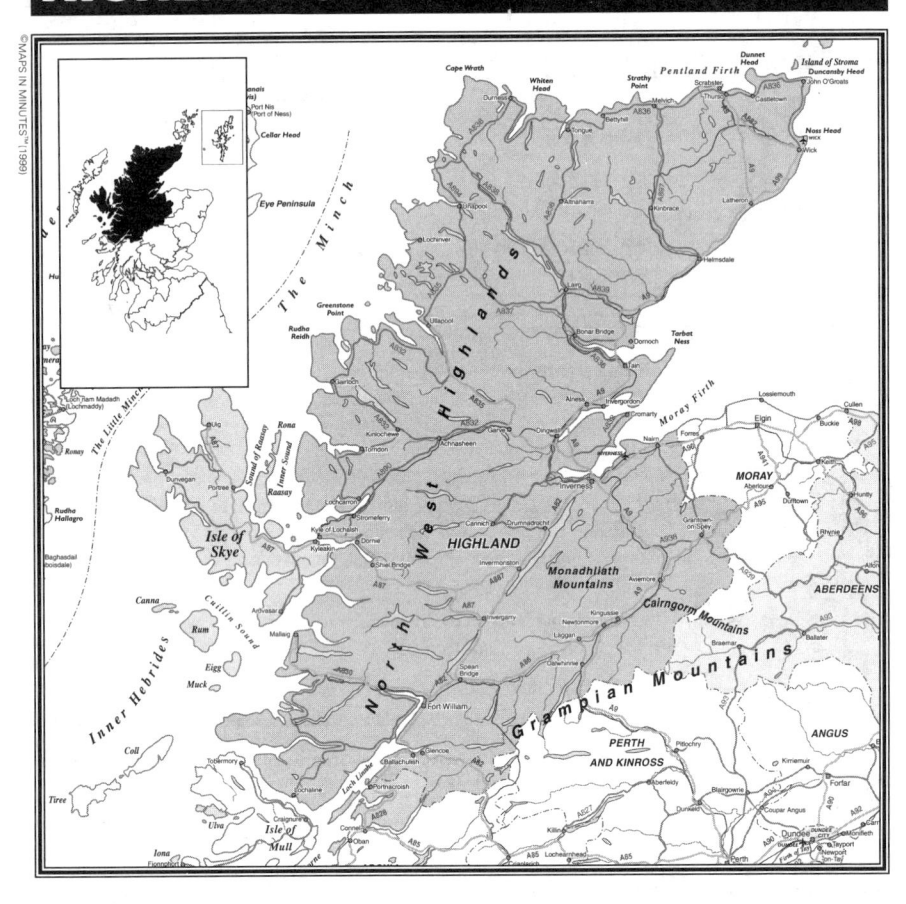

## Visit the
## ORKNEY ISLANDS
### Daily from John O'Groats and Inverness.

Exciting full Day Tours of these fascinating Islands leave Inverness at 7.30am and from John O'Groats at 9am and 10.30am.
Every Day All Summer

**Phone Now For Full Details**

**DAY TRIPS**

Tel: **01955 611353**
Website: www.jogferry.co.uk

John O'Groats Ferries, Ferry Office, John O'Groats, Caithness, Scotland KW1 4YR   Fax: 01955 611301

# HIGHLANDS (Mid)

## ROYAL HOTEL  Union Street, Fortrose, Ross-shire IV10 8TD

This family-run hotel is located in the centre of Fortrose, serving food and refreshments locally produced. Various activities catered for including golf, cycling, horseriding or simply peace to relax. Open all year.

**STB ★★ HOTEL**

*Tel & Fax: 01381 620236*
*websites: www.fortrosehotel.co.uk*
*www.royalhotel-fortrose.co.uk*
*e-mail: royalfortrose@cali.co.uk*

---

**AULTBEA. Margaret Mortimer, Cartmel Guesthouse, Birchburn Road, Aultbea IV22 2HZ (01445 731375).** Cartmel is a bungalow set in half-an-acre of mature woodland garden, in the West Highland village of Aultbea. The famous Inverewe Garden is six miles away. To the North is Ullapool (50 miles) and to the south is the Ben Eigh Nature Reserve and the Torridon Mountains. Close by are beautiful sandy beaches. There are two en suite bedrooms and two standard rooms, all with washbasins and tea/coffee making facilities. There is a comfortable lounge with colour TV and separate diningroom, where breakfast and home cooked evening meals are served. Non-smoking. Dogs welcome. Bed and Breakfast from £19 to £23; Dinner £12.50. **STB ★★★** *GUEST HOUSE.*

---

**BALINTORE. Mrs J. Palfreman, Rowchoish, East Street, Balintore, Near Tain IV20 1UE (01862 832422).** Bed and Breakfast in Balintore overlooking the Moray Firth, north-east of Inverness. Comfortable homely accommodation in one double and one twin room with tea making facilities; separate shower and toilet. Visitors' lounge. Packed lunches available. Guests can enjoy sea angling, golf and riding in the area, plus the unique Dolphin Watch. Bed and Breakfast from £17.50 per person per night. Longer stay reductions. Brochure on request. *WELCOME HOST AWARD.*
**e-mail: jackie@freeserve.co.uk**
**website: www.rowchoish.freeserve.co.uk**

---

**GAIRLOCH. Miss McKenzie, "Duisary", 24 Strath, Gairloch IV21 2DA (01445 712252).** A true Highland welcome awaits you in this modernised croft house situated on the outskirts of the village. Superb views of the sea and Torridon Hills. Close to the famous Inverewe Gardens. Idyllic setting with beaches, watersports, golf course, swimming pool and leisure centre all nearby. Ideal spot for hill walking, bird watching, fishing or just relaxing. Lounge with colour TV. Full central heating. TV in all bedrooms. Open April to October. Further details available on request. **STB ★★★** *B&B*
**e-mail: isobel@duisary.freeserve.co.uk**

**INVERGORDON. Jo Brown, Craigaron, 17 Saltburn, Invergordon IV18 0JX (01349 853640; Fax: 01349 853619).** Situated on seafront, overlooking Cromarty Firth, five minutes from town centre. Friendliness, warmth and comfort in bright, pleasant surroundings. Abundant sea life and bird life, visiting cruise liners, and 20 golf courses (two championship) within an hour's drive. Ground floor bedrooms, central heating, colour TV and tea/coffee tray. **STB** ★★★ *B&B*

**PLOCKTON. Mrs Janet MacKenzie Jones, "Tomacs", Frithard Road, Plockton (01599 544321).** Fine views overlooking Loch Carron and Applecross Hills. Double and twin bedrooms. One room has en suite facilities and one has private facilities; all have washbasin, central heating, TV and tea/coffee making facilities. Bed and Breakfast from £16. **STB** ★★★ *GUEST HOUSE.*

**STRATHPEFFER. Dunraven Lodge, Golf Course Road, Strathpeffer IV14 9AS (01997 421210).** Beautiful Listed period house with all rooms en suite; recently refurbished to a very high standard of comfort and design. Guest lounge, dining room, full-size snooker room and lovely gardens provide an excellent base for your holiday or business trip. Open all year with many seasonal specials. Golf course, restaurants, bars and shops are just a short distance away, and we are ideally situated for exploring both the East and West coasts of the Highlands, Aviemore, Ullapool, Dornoch, Inverness, the Isle of Skye and Loch Ness. **STB** ★★★★
e-mail: iddon@freeuk.com
website: www.milford.co.uk/scotland/accom/h-a-1865.html

**ULLAPOOL. Eilean Donan Guest House, 14 Market Street, Ullapool (01854 612524).** Eilean Donan is a guest house and restaurant situated in a conservation area within the village. John and Mary Macrae extend a warm welcome to visitors, offering comfortable, quality accommodation in a relaxed family atmosphere. All rooms are en suite, have hospitality tray and colour TV. There is a private car park and drying facilities available. We are within easy reach of all the amenities in Ullapool including the sports centre with indoor pool, golf course, pubs, daily cruises and walking amongst some of the most spectacular scenery in the Highlands.

**FHG**
Visit the FHG website
**www.holidayguides.com**
for details of the wide choice of accommodation
featured in the full range of FHG titles

# HIGHLANDS (South)

**AVIEMORE. Mrs Margaret Hall, Kinapol Guest House (Est 1975), Dalfaber Road, Aviemore PH22 1PY (Tel & Fax: 01479 810513).** Small modern Guest House in quiet situation, only five minutes' walk to station, buses and all amenities in centre of Aviemore. Three double and two family rooms, all with TV, washbasin and tea/coffee trays etc., and most have views of Cairngorm Mountains. There is a large bright lounge for guests with TV and hot drinks trolley. The garden has access to the River Spey and riverside walks. Drying cupboard, ski store, off-road parking. Mountain bikes for hire. Bed and Breakfast from £15 per night. Reduced rates for weekly bookings. Major credit cards accepted. **STB ★★** *GUEST HOUSE*.
e-mail: kinapol@aol.com
website: www.aviemore.co.uk/kinapol

**CULLODEN MOOR. Mrs Margaret Campbell, Bay View, Westhill, By Inverness IV1 2BP (01463 790386).** Bay View is set in a rural area on famous Culloden Moor, offering comfortable homely accommodation in one twin-bedded room with en suite shower, one double room with en suite bathroom, and one double room with private bathroom. An excellent touring base for the Highlands of Scotland and many famous historic sites. All home made food, local produce used. Bed and Breakfast from £16. **STB ★★★** *B&B*.

**DRUMNADROCHIT. Mrs Sandra Silke, Westwood, Lower Balmacaan, Drumnadrochit IV63 6WU (Tel & Fax: 01456 450826).** Westwood is a warm comfortable bungalow in the village of Drumnadrochit on the side of Loch Ness and has wonderful views towards the hills. Urquhart Castle and the "Nessie" exhibitions are close by. The house is only 20 minutes from Glens Cannich, Affric and Strathfarrar; Inverness 14 miles. Westwood is well placed for touring or hillwalking in the Highlands. Accommodation comprises one double en suite, one twin en suite and one single bedroom, with colour TV, tea/coffee making facilities and hairdryer. Full central heating, guest lounge with colour TV. Evening Meals available by arrangement. Open all year. Further details on request. **STB ★★★** *B&B*.
e-mail: sandra@westwoodbb.freeserve.co.uk
website: www.westwoodbb.freeserve.co.uk

**FORT AUGUSTUS. Brenda Graham, Caledonian Cottage, Station Road, Fort Augustus PH32 4AY (01320 366401; Mobile: 07967 740329).** Offering a warm Highland welcome, the cottage is set in the quiet picturesque village of Fort Augustus, where the five lochs flow into Loch Ness. Beautiful landscape, a walker's paradise; fishing, boating, canoeing in season. The village is just steps away from pubs and eateries. Comfortable modern accommodation with TV, tea and coffee facilities. Non-smoking. Double/twin (sleeps three) en suite; family room en suite; double with private facilities. Pleasant garden to relax in and take in the view. Private parking. Children and pets welcome. Single supplement; short break supplement. Rates from £15 according to season.
e-mail: cal@ipw.com

---

*Please mention Bed & Breakfast Stops when writing to enquire about accommodation*

**FORT WILLIAM. Mrs F. A. Cook, Melantee, Achintore Road, Fort William PH33 6RW (01397 705329; Fax: 01397 700453).** Melantee is a bungalow situated one-and-a-half miles south of the town on the A82 with views of Loch Linnhe. Ideal centre for touring the Highlands, Inverness, Aviemore, Oban, Mallaig, Kyle of Lochalsh, Skye or walk to the top of Britain's highest mountain, Ben Nevis, via the tourist path. One double, one twin, two family rooms with washbasins, shaver points. Tea and coffee facilities in all bedrooms. Access to house at all times, ample parking, open all year round. Terms from £15.50 per adult for Bed and Breakfast. Reductions for children in family rooms. Fire Certificate held. **STB ★★ B&B, WELCOME HOST.**

**FORT WILLIAM. Mrs Catriona Morrison, Torlinnhe, Achintore Road, Fort William PH33 6RN (Tel & Fax: 01397 702583).** Friendly family run Bed and Breakfast with ample parking. Five rooms en suite, one with private bathroom. All with colour TV and hospitality trays. Two double rooms, one twin room, two family rooms and one single, most have views over Loch Linnhe and the hills beyond. Full fire certificate. Torlinnhe is situated one mile south of the town on the main A82 and is an excellent base for touring or enjoying a pleasant walk into town. New and return guests always welcome. Prices range from £16 to £22. **STB ★★★ B&B.**

**FORT WILLIAM. Mrs Mary MacLean, Innishfree, Lochyside, Fort William PH33 7NX (01397 705471).** Set against the background of Ben Nevis, this spacious Bed and Breakfast house offers a high level of service. Just two miles from the town centre and three miles from Glen Nevis. Visitors are guaranteed a warm friendly welcome and excellent accommodation. All rooms have en suite facilities and also offer remote-control colour TV and tea/coffee making facilities. Breakfast is served in the conservatory, which is overlooked by panoramic views. Enthusiastic advice on pursuits and activities are given. Access to private car park is available. This house has a non-smoking policy and pets are not allowed. Open all year. Prices range from £19 to £25 per person per night. **STB ★★★★ B&B**

**FORT WILLIAM. Mr and Mrs McQueen, Stronchreggan View Guest House, Achintore Road, Fort William PH33 6RW (Tel & Fax: 01397 704644).** Our guest house is on the A82, one mile south of Fort William, overlooking Loch Linnhe with views to the Argour Hills. Accommodation offers an excellent guest lounge, full central heating, five bedrooms en suite, two with private facilities. Parking within grounds. Fort William is a good touring centre with the Isle of Skye, Oban and Inverness, etc. all within easy reach. Bed and Breakfast from £18 to £24.

**FORT WILLIAM. Thistle Cottage, Torlundy, Fort William (01397 702428).** In a rural area three-and-a-half miles north of Fort William in a beautiful quiet valley below Aonach Mor Ski Centre. Central for touring the Highlands. Warm and friendly welcome. Double and family rooms with TV and tea/coffee making facilities. En suite available. Ample parking. Pets welcome in bedroom. Open all year. Contact Mrs Matheson for details. Bed and Breakfast from £13 per night per person. **STB ★★ B&B**

# Highlands (South)

**FORT WILLIAM. Mrs Wallace, Ossian's Hotel, High Street, Fort William PH33 6DH (01397 700857).** Ossian's can provide the traveller to the Scottish Highlands a comfortable, friendly and informal hotel, right in the centre of town. Shops, pubs and entertainment are just outside our front door. Relax and enjoy some of our good home cooking. All rooms are en suite. Budget/family rooms available. Some rooms have loch views. Lift access to all floors. Well behaved pets and children are welcome. We are only a four minute walk from train or bus stations. Fort William makes an excellent base for touring the West Highlands, and with some of the best climbing in Britain, walkers and climbers are very welcome here. Bed and Breakfast from £16 to £28.

**FORT WILLIAM. Mrs Grant, Glen Shiel Guest House, Achintore Road, Fort William PH33 6RW (Tel & Fax: 01397 702271).** Modern purpose-built guest house situated near the shore of Loch Linnhe with panoramic views of the surrounding mountains. Accommodation comprises three en suite double bedrooms, one twin-bedded room and one family room, all with colour TV and tea making facilities. Non smoking. Large car park. Garden. Directions: on the A82 one-and-a-half-miles south of Fort William. Bed and Breakfast from £16 to £20. **STB** ★★ *GUEST HOUSE*

**FORT WILLIAM. Mabel Wallace, "The Wallace" 6 Kinross Place, Upper Achintore, Fort William PH33 6UN (Tel & Fax: 01397 703635).** Quality Bed and Breakfast in quiet cul-de-sac within 10/15 minutes' walk from Town Centre. (Close to local bus route). One double and two twin rooms all shower/en suite, central heating, colour TV, radio alarm, hospitality tray, private parking. Follow Upper Achintore sign from West End roundabout, take fifth turning on left, Sutherland Ave, along to right turn for Lochaber Rd, follow road to bus turning point, straight through, Perth Place on left, Kinross Place on right. "The Wallace" third property on right. We look forward to meeting guests and strive to do our best to ensure an enjoyable stay with us. Always look forward to welcoming them on return visits. 'Haste ye back'. Open all year. No Smoking. Bed and Breakfast from £19. **STB** ★★★ *B&B.*

**FORT WILLIAM. Allt-Nan-Ros Hotel, Onich, By Fort William PH33 6RY (01855 821210; Fax: 01855 821462).** Named in Gaelic after the cascading stream that runs through the beautiful and colourful four acres of gardens, this fine hotel will hold special appeal for lovers of wild and romantic mountain and loch scenery. Situated on the A82 in the crofting village of Onich, Allt-nan-Ros is an imposing building of Victorian origin that has been modernised with skill and imagination. Guest rooms have magnificent views, and are appointed with private bath and toilet facilities, radio, central heating, electric blankets and tea and coffee makers. Under the attentive care of an expert chef, the cuisine is superbly prepared and presented, from the full Scottish breakfast to dinner which features many imaginative specialities. **STB** ★★★★ *HOTEL*, **AA** ★★★ *AND TWO ROSETTES*, **RAC** ★★★ *AND THREE DINING AWARDS*
e-mail: fhg@allt-nan-ros.co.uk
website: www.allt-nan-ros.co.uk

**FORT WILLIAM. J. & E. Rosie, Guisachan Guest House, Alma Road, Fort William PH33 6HA (Tel & Fax: 01397 703797).** Delightfully situated in own grounds overlooking Loch Linnhe and Ardgour Hills, yet within five minutes walking of bus and railway stations and town centre, well-placed for day trips to Inverness, Isle of Skye, Oban, Inveraray, Pitlochry etc. For the more energetic there is excellent walking, climbing and fishing and skiing in winter and early spring. Rooms are en suite with tea/coffee, colour TV, hairdryers and clock radio. A warm welcome awaits you. Open January - December. Prices £18 - £28 per person. **STB** ★★★ *GUEST HOUSE.*

### Highland Hospitality at the
# 𝕴𝖛𝖆𝖓𝖍𝖔𝖊 GUEST HOUSE
**68 Lochalsh Road, Inverness IV3 6HW**
**Tel/Fax: 01463 223020**

Small, friendly Guest House situated near town centre, 10 minutes from bus and train stations. Clean, comfortable rooms, with washbasins, colour TV and hospitality trays. En suite available. Visit the Capital of the Highlands, enjoy the many splendid sights, and stay in a relaxing and comfortable atmosphere with us at the Ivanhoe.

---

**INVERNESS. Mrs F. McKendrick, Lyndale Guest House, 2 Ballifeary Road, Inverness IV3 5PJ (01463 231529).** Lyndale Guest House, adjacent to the A82 on entering Inverness from Loch Ness, is delightfully situated in an exclusive residential area close to the River Ness and within eight minutes' walk from town centre. Eden Court Theatre and Restaurant 200 yards, the municipal golf course and Loch Ness Cruise departure point five minutes' walk. Standing in private grounds Lyndale is well appointed, with an attractive diningroom; all bedrooms with colour TV and tea/coffee facilities; several en suite. Guests have full use of amenities of the house all day. Private parking in grounds. Bed and Breakfast from £16; en suite £22.

**INVERNESS. Mrs A. MacLean, Waternish, 15 Clachnaharry Road, Inverness IV3 8QH (01463 230520).** Delightful bungalow in beautiful setting overlooking Moray Firth and Black Isle. On main A862 road to Beauly, and just five minutes to Inverness town centre. Ideal touring centre for North and West. Canal cruises and golf course nearby and lovely walks by banks of Caledonian Canal. Loch Ness is just 15 minutes' drive. Accommodation comprises three double/twin rooms, one en suite, all with tea/coffee making facilities and colour TV. Comfortable lounge. Full Scottish breakfast. Private car park. Open March to October. Bed and Breakfast from £14.

**INVERNESS. Miss Storrar, Abb Cottage, 11 Douglas Row, Inverness IV1 1RE (01463 233486).** A historic Listed, riverside, terraced cottage in a quiet central street. Within easy walking distance of coach and train stations. Three twin bedrooms have washbasins, shaver points; lounge/dining room has books, puzzles, games, tourist information and time tables, etc. All ground floor rooms are wheelchair accessible, one step is at the front door. Vegetarians and special diets catered for. Packed breakfasts are provided for early departures. Children over 12 welcome, sorry, no pets, no smoking. Private car parking.

**INVERNESS. Mrs S. Chalmers, 'Tamarue', 70A Ballifeary Road, Inverness IV3 5PF (01463 239724).** Comfortable Bed and Breakfast base whilst you tour the many beauty spots and places of interest in the Highlands, or if you are simply passing through. Guests are accommodated in one double en suite and one double and one twin; all rooms overlook attractive garden to rear and have washbasins and tea-making facilities; central heating; TV lounge; separate shower for visitors' use. Near to riverside walks, golf course and Loch Ness cruises; 10 minutes' walk to Eden Court Theatre and 15 minutes to shops, restaurants, bus and railway station. Ample parking. Long established reputation for cleanliness and attractive surroundings. Completely non-smoking house. Bed and Breakfast from £15 to £20, no VAT. **STB** ★★ *B&B*

**INVERNESS. Mrs E. MacKenzie, The Whins, 114 Kenneth Street, Inverness IV3 5QG (01463 236215).** Comfortable, homely accommodation awaits you here 10 minutes' walking distance from town centre, bus and railway stations, Inverness being an excellent touring base for North, West and East bus and rail journeys. Bedrooms have TV and tea-making facilities, washbasin and heating off-season. Bathroom has a shared shower and toilet. Two double/twin rooms from £15 per person per night. Non-smoking. Write or phone for full details.

**MALLAIG. Jill and Tom Smith, Springbank Guest House, East Bay, Mallaig PH41 4QF (Tel & Fax: 01687 462459).** Overlooking the harbour and the Sound of Sleat to Skye. Five minutes' walk from railway station at the end of the world-famous West Highland Line and from ferry terminal to Skye, the Small Isles and Knoydart. The house is fully centrally heated and double glazed. Evening Dinner is available by arrangement. Children and pets welcome. From £16 - £17 per night. Telephone for brochure. **STB ★** *B&B*.

**MORAR (by Mallaig). Mrs U. Clulow, Sunset Guest House, Morar, by Mallaig PH40 4PA (Tel & Fax: 01687 462259).** Situated in the peaceful west coast village of Morar, overlooking the renowned silver sands and the beautiful Inner Hebrides. With the island studded Atlantic in front and backdrop of the mountain wilds of Knoydart, Sunset is superbly placed for those wishing to find the tranquillity, scenic beauty and romantic history for which this part of Scotland is famous. AUTHENTIC THAI FOOD is also on the menu to provide some inner warmth after a long and energetic day. Children welcome. Prices from £12.50.
e-mail: sunsetgh@aol.com

See also Colour Display Advertisement

**SPEAN BRIDGE. Dreamweavers, Earendil, Mucomir, By Spean Bridge PH34 4EQ (Tel & Fax: 01397 712548).** Come to the heart of the Hghlands and experience the ultimate in Scottish hospitality. Comfortable spacious accommodation, plentiful home cooking and beautiful surroundings. Artists, birdwatchers, photographers and walkers all welcome, with plenty to do, see and inspire you. We are the ideal centre for all mountain and water sports and golf is available nearby. Special Theme Weekends available. Children welcome. Specially adapted to meet the needs of all disabled with easy access and a range of aids available. Please contact for further details.
e-mail: helen@dreamweavers.co.uk

**TOMATIN. Kevin and Maureen Ellerbeck, Glenan Lodge (Licensed), Tomatin IV13 7YT (01808 511217; Fax: 01808 511356).** The Glenan Lodge is a typical Scottish Lodge situated in the midst of the Monadhliath Mountains in the valley of the Findhorn River, yet only one mile from the A9. It offers typical Scottish hospitality, home cooking, warmth and comfort. The nine bedrooms all have central heating, tea making facilities and washbasins; five have en suite facilities. There is a large comfortable lounge and a homely dining room. The licensed bar is well stocked with local malts for the guests. Glenan Lodge caters for the angler, birdwatcher, hillwalker, stalker and tourist alike whether passing through or using as a base. Open all year round. Bed and Breakfast; Dinner optional. Eurocard and Visa accepted

---

# FREE or REDUCED RATE entry to Holiday Visits and Attractions — see our READERS' OFFER VOUCHERS on pages 43-60

# LANARKSHIRE

**BROUGHTON. Neil Robinson & Fiona Burnett, The Glenholm Centre, Broughton, By Biggar ML12 6JF (Tel & Fax: 01899 830408).** A warm welcome awaits you at our family-run guest house set on a farm at the heart of Glenholm in the Scottish Borders. Just 30 miles south of Edinburgh, it is an ideal stop on a journey to/from Scotland, or the perfect centre to explore the hills and glens of the Upper Tweed valley. Accommodation is available in three twin/double rooms, each with en suite shower and toilet, colour TV, fridge and tea/coffee making facilities; one room adapted for wheelchair access. Family suite available in adjacent cottage. The Centre provides excellent farmhouse cooking, with meals served buffet-style in the dining room, and there is a small residents' bar. Non-smoking. Reductions for children. **STB ★★★** *GUEST HOUSE.* **AA** *QQQQ.*
e-mail: glenholm@dircon.co.uk
website: www.glenholm.dircon.co.uk

**CALDERBANK. Mrs Betty Gaines, Calder Guest House, 13 Main Street, Calderbank ML6 9SG (01236 769077; Fax: 01236 750506).** Calder Guest House is a spacious Victorian house which is over 100 years old and has recently been tastefully refurbished. With its close proximity to the motorway network, and within two miles of the railway station, it is ideally situated for the holiday or business traveller, as a convenient stopover or as a base to tour or visit the surrounding countryside. The spacious accommodation has a choice of bedrooms to suit the family or the person travelling alone, some are en suite, and all are equipped with colour TV and tea/coffee making facilities. The conservatory to the rear of the house, overlooking the garden and the children's play area, contains the diningroom and lounge, giving a bright and cheerful setting to enjoy a hearty Scottish breakfast, or to relax in the evening after a hard day. There is ample off-road parking. Games room with pool and darts or watch "the big match", golf or cricket on television. **STB ★★★** *GUEST HOUSE.*

**HARTHILL. Mrs H. Stephens, Blair Mains Farm, Harthill ML7 5TJ (01501 751278; Fax: 01501 753383).** Attractive farmhouse on small farm – 72 acres. Immediately adjacent to Junction 5 of M8 motorway. Ideal centre for touring, with Edinburgh, Glasgow, Stirling 30 minutes' drive. Fishing (trout and coarse) and golf nearby. One double, three twin, two single (three en suite) bedrooms; bathroom; sittingroom, diningroom; sun porch. Central heating. Children welcome – babysitting offered. Pets welcome. Car essential – parking. Bed and Breakfast from £16; weekly rates available. Reduced rates for children. Open all year.
e-mail: heather@blairmains.freeserve.co.uk

---

# FHG

### PLEASE MENTION THIS GUIDE WHEN YOU WRITE OR PHONE TO ENQUIRE ABOUT ACCOMMODATION

### IF YOU ARE WRITING, A STAMPED, ADDRESSED ENVELOPE IS ALWAYS APPRECIATED

# PERTH & KINROSS

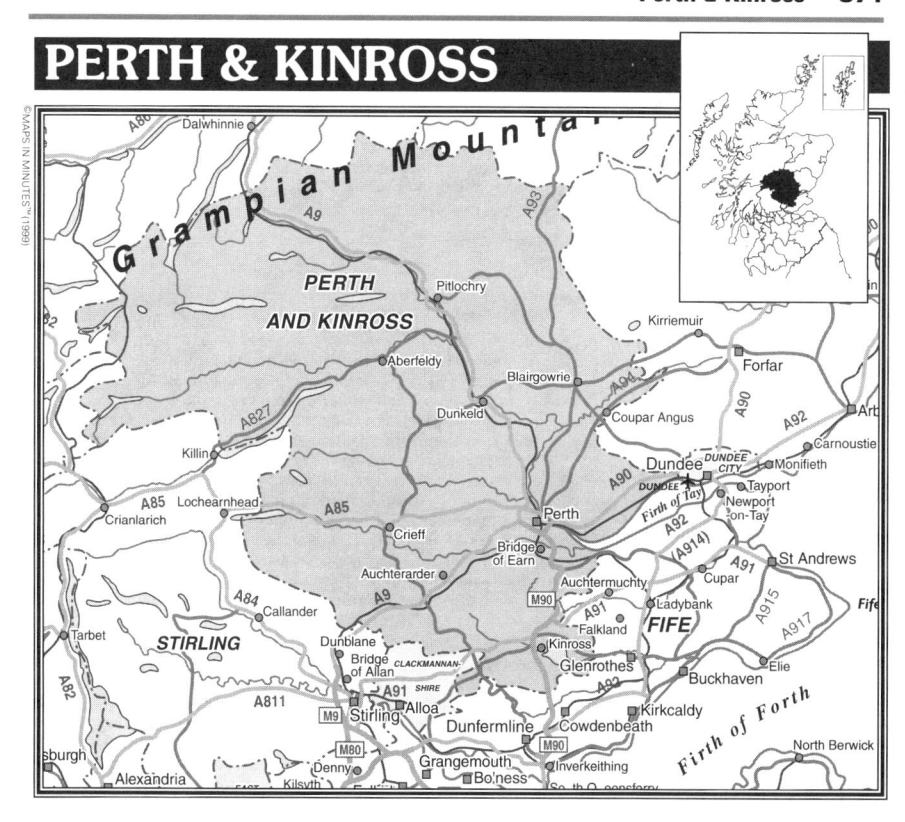

**ABERNETHY near. Mrs Kathleen Baird, Easter Clunie Farmhouse, Easter Clunie, Newburgh KY14 6EJ (01337 840218; Fax: 01337 842226). Working farm.** David and Kathleen Baird warmly welcome you to their 18th century centrally heated farmhouse. Easter Clunie is an arable farm with stock, situated on the A913 between Abernethy and Newburgh. Home baking and tea served on arrival in the residents' lounge. All rooms have private facilities or are en suite; tea/coffee making facilities. Relax in the walled garden, enjoy panoramic views of the River Tay. Ideal touring base for Fife and Perthshire, only 45 minutes from Edinburgh. Children welcome. Bed and Breakfast from £18 to £20. Open April to October. **STB** ★★★ *B&B*.
e-mail: cluniefarm@aol.com

**AUCHTERARDER. Mrs Brodie, Allandale House, 17 High Street, Auchterarder PH3 1DB (01764 663329; Mobile: 07801 479056; Fax: 01764 664451).** Allandale House is a stylish bed and breakfast of great comfort and character, which has been refurbished to a very high standard, yet still retains many of its original features. Each spacious bedroom has tea/coffee making facilities, colour TV and central heating. Most rooms have private facilities, one of which is a family room. Auchterarder is perfectly situated as a base for touring Scotland. Perth, Stirling, Pitlochry, The Trossachs, Loch Lomond and Edinburgh are all less than one hour away and Gleneagles is only two miles away. Highchairs and cots provided. Car parking available. **STB** ★★★ *B&B*, **AA** ◆◆◆◆
e-mail: AllandaleHouse@aol.com
website: http://freespace.virgin.net/allandale.house/

**AUCHTERARDER. Mrs Henderson, Ashford House, 59 High Street, Auchterarder PH3 1BN (01764 663602).** Ashford House is situated in the heart of Auchterarder and is an ideal base for touring the local countryside and historic attractions of Perthshire or to take advantage of the golf, fishing, birdwatching and skiing facilities nearby. Four bedrooms are available (two en suite, two with private facilities) with colour TV, tea/coffee making facilities and heating. Pets welcome. Open all year. Bed and Breakfast from £18.

**BLAIRGOWRIE. Rosalind Young, Holmrigg, Wester Essendy, Blairgowrie PH10 6RD (Tel & Fax: 01250 884309).** One double/family, one double four-poster and one twin/double on ground floor. All rooms are en suite with tea/coffee making facilities, radio and TV; ironing and hair drying facilities. Comfortable lounge with open fire and colour TV; diningroom. Heating throughout. Vegetarian meals and packed lunches; home cooking and baking; full cooked breakfast. Places of interest range from Scott's Discovery in Dundee to Edinburgh Castle. Also golf, fishing and walking. Pets by arrangement. Putting; parking. Non-smoking house. Bed and Breakfast from £16–£20; with Evening Meal £26–£30. Discounts for children and Senior Citizens.
e-mail: info@holmrigg.co.uk
website: www.holmrigg.co.uk

**BRIDGE OF CALLY. Mrs Josephine MacLaren, Blackcraig Castle, Bridge of Cally PH10 7PX (01250 886251 or 0131-551 1863).** A beautiful castle of architectural interest situated in spacious grounds. Free trout fishing on own stretch of River Ardle. Excellent centre for hill walking, golf and touring - Braemar, Pitlochry (Festival Theatre), Crieff, Dunkeld, etc., Glamis Castle within easy reach by car. Four double, two twin, two family and two single bedrooms, eight with washbasin; two bathrooms, three toilets. Cot, highchair. Dogs welcome free of charge. Car essential, free parking. Open for guests from 1st July to 7th September. £24 per person per night includes full breakfast plus tea/coffee and home baking at 10pm in the beautiful drawing room which has a log fire. Reduced rates for children under 14 years. Enquiries November to end June to **1 Inverleith Place, Edinburgh EH3 5QE.**

**CALLANDER. Annfield Guest House, North Church Street, Callander FK17 8EG (01877 330204; Fax: 01877 330674).** Annfield is situated in a quiet spot a few minutes walk from shops and restaurants. Ideal as an overnight stop or as a centre for visiting the surrounding Scottish Highlands. You will receive the warmest of welcomes from your hosts, Janet and Mike Greenfield, to their fine Victorian family home. All bedrooms have en suite facilities or private bathroom, hospitality tray and hairdryer. Guests' lounge with colour TV. Non-smokers preferred. Private parking. Open all year. Major credit cards accepted. **STB ★★★ B&B. AA ◆◆◆.WELCOME HOST AWARD.**

---

**FHG**

Visit the FHG website
**www.holidayguides.com**
for details of the wide choice of accommodation
featured in the full range of FHG titles

See also Colour Display Advertisement

**CALLANDER. Riverview Guest House, Leny Road, Callander FK17 8AL (Tel & Fax: 01877 330635).** Excellent value for money accommodation in the Trossachs area which forms the most beautiful part of Scotland's first proposed National Park. Ideal centre for walking and cycling holidays with cycle storage being available. GUEST HOUSE - all rooms en suite, TV and tea making facilities. Bed and Breakfast from £21, dinner by arrangement £10. Low season and long stay discounts available. Private parking. SELF CATERING - stone cottages sleep three or four from £225 per week. Call Drew or Kathleen Little for details. Sorry no smoking and no pets. STB ★★★ *B&B*, STB ★★★★ *SELF-CATERING.*
e-mail: auldtoll@netscapeonline.co.uk
website: www.nationalparkscotland.co.uk

**CRIANLARICH. Mr & Mrs A. Chisholm, Tigh Na Struith, The Riverside Guest House, Crianlarich FK20 8RU (01838 300235; Fax: 01838 300268).** Voted the Best Guest House in Britain by the British Guild of Travel Writers in 1984, this superbly sited Guest House comprises six bedrooms, each with unrestricted views of the Crianlarich Mountains. The three-acre garden leads down to the River Fillan, a tributary of the River Tay. Personally run by the owners, Janice and Sandy Chisholm, Tigh Na Struith allows visitors the chance to relax and enjoy rural Scotland at its best. To this end, each bedroom is centrally heated, double glazed, with colour TV and tea/coffee making facilities. Open March to November. Bed and Breakfast from £16 per person.

See also Colour Display Advertisement

**GLENFARG. Peter and Marion Dickson, Hayfield Cottage, Hayfield Road, Glenfarg PH2 9QH (01577 830431).** We would like to welcome you to Hayfield Cottage. Situated in our tranquil four acre garden with the River Farg flowing through, 'The Garden Room' provides self-contained twin-bedded room with sitting area round a wood-burning stove. Facilities include colour TV, radio, tea-making and a separate en suite shower room. Breakfast is served in our conservatory at a time to suit you. The 'Best Kept' award winning village of Glenfarg is ideally situated for easy tourist access, central for Edinburgh, St Andrews and the Highlands, and is less that five minutes from the motorway. The village also boasts the highly acclaimed Glenfarg Hotel to supply your dinner/supper requirements. Come and breathe a sense of peace and history with a walk around our idyllic garden which contains its very own derelict corn-mill and say 'hello' to the ducks, goose and hens. The price of £20 per person includes the provision of home-baking to welcome you.
e-mail: pdickson@talk21.com

---

*The* **FHG**
**GOLF**
**GUIDE**
*Where to Play*
*Where to Stay*
***2001***

Available from most bookshops, the 2001 edition of **THE GOLF GUIDE** covers details of every UK golf course – well over 2500 entries – for holiday or business golf. Hundreds of hotel entries offer convenient accommodation, accompanying details of the courses – the 'pro', par score, length etc.

*In association with 'Golf Monthly' and including the Ryder Cup Report as well as Holiday Golf in Ireland, France, Portugal, Spain, The USA, South Africa and Thailand .*

**£9.99 from bookshops or £10.50 including postage (UK only) from FHG Publications, Abbey Mill Business Centre, Paisley PAI ITJ**

## Perth & Kinross

**KINROSS. Mrs M Sneddon, St Serf's Bed and Breakfast, 35 The Muirs, Kinross KY13 8AS (01577 862183/864340).** A warm Scottish welcome awaits you in our charming guest house situated in a quiet residential area of the town. Kinross is an ideal centre for touring Perthshire, Stirling and The Kingdom of Fife, with the express bus route to Edinburgh close by should you decide to leave your car. Golf, fishing, gliding and birdwatching are available in the area, while walking enthusiasts will be delighted with the Vane Farm Nature Reserve. A visit to historic Loch Leven Castle, where Mary Queen of Scots was imprisoned, is a must, while an abundance of shops, pubs and restaurants offer more leisurely pursuits. Enjoy a traditional Scottish Breakfast each morning when individual tastes are also catered for. Comfortable residential lounge where you can just relax, read or watch television. Three attractive spacious family bedrooms, two en suite, one private bathroom. All with colour TV and tea/coffee available. Non-smoking establishment. **STB ★★★** *B&B.*

**KIRKMICHAEL. Log Cabin Hotel, Kirkmichael PH10 7NA (01250 881288; Fax: 01250 881206).** Unique, family-run hotel, set in the picturesque hills of Perthshire, less than half-an-hour from Glenshee, Pitlochry and Blairgowrie. The bar is fully licensed, with a good range of malt whiskies; guests can enjoy panoramic views of Strathardle from the dining room. All bedrooms are en suite. A good central base for touring Perthshire and beyond; many golf courses are within easy reach; skiing at Glenshee in the winter; ideal for walking holidays. Please call for brochure or further information. Pets and children welcome. **STB ★★** *HOTEL.*

**PERTH. Eleanor Marshall, Comely Bank Cottage, 19 Pitcullen Crescent, Perth PH2 7HT (01738 631118; Fax: 01738 571245).** Enjoy true Scottish hospitality and personal attention in this friendly, comfortable, well-appointed family home, only 10 minutes' walk from Perth city centre. Comely Bank Cottage is a Victorian semi villa situated on the A94, a main tourist route. Ideally located for visits to Perth races and Scone Palace and as a base for touring. Edinburgh, Stirling and St. Andrews are less than an hour's drive away as are many of Scotland's famous castles, palaces and golf courses. All rooms have central heating, TV, hospitality tray, en suite or private facilities; guest lounge and private parking. Bed and Breakfast from £18 per person. However long or short your stay at Comely Bank Cottage you can be assured of a warm welcome and friendly service.
e-mail:comelybankcott@hotmail.com
website: www.SmoothHound.co.uk/hotels/comelyba.html

**PERTH. Mrs Mary Fotheringham, Craighall Farmhouse, Forgandenny, Near Bridge of Earn, Perth PH2 9DF (01738 812415). Working farm.** Come and stay in a modern and warm farmhouse with a cheerful, friendly atmosphere situated in lovely Earn Valley, half-a-mile west of village of Forgandenny on B935 and only six miles south of Perth. True Highland hospitality and large choice for breakfast served in diningroom overlooking fields where a variety of cattle, sheep and lambs graze. Farm produce used. Open all year, the 1000 acre arable and stock farm is within easy reach of Stirling, Edinburgh, St. Andrews, Glasgow and Pitlochry. Fishing, golf, tennis, swimming locally. Hillwalking amid lovely scenery. All rooms en suite. Tea making facilities. Sittingroom. Cot and reduced rates for children. Sorry, no pets. Central heating. Car not essential, parking. Bed and Breakfast from £19.50. Mid-week bookings taken. AA/RAC Acclaimed. **STB ★★★** *B&B.*

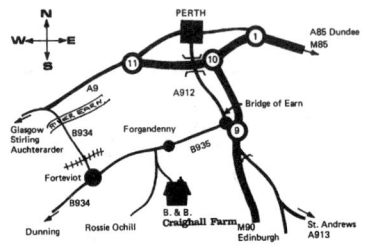

---

*Terms quoted in this publication may be subject to increase if rises in costs necessitate*

**PERTH. Stuart and Trisha Honeyman, Auld Manse Guest House, Pitcullen Crescent, Perth PH2 7HT (Tel & Fax: 01738 629187).** Victorian semi-villa, former manse just a short walk from city centre, parks and sport amenities. Situated on the A94 Coupar Angus road the Manse offers comfortable rooms all with private facilities, colour TV and hospitality tray. Guest lounge with satellite TV. Payphone and fax for guests' use. Ample car parking. Fire and Food Hygiene Certificates. Perth is an ideal base for touring and is only a short drive from most major cities; or try our many beautiful golf courses with a choice of nine or 18 hole play. Open all year. Bed and Breakfast from £18.50. Reductions for party bookings. **STB ★★** *GUEST HOUSE*.
e-mail: trisha@auldmanse.fsnet.co.uk

**PITLOCHRY. Mrs Ruth MacPherson-MacDougall, Dalnasgadh House, Killiecrankie, By Pitlochry PH16 5LN (01796 473237).** Attractive country house in grounds of two acres amidst magnificent Highland scenery. Close to National Trust Centre in Pass of Killiecrankie, historic Blair Castle nearby. Only seven minutes from Pitlochry with its famous Festival Theatre. Easy touring distance to Queen's View, Loch Tummel, Balmoral, Braemar, Glamis Castle, Scone Palace and Aviemore. Only six guests accommodated at one time. All bedrooms have wasbasins, shaver points, electric blankets and tea/coffee making facilities. Lounge with colour TV. Shower room with toilet and washbasin; bathroom with bath, shower, toilet and washbasin. Centrally heated throughout. Sorry no pets. No smoking. Open Easter to October. Fire Certificate Awarded. Write, telephone or please call in to enquire about terms. **AA/RAC ◆◆.**

**STANLEY. Mrs Ann Guthrie, Newmill Farm, Stanley PH1 4QD (01738 828281).** This 330 acre farm is situated on the A9, six miles north of Perth. Accommodation comprises twin and double en suite rooms and a family room with private bathroom; lounge, sittingroom, diningroom; bathroom, shower room and toilet. Bed and Breakfast from £18; Evening Meal on request. The warm welcome and supper of excellent home baking is inclusive. Reductions and facilities for children. Pets accepted. The numerous castles and historic ruins around Perth are testimony to Scotland's turbulent past. Situated in the area known as "The Gateway to the Highlands" the farm is ideally placed for those seeking some of the best unspoilt scenery in Western Europe. Many famous golf courses and trout rivers in the Perth area. **STB ★★★** *B&B*.
e-mail: guthrienewmill@sol.co.uk
website: www.newmillfarm.com

**STRATHYRE. Mrs Harley, Coire Buidhe, Strathyre FK18 8NA (01877 384288).** Coire Buidhe sits in the beautiful valley of Strathyre, nine miles from Callander, an excellent base for touring Loch Lomond, Trossachs, Stirling and Edinburgh, with both east and west coasts within easy reach. Two double en suite, one triple en suite, one single, one twin and one family room. Tea making facilities. Sitting and dining rooms. Open all year. Parking. Dogs permitted. Children welcome at reduced rates - cot, highchair and babysitting offered. All water sports and shooting available, plus trekking, tennis, hill walking, golf and putting. Bed and Breakfast from £17. Bar and restaurant meals available 50 yards. Special diets catered for. Full Fire Certificate. Garden patio available for guests' use.

---

Please mention *Bed and Breakfast Stops* when making enquiries about accommodation featured in these pages.

# STIRLING & DISTRICT

**BLAIRLOGIE. Mrs Margaret Logan, Blairmains Farm, Manor Loan, Blairlogie, Stirling FK9 5QA (01259 761338). Working farm.** Charming, traditional stone farmhouse set in attractive gardens on a working dairy farm with a herd of pedigree Holstein cattle. Adjacent to a picturesque conservation village and close to the Wallace Monument and Stirling University. Three-and-a-half miles from Stirling. Edinburgh airport is 30 minutes' drive and Glasgow airport 45 minutes. Ideal base for touring and walking. Accommodation is in one double and two twin rooms with shared bathroom. Very comfortable TV lounge. Ample private parking at this non-smoking establishment. Children welcome. Sorry no pets. Bed and Breakfast terms – double or twin £18 to £20; single £20 to £22. Room only £16. A warm Scottish welcome awaits you.

**DENNY. Mrs Jennifer Steel, The Topps Farm, Fintry Road, Denny FK6 5JF (01324 822471; Fax: 01324 823099)** A modern farmhouse guesthouse in a beautiful hillside location with stunning, panoramic views. Family, double or twin-bedded rooms available, all en suite with tea/coffee, shortbread, TV, radio, telephone. Food a speciality ("Taste of Scotland" listed). Restaurant open to all non-residents. A la carte menu only. Easy access to all major tourist attractions. Your enjoyment is our aim and pleasure! Children welcome, pets by arrangement. Open all year. Bed and Breakfast from £20; Evening Meal from £12. **STB ★★** *GUEST HOUSE*

*See also Colour Display Advertisement*

**DUNBLANE. Jim and Judy Bennett, "Mossgiel" Doune Road, Dunblane FK15 9ND (01786 824325).** Jim and Judy Bennett welcome you to Mossgiel. We are situated in a beautiful countryside setting between the Cathedral City of Dunblane and Doune Castle, yet conveniently placed for access to the A9 and M9 motorway. Mossgiel is an ideal base for touring Stirling, Loch Lomond and the Trossachs. Perth, Glasgow and Edinburgh are also within easy reach. The house is furnished to a high standard and all bedrooms are equipped with hair dryer, clock/radio and tea/coffee making facilities. We have one double and one family room with en suite facilities, and one twin room with private facilities. The guest lounge has a colour TV and is available at all times. All rooms are on the ground floor, and there is safe off-road parking within spacious grounds. Centrally heated throughout and operating a non-smoking policy, we are ensured a comfortable, relaxing holiday.
e-mail: judy@mossgiel.com

**FALKIRK. Mrs E. Strain, "Hawthorndean", Wallacestone Brae, Reddingmuirhead, Falkirk FK2 0DQ (Tel & Fax: 01324 715840).** Come and stay at "Hawthorndean" situated in an area surrounded by local history. Centrally situated for touring Edinburgh, Glasgow and Stirling; near M9 motorway and train station. Open all year; traditional accommodation to suit all. Centrally heated double en suite, family, single and twin rooms with TV, radio-alarm clock, hairdryer, hospitality trays and ironing facilities. Relax in the guest lounge with 32" digital TV or stroll in our garden down to the stream. Ample parking. Traditional Scottish Breakfast or special dietary needs catered for. We look forward to meeting you. Please send for our brochure. Prices from £16 to £25. **STB ★★** *B&B*.

---

*Please mention Bed & Breakfast Stops when writing to enquire about accommodation*

# SCOTTISH ISLANDS

## Isle of Lewis

**NESS. Catriona MacLeod, Eisdean, 12 Coig Peighinnean, Ness HS2 0XG (01851 810240).** Surrounded by impressive coastline with beautiful beaches and interesting birdlife. High standard of cooking; special diets catered for. Accommodation available in single, twin and family rooms. Open all year. Bed and Breakfast from £18; Evening Meal available. Children welcome. **STB** ★★ *B&B*

**STORNOWAY. Mrs C. MacKay, Blackburn, 109 Newmarket, Stornoway HS2 0DU (01851 705232).** A warm welcome in peaceful surroundings. Beautiful view of Broadbay Sea, 20 minutes to the Calanish Stones, Broch and Gearrannan Black House Village, etc. Beautiful beaches on this beautiful island, also wildlife to be admired. Bed and Breakfast from £18 - £19 per person per night. All rooms have tea/coffee making facilities. **STB** ★★★

**STORNOWAY. Lisbeth and Michael Dunne, 3 Sand Street, Stornoway HS1 2UE (Tel & Fax: 01851 702943).** Friendly, comfortable Bed and Breakfast in quiet road leading to the beach but within walking distance of Stornoway town centre. One twin room and one single room each with TV/video, tea and coffee making facilities, hair dryer and shaver adaptor. Bathroom/toilet available for sole use of guests. Use of sun lounge for guests. This is a no smoking establishment. Bed and Breakfast at £15 per person, room only rate £12 per person.

**STORNOWAY. Mr G. Lowder, Hal 'O' The Wynd Guest House, Newton Street, Stornoway HS1 2RE (01851 706073).** Hal 'O' The Wynd is a large three storey building painted white and dates back some 300 years. The property has four large bedrooms, two en suite and two standard. All rooms have a sea view and a panoramic view of Lewis Castle grounds and beyond to Arnish Point. It also has a comfortable guest lounge and a well laid out diningroom. There is also a public payphone in the front hall. All rooms are centrally heated with a thermostatic control, colour teletext TV and tea/coffee making facilities. The town centre is a five minute walk where you will find the bus station which has a good service to all major attractions on the island. We can arrange guided tours of the island. We also have an attractive rear garden that you may wish to use for a barbecue to taste our local fresh seafood etc. Whatever you decide to do on your holiday we will try to make it a pleasant and happy one to remember and hope you enjoy your stay with us. **STB** ★★★ *GUEST HOUSE*

---

Terms quoted in this publication may be subject to increase if rises in costs necessitate

**Scottish Islands**

**STORNOWAY Near. Mrs Rachel Dowie, 74 Newmarket, Stornoway HS2 0DU (01851 704728).** A warm welcome awaits you here with comfortable ground floor accommodation. Two double rooms en suite, one twin with private bathroom. All rooms have tea/coffee making facilities, TV, clock/radio, hairdryer, electric blankets and central heating. We are only two miles from the town of Stornoway and the golf course. The nearest beach is three miles away. Trout and sea fishing. Ample private parking. Restricted smoking. Pets welcome. Reduced rates for children. Bed and Breakfast from £17. **STB** ★★★ *B&B*.

## Orkney Islands

**KIRKWALL. John D. Webster, Lav'rockha Guest House, Inganess Road, Kirkwall KW15 1SP (Tel & Fax: 01856 876103).** Situated a short walk from the Highland Park Distillery and Visitor Centre, and within reach of all local amenities. Lav'rockha is the perfect base for exploring and discovering Orkney. We offer high quality accommodation at affordable rates. All our rooms have en suite WC and power shower, tea/coffee tray, hairdryer, radio alarm clock and remote-control colour TV. Those with young children will appreciate our family room with reduced children's rates, children's meals and child minding service. We also have facilities for the disabled, with full unassisted wheelchair access from our private car park. All our meals are prepared to a high standard using fresh produce as much as possible. Bed and Breakfast from £22 per person. Special winter break prices available. **STB** ★★★★ *GUEST HOUSE, WINNER OF BEST B&B ORKNEY; FOOD AWARDS*. 
e-mail: lavrockha@orkney.com
website: www.orkneyislands.co.uk/lavrockha/

## Shetland

**BRAE. Mrs E. Wood, Westayre Bed and Breakfast, Muckle Roe, Brae ZE2 9QW (01806 522368).** A warm welcome awaits you at our working croft on the picturesque island of Muckle Roe, where we have breeding sheep, pet lambs, ducks and cats. The island is joined to the mainland by a small bridge and is an ideal place for children. The accommodation is of a high standard and has en suite facilities. Guests can enjoy good home cooking and baking. In the evening sit by the open peat fire and enjoy the views looking out over Swarbacks Minn. Spectacular cliff scenery and clean safe sandy beaches, bird watching and hill walking and also central for touring North Mainland and North Isles. Bed and Breakfast from £20 - £22; Dinner, Bed and Breakfast from £30 - £32. **STB** ★★★★ *B&B*.
e-mail: westayre@ukonline.co.uk
website: www.westayre.shetland.co.uk

---

Please mention ***Bed and Breakfast Stops*** when making enquiries about accommodation featured in these pages.

# Isle of Skye

**BROADFORD. Kathie McLoughlin, Lime Stone Cottage, 4 Lime Park, Broadford IV49 9AG (01471 822142).** A truly warm welcome awaits you at this original stone built crofter's cottage. Feel the romantic atmosphere with exposed beams, glazed stone walls, and the inviting open fire in the cosy sitting/breakfast room. All bedrooms are en suite and fully fitted to the highest standards, affording maximum comfort, coupled with breathtaking views over Broadford Bay and Wester Ross Torridon Mountain Range. Within close walking distance there are many local amenities, excellent shops, cafe, restaurants, public houses, bank, post office, churches, 24 hour garage, cycle hire, boat trips, guided bus tours, numerous hill and coastal walks. Something for everyone. **STB** ★★★ *B&B*. 
e-mail: kathie.mc.limecottage@tinyworld.co.uk

**KYLEAKIN. Blairdhu House, Kyle Farm Road, Kyleakin IV41 8PR (01599 534760; Fax: 01599 534623).** Blairdhu House is situated amidst beautiful scenery, offering panoramic views, and is an ideal base for hill walking and bird watching. Just five minutes from the picturesque fishing village of Kyleakin and two minutes' walk from the Skye Bridge. Luxury accommodation in double, twin or family rooms, all en suite, with TV, radio, hairdryer and tea/coffee making facilities. From £28. **STB** ★★★★ *B&B*
website: ourworld.compuserve.com/homepages/blairdhuskye

**PORTREE. The Shielings Guest House, 7 Torvaig, Portree IV51 9HY (01478 613024).** Family-run guest house situated in a crofting area north of Portree off the Staffin Road. Our guests are free to stroll in our own garden, enjoying the fine scenery and our "four-legged neighbours", or they may wish to take advantage of some of our fine local walks. This traditional stone house affords spectacular views of the Cuillins, MacLeod's Tables etc. Only a short walk from the town centre, or just five minutes by car. Accommodation comprises four rooms, all en suite; three doubles and one twin, each with TV. Bedrooms are pine-clad with tea/coffee making facilities. There is a residents' lounge and a separate diningroom. Bed and Breakfast from £18. Evening Meal £10.00. **STB** ★★ *GUEST HOUSE.*

**STAFFIN. Mrs MacDonald, Gairloch View, 3 Digg, Staffin IV51 9LA (01470 562718).** Built in 1997 "Gairloch View" is a modern bungalow on the north coast of Skye with magnificent sea and mountain views overlooking Gairloch on the mainland and nestling below the famous Quiraing Mountain. An ideal base for touring, walking, fishing (sea and loch), golf and beach. Day trips to Outer Isles from Uig (eight miles). Hotels and restaurants nearby. One en suite family room sleeping up to four persons, one en suite family room sleeping up to three persons. Central heating, tea/coffee making facilities. Large guest lounge with sea views, open fire, TV and video. Private car park. Double/twin/family from £18 per person per night. Reduced rates for children.
website: www.gairlochview.co.uk

---

Visit the **FHG** website
# www.holidayguides.com
for details of the wide choice of accommodation featured in the full range of FHG titles

# THE FHG DIPLOMA

## HELP IMPROVE BRITISH TOURIST STANDARDS

You are choosing holiday accommodation from our very popular FHG Publications.
Whether it be a hotel, guest house, farmhouse or self-catering accommodation, we think you will find it hospitable, comfortable and clean, and your host and hostess friendly and helpful.

Why not write and tell us about it?

As a recognition of the generally well-run and excellent holiday accommodation reviewed in our publications, we at FHG Publications Ltd. present a diploma to proprietors who receive the highest recommendation from their guests who are also readers of our Guides. If you care to write to us praising the holiday you have booked through FHG Publications Ltd. – whether this be board, self-catering accommodation, a sporting or a caravan holiday, what you say will be evaluated and the proprietors who reach our final list will be contacted.

The winning proprietor will receive an attractive framed diploma to display on his premises as recognition of a high standard of comfort, amenity and hospitality. FHG Publications Ltd. offer this diploma as a contribution towards the improvement of standards in tourist accommodation in Britain. Help your excellent host or hostess to win it!

---

## FHG DIPLOMA

We nominate ..............................................................................................................................

..................................................................................................................................................

Because

Name ........................................................................................................................................

Address.....................................................................................................................................

..................................................................................................................................................

Telephone No.............................................................

# WALES

# Anglesey & Gwynedd

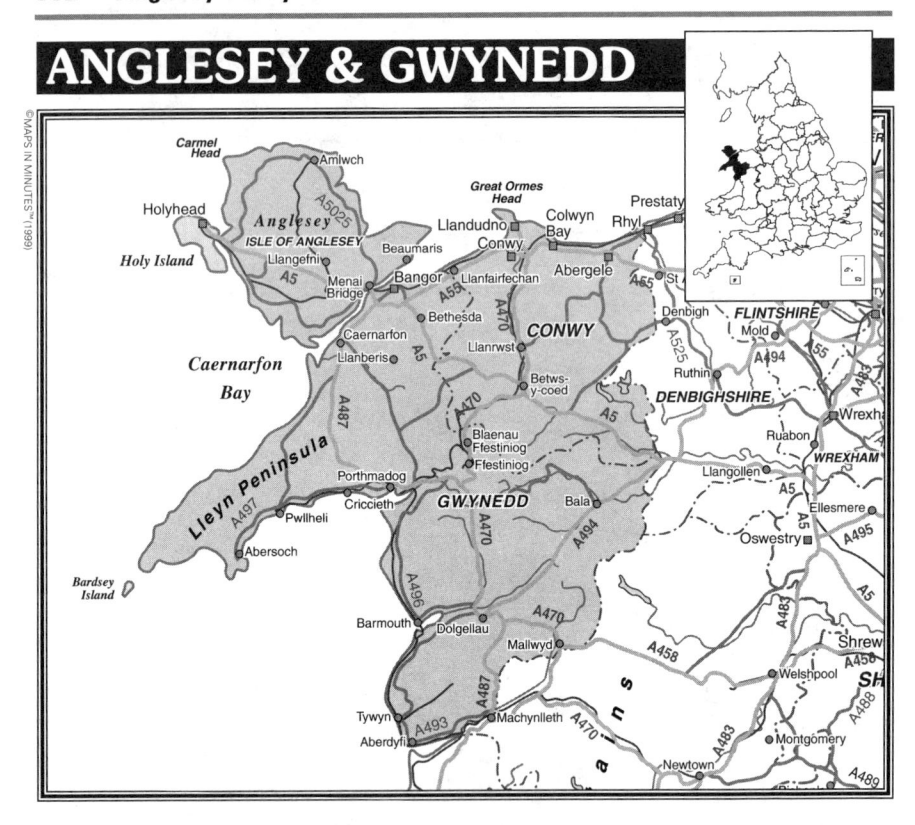

**ABERDARON. Mrs V. Bate, Bryn Mor, Aberdaron LL53 8BS (01758 760344).** Bryn Mor is a family-run Guest House. Full English breakfast, evening meal optional. Comfortable lounge and separate diningroom. Access to rooms at all times. TV and tea making facilities in all rooms. Bathroom and shower facilities. The house overlooks the bay a few minutes from village and beach. Ample parking space in our own grounds. Bryn Mor is situated in the village of Aberdaron at the tip of the Lleyn Peninsula. Around the bay are numerous walks with panoramic views, also fishing, sailing and golf in the locality. Assuring you of our best endeavours to make your holiday a pleasant one. Sorry, no pets. Bed and Breakfast £17, Evening Meal £10.

**ANGLESEY. Mrs Ritson, "Ger-y-Coed", Gaerwen, Anglesey LL60 6BS (01248 421297; Fax: 01248 421400).** Homely guest house situated six miles from Bangor on main Holyhead road (A5). Comfortably furnished. Tea/coffee making facilities, washbasins, shaver points and colour TVs in all rooms. Some rooms en suite. Sky TV. Nice garden, with off-road parking. Good and plentiful food. Double, twin and family rooms available. Central heating. Open all year. Close to all amenities and ferry. Ideal for touring and discovering Snowdonia. Warm welcome assured. Bed and Breakfast from £17.50. Access and Visa accepted. Full Fire Certificate. **WTB ★★** *GUEST HOUSE.*

**BALA. Mrs C. A. Morris, Tai'r Felin Farm, Frongoch, Bala LL23 7NS (01678 520763). Working farm.** 
Tai'r Felin Farm is a working farm, situated three miles north of Bala (A4212 and B4501). Double and twin bedrooms available with beverage tray and clock radio. Beamed lounge with colour TV and log fire when the weather is cooler. Excellent base for touring Snowdonia National Park, watersports, walking, fishing, etc. National White Water Centre is nearby. Hearty breakfast, with packed lunches and snacks available on request. Recommended for excellent cooking and friendly atmosphere. Relax and enjoy a homely welcome. Bed and Breakfast from £16. Walkers and cyclists welcome. Reductions for longer stays. **WTB ★★** *FARM*

**BANGOR. Penhower Uchaf Newydd, Caerhun, Bangor LL57 4DT (01248 362427).** Ingrid and David Farrar look forward to welcoming you to Penhower with its wonderful panoramic views of Snowdonia and Anglesey. A single-storey home set in a spacious garden with ample and secure parking and within easy reach of Bangor, Caernarfon, Llanberis, castles, beaches and many other amenities. We are also convenient for the A5/A55 to Holyhead. A non-smoking establishment with all of our de luxe rooms en suite with showers, we take great pride in offering warm and friendly hospitality and acclaimed home cooking. A brochure is available. Bed and Breakfast from £18 to £22.50. **WTB ★★★★** *B&B*.

**CAERNARFON. Gwyndaf and Jane Lloyd Rowlands, Pengwern, Saron, Llanwnda, Caernarfon LL54 5UH (Tel & Fax: 01286 831500; Mobile: 07778 411780).**
Charming spacious farmhouse of character, situated between mountains and sea. Unobstructed views of Snowdonia. Well-appointed bedrooms, all en suite. Set in 130 acres of land which runs down to Foryd Bay. Jane has a cookery diploma and provides excellent meals with farmhouse fresh food, including home-produced beef and lamb. Excellent access. Children welcome. Open February to November. Bed and Breakfast from £22 to £28; Evening Meal from £13. **WTB ★★★★** *FARM*.

**CAERNARFON near. Paula and David Foster, Tan y Gaer, Rhosgadfan, Near Caernarfon LL54 7LE (01286 830943).** Set in spectacular scenery with views to the top of Snowdon and over the Irish Sea, this farmhouse with beams and open fires offers a restful atmosphere from which to enjoy beautiful North Wales. Riding, climbing, walking and beaches are all close by. The home-made bread and farmhouse cooking are done on the 'Aga' and much of the food is home produced. Guests have their own diningroom and lounge with TV, books, etc. and the en suite bedrooms are spacious. Bed and Breakfast from £20, Evening Meal optional. Reductions for weekly stays. Telephone for details, brochure on request.

---

Readers are requested to mention this guidebook when seeking accommodation (and please enclose a stamped addressed envelope).

# Anglesey & Gwynedd

**DOLGELLAU. Mr and Mrs J. S. Bamford, Ivy House, Finsbury Square, Dolgellau LL40 1RF (01341 422535; Fax: 01341 422689).** A country town guesthouse offering a welcoming atmosphere and good homemade food. Guest accommodation consists of six double rooms, three with en suite toilet facilities, all with colour TV, tea/coffee making facilities and hair dryer. The diningroom, which is licensed, has a choice of menu, including vegetarian dishes. The lounge has tourist information literature and there are maps available to borrow. Dolgellau is an ideal touring, walking and mountain biking region in the southern area of the Snowdonia National Park. Bed and Breakfast from £18.50. **WTB ★★** *GUEST HOUSE*. **AA ♦♦♦**.
e-mail: ivy.hse.dolgellau@ic24.net

**DOLGELLAU. Mrs G.D. Evans, "Y Goedlan", Brithdir, Dolgellau LL40 2RN (Tel and Fax: 01341 423131).** Guests are welcome at "Y Goedlan" from February to October. This old Vicarage with adjoining farm offers peaceful accommodation in pleasant rural surroundings. Three miles from Dolgellau on the B4416 road, good position for interesting walks (Torrent, 400 yards from the house), beaches, mountains, narrow gauge railways and pony trekking. All bedrooms are large and spacious; one double, one twin and one family room, all with colour TV, tea/coffee facilities and washbasins. Bathroom, two toilets; shower; lounge with colour TV; separate tables in dining room. Reduced rates for children under 10 years. Central heating. Car essential, parking. Comfort, cleanliness and personal attention assured, with a good hearty breakfast; Bed and Breakfast from £16.50. **WTB ★★** *B&B*.

**DOLGELLAU. Mrs Jones, Fronoleu Farm Hotel, Tabor, Dolgellau LL40 2PS (01341 422197/422361; Fax: 01341 422361).** Secretly secluded, surrounded by wild Welsh beauty, stands Fronoleu. This converted, family-run Welsh farmhouse overlooks the magnificent Mawddach Estuary and combines traditional Welsh warmth with modern excellence. Log-fired lounges, an award-winning Stable Restaurant offering à la carte and bar meals, four-poster beds and a Celtic harpist most evenings enhance Fronoleu's cosy, friendly atmosphere. Free fishing licences. Very lively at weekends and idyllically peaceful during the week. Non-smoking. **WTB ★★** *HOTEL*.

**FAIRBOURNE. John and Ann Waterhouse, Einion House, Friog, Fairbourne LL38 2NX (01341 250644).** Lovely old house between mountains and sea, set in beautiful scenery. Comfortable rooms, double, twin or single, en suite available. Reputation for good home cooking - vegetarians catered for. All rooms with colour TVs, clock/radios, hairdryers, teamakers, sea or mountain views. Separate dining tables. Guests' TV lounge. Restaurant and residential licence. Wonderful sunsets, marvellous walking - maps and Land Rover lifts available. Pony trekking, fishing and bird watching. Good centre for Narrow Gauge Railways. Castle within easy reach. Safe sandy beach few minutes' walk from house. Bed and Breakfast from £20 - £50; optional three-course Dinner £11. Weekly terms. **WTB ★★** *GUEST HOUSE*.

---

# FREE or REDUCED RATE entry to Holiday Visits and Attractions — see our READERS' OFFER VOUCHERS on pages 43-60

**Anglesey & Gwynedd** 385

**MENAI BRIDGE. Ms. Rosemary Ann Abas, Bwthyn, Brynafon, Menai Bridge, Isle of Anglesey LL59 5HA (Tel & Fax: 01248 713119).** Warm, welcoming, non-smoking Bed and Breakfast one minute from beautiful Menai Straits and bowling green, close by Telford's elegant Suspension Bridge. Bwthyn ("dear little house" in Welsh), a former quarryman's terraced cottage offers character, comfort, genuine hospitality. Two very pretty en suite double rooms, power showers, etc (one plus bath), colour TV, tea/coffee makers, scrumptious home cooking. Bed and Breakfast £17.50 per person per night (double) single nights; £17.00 per person per night two/three nights; £16.00 per person per night four nights or more. Delicious four-course dinner £14.00 per person (double). Special Breaks for over 45's: three nights Bed and Breakfast £49 per person; Dinner, Bed and Breakfast £89.00 per person. Ideal base for coast, country, castles, Snowdonia; one-and-a-half miles A5/A55, two miles rail, coaches, 35 minutes Holyhead ferry. Come as guests, leave as friends. **WTB ★★★★** *B&B.*

**NEFYN. Mrs E. Jones, "Terfyn", Morfa Nefyn, Pwllheli LL53 6BA (01758 721332).** Detached house situated at the end of quiet seaside village, only seven miles from Pwllheli, popular market town. Beach and 26 hole golf course 10 minutes' walk away. Caernarfon Castle, Portmeirion Italian Village and Anglesey only 30/40 minutes' drive away. Tea and coffee making facilities in all rooms. TV in sitting room. Light refreshments served at 9pm included in the price. Table and chairs in garden. Open all year except family holidays. Children welcome. Private parking. Sorry no pets. Bed and full cooked Breakfast from £15 adults, children under five years FREE, up to 13 years £7.50.

# FHG

Other specialised

# FHG PUBLICATIONS

Published annually: Please add 50p postage (UK only) when ordering from the publishers

- Recommended COUNTRY HOTELS OF BRITAIN   £4.99
- Recommended WAYSIDE & COUNTRY INNS OF BRITAIN   £4.99
- PETS WELCOME!   £5.99
- B&B IN BRITAIN   £3.99
- THE GOLF GUIDE Where to Play / Where to Stay   £9.99

## FHG PUBLICATIONS LTD
### Abbey Mill Business Centre,
### Seedhill, Paisley, Renfrewshire PA1 1TJ

Tel: 0141-887 0428 • Fax: 0141-889 7204
e-mail: fhg@ipcmedia.com • website: www.holidayguides.com

# NORTH WALES

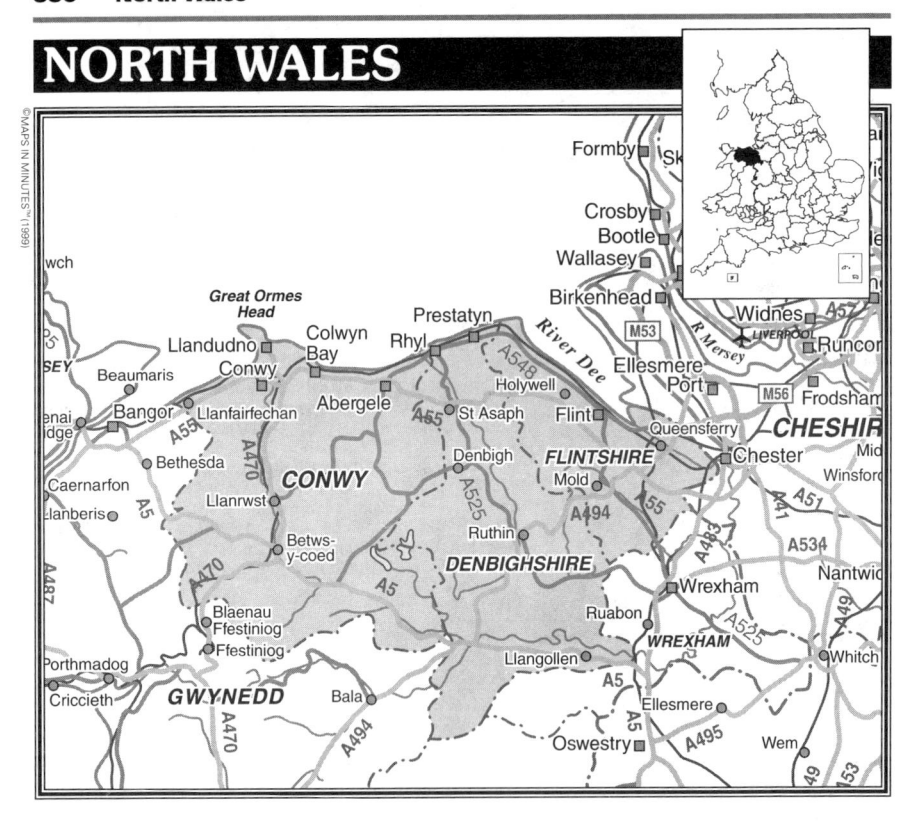

**BETWS-Y-COED. Mrs Margaret Martin, Mairlys Guest House, Holyhead Road, Betws-y-Coed LL24 0AN (01690 710190).** Situated in the picturesque village of Betws-y-Coed, Mairlys is a totally non-smoking, well-appointed Victorian residence which offers the visitor a high standard of comfort. All bedrooms have colour TV and tea/coffee making facilities. Double rooms have full en suite facilities, the twin and single rooms are semi en suite. There is a very comfortable guest lounge and ample car parking. Whether it be walking or touring, Betws-y-Coed is an ideal base from which to explore. Golfers are also well catered for with several courses in the area. Sorry, no pets or children. Bed and Breakfast from £21 to £24 per person. **WTB ★★★** *GUEST HOUSE.*

**BETWS-Y-COED. Mrs E.A. Jones, Pant Glas, Padoc, Pentrefoelas Road, Betws-y-Coed LL24 0PG (01690 770248).** Peaceful and quiet, but with a friendly atmosphere, this beef and sheep farm of 181 acres, with scenic views, is situated five miles from Betws-y-Coed. Ideal for touring, within easy reach of Snowdon, Bodnant Gardens, Caernarvon Castle, Llandudno, Black Rock Sands, Ffestiniog Railway, Llechwedd Slate Mines, Swallow and Conwy Falls and woollen mills. Accommodation comprises two double and one twin bedrooms, all with washbasins and tea/coffee making facilities; bath and shower, two toilets. Use of colour TV lounge. Sorry no pets. Car essential, parking for three/four cars. Bed and Breakfast from £14. Open Easter to November.

## Fron Heulog Country House

Betws-y-Coed, North Wales LL24 0BL
Tel: 01690 710736; Fax: 01690 710920
e-mail: jean&peter@fronheulog.co.uk
website: www.fronheulog.co.uk

*Jean & Peter Whittingham welcome house guests*

*"The Country House in the Village !"*

### *Betws-y-Coed – "Heart of Snowdonia"*

We invite you to visit our home where you will enjoy real hospitality. Fron Heulog is an elegant Victorian stone-built house facing south in quiet, peaceful, wooded riverside scenery, which offers de luxe accommodation, completely non-smoking, with full facility bedrooms, en suite bathrooms, spacious lounges, a pleasant dining room and private parking. Sorry, no pets. Highly recommended for friendly atmosphere, warmth, comfort, and hostess' home cooking. Full central heating. In Betws-y-Coed, in the heart of the wonderfully picturesque Snowdonia National Park – with so much to see and do – Fron Heulog is an ideal touring and walking centre. Bed and Breakfast from £20 – £28

**WTB ★★★ Country House**

*Fron Heulog has been highly commended by WTB. Tourism Award. Welcome Host Gold. Recommended by "Which". Welcome – Croeso!*

*See also colour advertisement*

---

**BETWS-Y-COED. Mrs B. Youe. Fairy Glen Hotel, Dolwyddelan Road, Betws-y-Coed LL24 0SH (Tel & Fax: 01690 710269).** At Fairy Glen Hotel we offer you a warm and friendly welcome, comfortable accommodation and excellent home-cooked food, in a relaxed and convivial atmosphere. All our rooms are well equipped with central heating, colour TV, alarm clock-radio, hair dryer and tea/coffee making facilities. Most rooms have en suite bathrooms or shower rooms. We have a TV lounge, and cosy licensed cocktail bar for our residents to relax in. Our private car park is for guests only. Packed lunches and vegetarian meals are available. Bed and Breakfast from £21 per person per night. **WTB ★★ HOTEL. AA ★**

---

**BETWS-Y-COED. Mrs Eirian Ifan, Llannerch Goch 17th Century Country House, Capel Garmon, Betws-y-Coed LL26 0RL (01690 710261).** A charming no smoking 17th century former rectory with character. Panoramic views of the Snowdonia range, ideal for touring, walking, trekking, visiting National Trust properties or for simply relaxing in our mature garden by the pond. This smallholding is situated two miles from the picturesque village of Betws-y-Coed in the Snowdonia National Park. Llannerch Goch has retained many features of its past together with traditional Welsh furniture. We offer three double bedrooms, all en suite, two with canopy bed. Two large sittingrooms and a conservatory for guests' use. Pool room. Central heating throughout. Beverage trays. TV in bedrooms. Also newly renovated self-catering Old Coach House sleeping four/six available. Ample parking. 400 yards from traditional country pub/restaurant. Please telephone for further details. 25% off golfing green fees. **WTB ★★★★ COUNTRY HOUSE.**
e-mail: eirianifan@talk21.com
website: www.croeso-betws.org.uk/acc/bb/llangoch.htm

---

**BETWS-Y-COED. David and Jean Pender, Bryn Bella Guest House, Llanrwst Road, Betws-y-Coed LL24 0HD (Tel & Fax: 01690 710627).** Bryn Bella is a small but select Victorian guest house enjoying an elevated position overlooking the beautiful village of Betws-y-Coed and the surrounding mountains of the Snowdonia National Park. All rooms are beautifully furnished and most have en suite shower rooms. All rooms have colour TV and tea/coffee making facilities. The house enjoys glorious views of the village and surrounding mountains and there is ample private parking. Garaging for motorcycles and mountain bikes is also available. If travelling by train or bus there is a free pick-up service from the local station. Non-smoking throughout. Bed and Breakfast from £22 per person. **WTB ★★★ GUEST HOUSE.**
e-mail: brynbella@clara.net
website: www.brynbella.co.uk

**BETWS-Y-COED. Summer Hill Non-Smokers' Guest House, Coedcynhelier Road, Betws-y-Coed LL24 0BL (01690 710306).** Especially for the non-smoker, Summer Hill is delightfully situated in a quiet, sunny location overlooking the River Llugwy and Fir Tree Island; 150 yards from main road, shops and restaurants. Seven comfortable bedrooms (four en suite), washbasin and tea/coffee making facilities. Residents' lounge with colour TV. Ideal for walkers. Flasks filled. Vegetarians, special diets catered for. Private car parking. Betws-y-Coed is the gateway to Snowdonia, with spectacular mountains, forests and rivers. Golf, fishing, gardens, castles all accessible. Bed and Breakfast from £17.50. **WTB ★★** *GUEST HOUSE.* **AA ♦♦♦**

**BETWS-Y-COED. Mrs Florence Jones, Maes Gwyn Farm, Pentrefoelas, Betws-y-Coed LL24 0LR (01690 770668).** Maes Gwyn is a mixed farm of 90-97 hectares, situated in lovely quiet countryside, about one mile from the A5, six miles from the famous Betws-y-Coed. The sea and Snowdonia Mountains about 20 miles. Very good centre for touring North Wales, many well-known places of interest. House dates back to 1665. It has one double and one family bedrooms with washbasins and tea/coffee making facilities; bathroom with shower, toilet; lounge with colour TV and diningroom. Children and Senior Citizens are welcome at reduced rates and pets are permitted. Car essential, ample parking provided. Good home cooking. Six miles to bus/railway terminal. Open May/November for Bed and Breakfast from £16. SAE, please, for details.

**BETWS-Y-COED. Jim and Lilian Boughton, Bron Celyn Guest House, Lon Muriau, Llanrwst Road, Betws-y-Coed LL24 0HD (01690 710333; Fax: 01690 710111).** A warm welcome awaits you at this delightful guest house overlooking the Gwydyr Forest and Llugwy/Conwy Valleys and village of Betws-y-Coed in Snowdonia National Park. Ideal centre for touring, walking, climbing, fishing and golf. Also excellent overnight stop en-route for Holyhead ferries. Easy walk into village and close to Conwy/Swallow Falls and Fairy Glen. Most rooms en suite, all with colour TV and beverage makers. Lounge. Full central heating. Garden. Car park. Open all year. Full hearty breakfast, packed meals, snacks, evening meals - special diets catered for. Bed and Breakfast from £19 to £26, reduced rates for children under 12 years. Special out of season breaks. **WTB ★★★** *GUEST HOUSE.*
e-mail: broncelyn@betws-y-coed.co.uk
website: www.betws-y-coed.co.uk/broncelyn

**BETWS-Y-COED. Mrs E. Jones, Maes-y-Garnedd Farm, Capel Garmon, Llanrwst, Betws-y-Coed (01690 710428). Working farm.** This 140-acre mixed farm is superbly situated on the Rooftop of Wales as Capel Garmon has been called, and the Snowdonia Range, known to the Welsh as the "Eyri", visible from the land. Two miles from A5. Surrounding area provides beautiful country scenery and walks. Safe, sandy beaches at Llandudno and Colwyn Bay. Salmon and trout fishing (permit required). Mrs Jones serves excellent home-produced meals with generous portions including Welsh lamb and roast beef. Gluten-free and coeliacs' wheat-free diets can be arranged. Packed lunches, with flask of coffee or tea. One double and one family bedrooms with washbasins; bathroom, toilet; sittingroom, dining room. Children welcome; cot, high chair and babysitting available. Regret, no pets. Car essential, ample parking. Open all year. Bed and Breakfast; Evening Meal optional. SAE brings prompt reply with details of terms. Reductions for children. Bala Lakes, Bodnant Gardens, Ffestiniog Railway, slate quarries, Trefriw Woollen Mills nearby. Member of AA. **WTB ★** *FARM*

*When making enquiries or bookings, a stamped addressed envelope is always appreciated*

## North Wales

**CHESTER near. Mrs Christine Whale, Brookside House, Brookside Lane, Northop Hall, Mold CH7 6HN (01244 821146).** Relax and enjoy the hospitality of our recently refurbished 18th century Welsh stone cottage. The home-from-home accommodation offers a double, twin or family room, en suite upon request. All rooms have colour TV and tea-making facilities. Within a short walk the village has an excellent restaurant and two pubs (one of which serves bar meals). Suitable for touring North Wales and Chester or just a short break away from it all. Bed and Breakfast from £20. **WTB ★★★** B&B.
e-mail: christine@BrooksideHouse.fsnet.co.uk
website: www.brooksidehouse.fsnet.co.uk/

**CONWY. Glan Heulog Guest House, Llanrwst Road, Conwy LL32 8LT (01492 593845).** Spacious Victorian house, tastefully decorated. With off-road parking. Short walk from historic castle and town walls of Conwy. Ideally situated for touring Snowdonia and North Wales with its many attractions. We have a selection of twin, double and family rooms with en suite facilities, TV and tea/coffee making facilities. There is a large garden with seating to enjoy the far-reaching views. Children welcome. Pets by arrangement. Vegetarians catered for. Bed and Breakfast from £15–£20 per person. **WTB ★★** GUEST HOUSE. **AA ♦♦♦**

**CONWY. Park Hill Hotel/Gwesty Bryn Parc, Llanrwst Road, Betws-y-Coed, Conwy LL24 0HD (Tel & Fax: 01690 710540).** OUR HOTEL IS YOUR CASTLE. Family-run country house hotel. Ideally situated in Snowdonia National Park. Breathtaking views of Conway/Llugwy Valleys. Renowned for excellent service, cuisine and its teddy bear collection. Indoor heated swimming pool with sauna free and exclusively for our guests. Secluded free car park. Golf course and village within six minutes' walking distance. Walkers welcome; guided walks on request. Free shuttle service to nearest railway stations. All our rooms with en suite bathroom facilities, coffee/tea tray, CTV etc. Full cooked English Breakfast. Multilingual staff. Bed and Breakfast from £27.50 per person per night. Special Hospitality Award. ASHLEY COURTENAY AND WHICH? RECOMMENDED. **WTB ★★★** HOTEL. **AA/RAC ★★**
e-mail: Parkhill.Hotel@virgin.net
website: www.betws-y-coed.co.uk/acc/parkhill/

**CONWY. Mrs Sylvia Baxter, Glyn Uchaf, Conwy Old Road, Dwygyfyichi, Penmaenmawr, Conwy, LL34 6YS (Tel & Fax: 01492 623737).** Enjoy a quiet, peaceful holiday at this old mill house set in 11 acres of National Parkland in beautiful mountainous countryside. Ideal touring centre for Snowdonia. Accommodation comprises three bedrooms, all en suite and having lovely views. Lounge with colour TV; diningroom. Excellent cuisine with varied menus and home produce. Tea/coffee making facilities, and colour TV in bedrooms. Children welcome. Two-and-a-half miles to Conwy, five to Llandudno and Colwyn Bay– three minutes' walk to village. Pony trekking, golf and fishing locally. Ample parking. Guests have access to house at all times. Bed and Breakfast from £20. Reductions for children under 12. Highly recommended. SAE or phone please. **WTB ★★★** GUEST HOUSE.

---

**FHG**

Visit the FHG website
**www.holidayguides.com**
for details of the wide choice of accommodation
featured in the full range of FHG titles

**CONWY. Heather and Alex Sexton, Gaynor House, Trefriw, Conwy LL27 0JH (01492 640208).** Heather and Alex welcome you to this quiet seven-bedroom house in the beautiful Conwy Valley, built as part of the estate of LLewellyn, Prince of Wales. Four miles from Betws-y-Coed, 17 miles from the coast. Enjoy fishing, walking, climbing, cycling or just relaxing in Snowdonia. All rooms have washbasins. Guest bathroom with shower. Good home-cooked evening meals, packed lunches by request. Diningroom/residents' lounge. Car park. Open all year. Bed and Breakfast £16 per person. Children five to eight years £8; under five free.

**CONWY. Mrs Janet Shaw, Bryn, Sychnant Pass Road, Conwy LL32 8NS (01492 592449).** In a unique position at the foot of Sychnant Pass, adjacent to the 13th century town walls, Bryn is a comfortable 150-year-old family house in a large attractive garden. Two minutes' walk to the town and within easy reach of Conwy Mountain, Castle and Marina. Ideally situated for walking in Snowdonia and en route for Holyhead ferry. All rooms have colour TV and tea/coffee making facilities, with en suite or private bathroom. Extensive breakfast menu, including our own honey. Parking in large yard at rear. No smoking or pets. Open all year. Bed and Breakfast from £18. **WTB ★★** *B&B*.
e-mail: b&b@bryn.org.uk

**CORWEN. Bob and Kit Buckland, Corwen Court Private Hotel, London Road, Corwen LL21 0DP (01490 412854).** Situated on the main A5, this converted old police station and courthouse has six prisoners' cells turned into single bedrooms. Hot and cold in each, with a bathroom to service three on the first floor and a shower room for three on the ground floor. All double bedrooms have bathrooms en suite. The dining room in the old courthouse is where the local magistrates presided, and the comfortable lounge spreads over the rest of the court. Central heating throughout and colour TV in the lounge. Fire Certificate. Bed and Breakfast from £16; Evening Meal £9. Children and pets welcome. Convenient base for touring North Wales.

**CORWEN. Mr Bob Wivell, Pen-y-Bont Fawr, Cynwyd, Near Corwen LL21 0ET (01490 412663).** Pen-y-Bont Fawr is situated on the outskirts of Cynwyd village, near Corwen. Convenient for the A5, with Llangollen, Bala, Betws-y-Coed and Snowdonia all nearby. An ideal area for walking, cycling, fishing and watersports in Bala. Horse riding can be arranged and you can be assured of the legendary Welsh hospitality. Converted barn has a choice of twin or double bedroom, one twin with vanity unit and use of shower and toilet facilities, two double en suite. Shared dining and livingroom. Tea and coffee facilities available. Children welcome. Regret, no pets. Evening meal on request, special diets catered for. Bed and Breakfast from £15.00. Special three day break with Evening Meal £63 per person. **WTB ★★★** *B&B*.

**LLANDUDNO. Mrs Ruth Hodkinson, Cranleigh, Great Orme's Road, West Shore, Llandudno LL30 2AR (01492 877688).** A comfortable, late Victorian private residence and family home situated on the quieter West Shore of Llandudno. Only yards from beach and magnificent Great Orme Mountain. Parking: no problem. Town centre is a short pleasant walk away. Many places of interest in surrounding area, and opportunities for sports and recreational activities. Excellent home cooked food. Two en suite rooms available, both with views of sea and mountains. Conforms to high standards of S.I. 1991/474. Most highly recommended.

**LLANDUDNO. Roger and Merril Pitblado, Chilterns, 19 Deganwy Avenue, Llandudno LL30 2YB (Tel & Fax: 01492 875457).** Chilterns is entirely non-smoking with full central heating, near the Great Orme, promenade, beach and shops. Our forecourt provides invaluable parking in this busy seaside town. This family-run guest house has just six trading bedrooms - double, family and twin rooms with en suite facilities, colour television, beverage tray and some with king size bed. Our basic tariff is £18 per person per night, with reductions for stays of three or more nights. Children stay at a reduced rate. We look forward to welcoming you to our home. **WTB ★★★** *GUEST HOUSE*.

**\LLANDUDNO. Mr and Mrs Collings, The Wellington Hotel, 12 North Parade, Llandudno LL30 2LP (01492 876709; Fax: 01492 871160).** Set between the Great and Little Ormes in Llandudno Bay, opposite the Victorian pier, is the Wellington Hotel, offering fully en suite rooms, with evening meals on request. Come and enjoy the splendour of this fully licensed hotel which offers a warm welcome all year round. Rooms have TV, radio alarms and much more. Enjoy the local attractions or explore the surrounding areas such as Snowdonia. A warm welcome is assured from Chris and Pamela Collings. Bed and Breakfast from £23 per person per night. Four-course evening meal £10. Special rates for seven-day bookings.

**LLANGOLLEN. Joan and Colin Lloyd, Hillcrest Guest House, Hill Street, Llangollen LL20 8EU (Tel & Fax: 01978 860208).** Hillcrest lies in a quiet area of the town. Bedrooms are attractively furnished and decorated and all have colour television and tea/coffee making facilities; one is on the ground floor. The cosy lounge has an original 1890's fireplace. At the rear of the house are gardens; safe parking. Licensed. Open all year. Bed and Breakfast from £42 (double room). Welcome Host Award Winner 1996 and 1998. **WTB ★★★** *GUEST HOUSE.*
e-mail: colin@hillcrest-llangollen.freeserve.co.uk

**LLANSILIN. Mrs G. Jones, Lloran Ganol Farm, Llansilin, Oswestry SY10 7OX (01691 791287; mobile: 07779 935009). Working farm, join in.** A friendly welcome is assured at this modern farm set in 300 acres in Welsh valley. A busy working farm of dairy, sheep and cattle, it has surrounding garden and lawns. Fly fishing available locally and horse riding available on the farm. Tastefully furnished farmhouse has three bedrooms – one double, one twin and one single, each with washbasin, TV and tea/coffee facilities; modern bathroom. Large lounge, dining room and conservatory; colour TV. English Breakfast and Evening Meal. Bed and Breakfast from £15; Dinner, Bed and Breakfast (by arrangement) from £24. Weekly self catering from £80.

**RHOS-ON-SEA, Conwy. Mr and Mrs Mike Willington, Sunnydowns Hotel, 66 Abbey Road, Rhos-on-Sea, Conwy LL28 4NU (01492 544256; Fax: 01492 543223).** A family-run hotel. All rooms en suite with colour TV, video and satellite channels, clock radio, tea/coffee facilities, hairdryer, mini-bar refrigerator, direct-dial telephone and central heating. Hotel facilities also include bar, pool room, restaurant, sauna and car park. Situated just a five minute walk from Rhos-on-Sea Golf Club and with four more Championship courses close by. Five minutes' drive to Llandudno. Telephone or fax for brochure and special group terms. **WTB ★★★** *HOTEL.*
website: www.hotelnorthwales.co.uk

**RHYL. The Kensington House Hotel, 17 East Parade, Rhyl LL18 3AG (01745 331868).** Prominent seafront and central location in this traditional family resort. The Kensington is a small family-run hotel which has been established for over ten years. Our ten en suite bedrooms are kept warm and clean; each has full en suite facilities, colour TV, iron and board, tea and coffee, clean towels daily, central heating, comfortable beds with good linen. Our many regular visitors revere the standards we keep as much as the extensive breakfast menu. Close to all amenities and shops, ideal for a rest or as a base for touring North Wales. Prices range from £18 to £35 per person per night.

**WTB ★★★**

**Crafnant GUEST HOUSE**

Mike and Jan Bertenshaw, Crafnant Guest House, Trefriw LL27 0JH • Telephone: 01492 640809
Website: www.trefriw.co.uk • E-mail: crafnant@tesco.net

You can rest assured of a warm welcome at our beautifully appointed guest house in an unspoilt and picturesque village. Cast-iron beds with fresh white linen. Two guest lounges. Ideal base for forest walks, fishing, touring or simply relaxing. Good food and village pubs on doorstep. Three mountain lakes within three miles. Private parking. Bed and Breakfast from £20 to £22 per person per night. Open February to November. Discounts for three nights.

*See also Colour Display Advertisement*

**RUTHIN. Mrs Ella Williams, Tyddyn Chambers, Pwllglas, Ruthin LL15 2LS (01824 750683).** A traditional sheep and dairy working farm set in scenic countryside with close proximity to Snowdonia and many other North Wales attractions. Your hosts are a typical Welsh-speaking musical family. Your stay will be enhanced by tasting our home-fare cooking and enjoyment of the peaceful surroundings. One double room, one twin room and one family room all en suite. Croeso/welcome. Open all year except Christmas and New Year. Bed and Breakfast from £18 to £22, Evening Meal from £10. **WTB ★★** *FARM*.

**ST. ASAPH. Mrs N. Price, Plas Penucha, Caerwys, Mold CH7 5BH (01352 720210).** One family has owned this unique farmhouse for over 400 years. Over the centuries it has been altered and modernised, but always with the aim of retaining its sense of history and serenity. Extensive gardens overlook the Clwydian Hills. A spacious lounge with large library. Full central heating. There are four bedrooms, two en suite, all with washbasins, shaver points, hairdryers and tea/coffee making facilities. Two miles from A55 expressway - 30 minutes Chester and North Wales Coast - one hour Snowdonia, ideal for walkers. Open all year. Bed and Breakfast £21 to £25; Evening Meal from £11. Discounts available. Brochure on request. **WTB ★★★** *COUNTRY HOUSE.*

**TREFRIW. Mrs B. Cole, Glandwr, Trefriw, Near Llanrwst LL27 0JP (01492 640 431).** Large country house on the outskirts of Trefriw Village overlooking the Conwy River and its Valley, with beautiful views towards the Clwydian Hills. Good touring area; Llanrwst, Betws-y-Coed and Swallow Falls five miles away. Fishing, walking, golfing and pony trekking all close by. Comfortable rooms, lounge with TV, dining room. Good home cooking using local produce whenever possible. Parking. Bed and Breakfast from £18.

Please mention ***Bed and Breakfast Stops*** when making enquiries about accommodation featured in these pages.

# CARDIGANSHIRE

**ABERAERON. Mr and Mrs J. Lewis, Hazeldene Guest House, South Road, Aberaeron SA46 0DP (01545 570652; Fax: 01545 571012).** Jackie and John Lewis offer you a warm and distinctively Welsh welcome with good home cooking. Hazeldene has a substantial, dignified character, in keeping with its original role as home to an affluent sea captain. Dating from 1906 its spacious rooms display a wealth of architectural detail - stained glass windows, impressive fireplaces and ceilings. Immaculately refurbished and spotless throughout. The en suite bedrooms are comfortable and very well equipped including TV and beverage facilities. Fishing, riverside and coastal walks, tennis courts, swimming pool and leisure centre nearby. Aberaeron is a delightful coastal town on Cardigan Bay renowned for its Georgian-style architecture and picturesque harbour. Bed and Breakfast from £20. Sorry no children or pets. **WTB ★★★★** *GUEST HOUSE, TOP 20 "WHICH" GOOD B & B GUIDE.* 
e-mail: hazeldeneaberaeron@tesco.net
website: aberaeron.co.uk/hazeldene.htm

**ABERAERON. Mrs Christine Jones, Frondolau Farm Guest House, Heol Llain Prysg, Llanon SY23 5HZ (01974 202354).** Frondolau is a period house in a quiet location and is part of a working dairy farm. Situated five miles north of Aberaeron and ten miles south of Aberystwyth we are ideally placed for visiting Ceredigion's many beautiful beaches and mountains. Bedrooms have tea/coffee facilities, clock radio, double glazing and central heating. A large sitting room with wood fire is available for your use. Relax and enjoy being a welcome guest with home-produced food from the farm and garden. Bed and Breakfast from £16 per person with special rates available for short breaks (five days plus). Open all year. Brochure available. **WTB ★★** *B&B. WELCOME HOST AWARD. MEMBER OF TASTE OF WALES.*

**ABERYSTWYTH. Blue Grass Cottages.** Bed and Breakfast with a difference – a unique experience. Your own cottage with the breakfast being served therein. Blue Grass Cottages are situated on Brynglas Farm, Chancery – a little hamlet in rural countryside along the main A487; just four miles south of Aberystwyth and set in lovely panoramic views. A small family run working farm. The cottages are of a very high standard and fully equipped with a few little extras to make you feel at home. Ideal for children. Dogs welcomed. Come and discover our lovely country location and enjoy the tranquillity – away from the hustle and bustle of city life. Brochure available on request. Contact - **Mrs Lisa Bumford, Brynglas Farm, Chancery, Aberystwyth SY23 4DF (01970 612799; Fax: 01970 615099).**
e-mail: blue.grass@lineone.net

**ABERYSTWYTH. Y Gelli, Lovesgrove, Aberystwyth SY23 3HP (01970 617834).** Luxury Scandinavian style house on a 22-acre smallholding in a peaceful country setting with abundant wildlife. Just three miles from Aberystwyth and 200 yards off the A44. Centrally heated bedrooms with colour TV, tea and coffee making facilities etc. Also, group accommodation available in nearby mansion. Terms from £18 per night. **WTB ★★** *GUEST HOUSE.*

*Please mention Bed & Breakfast Stops when writing to enquire about accommodation*

**LAMPETER. Mrs Eleanor Marsden-Davies, Brynog Mansion, Felinfach, Lampeter SA48 8AQ (01570 470266).** Enjoy a relaxing holiday in the friendly atmosphere of this spacious 250-year-old country mansion. Brynog is a 170 acre grazing farm situated in the beautiful Vale of Aeron, midway between Lampeter market town and the unique Aberaeron seaside resort, just 10 minutes by car. The mansion is approached by a three-quarter-mile rhododendron-lined drive. Spacious en suite bedrooms with bathroom or shower, other room with washbasin, near bathroom. Tea making facilities on request. Central heating. Full Welsh breakfast provided, served in the grand old well-furnished diningroom. There is a spacious comfortable lounge with TV. Rough shooting, private fishing, bird-watching and riverside walk nearby. Children over six years welcome. Sorry, no dogs. Bed and Breakfast from £20 to £25. **WTB ★★★** *B&B. TOURIST BOARD "WELCOME HOST" AWARD.*

See also Colour Display Advertisement

**LLANRHYSTUD. Penycastell Farm Hotel, Llanrhystud SY23 5BZ (01974 272622).** Penycastell has a fantastic central location in Wales which makes it an ideal place for exploring the Cardigan Bay Marine Heritage Coast, Aberystwyth and Aberaeron. Situated well above sea level the farm enjoys spectacular panoramic views. Cosy and relaxing atmosphere, antiques and paintings abound, along with beams and old panelling. All bedrooms are en suite and centrally heated, and each is individually designed with lots of little extras. One twin available on ground floor, suitable for partially disabled. One four-poster room. Car parking. Sorry, no children or pets. Bed and Breakfast £25 to £45. Special Breaks available.

# CARMARTHENSHIRE

**CARMARTHEN. Mrs Margaret Thomas, Plas Farm, Llangynog, Carmarthen SA33 5DB (Tel & Fax: 01267 211492). Working farm.** "Welcome Host". Situated six miles west of Carmarthen town along the A40 towards St. Clears. Quiet location, ideal touring base. Working farm run by the Thomas family for the past 100 years. Very spacious, comfortable farmhouse. All rooms en suite, with tea/coffee making facilities, colour TV and full central heating. TV lounge. Evening meals available at local country inn nearby. Good golf course minutes away. Plas Farm is en route to Fishguard and Pembroke Ferries. Ample safe parking. Bed and Breakfast from £18 per person. Children under 16 years sharing family room half price. Special mid-week breaks available. A warm welcome awaits. **WTB ★★★** *FARM.*

---

# FREE or REDUCED RATE entry to Holiday Visits and Attractions — see our READERS' OFFER VOUCHERS on pages 43-60

# PEMBROKESHIRE

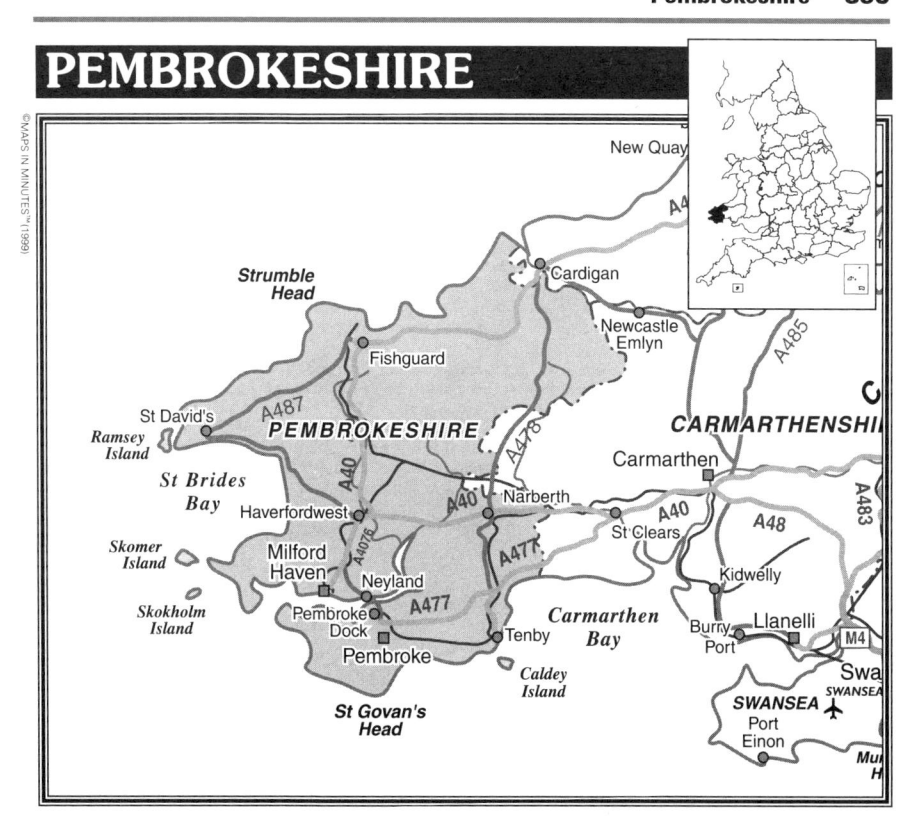

**BLAENFFOS. Castellan House, Blaenffos, Boncath SA37 0HZ (01239 841644).** Castellan nestles on the edge of the Preseli Hills with spectacular panoramic views and our own valley with badger setts, fox and buzzard lairs. We are 10 minutes from Cardigan market town and Cardigan Bay, home of the famous bottle nose dolphins. We have salmon, sewin and trout fishing within five miles, several golf courses within 10 miles, beaches rivalling the Mediterranean, National Trust walks and delightful gardens. Quality ground floor bedrooms with own front door, en suite, central heating, TV, tea-making facilities. Pets welcome. Bed and Breakfast from £17 per person; optional Evening Meal £14. Reductions for children.

**BROADHAVEN. The Bower Farm, Little Haven, Haverfordwest SA62 3TY (01437 781554; Fax: 01437 781940).** Friendly farmhouse run by historic local family. Fantastic views over bay and islands. Fine country cuisine. Walking distance of sandy beaches. Superb riding facilities, all types of sailing, windsurfing, diving, sea and fresh water fishing and numerous golf courses all close by. Full en suite facilities. Colour TV and comfortable lounge. Tray with tea, coffee, chocolate and biscuits. Private safe parking outside the door. Pets and children welcome. Bed and Breakfast from £20 per person per night. **WTB ★★★ FARM**
e-mail: bowerfarm@lineone.net
website: www.a1tourism.com/uk/bower.html

**BROADHAVEN near. Sandra Davies, Barley Villa, Walwyns Castle, Near Broadhaven, Haverfordwest SA62 3EB (01437 781254).** Our 20 acre smallholding with friendly horses offers peace, tranquillity and walks and overlooks Rosemoor Nature Reserve in Pembrokeshire's National Park. Our spacious house, furnished for the comfort of our guests, has three bedrooms, two of which are en suite, complete with hospitality trays; lounge/dining room with colour TV, coal fire and board games for restful evenings. We are centrally situated for visiting Pembokeshire's many sandy bays, famous bird islands, coastal paths and historic places. Many sport and leisure activities within easy travelling distance. We offer hearty breakfasts, packed lunches, special diets and dinner by prior arrangement. Private car parking. No smoking. Bed and Breakfast from £18 to £22 en suite. Comfortable two-bedroomed caravan also available for hire. **WTB ★★★** *FARM*

**FISHGUARD near. Heathfield Mansion, Letterston, Near Fishguard SA62 5EG (01348 840263).** A Grade II Listed Georgian country house in 16 acres of pasture and woodland, Heathfield is the home of former Welsh rugby international, Clive Rees and his wife Angelica. This is an ideal location for the appreciation of Pembrokeshire's many natural attractions. There is excellent golf, riding and trout fishing in the vicinity and the coast is only a few minutes' drive away. The accommodation is very comfortable and two of the three bedrooms have en suite bathrooms. The cuisine and wines are well above average. This is a most refreshing venue for a tranquil and wholesome holiday. Bed and Breakfast from £20 to £24 per person per night; Dinner by prior arrangement. **WTB ★★★** *GUEST HOUSE*.

**GOODWICK. Mrs M. P. Miller, Siriole Guest House, 2 Siriole, Quay Road, Goodwick SA64 0BS (01348 872375).** Beautifully run Bed and Breakfast with spacious accommodation overlooking Fishguard Bay and the Preseli Hills. In a quiet location with ample parking and close to Goodwick village and a short walk to the main ferry terminal to Rosslare - ideal for day trips to Ireland. We are centrally located for walks along the splendid Pembrokeshire National Coastal Path and numerous attractions. All rooms are en suite with shower/toilet, tea/coffee facilities and colour TV; some have sea views. Children and pets welcome. Prices for Bed and Breakfast £19 per person seaview rooms, £17 per person for back rooms. Reductions for longer stays. Open all year.

**GOODWICK. Miss S. Philipps, Ivybridge, Drim Mill, Dyffryn, Goodwick SA64 0FT (01348 875366 or 872623; Fax: 01348 872338).** Situated down a leafy lane, Ivybridge waits to welcome you. Heated indoor pool, licensed bar. En suite bedrooms with colour TV and hot drinks tray. Home cooking, vegetarian and special diets catered for. Half-a-mile from port, ferry travellers welcome. Ample car parking. Please ring for brochure. Tariff as from June 2001: Bed and Breakfast £20.50 to £24.50 per person. Two-night break Dinner, Bed and Breakfast £67 to £75 per person. **WTB ★★** *GUEST HOUSE*
e-mail: ivybridge@cwcom.net
website: www.ivybridge.cwc.net

**HAVERFORDWEST. Mrs M.E.Davies, Cuckoo Mill Farm, Pelcomb Bridge, St David's Road, Haverfordwest SA62 6EA (01437 762139). Working farm.** There is a genuine welcome to our mixed working family farm. Quietly set in beautiful countryside surrounded by animals and wildlife. Comfortable, well-appointed accommodation. Bedrooms with tea/coffee tray, radio, TV and en suite. Excellent quality food using home and local produce. Families welcome. Deductions for children and senior citizens. Open January to December. Pretty flowers and lawns in relaxed surroundings. Personal attention. Unrestricted access. Ideally situated for central Pembrokeshire, coastline walks, sandy beaches, bird islands, castles, City of St Davids and Tenby. Bed and Breakfast, Evening Meal available. **WTB ★★★** *FARM. GOLD WELCOME HOST AWARD. TASTE OF WALES.*

**HAVERFORDWEST. Mr and Mrs Patrick, East Hook Farm, Portfield Gate, Haverfordwest, Pembroke SA62 3LN (01437 762211).** Howard and Jen welcome you to their Georgian Farmhouse surrounded by beautiful countryside, four miles from the coastline and three miles from Haverfordwest. Double, twin and family suite available, all en suite. Pembrokeshire produce used for dinner and breakfast. Dinner £14 per person. Bed and Breakfast from £20 to £22 per person. **WTB ★★★** *FARMHOUSE.*

**HAVERFORDWEST. Joyce Canton, Nolton Haven Farm, Nolton Haven, Haverfordwest SA62 1NH (01437 710263).** The farmhouse is beside the beach on a 200 acre mixed farm, with cattle, calves and lots of show ponies. It has a large lounge which is open to guests all day as are all the bedrooms. Single, double and family rooms; two family rooms en suite, four other bathrooms. Pets and children most welcome, babysitting free of charge. 50 yards to the beach, 75 yards to the local inn/restaurant. Pony trekking, surfing, fishing, excellent cliff walks, boating and canoeing are all available nearby. Riding holidays and short breaks all year a speciality. Colour brochure on request.

**SAUNDERSFOOT. Bob & Jayne King, Jalna Hotel, Stammers Road, Saundersfoot SA69 9HH (Tel & Fax: 01834 812282).** Saundersfoot is a delightfully sunny village with golden beaches offering miles of safe bathing. The popular harbour caters for those wishing to sail or fish. Picturesque cliff tops and woodlands are there for all. The Jalna Hotel is situated in a superb position for easy access to the sea front and harbour. The Hotel's 14 en suite bedrooms are on ground and first floor levels, some bedrooms are designated non-smoking. All are comfortably furnished with colour TVs, beverage trays, hairdryers, radio alarm clocks and full central heating. Two-bedroom suite on the lower ground floor, ideal for those who cannot manage stairs. Bob and Jayne have the experience to make your holiday as relaxing as you want. Comfortable lounge bar. **WTB/AA ★★** *HOTEL.*

**TENBY. Jeff and Yvonne Hurton, Pen Mar, New Hedges, Tenby SA70 8TL (01834 842435).** Situated between Tenby (one mile) and Saundersfoot (one-and-a-half miles) in Pembrokeshire National Park, having sea views of Carmarthen Bay. Waterwynch Bay is just a few minutes' walk. South Pembrokeshire with its beautiful coastline, unspoiled beaches, golden sands and sheltered bays is ideal for sailing, sea fishing, horse riding, golfing or touring. There are many interesting walks along the coastal paths. Comfortable, relaxing atmosphere awaits at Pen Mar, our friendly fully licensed family-run Hotel. We have a pleasant diningroom with separate tables, a well stocked bar, table d'hôte and à la carte menus offering a wide choice of English and Continental cuisine. Open all year. Reductions for children. Bed and Breakfast £18.50 to £25. Most rooms en suite. Private car park. All credit cards accepted. **WTB ★★★** *HOTEL*, **RAC ◆◆◆**
e-mail: penmarhotel@jhurton.freeserve.co.uk

# FHG
## Visit the FHG website
### www.holidayguides.com
for details of the wide choice of accommodation featured in the full range of FHG titles

# POWYS

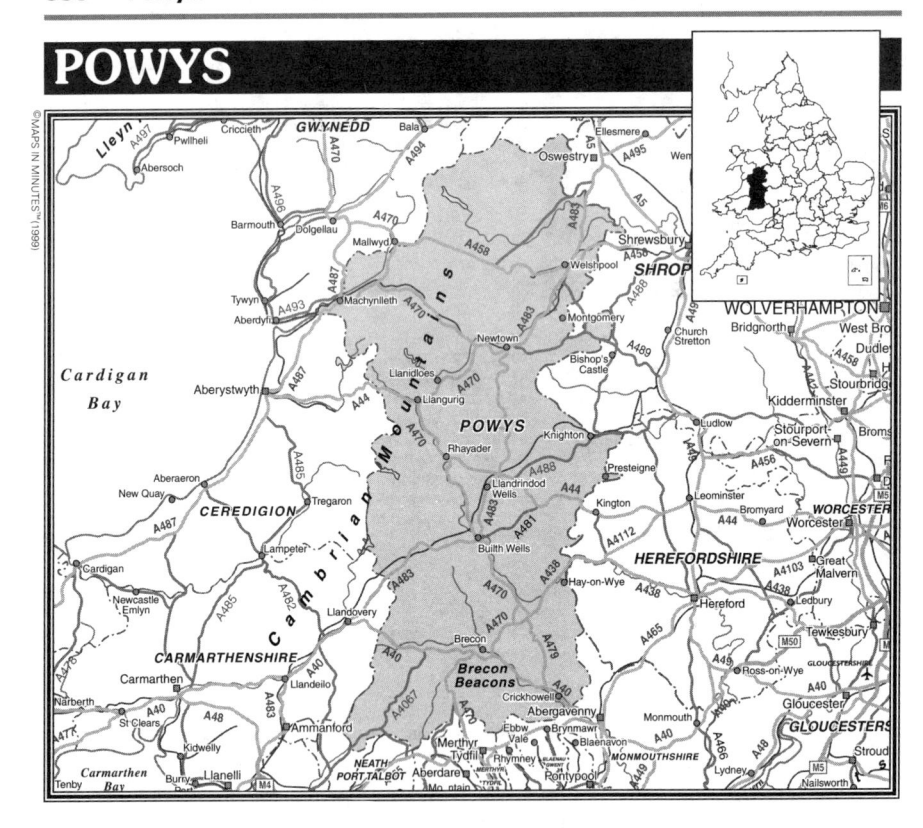

**BRECON. Peter and Barbara Jackson, The Beacons Restaurant & Accommodation, 116 Bridge Street, Brecon LD3 8AH, (Tel & Fax: 01874 623339).** A recently restored Georgian house situated close to the river in the historic small market town of Brecon. Surrounded by magnificent scenery in the heart of the National Park. This 17th/18th century house is full of warmth and character, and offers a variety of individually styled, well equipped bedrooms including four-poster and king-size luxury period rooms. Elegant lounge, cosy cellar bar and a candlelit restaurant serving fine food and wines (five nights) in a relaxed and informal atmosphere. Private parking and secure bike store. **WTB** ★★★ *GUEST HOUSE*. **AA/RAC** ♦♦♦.
e-mail: beacons@brecon.co.uk
website: www.beacons.brecon.co.uk

**BRECON. Mrs Marion Meredith, Lodge Farm, Talgarth, Brecon LD3 0DP (Tel & Fax: 01874 711244).** Warm Welsh hospitality guaranteed in this Georgian farmhouse in the eastern section of the Brecon Beacons National Park with direct access to the Black Mountains. Situated in a quiet rural position with many walks from the front door. The house with original oak beams, inglenook fireplace and flagstone floor, offers quality en suite period furnished bedrooms with tea making facilities. Lounge with TV. Dining room with separate tables serving quality freshly prepared "real food" including vegetarian choice using local and home grown produce is a speciality, also hearty breakfast choice. The house enjoys mountain views set in a country style garden where guests are welcome to relax. Talgarth one-and-a-half miles, Hay-on-Wye and Brecon eight miles. Bed and Breakfast £21 to £23 per person per night. Evening Dinner by arrangement. Weekly rates. Brochure. No smoking. **WTB** ★★★ *FARM*.

**BRECON. Nicola and Bob Atkins, Cambrian Cruisers, Ty-Newydd, Pencelli, Brecon LD3 7LJ (01874 665315).** Our farmhouse, built in 1720 and three miles south of Brecon, offers excellent accommodation for people wishing to enjoy the Brecon Beacons National Park. We are adjacent to the Mon and Brec Canal and also have a modern fleet of narrow boats for daily and weekly hire. We have very comfortable rooms, all en suite with superb views from every window - all with TV, central heating and tea making facilities. Guests have their own entrance, breakfast room and conservatory. For the comfort and safety of our guests we do not permit smoking or pets. We are open March to October and Bed and Breakfast is from £20 per person. **WTB ★★★** *FARMHOUSE*. **AA ♦♦♦♦**
e-mail: cambrian@talk21.com

**BRECON near. Gwyn and Hazel Davies, Caebetran Farm, Felinfach, Brecon LD3 0UL (Tel & Fax: 01874 754460). Working farm, join in**. "Welcome Host". A warm welcome, a cup of tea and home-made cakes await you when you arrive at Caebetran. Visitors are welcome to see the cattle and sheep on the farm. There are breathtaking views of the Brecon Beacons and the Black Mountains and across a field is a 400 acre common, ideal for relaxing. Ponies and sheep graze undisturbed, while buzzards soar above you. The farmhouse dates back to the 17th century and has been modernised to give the quality and comfort visitors expect. There are extras in the rooms to give that special feel to your holiday. The rooms are all en suite and have colour TV and tea making facilities. The diningroom has separate tables, there is also a comfortable lounge with colour TV for guests' use. Caebetran is an ideal base for exploring this beautiful unspoilt part of the country with pony trekking, walking, bird-watching, wildlife, hang-gliding and so much more. For a brochure and terms please write, telephone or fax. "Arrive as visitors and leave as friends". Winner of the FHG Diploma for Wales 1998 and 1999.

**BUILTH WELLS. C. Davies, Gwern-y-Mynach, Llanafan Fawr, Builth Wells LD2 3PN (01597 860256). Working farm.** Gwern-y-Mynach Farm is a working hill sheep farm near Builth Wells in mid-Powys where golf, rugby, bowls, cricket and a new sports hall are all available. Our house is centrally heated throughout. Guest accommodation comprises one single room and one double room with bathroom en suite. Situated in a lovely area, ideal for walking, enjoying the open mountains and watching the Red Kites in flight. Close to the farm in the forest we have Greenwood chair making, steam bending and coracle making, which attract people from overseas to the classes. Also nearby the oldest pub in Powys – The Red Lion, voted best pub in Powys for food. Please write or telephone for further information and tariff.

**BUILTH WELLS near. Mrs Margaret Davies, The Court Farm, Aberedw, Near Builth Wells LD2 3UP (01982 560277).** Non-smokers please. We welcome guests into our home on a family-run livestock farm situated away from traffic in a peaceful, picturesque valley surrounded by hills. Lovely walking, wildlife area, central to Hay-on-Wye, Brecon Beacons, Elan Valley and very convenient for Royal Welsh Showground. We offer comfort, care and homeliness in our spacious stone-built farmhouse with traditional cooking using home produce where possible. Bedrooms have adjustable heating, hospitality trays and electric blankets. En suite or private bathroom available. Guests' lounge with TV. Bed and Breakfast from £18. Good food available at nearby village inn.

# FREE or REDUCED RATE entry to Holiday Visits and Attractions — see our READERS' OFFER VOUCHERS on pages 43-60

**HAY-ON-WYE. Annie and John McKay, Hafod-y-Garreg, Erwood, Builth Wells LD2 3TQ (01982 560400).** A late medieval farmhouse, nestling on a wooded hillside in an Area of Special Scientific Interest, well off the beaten track, above, reputedly, the most picturesque part of the River Wye. A short drive from Hay-on-Wye 'Town of Books', and Brecon and the Beacons National Park. Alternatively, leave your car and step through our gate into a walkers' paradise, steeped in ancient Celtic history. Drink spring water from the tap, and have an enormous breakfast with our free-range eggs. Enjoy a delicious candlelit supper with log fires in the massive inglenook. Bed and Breakfast from £17.50.

**LLANDRINDOD WELLS. The Park Motel, Crossgates, Llandrindod Wells LD1 6RF (Tel & Fax: 01597 851201).** Set in three acres, amidst beautiful mid Wales countryside, yet conveniently situated on the A44. The centrally heated units are available for Bed and Breakfast or self-catering. Each unit has a twin-bedded room, shower room with toilet and a fully fitted kitchenette. The dining area converts to a double bed. Equipped with colour TV, tea/coffee making facilities. The Motel has several advantages over a conventional hotel or bed and breakfast accommodation, being completely self-contained with a front and back door, giving the freedom to come and go as you please. Fully licensed restaurant open all day, offering a good selection of reasonably priced meals, including vegetarian or takeaway. Pets welcome. Bed and Breakfast £22 to £25 per person per night. Self-catering from £35 to £40 per unit per night. **WTB ★★** *COUNTRY LODGE.*

**LLANIDLOES. Jean Bailey, Glangwy, Llangurig, Llanidloes SY18 6RS (01686 440697).** Local river stone (Wye) built house offering comfortable Bed and Breakfast accommodation in beautiful countryside. Traditional English breakfast served with all home cooked evening meals; special diets catered for, vegetarians included. Accommodation comprises two doubles (can be used as family rooms as single bed also in each) and one twin bedroom with washbasin, tea/coffee facilities and storage heater (all beds have electric underblanket); bathroom, separate shower room; diningroom (separate tables per party); lounge with colour TV. Pets welcome. Parking. Central for touring and local walks. Bed and Breakfast £14 per person; reductions for children under nine years.

**LLANIDLOES. Mrs Janet Evans, Dyffryn Glyn, Llanidloes SY18 6NE (01686 412129).** Dyffryn is centrally situated in an Area of Natural Beauty two miles from the friendly market town of Llanidloes, one mile from Clywedog Lake with its spectacular views where sailing, fishing, birdwatching and walking can be pursued. Ideal area for touring. Accommodation comprises one en suite room and one double and one twin-bedded room with washbasin and use of bathroom; both rooms have towels and tea making facilities. Visitors' own sitting room with TV, separate dining room. Ample parking. Bed and Breakfast from £18. **WTB ★★**

**NEWTOWN. Mrs Vi Madeley, Greenfields, Kerry, Newtown SY16 4LH (01686 670596; Fax: 01686 670354).** A warm welcome awaits you at Greenfields. All rooms are tastefully decorated and are spacious in size, each having panoramic views of the rolling Kerry hills. There is a good choice of breakfast menu and evening meals can be provided by prior arrangement; packed lunches are also available. Licensed for residents. Accommodation available in one double and two twin-bedded rooms, all en suite (twin rooms let as singles if required). Hostess tray and TV in all rooms. The diningroom has individual tables. A good place for stopping for one night, a short break or longer holiday. Excellent off-road parking. Bed and Breakfast from £20 to £22 per person; Evening Meal £4.50 to £10. Brochure available. **WTB ★★** *GUEST HOUSE.*

**RHAYADER. Mrs Lena Powell, Gigrin Farm, South Road, Rhayader LD6 5BL (01597 810243; Fax: 01597 810357).** Gigrin is a 17th century longhouse, retaining original oak beams and cosy atmosphere. Peacefully situated overlooking the Wye Valley and half-a-mile from the market town of Rhayader with its numerous inns and leisure centre. The spectacular Elan Valley dams, which supply Birmingham with water are three miles away (home of the Red Kite). The sea is only an hour's drive over the Cambrian Mountains to Aberystwyth. A two mile Nature Trail on the farm; Red Kite feeding daily. The farmhouse is centrally heated and guests have shared use of a bathroom with shower. There are two bedrooms, each with double bed, washbasin and hospitality tray. Residents' sittingroom and diningroom. Bed and Breakfast from £17.50. Non-smoking. Restaurant nearby (200 yards) for Evening Meals. Children welcome. Self-catering accommodation also available. Brochure on request. **WTB ★★** *B&B*.
e-mail: accomm@gigrin.co.uk
website: www.gigrin.co.uk

**TALGARTH. Mrs Bronwen Prosser, Upper Genffordd Farm Guest House, Talgarth LD3 0EN (01874 711360).** Set amongst the most spectacular scenery of the Brecon Beacons National Park, Upper Genfford Farm is an ideal base for exploring the Black Mountains, Wye Valley and the Brecon Beacons, an area of outstanding beauty, rich in historical and archaeological interest, with Roman camps and Norman castles. Picturesque mountain roads will lead you to reservoirs, the Gower coast with its lovely sandy beaches and Llangorse Lake - well known for all kinds of water sports. The charming Guest House accommodation includes one double and one twin-bedded room, both with en suite facilities. they are beautifully decorated and furnished, including tea/coffee making facilities, central heating, colour TV and hairdryer. the cosy lounge has a wealth of personal bric-a-brac, maps and paintings. Very much a home from home, with colour TV and books. Guests are made welcome with home-made cakes and tea on arrival. The local pub and restaurant is nearby and Hay-on-Wye, 'The Town of Books', is a short distance away. bed and Breakfast from £18 to £20 per person. Also fully equipped self-catering cottage with microwave. Bathroom with shower. Ample parking on attractive patio adjacent to cottage. Play area for children, also a friendly pony. Terms from £150 to £180 weekly. Awarded Plaque of Recommendation from the Welsh Tourist Board. Nominated "Landlady of the Year" 1999. Winner of FHG Diploma. **AA ◆◆◆ AA** *QQQQ*.

**WELSHPOOL near. Mrs E.E. Sheridan, Cross Lane Farm, Berriew, Near Welshpool SY21 8AU (01686 640233).** Bill and Lucy welcome you with tea, scones and a friendly chat when you visit them at their spacious farmhouse near the best kept village in Wales, just five miles from the market town of Welshpool. We have enjoyed 28 years of providing accommodation in unspoilt countryside, ideal for walking, golfing, fishing, etc. Accommodation comprises two large double and one single bedrooms; visitors' lounge. Ample parking. Children welcome, cot available. Good plain home cooking comes recommended. Bed and Breakfast from £16. Reduced rates for children under 11 years. Packed lunches by prior request.

**WELSHPOOL Mrs Freda Emberton,Tynllwyn Farm, Welshpool SY21 9BW (01938 553175/553054).** *Working farm.* A warm welcome is assured at Tynllwyn Farm, built 1861, which stands on a hillside with breathtaking views of the Long Mountain and Severn Valley. We are a working beef farm. Large comfortable lounge with open fires in winter. Also licensed bar. All bedrooms have colour TV, tea/coffee facilities and central heating. All home cooking. Large parking area. Nearby are the lovely market town of Welshpool, Powys Castle, Welshpool and Llanfair Steam Railway, canal trips, also exciting quad trekking and mountain bike hire. Easy reach of the lakes and mountains of Mid Wales. Children welcome, pets by arrangement. Bed and Breakfast from £16 to £23. Two self catering cottages available. **WTB ★★★** *FARM*.

---

Visit the **FHG** website
# www.holidayguides.com
for details of the wide choice of accommodation featured in the full range of FHG titles

# SOUTH WALES

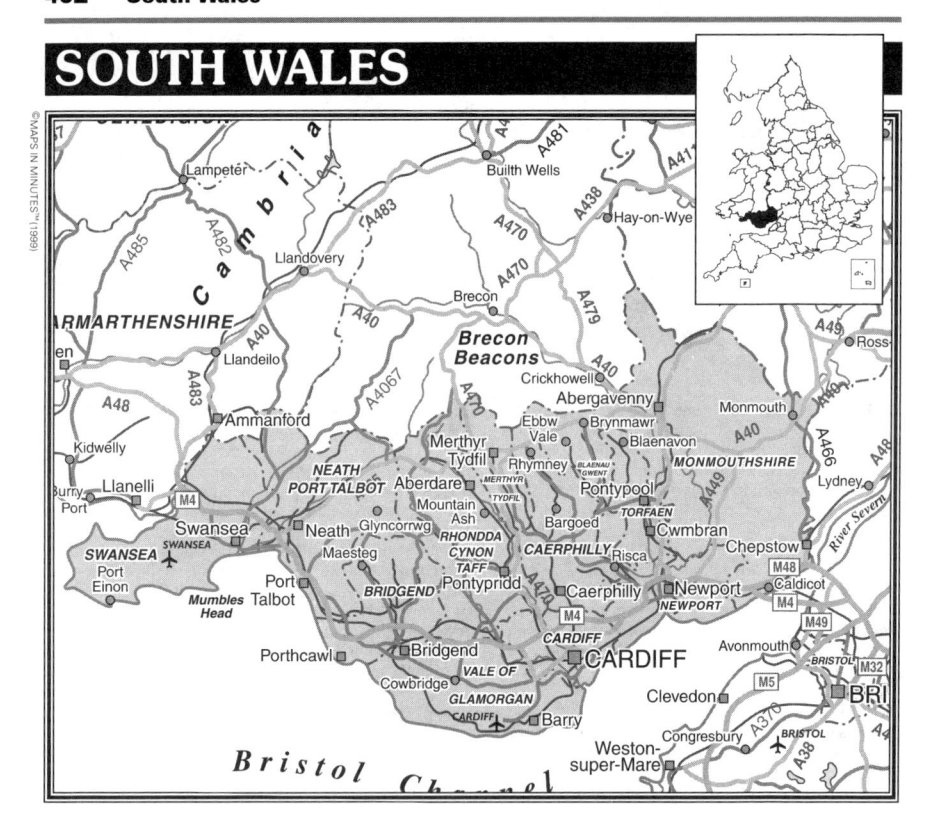

**CARDIFF. Mrs Sarah Nicholls, Preste Gaarden Hotel, 181 Cathedral Road, Cardiff CF11 9PN (029 2022 8607; Fax: 029 2037 4805).** This spacious Victorian family home offers olde worlde charm with modern amenities, including en suite facilities in most rooms. You will immediately feel relaxed by the warm welcome given by Sarah. Situated in the heart of the City, close to the Castle, museums, shops and an international array of restaurants and only 100 yards from Sophia Gardens offering walking, fishing and horse riding. Bed and Breakfast from £18 to £27 per person includes tea/coffee and biscuits in your room. Well established and independently recommended. **WTB** ★★ *HOTEL*, *WELCOME HOST GOLD.*
e-mail: cardiff.hotel@btinternet.com
website: www.cardiff.hotel.btinternet.co.uk

**CARDIFF. Austins Hotel, 11 Coldstream Terrace, City Centre, Cardiff CF11 6LJ (02920 277148).** Situated in the centre of Cardiff, 300 yards from the Castle. Five single and six twin-bedded rooms, five with full en suite facilities, all with washbasins, shaver points, fixed heating, colour TV and tea/coffee making facilities. Full English Breakfast. Only 10 minutes' walk from central bus and train stations. Fire Certificate held. Warm welcome offered to all. Bed and Breakfast from £20. Reduced rates for children and Senior Citizens. **WTB** ★★ *HOTEL*
e-mail: stephen.hopkins1@virgin.net

## South Wales 403

**COWBRIDGE near. Mrs Sue Beer, Plas Llanmihangel, Llanmihangel, Near Cowbridge CF71 7LQ (01446 774610).** Plas Llanmihangel is the finest medieval Grade 1 Listed manor house in the beautiful Vale of Glamorgan. We offer a genuine warmth of welcome, delightful accommodation, first class food and service in our wonderful home. The baronial hall, great log fires, the ancient tower and acres of beautiful historic gardens intrigue all who stay in this fascinating house. Its long history and continuous occupation have created a spectacular building in romantic surroundings unchanged since the 16th century. A great opportunity to experience the ambience and charm of a past age. Featured in "Distinctly Different". Three double rooms. Bed and Breakfast from £28. High quality home cooked evening meal on request. **WTB ★★** *GUEST HOUSE.*

**GOWER PENINSULA. Mrs M. Valerie Evans, The Old Rectory, Reynoldston, Swansea SA3 1AD (01792 390129; Fax 01792 390764).** A warm welcome awaits visitors to our home in this beautiful peninsula. The village is 12 miles west of Swansea and the area offers lovely coast and hill walks, wild flowers, bird-watching, pony trekking, golf and sea activities. We offer comfort, peace and quiet, a lovely secluded garden and good food grown in our own garden or locally. (Under one hour from the National Botanic Gardens and Aberglasney). Tea/coffee facilities in all bedrooms. Central heating. Open most of the year. Bed and Breakfast £20. Non-smokers preferred.

**GOWER PENINSULA. Joanne and Chris Allder, Heathfield, Llethryd, Gower SA2 7LH (01792 390198).** All guests are welcomed by a friendly atmosphere. Our house is set in an acre of mature garden with a heated swimming pool that visitors are welcome to use by arrangement. Llethryd village is a quiet hamlet on the B4271 on the Gower Peninsula which is an Area of Outstanding Natural Beauty. From our house there are lovely tranquil woodland walks and sandy beaches. We are close to restaurants serving locally caught fish and home grown produce. We are approximately 20 minutes from Swansea's extensive shopping centre and theatres. All rooms have TV and tea/coffee making facilities. Children welcome. Non-smokers preferred. Bed and Breakfast from £20 per person.

**MONMOUTH. Rosemary and Derek Ringer, Church Farm Guest House, Mitchel Troy, Monmouth NP25 4HZ (01600 712176)** A spacious and homely 16th century former farmhouse with oak beams and inglenook fireplaces, set in large attractive garden with stream. An excellent base for visiting the Wye Valley, Forest of Dean and Black Mountains. All bedrooms have washbasin, tea/coffee making facilities and central heating; most are en suite. Own car park. Terrace, barbecue. Colour TV. Non-smoking. Bed and Breakfast from £20 to £23.50 per person, Evening Meals by arrangement. We also offer a programme of guided and self-guided walking holidays and short breaks. Separate "Wysk Walks" brochure on request. **WTB ★★** *GUEST HOUSE.* AA ♦♦♦

---

# NOTE

All the information in this book is given in good faith in the belief that it is correct. However, the publishers cannot guarantee the facts given in these pages, neither are they responsible for changes in policy, ownership or terms that may take place after the date of going to press. Readers should always satisfy themselves that the facilities they require are available and that the terms, if quoted, still apply.

**NEATH. Mrs S. Brown, Green Lantern Guest House, Hawdref Ganol Farm, Cimla, Neath SA12 9SL (01639 631884).** West Glamorgan's only AA QQQQQ Premier Selected family-run 18th century luxury centrally heated farmhouse, set in its own 45 acres with beautiful scenic views over open countryside. Close to Afan Argoed and Margam Parks; 10 minutes from M4; one mile from birthplace of Richard Burton. Ideal for walking, cycling, horse riding from farm. Colour TV. Tea/coffee making facilities in all rooms, en suite availability. Pets welcome by arrangement. We offer luxury accommodation at an affordable price. Safe off-road parking. Central for Swansea, Neath and Port Talbot. Want to be impressed, try us. Terms from £23, reductions for children. **WTB ★★★★** *GUEST HOUSE.*
e-mail: stuart.brown7@virgin.net
website: http://freespace.virgin.net/stuart.brown7/

**NEWPORT. Mrs M. Evans, "Westwood Villa Guest House", 59 Risca Road, Crosskeys, Newport NP1 7BT (01495 270336).** Six miles M4; close Newport, Cardiff, Wye Valley. Brecon Beacons one hour's drive, Ebbw Vale 20 minutes. Scenic drives, walks, sport and leisure entertainment. Guest House has central heating and is double glazed. Single, double and family rooms available, en suite rooms available, all with colour TV, washbasin, tea/coffee making facilities, radio alarm clocks; two bathrooms. Tasty home cooking; evening meals. Licensed bar. Children, contractors and pets very welcome. Set in beautiful valleys with outstanding scenery "Westwood Villa", originally a manse, offers beautiful accommodation with that personal touch which makes all the difference and a holiday to remember. Bed and Breakfast from £24 single, £36 double. Bar meals from £5 served 6pm to 8pm. A warm welcome from host Maureen awaits guests. Visa accepted. **WTB ★★★** *GUEST HOUSE.*

**ST. BRIDES WENTLOOG (Near Newport). Mr David W. Bushell, Chapel Guest House, Church Road, St. Brides Wentloog, Near Newport NP10 8SN (01633 681018; Fax: 01633 681431)** Comfortable accommodation in a converted chapel situated in a village between Newport/Cardiff, near Tredegar House. Restaurant and inn adjacent, car park available. Guest lounge with TV. Single, double and twin rooms en suite or private bathroom. Beverage trays, TV, shaver points in all rooms. From £19. Children under three years FREE, three to 12 year olds half price sharing parents' room. Pets by arrangement. Leave M4 at Junction 28, take A48 towards Newport, at roundabout take third exit signposted St. Brides, B4239. Drive to centre of village, turn right into Church Road and left into Church House Inn car park; the guest house is on the left and a warm welcome awaits. **WTB ★★★** *GUEST HOUSE.*

**SWANSEA. Fairyland, Ken and Jan's B&B, 91-93 Alexandra Road, Gorseinon, Swansea SA4 4NU (01792 897940; Fax: 01792 542078).** Family-run guest house, artistically decorated with each room themed on a Flower Fairy. Fairy Grotto; Victorian-style beamed lounge with log stove and massage chair; Wales's first 'Relaxarium' for the ultimate in relaxation. Some rooms self-catering. Laundry facilities. Small pets welcome. All bedrooms with colour TV, tea and coffee tray, washbasins; some en suite. Two jacuzzi bath en suite family rooms. Large car park. Discounts for children and 10% discount offered to members of Vegetarian Society. Two minutes many restaurants, pubs, takeaways, shops. Situated close to Swansea and Gower, ideal touring area for beautiful beaches, waterfalls, mountains, on foot, cycling or by car. Spanish and French spoken. Terms from £16 per person per night Bed and Breakfast, £19 en suite. **WTB ★★** *B&B.*
e-mail: jmurphy@net.ntl.com
website: websites.ntl.com/~jmurphy/

**TINTERN. Anne and Peter Howe, Valley House, Raglan Road, Tintern, Near Chepstow NP6 6TH (01291 689652).** Valley House is a fine Georgian residence situated in the tranquil Angidy Valley 800 yards from the A466 Chepstow to Monmouth road and within a mile of Tintern Abbey. Numerous walks through picturesque woods and valleys right from our doorstep. The accommodation is of a very high standard; all rooms are en suite, have tea/coffee making facilities and colour TV, whilst the guests' lounge and diningroom have a unique arched stone ceiling. Numerous places to eat nearby. Bed and Breakfast from £22.50 per person. Open all year. Non-smoking. **WTB ★★** *GUEST HOUSE*, **AA ♦♦♦**, **RAC** *ACCLAIMED.*

# NORTHERN IRELAND

## COUNTY DOWN

**BALLYWALTER.** Alison Baird, Ganaway House, 12 Ganaway Road, Ballywalter, Newtownards BT22 2LG 7LQ (Tel & Fax: 028 4275 7096). Recently built house with old charm in quiet rural setting overlooking the Irish Sea. Three en suite bedrooms with TV and tea/coffee making facilities. Near to Mount Stewart, Kirkistown, aquarium, sailing and golf (special rates available). Good food. Safe parking. Newtownards 10 miles, Bangor nine miles. Bed & Breakfast from £18 twin/double, £20 single. Evening meal from £10. Half mile from main Ballywalter Road. 
e-mail: ganawayhouse@hotmail.com
website: www.visitcoastofdown.com/ganawayhouse

**BELFAST.** Jean Dornan, Enler Cottage, 385 Comber Road, Dundonald, Belfast BT16 0XB (01247 873240) Comfortable, friendly accommodation in rural surroundings. Convenient to Belfast, Bangor and the Ards Peninsula. Accommodation comprises two rooms with en suite facilities, central heating and television. Children welcome. Parking available. Bed and Breakfast from £17.50 per person.

---

*The* **FHG**
**GOLF GUIDE**
*Where to Play Where to Stay*
**2001**

Available from most bookshops, the 2001 edition of **THE GOLF GUIDE** covers details of every UK golf course – well over 2500 entries – for holiday or business golf. Hundreds of hotel entries offer convenient accommodation, accompanying details of the courses – the 'pro', par score, length etc.

*In association with 'Golf Monthly' and including the Ryder Cup Report as well as Holiday Golf in Ireland, France, Portugal, Spain, The USA, South Africa and Thailand .*

**£9.99 from bookshops or £10.50 including postage (UK only) from FHG Publications,
Abbey Mill Business Centre, Paisley PAI ITJ**

# REPUBLIC OF IRELAND

## Co. KERRY

**TRALEE. Mrs McCarthy, Springmount, Killeen, Ballybunion Road, Tralee (00353 6626146).** Detached two storey house on own grounds with large gardens. Two minutes' drive from town centre and close to all amenities – pitch and putt, aquadrome, museum, sports facilities, equestrian centre, golf courses, greyhound track, safe sandy beaches. Ideal touring base for Kerry, Ring of Kerry, Dingle Peninsula and Killarney. All rooms are en suite with tea/coffee facilities and TV. Breakfast menu. Private safe parking.

## Co. KILDARE

**CASTLEDERMOT. Mr G. D. Greene, Kilkea Lodge Farm, Castledermot (00 353 50345112).** Kilkea Lodge has belonged to the Greene family since 1740. Set in 260 acres of prime tillage and rolling parklands this tranquil setting offers guests the opportunity to relax in the comfort of log fires and traditional Irish hospitality. Accommodation comprises two double and one twin-bedded rooms en suite, and one single room and one family suite. First class traditional home-cooking. Riding Centre on site run by Marion Greene and offering a variety of instructional and fun holidays under qualified supervision. Children welcome. French spoken. Open all year round except Christmas. Bed and Breakfast from £30 to £35 per person; single supplement £5. Dinner from £15 to £20 Advance booking essential. Brochure available.

---

**FHG**

Visit the FHG website
**www.holidayguides.com**
for details of the wide choice of accommodation
featured in the full range of FHG titles

# SPECIAL WELCOME SUPPLEMENT

Are you looking for a guest house where smoking is banned, a farmhouse that is equipped for the disabled, or a hotel that will cater for your special diet? If so, you should find this supplement useful. Its three sections, NON-SMOKERS, DISABLED, and SPECIAL DIETS, list accommodation where these particular needs are served. Brief details of the accommodation are provided in this section; for a fuller description you should turn to the appropriate place in the main section of the book.

## Non-smoking • England

**LONDON, HAMMERSMITH. Anne and Sohel Armanios, 67 Rannoch Road, Hammersmith, London W6 9SS (020 7385 4904; Fax: 020 7610 3235).** Comfortable, centrally located Edwardian family home. Great base for sightseeing. Excellent transport access. Bed and Continental Breakfast £22 nightly. Smoking only in garden.

**LONDON, KENSINGTON. Mowbray Court Hotel, 28-30 Penywern Road, Earls Court, London SW5 9SU (0207-370 3690; Fax: 0207-370 5693).** Listed Bed and Breakfast Tourist Class Hotel. Non-smoking rooms available. The hotel is close to all major shopping areas and tourist sights. We accept well behaved pets.

**CAMBRIDGESHIRE, CAMBRIDGE. Cristina's Guest House. 47 St Andrews Road, Cambridge CB4 1DH (01223 365855; Fax: 01223 365855).** Only 15 minutes' walk from the City Centre and colleges. All rooms have colour TV, hair dryer, alar/clock-radio and tea/coffee making equipment. Centrally heated with comfortable TV lounge. Private car park, locked at night.

**CAMBRIDGESHIRE, HEMINGFORD GREY. Maureen and Tony Webster, The Willow Guest House, 45 High Street, Hemingford Grey, St. Ives, Cambs PE28 9BJ (01480 494748; Fax: 01480 464456).** Large private guest house in centre of this picturesque village. Family, twin, double and single rooms available. All bedrooms en suite and non-smoking. Sorry no pets.

**CHESHIRE, CHESTER. Brian and Hilary Devenport, White Walls, Village Road, Christleton CH3 7AS (Tel & Fax: 01244 336033).** Converted stables in heart of village two miles from Chester, double en suite and twin. Colour TV, tea/coffee making facilities, Bed and Full English Breakfast from £18-£25. Near village pub, pond, church, bus stop and post office. A rural heaven.

**CORNWALL, FALMOUTH. Bos-Sclewys Guest House, 97 Dracaena Avenue, Falmouth TR11 2EP (01326 314592).** A friendly, Cornish family-run guest house. Bed and Breakfast from £18. Reductions for weekly bookings. Cornwall Tourist Board Approved Accommodation. Please write or phone for brochure to Yvonne Eddy.

**CORNWALL, FALMOUTH (Near). Mrs A. Hunter, 'Broad Reach', Trewen Road, Budock Water, Near Falmouth TR11 5EB (01326 313469).** 'Broad Reach' is situated two miles from Falmouth. All rooms are comfortable, light and well equipped. There is a large garden to enjoy, and ample parking. Pets welcome, reductions for children.

**CORNWALL, HELSTON. Mrs Moira Bevan, The Manse, St. Keverne, Helston TR12 6LY (Tel & Fax: 01326 281025).** The Manse is an ideal base for walking, including the south west coast path, diving, fishing and exploring the beautiful Lizard Peninsula. Double rooms (one en suite) have vanity unit, colour TV and beverage tray. The Manse is a non-smoking house.

**CORNWALL, NEWQUAY. Margaret and Alan Bird, The Philadelphia, 19 Eliot Gardens TR7 2QE (01637 877747; Fax: 01637 876860).** Newquay's premier smoke free guest house. Bright and spacious qaulity accommodation in six individually themed rooms, superbly refurbished and decorated with luxury en suite facilities, colour TV and complimentary beverages.

**CORNWALL, ST IVES. Miss B. Delbridge, Bella Vista Guest House, St. Ives Road, Carbis Bay, St. Ives TR26 2SF (01736 796063).** First class accommodation, highly recommended, satisfaction guaranteed. Washbasins, colour TV, central heating in all rooms. Own key to room. Free parking on premises. Open all year. Non-smokers welcome. SAE for brochure.

**CORNWALL, TINTAGEL. Cate West, Chilcotts, Bossiney. Tintagel PL34 0AY (Tel & Fax: 01840 770324).** Friendly, old, listed cottage with beamed ceilings. Bed and Breakfast from £16.

**SPECIAL WELCOME**     Non-Smokers

**CORNWALL, TRURO. Mrs Shirley Wakeling, Rock Cottage, Blackwater, Truro TR4 8EU (01872 560252).** 18th century beamed cob cottage, two double, one twin, all en suite. Haven for non-smokers. Mastercard/Visa/Switch/Delta/JCB. Closed Christmas/New Year. **ETC/AA** ♦♦♦♦

**CUMBRIA, ALSTON. Clare and Mike Le Marie, Brownside House, Leadgate, Alston CA9 3EL (01434 382169 or 01434 382100).** Ideal centre for walking, cycling, birdwatching and exploring old lead mines. Easy reach for Lake District, Hadrian's Wall, Northumberland. Children and pets welcome (babysitting available).

**CUMBRIA, AMBLESIDE. Elder Grove, Lake Road, Ambleside LA22 0DB (015394 32504).** Our Victorian house welcomes non-smokers, children, dogs and walkers. We are also motorcyclist friendly and do special diets. Secure storage for bikes. Packed lunches and drying-room available.

**CUMBRIA, KESWICK. Clarence House, Linda & Stuart Robertson, 14 Eskin Street, Keswick CA12 4DQ (017687 73186; Fax: 017687 72317).** Lovely Victorian house; bedrooms with full en suite facilities, colour TV etc. Evening meals available in licensed diningroom. Major credit/debit cards accepted. Non-smoking. **ETC** ♦♦♦.

**CUMBRIA, KESWICK. Annie Scally and Ian Townsend, Latrigg House, St. Herbert Street, Keswick CA12 4DF (017687 73068).** An attractive detached Victorian house situated in a quiet area, only a few minutes' walk from the town centre and Lake, offering a non-smoking environment for the well-being and comfort of guests. **ETC** ♦♦♦♦

**CUMBRIA, LOWESWATER. Mrs Vickers, Askhill Farm, Loweswater, Cockermouth CA13 0SU (01946 861640).** Askhill is a family-run farm which has beef and sheep. Situated on the hillside over looking Loweswater Lake. The area is ideal for fell-walkers; there are plenty of walks. Non-smoking.

**CUMBRIA, PENRITH. Brookland Guest House, 2 Portland Place, Penrith CA11 7QN (Tel: 01768 863395).** Charming and elegant surroundings await any visitor to Brooklands Guest House in the heart of historic Penrith. Ideal base for exploring the many and various delights of the English Lakes. Non-smoking.

**CUMBRIA, PENRITH. Norcroft Guest House, Graham Street, Penrith CA11 9LQ (Tel & Fax: 01768 862365).** Convenient for M6 and just five minutes' walk from town centre. Single to family rooms all en suite. Ground floor room with disabled access. Non-smoking. Private parking. Credit cards accepted. Contact **Mrs Sylvia Jackson**. **ETC/RAC** ♦♦♦♦ Warm Welcome Award.

**CUMBRIA, TROUTBECK. Gwen and Peter Parfitt, Hill Crest, Troutbeck, Penrith CA11 0SH (017684 83935).** A unique warm and friendly Lakeland home. Non-smoking establishment where children and dogs are welcome. En suite rooms available.

**CUMBRIA, ULLSWATER. Geoff and Steph Mason, Knotts Mill Country Lodge, Watermillock, Penrith CA11 0JN (Tel & Fax: 017684 86699).** Spacious guesthouse close to magical Ullswater, in peaceful, scenic surroundings. Ideal for walking, boating or touring the Lake District. Eight en suite bedrooms with stunning views, including family rooms and facilities for the disabled. **ETC** ♦♦♦

**CUMBRIA, WINDERMERE. Mr and Mrs Mick and Fiona Rooney, Villa Lodge, Cross Street, Windermere LA23 1AE (Tel & Fax: 015394 43318).** Extremely comfortable non-smoking accommodation in peaceful area overlooking Windermere village. Open all year. Non-smokers welcomed. **ETC** ♦♦♦♦.

**CUMBRIA, WINDERMERE. John and Pauline MacDonald, Boston House, The Terrace, Windermere LA23 1AJ (015394 43654).** Boston House, the perfect choice for sincere attentive hospitality. Romantic en suite bedrooms with four-poster beds. Exclusively for non-smokers. **ETC** ♦♦♦♦

**DERBYSHIRE, ASHBOURNE. A. and D. Harris, Dairy House Farm, Alkmonton, Longford, Ashbourne DE6 3DG (Tel & Fax: 01335 330359).** Warm welcome and hospitality guaranteed in a comfortable atmosphere with good food and a residential licence. Sorry, no pets, no smokers and no children under 16. **ETC/AA** ♦♦♦♦.

**DERBYSHIRE, ASHBOURNE. The Courtyard, Dairy House Farm, Alkmonton, Longford, Ashbourne DE6 3DG (Tel & Fax: 01335 330187).** Stay in one of our seven rooms - five double, twin and one family, all with en suite facilities. Good farmhouse fare. Children welcome. Regret, no pets. **RAC/AA** ♦♦♦♦

**DERBYSHIRE, BAKEWELL. Mrs Julia Finney, Mandale House, Haddon Grove, Bakewell DE45 1JF (01629 812416).** Relax in the warm and friendly atmosphere of our peaceful farmhouse situated on the edge of Lathkill Dale. Completely non-smoking. Telephone for brochure. **ETC** ♦♦♦♦

**DERBYSHIRE, BUXTON. Mrs Ann Oliver, "Westlands", Bishop's Lane, St. John's Road, Buxton SK17 6UN (01298 23242).** Close to Staffordshire and Cheshire borders, this well established Bed and Breakfast is for non-smokers. Situated on country lane one mile from town centre. Special diets catered for by arrangement.

**DEBYSHIRE, MATLOCK. Mrs Whitehead, Mount Tabor House, Bowns Hill, Crich, Matlock DE4 5DG (01773 857008; Mobile: 07977 078266).** A former Methodist chapel. Comfortable guest accommodation with a homely atmosphere. Fay uses local and organic produce in the freshly prepared meals. Non-smoking throughout. Double room £25 per person; £30 single; three-course dinner £17. **AA** ♦♦♦♦

**DERBYSHIRE, TIDESWELL. Mrs Pat Harris, Laurel House, The Green. Litton, Tideswell, Near Buxton SK17 8QP (01298 871971).** Overlooking the village green. One double with en-suite facilities and a twin room with washbasin and private use of bathroom and toilet; tea/coffee making facilities in both. Private lounge. No smoking. **ETC** ♦♦♦♦

**Non-Smokers**  SPECIAL WELCOME

**DERBYSHIRE, TIDESWELL.** Mr D.C. Pinnegar, "Poppies", Bank Square, Tideswell, Buxton SK17 8LA (01298 871083). Situated in attractive Derbyshire village. Bed, Breakfast and Evening Meal available. Non- smoking establishment.

**DEVON, CLOVELLY.** Mrs D. Vanstone, The Old Smithy, Sierra Hill, Clovelly, Bideford EX39 5ST (01237 431202). A 16th century cottage and converted forge, situated one mile from the sea and the unspoilt picturesque village of Clovelly. No smoking in public rooms, i.e. dining room.

**DEVON, CROYDE BAY.** Paul and Faith Davis, Moorsands, 34 Moor Lane, Croyde Bay EX33 1NP (01271 890781). We have six en suite bedrooms, double, single, twin or family. All rooms have a basket of beverages, central heating, clock radio and colour TV. Non smoking. No pets.

**DEVON, DARTMOUTH.** Rhoda West, Little Weeke House, Weeke Hill, Dartmouth TQ6 0JT (01803 832380; Fax: 01803 832342). Superb views and peaceful location. All bedrooms en suite with colour TV, tea and coffee making facilities and hairdryer. Dogs welcome. Private parking. Please contact for brochure or reservations.

**DEVON, DITTISHAM.** Mr & Mrs H.S. Treseder, The White House, Manor Street, Dittisham TQ6 0EX (Tel & Fax: 01803 722355). Situated on the western bank of the River Dart three miles north of Dartmouth. En suite available. Special diets catered for. No smoking.

**DEVON, EXETER.** Mrs Heather Glanvill, Holbrook Farm, Clyst Honiton, Exeter EX5 2HR (Tel & Fax: 01392 367000). The spacious en suite rooms are furnished to a high standard with TV and hot drinks facilities, enjoying beautiful views. Bed and Breakfast £19 to £21. **ETC/AA** ♦♦♦♦.

**DEVON, HOLSWORTHY.** Pat and Phil Jennings, Leworthy Farmhouse, Lower Leworthy, Pyworthy, Holsworthy EX22 6SJ (01409 259469). A charming Georgian farmhouse nestling in an unspoilt backwater, with lawns, orchard, meadow, fishing lake. Nearby spectacular north Cornish coast (20 minutes), good walking, fishing, cycling. Quiet pastoral enjoyment. Non-smoking. No pets.

**DEVON, ILFRACOMBE.** Mr & Mrs Holdsworth, Lyncott, 56 St. Brannocks Road, Ilfracombe (Tel & Fax: 01271 862425). David and Marianna invite you to relax, smoke-free in the comfort of their elegant, lovingly restored period Victorian house. We offer delightful spacious, individually designed, en suite bedrooms. We also have a reputation for scrumptious homemade fare. Private car park. **ETC** ♦♦♦♦

**DEVON, PAIGNTON.** Freda Dwane and Steve Bamford, Clifton Hotel, 9-10 Kernou Road, Paignton TQ4 6BA (Tel & Fax: 01803 556545). Friendly, licensed, non-smoking hotel in ideal level location just off seafront. All rooms en suite with TV and beverages. Superb evening meals available. Open Easter to end October.

**DORSET, BEAMINSTER.** Caroline and Vincent Pielesz, The Walnuts, 2 Prout Bridge, Beaminster DT8 3AY (01308 862211). Very well situated in this medieval town, the house has been very tastefully refurbished with en suite rooms, tea and coffee making facilities, all the comforts of home. Totally non-smoking. **ETB Listed** *HIGHLY COMMENDED.*

**DORSET, BOURNEMOUTH.** Mr S. Goodwin, Cransley Hotel, 11 Knyveton Road, East Cliff, Bournemouth BH1 3QG (01202 290067). A licensed hotel for non-smokers. Rooms are en suite with colour TV and hospitality tray. Open all year. Ground floor accommodation for the less mobile guest. Evening Meals available. **ETC/AA** ♦♦♦.

**DORSET, BOURNEMOUTH.** Amitie Guest House, 1247 Christchurch Road, Bournemouth BH7 6BP (01202 427255; Fax: 01202 461488). Please contact Jenny or Paul for details. **AA** ♦♦♦♦.

**DORSET, LYME REGIS.** Mrs L. Brown, Providence House, Lyme Road, Uplyme DT7 3TH (01297 445704). Character house in village location on edge of historic Lyme Regis. Accommodation comprises one single, one double, one double en suite, all with TV and tea/coffee making facilities.

**DORSET, MARNHULL.** Robin and Sarah Hood, The Old Bank, Burton Street, Marnhull, Sturminster Newton, DT10 1PH (Tel & Fax: 01258 821019). The Old Bank is a comfortable, friendly 18th century house in the centre of an attractive Dorset village. Two double, one twin, one family bedroom, shared bathroom and shower-room. £20 per person, per night.

**GLOUCESTERSHIRE, MORETON-IN-MARSH (Near).** Mrs. Susan Woolston, Farriers Cottage, 44 Todenham, GL56 9PF (01608 652664; Fax: 01608 652668) Lovely Cotswold stone cottage, recently restored with central heating, en suite accommodation and ample parking. Sorry no pets and no smoking.

**GLOUCESTERSHIRE, NAILSWORTH.** Mrs Lesley Williams-Allen, The Laurels at Inchbrook, Nailsworth GL5 5HA. (Tel & Fax: 01453 834021). A lovely rambling house, part cottage-style and part Georgian. RAC Acclaimed. The emphasis is on relaxation and friendly hospitality. Disabled accommodation available.

**GLOUCESTERSHIRE, NEWLAND.** Ann Edwards, Rookery Farmhouse, Newland GL16 8NJ (01594 832432). Ideal walking and fishing country with stables, cycle paths and golf courses nearby. Spacious en suite rooms with bath and shower. Dogs welcome by prior arrangement. Self catering cottages also available. No smoking. **ETC** ♦♦♦.

**GLOUCESTERSHIRE, STOW-ON-THE-WOLD.** Mrs F.J. Adams, Aston House, Broadwell, Moreton-in-Marsh GL56 0TJ (01451 830475) Chalet bungalow in peaceful village overlooking fields. Bed and good English Breakfast, bedtime drinks. Non- smoking. Car essential - parking. **ETC** ♦♦♦♦.

## 410 SPECIAL WELCOME — Non-Smokers

**GLOUCESTERSHIRE, STROUD.** Monica, Iain and Niall McRiner, Glenfinlas, 5 Castle Villas, Castle Street, Stroud GL5 2HP (01453 759256). Enjoy the warm, friendly atmosphere in this family home, an early Victorian stone villa, situated in a secluded part of Stroud. One twin-bedded room with private facilities, with additional single room available on request. Non-smoking. Continental or English Breakfast.

**HAMPSHIRE, FAREHAM.** Ian & Sarah Pike, Bembridge House, 32 Osborn Road, Fareham PO16 7DS (Tel & Fax: 01329 317050). A variety of character rooms is available all with colour television, coffee and tea making facilities and welcome tray. Ample off road private parking, and our five course breakfast is sumptuous! RAC ♦♦♦♦ *SPARKLING DIAMOND AWARD.*

**HAMPSHIRE, LYMINGTON,** Our Bench, Lodge Road, Lymington SO41 8HH (Tel & Fax: 01590 673141). Large non-smoking bungalow and no children, situated between New Forest and Coast. Full English Breakfast. Indoor heated pool, jacuzzi and sauna. Mountain bikes. National Accessibility Scheme 3. ETC ♦♦♦♦ *GOLD AWARD.* ENGLAND FOR EXCELLENCE WINNER. FHG DIPLOMA WINNER.

**HAMPSHIRE, RINGWOOD (New Forest).** Margaret and Steve Willis, 1 Hiltom Road, Ringwood BH24 1PW (01425 461274). A warm and friendly welcome awaits you in our quiet old modernised cottage. Comfortable accommodation. Good English Breakfast. Garden smoking only. Ample parking. Terms from £17 per person. Open all year. ETC ♦♦♦

**HAMPSHIRE, WINCHESTER.** Mrs S. Buchanan, "Acacia", 44 Kilham Lane, Winchester SO22 5PT (01962 852259; 07885 462993 mobile).. Accommodation consists of one double and two twin bedrooms, all of which have en suite or private bathroom, plus tea and coffee making facilities. Off-street parking. Non-smokers only. ETC/AA ♦♦♦♦

**HAMPSHIRE, WINCHESTER.** Susan and Richard Pell, The Lilacs, 1 Harestock Close, off Andover Road North, Winchester SO22 6NP (01962 884122). A non-smoking family home offering an excellent English Breakfast, including vegetarian meals. Country views.

**HEREFORDSHIRE, HEREFORD.** Heron House, Canon Pye Road, Portway, Burghill, Hereford HR4 8NG (01432 761111; Fax: 01432 760603). Friendly welcome at rural location four miles north of Hereford. En suite, vanity units, tea making facilities, colour TV, log fire, parking. Non-smoking. ETC ♦♦♦

**HEREFORDSHIRE, VOWCHURCH.** The Old Vicarage. Vowchurch HR2 0QD (Tel & Fax: 01981 550357). Highly praised quality breakfasts. Delightful candlelit dinners by arrangement, with local home grown produce. Attractive en suites, private bathrooms. Completely non-smoking. ETC ♦♦♦♦ *SILVER AWARD.*

**KENT, ASHFORD near.** Pam and Arthur Mills, Cloverlea, Bethersden, Ashford TN26 3DU (01233 820353; mobile: 07711 739690). Spacious new country bungalow in peaceful location. Suberb accommodation in two twin rooms, both en suite, one family. Excellent breakfasts. No smoking. ETC ♦♦♦

**KENT, FOLKESTONE.** Mrs L. Dowsett, Sunny Lodge Guest House, 85 Cheriton Road, Folkestone CT20 2QL (01303 251498; Fax: 01303 258267). Comfortable family-run Guesthouse and lovely garden. Close to town centre, railway station, Seacat, Channel Tunnel, 20 minutes to Dover. Bed and Breakfast from £18.00, Children welcome. No-smoking.

**LANCASHIRE. BLACKPOOL.** Elsie and Ron Platt, Sunnyside and Holmesdale Guest House, 25-27 High Street, North Shore, Blackpool FY1 2BN (01253 623781). Two minutes from North Station, five minutes from Promenade. Special diets catered for. Bed and Breakfast from £18. No smoking.

**LANCASHIRE, BLACKPOOL (NORTH SHORE).** Barbara and Steve Hornby, The Birchley Hotel, 64 Holmfield Road, Blackpool FY2 9RT (01253 354174). You are assured of a warm welcome in our friendly, relaxed and totally "smoke free" hotel. We offer personal attention and service normally associated with much larger hotels. Please telephone for a brochure.

**LANCASHIRE, SOUTHPORT.** The Sidbrook Private Hotel, 14 Talbot Street, Southport PR8 1HP (01704 530608). All our bedrooms are en suite and have remote control colour TV, clock radio, hairdryer, hospitality tray and toiletries. Secluded garden, free parking and access at all times. No smoking. ETC/AA ♦♦♦

**LINCOLNSHIRE, LINCOLN.** South Park Guest House, 11 South Park, Lincoln LN5 8EN (01522 528243; Fax: 01522 524603). Fine Victorian detached house, only a short walk to shops, restaurants, pubs, city centre and tourist attractions. All rooms en suite. Private parking with security lighting.

**LINCOLNSHIRE, NORTH HYKEHAM.** Mrs J. Henry, Loudor Hotel, 37 Newark Road, Lincoln LN6 8RB (01522 680333; Fax: 01522 680403). All rooms are en-suite with TV, tea/coffee making facilities, direct dial telephones, licensed bar and ample parking. Single £34 per night Bed and Breakfast, Double/Twin £45, Family £50. Non-smoking. AA ★★

**NORFOLK, HOLME-NEXT-THE-SEA.** Mary & Robbie Burton, Meadow Springs, 15 Eastgate Road, Holme-next-the Sea PE36 6LL (01485 525279). Modern, attractively furnished rooms - one double, one twin - both with en-suite bathrooms, CTV, radio and tea/coffee making facilities. There are sandy beaches, nature reserves and championship golf courses nearby. Non-smoking.

**NORFOLK, HORSEY CORNER.** The Old Chapel, Horsey Corner NR29 4EH (01493 393498). Tranquil and traditional English Bed and Breakfast, from £18. Ground floor en suite rooms (Category Three National Accessible Scheme for wheelchair users). Non-smoking. ETC ♦♦♦♦

**Non-Smokers**     **SPECIAL WELCOME 411**

**NORFOLK, KING'S LYNN. Mrs M. Howard, Jubilee Lodge, Station Road, Docking, King's Lynn PE31 8LS (Tel & Fax: 01485 518473).** High standard bed and breakfast accommodation. All bedrooms en suite with colour TV. Choice of English or continental breakfasts. Packed lunches are also available on request. Smoke and pet free establishment. **ETC** ◆◆◆

**NORFOLK, WELLS-NEXT-THE-SEA. Oyster Cottage B&B, 20 High Street, Wells-next-the-Sea NR23 1EP (01328 711997).** An ideal retreat for families, couples and friends. En suite rooms with TV and tea/coffee making; amenities include central heating, laundry service, baby equipment, room service and cycle storage. Wide breakfast menu.

**OXFORDSHIRE, OXFORD. Diana and Richard Mitchell, Highfield West, 188 Cumnor Hill, Oxford OX2 9PJ (01865 863007).** Comfortable home in quiet residential area. Well appointed rooms with colour TV, central heating and refreshment trays. Large outdoor pool. No smoking. Vegetarians welcome. **ETC** ◆◆◆

**OXFORDSHIRE, TACKLEY. June and George Collier, 55 Nethercote Road, Tackley, Kidlington OX5 3AT (01869 331255; mobile: 07990 338225; Fax: 01869 331670).** An excellent Bed and Breakfast. Ideal base for touring, walking and riding. Central for Oxford, the Cotswolds and Stratford upon Avon. Dogs and horses made especially welcome.

**OXFORDSHIRE, WITNEY. Mrs Elizabeth Simpson, Field View, Wood Green, Witney OX8 6DE (01993 705485; Mobile: 0468 614347).** Set in two acres and situated on picturesque Wood Green, yet only ten minutes from the centre of town. Non-smoking. **ETC** ◆◆◆◆ *SILVER AWARD*

**OXFORDSHIRE, WOODSTOCK. Mrs Mandy Buck, Elbie House, East End, North Leigh, Near Witney OX8 8PZ (01993 880166).** Two en suite rooms, one with four-poster bed. English or Continental/vegetarian breakfasts served in rooms. Ground floor accommodation allows easy access for less able visitors. **ETC** ◆◆◆◆

**SHROPSHIRE, BRIDGNORTH. Jutta and Alan Ward, Linley Crest, Linley Brook, Near Bridgnorth WV16 4SZ. (Tel & Fax: 01746 765527).** Extremely comfortable accommodation; quiet and pretty location; excellent base for exciting tourist attractions; wholesome breakfasts, almost every wish granted, however, most definitely no smoking in the house. **ETC** ◆◆◆◆ *SILVER AWARD*.

**SHROPSHIRE, CHURCH STRETTON. Willowfield Guest House, Lower Wood, All Stretton, Church Stretton. (01694 751471).** Quiet and idyllic, in its own grounds with beautiful rural views. All bedrooms en suite with posture sprung beds, settee, TV and beverages. Delicious home-cooking, homegrown and local produce. Licensed. Non-smoking. No pets. **ETC/AA** ◆◆◆◆◆.

**SHROPSHIRE, DORRINGTON. Ron and Jenny Repath. Meadowlands, Lodge Lane, Frodesley, Dorrington SY5 7HD (01694 731350).** Former farmhouse attractively decorated. Quiet location in delightful hamlet with panoramic views to Stretton Hills. Central heating. Parking. Colour TV in bedrooms. Guests' lounge. En suite available. Non-smoking. Brochure available. **ETC** ◆◆◆.

**SHROPSHIRE, NEWPORT. Mrs Green, Peartree Farmhouse, Farm Grove, Newport TF10 7PX (01952 811193).** Charming farmhouse set in picturesque gardens. Immaculate modern accommodation, non-smoking environment, TV lounge. All rooms satellite TV, tea/coffee making facilities, controllable central heating, mostly en suite. Ample private parking. Bed and Breakfast from £25 per person.

**SHROPSHIRE, TELFORD. Mrs Hazel Miller, The Old Rectory, Stirchley Village, Telford TF3 1DY (01952 596308).** Set in an acre of quiet, secluded gardens and adjacent to Telford Town Park. All bedrooms have either en suite facilities or private bathrooms, TV, clock radio, tea/coffee making facilities and central heating. We do ask guests not to smoke in the house please.

**SOMERSET, BATH. Michael and Carole Bryson, Walton Villa, 3 Newbridge Hill, Bath BA1 3PW (01225 482792; Fax: 01225 313093).** All bedrooms tastefully decorated and furnished with en suite facilities, hospitality tray, colour TV, hairdryer and central heating. No smoking policy throughout. **ETC** ◆◆◆◆

**SOMERSET, BATH. Jan and Bryan Wotley, The Albany Guest House, 24 Crescent Gardens, Bath BAI 2NB (01225 313339).** Non smoking accommodation at our friendly Victorian home. Just five minutes' walk from city centre.

**SOMERSET, BURNHAM-ON-SEA. Mrs F. Alexander, Priors Mead, 23 Rectory Road, Burnham-on-Sea TA8 2BZ (Tel & Fax: 01278 782116; Mobile: 07990 595585).** Peter and Fizz welcome guests to enjoy their enchanting Edwardian home. En suite or private facilities available. Bed and Breakfast from £17 to £18. **ETC** ◆◆◆. *"WHICH?" RECOMMENDED.*

**SOMERSET, CHURCHILL (Bristol near). Ms Susan Lewis, The Mendip Gate Guest House, Bristol Road (A38), Churchill BS25 5NL (01934 852333; Fax: 01934 852001).** Handy hostelries for tasty Evening Meals and comfortable rooms for a convenient overnight stop on longer journeys. Ideal for visiting Wells, Bristol or Bath.

**STAFFORDSHIRE, BUTTERTON, near Newcastle. Ms. S. Jealouse, Butterton House, Park Road, Butterton, Newcastle-Under-Lyme ST5 4DZ (01782 619085).** Ideal for visiting pottery factory shops, Alton Towers, Chester and the Peak District, etc. Large comfortable en suite rooms. Great English Breakfast - vegetarians catered for. **ETC** ◆◆◆ *VOTED "BEST B&B IN ENGLAND" BY COUNTRY ROVER BROCHURE GUESTS.*

## 412 SPECIAL WELCOME — Non-Smokers

**STAFFORDSHIRE, ECCLESHALL. Mrs Sue Pimble, Cobblers Cottage, Kerry Lane, Eccleshall ST21 6EJ (01785 850116).** A five minute walk from the centre of Eccleshall situated within the conservation area. Children and pets welcome but we are non-smoking. **ETC** ◆◆◆◆

**STAFFORDSHIRE, ECCLESHALL. Mrs Helen Bonsall, Slindon House Farm, Slindon, Eccleshall ST21 6LX (01782 791237).** Working dairy, arable and sheep farm. Large attractive garden and offers excellent accommodation, comfortable, spacious and well equipped rooms. No smoking. **ETC** ◆◆◆◆.

**SUSSEX (EAST), BRIGHTON. Mrs M.A. Daughtery, Ma'on Hotel, 26 Upper Rock Gardens, Brighton BN2 1QE (01273 694400).** Completely non-smoking Grade II Listed building. Two minutes from the sea and within easy reach of conference and main town centres. Access to rooms at all times. Brochure on request with SAE.

**SUSSEX (EAST), HASTINGS. Peter Mann, Grand Hotel, Grand Parade, St. Leonards, Hastings TN38 0DD (Tel & Fax: 01424 428510)** Seafront family-run hotel; all rooms with colour TV, radio; some en suite. Unrestricted/disabled parking. Non-smoking restaurant. Licensed bar. **ETC** ◆◆◆.

**WARWICKSHIRE, ALCESTER. Mrs Margaret Kember, Orchard Lawns, Wixford, Alcester B49 6DA (01789 772668).** A warm welcome awaits you at our totally non-smoking establishment. Three bedrooms (one en suite). Bed and Breakfast from £20 per person. **ETC** ◆◆◆◆ *SILVER AWARD.*

**WARWICKSHIRE, STRATFORD-UPON-AVON. Mrs Karen Cauvin, Penshurst Guest House, 34 Evesham Place, Stratford-upon-Avon CV37 6HT (01789 205259; Fax: 01789 295322).** Prettily refurbished Victorian townhouse. Town centre five minutes' walk. Bed and Breakfast from £16. Totally non-smoking establishment. **ETC** ◆◆◆

**WARWICKSHIRE, STRATFORD-UPON-AVON. Hampton Lodge, 38 Shipston Road, Stratford-upon-Avon CV37 7LP (Tel/Fax: 01789 299374).** The perfect base for exploring Shakespeares' Country and the north Cotswolds. Seven spacious rooms, individually decorated, en suite facilities, direct dial telephone, colour television, tea and coffee trays and hair dryers. **ETC/RAC** ◆◆◆, RAC DINING AWARD, WARM WELCOME, SPARKLING DIAMOND

**WARWICKSHIRE, WARWICK. Mr and Mrs D. Clapp, The Croft, Haseley Knob, Warwick CV35 7NL (Tel & Fax: 01926 484447).** Friendly family atmosphere, picturesque rural surroundings, home cooking and very comfortable accommodation. Ground floor en-suite bedrooms available. No smoking inside. **ETC** ◆◆◆◆

**WILTSHIRE, LANDFORD. Mr and Mrs Westlake, Springfields, Lyndhurst Road, Landford, Salisbury SP5 2AS (01794 390093).** Springfields offers two double rooms and one single each able to accommodate an extra bed for accompanying children and with colour TV, radio and tea/coffee making facilities. Payphone. Garden. Off road parking. Non-smoking. Bed and Breakfast from £18 per person per night. **AA** ◆◆◆◆

**YORKSHIRE (NORTH), EASINGWOLD. Mrs Lorna Huxtable, Dimple Wells, Thormanby, Easingwold YO61 4NL (Tel & Fax: 01845 501068).** Secluded country house betwixt Yorkshire Moors and Dales. En suite rooms with colour TV, tea/coffee tray. Ample parking. No smoking throughout. **ETC** ◆◆◆◆

**YORKSHIRE (NORTH), SCARBOROUGH. Sue and Tony Hewitt, Harmony Country Lodge, Limestone Road, Burniston, Scarborough YO13 0DG (0800 2985840).** Relaxing octagonal retreat, superb 360° views of the National Park and sea. Licensed, private parking, completely non-smoking. Warm and friendly. **ETC** ◆◆◆◆.

**YORKSHIRE (NORTH),SCARBOROUGH. Mrs D.M. Medd, Hilford House, Crossgates, Scarborough YO12 4JU (01723 862262).** Three double, one single and one family bedrooms all with washbasins and central heating. En suite available. Non-smoking accommodation available. Private car parking.

**YORKSHIRE (NORTH), THIRSK. Joyce Ashbridge, Mount Grace Farm, Cold Kirby, Thirsk YO7 2HL (Tel: 01845 597389; Fax: 01845 597872).** Ideal location for touring or exploring the many walks in the area. Luxury en suite bedrooms with tea/coffee facilities. Children from 12 years plus. No smoking. No pets. Open all year except Christmas. **ETC** ◆◆◆◆

**YORKSHIRE (NORTH), YORK.** The Kismet Guest House, 147 Haxby Road, York YO31 8JZ (01904 621056). Close to city centre, Yorkshire Dales and coast. Vegetarians catered for. non-smoking.

**YORKSHIRE (NORTH), YORK. Jenny Clark, Cumbria House, 2 Vyner Street, Haxby Road, York YO31 8HS (01904 636817).** Elegant, tastefully decorated Victorian guest house. Rooms have colour TV, radio alarms and tea/coffee facilities. Most are en suite or have certain private facilities. Central heating. Fire Certificate. Guests' car park. Full English breakfast or vegetarian alternative. **AA** QQQ

**YORKSHIRE (NORTH), YORK. Mr Ian McNabb, The Hazelwood, 24-25 Portland Street, Gillygate, York YO31 7EH (01904 626548; Fax: 01904 628032).** Victorian townhouse retaining many original features. Friendly and informal. Wide choice of high quality breakfasts including vegetarian, ranging from traditional English to croissants and Danish pastries. Completely non smoking. **ETC/AA/RAC** ◆◆◆◆

---

**PLEASE SEND A STAMPED ADDRESSED ENVELOPE WITH ENQUIRIES**

## Non-smoking • Scotland

**ARGYLL, INVERARAY. Mr R. Gayre, Minard Castle, Minard, Argyll PA32 8YB (Tel & Fax: 01546 886272).** Stay in exclusive style in our 19th Century Scottish castle which stands in its own grounds in beautiful countryside. The three comfortable bedrooms have colour television, tea/coffee making facilities and en suite bathrooms. No smoking in the house.

**ARGYLL, OBAN near. Margaret and Norman Hill, Lerags House, Lerags, By Oban PA34 4SE (01631 563381).** Set in the tranquil and picturesque Lerags Glen. Good quality accommodation, food and service at value for money prices in a warm and relaxing atmosphere. Bed and Breakfast from £22.50, Bed, Breakfast and Evening Meal from £35. We are a non-smoking establishment.

**DUMFRIES & GALLOWAY, DUMFRIES. The Maxwell Family, Southpark Guest House, Quarry Road, Locharbriggs, Dumfries DG1 1QG (Tel & Fax: 01387 711188).** Excellent value for money balanced with home from home comfort and fine hospitality. No smoking establishment. STB ★★★ B&B, AA ◆◆◆◆.

**EDINBURGH & LOTHIANS, EDINBURGH (14 miles). Mrs Janet Burke, Patieshill Farm, Carlops, Penicuik EH26 9ND (01968 660551; Fax: 01968 661162).** Working hill sheep and cattle farm set in the midst of the Pentland Hills offering Bed and Breakfast. No smoking. STB ★★★ B&B.

**EDINBURGH & LOTHIANS, LIVINGSTON. Ms M. Easdale, 3 Cedric Rise, Dedridge East, Livingston EH54 6JR (Tel & Fax: 01506 413095).** A friendly welcome is assured. Accommodation comprises one twin-bedded, one single, one room with double and single beds and a triple bedded room (these rooms are located on the first and second floors).

**HIGHLANDS SOUTH, AVIEMORE. Mrs Margaret Hall, Kinapol Guest House (Est 1975), Dalfaber Road, Aviemore PH22 1PY (Tel & Fax: 01479 810513).** Small modern Guest House in quiet situation, only five minutes' walk to centre of Aviemore. Three double and two family rooms, all with TV, washbasin and tea/coffee trays etc. STB ★★ GUEST HOUSE.

**HIGHLANDS SOUTH, FORT AUGUSTUS. Caledonian Cottage, Station Road, Fort Augustus PH32 4AY (01320 366401; Mobile: 07967 740329)** Set in a quiet village, offering comfortable modern accommodation. Non-smoking. Rooms en suite or with private facilities. Children and pets welcome.

**PERTH & KINROSS, CALLANDER. Annfield Guest House, North Church Street, Callander FK17 8EG (01877 330204; Fax: 01877 330674).** Ideal as an overnight stop or as the centre for visiting the surrounding Scottish Highlands. All bedrooms have en suite facilities or private bathroom, hospitality tray and hairdryer. Non smokers preferred. Private parking. AA ◆◆◆. STB ★★★ B&B. Welcome Host Award.

## Non-smoking • Wales

**ANGLESEY & GWYNEDD, BANGOR. Penhower Uchaf Newydd, Caerhun, Bangor LL57 4DT (01248 362427).** Single storey home set in a spacious garden with ample and secure parking. A non-smoking establishment with all of our de luxe rooms en suite with showers, we take great pride in offering warm and friendly hospitality and acclaimed home cooking. WTB ★★★★.

**NORTH WALES, BETWS-Y-COED. Summer Hill Non-Smokers' Guest House, Betws-y-Coed LL24 0BL (01690 710306).** Especially for the non-smoker, Summer Hill is delightfully situated in a quiet sunny location. Bed and Breakfast. Ideal for walkers.

**NORTH WALES, CONWY. Mrs Janet Shaw, Bryn, Sychnant Pass Road, Conwy LL32 8NS (01492 592449).** Beside the town walls, large garden, parking. Five rooms, en suite or private bathroom. Extensive breakfast menu. Completely non smoking.

**NORTH WALES, LLANDUDNO. Roger and Merril Pitblado, Chilterns, 19 Deganwy Avenue, llandudno LL30 2YB (Tel & Fax: 01492 875457).** Chilterns is entirely non-smoking with full central heating. Double, family and twin rooms with en suite facilities, colour televisions, beverage trays and some with king size beds. WTB ★★★

**POWYS, BRECON. Cambrian Cruisers, Ty Newydd, Pencelli, Brecon LD3 7LJ (01874 665315).** 17th century farmhouse with en suite bedrooms all with stunning views of Brecon Beacons. Non-smoking. No pets. Please see main entry for further details.

**POWYS, RHAYADER. Mrs Lena Powell, Gigrin Farm, South Road, Rhayader LD6 5BL (01597 810243).** Gigrin is a 17th century longhouse, retaining original oak beams and cosy atmosphere. Non-smoking. Children welcome. Self-catering accommodation also available. Brochure on request. WTB ★★ B&B.

**SOUTH WALES, ST. BRIDES WENTLOOG (Near Newport). Mr David W. Bushell, Chapel Guest House, Church Road, St. Brides Wentloog, Near Newport NP10 8SN (01633 681018; Fax: 01633 681431)** Comfortable accommodation in a converted chapel. Guest lounge with TV. Single, double and twin rooms en suite or private bathroom. Beverage trays, TV, shaver points in all rooms. From £19. WTB ★★★ GUEST HOUSE.

**SOUTH WALES, TINTERN. Anne and Peter Howe, Valley House, Raglan Road. Tintern, Near Chepstow NP6 6TH (01291 689652).** Accommodation of a very high standard in a fine Georgian residence. Open all year. Non-smoking. WTB ★★ GUEST HOUSE. AA ◆◆◆◆, RAC ACCLAIMED.

## Disabled • England

**BEDFORDSHIRE, PULLOXHILL.** Mrs A. Lawrence, "Tower House", 74 Church Road, Pulloxhill MK45 5HE (01525 714818). Situated in a quiet lane backing onto open countryside. All rooms en suite. Full English and continental breakfasts are served in a farmhouse style kitchen. Ground floor room with wheelchair access.

**CAMBRIDGESHIRE, ELY.** Val Pickford, Rosendale Lodge, Witchford, Ely CB6 2HT (Tel & Fax: 01353 667700). Relax in our home with level wheelchair access to house/gardens with ground floor bedroom en suite specially adapted for disabled guests with twin beds, colour TV, sofa and generous beverage tray. An ideal touring base for East Anglia and Ely's many attractions. Non-smoking.

**CUMBRIA, PENRITH.** Norcroft Guest House, Graham Street, Penrith CA11 9LQ (Tel & Fax: 01768 862365). Convenient for M6 and just five minutes' walk from town centre. Single to family rooms all en suite. Ground floor room with disabled access. Non-smoking. Private parking. Credit cards accepted. Contact **Mrs Sylvia Jackson**. ETC/RAC ◆◆◆◆ Warm Welcome Award.

**CUMBRIA, ULLSWATER.** Geoff and Steph Mason, Knotts Mill Country Lodge, Watermillock, Penrith CA11 0JN (Tel & Fax: 017684 86699). Spacious guesthouse close to magical Ullswater, in peaceful, scenic surroundings. Ideal for walking, boating or touring the Lake District. Eight en suite bedrooms with stunning views, including family rooms and facilities for the disabled. **ETC** ◆◆◆

**DERBYSHIRE, ASHBOURNE.** The Courtyard, Dairy House Farm, Alkmonton, Longford, Ashbourne DE6 3DG (Tel & Fax: 01335 330187). Stay in one of our seven rooms - five double, twin and one family, all with en suite facilities. Children welcome. Regret, no pets. **AA/RAC** ◆◆◆◆ CATEGORY 1 WHEELCHAIR ACCESS.

**DERBYSHIRE, BAKEWELL.** Mrs Julia Finney, Mandale House, Haddon Grove, Bakewell DE45 1JF (01629 812416). Peaceful farmhouse offers bedrooms with colour TV and tea-making facility. Two rooms on the ground floor with en suite facilities suitable for disabled guests. **ETC** ◆◆◆◆

**DEVON, CLOVELLY.** Mrs D. Vanstone, The Old Smithy, Sierra Hill, Clovelly, Bideford EX39 5ST (01237 431202). A 16th century cottage and converted forge, situated one mile from the sea and the village of Clovelly. One ground floor en suite double/twin/family room. Not suitable for wheelchair in bathroom.

**DEVON, EXETER.** Mrs Heather Glanvill, Holbrook Farm, Clyst Honiton, Exeter EX5 2HR (Tel & Fax: 01392 367000). The spacious en suite rooms are furnished to a high standard with TV and hot drinks facilities, enjoying beautiful views. Bed and Breakfast £19 to £21. **ETC/AA** ◆◆◆◆

**GLOUCESTERSHIRE, NAILSWORTH.** Mrs Lesley Williams-Allen, The Laurels at Inchbrook, Nailsworth GL5 5HA. (Tel & Fax: 01453 834021). A lovely rambling house, part cottage-style and part Georgian. RAC Acclaimed. The emphasis is on relaxation and friendly hospitality. Disabled accommodation available.

**HAMPSHIRE, LYMINGTON,** Our Bench, Lodge Road, Lymington SO41 8HH (Tel & Fax: 01590 673141). Large non-smoking bungalow and no children, situated between New Forest and Coast. Full English Breakfast. Indoor heated pool, jacuzzi and sauna. Mountain Bikes. National Accessibility Scheme 3. **ETC** ◆◆◆◆.*ENGLAND FOR EXCELLENCE WINNER. FHG DIPLOMA WINNER.*

**LINCOLNSHIRE, CLEETHORPES.** Mr D. Turner, Clee House, 31/33 Clee Road, Cleethorpes DN35 8AD (Tel & Fax: 01472 200850). Magnificent Edwardian property just a few minutes' walk from the sea front. Three guest bedrooms en suite with wheelchair access. **ETC/AA** ◆◆◆◆

**NORFOLK, HOLME-NEXT-THE-SEA** Mary & Robbie Burton, Meadow Springs, 15 Eastgate Road, Holme-next-the-Sea PE36 6LL. (01485 525279). Modern, attractively furnished rooms - one double, one twin - both with en-suite bathrooms, CTV, radio and tea/coffee making facilities. Suitable for disabled guests.

**OXFORDSHIRE, WOODSTOCK.** Mrs Mandy Buck, Elbie House, East End, North Leigh, Near Witney OX8 6PZ (01993 880166). Two en suite rooms, one with four-poster bed. English or Continental/vegetarian breakfasts served in rooms. Ground floor accommodation allows easy access for less able visitors. **ETC** ◆◆◆◆

**SHROPSHIRE, BRIDGNORTH.** Jutta and Alan Ward, Linley Crest, Linley Brook, Near Bridgnorth WV16 4SZ (Tel & Fax: 01746 765527). Welcome to our attractive rural retreat. Two of our double bedrooms have ground floor access for guests with restricted mobility, en suite shower, TV, radio/alarm, beverage tray, hair dryer etc. We offer multiple choice breakfasts and cater for special requirements. **ETC** ◆◆◆ *SILVER AWARD.*

**SHROPSHIRE, TELFORD.** Mrs Hazel Miller, The Old Rectory, Stirchley Village, Telford TF3 1DY (01952 596308). Set in an acre of quiet, secluded gardens and adjacent to Telford Town Park. All bedrooms have either en suite facilities or private bathrooms, TV, clock radio, tea/coffee making facilities and central heating. One ground floor bedroom is suitable for wheelchair users (Category 1).

**SUSSEX (EAST), HASTINGS.** Peter Mann, Grand Hotel, Grand Parade, St. Leonards, Hastings TN38 0DD (Tel & Fax: 01424 428510). Seafront family-run hotel; all rooms with colour TV, radio; some en suite. Unrestricted/disabled parking. Non-smoking restaurant. Licensed bar. **ETC** ◆◆◆.

**SUSSEX (WEST), ARUNDEL.** Mrs Vicki Richards, Woodacre, Arundel Road, Fontwell, Arundel BN18 0SD (01243 814301). Bed and breakfast in a traditional family home with accommodation for up to 10/12 guests. Well positioned for Chichester, Arundel, Goodwood and the seaside and easily accessible from the A27. Our rooms are clean and spacious and two are on the ground floor.

**WARWICKSHIRE, STRATFORD-UPON-AVON. Hampton Lodge, 38 Shipston Road, Stratford-upon-Avon CV37 7LP (Tel/Fax: 01789 299374).** The perfect base for exploring Shakespeare Country and the north Cotswolds. Seven spacious rooms, individually decorated, en suite facilities, direct dial telephone, colour television, tea and coffee trays and hair dryers. **ETC/RAC** ◆◆◆◆, RAC DINING AWARD, WARM WELCOME, SPARKLING DIAMOND

**WARWICKSHIRE, STRATFORD-UPON-AVON. Mrs Karen Cauvin, Penshurst Guest House, 34 Evesham Place, Stratford-upon-Avon CV37 6HT (01789 205259; Fax: 01789 295322).** Prettily refurbished Victorian townhouse. One ground floor en suite room specially adapted for disabled guests. ETB Category 2 Accessibility symbol awarded. **ETC** ◆◆◆

## Disabled • Scotland

**DUMFRIES & GALLOWAY, DUMFRIES. The Maxwell Family, Southpark Guest House, Quarry Road, Locharbriggs, Dumfries DG1 1QG (Tel & Fax: 01387 711188).** Excellent value for money balanced with home from home comfort and fine hospitality. Ground floor en suite rooms being built for 2001. **STB** ★★★ *B&B*, **AA** ◆◆◆◆.

**EDINBURGH & LOTHIANS, EDINBURGH (14 miles). Mrs Janet Burke, Patieshill Farm, Carlops, Penicuik EH26 9ND (01968 660551; Fax: 01968 661162).** A very warm and friendly welcome is extended to all guests. Ground floor accommodation available. **STB** ★★★ *B&B*.

## Disabled • Wales

**NORTH WALES, CONWY. Mrs Janet Shaw, Bryn, Sychnant Pass Road, Conwy LL32 8NS (01492 592449).** One double en suite room on ground floor suitable for mobile partially disabled or elderly guests. Parking, no steps. No smoking.

**SOUTH WALES, ST. BRIDES WENTLOOG (Near Newport). Mr David W. Bushell, Chapel Guest House, Church Road, St. Brides Wentloog, Near Newport NP10 8SN (01633 681018; Fax: 01633 681431)** Comfortable accommodation in a converted chapel. Guest lounge with TV. Single, double and twin rooms en suite or private bathroom. Beverage trays, TV, shaver points in all rooms. From £19. **WTB** ★★★ *GUEST HOUSE*.

# RADAR
the disability network

## Holidays in Britain & Ireland 2000 - a Guide for Disabled People

If you're looking for information on accessible hotels or self-catering accommodation in the British Isles, for holiday places which can offer personal assistance if needed, for activity centres which can cater for disabled people, or for details of organisations which run specialised holidays, then "Holidays in Britain & Ireland 2000 - A Guide for Disabled People" will be for you. The guide, which aims to give information that will be useful to people with as wide a range of disabilities as possible, has been produced annually for over 20 years by RADAR, the national disability charity. The guide includes information on over 1300 places to stay, and includes access details for each, plus indications of facilities and service (such as special diets or whether feather-free bedding is available, for example). The guide also gives information on advice services, relevant voluntary and commercial organisations, and transport.

## For details see our website: www.radar.org.uk

## Special Diets • England

**LONDON, HAMMERSMITH.** Anne and Sohel Armanios, 67 Rannoch Road, Hammersmith, London W6 9SS (020 7385 4904; Fax: 020 7610 3235). Comfortable, centrally located Edwardian family home. Great base for sightseeing. Excellent transport access. Bed and Continental Breakfast £22 nightly. Smoking only in garden.

**BEDFORDSHIRE, PULLOXHILL.** Mrs A. Lawrence, "Tower House", 74 Church Road, Pulloxhill MK45 5HE (01525 714818). Situated in a quiet lane backing onto open countryside. All rooms en suite. Full English and continental breakfasts are served in a farmhouse style kitchen. Special Diets catered for.

**CORNWALL, HELSTON.** Mrs Moira Bevan, The Manse, St. Keverne, Helston TR12 6LY (Tel & Fax: 01326 281025). Double rooms (one en suite) have vanity unit, colour TV and beverage tray. Food is home-cooked using mainly local and/or organic produce. Vegetarian options. An Evening Meal is available, also Packed Lunches on request. Bed and Breakfast from £17.50 to £20. Brochure on request. Cornwall Tourist Board Approved.

**CORNWALL, PORTHLEVEN.** Mrs Mary Fuhrmann, Tamarind, Shrubberies Hill, Porthleven, Helston TR13 9EA (01326 574293). Five minutes' walk from harbour, shops, restaurants and inns. Colour TV, tea and coffee making facilities in bedroom. Smoking in sun lounge only.

**CORNWALL, TINTAGEL.** Cate West, Chilcotts, Bossiney. Tintagel PL34 0AY (Tel & Fax:01840 770324). Friendly, old, listed cottage with beamed ceilings. Vegetarian, vegan, wholefood or special diet breakfasts.

**CUMBRIA, ALSTON.** Clare and Mike Le Marie, Brownside House, Leadgate, Alston CA9 3EL (01434 382169 or 01434 382100). Ideal centre for walking, cycling, birdwatching and exploring old lead mines. Easy reach for Lake District, Hadrian's Wall, Northumberland. Children and pets welcome (babysitting available). **ETC** ◆◆◆

**CUMBRIA, KESWICK.** Annie Scally and Ian Townsend, Latrigg House, St. Herbert Street, Keswick CA12 4DF (017687 73068). We promise a very warm welcome, good food, comfort and hospitality; vegetarian and vegan meals provided if required. **ETC** ◆◆◆◆

**CUMBRIA, PENRITH.** Brookland Guest House, 2 Portland Place, Penrith CA11 7QN (Tel: 01768 863395). Charming and elegant surroundings await any visitor to Brooklands Guest House in the heart of historic Penrith. Ideal base for exploring the many and various delights of the English Lakes. Non-smoking. Special diets catered for.

**CUMBRIA, PENRITH.** Norcroft Guest House, Graham Street, Penrith CA11 9LQ (Tel & Fax: 01768 862365). Conveniently for M6 and just five minutes' walk from town centre. Single to family rooms all en suite. Renowned for our delicious Cumbrian breakfast. Non-smoking. Private parking. Credit cards accepted. For brochure and details please contact **Mrs Sylvia Jackson**. **ETC/RAC** ◆◆◆◆ Warm Welcome Award.

**CUMBRIA, TROUTBECK.** Gwen and Peter Parfitt, Hill Crest, Troutbeck, Penrith CA11 0SH (017684 83935). A unique warm and friendly Lakeland home with vegetarian and healthy eating menus, where children and dogs are welcome, En suite rooms available. No smoking.

**CUMBRIA, ULLSWATER.** Geoff and Steph Mason, Knotts Mill Country Lodge, Watermillock, Penrith CA11 0JN (Tel & Fax: 017684 86699). Spacious guesthouse close to magical Ullswater, in peaceful, scenic surroundings. Ideal for walking, boating or touring the Lake district. Eight en suite bedrooms with stunning views, including family rooms and facilities for the disabled. **ETC** ◆◆◆

**CUMBRIA, WINDERMERE.** Mr and Mrs Mick and Fiona Rooney, Villa Lodge. Cross Street, Windermere LA23 1AE (Tel & Fax: 015394 43318). Extremely comfortable accommodation in peaceful area overlooking Windermere village. Vegetarian/Special diets catered for. **ETC** ◆◆◆◆

**CUMBRIA, WINDERMERE.** John and Pauline MacDonald, Boston House, The Terrace, Windermere LA23 1AJ (015394 43654). Boston House, the perfect choice for sincere attentive hospitality. Romantic en suite bedrooms with four-poster beds. AGA cooked breakfasts. Short stroll to all amenities. **ETC** ◆◆◆◆

**DERBYSHIRE, ASHBOURNE.** The Courtyard, Dairy House Farm, Alkmonton, Longford, Ashbourne DE6 3DG (Tel & Fax: 01335 330187). Stay in one of our seven rooms - five double, twin and one family, all with en suite facilities. Good farmhouse fare. Children welcome. Regret, no pets. **AA/RAC** ◆◆◆◆

**DERBYSHIRE, ASHBOURNE.** A. and D. Harris, Dairy House Farm, Alkmonton, Longford, Ashbourne. DE6 3DG (Tel & Fax: 01335 330359). Warm welcome and hospitality guaranteed in a comfortable atmosphere with good food and a residential licence. Sorry, no pets, no smokers and no children under 16. **ETC/AA** ◆◆◆◆.

**DERBYSHIRE, BAKEWELL.** Mrs Julia Finney. Mardale House, Haddon Grove, Bakewell DE45 1JF (01629 812416). Vegetarians catered for, other special diets by arrangement. **ETC** ◆◆◆

**DERBYSHIRE, BUXTON.** Mrs Ann Oliver, "Westlands", Bishop's Lane, St. John's Road, Buxton SK17 6UN (01298 23242). Close to Staffordshire and Cheshire borders, this well established Bed and Breakfast is for non-smokers. Situated on country lane one mile from town centre. Special diets catered for by arrangement.

**DEBYSHIRE, MATLOCK.** Mrs Whitehead, Mount Tabor House, Bowns Hill, Crich, Matlock DE4 5DG (01773 857008; Mobile: 07977 078266). A former Methodist chapel. Comfortable guest accommodation with a homely atmosphere. Fay uses local and organic produce in the freshly prepared meals. Non-smoking throughout. **AA** ◆◆◆◆

**Special Diets**  SPECIAL WELCOME 417

**DERBYSHIRE, TIDESWELL. Mrs Pat Harris, Laurel House, The Green, Litton,Tideswell, Near Buxton SK17 8QP (01298 871971).** Overlooking the village green. One double with en-suite facilities, and a twin room with washbasin and private use of bathroom and toilet. Tea/coffee making facilities in both. Private lounge. Special diets catered for. **ETC** ◆◆◆◆.

**DERBYSHIRE, TIDESWELL. Mr D.C. Pinnegar, Poppies, Bank Square, Tideswell, Buxton SK17 8LA (01298 871083).** Comfortable accommodation. Vegetarians/vegans, diabetics catered for, other diets by arrangement.

**DEVON, CLOVELLY. Mrs D. Vanstone, The Old Smithy, Sierra Hill, Clovelly, Bideford EX39 5ST (01237 431202).** A 16th century cottage and converted forge, situated one mile from the sea and the unspoilt picturesque village of Clovelly. Vegetarian breakfast if notified in advance.

**DEVON, HOLSWORTHY. Pat and Phil Jennings, Leworthy Farmhouse, Lower Leworthy, Pyworthy, Holsworthy EX22 6SJ (01409 259469).** A genuinely warm, friendly and discreet peaceful haven. Breakfast traditional farmhouse, or prunes, porridge, fresh fruit, yoghurt, free range eggs, kippers, black pudding. Nearby spectacular North Cornish Coast. Non-smoking. No pets.

**DORSET, BOURNEMOUTH. Mr S. Goodwin, Cransley Hotel, 11 Knyveton Road, East Cliff, Bournemouth BH1 3QG (01202 290067).** You are assured of a warm welcome at the Cransley – a licensed hotel for non-smokers. Rooms are en suite with colour TV and hospitality tray. Open all year. Evening Meals available. Special diets catered for. **ETC/AA** ◆◆◆.

**DORSET, BOURNEMOUTH. Amitie Guest House, 1247 Christchurch Road, Bournemouth BH7 6BP (01202 427255; Fax: 01202 461488).** All diets catered for with prior notice. Please contact Jenny or Paul for details. **AA** ◆◆◆◆.

**DORSET, BRIDPORT. Mrs Sally Long, Old Dairy House, Walditch, Bridport DT6 4LB (01308 458021).** One twin, one double (non smoking) bedrooms. Hearty full English breakfast with home-made preserves.

**DORSET, LYME REGIS. Mrs L. Brown, Providence House, Lyme Road, Uplyme DT7 3TH (01297 445704).** Accommodation comprises one single, one double, one double en suite, all with TV and tea/coffee making facilities. Full English Breakfast and vegetarian option.

**GLOUCESTERSHIRE, NEWLAND. Ann Edwards, Rookery Farmhouse, Newland GL16 8NJ (01594 832432).** Ideal walking and fishing country with stables, cycle paths and golf courses nearby. En suite rooms with bath and shower, colour TV and tea/coffee making facilities. Dogs welcome by prior arrangement. Self catering cottages also available. **ETC** ◆◆◆.

**HAMPSHIRE, FAREHAM. Ian & Sarah Pike, Bembridge House, 32 Osborn Road, Fareham PO16 7DS (Tel & Fax: 01329 317050).** Within a quarter of a mile from Bembridge House there are many pleasant places to dine: Italian , Indian, French, Chinese cuisine or good British food restaurants and some excellent local pubs. Ample off road private parking, and our five course breakfast is sumptuous! **RAC** ◆◆◆◆ Sparkling Diamond Award.

**HAMPSHIRE, LYMINGTON, Our Bench, Lodge Road, Lymington SO41 8HH (Tel & Fax: 01590 673141).** Large non-smoking bungalow and no children, situated between New Forest and Coast. Full English Breakfast. Indoor heated pool, jacuzzi and sauna. Mountain Bikes. National Accessibility Scheme 3. **ETC** ◆◆◆. *ENGLAND FOR EXCELLENCE WINNER. FHG DIPLOMA WINNER.*

**HAMPSHIRE, WINCHESTER. Mrs S. Buchanan, "Acacia', 44 Kilham lane, Winchester SO22 5PT (01962 852259; 07885 462993 mobile)..** Accommodation consists of one double and two twin bedrooms, all of which have en suite or private bathroom, plus tea and coffee making facilities. Off-street parking. Excellent choice of breakfast. **ETC/AA** ◆◆◆◆

**HAMPSHIRE, WINCHESTER. Susan and Richard Pell, The Lilacs, 1 Harestock Close, off Andover Road North, Winchester S022 6NP (01962 884122).** A non-smoking family home offering an excellent English Breakfast, including vegetarian meals. Country views.

**HEREFORDSHIRE, VOWCHURCH. The Old Vicarage. Vowchurch HR2 0QD (Tel & Fax: 01981 550357).** Highly praised quality breakfasts. Award winner for creative cooking with local foods. Discuss your needs with us. Completely non-smoking. **ETC** ◆◆◆◆ *SILVER AWARD*.

**LANCASHIRE, SOUTHPORT. The Sidbrook Private Hotel, 14 Talbot Street, Southport PR8 1HP (01704 530608).** All our bedrooms are en suite and have remote control colour TV, clock radio, hairdryer, hospitality tray and toiletries. Secluded garden, free parking and access at all times. Three course breakfast - special diets catered for. **ETC/AA** ◆◆◆

**NORFOLK, WELLS-NEXT-THE-SEA. Oyster Cottage B&B, 20 High Street, Wells-next-the-Sea NR23 1EP (01328 711997).** An ideal retreat for families, couples and friends. En suite rooms with TV and tea/coffee making; amenities include central heating, laundry service, baby equipment, room service and cycle storage.Vegetarian and other special diets catered for.

**OXFORDSHIRE, OXFORD. Diana and Richard Mitchell, Highfield West, 188 Cumnor Hill, Oxford OX2 9PJ (01865 863007).** Comfortable home in quiet residential area. Well appointed rooms with colour TV, central heating and refreshment trays. Large outdoor pool. No smoking. Vegetarians welcome. **ETC** ◆◆◆.

# 418 SPECIAL WELCOME    Special Diets

**OXFORDSHIRE, WOODSTOCK. Mrs Mandy Buck, Elbie House, East End, North Leigh, Near Witney OX8 6PZ (01993 880166).** Two spacious en suite rooms, one with four-poster bed. English or Continental/vegetarian breakfasts served in rooms. Ground floor accommodation allows easy access for less able visitors. **ETC ♦♦♦♦**.

**SHROPSHIRE, BRIDGNORTH. Jutta and Alan Ward, Linley Crest, Linley Brook, Near Bridgnorth WV16 4SZ (Tel & Fax: 01746 765527).** The setting is tranquil and pleasing. The cosy bedrooms have king-sized beds and every home comfort. The breakfasts are generous, wholesome and varied. We happily cater for special dietary requirements. **ETC ♦♦♦♦ SILVER AWARD.**

**SOMERSET, BATH. Jenny and David Nixon, Footman's Cottage, High Street, Wellow, Bath BA2 8QQ (Tel & Fax: 01225 837024).** A warm welcome awaits you at our 18th century cottage in an area ideal for walking or trekking. Homemade bread and preserves are served with an excellent breakfast and we are happy to cater for special diets, with prior notice.

**SOMERSET, BATH. Jan and Bryan Wotley, The Albany Guest House, 24 Crescent Gardens, Upper Bristol Road, Bath BA1 2NB (01225 313339).** Welcoming accommodation at our Victorian home, just five minutes from city centre. Vegetarians, vegans and special diets happily catered for.

**STAFFORDSHIRE, ECCLESHALL. Mrs Sue Pimble, Cobblers Cottage, Kerry Lana, Eccleshall ST21 6EJ (01785 850116).** Eccleshall is ideally situated for the Potteries, Alton Towers and other attractions. Children and pets welcome. Special diets can be accommodated. Non-smoking. **ETC ♦♦♦♦**

**SUSSEX (EAST), HASTINGS. Peter Mann, Grand Hotel, Grand Parade, St. Leonards, Hastings TN38 0DD (Tel & Fax: 01424 428510)** Seafront family-run hotel; all rooms with colour TV, radio; some en suite. Unrestricted/disabled parking. Non-smoking restaurant. Licensed bar. **ETC ♦♦♦**.

**SUSSEX (WEST), ARUNDEL. Mrs Vicki Richards, Woodacre, Arundel Road, Fontwell, Arundel BN18 0SD (01243 814301).** Bed and breakfast in a traditional family home with accommodation for up to 10/12 guests. Well positioned for Chichester, Arundel, Goodwood and the seaside and easily accessible from the A27. Full English breakfast in our conservatory or dining room overlooking the garden. Evening meals are available by arrangment.

**WARWICKSHIRE, ALCESTER. Mrs Margaret Kember, Orchard Lawns, Wixford, Alcester B49 6DA (01789 772668).** A warm welcome awaits you at our totally non-smoking establishment. Three bedrooms (one en suite). Bed and Breakfast from £20 per person. **ETC ♦♦♦♦ SILVER AWARD.**

**WARWICKSHIRE, STRATFORD-UPON-AVON. Hampton Lodge, 38 Shipston Road, Stratford-upon-Avon CV37 7LP (Tel/Fax: 01789 299374).** The perfect base for exploring Shakespeares' Country and the north Cotswolds. Seven spacious rooms, individually decorated, en suite facilities, direct dial telephone, colour television, tea and coffee trays and hair dryers. **ETC/RAC ♦♦♦♦**, RAC DINING AWARD, WARM WELCOME, SPARKLING DIAMOND

**WARWICKSHIRE, STRATFORD-UPON-AVON. Mrs Karen Cauvin, Penshurst Guest House, 34 Evesham Place, Stratford-upon-Avon CV37 6HT (01789 205259; Fax: 01789 295322).** Prettily refurbished Victorian townhouse. Town centre five minutes' walk. Will cater for any special diet, including vegetarian. **ETC ♦♦♦**

**WARWICKSHIRE, STRATFORD-UPON-AVON. Hampton Lodge, 38 Shipston Road, Stratford-upon-Avon CV37 7LP (Tel/Fax: 01789 299374).** Seven spacious rooms, individually decorated, en suite facilities, direct dial telephone, colour television, tea and coffee trays and hair dryers. Home-cooked, traditional dinner is served in the conservatory at 6.30pm with earlier pre-theatre dinners available on request. **ETC/RAC ♦♦♦♦**, RAC DINING AWARD, WARM WELCOME, SPARKLING DIAMOND

**YORKSHIRE (NORTH), EASINGWOLD. Mrs Lorna Huxtable, Dimple Wells, Thormanby, Easingwold YO61 4NL (Tel & Fax: 01845 501068).** Secluded country house betwixt Yorkshire Moors and Dales. En suite rooms with colour TV, tea/coffee tray. Ample parking. Special diets/vegetarian breakfasts upon request. **ETC ♦♦♦♦**.

**YORKSHIRE (NORTH), YORK. Jenny Clark, Cumbria House, 2 Vyner Street, Haxby Road, York YO31 8HS (01904 636817).** An elegant, tastefully decorated Victorian guest house, where comfort and quality are assured. All rooms have colour TV, radio alarms and tea/coffee facilities. Central heating. Fire Certificate. Guests' car park. Full English breakfast or vegetarian alternative. **AA** *QQQ*.

**YORKSHIRE, (NORTH ), YORK. Mr Ian McNabb, The Hazelwood, 24-25 Portland Street, Gillygate, York YO31 7EH (01904 626548; Fax: 01904 628032).** Victorian townhouse retaining many original features. Friendly and informal. Wide choice of high quality breakfasts including vegetarian, ranging from traditional English to croissants and Danish pastries. Completely non smoking. **ETC/AA/RAC ♦♦♦♦**

**YORKSHIRE (NORTH), YORK. The Kismet Guest House, 147 Haxby Road, York YO31 8JZ (01904 621056).** Close to city centre, Yorkshire Dales and coast. Vegetarians catered for. non-smoking.

---

*Please mention Bed & Breakfast Stops when writing
to enquire about accommodation*

## Special Diets • Scotland

**DUMFRIES & GALLOWAY, DUMFRIES. The Maxwell Family, Southpark Guest House, Quarry Road, Locharbriggs, Dumfries DG1 1QG (Tel & Fax: 01387 711188).** Excellent value for money balanced with home from home comfort and fine hospitality. Hearty Scottish breakfasts, special diets catered for on request. **STB ★★★** B&B, **AA ♦♦♦♦**.

**EDINBURGH & LOTHIANS, EDINBURGH (14 miles). Mrs Janet Burke, Patieshill Farm, Carlops, Penicuik EH26 9ND (01968 660551; Fax: 01968 661162).** A very warm and friendly welcome is extended to all guests. Special diets catered for by arrangement. **STB ★★★** B&B.

**HIGHLANDS SOUTH, FORT AUGUSTUS. Caledonian Cottage, Station Road, Fort Augustus PH32 4AY (01320 366401; Mobile: 07967 740329)** Set in a quiet village, offering comfortable modern accommodation. Non-smoking. Rooms en suite or with private facilities. Children and pets welcome.

## Special Diets • Wales

**ANGLESEY & GWYNEDD, BANGOR. Penhower Uchaf Newydd, Caerhun, Bangor LL57 4DT (01248 362427).** Single storey home set in a spacious garden with ample and secure parking. A non-smoking establishment with all of our de luxe rooms en suite with showers, we take great pride in offering warm and friendly hospitality and acclaimed home cooking. **WTB ★★★★**.

**NORTH WALES, BETWS-Y-COED. Jim and Lilian Boughton, Bron Celyn Guest House, Lon Muriau, Llanrwst Road, Betws-y-Coed LL24 0HD (01690 710333; Fax: 01690 710111).** A warm welcome awaits you at this delightful guest house. Ideal centre for touring, walking, climbing, fishing and golf. Car park. Open all year. Evening meals - special diets catered for. Bed and Breakfast from £19 to £26. **WTB ★★★** GUEST HOUSE.

**SOUTH WALES, ST. BRIDES WENTLOOG (Near Newport). Mr David W. Bushell, Chapel Guest House, Church Road, St. Brides Wentloog, Near Newport NP10 8SN (01633 681018; Fax: 01633 681431)** Comfortable accommodation in a converted chapel. Guest lounge with TV. Single, double and twin rooms en suite or private bathroom. Beverage trays, TV, shaver points in all rooms. From £19. **WTB ★★★** GUEST HOUSE.

**SOUTH WALES, SWANSEA. Fairyland, Ken and Jan's B&B, 89-93 Alexandra Road, Gorseinon, Swansea SA4 4NU (01792 897940; Fax: 01792 542078).** Family-run guest house, artistically decorated with each room themed on a Flower Fairy. Some rooms self-catering. Discount for children and 10% discount offered to members of Vegetarian Society. **WTB ★★★** B&B

# FHG

Other specialised

# FHG PUBLICATIONS

Published annually: Please add 50p postage (UK only) when ordering from the publishers

- Recommended COUNTRY HOTELS OF BRITAIN    £4.99
- Recommended WAYSIDE & COUNTRY INNS OF BRITAIN    £4.99
  - PETS WELCOME!    £5.99
  - B&B IN BRITAIN    £3.99
- THE GOLF GUIDE Where to Play / Where to Stay    £9.99

## FHG PUBLICATIONS LTD
Abbey Mill Business Centre,
Seedhill, Paisley, Renfrewshire PA1 1TJ

Tel: 0141-887 0428 • Fax: 0141-889 7204
e-mail: fhg@ipcmedia.com • website: www.holidayguides.com

# Website Directory

A quick-reference guide to holiday accommodation with an e-mail address and website, conveniently arranged by country and county, with full contact details

## • LONDON

*Hotel*
Stanley House Hotel, 19 – 21 Belgrave Road, VICTORIA, London SW1V 1RB
020 7834 5042
- e-mail: cmahotel@aol.com
- website: www.affordablehotelsonline.com

*Hotel*
St Georges Hotel, 23 Belgrave Road, LONDON SW1V 1RD
020 7828 2061
- e-mail: cmahotel@aol.com
- website: www.affordablehotelsonline.com

*Hotel*
Colliers Hotel, 97 Warwick Way, LONDON SW1V 1QL
020 7834 6931
- e-mail: cmahotel@aol.com
- website: www.affordablehotelsonline.com

## • CORNWALL

*Guest House*
Mrs C. Carruthers, The Clearwater, 50 Melvill Road, FALMOUTH, Cornwall TR11 4DF
01326 311344
- e-mail: clearwater@lineone.net
- website: www.clearwaterhotel.co.uk

*Hotel*
Parc-An-Ithan House Hotel, Sithney, NEAR HELSTON, Cornwall TR13 0RN
01326 572565
- e-mail: parc-hotel@btinternet.com
- website: www.visitweb.com/parc

*Self-Catering*
Mr & Mrs Cotter, Trewalla Farm, Minions, LISKEARD, Cornwall PL14 6ED
01579 342385
- e-mail: cotter.trewalla@virgin.net
- website: www.selfcateringcornwall.net

*Lodge*
Jan & Jeff Loveridge, Harescombe Lodge, Watergate, NEAR LOOE, Cornwall PL13 2NE
01503 263158
- e-mail: harescombe@dial.pipex.com
- website: www.harescombe.dial.pipex.com

*Hotel*
Lostwithiel Hotel, Golf & Country Club, Lower Polscoe, LOSTWITHIEL, Cornwall PL22 0HQ
01208 873550
- e-mail: reception@golf-hotel.co.uk
- website: www.golf-hotel.co.uk

*Hotel*
Seavista Hotel, Mawgan Porth, NEAR NEWQUAY Cornwall TR8 4AL
01637 860276
- e-mail: crossd@supanet.com
- website: www.seavistahotel.co.uk

*Self-Catering*
Cornish Horizons Holiday Cottages, Higher Trehenborne, St Merryn, PADSTOW Cornwall PL28 8JU
01841 520889
- e-mail: cottages@cornishhorizons.co.uk
- website: www.cornishhorizons.co.uk

*Self-Catering*
Angela Clark, Darrynane Cottages, Darrynane, ST BREWARD, Bodmin Moor, Cornwall PL30 4LZ
01208 850885
- e-mail: darrynane@eclipse.co.uk
- website: www.darrynane.co.uk

*Guest House*
Mr & Mrs Clark, Trewerry Mill, Trerice, ST NEWLYN EAST, Cornwall TR8 5HGS
01872 510345
- e-mail: trewerry.mill@which.net
- website: www.connexions.co.uk\trewerry.mill

*B & B*
Mrs Lynda Spring, Trethevy Manor, Trethevy, TINTAGEL, Cornwall PL34 0BG
01840 770636
- e-mail: manor1151@talk21.com
- website: www.cornwall-online.co.uk/trethevy-manor

## CORNWALL (Contd)

*Hotel*
Rosevine Hotel, Porthcurnick Beach, St Mawes, TRURO, Cornwall TR2 5EW
01872 580206
• e-mail: info@rosevine.co.uk
• website: www.rosevine.co.uk

*B&B / Self-Catering*
Mrs. Pamela Carbis, Trenona Farm, Ruan High Lanes, TRURO, Cornwall TR2 5JS
01872 501339
• e-mail: pcarbis@compuserve.com
• website: www.connexions.co.uk/trenona

## •CUMBRIA

*Self-Catering*
Mr and Mrs P. Hart, Bracken Fell, Outgate, AMBLESIDE, Cumbria LA22 0NH
015394 36289
• e-mail: hart.brackenfell@virgin.net
• website: www.brackenfell.com

*B & B, Self-Catering*
Mrs Cotton, Glebe House, Bolton APPLEBY-IN-WESTMORLAND, Cumbria CA16 6AW
017683 61125
• e-mail: derick.cotton@btinternet.com

*Self-Catering*
Lakelovers, The New Toffee Loft, Kendal Road, BOWNESS, Cumbria LA23 3RA
01539 488855
• e-mail: bookings@lakelovers.co.uk
• website: www.lakelovers.co.uk

*Self-Catering*
Mr P. Johnston, The Coppermines at Coniston, The Estate Office, The Bridge, CONISTON Cumbria LA21 8HX
01539 441765
• e-mail: bookings@coppermines.co.uk
• website: www.coppermines.co.uk

*Self-Catering*
Mr and Mrs E.D. Robinson, 1 Field End, Patton, KENDAL, Cumbria LA8 9DU
01539 824220
• e-mail: fshawend@globalnet.co.uk
• website: www.diva-web.co.uk/fsendhols

*B & B*
Mr & Mrs M. Rooney, Villa Lodge, Cross Street, WINDERMERE, Cumbria LA23 1AE
01539 443318
• e-mail: rooneym@btconnect.com
• website: www.villa-lodge.co.uk

*Self-Catering*
Mr and Mrs F. Legge, Pinethwaite Holiday Cottages, Luckbarrow Road, WINDERMERE Cumbria LA23 2NQ
01539 444558
• e-mail: legge@pinethwaite.freeserve.co.uk
• website: www.pinecottages.co.uk

*Guest House*
Mr Brian Fear, Cambridge House, 9 Oak Street, WINDERMERE, Cumbria LA23 1EN
01539 443846
• e-mail: reservations@cambridge-house.fsbusiness.co.uk
• website: www.cambridge-house.fsbusiness.co.uk

## •DEVON

*B & B*
Mr C.D. Moore, Gages Mill, Buckfastleigh Road, ASHBURTON, Devon TQ13 7JW
01364 652391
• e-mail: moore@gagesmill.co.uk
• website: www.gagesmill.co.uk

*Farmhouse B&B*
Jaye Jones & Helen Asher, Twitchen Farm, Challacombe, BARNSTAPLE, Devon EX31 4TT
01598 763568
• e-mail: holidays@twitchen.co.uk
• website: www.twitchen.co.uk

*Self-Catering*
Mrs L. Nash, Swincombe Farm, Challacombe, NEAR BARNSTAPLE, Devon EX31 4TV
01598 763506
• e-mail: nash@lineone.com
• website: www.jcjdatacomm.co.uk\nash

*Hotel*
Fingals at Old Coombe Manor, Dittisham, NEAR DARTMOUTH, Devon TQ6 0JA
01803 722398
• e-mail: richard@fingals.co.uk
• website: www.fingals.co.uk

---

*Please mention FHG Publications when enquiring about accommodation featured in this Website Directory*

## 422 WEBSITE DIRECTORY

*Self-Catering*
Paul and Julia Hardy, Treaslake Holiday Cottages, Buckerell, HONITON, Devon EX14 3EP
01404 850292
- e-mail: treaslake_cottages@breathemail.net
- website: www.devoncottage.com

*Self-Catering*
Mrs Sue Horn, Narramore Farm Cottages, Narramore Farm, MORETONHAMPSTEAD, Devon TQ13 8QT
01647 440455
- e-mail: narramore@btinternet.com
- website: www.narramorefarm.co.uk

*Self-Catering*
Mr Tromans, Hope Barton Barns, Hope Cove, NEAR SALCOMBE, Devon TQ7 3HT
01548 561393
- e-mail: info@hopebarton.co.uk
- website: www.hopebarton.co.uk

*Hotel*
Lodge Hill Farm Hotel, TIVERTON, Devon EX16 5PA
01884 251200
- e-mail: lodgehill@dialpipex.com
- website: www.lodgehill.co.uk

## •DORSET

*Country House B&B*
Mrs Martine Tree, The Old Rectory, Winterbourne Steepleton, DORCHESTER, Dorset DT2 9LG
01305 889468
- e-mail: trees@eurobell.co.uk
- website: www.trees.eurobell.co.uk

*Guest House*
Lydwell Guest House, Lyme Road, Uplyme, LYME REGIS, Dorset DT7 3TJ
- e-mail: lydwell@britane16.fsbusiness.co.uk
- website: www.SmoothHound.co.uk

## •GLOUCESTERSHIRE

*B & B*
Mr S. D. Gwilliam, Dryslade Farm, English Bicknor, COLEFORD, Gloucestershire GL16 7PA
01594 860259
- e-mail: gwilliam@dryslade.freeserve.co.uk
- website: www.fweb.org.uk/dryslade

*Lodge*
Mr Paul Korn, Symonds Yat Rock Lodge, Hillersland, NEAR COLEFORD, Gloucestershire GL16 7NY
01594 836191
- e-mail: enquiries@rocklodge.co.uk
- website: www.rocklodge.co.uk

*Hotel*
Speech House Hotel, COLEFORD, Forest of Dean, Gloucestershire GL16 7EL
01594 822607
- e-mail: relax@thespecchouse.co.uk
- website: www.thespeechhouse.co.uk

## •HAMPSHIRE

*Guest House*
Mrs Lewis, Our Bench, Lodge Road, Pennington, LYMINGTON, Hampshire SO41 8HH
01590 673141
- e-mail: enquiries@ourbench.co.uk
- website: www.ourbench.co.uk

*B & B*
Graham & Sandra Tubb, Hamilton House, 95 Victoria Road North, Southsea, PORTSMOUTH, Hampshire PO5 1PS
02392 823502
- e-mail: sandra@hamiltonhouse.co.uk
- website: www.hamiltonhouse.co.uk

## •LANCASHIRE

*B & B*
Mr & Mrs M. Smith, The Old Coach House, 50 Dean St, BLACKPOOL, Lancashire FY4 1BP
01253 349195
- e-mail: blackpool@theoldcoachhouse.freeserve.co.uk
- website: www.theoldcoachhouse.freeserve.co.uk

*B & B*
Mrs Melanie Smith, Capernwray House, Capernwray, CARNFORTH, Lancashire LA6 1AE
01524 732363
- e-mail: thesmiths@capernwrayhouse.com
- website: www.capernwrayhouse.com

*Hotel*
Rosedale Hotel, 11 Talbot Street, SOUTHPORT, Lancashire PR8 1HP
0800 0738133
- e-mail: info@rosedalehotelsouthport.co.uk
- website: www.rosedalehotelsouthport.co.uk

## •LEICESTERSHIRE

*B & B*
Mrs A.T. Hutchinson and Mrs A.M. Knight
The Greenway and Knaptoft House Farm,
Bruntingthorpe Road, Near Shearsby,
LUTTERWORTH, Leicestershire LE17 6P
011624 78388
- e-mail: info@knaptoft.com
- website: www.knaptoft.com

## •LINCOLNSHIRE

*Guest House*
Edward King House, The Old Palace,
LINCOLN, Lincolnshire LN2 1PU
01522 528778
- e-mail: ekh@oden-org.ok
- website: www.lincoln.anglican.org/ekh

*B&B*
Mrs B. Moss, Keddington House,
5 Keddington Road, LOUTH, Lincolnshire
LN11 0AA
01507 603973
- e-mail: beverly@keddingtonhouse.co.uk
- website: www.keddingtonhouse.co.uk

## •NORFOLK

*Hotel*
Ffolkes Arms Hotel, Lynn Road, Hillington,
KING'S LYNN, Norfolk PE31 6BJ
01485 600210
- e-mail: ffolkespub@aol.com
- website: www.ffolkes-arms-hotel.co.uk

*B&B*
Mrs M.A. Hemnant, Poplar Farm, Sisland,
Loddon, NORWICH, Norfolk NR14 6EF
01508 520706
- e-mail: milly@hemnant.myhome.org.uk
- website: www.farm-holidays.co.uk

## •NORTHUMBERLAND

*Self-Catering*
Mrs Vicki Taylor, Quality Self Catering,
Letton Lodge, ALNMOUTH,
Northumberland NE66 2RJ
01665 830633
- e-mail: lettonlodge@aol.com
- website: www.alnmouth.co.uk

*Self-catering*
Northumbria Coast and Country Cottages,
Riverbank Road, ALNMOUTH,
Northumberland NE66 2RH
01665 830783
- e-mail: cottages@nccc.demon.co.uk
- website: www.northumbriacottages.com

## •OXFORDSHIRE

*Self-Catering*
Mrs W. Church, Cottage in the Country,
Forest Gate, Forge Lane, MILTON-UNDER-
WYCHWOOD, Oxfordshire OX7 6JZ
01993 831495
- e-mail: cottage@cottageinthecountry.co.uk
- website: www.cottageinthecountry.co.uk

## •SOMERSET

*Farm*
Mr & Mrs Rowe, Wembdon Farm, Hollow
Lane, Wembdon, BRIDGWATER, Somerset
TA5 2BD
01278 453097
- e-mail: mary.rowe@btinternet.com
- website: www.farmaccommodation.co.uk

*Hotel*
Braeside Hotel, 2 Victoria Park, WESTON-
SUPER-MARE, Somerset BS23 2HZ
01934626642
- e-mail: info@thebraesidehotel.co.uk
- website: www.braesidehotel.co.uk

---

**FHG**

Visit the **FHG** website
**www.holidayguides.com**
for details of the wide choice of accommodation
featured in the full range of FHG titles

## •STAFFORDSHIRE

*Guest House*
Mrs Griffiths, Prospect House Guest House, 334 Cheadle Road, Cheddleton, LEEK, Staffordshire ST13 7BW
01782 550639
• e-mail: prospect@talk21.com
• website: www.touristnetuk.com/wm/prospect/index.htm

## •SUFFOLK

*Guest House*
Kay Dewsbury, Manor House Guest House, The Green Beyton, BURY ST EDMUNDS, Near Suffolk IP30 9AF
01359 270960
• e-mail: manorhouse@thegreenbeyton.com
• website: www.beyton.com

*Guest House/Tearoom*
Mr & Mrs Bowles, Ship Stores, 22 Callis St, CLARE, Sudbury, Suffolk CO10 8DX
01787 277834
• e-mail: shipclare@aol.co.uk
• website: www.ship-stores.co.uk

*Guest House*
Chippenhall Hall, Fressingfield, EYE, Suffolk IP21 5TD
01379 558180 or 586733
• e-mail: info@chippenhall.co.uk
• website: www.chippenhall.co.uk

*Self-Catering*
Melanie Reiger, Mill House, Water Run, Hitcham, IPSWICH, Suffolk IP7 7LN
01449 740315
• e-mail: hitcham@aol.com
• website: www.millhouse-hitcham.co.uk

*Hotel*
Pakefield Pet Hotel, London Road, Pakefield, LOWESTOFT, Suffolk NR33 7PG
01502 563399
• e-mail: marion@pakefieldpethotel.fsnet.co.uk
• website: www.pakefieldpethotel.co.uk

## •SURREY

*Guest House*
Mr. A. Grinsted, The Lawn Guest House, 30 Massetts Road, HORLEY, Surrey, RH5 7DE
01293 775751
• e-mail: info@lawnguesthouse.co.uk
• website: www.lawnguesthouse.co.uk

*Hotel*
Chase Lodge Hotel, 10 Park Road, Hampton, Wick, KINGSTON UPON THAMES, Surrey KT1 4AS
02089 431862
• e-mail: chaselodgehotel@aol.com
• website: www.chaselodgehotel.com

## •EAST SUSSEX

*B & B*
Mr Mundy, The Homestead, Homestead Lane, Valebridge Road, BURGESS HILL, East Sussex RH15 0RQ
01444 246899
• e-mail: homestead@burgess-hill.co.uk
• website: www.burgess-hill.co.uk

*Guest House*
Mrs J. P. Hadfield, Jeake's House, Mermaid Street, RYE, East Sussex TN31 7ET
01797 222828
• e-mail: jeakeshouse@btinternet.com
• website: www.jeakeshouse.com

## •WEST SUSSEX

*B & B*
Deborah S. Collinson, The Old Priory, 80 North Bersted Street, BOGNOR REGIS, West Sussex PO22 9AQ
01243 863580
• e-mail: old.priory@mcmail.com
• website: www.old.priory.mcmail.com

## •WARWICKSHIRE

*Guest House*
Mr & Mrs K Wheat, Hollyhurst Guest House, 47 Priory Road, KENILWORTH, Warwickshire CV8 1LL
01926 853882
• e-mail: admin@hollyhurstguesthouse.co.uk
• website: www.hollyhurstguesthouse.co.uk

**FHG**

# •NORTH YORKSHIRE

*Guest House*
Mr Kingsley, Arbutus Guest House, Riverside, CLAPHAM, Near Settle, North Yorkshire LA2 8DS
01524 251240
• e-mail: info@arbutus.co.uk
• website: www.arbutus.co.uk

*Guest House*
Mr & Mrs R. Joyner, Anro Guest House, 90 Kings Road, HARROGATE, North Yorkshire HG1 5JX
01423 503087
• e-mail: info@theanro.harrogate.net
• website: www.theanro.harrogate.net

*B & B*
Mr & Mrs C. Richardson, The Coppice, 9 Studley Road, HARROGATE, North Yorkshire HG1 5JU
01423 569626
• e-mail: coppice@harrogate.com
• website: www.harrogate.com/coppice

*Guest House B&B*
Mrs S. Robinson, Valley View Farm, Old Byland, HELMSLEY, North Yorkshire YO6 5LG
01439 798221
• e-mail: sally@valleyviewfarm.com
• website: www.valleyviewfarm.com

*Hotel*
Mrs Ella Bowes, Banavie, Roxby Road, Thornton-Le-Dale, PICKERING, North Yorkshire YO18 7SX
01751 474616
• e-mail: ella@banavie-fsbusiness.co.uk
• website: www.smoothhound.co.uk/hotels/banavie.html

*Hotel / Inn*
Mr N. Thompson, The Queens Arms, Litton, NEAR SKIPTON, North Yorkshire BD23 5QJ
01756 770208
• e-mail: queensarms.litton@amserve.net
• website: www.yorkshiredales.net/stayat/queens

*Caravans*
Mr & Mrs Tyerman, Partridge Nest Farm, Eskdaleside, Sleights, WHITBY, North Yorkshire YO22 5ES
01947 810450
• e-mail: pnfarm@aol.com
• website: www.tmis.uk.com/partridge-nest/

*Self-Catering*
Mr Eddleston, Greenhouses Farm Cottages Lealholm, NEAR WHITBY, North Yorkshire YO21 2AD
01947 897486
• e-mail: n_eddleston@yahoo.com
• website: www.greenhouses-farm-cottages.co.uk

## SCOTLAND

# •ARGYLL & BUTE

*Hotel*
Willowburn Hotel, Clachan Seil, BY OBAN, Argyll PA34 4TJ
01852 300276
e-mail: willowburnhotel@virgin.net
• website: www.willowburn.co.uk

# •DUNDEE & ANGUS

*Self-Catering*
Mrs M. Marchant, The Welton of Kingoldrum, Welton Farm, KIRRIEMUIR, Angus DD8 5HY
01575 574743
• e-mail: weltonholidays@btinternet.com
• website:
http://homepages.go.com/~thewelton/index.htm

# •EDINBURGH & LOTHIANS

*Guest House*
Irene Cheape, Crion Guest House, 33 Minto Street, EDINBURGH, Lothians EH9 2BT
0131 667 2708
• e-mail: wcheape@gilmourhouse.freeserve.co.uk
• website: www.edinburghbedbreakfast.com

---

*Please mention FHG Publications when enquiring about accommodation featured in this Website Directory*

*Guest House*
John and Muriel Hamilton, Southdown Guest House, 20 Craigmillar Park, EDINBURGH, Lothians EH16 5PS
0131 667 2410
- e-mail: ham120@aol.com
- website: www.smoothhound.co.uk/hotels/southdow.html

*Self-Catering*
Premier Vacations, 5 St Peters Buildings, EDINBURGH, East Lothian EH3 9PG
0131 221 9001
- e-mail: reservations@premiervacations.net
- website: www.premiervacations.net

*Guest House*
Mr David Martin, Spylaw Bank House, 2 Spylaw Ave, Colinton, EDINBURGH, Lothians EH13 0LR
0131 441 5022
- e-mail: angelaatspylawbank.freeserve.co.uk
- website: www.spylawbank.freeserve.co.uk

*Guest House*
Mrs Vidler, Rowan Guest House, 13 Glenorchy Terrace, EDINBURGH EH9 2DQ
0131-667 2463
- e-mail: rowanhouse@hotmail.com
- website: www.rowan-house.co.uk

*B & B*
The Stuarts, 17 Glengyle Terrace, EDINBURGH, Lothians EH3 9LN
0131 229 9559
- e-mail: fhg@the-stuarts.com
- website: www.the-stuarts.com

*Guest House*
Ben Doran Guest House, 11 Mayfield Gardens, EDINBURGH EH9 2AX
0131-667 8488
- e-mail: info@bendoran.com
- website: www.bendoran.com

*Guest House*
Elizabeth Scott, Ashcroft Farmhouse, East Calder, NEAR EDINBURGH
01506 881810
- e-mail: ashcroftfa@aol.com
- website: www.ashcroft-farmhouse.com

*Guest House*
Mrs Lamb, Priory Lodge, 8 The Loan, SOUTH QUEENSFERRY, West Lothian EH30 9NS
0131 331 4345
- e-mail: calmyn@aol.com
- website: www.queensferry.com

# • FIFE

*Self-Catering*
Mr Potter, Carvenom Farm Cottage, Carvenom House, BY ANSTRUTHER, Fife KY10 3JU
01333 311823
- e-mail: gtpotter@aol.com
- website: www.carvenom.btinternet.co.uk

*Hotel*
The Golf Hotel, The Golf Hotel, ELIE, Fife KY9 1EF
01333 330209
- e-mail: golf@standrews.co.uk
- website: www.golfhotel.co.uk

# • HIGHLANDS

*Guest House B&B*
Mrs Sandra Silke, Westwood, Lower Balmacaan, DRUMNADROCHIT, Inverness-shire IV63 6WU
01456 450826
- e-mail: sandra@westwoodbb.freeserve.co.uk
- website: www.westwoodbb.freeserve.co.uk

*B&B/Self-Catering*
Mr A. Allan, Torguish House & Holiday Homes, DAVIOT, Inverness-shire IV1 2XQ
01463 772308
- e-mail: torguish@torguish.com
- website: www.torguish.com

*Farm/Croft*
Ian & Pamela Grant, Greenfield Croft, Insh, By KINGUSSIE, Inverness-shire PH21 1NT
01540 661010
- e-mail: farmhouse@kincraig.com
- website: www.kincraig.com/greenfield.htm

*Self-Catering*
Mr J. Fleming, Dell of Abernethy Cottages, NETHYBRIDGE, Inverness-shire PH25 3DL
01463 224358
- e-mail: dellofabernethy.htm
- website: www.nethybridge.com

*Self-Catering*
Mrs Dean, Fhuarain Forest Cottages & Lazy Duck Hostel, Badanfhuarain, NETHYBRIDGE, Inverness-shire PH25 3ED
01479 821642
- e-mail: lazy.duck@virgin.net
- website: www.forestcottages.com

*Guest House*
Dreamweavers, Earendil, Mulomir, BY SPEAN BRIDGE, Inverness-shire PH34 4EQ
01397 712548
* e-mail: helen@dreamweavers.co.uk
* website: www.dreamweavers.co.uk

*Self-Catering*
Mr & Mrs Allen, Wildside Highland Lodges. WHITEBRIDGE, Inverness-shire IV1 2UN
01456 486373
* e-mail: info@wildside lodges.com
* website: www.wildsidelodges.com

Mr Anderson, Killiecrankie Hotel, Pass of Killiecrankie, BY PITLOCHRY, Perthshire PH16 5LG
01796 473220
* e-mail: enquiries@killiecrankiehotel.co.uk
* website: www.killiecrankiehotel.co.uk

*Guest House*
Mrs Hilary Pratt, Bonskeid House, PITLOCHRY, Perthshire PH16 5NP
01796 473208
* e-mail: bonskeid@aol.com
* website: www.bonskeid-house.co.uk

## •PERTH & KINROSS

*Self-Catering*
Mr Alastair Steeple, Altamount Chalets, Coupar Angus Road, BLAIRGOWRIE, Perthshire PH10 6JN
01250 873324
* e-mail: alastair@altamountchalets.co.uk
* website: www.altamountchalets.co.uk

*Hotel*
The Highland House Hotel, South Church Street, CALLANDER, Perth FK17 8BN
01877 330269
* e-mail: highland.house.hotel@lineone.net
* website: www.highlandhousehotel.co.uk

*Self-Catering*
The Birnam House Hotel, Birnam, DUNKELD, Perthshire PH8 0BQ
01350 727462
* e-mail: email@birnamhousehotel.co.uk
* website: www.birnhamhousehotel.co.uk

*Self-Catering*
Mrs F. Bruges, Laighwood Holidays, Butterstone, BY DUNKELD, Perthshire PH8 0HB
01350 724241
* e-mail: holidays@laighwood.co.uk
* website: www.laighwood.co.uk

*Self-Catering*
Mrs W. Marshall, Duncrub Holidays, Dalreoch, DUNNING, Perthshire PH12 0QJ
01764 684368
* e-mail: info@duncrub-holidays.com
* website: www.duncrub-holidays.com*Hotel*

## •ORKNEY ISLANDS

*Hotel*
Cleaton House Hotel, Cleaton, WESTRAY, Orkney KW17 2DB
01857 677508
* e-mail: cleaton@orkney.com
* website: www.orkneyhotel.com

## WALES

## •ANGLESEY & GWYNEDD

*Guest House*
Mr & Mrs D. Pender, Bryn Bella Guest House, Llanrwst Road, BETWS-Y-COED, Gwynedd LL24 0HD
01690 710627
* e-mail: brynbella@clara.net
* website: www.brynbella.co.uk

## •NORTH WALES

*B & B*
Mrs Janet Shaw, Bryn, Sychnant Pass Road, CONWY, North Wales LL32 8NS
01492 592449
* e-mail: b&b@bryn.org.uk
* website: www.bryn.org.uk

*Hotel*
Caerlyr Hall Hotel, Conwy Old Road, Penmaenmawr, CONWY, North Wales LL34 6SW
01492 623518
* website: nwi.co.uk/snowdonia/caerlyrhall

*Please mention FHG Publications when enquiring about accommodation featured in this Website Directory*

## • PEMBROKESHIRE

*B & B*
Mrs Lort Philips, Knowles Farm,
LAWRENNY, Pembrokeshire SA68 0PX
01834 891221
• e-mail: ginilp@lawrenny.org.uk
• website: www.lawrenny.org.uk

## •POWYS

*Guest House*
Mr & Mrs Jackson, Beacons Guest House,
16 Bridge Street, BRECON, Powys LD3 8AH
01874 623339
• e-mail: beacons@brecon.co.uk
• website: www.beacons.brecon.co.uk

*B&B*
N. Atkins, Cambrian Cruisers, Marina, Ty
Newydd, Pencelli, BRECON, Powys LD3 7LJ
01874 665315
• e-mail: cambrian@talk21.com
• website: www.cambriancruisers.co.uk*B & B*

Mr & Mrs P. Roberts, York House, Cusop,
HAY-ON-WYE, Powys HR3 5QX
01497 820705
• e-mail: roberts@yorkhouse59.fsnet.co.uk
• website: www.hay-on-wye.co.uk/yorkhouse

## IRELAND

*Caravan & Camping/Self-catering*
Belleek Caravan & Camping Park, BALLINA,
Co. Mayo
00353 9671533
• e-mail: lenahan@indigo.ie
• website: http://indigo.ie/~lenahan

---

Other specialised
# FHG PUBLICATIONS

Published annually: Please add 50p postage (UK only)
when ordering from the publishers

• Recommended COUNTRY HOTELS OF BRITAIN   £4.99

• Recommended WAYSIDE & COUNTRY INNS OF BRITAIN   £4.99

• PETS WELCOME!   £5.99

• B&B IN BRITAIN   £3.99

• THE GOLF GUIDE Where to Play / Where to Stay   £9.99

**FHG PUBLICATIONS LTD**
Abbey Mill Business Centre,
Seedhill, Paisley, Renfrewshire PA1 1TJ

Tel: 0141-887 0428 • Fax: 0141-889 7204
e-mail: fhg@ipcmedia.com • website: www.holidayguides.com

# Index of towns and counties.
## Please also refer to Contents pages 38-39

| | |
|---|---|
| Abbotsbury | DORSET |
| Aberaeron | CARDIGANSHIRE |
| Aberdaron | ANGLESEY & GWYNEDD |
| Aberdeen | ABERDEEN, BANFF & MORAY |
| Abernethy | PERTH & KINROSS |
| Aberystwyth | CARDIGANSHIRE |
| Acle | NORFOLK |
| Alcester | WARWICKSHIRE |
| Aldborough | NORFOLK |
| Allendale | NORTHUMBERLAND |
| Allerford | SOMERSET |
| Alnmouth | NORTHUMBERLAND |
| Alnwick | NORTHUMBERLAND |
| Alston | CUMBRIA |
| Alton | STAFFORDSHIRE |
| Altrincham | CHESHIRE |
| Ambergate | DERBYSHIRE |
| Ambleside | CUMBRIA |
| Ampleforth | NORTH YORKSHIRE |
| Anglesey | ANGLESEY & GWYNEDD |
| Appleby | CUMBRIA |
| Appleby-in-Westmorland | CUMBRIA |
| Arbroath | DUNDEE & ANGUS |
| Arrochar | ARGYLL & BUTE |
| Arundel | WEST SUSSEX |
| Ascot | BERKSHIRE |
| Ashbourne | DERBYSHIRE |
| Ashbrittle | SOMERSET |
| Ashburton | DEVON |
| Ashford | KENT |
| Ashkirk | BORDERS |
| Askrigg | NORTH YORKSHIRE |
| Atherington | DEVON |
| Attleborough | NORFOLK |
| Auchterarder | PERTH & KINROSS |
| Aultbea | HIGHLANDS (MID) |
| Aviemore | HIGHLANDS (SOUTH) |
| Axminster | DEVON |
| Aylesbury | BUCKINGHAMSHIRE |
| Aylsham | NORFOLK |
| Ayr | AYRSHIRE & ARRAN |
| Bakewell | DERBYSHIRE |
| Bala | ANGLESEY & GWYNEDD |
| Baldersby | NORTH YORKSHIRE |
| Balintore | HIGHLANDS (MID) |
| Ballachulish (near Glencoe) | ARGYLL & BUTE |
| Ballywalter | COUNTY DOWN |
| Balterley | CHESHIRE |
| Bampton | DEVON |
| Banbury | OXFORDSHIRE |
| Banbury/Warmington | WARWICKSHIRE |
| Bangor | ANGLESEY & GWYNEDD |
| Barnard Castle | DURHAM |
| Barnstaple | DEVON |
| Bath | GLOUCESTERSHIRE |
| Bath | SOMERSET |
| Beaconsfield | BUCKINGHAMSHIRE |
| Beaminster | DORSET |
| Beaulieu | HAMPSHIRE |
| Beccles | NORFOLK |
| Beckington | SOMERSET |
| Bedale | NORTH YORKSHIRE |
| Beith | AYRSHIRE & ARRAN |
| Belfast | CO DOWN |
| Belton-in-Rutland | LEICESTERSHIRE |
| Benniworth | LINCOLNSHIRE |
| Berwick-Upon-Tweed | NORTHUMBERLAND |
| Betws-y-Coed | NORTH WALES |
| Bewdley | WORCESTERSHIRE |
| Biddenden | KENT |
| Bideford | DEVON |
| Bideford Quay | DEVON |
| Bigbury-on-Sea | DEVON |
| Biggar | BORDERS |
| Binham | NORFOLK |
| Birdlip | GLOUCESTERSHIRE |
| Birmingham | WEST MIDLANDS |
| Bishop's Castle | SHROPSHIRE |
| Blackburn | LANCASHIRE |
| Blackpool | LANCASHIRE |
| Bladon | OXFORDSHIRE |
| Blaenffos | PEMBROKESHIRE |
| Blairgowrie | PERTH & KINROSS |
| Blairlogie | STIRLING & DISTRICT |
| Blandford | DORSET |
| Bodmin | CORNWALL |
| Bognor Regis | WEST SUSSEX |
| Boscastle | CORNWALL |
| Bournemouth | DORSET |
| Bovey Tracey | DEVON |
| Bowness-on-Windermere | CUMBRIA |
| Boxford | SUFFOLK |
| Brackley | NORTHAMPTONSHIRE |
| Brae | SHETLAND ISLES |
| Brailes | OXFORDSHIRE |
| Braintree | ESSEX |
| Brampton | CUMBRIA |
| Braunton | DEVON |
| Brean | SOMERSET |
| Brecon | POWYS |
| Bridge of Cally | PERTH & KINROSS |
| Bridgnorth | SHROPSHIRE |
| Bridgwater | SOMERSET |
| Bridlington | EAST YORKSHIRE |
| Bridport | DORSET |
| Brighton | EAST SUSSEX |
| Bristol | GLOUCESTERSHIRE |

# 430 INDEX OF TOWNS/COUNTIES

| | |
|---|---|
| Bristol | SOMERSET |
| Broad Haven | PEMBROKESHIRE |
| Broadford | ISLE OF SKYE |
| Brodick | AYRSHIRE & ARRAN |
| Broughton | LANARKSHIRE |
| Broughty Ferry | DUNDEE & ANGUS |
| Buckfastleigh | DEVON |
| Bucknell | SHROPSHIRE |
| Bude | CORNWALL |
| Budleigh Salterton | DEVON |
| Builth Wells | POWYS |
| Burgess Hill | EAST SUSSEX |
| Burley | HAMPSHIRE |
| Burnham-on-Sea | SOMERSET |
| Burton Joyce | NOTTINGHAMSHIRE |
| Burwash | EAST SUSSEX |
| Bury St Edmunds | SUFFOLK |
| Butterton | STAFFORDSHIRE |
| Buxton | DERBYSHIRE |
| Cadgwith Cove | CORNWALL |
| Cadnam | HAMPSHIRE |
| Caernarfon | ANGLESEY & GWYNEDD |
| Caldbeck | CUMBRIA |
| Caldecott | LEICESTERSHIRE |
| Calderbank | LANARKSHIRE |
| Callander | PERTH & KINROSS |
| Callington | CORNWALL |
| Cambridge | CAMBRIDGESHIRE |
| Canonbie | DUMFRIES & GALLOWAY |
| Canterbury | KENT |
| Cardiff | SOUTH WALES |
| Carlisle | CUMBRIA |
| Carmarthen | CARMARTHENSHIRE |
| Carnforth | LANCASHIRE |
| Carradale | ARGYLL & BUTE |
| Castle Douglas | DUMFRIES & GALLOWAY |
| Castledermot | COUNTY KILDARE |
| Castleton | DERBYSHIRE |
| Catacol/Arran | AYRSHIRE & ARRAN |
| Cerne Abbas | DORSET |
| Chagford | DEVON |
| Charmouth | DORSET |
| Cheddar | SOMERSET |
| Cheltenham | GLOUCESTERSHIRE |
| Chester | CHESHIRE |
| Chester | NORTH WALES |
| Chester City | CHESHIRE |
| Chesterfield | DERBYSHIRE |
| Chippenham | WILTSHIRE |
| Chipping Campden | GLOUCESTERSHIRE |
| Chorley | LANCASHIRE |
| Chudleigh | DEVON |
| Church Minshull | CHESHIRE |
| Church Stretton | SHROPSHIRE |
| Churchill | SOMERSET |
| Clare | SUFFOLK |
| Cleethorpes | LINCOLNSHIRE |
| Cleobury Mortimer | SHROPSHIRE |
| Clitheroe | LANCASHIRE |
| Clovelly | DEVON |
| Clun | SHROPSHIRE |
| Coaltown of Wemyss | FIFE |
| Cockermouth | CUMBRIA |
| Colchester | ESSEX |
| Coldstream | BORDERS |
| Colebrooke | DEVON |
| Compton Abbas | DORSET |
| Congleton | CHESHIRE |
| Conwy | NORTH WALES |
| Coombe Martin | DEVON |
| Corbridge | NORTHUMBERLAND |
| Cornforth | DURHAM |
| Corwen | NORTH WALES |
| Cotswolds | GLOUCESTERSHIRE |
| Coventry | WARWICKSHIRE |
| Coverdale | NORTH YORKSHIRE |
| Cowbridge | SOUTH WALES |
| Cowdenbeath | FIFE |
| Craven Arms | SHROPSHIRE |
| Crawley | WEST SUSSEX |
| Crediton | DEVON |
| Crewe | CHESHIRE |
| Crewkerne | SOMERSET |
| Crianlarich | PERTH & KINROSS |
| Cromer | NORFOLK |
| Croyde Bay | DEVON |
| Culloden Moor | HIGHLANDS (SOUTH) |
| Cullompton | DEVON |
| Cupar | FIFE |
| Dalton-in-Furness | CUMBRIA |
| Danby | NORTH YORKSHIRE |
| Dartmouth | DEVON |
| Denny | STIRLING & DISTRICT |
| Derby | DERBYSHIRE |
| Dereham | NORFOLK |
| Devizes | WILTSHIRE |
| Didmarton | GLOUCESTERSHIRE |
| Diss | NORFOLK |
| Dittisham | DEVON |
| Dolgellau | ANGLESEY & GWYNEDD |
| Dorchester | DORSET |
| Dorrington | SHROPSHIRE |
| Dover | KENT |
| Downham Market | NORFOLK |
| Driffield | EAST YORKSHIRE |
| Droitwich | WORCESTERSHIRE |
| Drumnadrochit | HIGHLANDS SOUTH |
| Dulverton | SOMERSET |
| Dumfries | DUMFRIES & GALLOWAY |
| Dunblane | STIRLING & DISTRICT |
| Dundee | DUNDEE & ANGUS |
| Dunfermline | FIFE |
| Dunlop | AYRSHIRE & ARRAN |
| Dunoon | ARGYLL & BUTE |
| Duns | BORDERS |
| Durham | DURHAM |
| Dursley | GLOUCESTERSHIRE |
| Dymock | GLOUCESTERSHIRE |
| Easingwold | NORTH YORKSHIRE |

## INDEX OF TOWNS/COUNTIES 431

| | | | |
|---|---|---|---|
| East Calder | EDINBURGH & LOTHIAN | Hailsham | EAST SUSSEX |
| East Lambrook | SOMERSET | Haltwhistle | NORTHUMBERLAND |
| East Looe | CORNWALL | Hammersmith | GREATER LONDON |
| East Prawle | DEVON | Hampton Court | SURREY |
| Eastbourne | EAST SUSSEX | Harleston | NORFOLK |
| Eastleigh | HAMPSHIRE | Harrogate | NORTH YORKSHIRE |
| Eccleshall | STAFFORDSHIRE | Harrow | GREATER LONDON |
| Edinburgh | EDINBURGH & LOTHIAN | Hartfield | EAST SUSSEX |
| Edwinstowe | NOTTINGHAMSHIRE | Harthill | LANARKSHIRE |
| Edzell | DUNDEE & ANGUS | Hartington | DERBYSHIRE |
| Ely | CAMBRIDGESHIRE | Hassocks | WEST SUSSEX |
| Exeter | DEVON | Hastings | EAST SUSSEX |
| Exford | SOMERSET | Hathersage | DERBYSHIRE |
| Exmoor | SOMERSET | Haverfordwest | PEMBROKESHIRE |
| | | Hawkhurst | KENT |
| Fairbourne | ANGLESEY & GWYNEDD | Hawkshead | CUMBRIA |
| Falkirk | STIRLING & DISTRICT | Hay-On-Wye | POWYS |
| Falkland | FIFE | Headcorn | KENT |
| Falmouth | CORNWALL | Heathfield | EAST SUSSEX |
| Fareham | HAMPSHIRE | Helmsley | NORTH YORKSHIRE |
| Faringdon | OXFORDSHIRE | Helston | CORNWALL |
| Farnham | SURREY | Hemel Hempstead | HERTFORDSHIRE |
| Farnsfield | NOTTINGHAMSHIRE | Hemingford Grey | CAMBRIDGESHIRE |
| Felton | HEREFORDSHIRE | Hemsby | NORFOLK |
| Fenny Compton | WARWICKSHIRE | Henfield | WEST SUSSEX |
| Ferndown | DORSET | Henley-On-Thames | OXFORDSHIRE |
| Filey | NORTH YORKSHIRE | Henstridge | SOMERSET |
| Fishguard | PEMBROKESHIRE | Hereford | HEREFORDSHIRE |
| Folkestone | KENT | Herstmonceux | EAST SUSSEX |
| Fort Augustus | HIGHLANDS SOUTH | Hexham | NORTHUMBERLAND |
| Fort William | HIGHLANDS (SOUTH) | Highampton | DEVON |
| Fortrose | HIGHLANDS MID | Highbridge | SOMERSET |
| Framlingham | SUFFOLK | Hingham | NORFOLK |
| Frampton-on-Severn | GLOUCESTERSHIRE | Hinton-St-Mary | DORSET |
| Freeland | OXFORDSHIRE | Holbeach | LINCOLNSHIRE |
| Freshwater | ISLE OF WIGHT | Holme-Next-The-Sea | NORFOLK |
| Frodsham | CHESHIRE | Holsworthy | DEVON |
| Furzehill | DORSET | Holt | NORFOLK |
| | | Honiton | DEVON |
| Gairloch | HIGHLANDS MID | Hook | HAMPSHIRE |
| Gatwick | SURREY | Horncastle | LINCOLNSHIRE |
| Gatwick | WEST SUSSEX | Horsey Corner | NORFOLK |
| Glasgow | GLASGOW | Huntingdon | CAMBRIDGE |
| Glastonbury | SOMERSET | Hyde | CHESHIRE |
| Glenfarg | PERTH & KINROSS | Hythe | HAMPSHIRE |
| Glossop | DERBYSHIRE | | |
| Gloucester | GLOUCESTERSHIRE | Ilam | DERBYSHIRE |
| Goathland | NORTH YORKSHIRE | Ilfracombe | DEVON |
| Golden Valley | HEREFORDSHIRE | Ilkley | WEST YORKSHIRE |
| Goodwick | PEMBROKESHIRE | Ilminster | SOMERSET |
| Gower Peninsula | SOUTH WALES | Ingleton | NORTH YORKSHIRE |
| Grange-Over-Sands | CUMBRIA | Instow | DEVON |
| Grantham | LINCOLNSHIRE | Inveraray | ARGYLL & BUTE |
| Grasmere | CUMBRIA | Inveresk | EDINBURGH & LOTHIANS |
| Great Malvern | WORCESTERSHIRE | Invergordon | HIGHLANDS (MID) |
| Great Yarmouth | NORFOLK | Inverness | HIGHLANDS (SOUTH) |
| Gullane | EDINBURGH & LOTHIAN | Ipswich | SUFFOLK |
| | | Ironbridge/Telford | SHROPSHIRE |
| Hadleigh | SUFFOLK | Ivybridge | DEVON |
| Hadrian's Wall | CUMBRIA | | |
| Hadrian's Wall | NORTHUMBERLAND | | |

## INDEX OF TOWNS/COUNTIES

| | |
|---|---|
| Kelvedon | ESSEX |
| Kendal | CUMBRIA |
| Kenilworth | WARWICKSHIRE |
| Kensington | GREATER LONDON |
| Keswick | CUMBRIA |
| Kew Gardens | GREATER LONDON |
| Kilmarnock | AYRSHIRE & ARRAN |
| Kimbolton | HEREFORDSHIRE |
| Kings Cross | GREATER LONDON |
| King's Lynn | NORFOLK |
| Kingsbridge | DEVON |
| Kingsley | CHESHIRE |
| Kinross | PERTH & KINROSS |
| Kirkby Lonsdale | CUMBRIA |
| Kirkby Stephen | CUMBRIA |
| Kirkcaldy | FIFE |
| Kirkmichael | PERTH & KINROSS |
| Kirkwall | ORKNEY |
| Knapton | NORFOLK |
| Kyleakin | ISLE OF SKYE |
| Lake District/Hawkshead | CUMBRIA |
| Lampeter | CARDIGANSHIRE |
| Lancaster | LANCASHIRE |
| Landford | WILTSHIRE |
| Land's End | CORNWALL |
| Langton-in-Wragby | LINCOLNSHIRE |
| Launceston | CORNWALL |
| Lechlade | GLOUCESTERSHIRE |
| Ledbury | HEREFORDSHIRE |
| Leeds | NORTH YORKSHIRE |
| Leek | STAFFORDSHIRE |
| Leominster | HEREFORDSHIRE |
| Letham | DUNDEE & ANGUS |
| Leven | FIFE |
| Lighthorne | WARWICKSHIRE |
| Lillington | DORSET |
| Lincoln | LINCOLNSHIRE |
| Lingfield | SURREY |
| Linlithgow | EDINBURGH & LOTHIAN |
| Liskeard | CORNWALL |
| Livingston | EDINBURGH & LOTHIANS |
| Lizard Peninsula | CORNWALL |
| Llandrindod Wells | POWYS |
| Llandudno | NORTH WALES |
| Llangollen | NORTH WALES |
| Llanidloes | POWYS |
| Llanrhystud | CARDIGANSHIRE |
| Llansilin | NORTH WALES |
| Loch Lomond | DUNBARTONSHIRE |
| Lochgoilhead | ARGYLL & BUTE |
| Loddon | NORFOLK |
| London | GREATER LONDON |
| Long Hanborough | OXFORDSHIRE |
| Longtown | HEREFORDSHIRE |
| Looe | CORNWALL |
| Loughborough | LEICESTERSHIRE |
| Louth | LINCOLNSHIRE |
| Lowestoft | SUFFOLK |
| Loweswater | CUMBRIA |
| Ludlow | SHROPSHIRE |
| Lulworth Cove | DORSET |
| Luss | DUNBARTONSHIRE |
| Lydbury North | SHROPSHIRE |
| Lydney | GLOUCESTERSHIRE |
| Lyme Regis | DORSET |
| Lymington | HAMPSHIRE |
| Lyndhurst | HAMPSHIRE |
| Lynmouth | DEVON |
| Lynton | DEVON |
| Lytham St. Annes | LANCASHIRE |
| Macclesfield | CHESHIRE |
| Maidstone | KENT |
| Malham | NORTH YORKSHIRE |
| Mallaig | HIGHLANDS (SOUTH) |
| Malmesbury | WILTSHIRE |
| Malton | NORTH YORKSHIRE |
| Malvern | WORCESTERSHIRE |
| Malvern Wells | WORCESTERSHIRE |
| Manchester | LANCASHIRE |
| Mansel Lacy | HEREFORDSHIRE |
| Mansfield | NOTTINGHAMSHIRE |
| Marazion | CORNWALL |
| Margate | KENT |
| Mark | SOMERSET |
| Market Drayton | SHROPSHIRE |
| Marnhull | DORSET |
| Matlock | DERBYSHIRE |
| Mattishall | NORFOLK |
| Mauchline | AYRSHIRE & ARRAN |
| Medbourne | LEICESTERSHIRE |
| Melksham | WILTSHIRE |
| Melton Mowbray | LEICESTERSHIRE |
| Menai Bridge | ANGLESEY & GWYNEDD |
| Mere | WILTSHIRE |
| Mevagissey | CORNWALL |
| Milford-on-Sea | HAMPSHIRE |
| Minchinhampton | GLOUCESTERSHIRE |
| Minster Lovell | OXFORDSHIRE |
| Minsterley | SHROPSHIRE |
| Moffat | DUMFRIES & GALLOWAY |
| Monmouth | SOUTH WALES |
| Monnington-on-Wye | HEREFORDSHIRE |
| Montacute | SOMERSET |
| Morar | HIGHLANDS (SOUTH) |
| Morecambe | LANCASHIRE |
| Moreton in Marsh | GLOUCESTERSHIRE |
| Musselburgh | EDINBURGH & LOTHIANS |
| Nailsworth | GLOUCESTERSHIRE |
| Nantwich | CHESHIRE |
| Neath | SOUTH WALES |
| Nefyn | ANGLESEY & GWYNEDD |
| Ness | ISLE OF LEWIS |
| New Forest | HAMPSHIRE |
| New Milton | HAMPSHIRE |
| New Romney | KENT |
| Newbiggin-on-Lune | CUMBRIA |
| Newby Bridge | CUMBRIA |
| Newcastle-under-Lyme | STAFFORDSHIRE |

## INDEX OF TOWNS/COUNTIES 433

| | |
|---|---|
| Newland | GLOUCESTERSHIRE |
| Newport | SHROPSHIRE |
| Newport | SOUTH WALES |
| Newquay | CORNWALL |
| Newton Ferrers | DEVON |
| Newton Poppleford | DEVON |
| Newton Stewart | DUMFRIES & GALLOWAY |
| Newtown | POWYS |
| North Cadbury | SOMERSET |
| North Hykeham | LINCOLNSHIRE |
| North Tawton | DEVON |
| Norwich | NORFOLK |
| Nottingham | NOTTINGHAMSHIRE |
| Oban | ARGYLL & BUTE |
| Okehampton | DEVON |
| Ombersley | WORCESTERSHIRE |
| Oswestry | SHROPSHIRE |
| Otley | NORTH YORKSHIRE |
| Ottery St Mary | DEVON |
| Over | CAMBRIDGESHIRE |
| Oxford | OXFORDSHIRE |
| Oxted | SURREY |
| Padstow | CORNWALL |
| Paignton | DEVON |
| Par | CORNWALL |
| Patthead | EDINBURGH & LOTHIANS |
| Peldon | ESSEX |
| Penrith | CUMBRIA |
| Penzance | CORNWALL |
| Perranporth | CORNWALL |
| Perth | PERTH & KINROSS |
| Peterborough | LINCOLNSHIRE |
| Peterhead | ABERDEEN, BANFF & MORAY |
| Petersfield | HAMPSHIRE |
| Petworth | WEST SUSSEX |
| Pickering | NORTH YORKSHIRE |
| Pillerton Hersey | WARWICKSHIRE |
| Pilling | LANCASHIRE |
| Pinwherry | AYRSHIRE & ARRAN |
| Pitlochry | PERTH & KINROSS |
| Plockton | HIGHLANDS (MID) |
| Pluckley | KENT |
| Plymouth | DEVON |
| Polzeath | CORNWALL |
| Pontefract/Wentbridge | WEST YORKSHIRE |
| Poole | DORSET |
| Porlock | SOMERSET |
| Port Isaac | CORNWALL |
| Porthleven | CORNWALL |
| Portpatrick | DUMFRIES & GALLOWAY |
| Portree | ISLE OF SKYE |
| Portsmouth | HAMPSHIRE |
| Praa Sands | CORNWALL |
| Pulloxhill | BEDFORDSHIRE |
| Quantock Hills | SOMERSET |
| Rackheath | NORFOLK |
| Ravenscar | NORTH YORKSHIRE |
| Reading | BERKSHIRE |
| Redhill | SURREY |
| Reeth | NORTH YORKSHIRE |
| Rhayader | POWYS |
| Rhos-on-Sea | NORTH WALES |
| Rhyl | NORTH WALES |
| Richmond | NORTH YORKSHIRE |
| Rickmansworth | HERTFORDSHIRE |
| Ringwood (New Forest) | HAMPSHIRE |
| Ripon | NORTH YORKSHIRE |
| Robin Hood's Bay | NORTH YORKSHIRE |
| Rochdale/Bury | LANCASHIRE |
| Romsey/New Forest | HAMPSHIRE |
| Ropley | HAMPSHIRE |
| Rosedale East | NORTH YORKSHIRE |
| Roseland Peninsula | CORNWALL |
| Ross-on-Wye | HEREFORDSHIRE |
| Royal Deeside | ABERDEEN, BANFF & MORAY |
| Ruthin | NORTH WALES |
| Ryde | ISLE OF WIGHT |
| Rye | EAST SUSSEX |
| St Abbs | BORDERS |
| St Agnes | CORNWALL |
| St Andrews | FIFE |
| St Asaph | NORTH WALES |
| St Austell | CORNWALL |
| St Brides Wentloog | SOUTH WALES |
| St Ives | CORNWALL |
| St.Neots | CAMBRIDGESHIRE |
| Salisbury | WILTSHIRE |
| Saltburn-By-Sea | DURHAM |
| Sandy | BEDFORDSHIRE |
| Saundersfoot | PEMBROKESHIRE |
| Scarborough | NORTH YORKSHIRE |
| Seaford | EAST SUSSEX |
| Seaton | DEVON |
| Sennen | CORNWALL |
| Shanklin | ISLE OF WIGHT |
| Shap | CUMBRIA |
| Shepton Mallet | SOMERSET |
| Sherborne | DORSET |
| Sheringham | NORFOLK |
| Shillingstone | DORSET |
| Shipston-on-Stour | WARWICKSHIRE |
| Shrewsbury | SHROPSHIRE |
| Sidmouth | DEVON |
| Sittingbourne/Lynsted | KENT |
| Sixpenny Handley | DORSET |
| Skegness | LINCOLNSHIRE |
| Skipton | NORTH YORKSHIRE |
| Slapton | DEVON |
| Solihull | WEST MIDLANDS |
| Souldern | OXFORDSHIRE |
| South Molton | DEVON |
| South Queensferry | EDINBURGH & LOTHIAN |
| Southampton | HAMPSHIRE |
| Southport | LANCASHIRE |
| Spalding | LINCOLNSHIRE |
| Spean Bridge | HIGHLANDS (SOUTH) |

# 434 INDEX OF TOWNS/COUNTIES

| | |
|---|---|
| Spennymoor | DURHAM |
| Staffin | ISLE OF SKYE |
| Stamford | LINCOLNSHIRE |
| Stanley | PERTH & KINROSS |
| Stanley | DURHAM |
| Steyning | WEST SUSSEX |
| Stockbridge | HAMPSHIRE |
| Stoke-on-Trent | STAFFORDSHIRE |
| Stonehaven | ABERDEEN, BANFF & MORAY |
| Stonehouse | GLOUCESTERSHIRE |
| Stornoway | ISLE OF LEWIS |
| Storrington/Pulborough | WEST SUSSEX |
| Stow-on-the-Wold | GLOUCESTERSHIRE |
| Stratford-Upon-Avon | WARWICKSHIRE |
| Strathpeffer | HIGHLANDS (MID) |
| Strathyre | PERTH & KINROSS |
| Stroud | GLOUCESTERSHIRE |
| Sturminster Marshall | DORSET |
| Sturminster Newton | DORSET |
| Sudbury | SUFFOLK |
| Sutton-In-Ashfield | NOTTINGHAMSHIRE |
| Swaffham | NORFOLK |
| Swanage | DORSET |
| Swansea | SOUTH WALES |
| Swindon | WILTSHIRE |
| Tackley | OXFORDSHIRE |
| Talgarth | POWYS |
| Tanworth in Arden | WARWICKSHIRE |
| Tattenhall | CHESHIRE |
| Taunton | SOMERSET |
| Tayport | FIFE |
| Tebay | CUMBRIA |
| Teign Valley | DEVON |
| Teignmouth | DEVON |
| Telford | SHROPSHIRE |
| Tenby | PEMBROKESHIRE |
| Tenterden/Biddenden | KENT |
| Tetsworth | OXFORDSHIRE |
| Tewkesbury | GLOUCESTERSHIRE |
| Theale | SOMERSET |
| Thirsk | NORTH YORKSHIRE |
| Thornton-Le-Dale | NORTH YORKSHIRE |
| Thorpe Fendykes | LINCOLNSHIRE |
| Threshfield | NORTH YORKSHIRE |
| Thursford | NORFOLK |
| Tideswell | DERBYSHIRE |
| Tintagel | CORNWALL |
| Tintern | SOUTH WALES |
| Tiverton | DEVON |
| Tolpuddle | DORSET |
| Tomatin | HIGHLANDS (SOUTH) |
| Tonbridge | KENT |
| Torquay | DEVON |
| Totland Bay | ISLE OF WIGHT |
| Totnes | DEVON |
| Tralee | COUNTY KERRY |
| Trefriw | NORTH WALES |
| Tregony | CORNWALL |
| Troutbeck | CUMBRIA |
| Truro | CORNWALL |
| Tunbridge Wells | KENT |
| Ullapool | HIGHLANDS (MID) |
| Ullswater | CUMBRIA |
| Umberleigh | DEVON |
| Wadebridge | CORNWALL |
| Walton-on-Thames | SURREY |
| Wareham | DORSET |
| Warkworth | NORTHUMBERLAND |
| Warwick | WARWICKSHIRE |
| Washford | SOMERSET |
| Watchet | SOMERSET |
| Watton | NORFOLK |
| Wells | SOMERSET |
| Wells-Next-The-Sea | NORFOLK |
| Welshpool | POWYS |
| Wem | SHROPSHIRE |
| Wenhaston | SUFFOLK |
| Wensleydale | NORTH YORKSHIRE |
| Westcliff-on-Sea | ESSEX |
| Weston-Super-Mare | SOMERSET |
| Westonzoyland | SOMERSET |
| Weymouth | DORSET |
| Whitby | NORTH YORKSHIRE |
| Whitchurch | SHROPSHIRE |
| Whitehaven | CUMBRIA |
| Whithorn | DUMFRIES & GALLOWAY |
| Wicken | CAMBRIDGESHIRE |
| Wimborne | DORSET |
| Winchcombe | GLOUCESTERSHIRE |
| Winchelsea | EAST SUSSEX |
| Winchester | HAMPSHIRE |
| Windermere | CUMBRIA |
| Windsor | BERKSHIRE |
| Winfrith Newburgh | DORSET |
| Wingham | KENT |
| Winkleigh | DEVON |
| Winster | DERBYSHIRE |
| Wisbech | CAMBRIDGE |
| Witney | OXFORDSHIRE |
| Woodchester | GLOUCESTERSHIRE |
| Woodhall Spa | LINCOLNSHIRE |
| Woodstock | OXFORDSHIRE |
| Woodton | NORFOLK |
| Woolacombe | DEVON |
| Worcester | WORCESTERSHIRE |
| Wrington | SOMERSET |
| Wroxham | NORFOLK |
| Wyton | CAMBRIDGESHIRE |
| Yeovil | SOMERSET |
| York | NORTH YORKSHIRE |
| Zennor | CORNWALL |

# ONE FOR YOUR FRIEND 2001

**FHG Publications** have a large range of attractive holiday accommodation guides for all kinds of holiday opportunities throughout Britain. They also make useful gifts at any time of year. Our guides are available in most bookshops and larger newsagents but we will be happy to post you a copy direct if you have any difficulty. We will also post abroad but have to charge separately for post or freight. **The inclusive cost of posting and packing the guides to you or your friends in the UK is as follows:**

Recommended
SHORT BREAK HOLIDAYS
in Britain.
'Approved' accommodation for quality bargain breaks
£5.50 inc p&p

SELF-CATERING HOLIDAYS
in Britain
Over 1000 addresses throughout for Self-catering and caravans
in Britain.
£5.50 inc p&p.

BRITAIN'S BEST HOLIDAYS
A quick-reference general guide for all kinds of holidays.
£4.50 inc p&p.

FARM HOLIDAY GUIDE
England, Scotland, Wales, Ireland and Channel Islands
Board, Self-catering, Caravans/Camping, Activity Holidays.
£6.00 inc p&p.

Recommended
WAYSIDE AND COUNTRY INNS
of Britain
Pubs, Inns and small hotels.
£5.50 inc p&p.

Recommended
COUNTRY HOTELS OF BRITAIN
Including Country Houses, for the discriminating
£5.50 inc p&p

**GOLF GUIDE –**
Where to play. Where to stay.
In association with GOLF MONTHLY.
Over 2500 golf courses in Britain
with convenient accommodation.
Holiday Golf in France, Portugal,
Spain, USA, South Africa and
Thailand.
£10.50 inc p&p. ☐

The FHG Guide to CARAVAN &
CAMPING HOLIDAYS
Caravans for hire, sites and
holiday parks and centres.
£4.50 inc p&p. ☐

B&B in Britain
Over 1000 choices for touring
and holidays throughout Britain.
Airports and Ferries Supplement.
£4.50 inc p&p. ☐

CHILDREN WELCOME! Family Holidays and Attractions guide.
Family holidays with details of amenities for children and babies. £5.50 inc p&p. ☐

PETS WELCOME!
The unique guide for holidays for pet owners and their pets. £6.50 inc p&p. ☐

Tick your choice and send your order and payment to

**FHG PUBLICATIONS, ABBEY MILL BUSINESS CENTRE,
SEEDHILL, PAISLEY PA1 1TJ
TEL: 0141- 887 0428; FAX: 0141- 889 7204**
e-mail: fhg@ipcmedia.com
Deduct 10% for 2/3 titles or copies; 20% for 4 or more.

Send to:  NAME..................................................................................................

ADDRESS ............................................................................................

..............................................................................................................

..............................................................................................................

POST CODE  ..............................

I enclose Cheque/Postal Order for £.................................................................

SIGNATURE .............................................DATE ...........................................

Please complete the following to help us improve the service we provide. How did you find out about our guides?:

☐ Press      ☐ Magazines      ☐ TV/Radio      ☐ Family/Friend      ☐ Other